Not For Tourists™ Guide to CHICAGO

2007

Not For Tourists Inc New York

published and designed by
Not For Tourists Inc
NFT$_{TM}$- Not For Tourists$_{TM}$- Guide to CHICAGO 2007
www.notfortourists.com

Publisher
Jane Pirone

Information Design
Jane Pirone
Rob Tallia
Scot Covey
Ben Bray

Managing Editor
Rob Tallia

Database Manager
Ben Bray

City Editor
Kathie Bergquist

Sales and Marketing
Alli Hirschman
Erin Hodson
Annie Holt

Writing and Editing
Mark Armstrong
Kathie Bergquist
Bathsheba Birman
Julia Borcherts
Chandra Clark
Brian Diebold
Max Grinnell
Emily Hauser
Jessica Herman
Darwyn Jones
Amy Kraft
Jeff Moyers
JT Newman
Lisa Shames
Andrea Weifurt

Contributor
Alice Tegtmeier

Research
Michael Dale
Manny Rodriguez
Sho Spaeth

Research Intern
Lily Chu

Graphic Design/Production
Chesley Andrews
Scot Covey
Lisette de Orbegoso
Jeanette Rodriguez

Graphic Design Intern
Aaron Schielke

Proofing
Dorothy Ball
Jennifer Keeney Sendrow

NFT would like to thank **Diana Pizzari** for her hard work and dedication over the past five years—best of luck!

Printed in China
ISBN#0-9778031-3-9 $16.95

Every effort has been made to ensure that the information in this book is as up-to-date as possible at press time. However, many details are liable to change—as we have learned. The publishers cannot accept responsibility for any consequences arising from the use of this book.

Not For Tourists does not solicit individuals, organizations, or businesses for listings inclusion in our guides, nor do we accept payment for inclusion into the editorial portion of our book; the advertising sections, however, are exempt from this policy. We always welcome communications from anyone regarding ANYTHING having to do with our books; please visit us on our website at www.notfortourists.com for appropriate contact information.

Dear NFT User,

The lakefront, the skyscrapers, the Sox and the Cubs, and (who woulda thunk it) the Bulls, the Southside St. Patty's Day Parade, Queen Oprah, Roger Ebert, Steppenwolf and Second City, the Mag Mile, the U of C, the Kennedy Expressway and O'Hare... Aldermen, silver shovels, and "the machine," the Pilsen murals, the giant jellybean and Gehry bandshell, trucks for hire, "Da Mare," Bud Billiken, Von Freeman, Smashing Pumpkins and the Metro, Charlie Trotter, the Uptown Poetry Slam, Superdawg, Thillens Field... Wind chill factors and heat waves, lawn chairs as parking space keepers, Jesse Jackson, Studs Terkel, V. I. Warshawsky, and Dorothy Tillman's hats. Whether you think Chicago is the City That Works, or the City That Works Your Nerves, these are the things that make Chicago the great, vibrant, boisterous, smelly, entirely American city that it is, and that is why we like it.

If this is your first time using the NFT Chicago guide (welcome aboard!), we are sure you will find it practical, enlightening, and entertaining, whether you are new to Chicago, a frequent business traveler, interested in exploring new neighborhoods, or taking a closer look at your own. Need a plumber at 3 am? Need to grab a bite to eat in Jefferson Park? If you want directions to the University of Chicago or help navigating Chicago's independent theater scene, NFT Chicago is the only resource you need.

If you are an already a devoted NFT user, you will be pleased with this newly revised edition. Besides completely updating and refurbishing all of the nightlife and restaurant listings, as well as the excellent neighborhood–by–neighborhood map coverage (all told we make over 1,000 changes to each edition every year!), we've brought the nearby suburb of Skokie into our fold and added sections on Continuing Education, self–storage rental listings, van and truck rental listings, and a new overview on sports in Chicago. In fact, we've done our best to make NFT Chicago as thorough and up–to–date as humanly possible.

And of course, we rely on your input as well. If you see room for improvement, know of any essential places we somehow missed, or you just want to say howdy and "keep up the good work" we encourage you to log on to our website, www.notfortourists.com, and tell us what's on your mind.

Cordially Yours,

Kathie, Jane & Rob

Chicago Neighborhoods

The Greater Loop

The South Side

The Near West Side

The Near North Side

The North Side

Greater Chicago

Parks & Places

Colleges & Universities

Sports

Transit

General Information

Arts & Entertainment

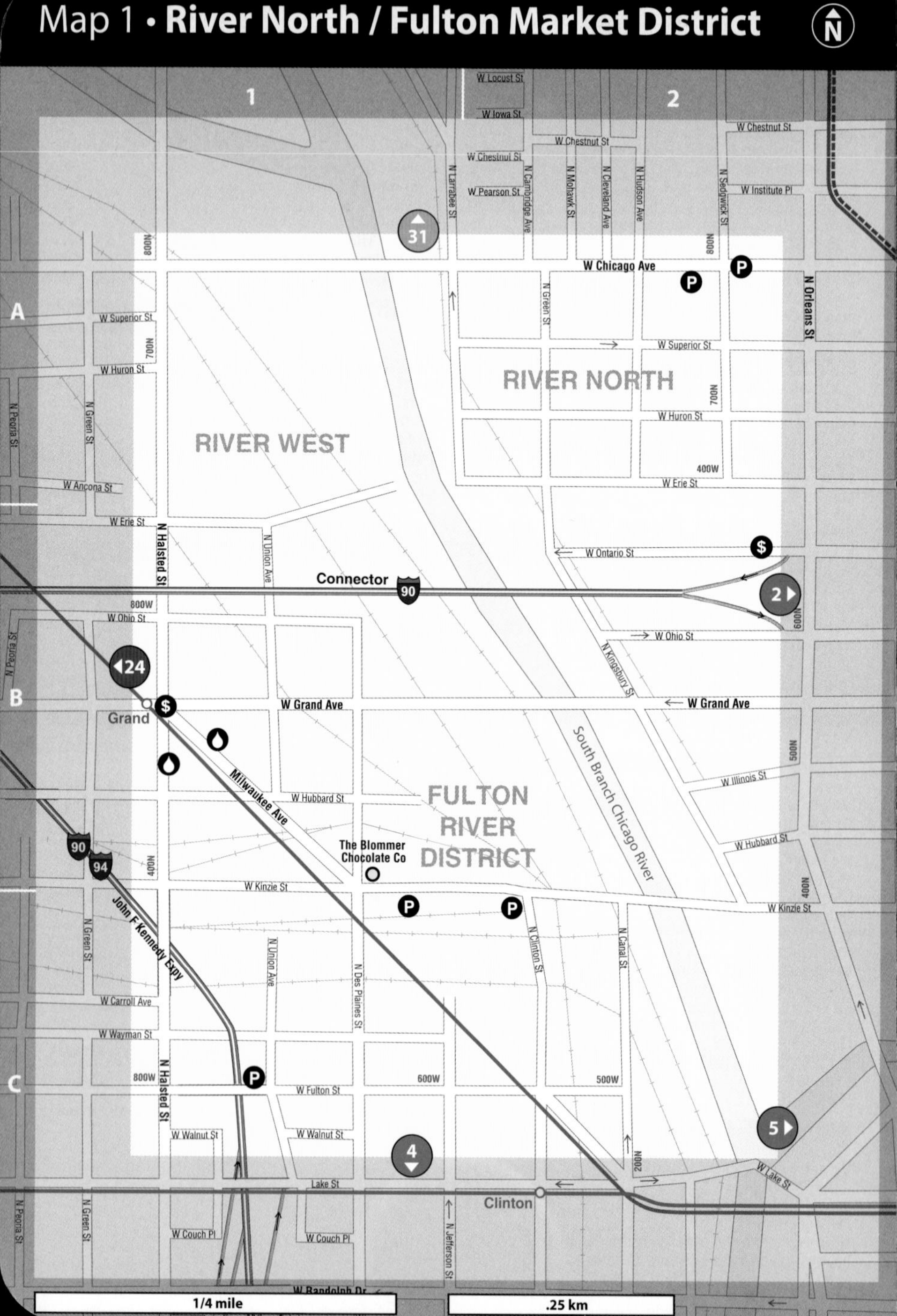
Map 1 • River North / Fulton Market District
N
1
2
A
B
C
W Locust St
W Iowa St
W Chestnut St
W Chestnut St
W Chestnut St
W Pearson St
W Institute Pl
N Larrabee St
N Cambridge Ave
N Mohawk St
N Cleveland Ave
N Hudson Ave
N Sedgwick St
31
800N
800N
W Chicago Ave
N Orleans St
W Superior St
700N
N Green St
W Superior St
W Huron St
RIVER NORTH
700N
W Huron St
N Peoria St
N Green St
RIVER WEST
400W
W Erie St
W Ancona St
W Erie St
N Halsted St
N Union Ave
W Ontario St
Connector
90
2
800W
600N
W Ohio St
W Ohio St
N Peoria St
N Kingsbury St
24
W Grand Ave
W Grand Ave
Grand
South Branch Chicago River
500N
Milwaukee Ave
W Illinois St
W Hubbard St
FULTON
RIVER
DISTRICT
W Hubbard St
90
The Blommer
Chocolate Co
94
400N
400N
W Kinzie St
W Kinzie St
John F Kennedy Expy
N Green St
N Union Ave
N Des Plaines St
N Clinton St
N Canal St
W Carroll Ave
W Wayman St
800W
N Halsted St
600W
500W
W Fulton St
5
W Walnut St
W Walnut St
4
200N
W Lake St
Lake St
Clinton
N Peoria St
N Green St
W Couch Pl
W Couch Pl
N Jefferson St
W Randolph Dr
1/4 mile
.25 km

Crisscrossed by rail tracks, I-90/94, and the Chicago River, this area is transitioning from industrial to residential as the loft-conversion craze in River North, Greek Town, and West Loop Gate expands. The Blommer Chocolate Company pumps sweet, chocolate-coated air into the streets all day. Diabetics, beware.

Banks

- **New Century** • 363 W Ontario St
- **Washington Mutual** • 501 N Milwaukee Ave

Car Washes

- **River West Hand Car Wash** • 478 N Milwaukee Ave
- **We Wash III** • 452 N Halsted St

Landmarks

- **The Blommer Chocolate Co** • 600 W Kinzie St

Parking

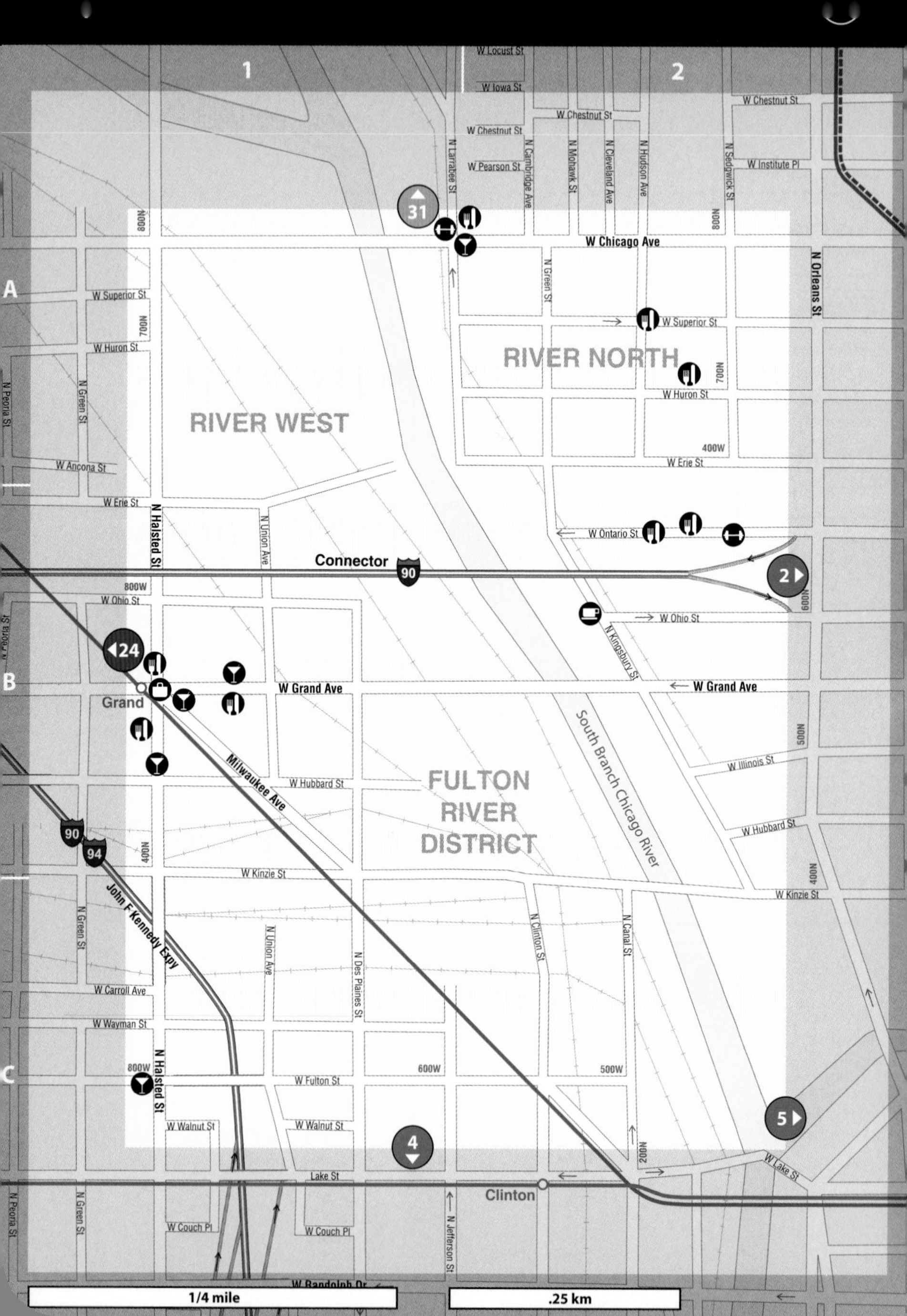
1
2
A
B
C
RIVER WEST
RIVER NORTH
FULTON RIVER DISTRICT
W Locust St
W Iowa St
W Chestnut St
W Pearson St
W Institute Pl
W Chicago Ave
W Superior St
W Huron St
W Ancona St
W Erie St
W Ontario St
Connector
90
W Ohio St
W Grand Ave
Grand
Milwaukee Ave
W Hubbard St
W Illinois St
W Kinzie St
South Branch Chicago River
John F Kennedy Expy
94
W Carroll Ave
W Wayman St
W Fulton St
W Walnut St
Lake St
W Lake St
Clinton
W Couch Pl
W Randolph Dr
N Larrabee St
N Cambridge Ave
N Mohawk St
N Cleveland Ave
N Hudson Ave
N Sedgwick St
N Orleans St
N Green St
N Peoria St
N Halsted St
N Union Ave
N Kingsbury St
N Clinton St
N Canal St
N Des Plaines St
N Jefferson St
800N
700N
600N
500N
400N
200N
800W
600W
500W
400W
31
24
2
4
5
1/4 mile
.25 km

Funky Buddha Lounge and Motel are the bars to scout out Mr. or Ms. Right (or Mr. or Ms. Right NOW). Have beer and burgers with your buddies at Emmit's. French-Japanese fusion restaurant Japonais is one of a handful of trendy concept restaurants pumping new blood into the Chicago restaurant scene.

Coffee

- **Caribou Coffee** • 600 N Kingsbury St

Gyms

- **David Barton Gym** • 600 W Chicago Ave
- **Sharper Fitness** • 401 W Ontario St

Nightlife

- **Emmit's Irish Pub & Eatery** • 495 N Milwaukee Ave
- **Funky Buddha Lounge** • 728 W Grand Ave
- **The Motel Bar** • 600 W Chicago Ave
- **Rednofive & Fifth Floor** • 440 N Halsted St
- **Rive Gauche** • 306 N Halsted St

Restaurants

- **Carnivale** • 702 W Fulton St
- **Iguana Café** • 517 N Halsted St
- **Japonais** • 600 W Chicago Ave
- **La Scarola** • 721 W Grand Ave
- **Reza's** • 432 W Ontario St
- **Scoozi!** • 410 W Huron St
- **Timo** • 464 N Halsted St
- **Tony Rocco's River North** • 416 W Ontario St
- **Zealous** • 419 W Superior St

Shopping

- **Doolin's** • 511 N Halsted St

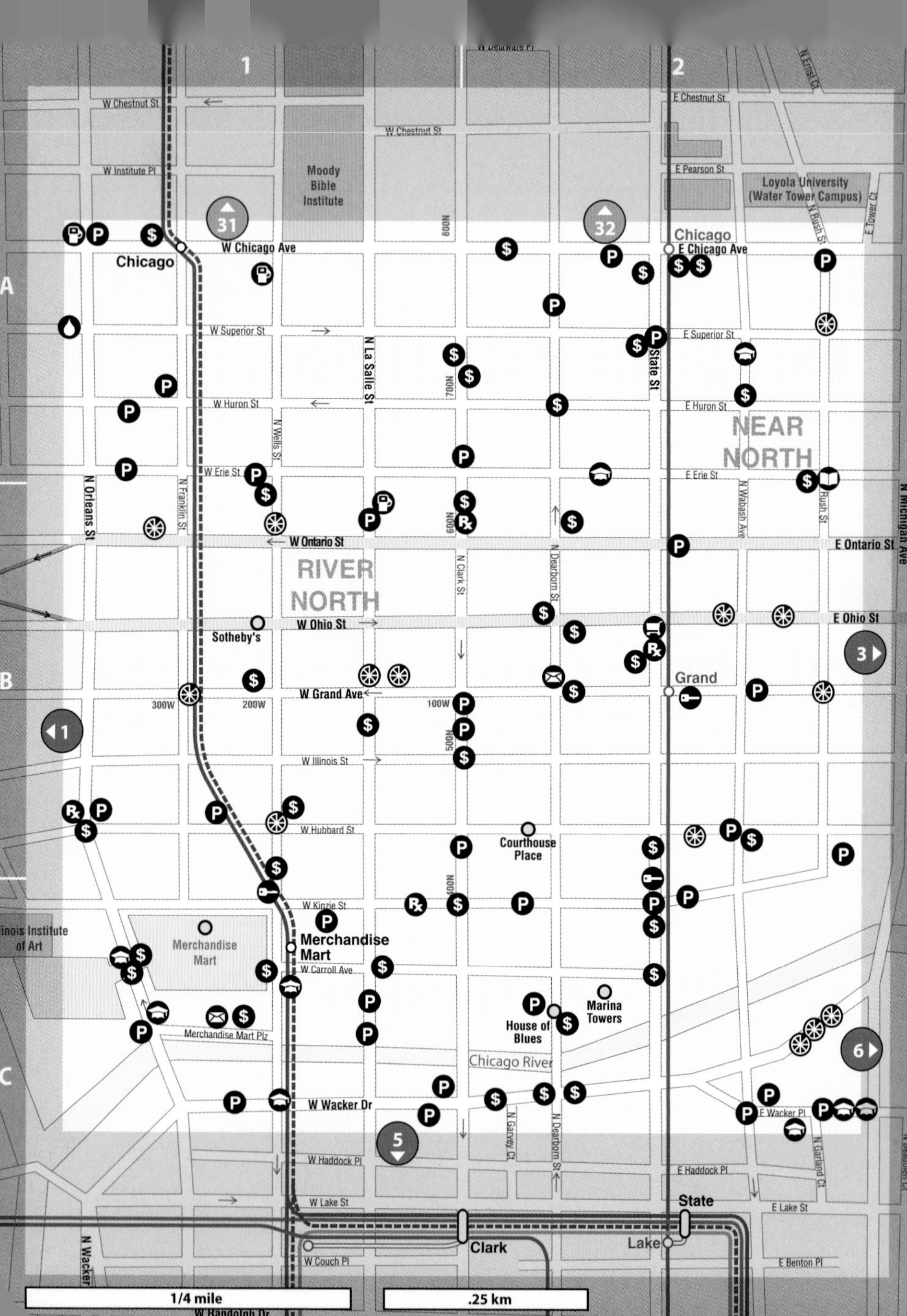
1
2
A
B
C
W Chestnut St
W Chestnut St
E Chestnut St
W Institute Pl
E Pearson St
Moody Bible Institute
Loyola University (Water Tower Campus)
31
32
800N
Chicago
W Chicago Ave
Chicago
E Chicago Ave
W Superior St
E Superior St
N La Salle St
700N
State St
W Huron St
E Huron St
NEAR NORTH
N Wells St
W Erie St
E Erie St
N Orleans St
N Franklin St
600N
N Wabash Ave
Rush St
N Michigan Ave
W Ontario St
E Ontario St
RIVER NORTH
N Clark St
N Dearborn St
W Ohio St
E Ohio St
Sotheby's
3
Grand
300W
200W
W Grand Ave
100W
1
500N
W Illinois St
W Hubbard St
Courthouse Place
400N
W Kinzie St
Illinois Institute of Art
Merchandise Mart
Merchandise Mart
W Carroll Ave
Merchandise Mart Plz
House of Blues
Marina Towers
Chicago River
6
W Wacker Dr
E Wacker Pl
5
N Garvey Ct
N Dearborn St
N Garland Ct
W Haddock Pl
E Haddock Pl
W Lake St
State
E Lake St
N Wacker
Clark
Lake
W Couch Pl
E Benton Pl
1/4 mile
.25 km
W Randolph Dr

Monolithic Merchandise Mart casts its shadow over River North, helping the area maintain its industrial edge even if a number of the former warehouse spaces are now upscale lofts or designer showrooms. A former art gallery haven, only the most successful (and staid) have persevered—edgier artistes have migrated to lower rents on the near west side.

Banks

- **Bank of America** • 49 E Chicago Ave
- **Bank of America** • 601 N Dearborn St
- **Bank of America (ATM)** • 320 N Wells St
- **Bank of America (ATM)** • 59 E Chicago Ave
- **Bank of America (ATM)** • 640 N Wells St
- **Charter One** • 33 W Grand Ave
- **Chase** • 230 W Grand Ave
- **Chase** • 340 N State St
- **Chase** • 35 W Wacker Dr
- **Chase** • 71 W Chicago Ave
- **Chase (ATM)** • 101 E Erie St
- **Chase (ATM)** • 321 N Clark St
- **Chase (ATM)** • 641 N Clark St
- **Citibank** • 400 N Clark St
- **Citibank (ATM)** • 1 W Superior St
- **Citibank (ATM)** • 751 N Clark St
- **Fifth Third** • 222 Merchandise Mart Plz
- **Fifth Third** • 350 Orleans St
- **Fifth Third (ATM)** • 401 N Wells St
- **Fifth Third (ATM)** • 431 N Wells St
- **Harris Trust & Savings** • 33 W Ohio St
- **Lakeside** • 55 W Wacker Dr
- **LaSalle** • 515 N La Salle St
- **MB Financial** • 1 E Wacker Dr
- **New Century (ATM)** • 306 W Chicago Ave
- **New Century (ATM)** • Holiday Inn • 350 N Orleans St
- **New Century (ATM)** • 441 N Wabash Ave
- **North** • 501 N Clark St
- **North Community** • 448 N Wells St
- **North Community** • 800 N State St
- **Oak Brook** • 33 W Huron St
- **TCF** • 635 N Dearborn St
- **TCF (ATM)** • 7-Eleven • 343 N La Salle St
- **TCF (ATM)** • 7-Eleven • 418 N State St
- **TCF (ATM)** • 550 N State St
- **TCF (ATM)** • 7-Eleven • 714 N Clark St
- **Washington Mutual** • 431 N Orleans St
- **Washington Mutual** • 710 N Wabash Ave

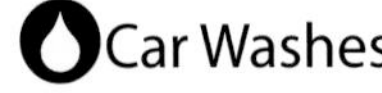

Car Washes

- **River North Hand Car Wash** • 356 W Superior St

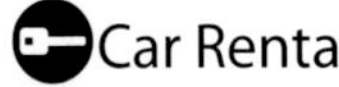

Car Rental

- **Enterprise** • 10 E Grand Ave • 312-670-7270
- **Enterprise** • 401 N Wells St • 312-494-3434
- **Hertz** • 401 N State St • 312-372-7600

Gas Stations

- **BP Connect** • 631 N La Salle Dr
- **Citgo** • 750 N Wells St
- **Shell** • 350 W Chicago Ave

Landmarks

- **Courthouse Place** • 54 W Hubbard St
- **House of Blues** • 329 N Dearborn St
- **Marina Towers** • 300 N State St
- **Merchandise Mart** • 222 Merchandise Mart Plz
- **Sotheby's** • 215 W Ohio St

Pharmacies

- **CVS Pharmacy** • 121 W Kinzie St
- **CVS Pharmacy** • 344 W Hubbard St
- **Jewel-Osco** • 550 N State St
- **Walgreens** • 641 N Clark St

Pizza

- **Alibi Restaurant** • 23 W Hubbard St
- **Bacino's on Wacker** • 75 E Wacker Dr
- **Bella Bacino's** • 75 E Wacker Dr
- **Buca Di Beppo** • 521 N Rush St
- **California Pizza Kitchen** • 52 E Ohio St
- **Delicious** • 308 W Erie St
- **Gino's East of Chicago** • 633 N Wells St
- **Giordano's** • 730 N Rush St
- **Leona's** • 646 N Franklin St
- **Lou Malnati's Pizzeria** • 439 N Wells St
- **Pizzeria Due** • 619 N Wabash Ave
- **Pizzeria Ora** • 545 N La Salle Dr
- **Pizzeria Uno** • 29 E Ohio St
- **Rizzata's Pizzeria** • 300 W Grand Ave
- **Rosati's Pizza and California Style Deli** • 126 W Grand Ave

Post Offices

- **US Post Office** • 222 Merchandise Mart Plz
- **US Post Office** • 540 N Dearborn St

Schools

- **Adler School of Professional Psychology** • 65 E Wacker Pl
- **Argosy University** • 350 N Orleans St
- **Associated Colleges of the Midwest** • 205 W Wacker Dr
- **Chicago School of Professional Psychology** • 325 N Wells St
- **Feltre** • 22 W Erie St
- **Frances Xavier Ward Middle** • 730 N Wabash Ave
- **Illinois Institute of Art** • 350 N Orleans St

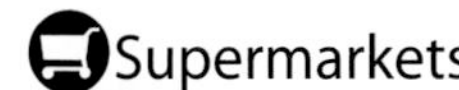

Supermarkets

- **Jewel-Osco** • 550 N State St
- **Whole Foods Market** • 30 W Huron St

Parking

W Delaware Pl
1
2
N Ernst Ct
W Chestnut St
E Chestnut St
W Chestnut St
W Institute Pl
E Pearson St
Moody Bible Institute
Loyola University (Water Tower Campus)
E Tower Ct
N Rush St
31
32
800N
Chicago
W Chicago Ave
Chicago
E Chicago Ave
A
W Superior St
E Superior St
N La Salle St
N State St
700N
W Huron St
E Huron St
NEAR NORTH
N Wells St
W Erie St
E Erie St
N Orleans St
N Franklin St
600N
N Wabash Ave
N Rush St
N Michigan Ave
W Ontario St
E Ontario St
RIVER NORTH
N Clark St
N Dearborn St
W Ohio St
E Ohio St
3
B
Grand
W Grand Ave
300W
200W
100W
1
500N
W Illinois St
W Hubbard St
400N
2
W Kinzie St
Illinois Institute of Art
Merchandise Mart
Merchandise Mart
W Carroll Ave
Merchandise Mart Plz
Chicago River
6
C
W Wacker Dr
E Wacker Pl
N Garvey Ct
N Dearborn St
5
W Haddock Pl
E Haddock Pl
N Garland Ct
W Lake St
State
E Lake St
Clark
Lake
N Wacker
W Couch Pl
E Benton Pl
1/4 mile
.25 km
W Randolph Dr

Dining options abound in River North, many of them catering to either tourists or to business travelers with expense accounts. Of the latter, Fulton's on the River serves up tasty (and pricey) prime steaks and scrumptious oysters. As for nightlife, Lincoln Park and Wicker Park cross paths at The Martini Ranch. Andy's jazz bar is a destination for aging beatniks.

Coffee

- **Cosi** • 55 E Grand Ave
- **Dunkin' Donuts** • 20 E Chicago Ave
- **Dunkin' Donuts** • 404 N Wabash Ave
- **Dunkin' Donuts** • 800 N State St
- **Dunkin' Donuts** • Merchandise Mart Plz
- **Ohio House Coffee Shop** • 600 N La Salle Dr
- **Starbucks** • 35 E Wacker Dr
- **Starbucks** • 414 N Orleans St
- **Starbucks** • 42 E Chicago Ave
- **Starbucks** • 430 N Clark St
- **Starbucks** • 470 Merchandise Mart Plz
- **Starbucks** • Embassy Suites • 600 N State St
- **Starbucks** • 750 N Franklin St

Copy Shops

- **FedEx Kinko's** • 350 N Clark St
- **Fedex Kinko's** • 444 N Wells St ㉔
- **Icon Printing** • 18 W Hubbard St
- **Office Depot** • 352 W Grand Ave
- **The UPS Store** • 40 E Chicago Ave
- **The UPS Store** • 446 N Wells St

Gyms

- **Crunch Fitness** • 350 N State St
- **Crunch Fitness** • 38 E Grand Ave
- **Executive Sports & Fitness Center** • 77 W Wacker Dr
- **Lakeshore Athletic Club** • 441 N Wabash Ave
- **Lawson YMCA** • 30 W Chicago Ave

Hardware Stores

- **Clark & Barlow Hardware** • 353 W Grand Ave
- **Gordon's Ace Hardware & Paint** • 440 N Orleans St
- **Katonah Architectural Hardware** • 222 Merchandise Mart Plz

Liquor Stores

- **Ben'z Liquors** • 15 E Ohio St
- **Binny's Beverage Depot** • 213 W Grand Ave
- **Copperfield's** • 70 W Huron St
- **Dalal Food & Liquor** • 414 N State St
- **Galleria Market** • 340 W Superior St
- **Holiday Wines & Spirits** • 6 W Chicago Ave
- **Marina Food & Liquor** • 300 N State St
- **Plaza Market** • 405 N Wabash Ave
- **Rossi's Liquors** • 412 N State St
- **Superior Liquor** • 750 N Clark St
- **White Hen Pantry** • 645 N State St

Nightlife

- **Andy's** • 11 E Hubbard St
- **Bin 36** • 339 N Dearborn St
- **Blue Chicago** • 736 N Clark St
- **Blue Frog Bar & Grill** • 676 N La Salle Dr
- **Brehon Pub** • 731 N Wells St
- **Excalibur** • 632 N Dearborn St
- **Gentry** • 440 N State St
- **Green Door Tavern** • 678 N Orleans St
- **House of Blues** • 329 N Dearborn St
- **Howl at the Moon** • 26 W Hubbard St
- **Martini Ranch** • 311 W Chicago Ave
- **Minx** • 111 W Hubbard St
- **Mother Hubbard's** • 5 W Hubbard St
- **Narcisse** • 710 N Clark St
- **Pippin's Tavern** • 806 Rush St
- **Pops for Champagne** • 601 N State St
- **Redhead Piano Bar** • 16 W Ontario St
- **Rock Bottom Restaurants & Brewery** • 1 W Grand Ave
- **Spy Bar** • 646 N Franklin St
- **Streeter's Tavern** • 50 E Chicago Ave
- **Vision** • 640 N Dearborn St

Restaurants

- **1492 Tapas Bar** • 42 E Superior St
- **Allen's New American Café** • 217 W Huron St
- **Avenues** • Peninsula Hotel • 108 E Superior St
- **Ballo** • 449 N Dearborn St
- **Ben Pao** • 52 W Illinois St
- **Bijan's Bistro** • 663 N State St
- **Bin 36** • 339 N Dearborn St
- **Brasserie Jo** • 59 W Hubbard St
- **Brett's Kitchen** • 233 W Superior St
- **Café Iberico** • 739 N La Salle Blvd
- **Carson's Ribs** • 612 N Wells St
- **Cerise** • Le Meridien Hotel • 521 N Rush St
- **Chicago Chop House** • 60 W Ontario St
- **Club Lago** • 331 W Superior St
- **Coco Pazzo** • 300 W Hubbard St
- **Crofton on Wells** • 535 N Wells St
- **Cyrano's Bistrot & Wine Bar** • 546 N Wells St
- **David Burke's Primehouse** • 616 N Rush St
- **F212** • 401 N Wells St
- **Fogo De Chao** • 661 N La Salle St
- **Frontera Grill** • 445 N Clark St
- **Fulton's on the River** • 315 N La Salle St
- **Gaylord Fine India Cuisine** • 678 N Clark St
- **Gene & Georgetti** • 500 N Franklin St
- **Gino's** • 633 N Wells St
- **Harry Caray's** • 33 W Kinzie St
- **House of Blues** • 329 N Dearborn St
- **India House** • 59 W Grand Ave
- **Joe's Seafood, Prime Steak & Stone Crab** • 60 E Grand Ave
- **Karyn's Cooked** • 738 N Wells St
- **Keefer's** • 20 W Kinzie St
- **Kevin** • 9 W Hubbard St
- **Kinzie Chophouse** • 400 N Wells St
- **Klay Oven** • 414 N Orleans St
- **L8** • 222 W Ontario St
- **Lawry's The Prime Rib** • 100 E Ontario St
- **Lou Malnati's Pizzeria** • 439 N Wells St
- **Maggiano's Little Italy** • 516 N Clark St
- **Meztiso** • 710 N Wells St
- **Mr Beef** • 666 N Orleans St
- **Nacional 27** • 325 W Huron St
- **Naha** • 500 N Clark St
- **Narcisse** • 710 N Clark St
- **Original Gino's East** • 633 N Wells St
- **Osteria Via Stato** • 620 N State St
- **Oysy** • 50 E Grand Ave
- **Pizzeria Due** • 619 N Wabash Ave
- **Pizzeria Uno** • 29 E Ohio St
- **Quartino** • 626 N State St
- **Redfish** • 400 N State St
- **Rosebud on Rush** • 720 N Rush St
- **Roy's** • 720 N State St
- **Rumba** • 351 W Hubbard St
- **Ruth's Chris Steak House** • 431 N Dearborn St
- **Shanghai Terrace** • Peninsula Hotel • 108 E Superior St
- **Shaw's Crab House & Blue Crab Lounge** • 21 E Hubbard St
- **Smith & Wollensky** • 318 N State St
- **Sorriso** • 321 N Clark St
- **Star of Siam** • 11 E Illinois St
- **Sullivan's Steakhouse** • 415 N Dearborn St
- **Sushi Naniwa** • 607 N Wells St
- **Sushisamba Rio** • 504 N Wells St
- **Tizi Melloul** • 531 N Wells St
- **Topolobampo** • 445 N Clark St
- **Vermillion** • 10 W Hubbard St
- **Vong's Thai Kitchen** • 6 W Hubbard St
- **Weber Grill** • Hilton Garden Inn • 539 N State St
- **Wildfire** • 159 W Erie St

Shopping

- **American Girl Place** • 11 E Chicago Ave
- **Jazz Record Mart** • 27 E Illinois St
- **Mig and Tig Furniture** • 540 N Wells St
- **Montauk** • 401 N Wells St
- **Orange Skin** • 223 W Erie St
- **Paper Source** • 232 W Chicago Ave

Video Rental

- **Blockbuster** • 700 N State St
- **Hubbard's Street Books** • 109 W Hubbard St

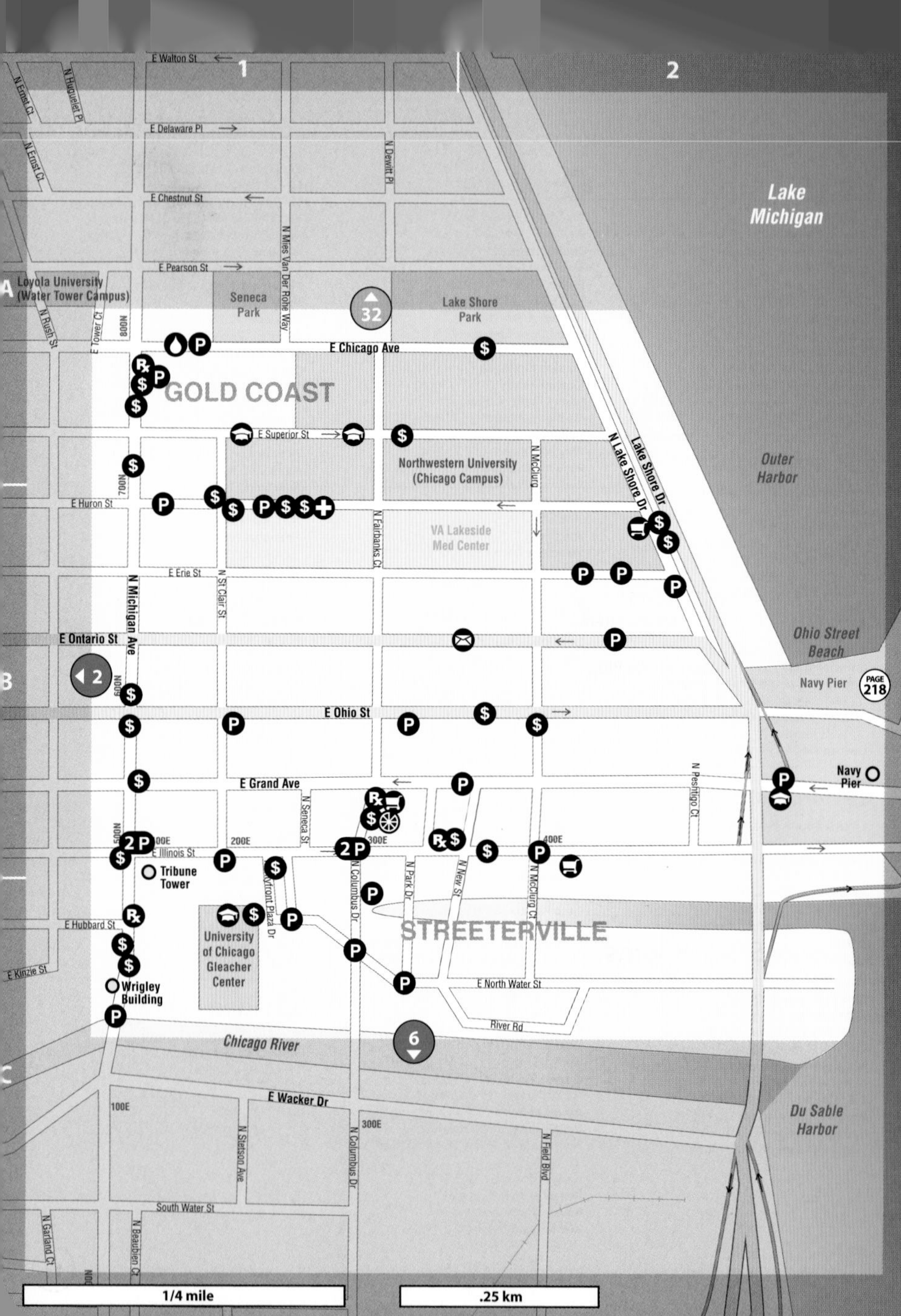
1
2
A
B
C
Lake Michigan
Outer Harbor
Ohio Street Beach
Du Sable Harbor
Chicago River
GOLD COAST
STREETERVILLE
E Walton St
E Delaware Pl
E Chestnut St
E Pearson St
E Chicago Ave
E Superior St
E Huron St
E Erie St
E Ontario St
E Ohio St
E Grand Ave
E Illinois St
E Hubbard St
E Kinzie St
E North Water St
River Rd
E Wacker Dr
South Water St
N Ernst Ct
N Hudson Pl
N Dewitt Pl
N Mies Van Der Rohe Way
N Rush St
N Tower Ct
N Michigan Ave
N St Clair St
N Fairbanks Ct
N McClurg Ct
N Lake Shore Dr
Lake Shore Dr
N Seneca St
N Columbus Dr
N Park Dr
N New St
N Peshtigo Ct
N Stetson Ave
N Field Blvd
N Garland Ct
N Beaubien Ct
Loyola University (Water Tower Campus)
Seneca Park
Lake Shore Park
Northwestern University (Chicago Campus)
VA Lakeside Med Center
Tribune Tower
Wrigley Building
University of Chicago Gleacher Center
Navy Pier
32
2
6
PAGE 218
800N
700N
600N
500N
100E
200E
300E
400E
1/4 mile
.25 km

The tiny, densely populated blocks of Streeterville are home to lots of big stores, lots of big restaurants, and lots of big hotels, as well as the maze that is the Northwestern University Medical campus. Hoity-toity residents of the premier high-rises sip their champagne and laugh at the overwhelmed tourists who look like ants so, so far below.

$ Banks

- **Associated (ATM)** • 401 E Illinois St
- **Banco Popular** • 717 N Michigan Ave
- **Bank of America** • 500 N Michigan Ave
- **Bank of America (ATM)** • 600 N Michigan Ave
- **Chase** • 605 N Michigan Ave
- **Chase (ATM)** • 251 E Huron St
- **Chase (ATM)** • 255 E Grand Ave
- **Chase (ATM)** • 342 E Illinois St
- **Chase (ATM)** • 430 N Michigan Ave
- **Chase (ATM)** • 757 N Michigan Ave
- **Citibank** • 539 N Michigan Ave
- **Harris Trust & Savings** • 352 E Illinois St
- **Harris Trust & Savings (ATM)** • 455 N Cityfront Plz Dr
- **Metropolitan (ATM)** • 680 N Lake Shore Dr
- **North** • 360 E Ohio St
- **Northern Trust** • 201 E Huron St
- **Northern Trust (ATM)** • Northwestern Hospital • 251 E Huron St
- **Northern Trust (ATM)** • Wrigley Bldg • 410 N Michigan Ave
- **US (ATM)** • 200 E Huron St
- **US (ATM)** • 320 E Superior St
- **US (ATM)** • Northwestern University • 357 E Chicago Ave
- **US (ATM)** • 710 N Lake Shore Dr

Car Washes

- **River North Experts** • 161 E Chicago Ave

Emergency Rooms

- **Northwestern Memorial** • 251 E Huron St

Landmarks

- **Tribune Tower** • 435 N Michigan Ave
- **Wrigley Building** • 400 N Michigan Ave

Pharmacies

- **Dominick's** • 255 E Grand Ave
- **Walgreens** • 342 E Illinois St
- **Walgreens** • 430 N Michigan Ave
- **Walgreens** • 757 N Michigan Ave

Pizza

- **Dominick's** • 255 E Grand Ave

Post Offices

- **US Post Office** • 227 E Ontario St

Schools

- **Near the Pier Development Center** • 540 N Lake Shore Dr
- **Northwestern University** • 211 E Superior St
- **University of Chicago Gleacher Center** • 450 N Cityfront Plz Dr

Supermarkets

- **Dominick's** • 255 E Grand Ave
- **Fox & Obel Food Store** • 401 E Illinois St
- **Treasure Island** • 680 N Lake Shore Dr

Parking

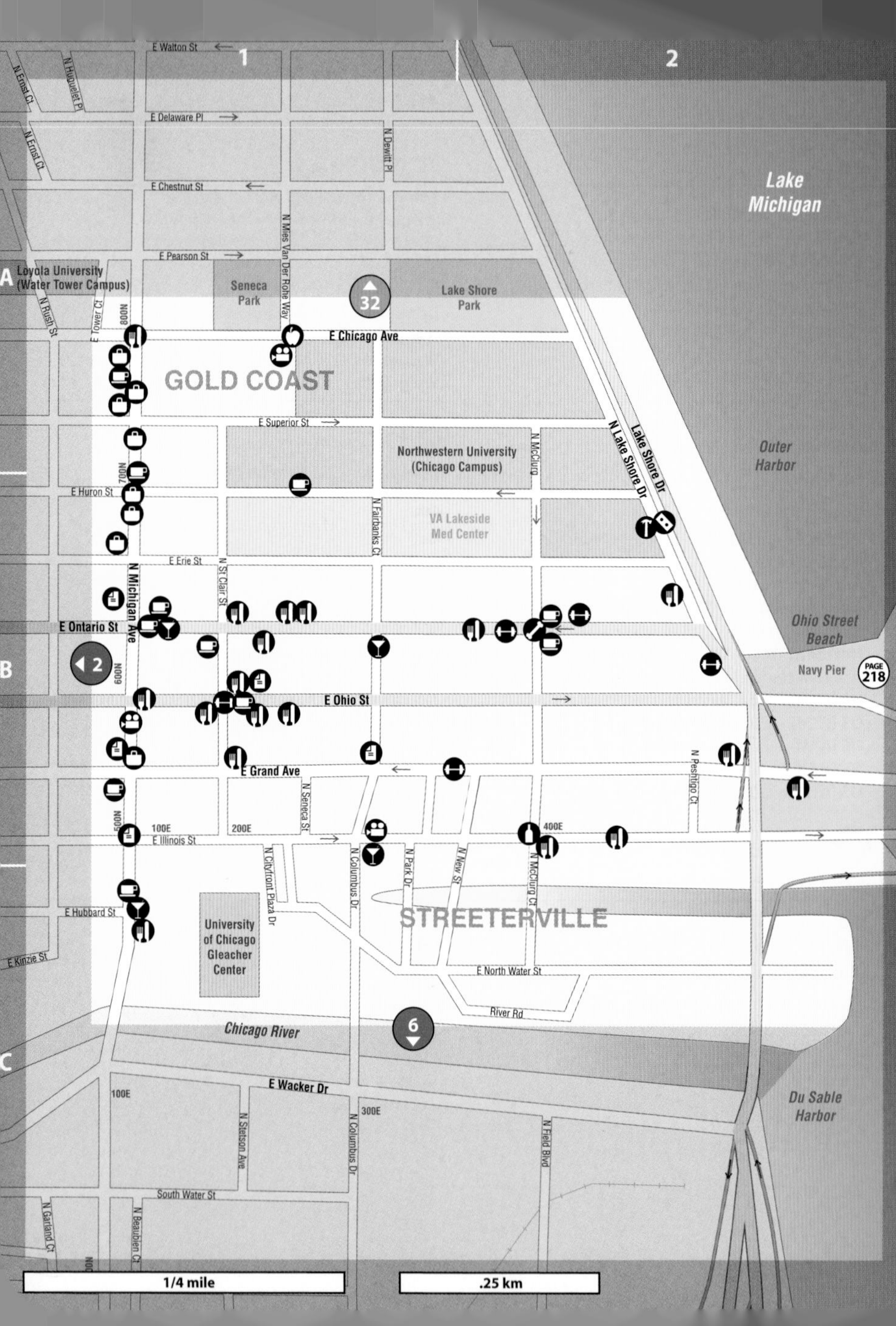

1
2
A
B
C
E Walton St
E Delaware Pl
E Chestnut St
E Pearson St
N Ernst Ct
N Huguelet Pl
N Dewitt Pl
N Mies Van Der Rohe Way
Lake Michigan
Loyola University (Water Tower Campus)
N Rush St
N Tower Ct
Seneca Park
32
Lake Shore Park
E Chicago Ave
GOLD COAST
E Superior St
Northwestern University (Chicago Campus)
N McClurg
Lake Shore Dr
N Lake Shore Dr
Outer Harbor
E Huron St
N Fairbanks Ct
VA Lakeside Med Center
E Erie St
N St Clair St
N Michigan Ave
E Ontario St
Ohio Street Beach
2
Navy Pier
PAGE 218
E Ohio St
E Grand Ave
N Peshtigo Ct
N Seneca St
100E
200E
400E
E Illinois St
N Cityfront Plaza Dr
N Columbus Dr
N Park Dr
N New St
N McClurg Ct
E Hubbard St
STREETERVILLE
University of Chicago Gleacher Center
E Kinzie St
E North Water St
River Rd
Chicago River
6
E Wacker Dr
100E
300E
Du Sable Harbor
N Stetson Ave
N Columbus Dr
N Field Blvd
South Water St
N Garland Ct
N Beaubien Ct
1/4 mile
.25 km

Young swingles pose artfully at the Museum of Contemporary Art's First Friday series, featuring a deejay, free finger food, and a cash bar. And speaking of cash, drop a wad of it dining at the posh French food emporium Les Nomades, or Rick Tramanto and Gale Gand's trendsetting Tru. For slumming, hit the Billy Goat.

Coffee

- **Dunkin' Donuts** • 200 E Ohio St
- **Dunkin' Donuts** • 401 E Ontario St
- **Starbucks** • Chicago Downtown Courtyard • 155 E Ontario St
- **Starbucks** • Northwestern Memorial Hospital • 251 E Huron St
- **Starbucks** • 401 E Ontario St
- **Starbucks** • 444 N Michigan Ave
- **Starbucks** • 670 N Michigan Ave

Copy Shops

- **AlphaGraphics** • 645 N Michigan Ave
- **Fedex Kinko's** • 540 N Michigan Ave
- **Kwik Kopy** • 500 N Michigan Ave
- **Press Type and Copy** • 541 N Fairbanks Ct
- **The UPS Store** • 207 E Ohio St

Farmer's Markets

- **Museum of Contemporary Art/Streeterville (Jun-Oct; Tues, 10am-6pm)** • E Chicago Ave & Mies Van der Rohe Wy

Gyms

- **Curves (women only)** • 200 E Ohio St
- **Holmes Place** • 355 E Grand Ave
- **Lakeshore Athletic Club** • 333 E Ontario St
- **North Pier Athletic Club** • 474 N Lake Shore Dr
- **Onterie Fitness Center** • 446 E Ontario St

Hardware Stores

- **Streeterville Ace Hardware** • 680 N Lake Shore Dr

Liquor Stores

- **Market Place Food** • 393 E Illinois St

Movie Theaters

- **AMC River East** • 322 E Illinois St
- **Loews** • 600 N Michigan Ave
- **Museum of Contemporary Art** • 220 E Chicago Ave

Nightlife

- **Billy Goat Tavern** • 430 N Michigan Ave
- **Dick's Last Resort** • 435 E Illinois St
- **O'Neill's Bar & Grill** • 152 E Ontario St
- **Timothy O'Toole's Pub** • 622 N Fairbanks Ct

Pet Shops

- **Streeterville Pet Spa and Boutique** • 401 E Ontario St

Restaurants

- **Bandera** • 535 N Michigan Ave
- **Benihana of Tokyo** • 166 E Superior St
- **Billy Goat Tavern** • 430 N Michigan Ave
- **Capital Grille** • 633 N St Clair St
- **City** • Lake Point Tower • 505 N Lake Shore Dr, 70th Fl
- **Copperblue** • 505 N Lake Shore Dr
- **Dick's Last Resort** • 435 E Illinois St
- **Emilio's Tapas Sol y Nieve** • 215 E Ohio St
- **Fox & Obel Café** • 401 E Illinois St
- **Heaven on Seven** • 600 N Michigan Ave
- **Hot Diggity Dogs** • 251 E Ohio St
- **Indian Garden** • 247 E Ontario St
- **Kamehachi** • 240 E Ontario St
- **Les Nomades** • 222 E Ontario St
- **Nomi Park Hyatt** • 800 N Michigan Ave
- **Ron of Japan** • 230 E Ontario St
- **Sayat Nova** • 157 E Ohio St
- **Tru** • 676 N St Clair St
- **Volare** • 201 E Grand Ave
- **Wave** • 644 N Lake Shore Dr

Shopping

- **Apple Store** • 679 N Michigan Ave
- **Chicago Place** • 700 N Michigan Ave
- **Disney Store** • 717 N Michigan Ave
- **Garrett Popcorn Shop** • 670 N Michigan Ave
- **Neiman-Marcus** • 737 N Michigan Ave
- **Niketown** • 669 N Michigan Ave
- **Ralph Lauren** • 750 N Michigan Ave
- **Tiffany & Co** • 730 N Michigan Ave
- **Virgin Megastore** • 540 N Michigan Ave

Video Rental

- **Hollywood Video** • 680 N Lake Shore Dr

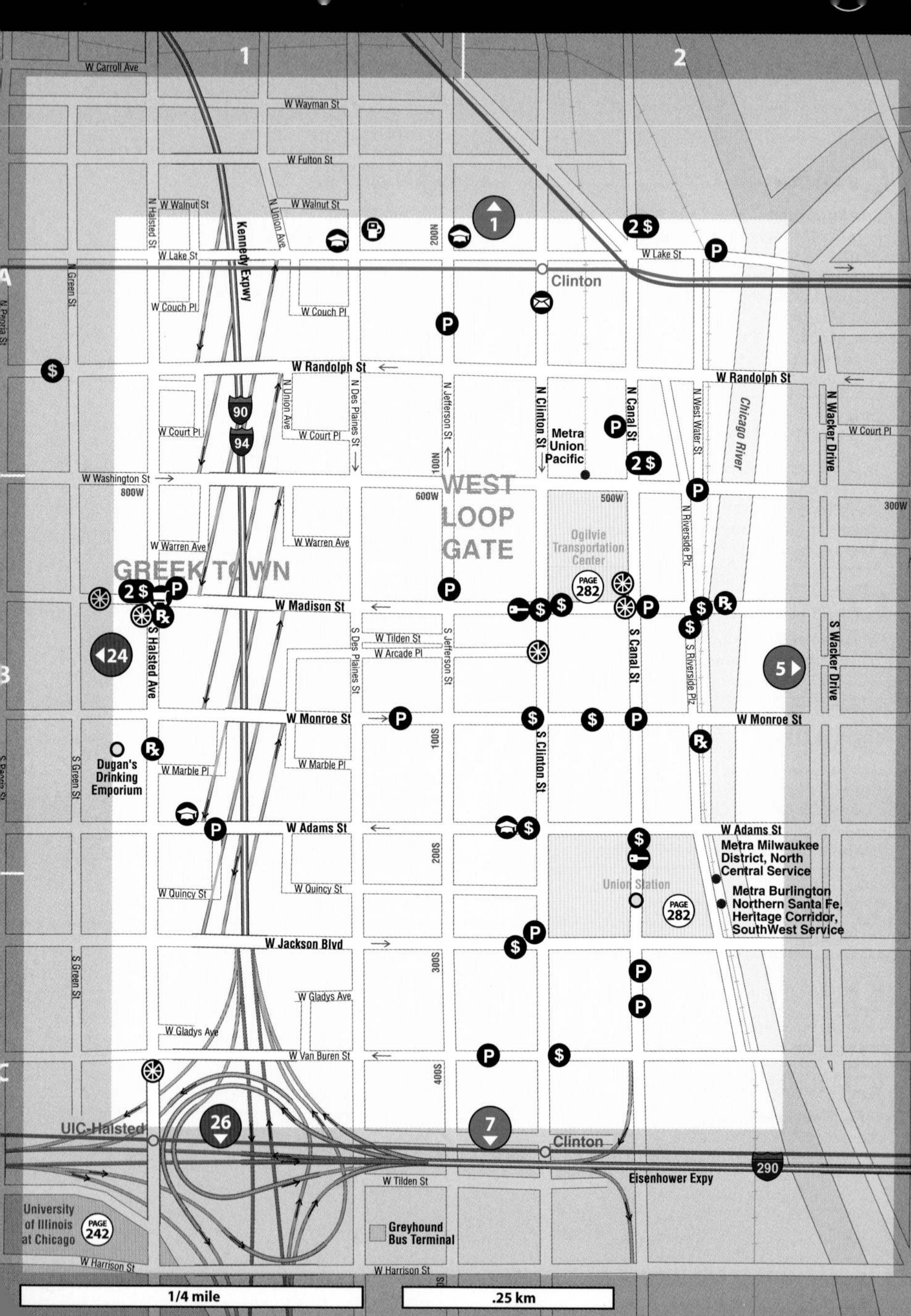

1
2
A
B
C
W Carroll Ave
W Wayman St
W Fulton St
N Halsted St
W Walnut St
N Union Ave
Kennedy Expwy
W Lake St
N Green St
N Peoria St
W Couch Pl
Clinton
W Randolph St
N Des Plaines St
N Jefferson St
N Clinton St
N Canal St
N West Water St
Chicago River
N Wacker Drive
W Court Pl
Metra Union Pacific
W Washington St
800W
600W
500W
300W
100N
200N
WEST LOOP GATE
Ogilvie Transportation Center
N Riverside Plz
W Warren Ave
GREEK TOWN
PAGE 282
W Madison St
S Halsted Ave
W Tilden St
W Arcade Pl
S Des Plaines St
S Jefferson St
S Canal St
S Riverside Plz
S Wacker Drive
24
5
W Monroe St
S Clinton St
S Green St
Dugan's Drinking Emporium
W Marble Pl
100S
200S
300S
400S
W Adams St
Metra Milwaukee District, North Central Service
Union Station
Metra Burlington Northern Santa Fe, Heritage Corridor, SouthWest Service
W Quincy St
W Jackson Blvd
W Gladys Ave
W Van Buren St
UIC-Halsted
26
7
Eisenhower Expy
290
90
94
W Tilden St
University of Illinois at Chicago
PAGE 242
Greyhound Bus Terminal
W Harrison St
1/4 mile
.25 km

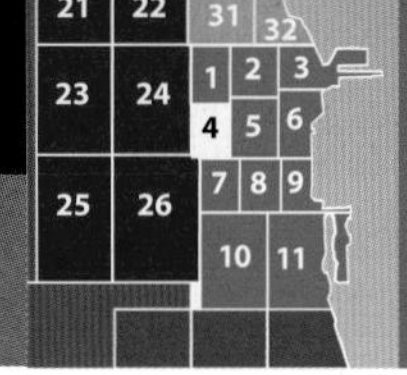

Trains, buses, gyros, and loft spaces define this transitioning 'hood. Proximity to the Loop, the Expressway, Union Station, Ogilvie Transportation Center, and the Greyhound Bus Depot make the area seem just right for hip urban commuters. Nonetheless, many pockets maintain a gritty vibe (particularly around said Greyhound station—isn't that always the case?).

Banks

- **American Chartered** • 932 W Randolph St
- **Bank of America** • 2 N Riverside Plz
- **Bank of America (ATM)** • Amtrack-Union Station • 225 S Canal St
- **Charter One** • 555 W Jackson Blvd
- **Chase** • 1 N Halsted St
- **Chase** • 300 S Riverside Plz
- **Chase (ATM)** • 111 N Canal St
- **Chase (ATM)** • 565 W Adams St
- **Citibank** • 500 W Madison St
- **Corus** • 10 S Riverside Plz
- **Fifth Third (ATM)** • Union Station • 225 S Canal St
- **Harris Trust & Savings (ATM)** • 555 W Madison St
- **La Salle** • 540 W Madison St
- **LaSalle (ATM)** • 130 S Canal St
- **LaSalle (ATM)** • 550 W Van Buren St
- **MB Financial** • 800 W Madison St
- **New Century (ATM)** • Union Station • 225 S Canal St
- **TCF** • 120 S Riverside Plz
- **TCF (ATM)** • 400 W Madison St
- **US (ATM)** • 111 N Canal St
- **Washington Mutual** • 555 W Monroe St

Car Rental

- **Enterprise** • 555 W Madison St • 312-906-8300
- **Hertz** • 210 S Canal St • 312-928-0538

Gas Stations

- **Fulton & Des Plaines** • 225 N Des Plaines St

Landmarks

- **Dugan's Drinking Emporium** • 128 S Halsted St
- **Union Station** • 200 S Canal St

Pharmacies

- **CVS Pharmacy** • 130 S Canal St
- **Dominick's** • 1 N Halsted St
- **Osco Drug** • 400 W Madison St
- **Walgreens** • 111 S Halsted St ㉔

Pizza

- **Bacino's** • 118 S Clinton St
- **Dominick's Finer Foods** • 1 N Halsted St
- **Giordano's** • 815 W Van Buren St
- **Leona's** • 848 W Madison St
- **Pizza Hut** • 500 W Madison St
- **Sbarro** • 500 W Madison St

Post Offices

- **US Post Office** • 168 N Clinton St

Schools

- **Chicago-Kent College of Law** • 565 W Adams St
- **The Frances Xavier Warde** • 700 W Adams St
- **KIPP Ascend Academy Charter** • 650 W Lake St, Ste 310
- **Uhlich Academy** • 217 N Jefferson St

Supermarkets

- **Dominick's** • 1 N Halsted St

Parking

Map 4 • West Loop Gate / Greek Town

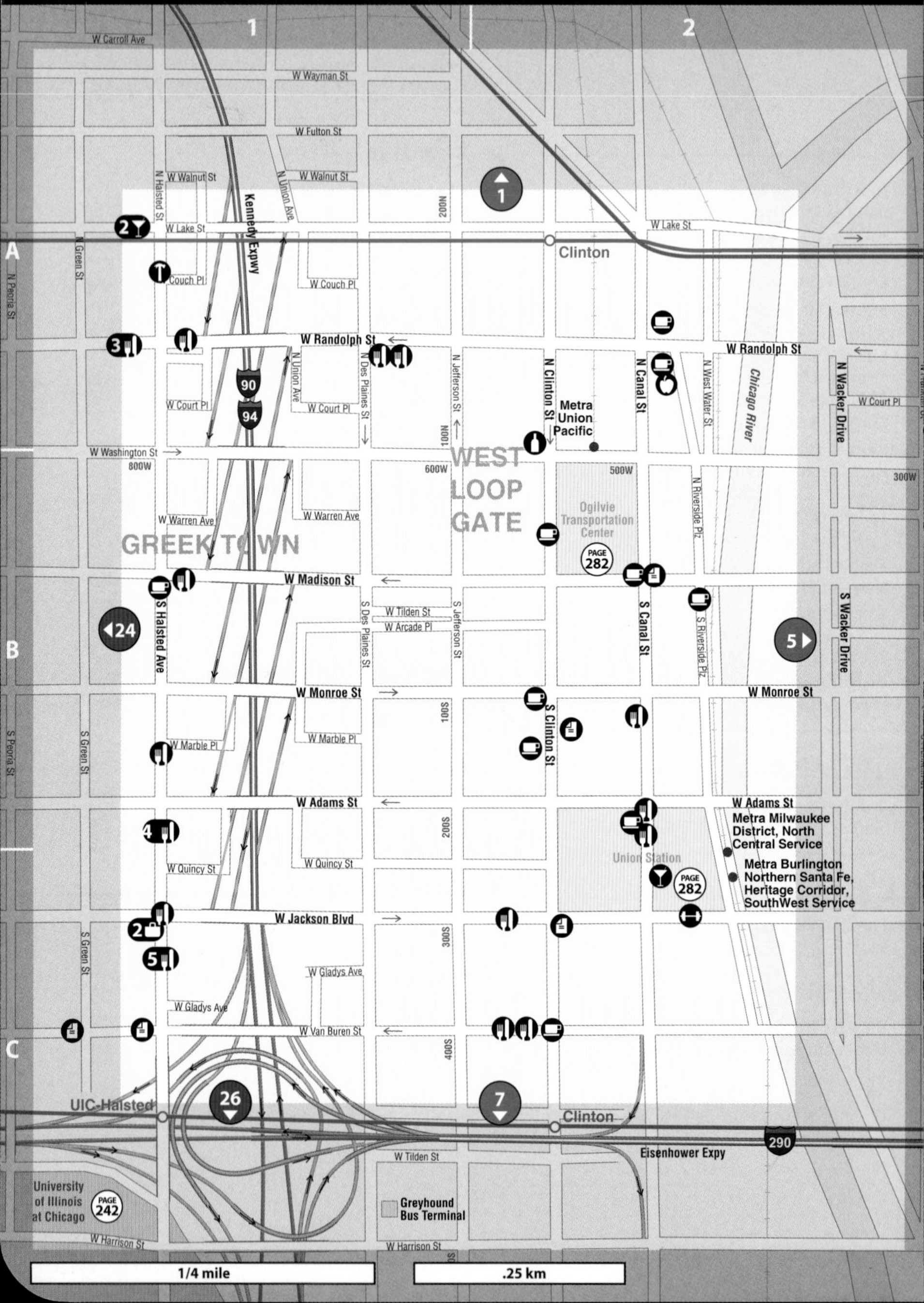

1
2
A
B
C

W Carroll Ave
W Wayman St
W Fulton St
W Walnut St
W Walnut St
N Halsted St
N Union Ave
Kennedy Expwy
200N
W Lake St
W Lake St
N Green St
N Peoria St
Clinton
Couch Pl
W Couch Pl
W Randolph St
W Randolph St
N Union Ave
N Des Plaines St
N Jefferson St
N Clinton St
N Canal St
N West Water St
Chicago River
N Wacker Drive
W Court Pl
W Court Pl
W Court Pl
90
94
100N
Metra Union Pacific
W Washington St
800W
600W
500W
300W
WEST LOOP GATE
N Riverside Plz
Ogilvie Transportation Center
PAGE 282
W Warren Ave
W Warren Ave
GREEK TOWN
W Madison St
S Halsted Ave
W Tilden St
W Arcade Pl
S Des Plaines St
S Jefferson St
S Canal St
S Riverside Plz
S Wacker Drive
24
5
W Monroe St
W Monroe St
S Clinton St
100S
S Peoria St
S Green St
W Marble Pl
W Marble Pl
W Adams St
W Adams St
200S
Metra Milwaukee District, North Central Service
Union Station
Metra Burlington Northern Santa Fe, Heritage Corridor, SouthWest Service
PAGE 282
W Quincy St
W Quincy St
W Jackson Blvd
300S
S Green St
W Gladys Ave
W Gladys Ave
W Van Buren St
400S
UIC-Halsted
26
7
Clinton
290
Eisenhower Expy
W Tilden St
University of Illinois at Chicago
PAGE 242
Greyhound Bus Terminal
W Harrison St
W Harrison St

1/4 mile
.25 km

Randolph Street's funky, contemporary restaurant row kicks off here and continues westward. Meanwhile, back in the old country, shouts of "opaa!" ring out on Halsted Street in Greek Town, especially in the summer, when many of the restaurants offer patio dining. Stop in at the Athenian Candle Co to stock up on "Law Be Gone" room spray and "Lover Come Back" floor wash.

Coffee

- **Bean Addiction** • 555 W Madison St
- **Caribou Coffee** • 500 W Madison St
- **Dunkin' Donuts** • 2 N Riverside Plz
- **Dunkin' Donuts** • 500 W Madison St
- **Krispy Kreme Doughnuts** • 210 S Canal St
- **Starbucks** • Dominick's • 1 N Halsted St
- **Starbucks** • 10 S Riverside Plz
- **Starbucks** • 139 S Clinton St
- **Starbucks** • 40 N Clinton St
- **Starbucks** • 400 W Madison St
- **Starbucks** • 550 W Van Buren St

Copy Shops

- **Comet Press** • 812 W Van Buren St
- **Fedex Kinko's** • 127 S Clinton St ⓩ
- **FedEx Kinko's** • 500 W Madison St
- **Fedex Kinko's** • 843 W Van Buren St
- **Sir Speedy** • 547 W Jackson Blvd

Farmer's Markets

- **Riverside Plaza (Jun–Oct; every other Thurs)** • 2 N Riverside Plz

Gyms

- **Union Station Multiplex** • 444 W Jackson Blvd

Hardware Stores

- **Chicago Wholesale Hardware** • 171 N Halsted St

Liquor Stores

- **Just Grapes (Wine only)** • 560 W Washington Blvd

Nightlife

- **Reserve** • 858 W Lake St
- **Reunion** • 811 W Lake St
- **Snuggery Saloon & Dining Room** • Union Station • 225 S Canal St

Restaurants

- **Artopolis Bakery & Café** • 306 S Halsted St
- **Athena** • 212 S Halsted St
- **Avec** • 615 W Randolph St
- **Blackbird** • 619 W Randolph St
- **Butter** • 130 S Green St
- **Costa's** • 340 S Halsted St
- **Dine** • 733 W Madison St
- **Extra Virgin** • 741 W Randolph St
- **Gold Coast Dogs** • Union Station • 225 S Canal St
- **Greek Islands** • 200 S Halsted St
- **J&C Inn** • 558 W Van Buren St
- **Lou Mitchell's** • 565 W Jackson Blvd
- **Nine** • 440 W Randolph St
- **Nine Muses** • 315 S Halsted St
- **Parthenon** • 314 S Halsted St
- **Pegasus Restaurant and Taverna** • 130 S Halsted St
- **Red Light** • 820 W Randolph St
- **Robinson's No 1 Ribs** • Union Station • 225 S Canal St
- **Rodity's** • 222 S Halsted St
- **Santorini** • 800 W Adams St
- **Starfish** • 804 W Randolph St
- **Sushi Wabi** • 842 W Randolph St

Shopping

- **Athenian Candle Co** • 300 S Halsted St
- **Greek Town Music** • 330 S Halsted St

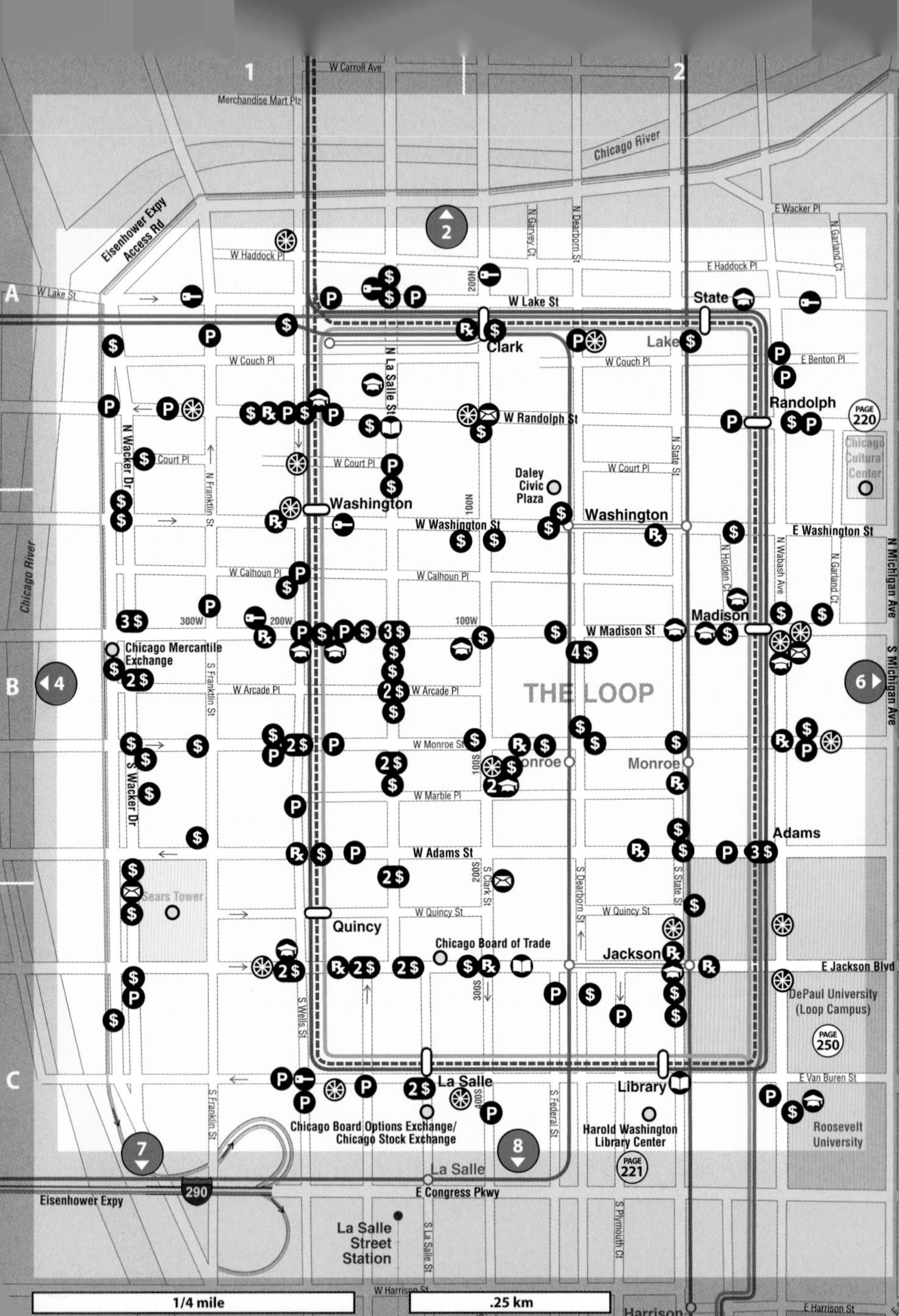

THE LOOP
Chicago River
W Carroll Ave
Merchandise Mart Plz
Eisenhower Expy Access Rd
W Haddock Pl
E Haddock Pl
E Wacker Pl
W Lake St
State
Clark
Lake
W Couch Pl
E Benton Pl
N La Salle St
Randolph
W Randolph St
PAGE 220
Chicago Cultural Center
N Wacker Dr
W Court Pl
N Franklin St
Daley Civic Plaza
N State St
Washington
W Washington St
E Washington St
W Calhoun Pl
N Holden Ct
N Wabash Ave
N Garland Ct
N Michigan Ave
Madison
W Madison St
Chicago Mercantile Exchange
W Arcade Pl
S Franklin St
S Michigan Ave
W Monroe St
Monroe
S Wacker Dr
W Marble Pl
Adams
W Adams St
Sears Tower
S Clark St
S Dearborn St
S State St
W Quincy St
Quincy
Chicago Board of Trade
Jackson
E Jackson Blvd
DePaul University (Loop Campus)
S Wells St
PAGE 250
E Van Buren St
La Salle
Library
S Federal St
Roosevelt University
Chicago Board Options Exchange/ Chicago Stock Exchange
Harold Washington Library Center
PAGE 221
E Congress Pkwy
Eisenhower Expy
290
La Salle Street Station
S La Salle St
S Plymouth Ct
W Harrison St
E Harrison St
Harrison
1/4 mile
.25 km

The Loop derives its moniker from the L tracks that lasso the city's heart. This here is the bustling financial and business district, where banks are plentiful and parking is pricey. The intersection of State and Madison is literally ground zero (0 east, 0 west, 0 north, 0 south) for Chicago's easy-to-follow street numbering grid.

Banks

- **Amalgamated** • 1 W Monroe St
- **Associated** • 200 N La Salle St
- **Banco Popular** • 415 N La Salle St
- **Bank of America** • 105 W Madison St
- **Bank of America** • 205 W Monroe St
- **Bank of America** • 231 S La Salle St
- **Bank of America** • 33 N Dearborn St
- **Bank of America (ATM)** • 110 N Wacker Dr
- **Bank of America (ATM)** • Sears Tower - Food Court • 233 S Wacker Dr
- **Bank of America (ATM)** • 300 S Wacker Dr
- **Bank of America (ATM)** • 302 W Adams St
- **Bank of America (ATM)** • 64 E Madison St
- **Charter One** • 150 S Wacker Dr
- **Charter One** • 2 S State St
- **Charter One** • 400 S La Salle St
- **Charter One** • 71 S Wacker Dr
- **Chase** • 10 S Dearborn St
- **Chase** • 120 S La Salle St
- **Chase** • 30 S Wacker Dr
- **Chase (ATM)** • 1 N La Salle St
- **Chase (ATM)** • 15 W Washington St
- **Chase (ATM)** • 191 N Clark St
- **Chase (ATM)** • 200 W Adams St
- **Chase (ATM)** • 201 W Madison St
- **Chase (ATM)** • 240 W Randolph St
- **Chase (ATM)** • 300 S State St
- **Chase (ATM)** • 425 S Wabash Ave
- **Chase (ATM)** • 60 E Monroe St
- **Chase (ATM)** • 66 W Washington St
- **Chase (ATM)** • 79 W Monroe St
- **Citibank** • 11 S La Salle St
- **Citibank** • 222 W Adams St
- **Citibank** • 69 W Washington St
- **Cole Taylor** • 111 W Washington St
- **Fifth Third** • 1 N Wacker Dr
- **Fifth Third** • 1 S Dearborn St
- **Fifth Third** • 175 W Jackson Blvd
- **Fifth Third** • Sears Tower • 233 S Wacker Dr
- **Fifth Third** • 57 E Randolph St
- **Fifth Third (ATM)** • 101 N Wacker Dr
- **First** • 161 N Clark St
- **First** • 20 N Wacker Dr
- **First American** • 33 W Monroe St
- **First American** • 50 E Adams St
- **Harris Trust & Savings** • 111 W Monroe St
- **Harris Trust & Savings** • 141 W Jackson Blvd
- **Harris Trust & Savings** • 99 W Washington St
- **Harris Trust & Savings (ATM)** • 115 S La Salle St
- **Harris Trust & Savings (ATM)** • 311 W Monroe St
- **Lakeside** • 141 W Jackson Blvd
- **LaSalle** • 100 S Wacker Dr
- **LaSalle** • 120 N La Salle St
- **LaSalle** • 135 S La Salle St
- **LaSalle** • 191 N Wacker Dr
- **LaSalle** • 201 S State St
- **LaSalle** • 203 N La Salle St
- **LaSalle** • 77 S Dearborn St
- **LaSalle (ATM)** • 175 W Jackson Blvd
- **LaSalle (ATM)** • 226 W Jackson Blvd
- **MB Financial** • 1 S Wacker Dr
- **MB Financial** • 2 S La Salle St
- **MB Financial (ATM)** • 177 N State St
- **MB Financial (ATM)** • 223 W Jackson Blvd
- **Northern Trust** • 50 S La Salle St
- **Northern Trust (ATM)** • 10 S La Salle St
- **Northern Trust (ATM)** • Deloitte Bldg • 111 S Wacker Dr
- **Northern Trust (ATM)** • 181 W Madison St
- **Shore** • 333 S State St
- **TCF** • 29 E Madison St
- **TCF (ATM)** • Osco • 111 W Jackson Blvd
- **TCF (ATM)** • 7-Eleven • 125 S Clark St
- **TCF (ATM)** • Osco • 137 S State St
- **TCF (ATM)** • 7-Eleven • 180 N Franklin St
- **TCF (ATM)** • 7-Eleven • 33 E Adams St
- **TCF (ATM)** • 7-Eleven • 343 S Dearborn St
- **TCF (ATM)** • 7-Eleven • 48 N Wells St
- **US** • 209 S La Salle St
- **US** • 25 E Washington St
- **US (ATM)** • 333 S Wabash Ave
- **Washington Mutual** • 200 W Randolph St
- **Washington Mutual** • 230 W Monroe St
- **Washington Mutual** • 247 S State St
- **Washington Mutual** • 311 S Wacker Dr
- **Washington Mutual** • 41 N Wabash Ave
- **Washington Mutual** • 70 W Madison St

Car Rental

- **Avis** • 214 N Clark St • 312-782-6825
- **Budget** • 65 E Lake St • 312-960-3100
- **Enterprise** • 201 W Madison St • 312-553-5230
- **Enterprise** • 303 W Lake St • 312-332-7783
- **Enterprise** • 425 S Wells St • 312-939-6001
- **Hertz** • 181 W Washington Blvd • 312-726-1476
- **National/Alamo** • 203 N La Salle St • 312-236-2581

Landmarks

- **Chicago Board of Trade** • 141 W Jackson Blvd
- **Chicago Board Options Exchange** • 400 S La Salle St
- **Chicago Cultural Center** • 78 E Washington St
- **Chicago Mercantile Exchange** • 20 S Wacker Dr
- **Chicago Stock Exchange** • 440 S La Salle St
- **Daley Civic Plaza** • 50 W Washington St
- **Harold Washington Library Center** • 400 S State St
- **Sears Tower** • 233 S Wacker Dr

Libraries

- **Harold Washington Public Library (Chicago Public Library Central Branch)** • 400 S State St
- **US Library** • 77 W Jackson Blvd

Pharmacies

- **CVS Pharmacy** • 105 S Wabash Ave
- **CVS Pharmacy** • 175 W Jackson Blvd
- **CVS Pharmacy** • 208 W Washington Blvd
- **Osco Drug** • 111 W Jackson Blvd
- **Osco Drug** • 137 S State St
- **Walgreens** • 15 W Washington St
- **Walgreens** • 16 W Adams St
- **Walgreens** • 191 N Clark St
- **Walgreens** • 200 W Adams St
- **Walgreens** • 201 W Madison St
- **Walgreens** • 240 W Randolph St
- **Walgreens** • 300 S State St
- **Walgreens** • 79 W Monroe St

Pizza

- **Bacci Pizzeria** • 120 N Wells St
- **Bonivino Restaurant** • 111 W Van Buren St
- **Exchequer Pub** • 226 S Wabash Ave
- **Giordano's** • 223 W Jackson Blvd
- **Giordano's** • 310 W Randolph St
- **Italian Village** • 71 W Monroe St
- **Jimmy John's-Washington** • 216 W Washington St
- **Mama Falco** • 125 S Clark St
- **Mama Falco's** • 5 N Wells St
- **Pizano's Pizza & Pasta** • 61 E Madison St
- **Pizza Broker** • 400 S Financial Pl
- **Ricobenes** • 222 N Wells St
- **Sbarro** • 100 W Randolph St
- **Sbarro** • 195 N Dearborn St
- **Sbarro** • 333 S State St

Post Offices

- **US Post Office** • 100 W Randolph St
- **US Post Office** • 211 S Clark St
- **US Post Office** • Sears Tower • 233 S Wacker Dr
- **US Post Office** • 5 S Wabash Ave

Schools

- **Alternative Safe Schools** • 125 S Clark St
- **Career Colleges of Chicago** • 11 E Adams St
- **Chicago City Colleges** • 226 W Jackson Blvd
- **Cosmopolitan Preparatory** • 188 W Randolph St
- **DePaul University** • 1 E Jackson Blvd
- **Harold Washington College** • 30 E Lake St
- **Harrington College of Design** • 200 W Madison St
- **International Academy of Design and Technology** • 1 N State St
- **John Marshall Law** • 315 S Plymouth Ct
- **Keller Graduate School of Management** • 225 W Washington St
- **LINC Alternative High** • 125 S Clark St
- **MacCormac College** • 29 E Madison St
- **Robert Morris College** • 401 S State St
- **School of the Art Institute** • 37 S Wabash Ave
- **State of IL Child Development** • 160 N La Salle St

Parking

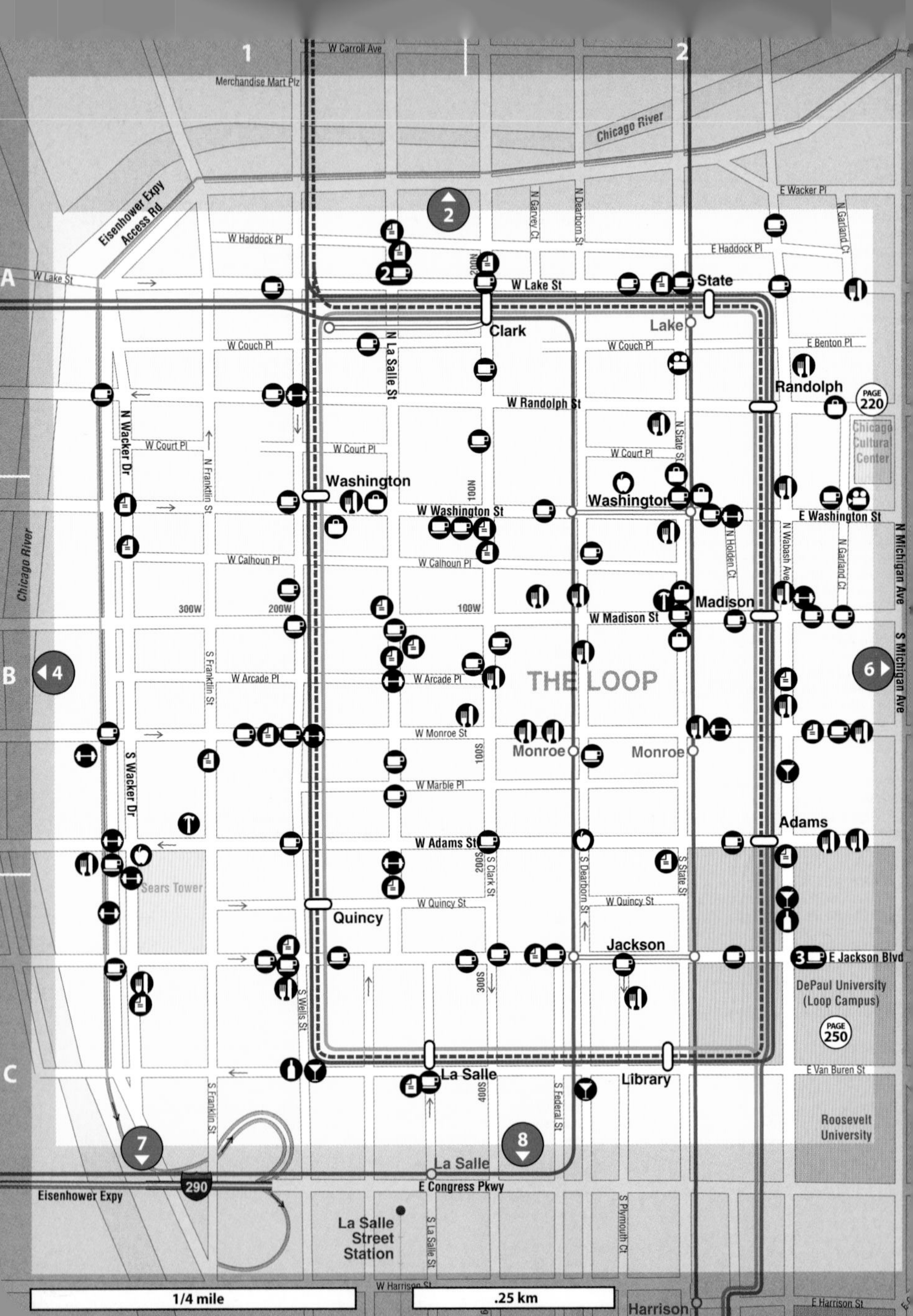
1
2
A
B
C
W Carroll Ave
Merchandise Mart Plz
Chicago River
E Wacker Pl
Eisenhower Expy Access Rd
W Haddock Pl
E Haddock Pl
N Garvey Ct
N Dearborn St
N Garland Ct
W Lake St
W Lake St
State
Lake
Clark
N La Salle St
W Couch Pl
W Couch Pl
E Benton Pl
Randolph
PAGE 220
W Randolph St
N Wacker Dr
N Franklin St
W Court Pl
W Court Pl
W Court Pl
N State St
Chicago Cultural Center
Washington
Washington
W Washington St
E Washington St
W Calhoun Pl
W Calhoun Pl
N Holden Ct
N Wabash Ave
N Garland Ct
N Michigan Ave
Chicago River
300W
200W
100W
Madison
W Madison St
S Michigan Ave
4
6
W Arcade Pl
W Arcade Pl
S Franklin St
THE LOOP
W Monroe St
Monroe
Monroe
S Wacker Dr
W Marble Pl
Adams
W Adams St
Sears Tower
S Clark St
S Dearborn St
S State St
W Quincy St
W Quincy St
Quincy
Jackson
E Jackson Blvd
S Wells St
DePaul University (Loop Campus)
PAGE 250
La Salle
Library
E Van Buren St
S Franklin St
S Federal St
Roosevelt University
7
8
La Salle
290
Eisenhower Expy
E Congress Pkwy
S Plymouth Ct
La Salle Street Station
S La Salle St
W Harrison St
E Harrison St
Harrison
1/4 mile
.25 km

Sundries/ Entertainment

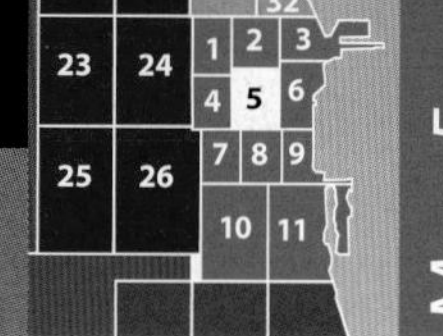

Marshall Fields, oh Marshall Fields…the State Street institution is now owned by Macy's and time will tell what changes are in store. Meanwhile, a revitalized theater district has kicked new energy in the Loop's after-hours scene. The three-restaurant Italian Village complex remains a popular spot for pre-and post-theatrics nosh.

Coffee

- **Capra's Café** • 46 S Clark St
- **Caribou Coffee** • 10 S La Salle St
- **Caribou Coffee** • 55 W Monroe St
- **The Coffee Grounds** • 203 N Wabash Ave
- **Cosi** • 203 N La Salle St
- **Cosi** • 230 W Monroe St
- **Cosi** • 230 W Washington St
- **Cosi** • 28 E Jackson Blvd
- **Cosi** • 33 N Dearborn St
- **Dunkin' Donuts** • 100 W Randolph St
- **Dunkin' Donuts** • 201 N Clark St
- **Dunkin' Donuts** • 201 N State St
- **Dunkin' Donuts** • 201 W Madison St
- **Dunkin' Donuts** • 203 N La Salle St
- **Dunkin' Donuts** • 205 Randolph St
- **Dunkin' Donuts** • 215 W Lake St
- **Dunkin' Donuts** • 229 W Jackson Blvd
- **Dunkin' Donuts** • 31 E Adams St
- **Dunkin' Donuts** • 39 W Jackson Blvd
- **Dunkin' Donuts** • 6 N Wabash Ave
- **Dunkin' Donuts** • 62 E Jackson Blvd
- **Dunkin' Donuts** • 75 E Washington St
- **Dunkin' Donuts** • 77 W Jackson Blvd
- **Intelligentsia Coffee & Tea** • 53 W Jackson Blvd
- **Java Java** • 2 N State St
- **Lavazza** • 111 W Jackson Blvd
- **Lavazza** • 134 N La Salle St
- **Lavazza** • 27 W Washington St
- **Liberty Coffee and Tea** • 401 S La Salle St
- **Starbucks** • 100 S Wacker Dr
- **Starbucks** • 105 W Adams St
- **Starbucks** • Marshall Fields • 111 N State St
- **Starbucks** • 111 W Washington St
- **Starbucks** • 131 S Dearborn St
- **Starbucks** • 150 N Wacker Dr
- **Starbucks** • CT&T Bldg• 161 N Clark St
- **Starbucks** • 175 W Jackson Blvd
- **Starbucks** • 180 N La Salle St
- **Starbucks** • 200 W Adams St
- **Starbucks** • 209 W Jackson Blvd
- **Starbucks** • 21 S Clark St
- **Starbucks** • AT&T Bldg • 227 W Monroe St
- **Starbucks** • Bank of America Bldg• 231 S La Salle St
- **Starbucks** • Sears Tower • 233 S Wacker Dr
- **Starbucks** • 25 E Washington Blvd
- **Starbucks** • 303 W Madison St
- **Starbucks** • 311 S Wacker Dr
- **Starbucks** • 40 W Lake St
- **Starbucks** • 55 E Jackson Blvd
- **Starbucks** • 66 W Washington St
- **Starbucks** • 68 E Madison St
- **Starbucks** • 70 W Madison St
- **Washington & Wells** • 220 W Washington St

Copy Shops

- **24 Seven Copies** • 222 N La Salle St ㉔
- **Acme Copy** • 218 S Wabash Ave
- **Advance Instant Printing** • 5 S Wabash Ave
- **AlphaGraphics** • 208 S La Salle St
- **Fastrac Printing** • 220 S State St
- **Fedex Kinko's** • 101 N Wacker Dr
- **FedEx Kinko's** • 111 W Washington St
- **FedEx Kinko's** • 2 N La Salle St
- **FedEx Kinko's** • 200 W Jackson Blvd
- **FedEx Kinko's** • 203 N La Salle St
- **Fedex Kinko's** • 227 W Monroe St
- **Fedex Kinko's** • 29 S La Salle St ㉔
- **FedEx Kinko's** • 400 S La Salle St
- **Fedex Kinko's** • 55 E Monroe St
- **Fedex Kinko's** • 6 W Lake St
- **Instant Printing** • 200 S Clark St
- **Kwik Kopy** • 11 S La Salle St
- **Sir Speedy** • 311 S Wacker Dr
- **The UPS Store** • 122 S Franklin St
- **The UPS Store** • 27 N Wacker Dr
- **Viking Printing & Copying** • 53 W Jackson Blvd

Farmer's Markets

- **Daley Plaza (May–Sep; Thurs 7 am–3 pm)** • W Washington St & S Dearborn St, N of W Washington St
- **Federal Plaza (May–Oct; Tues, 7 am–3 pm)** • Adams St & Dearborn St
- **The Park at Jackson & Wacker (May–Oct; Thurs, 7 am–3 pm)** • 311 S Wacker Dr at Sears Tower

Gyms

- **Bally Total Fitness** • 230 W Monroe St
- **Bally Total Fitness** • 25 E Washington St
- **Curves (women only)** • 39 S La Salle St
- **Equinox** • 200 W Monroe St
- **Executive Fitness Center** • Palmer House Hilton • 17 E Monroe St
- **Fitness Image Incorporated** • 9 N Wabash Ave, 4th Fl
- **Metropolitan Fitness Club** • Sears Tower • 233 S Wacker Dr
- **Randolph Athletic Club** • 188 W Randolph St
- **River Park Athletic Club** • 200 S Wacker Dr
- **Women's Workout World (Women only)** • 208 S La Salle St
- **World Gym Fitness Center** • 150 S Wacker Dr

Hardware Stores

- **Ace Hardware** • 312 W Adams St
- **Sears** • 2 N State St

Liquor Stores

- **Cal's Liquor Store** • 400 S Wells St
- **Wabash Food & Liquor** • 234 S Wabash Ave

Movie Theaters

- **Chicago Cultural Center** • 78 E Washington St
- **Gene Siskel Film Center** • 164 N State St

Nightlife

- **Cal's** • 400 S Wells St
- **Exchequer Pub** • 226 S Wabash Ave
- **Manhattans** • 415 S Dearborn St
- **Miller's Pub** • 134 S Wabash Ave

Restaurants

- **Atwood Café** • 1 W Washington St
- **Barro Cantina** • 73 E Lake St
- **Billy Goat Tavern** • 330 S Wells St
- **Everest** • 440 S La Salle St
- **Gold Coast Dogs** • 159 N Wabash Ave
- **Gold Coast Dogs** • 17 S Wabash Ave
- **Hannah's Bretzel** • 180 W Washington St
- **Heaven on Seven** • 111 N Wabash Ave
- **Italian Village** • 71 W Monroe St
- **Kamehachi** • 311 S Wacker Dr
- **La Cantina Enoteca** • Italian Village Restaurant Complex • 71 W Monroe St
- **La Rosetta** • 70 W Madison St
- **Miller's Pub** • 134 S Wabash Ave
- **Mrs Levy's Delicatessen** • Sears Tower • 233 S Wacker Dr
- **Nick's Fishmarket & Grill** • 51 S Clark St
- **Oasis Café** • 21 N Wabash Ave
- **Plymouth Restaurant** • 327 S Plymouth Ct ㉔
- **Rhapsody** • Symphony Ctr • 65 E Adams St
- **Russian Tea Time** • 77 E Adams St
- **Spa Café** • 112 W Monroe St
- **Trattoria No 10** • 10 N Dearborn St
- **The Village** • Italian Village Restaurant Complex • 71 W Monroe St
- **Vivere** • 71 W Monroe St

Shopping

- **American Music World** • 111 N State St
- **Carson Pirie Scott** • 1 S State St
- **Gallery 37 Store** • 66 E Randolph St
- **Kramer's Health Food Center** • 230 S Wabash Ave
- **Marshall Field's** • 111 N State St
- **Rock Records** • 175 W Washington St
- **Sears** • 2 N State St

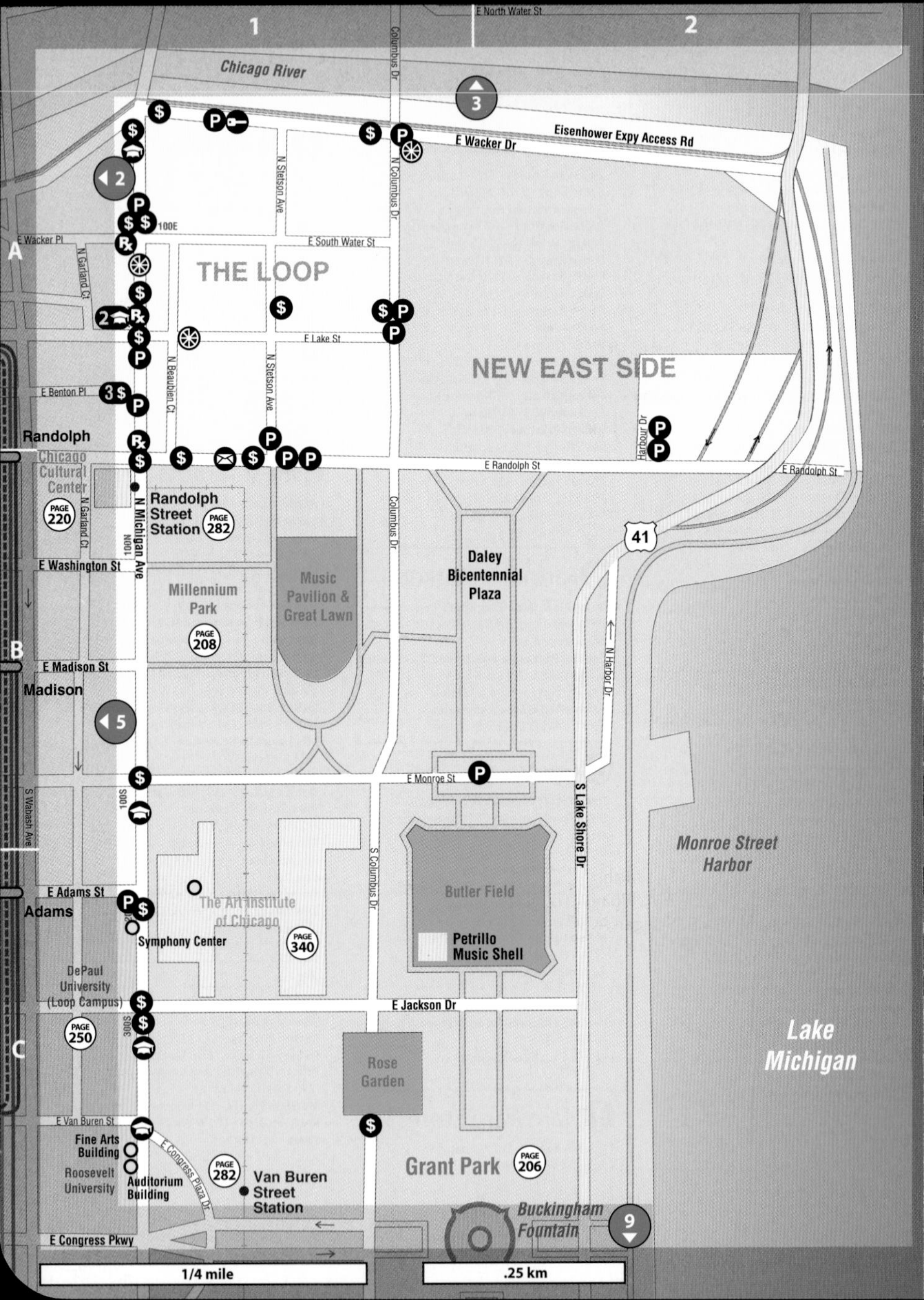

Map 6 • The Loop / Grant Park

1
2
A
B
C
E North Water St
Chicago River
Eisenhower Expy Access Rd
E Wacker Dr
E Wacker Pl
N Stetson Ave
N Columbus Dr
100E
E South Water St
N Garland Ct
THE LOOP
E Lake St
NEW EAST SIDE
E Benton Pl
N Beaubien Ct
Harbour Dr
Randolph
E Randolph St
Chicago Cultural Center
PAGE 220
Randolph Street Station
PAGE 282
N Michigan Ave
100N
41
Daley Bicentennial Plaza
E Washington St
Millennium Park
PAGE 208
Music Pavilion & Great Lawn
N Harbor Dr
E Madison St
Madison
E Monroe St
S Wabash Ave
100S
S Lake Shore Dr
S Columbus Dr
Monroe Street Harbor
E Adams St
Adams
The Art Institute of Chicago
Symphony Center
PAGE 340
Butler Field
Petrillo Music Shell
DePaul University (Loop Campus)
E Jackson Dr
PAGE 250
300S
Rose Garden
Lake Michigan
E Van Buren St
Fine Arts Building
Roosevelt University
Auditorium Building
E Congress Plaza Dr
PAGE 282
Van Buren Street Station
Grant Park
PAGE 206
Buckingham Fountain
E Congress Pkwy
1/4 mile
.25 km

High and low culture cross paths in Grant Park, where the famed Art Institute and Millennium Park's spectacular Gehry-designed bandshell compete with giant turkey legs and food-on-a-stick at summer festivals like Taste of Chicago and the Chicago Blues Festival. Architecture lovers should take a peek inside the landmark Fine Arts building and its spectacular neighbor, the Auditorium Theater.

Banks

- **Associated** • 130 E Randolph St
- **Associated** • 200 E Randolph St
- **Associated** • 225 N Michigan Ave
- **Chase (ATM)** • 300 N Michigan Ave
- **Chase (ATM)** • 307 N Michigan Ave
- **Citibank** • 100 S Michigan Ave
- **Citibank** • 233 N Michigan Ave
- **Citibank (ATM)** • 222 N Columbus Dr
- **MB Financial** • 303 E Wacker Dr
- **Midwest Bank & Trust Company** • 300 S Michigan Ave
- **Midwest Bank & Trust Company (ATM)** • 332 S Michigan Ave
- **New Century (ATM)** • 211 N Stetson Ave
- **North Community** • 180 N Michigan Ave
- **TCF (ATM)** • 150 N Michigan Ave
- **TCF (ATM)** • 174 N Michigan Ave
- **TCF (ATM)** • 224 S Michigan Ave
- **TCF (ATM)** • 500 S Columbus Dr
- **US** • 360 N Michigan Ave
- **US (ATM)** • 111 E Wacker Dr
- **Washington Mutual** • 206 N Michigan Ave

Car Rental

- **Enterprise** • 151 E Wacker Dr • 312-565-6518

Landmarks

- **Art Institute of Chicago** • 111 S Michigan Ave
- **Auditorium Building** • 430 S Michigan Ave
- **Fine Arts Building** • 410 S Michigan Ave
- **Symphony Center** • 220 S Michigan Ave

Pharmacies

- **CVS Pharmacy** • 205 N Michigan Ave
- **Osco Drug** • 150 N Michigan Ave
- **Walgreens** • 300 N Michigan Ave

Pizza

- **Giordano's** • 135 E Lake St
- **Mama Falco** • 303 E Wacker Dr
- **Sbarro** • 233 N Michigan Ave

Post Offices

- **US Post Office** • 200 E Randolph St

Schools

- **American Academy of Art** • 332 S Michigan Ave
- **Career Works Alternative** • 200 N Michigan Ave
- **Institute for Clinical Social Work** • 200 N Michigan Ave
- **Loop Lab** • 300 N Michigan Ave, Ste 300
- **National-Louis University** • 122 S Michigan Ave
- **Roosevelt University** • 430 S Michigan Ave

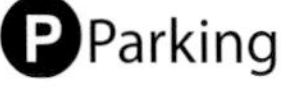

Parking

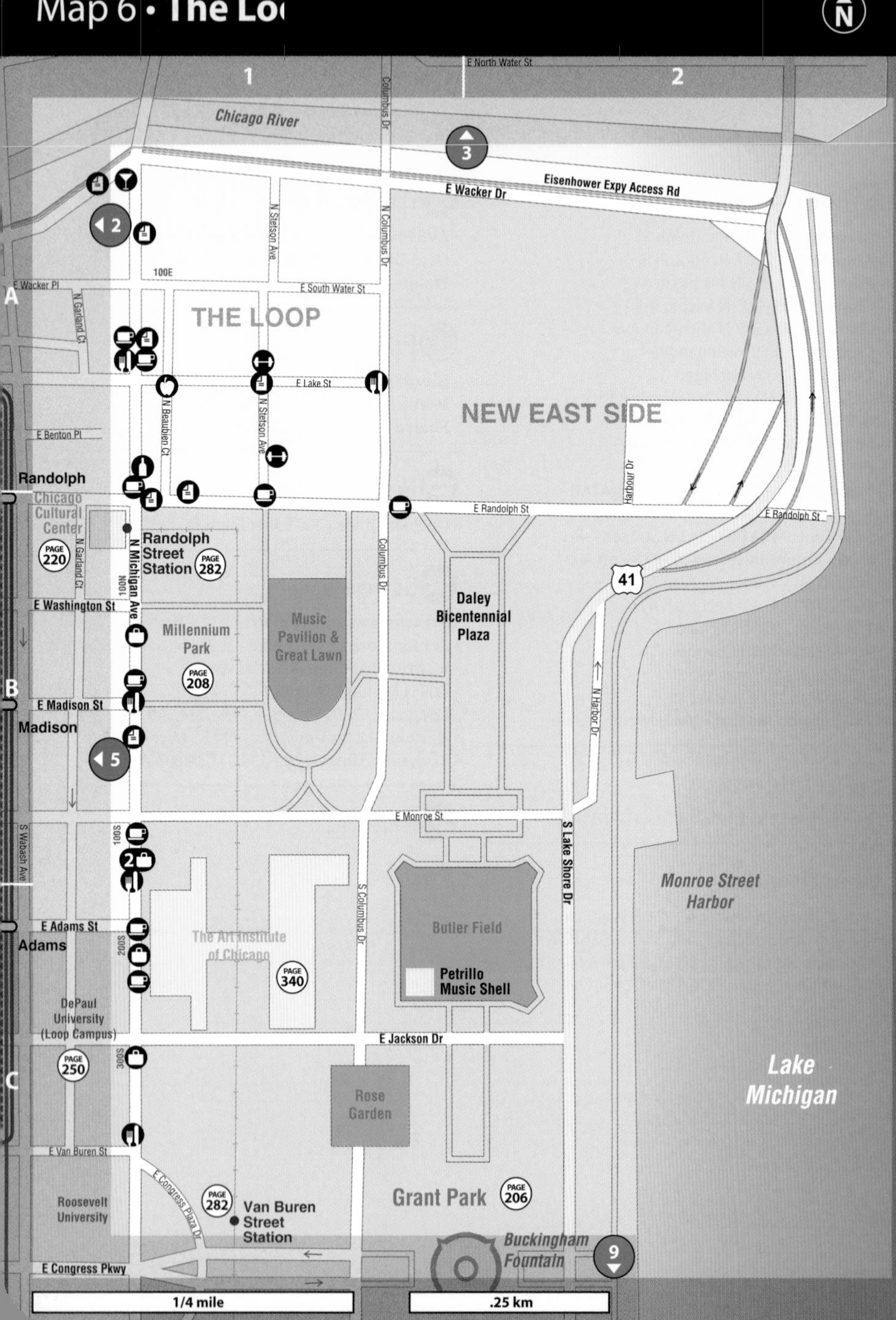
1
2
A
B
C
E North Water St
Columbus Dr
Chicago River
3
Eisenhower Expy Access Rd
E Wacker Dr
2
N Stetson Ave
N Columbus Dr
100E
E Wacker Pl
E South Water St
N Garland Ct
THE LOOP
E Lake St
NEW EAST SIDE
N Beaubien Ct
N Stetson Ave
E Benton Pl
Harbour Dr
Randolph
Chicago Cultural Center
E Randolph St
E Randolph St
N Garland Ct
Randolph Street Station
PAGE 220
PAGE 282
Columbus Dr
100N
N Michigan Ave
41
E Washington St
Daley Bicentennial Plaza
Millennium Park
Music Pavilion & Great Lawn
PAGE 208
N Harbor Dr
E Madison St
Madison
5
E Monroe St
S Wabash Ave
100S
S Columbus Dr
S Lake Shore Dr
Monroe Street Harbor
E Adams St
Adams
200S
The Art Institute of Chicago
Butler Field
PAGE 340
Petrillo Music Shell
DePaul University (Loop Campus)
E Jackson Dr
300S
PAGE 250
Rose Garden
Lake Michigan
E Van Buren St
E Congress Plaza Dr
Roosevelt University
PAGE 282
Van Buren Street Station
Grant Park
PAGE 206
Buckingham Fountain
9
E Congress Pkwy
1/4 mile
.25 km

It can be hard to get a table at Millennium Park's Park Grill when the weather is nice. Meanwhile, across the street, the Michigan Avenue Bennigan's is the world's busiest. The Chicago Symphony Orchestra's once-a-month Afterwork Masterwork program allows Loop workers to enjoy some of the world's greatest classical music at the commute-friendly time of 6:30 p.m.

Coffee

- **Caribou Coffee** • 20 N Michigan Ave
- **The Coffee Beanery** • 150 N Michigan Ave
- **Cosi** • 116 S Michigan Ave
- **Cosi** • 233 N Michigan Ave
- **Dunkin' Donuts** • 233 N Michigan Ave
- **Dunkin' Donuts** • 300 E Randolph St
- **Starbucks** • Amoco Bldg • 200 E Randolph St
- **Starbucks** • 202 N Michigan Ave
- **Starbucks** • Illinois Ctr • 225 N Michigan Ave

Copy Shops

- **AlphaGraphics** • 180 N Stetson Ave
- **Fedex Kinko's** • 111 E Wacker Dr
- **FedEx Kinko's** • 130 E Randolph St
- **FedEx Kinko's** • 225 N Michigan Ave
- **FedEx Kinko's** • 34 S Michigan Ave
- **Sir Speedy** • 130 E Randolph St
- **Swift Impressions** • 333 N Michigan Ave

Farmer's Markets

- **Prudential Plaza (Jun–Oct; Thurs, 7 am–3 pm)** • E Lake St & N Beaubien Ct

Gyms

- **Curves (women only)** • 180 N Stetson Ave
- **Lakeshore Athletic Club** • 211 N Stetson Ave

Liquor Stores

- **Gourmet Pantry** • 155 N Michigan Ave

Nightlife

- **Houlihan's** • 111 E Wacker Dr

Restaurants

- **Aria** • Fairmont Chicago Hotel • 200 N Columbus Dr
- **Artist's Café** • 412 S Michigan Ave
- **Bennigan's** • 150 S Michigan Ave
- **China Grill** • Hard Rock Hotel • 230 N Michigan Ave
- **Park Grill** • 11 N Michigan Ave

Shopping

- **Art & Artisans** • 108 S Michigan Ave
- **Museum Shop of the Art Institute** • 111 S Michigan Ave
- **Poster Plus** • 200 S Michigan Ave
- **Precious Possessions** • 28 N Michigan Ave
- **The Savvy Traveller** • 310 S Michigan Ave

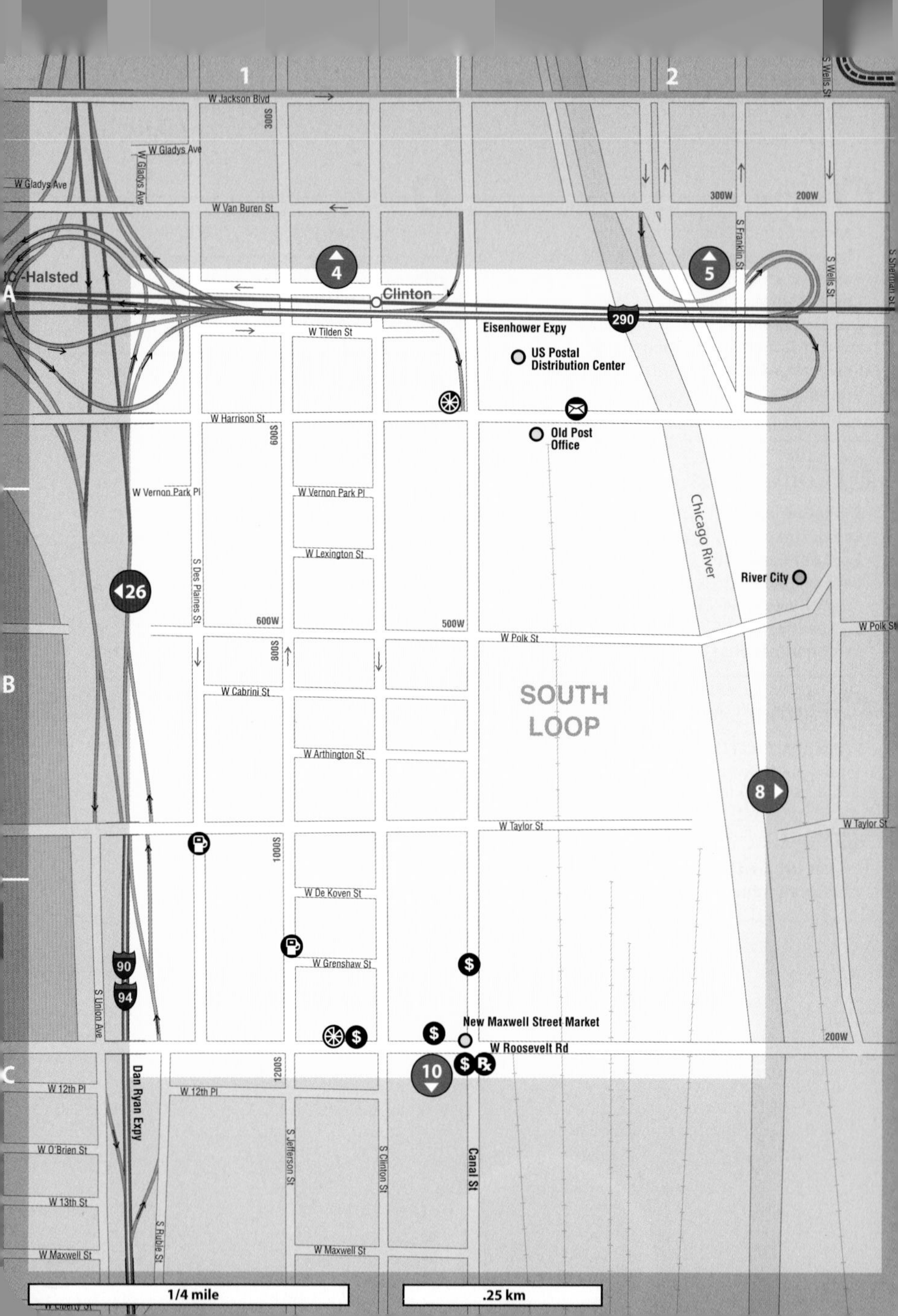

1
2
A
B
C
W Jackson Blvd
300S
W Gladys Ave
W Gladys Ave
W Gladys Ave
W Van Buren St
300W
200W
S Franklin St
S Wells St
S Wells St
S Sherman St
4
5
UC-Halsted
Clinton
W Tilden St
Eisenhower Expy
290
US Postal
Distribution Center
W Harrison St
600S
Old Post
Office
W Vernon Park Pl
W Vernon Park Pl
W Lexington St
Chicago River
River City
26
S Des Plaines St
600W
500W
W Polk St
W Polk St
800S
W Cabrini St
SOUTH
LOOP
W Arthington St
8
W Taylor St
W Taylor St
1000S
W De Koven St
W Grenshaw St
90
94
S Union Ave
New Maxwell Street Market
W Roosevelt Rd
200W
10
1200S
W 12th Pl
W 12th Pl
Dan Ryan Expy
W O'Brien St
S Jefferson St
S Clinton St
Canal St
W 13th St
S Ruble St
W Maxwell St
W Maxwell St
1/4 mile
.25 km

Bertrand Goldberg's brilliant River City, the sprawling condo development compound that hugs the eastern shore of the Chicago River, is just about all this area has going for it. With all those residents, you'd think more commercial endeavors might pop up here, but for now it's still mostly just warehouses, semi-trucks, and the flurry of activity that is the US Postal Distribution center.

Banks

- **Chase** • 1130 S Canal St
- **Chase (ATM)** • 501 W Roosevelt Rd
- **Harris Trust & Savings** • 522 W Roosevelt Rd
- **South Central** • 525 W Roosevelt Rd

Gas Stations

- **Citgo** • 1004 S Des Plaines St
- **Marathon** • 1121 S Jefferson St

Landmarks

- **New Maxwell Street Market** • 548 W Roosevelt Rd
- **Old Post Office** • 404 W Harrison St
- **River City** • 800 S Wells St
- **US Postal Distribution Center** • 433 W Harrison St

Pharmacies

- **Walgreens** • 501 W Roosevelt Rd

Pizza

- **Atinos Pizza** • 570 W Roosevelt Rd
- **Aurelio's Pizza** • 506 W Harrison St

Post Offices

- **US Post Office** • 433 W Harrison St

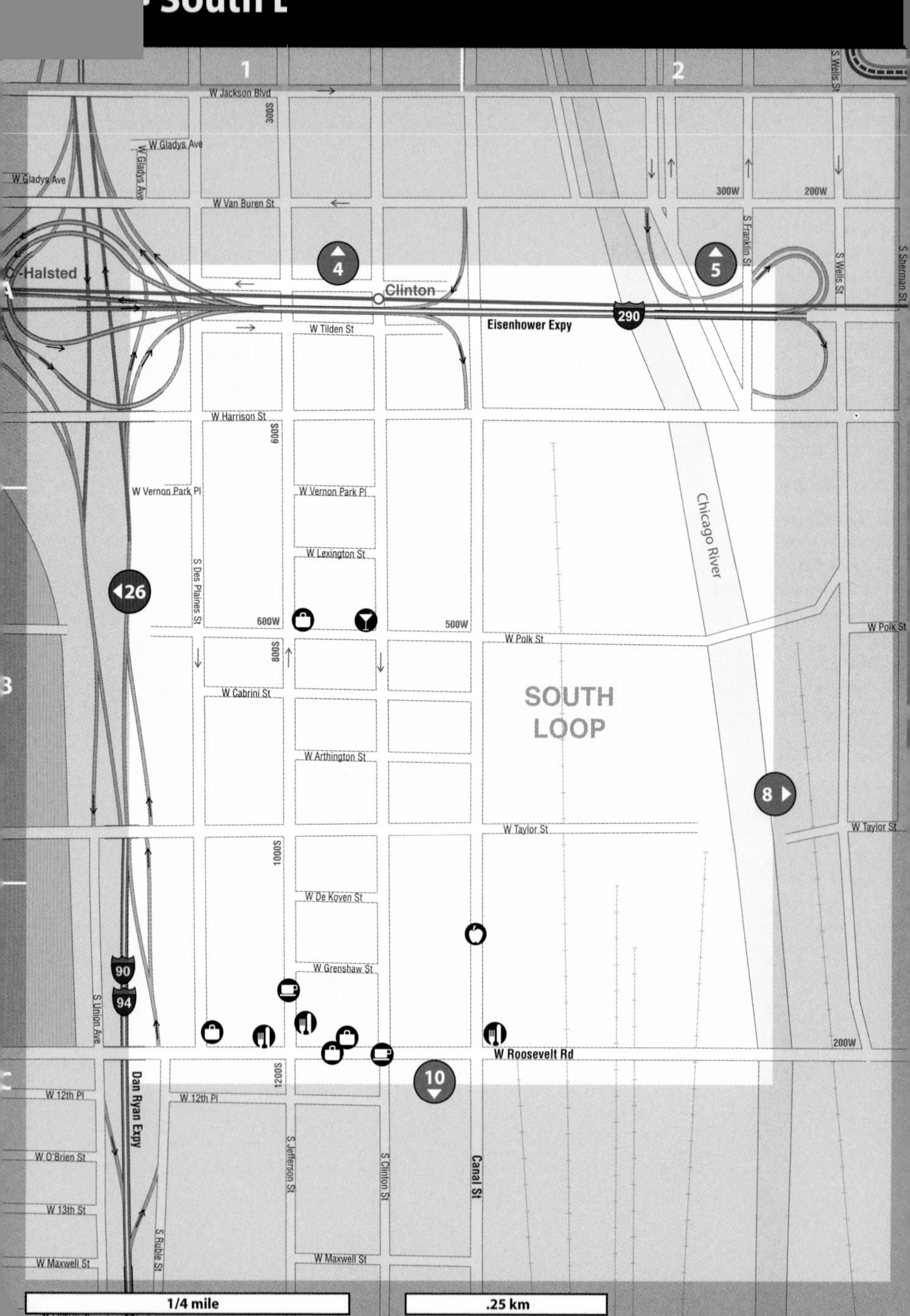
1
2
W Jackson Blvd
W Gladys Ave
W Van Buren St
Clinton
Halsted
Eisenhower Expy
290
W Tilden St
W Harrison St
W Vernon Park Pl
W Lexington St
S Des Plaines St
W Polk St
W Cabrini St
W Arthington St
SOUTH
LOOP
Chicago River
W Taylor St
W De Koven St
W Grenshaw St
W Roosevelt Rd
S Union Ave
W 12th Pl
W O'Brien St
W 13th St
W Maxwell St
Dan Ryan Expy
S Jefferson St
S Clinton St
Canal St
S Ruble St
S Franklin St
S Wells St
S Sherman St
90
94
4
5
8
10
26
1/4 mile
.25 km

Manny's famous coffee shop and deli is a popular breakfast and lunch spot for cops and politicians. Pack a wire just in case—you never know who you might end up sitting next to at the counter. Nearby, the 24-hour White Palace Grill has been sopping up late night booze since 1939. It may be a shadow of its former self, but the Maxwell Sunday Market on Canal is still one stop shopping for tube socks, cleaning supplies, churros, and trashy treasures.

Coffee

- **Dunkin' Donuts** • 1121 S Jefferson St
- **Dunkin' Donuts** • 500 W Roosevelt Rd

Farmer's Markets

- **Maxwell Sunday Market (Sun, 7 am–3 pm)** • Canal St b/w Taylor St & Roosevelt Rd

Nightlife

- **Scarlett's Gentleman's** • 750 S Clinton St

Restaurants

- **Bake for Me** • 608 W Roosevelt Rd
- **Manny's Coffee Shop** • 1141 S Jefferson St
- **White Palace Grill** • 1159 S Canal St

Shopping

- **Adam Joseph's Hats** • 544 W Roosevelt Rd
- **Fishman's Fabrics** • 1101 S Des Plaines St
- **Lee's Foreign Car Service** • 727 S Jefferson St
- **Morris & Sons** • 555 W Roosevelt Rd

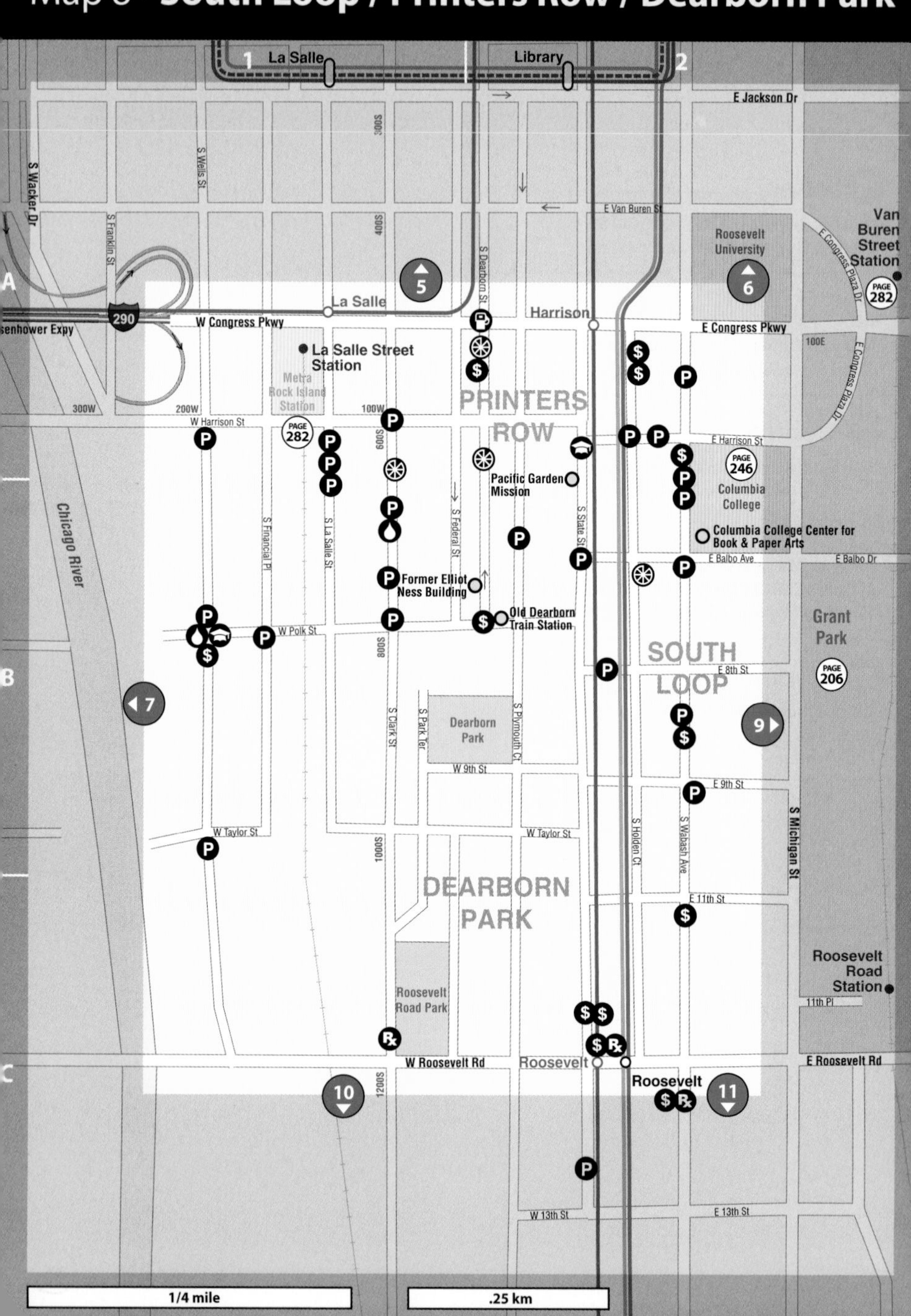
La Salle
Library
E Jackson Dr
S Wacker Dr
S Wells St
S Franklin St
E Van Buren St
Roosevelt University
Van Buren Street Station
E Congress Plaza Dr
PAGE 282
5
6
La Salle
Harrison
290
senhower Expy
W Congress Pkwy
E Congress Pkwy
S Dearborn St
100E
La Salle Street Station
Metra Rock Island Station
PRINTERS ROW
300W
200W
100W
W Harrison St
E Harrison St
PAGE 282
PAGE 246
Columbia College
Chicago River
Pacific Garden Mission
S Financial Pl
S La Salle St
S Federal St
S State St
Columbia College Center for Book & Paper Arts
E Balbo Ave
E Balbo Dr
Former Elliot Ness Building
Old Dearborn Train Station
W Polk St
Grant Park
SOUTH LOOP
E 8th St
PAGE 206
7
9
S Clark St
S Park Ter
Dearborn Park
S Plymouth Ct
W 9th St
E 9th St
W Taylor St
W Taylor St
S Holden Ct
S Wabash Ave
S Michigan St
E 11th St
DEARBORN PARK
Roosevelt Road Park
Roosevelt Road Station
11th Pl
W Roosevelt Rd
Roosevelt
E Roosevelt Rd
Roosevelt
10
11
W 13th St
E 13th St
1/4 mile
.25 km

The University Center, which houses students from nearby Columbia, Roosevelt, and DePaul, has injected a youthful flavor into this scrappy hood, for better or worse. The Dearborn Street corridor known as Printer's Row, once a publishing enclave, now sports student-friendly bars and restaurants. Look both ways before crossing Congress, as cars zip on and off the expressway like they're training for NASCAR.

Banks

- **Bank of America (ATM)** • 1104 S Wabash Ave
- **Bank of America (ATM)** • 623 S Wabash Ave
- **Charter One** • 1143 S State St
- **Chase** • 550 S Dearborn St
- **Chase** • 850 S Wabash Ave
- **Chase (ATM)** • 1167 S State St
- **Chase (ATM)** • 2 E Roosevelt Rd
- **Chase (ATM)** • 800 S Wells St
- **Chicago Community** • 47 W Polk St
- **MB Financial** • 557 S State St
- **TCF** • Jewel • 1224 S Wabash Ave
- **TCF (ATM)** • 7-Eleven • 525 S State St

Car Washes

- **Custom Hand Car Wash** • 700 S Clark St
- **River City Car Wash** • 800 S Wells St

Gas Stations

- **BP** • 50 W Congress Pkwy

Landmarks

- **Columbia College Center for Book & Paper Arts** • 1104 S Wabash Ave, 2nd Fl
- **Former Elliot Ness Building** • 618 S Dearborn St
- **Old Dearborn Train Station** • 47 W Polk St
- **Pacific Garden Mission** • 646 S State St

Pharmacies

- **Jewel-Osco** • 1224 S Wabash Ave
- **Target** • 1154 S Clark St
- **Walgreens** • 2 E Roosevelt Rd

Pizza

- **Edwardo's Natural Pizza** • 521 S Dearborn St
- **Pat's Pizzeria** • 638 S Clark St
- **Pizzeria** • 719 S State St
- **Trattoria Caterina** • 616 S Dearborn St

Schools

- **Daystar Education Association** • 800 S Wells St
- **Jones College Prep** • 606 S State St

Parking

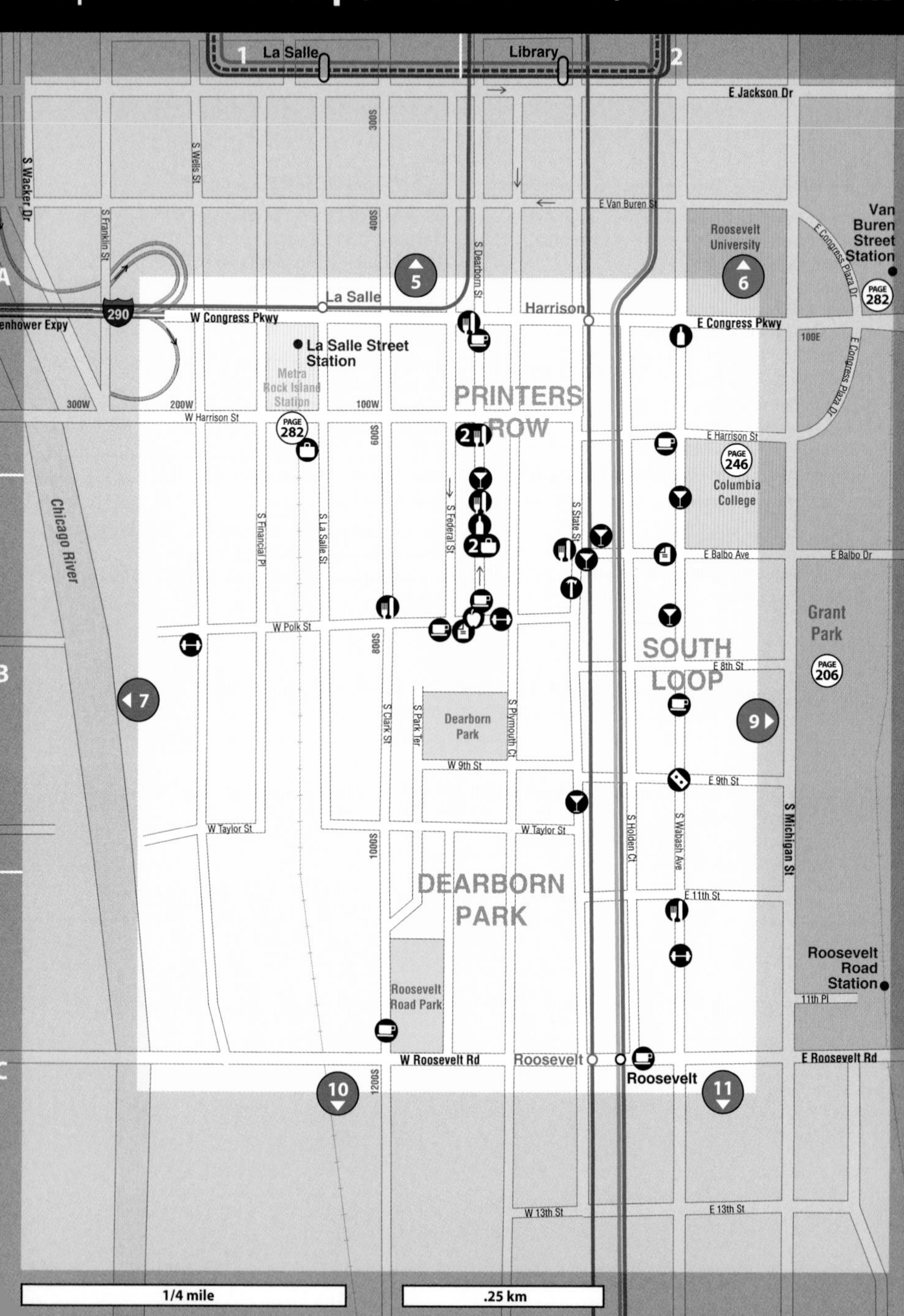

La Salle
Library
E Jackson Dr
S Wells St
S Wacker Dr
E Van Buren St
Roosevelt University
Van Buren Street Station
S Franklin St
S Dearborn St
La Salle
Harrison
290
W Congress Pkwy
E Congress Pkwy
E Congress Plaza Dr
enhower Expy
La Salle Street Station
Metra Rock Island Station
PRINTERS ROW
300W
200W
100W
100E
W Harrison St
E Harrison St
Columbia College
Chicago River
S Financial Pl
S La Salle St
S Federal St
S State St
E Balbo Ave
E Balbo Dr
W Polk St
Grant Park
SOUTH LOOP
E 8th St
S Clark St
S Park Ter
Dearborn Park
S Plymouth Ct
W 9th St
E 9th St
W Taylor St
S Holden Ct
S Wabash Ave
S Michigan St
DEARBORN PARK
E 11th St
Roosevelt Road Park
Roosevelt Road Station
11th Pl
W Roosevelt Rd
Roosevelt
E Roosevelt Rd
W 13th St
E 13th St
1/4 mile
.25 km

Sundries / Entertainment

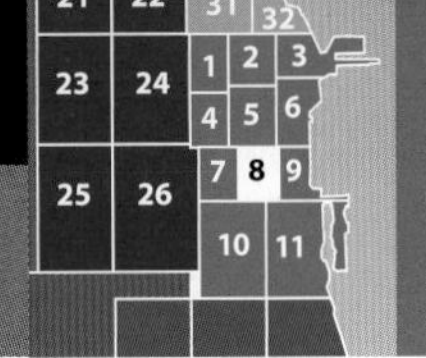

South Loop Club's bar food is way underrated. Stop here for juicy burgers served in a jiffy and sit by a window to take in the always-interesting street scene at this funky intersection. Down the block, not-for-profit HotHouse brings in some of the best in world music entertainment. Meanwhile, restaurateur Shawn McClain (Spring, Green Zebra) gets carnivorous at his latest venture, Custom House, in the old Prairie space.

Coffee

- **Caribou Coffee** • 800 S Wabash Ave
- **Dunkin' Donuts** • 600 S Wabash Ave
- **Gourmand** • 728 S Dearborn St
- **Printer's Roast Café** • 47 W Polk St
- **Starbucks** • Target • 1154 S Clark St
- **Starbucks** • 31 E Roosevelt Rd
- **Starbucks** • 555 S Dearborn St

Copy Shops

- **Fedex Kinko's** • 700 S Wabash Ave
- **The UPS Store** • 47 W Polk St

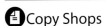

Farmer's Markets

- **Printer's Row (Jun–Oct; Sat, 7 am–2 pm)** • S Dearborn St & W Polk St

Gyms

- **Bally Total Fitness** • 800 S Wells St
- **Curves (women only)** • 47 W Polk St
- **Fitplex** • 1140 S Wabash Ave

Hardware Stores

- **South Loop Ace Hardware** • 725 S State St

Liquor Stores

- **George's Cocktail Lounge** • 646 S Wabash Ave
- **Printers Row Wine Shop** • 719 S Dearborn St
- **Warehouse Liquors** • 634 S Wabash Ave

Nightlife

- **Buddy Guy's Legends** • 754 S Wabash Ave
- **George's Cocktail Lounge** • 646 S Wabash Ave
- **HotHouse** • 31 E Balbo Ave
- **Kasey's Tavern** • 701 S Dearborn St
- **South Loop Club** • 701 S State St
- **Tantrum** • 1023 S State St

Restaurants

- **Blackie's** • 755 S Clark St
- **Custom House** • 500 S Dearborn St
- **Eleven City Diner** • 1112 S Wabash Ave
- **Hackney's** • 733 S Dearborn St
- **South Loop Club** • 701 S State St
- **SRO** • 610 S Dearborn St
- **Trattoria Caterina** • 616 S Dearborn St

Shopping

- **Kozy's Bike Shop** • 601 S La Salle St
- **Printer's Row Fine and Rare Books** • 715 S Dearborn St
- **Sandmeyer's Book Store** • 714 S Dearborn St

Video Rental

- **Movietime Home Video** • 900 S Wabash Ave

Map 9 • South Loop / South Michigan Ave

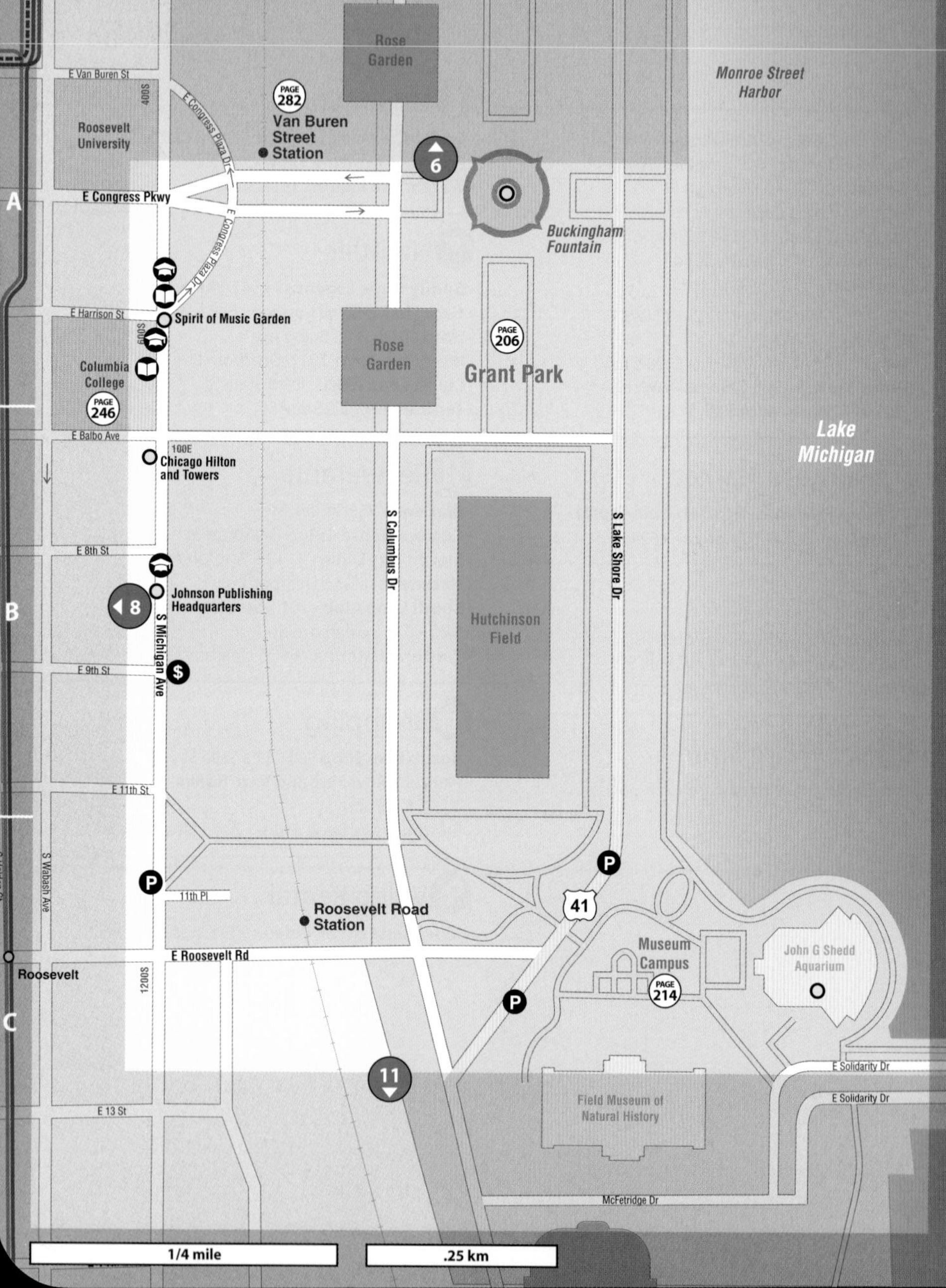

Essentials

The southern half of Chicago's front yard boasts gardens, tennis and volleyball courts, softball fields, and Shedd Aquarium (the world's largest indoor aquarium). While dancers of all skill levels gather at the Spirit of Music Park for the outdoor SummerDance series, Buckingham Fountain draws those out for a leisurely stroll. The skyrocketing water display, accompanied by lights and music, occurs every hour on the hour for twenty minutes until 11 pm daily from April to October.

$ Banks

- **New City** • 900 S Michigan Ave

o Landmarks

- **Buckingham Fountain** • Columbus Dr & E Congress Pkwy
- **Chicago Hilton and Towers** • 720 S Michigan Ave
- **Johnson Publishing Headquarters** • 820 S Michigan Ave
- **John G. Shedd Aquarium** • 1200 S Lake Shore Dr
- **Spirit of Music Garden** • 601 S Michigan Ave

Libraries

- **Asher Library-Spertus Institute** • 618 S Michigan Ave
- **Library of Columbia College** • 624 S Michigan Ave

Schools

- **Columbia College** • 600 S Michigan Ave
- **East-West University** • 816 S Michigan Ave
- **Spertus College** • 618 S Michigan Ave

Parking

Map 9 • South Loop / South Michigan Ave

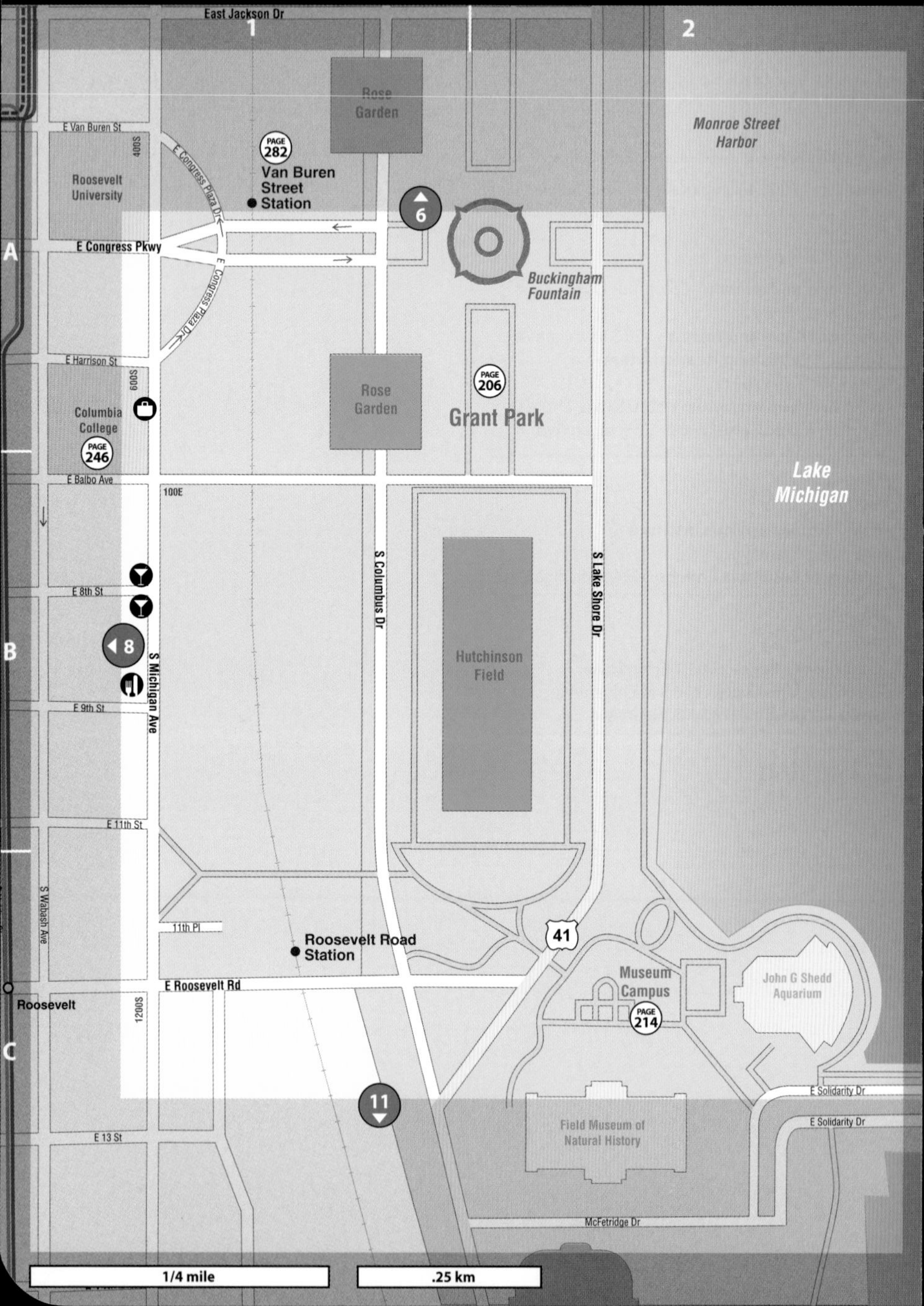

N

1
2
A
B
C

East Jackson Dr
Rose Garden
Monroe Street Harbor
E Van Buren St
400S
E Congress Plaza Dr
PAGE 282
Van Buren Street Station
Roosevelt University
6
E Congress Pkwy
E Congress Plaza Dr
Buckingham Fountain
E Harrison St
600S
Rose Garden
PAGE 206
Grant Park
Columbia College
PAGE 246
Lake Michigan
E Balbo Ave
100E
S Columbus Dr
S Lake Shore Dr
E 8th St
8
Hutchinson Field
S Michigan Ave
E 9th St
E 11th St
S Wabash Ave
11th Pl
41
Roosevelt Road Station
Museum Campus
John G Shedd Aquarium
E Roosevelt Rd
Roosevelt
1200S
PAGE 214
E Solidarity Dr
11
E Solidarity Dr
Field Museum of Natural History
E 13 St
McFetridge Dr

1/4 mile
.25 km

Built atop the rubble of the Great Chicago Fire of 1871, Grant Park is now affectionately known as Chicago's front yard. Spin around and you are guaranteed a view—Lake Michigan, Museum Campus, the city skyline, or the gardens of the park itself. While rather desolate in the winter, warm weather brings out Frisbee players, inline skaters, joggers, boaters, and sun-worshippers galore.

Nightlife

- **Kitty O'Shea's** • 720 S Michigan Ave
- **Savoy Bar and Grill** • 800 S Michigan Ave

Restaurants

- **Oysy** • 888 S Michigan Ave

Shopping

- **Bariff Shop** • 618 S Michigan Ave

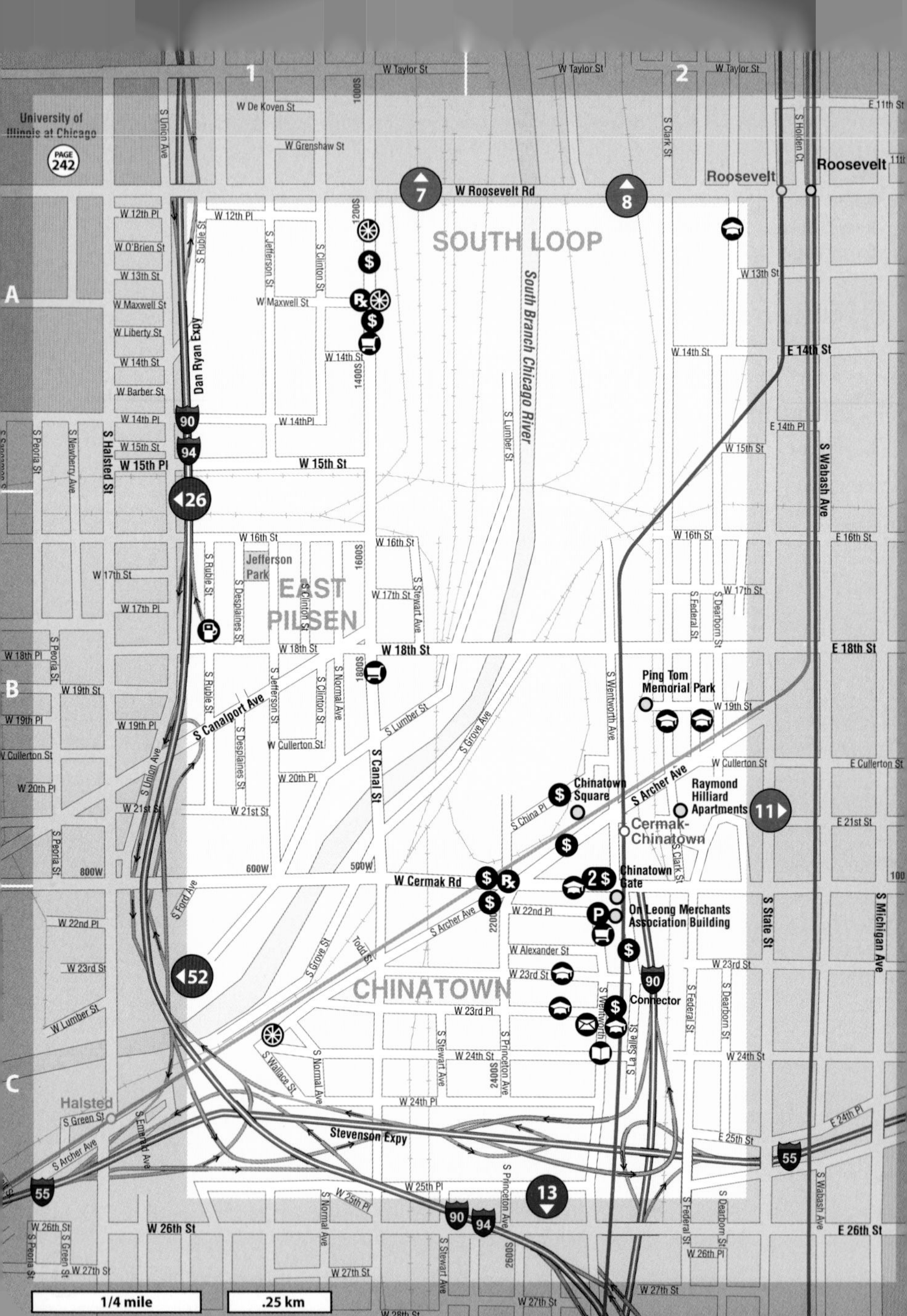

SOUTH LOOP
EAST PILSEN
CHINATOWN
University of Illinois at Chicago
PAGE 242
W Roosevelt Rd
Roosevelt
South Branch Chicago River
Dan Ryan Expy
Jefferson Park
Ping Tom Memorial Park
Chinatown Square
Raymond Hilliard Apartments
Cermak-Chinatown
Chinatown Gate
On Leong Merchants Association Building
Connector
Stevenson Expy
Halsted
W Cermak Rd
W 18th St
S Canal St
S Archer Ave
S Halsted St
S State St
S Wabash Ave
S Michigan Ave
W 26th St
1/4 mile
.25 km

Essentials

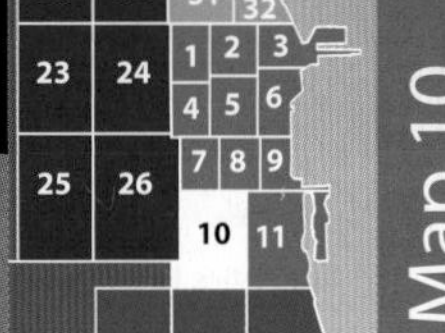

The developer John Podmajersky has a monopoly on the affordable loft rentals in East Pilsen that house so many of Chicago's working artists. Across the river in Chinatown, development continues to clip along with the same breakneck speed as the dim sum carts at the bustling expanse of Three Happiness during their popular Sunday brunch.

Banks

- **American Metro** • 2144 S Archer Ave
- **Charter One** • 2131 S China Pl
- **Charter One** • 2263 S Wentworth Ave
- **Chase** • 1340 S Canal St
- **Chase (ATM)** • 316 W Cermak Rd
- **International Bank of Chicago** • 208 W Cermak Rd
- **Lakeside** • 2200 S Archer Ave
- **New Asia** • 222 W Cermak Rd
- **New Asia** • 250 W Cermak Rd
- **South Central** • 2335 S Wentworth Ave
- **Washington Mutual** • 1226 S Canal St

Gas Stations

- **Shell** • 1741 S Ruble St

Landmarks

- **Chinatown Gate** • S Wentworth Ave & W Cermak Rd
- **Chinatown Square** • S Archer Ave
- **On Leong Merchants Association Building** • 2216 S Wentworth Ave
- **Ping Tom Memorial Park** • 300 W 19th St
- **Raymond Hilliard Apartments** • 2111 S Clark St

Libraries

- **Chinatown Public Library** • 2353 S Wentworth Ave

Pharmacies

- **Dominick's** • 1340 S Canal St
- **Walgreens** • 316 W Cermak Rd

Pizza

- **Connie's Pizza** • 2373 S Archer Ave
- **Dominick's Finer Foods** • 1340 S Canal St
- **Domino's** • 1234 S Canal St

Post Offices

- **US Post Office** • 2345 S Wentworth Ave

Schools

- **John C Haines Elementary** • 247 W 23rd Pl
- **National Teacher's Academy** • 55 W Cermak Rd
- **Perspectives Charter High** • 1915 S Federal St
- **Perspectives Charter High** • 1930 S Federal St
- **Pui Tak Christian** • 2301 S Wentworth Ave
- **South Loop Elementary** • 1212 S Plymouth Ct
- **St Therese** • 247 W 23rd St

Supermarkets

- **Dominick's** • 1340 S Canal St
- **Richwell Market** • 1835 S Canal St
- **Tai Wah Grocery** • 2226 S Wentworth Ave

Parking

Map 10 • **East Pilsen / Chinatown**

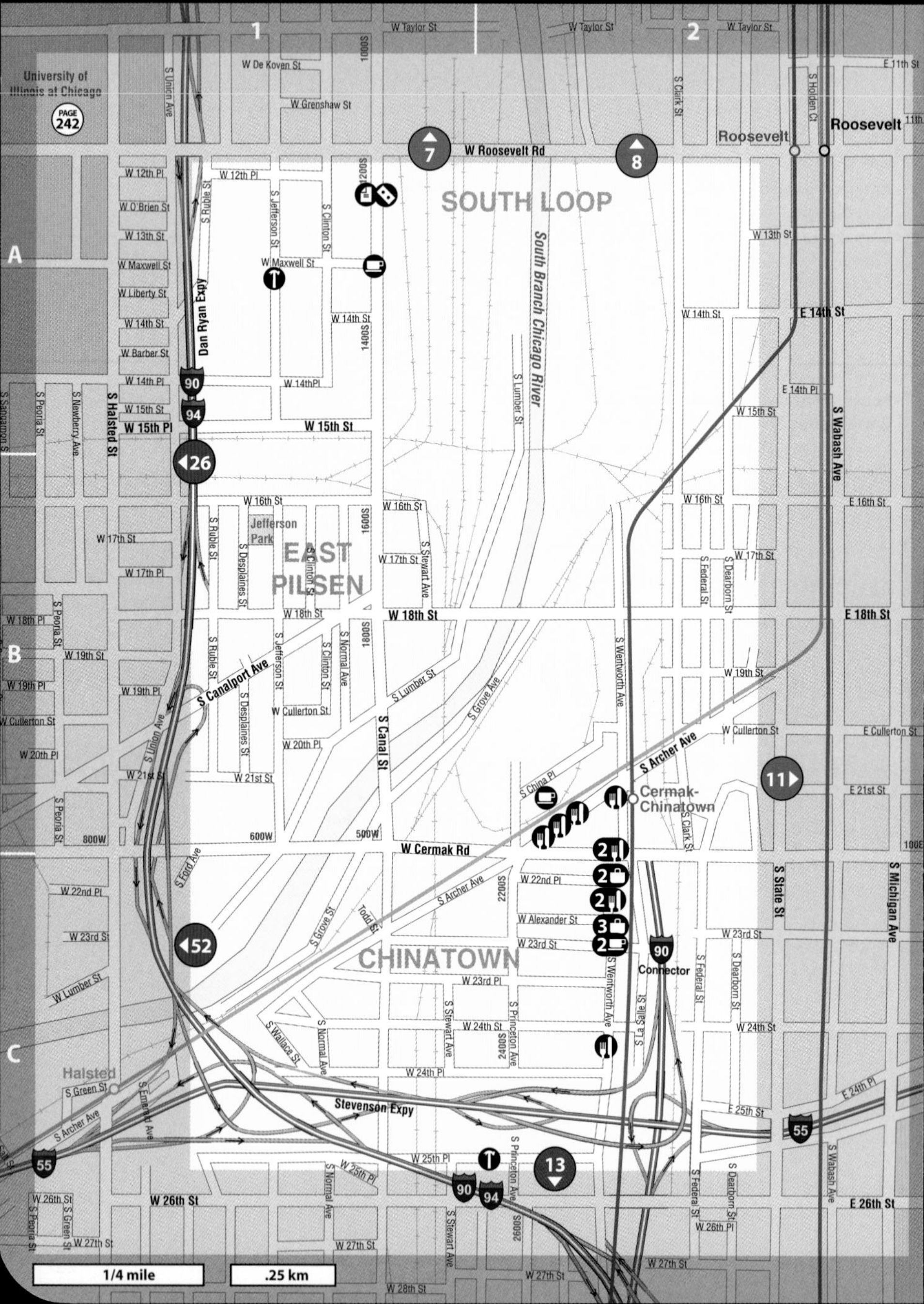

1
2
A
B
C

University of Illinois at Chicago

PAGE 242

SOUTH LOOP

EAST PILSEN

CHINATOWN

Jefferson Park

South Branch Chicago River

Dan Ryan Expy

Stevenson Expy

Connector

Roosevelt
Roosevelt
Cermak-Chinatown
Halsted

W Taylor St
W De Koven St
W Grenshaw St
W Roosevelt Rd
W 12th Pl
W O'Brien St
W 13th St
W Maxwell St
W Liberty St
W 14th St
W Barber St
W 14th Pl
W 15th St
W 15th Pl
W 16th St
W 17th St
W 17th Pl
W 18th St
W 18th Pl
W 19th St
W 19th Pl
W Cullerton St
W 20th Pl
W 21st St
W Cermak Rd
W 22nd Pl
W Alexander St
W 23rd St
W 23rd Pl
W 24th St
W 24th Pl
W 25th Pl
W 26th St
W 26th Pl
W 27th St
W 28th St
W Lumber St

E 11th St
E 14th St
E 14th Pl
E 16th St
E 18th St
E Cullerton St
E 21st St
E 24th Pl
E 25th St
E 26th St

S Union Ave
S Ruble St
S Jefferson St
S Clinton St
S Desplaines St
S Normal Ave
S Canal St
S Stewart Ave
S Lumber St
S Grove Ave
S Canalport Ave
S Archer Ave
S China Pl
S Wentworth Ave
S La Salle St
S Clark St
S Federal St
S Dearborn St
S State St
S Wabash Ave
S Michigan Ave
S Holden Ct
S Halsted St
S Peoria St
S Newberry Ave
S Sangamon St
S Green St
S Emerald Ave
S Ford Ave
S Grove St
Todd St
S Wallace St
S Princeton Ave

1000S
1200S
1400S
1600S
1800S
2200S
2400S
2600S
800W
600W
500W
100E

7
8
26
11
52
13
90
94
55

1/4 mile
.25 km

Sundries / Entertainment

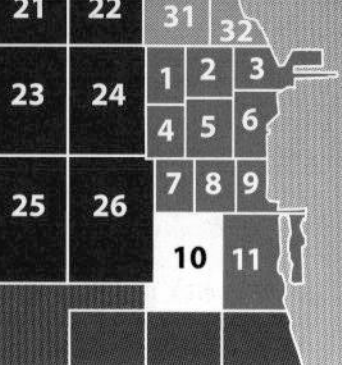

Twice a year the artist community of East Pilsen hosts a gallery crawl, where would-be collectors travel from funky space to funky space sipping wine and looking for the next Ed Paschke. Shopping in Chinatown is loads of fun, with cookware, utensils, finger traps, rice candy, and bamboo back-scratchers galore. Everyone has their favorite Chinatown restaurant they swear by, so we won't even bother making recommendations.

Coffee

- **Coco Café** • 2163 S China Pl
- **Starbucks** • Dominick's • 1340 S Canal St
- **Tasty Place** • 2339 S Wentworth Ave
- **Tea Leaf Café** • 2336 S Wentworth Ave

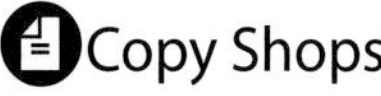

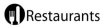

Copy Shops

- **Fedex Kinko's** • 1242 S Canal St

Hardware Stores

- **Turek & Sons True Value** • 1333 S Jefferson St
- **Zweifel True Value Hardware** • 345 W 25th Pl

Restaurants

- **Emperor's Choice** • 2238 S Wentworth Ave
- **Evergreen** • 2411 S Wentworth Ave
- **Happy Chef Dim Sum House** • 2164 S Archer Ave
- **Joy Yee's Noodle Shop** • 2159 Chinatown Sq
- **Lao Sze Chuan Spicy City** • 2172 S Archer Ave
- **Penang** • 2201 S Wentworth Ave
- **Phoenix** • 2131 S Archer Ave
- **Three Happiness** • 209 W Cermak Rd
- **Won Kow** • 2237 S Wentworth Ave

Shopping

- **Chinatown Bazaar** • 2221 S Wentworth Ave
- **Pacific Imports** • 2200 S Wentworth Ave
- **Sun Sun Tong** • 2260 S Wentworth Ave
- **Ten Ren Tea & Ginseng Co** • 2247 S Wentworth Ave
- **Woks 'n' Things** • 2234 S Wentworth Ave

Video Rental

- **Movie Gallery** • 1258 S Canal St

Map 11 • South Loop / McCormick Place

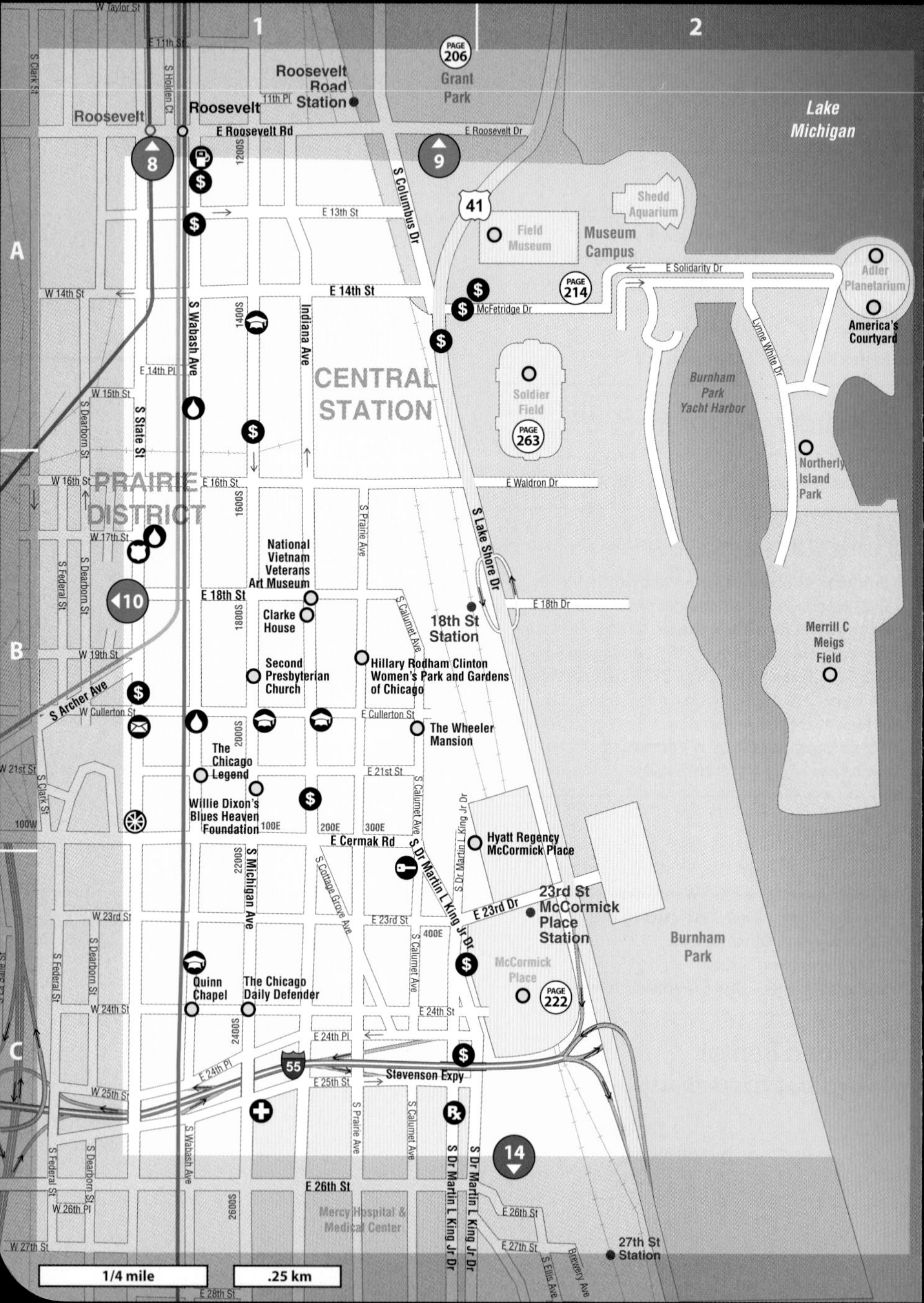

1
2
A
B
C
Lake Michigan
Roosevelt Road Station
PAGE 206
Grant Park
Roosevelt
E Roosevelt Rd
E Roosevelt Dr
W Taylor St
E 11th St
11th Pl
S Clark St
S Holden Ct
1200S
8
9
41
S Columbus Dr
E 13th St
Shedd Aquarium
Field Museum
Museum Campus
E Solidarity Dr
PAGE 214
Adler Planetarium
America's Courtyard
W 14th St
E 14th St
McFetridge Dr
1400S
Indiana Ave
S Wabash Ave
E 14th Pl
CENTRAL STATION
Soldier Field
PAGE 263
Lynne White Dr
Burnham Park Yacht Harbor
W 15th St
S State St
S Dearborn St
Northerly Island Park
W 16th St
E 16th St
E Waldron Dr
PRAIRIE DISTRICT
1600S
S Prairie Ave
S Lake Shore Dr
W 17th St
National Vietnam Veterans Art Museum
S Federal St
10
E 18th St
1800S
Clarke House
S Calumet Ave
18th St Station
E 18th Dr
Merrill C Meigs Field
W 19th St
Second Presbyterian Church
Hillary Rodham Clinton Women's Park and Gardens of Chicago
S Archer Ave
W Cullerton St
E Cullerton St
2000S
The Wheeler Mansion
The Chicago Legend
W 21st St
E 21st St
Willie Dixon's Blues Heaven Foundation
100W
100E
200E
300E
E Cermak Rd
S Dr Martin L King Jr Dr
Hyatt Regency McCormick Place
2200S
S Michigan Ave
S Cottage Grove Ave
23rd St McCormick Place Station
E 23rd Dr
W 23rd St
E 23rd St
400E
Burnham Park
McCormick Place
PAGE 222
Quinn Chapel
The Chicago Daily Defender
W 24th St
E 24th St
2400S
E 24th Pl
E 24th Pl
55
Stevenson Expy
E 25th St
W 25th St
S Wabash Ave
14
E 26th St
2600S
Mercy Hospital & Medical Center
W 26th Pl
E 26th St
W 27th St
E 27th St
S Ellis Ave
Brewery Ave
27th St Station
1/4 mile
.25 km
E 28th St

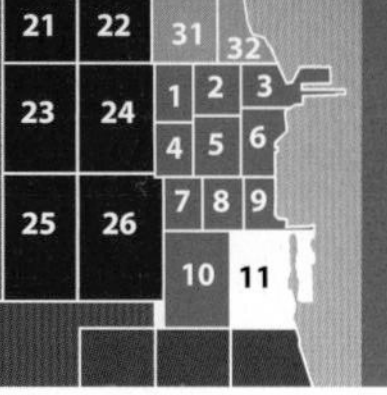

McCormick Place was once known as McCormick's Folly because most saw it as an obstruction to the Burnham Plan's clear lakefront view as opposed to the economic dynamo envisioned in the late 1940s by publisher Col. Robert R. McCormick. The convention and exhibition center is now the anchor and inspiration for a South Loop renaissance, characterized by a postmodern cubic crowning for Soldier Field's neoclassical Greek revivalism and the creation of the Museum Campus.

Banks

- **Chase** • 1934 S State St
- **Fifth Third (ATM)** • 1300 S Lake Shore Dr
- **First American** • 1241 S Wabash Ave
- **Harris Trust & Savings** • 1300 S Wabash Ave
- **La Salle (ATM)** • 1400 S Lake Shore Dr
- **La Salle (ATM)** • 2301 S Dr Martin L King Jr Dr
- **Lakeside** • 2141 S Indiana Ave
- **Lakeside (ATM)** • Stevenson Expy & Martin Luther King Dr
- **TCF (ATM)** • 425 E McFetridge Dr
- **Washington Mutual** • 1556 S Michigan Ave

Car Washes

- **State Street Hand Car Wash** • 1701 S State St
- **Strictly By Hand** • 2009 S Wabash Ave
- **Z-Wash** • 1522 S Wabash Ave

Car Rental

- **Hertz** • 2300 S Dr Martin L King Jr Dr • 312-567-0380

Gas Stations

- **BP** • 1221 S Wabash Ave

Emergency Rooms

- **Mercy** • 2525 S Michigan Ave

Landmarks

- **Adler Planetarium & Astronomy Museum** • 1300 S Lake Shore Dr
- **America's Courtyard** • South of Adler Planetarium on the lakefront
- **The Chicago Daily Defender** • 2400 S Michigan Ave
- **The Chicago Legend** • 2109 S Wabash Ave
- **Clarke House** • 1827 S Indiana Ave
- **Field Museum** • 1400 S Lake Shore Dr
- **Hillary Rodham Clinton Women's Park and Gardens of Chicago** • S Prairie Ave, b/w 18th St & 19th St
- **Hyatt Regency McCormick Place** • 2233 S Dr Martin L King Jr Dr
- **McCormick Place** • 2301 S Lake Shore Dr
- **Merill C Meigs Field** • n/a
- **National Vietnam Veterans Art Museum** • 1801 S Indiana Ave
- **Northerly Island Park** • Lakefront, south of Adler Planetarium
- **Quinn Chapel, African Methodist Episcopal Church** • 2401 S Wabash Ave
- **Second Presbyterian Church** • 1936 S Michigan Ave
- **Soldier Field** • 425 E McFetridge Dr
- **Willie Dixon's Blues Heaven Foundation** • 2120 S Michigan Ave
- **The Wheeler Mansion** • 2020 S Calumet Ave

Pharmacies

- **Osco Drug** • 2545 S Dr Martin L King Jr Dr

Pizza

- **Big Daddy's Pizzeria** • 2137 S State St

Police

- **1st District (Central)** • 1718 S State St

Post Offices

- **US Post Office** • 2035 S State St

Schools

- **ACE Tech Charter High** • 1455 S Michigan Ave, Ste 218
- **Detour 2 Discovery Day** • 2001 S Wabash Ave
- **Loop Learning Center** • 2001 S Michigan Ave
- **Ray Graham Training Center** • 2347 S Wabash Ave

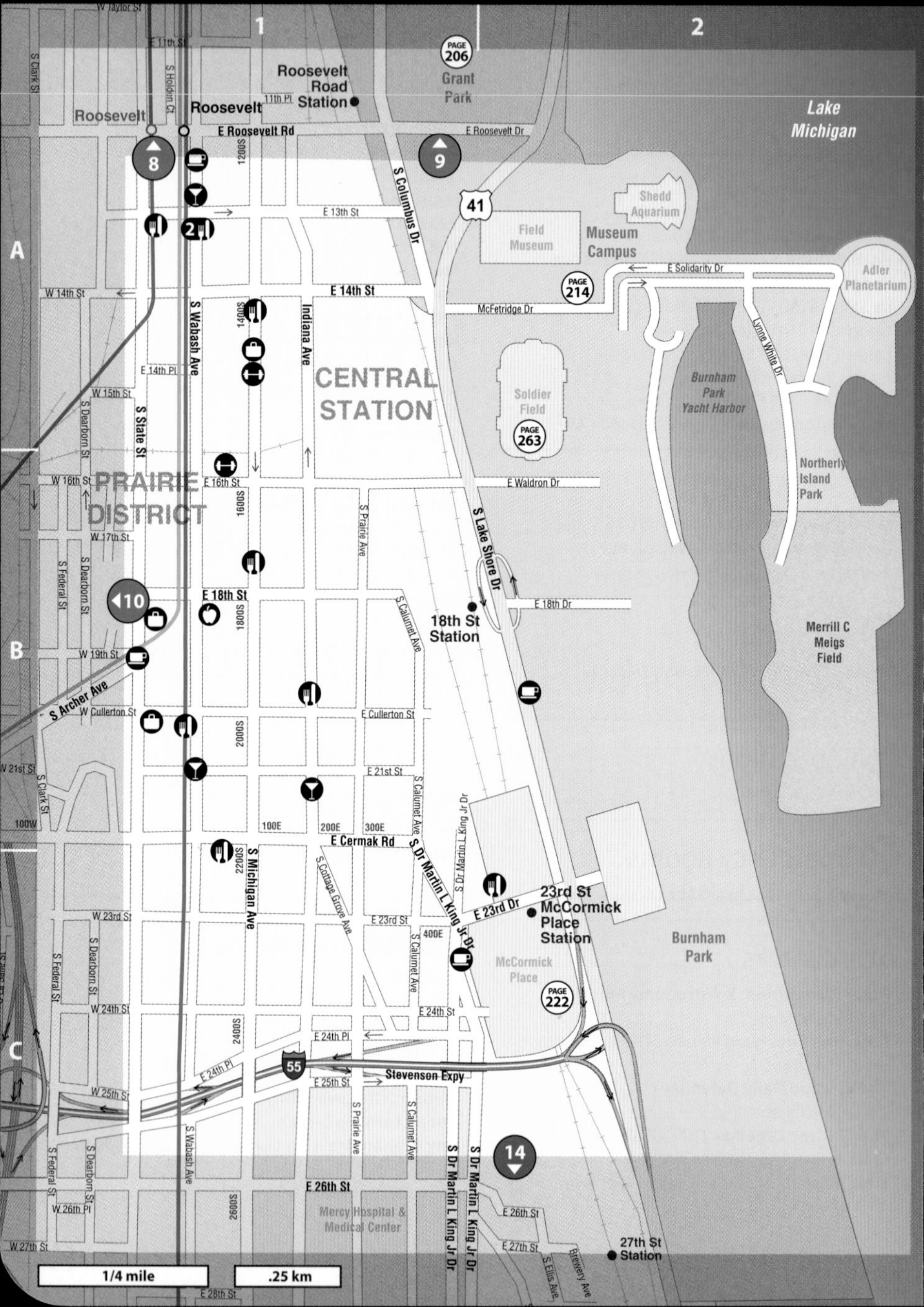

Map 11 • South Loop / McCormick Place

1
2
A
B
C

W Taylor St
E 11th St
S Clark St
S Holden Ct
11th Pl
Roosevelt Road Station
PAGE 206
Grant Park
Lake Michigan
Roosevelt
Roosevelt
E Roosevelt Rd
E Roosevelt Dr
1200S
8
9
S Columbus Dr
41
Shedd Aquarium
Field Museum
Museum Campus
E 13th St
2
E Solidarity Dr
Adler Planetarium
PAGE 214
W 14th St
E 14th St
McFetridge Dr
S Wabash Ave
1400S
Indiana Ave
Lynne White Dr
E 14th Pl
CENTRAL STATION
Soldier Field
PAGE 263
Burnham Park Yacht Harbor
W 15th St
S State St
S Dearborn St
Northerly Island Park
W 16th St
PRAIRIE DISTRICT
E 16th St
1600S
E Waldron Dr
S Prairie Ave
S Lake Shore Dr
W 17th St
S Federal St
S Dearborn St
10
E 18th St
1800S
S Calumet Ave
E 18th Dr
18th St Station
Merrill C Meigs Field
W 19th St
S Archer Ave
W Cullerton St
E Cullerton St
2000S
W 21st St
E 21st St
S Clark St
S Calumet Ave
S Dr Martin L King Jr Dr
100W
100E
200E
300E
E Cermak Rd
S Dr Martin L King Jr Dr
S Cottage Grove Ave
2200S
S Michigan Ave
E 23rd Dr
23rd St McCormick Place Station
W 23rd St
E 23rd St
400E
S Calumet Ave
S Dearborn St
S Federal St
Burnham Park
McCormick Place
PAGE 222
W 24th St
E 24th St
2400S
E 24th Pl
E 24th Pl
55
E 25th St
Stevenson Expy
W 25th St
S Wabash Ave
S Prairie Ave
S Calumet Ave
S Dr Martin L King Jr Dr
S Dr Martin L King Jr Dr
14
S Federal St
S Dearborn St
E 26th St
W 26th Pl
2600S
Mercy Hospital & Medical Center
E 26th St
W 27th St
E 27th St
S Ellis Ave
Brewery Ave
27th St Station
1/4 mile
.25 km
E 28th St

Although much of its Al Capone–related landmarks became casualties of gentrification in the '90s, the South Loop boasts attractions such as a burgeoning restaurant scene, making it more of a cultural gem in the formerly rough. While trendies dine at theatrical spots like Opera, old-schoolers placate themselves with live jazz at ramshackle institution The Velvet Lounge or toss back suds at Wabash Tap. History buffs and culture seekers take day trips to the prestigious addresses of the Prairie Avenue Historic District.

Coffee

- **Café Au Lait** • 1900 S State St
- **Dunkin' Donuts** • 1231 S Wabash Ave
- **Starbucks** • McCormick Con Ctr—Mezzanine • 2301 S Dr Martin L King Jr Dr
- **Starbucks** • McCormick Con Ctr— North Food Ct • 2301 S Lake Shore Dr

Farmer's Markets

- **South Loop Farmers Market (Jun–Oct; Sat, 7 am–2 pm)** • 18th St & Wabash Ave

Gyms

- **Curves (women only)** • 77 E 16th St
- **Phenomenal Fitness** • 1450 S Michigan Ave

Nightlife

- **Chicago Legends** • 2109 S Wabash Ave
- **Velvet Lounge** • 2128 1/2 S Indiana Ave
- **Wabash Tap** • 1233 S Wabash Ave

Restaurants

- **Chef Luciano** • 49 E Cermak Rd
- **Chicago Firehouse Resturant** • 1401 S Michigan Ave
- **Cuatro** • 2030 S Wabash Ave
- **Gioco** • 1312 S Wabash Ave
- **Kroll's** • 1736 S Michigan Ave
- **NetWorks** • Hyatt Regency • 2231 S Dr Martin L King Jr Dr
- **Opera** • 1301 S Wabash Ave
- **Triad** • 1933 S Indiana Ave
- **Wells on Wells** • 1617 N Wells St
- **Zapatista** • 1307 S Wabash Ave

Shopping

- **Blue Star Auto Stores** • 2001 S State St
- **Cycle Bicycle Shop** • 1465 S Michigan Ave
- **Waterware** • 1829 S State St

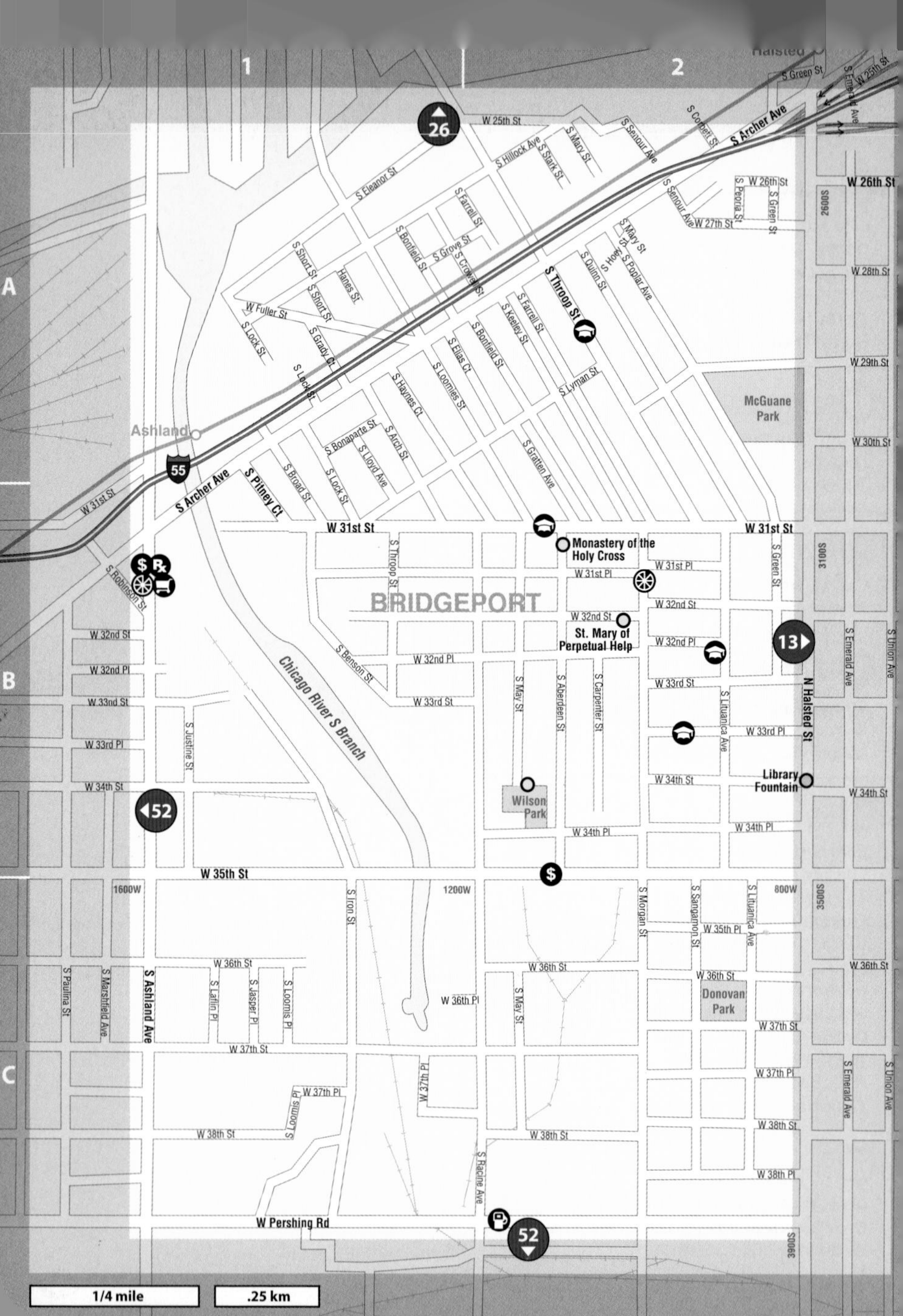

1
2
A
B
C
26
13
52
52
55
BRIDGEPORT
Halsted
Ashland
S Archer Ave
W 25th St
W 26th St
W 27th St
W 28th St
W 29th St
W 30th St
W 31st St
W 31st Pl
W 32nd St
W 32nd Pl
W 33rd St
W 33nd St
W 33rd Pl
W 34th St
W 34th Pl
W 35th St
W 35th Pl
W 36th St
W 36th Pl
W 37th St
W 37th Pl
W 38th St
W 38th Pl
W Pershing Rd
W Fuller St
S Eleanor St
S Hillock Ave
S Stark St
S Mary St
S Senour Ave
S Corbett St
S Green St
S Emerald Ave
S Union Ave
S Peoria St
S Farrell St
S Bonfield St
S Grove St
S Crowell St
S Short St
S Hanes St
S Lock St
S Grady Ct
S Throop St
S Quinn St
S Hoey St
S Poplar Ave
S Keeley St
S Elias Ct
S Loomis St
S Haynes Ct
S Lyman St
S Bonaparte St
S Arch St
S Lloyd Ave
S Broad St
S Pitney Ct
S Gratten Ave
S Robinson St
S Benson St
S Justine St
S May St
S Aberdeen St
S Carpenter St
S Lituanica Ave
N Halsted St
S Morgan St
S Sangamon St
S Iron St
S Racine Ave
S Paulina St
S Marshfield Ave
S Ashland Ave
S Laflin Pl
S Jasper Pl
S Loomis Pl
Chicago River S Branch
McGuane Park
Monastery of the Holy Cross
St. Mary of Perpetual Help
Library Fountain
Wilson Park
Donovan Park
1600W
1200W
800W
2600S
3100S
3500S
3900S
1/4 mile
.25 km

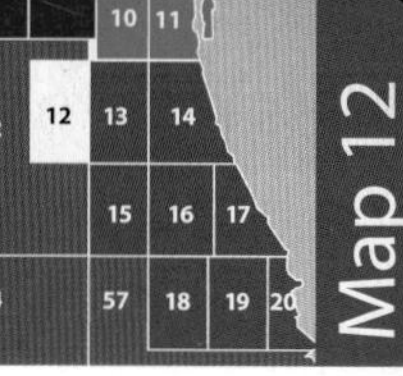

Once largely industrial and shunned by residents of Bridgeport proper, this area's jumbo land parcels and warehouses ripe for conversion have spurred pockets of development. Most notable is tony Bridgeport Village, set smack-dab on a stretch of the Chicago River known as Bubbly Creek. The waterway got its name because animal carcasses dumped by the former stockyards turned it into a gaseous stew and, despite the pricey homes along its banks, the bubbles still linger.

Banks

- **Chase** • 3145 S Ashland Ave
- **Chicago Community** • 1110 W 35th St

Gas Stations

- **Citgo** • 970 W Pershing Rd

Landmarks

- **Library Fountain** • W 34th St & Halsted St
- **Monastery of the Holy Cross** • 3111 S Aberdeen St
- **St Mary of Perpetual Help** • 1039 W 32nd St
- **Wilson Park** • S May St & W 34th Pl

Pharmacies

- **Dominick's** • 3145 S Ashland Ave

Pizza

- **Dominick's** • 3145 S Ashland Ave
- **Lina's Pizza** • 3132 S Morgan St

Schools

- **Armour Branch** • 911 W 32nd St
- **Charles N Holden Elementary** • 1104 W 31st St
- **Philip D Armour Elementary** • 950 W 33rd Pl
- **St Barbara Elementary** • 2867 S Throop St

Supermarkets

- **Dominick's** • 3145 S Ashland Ave

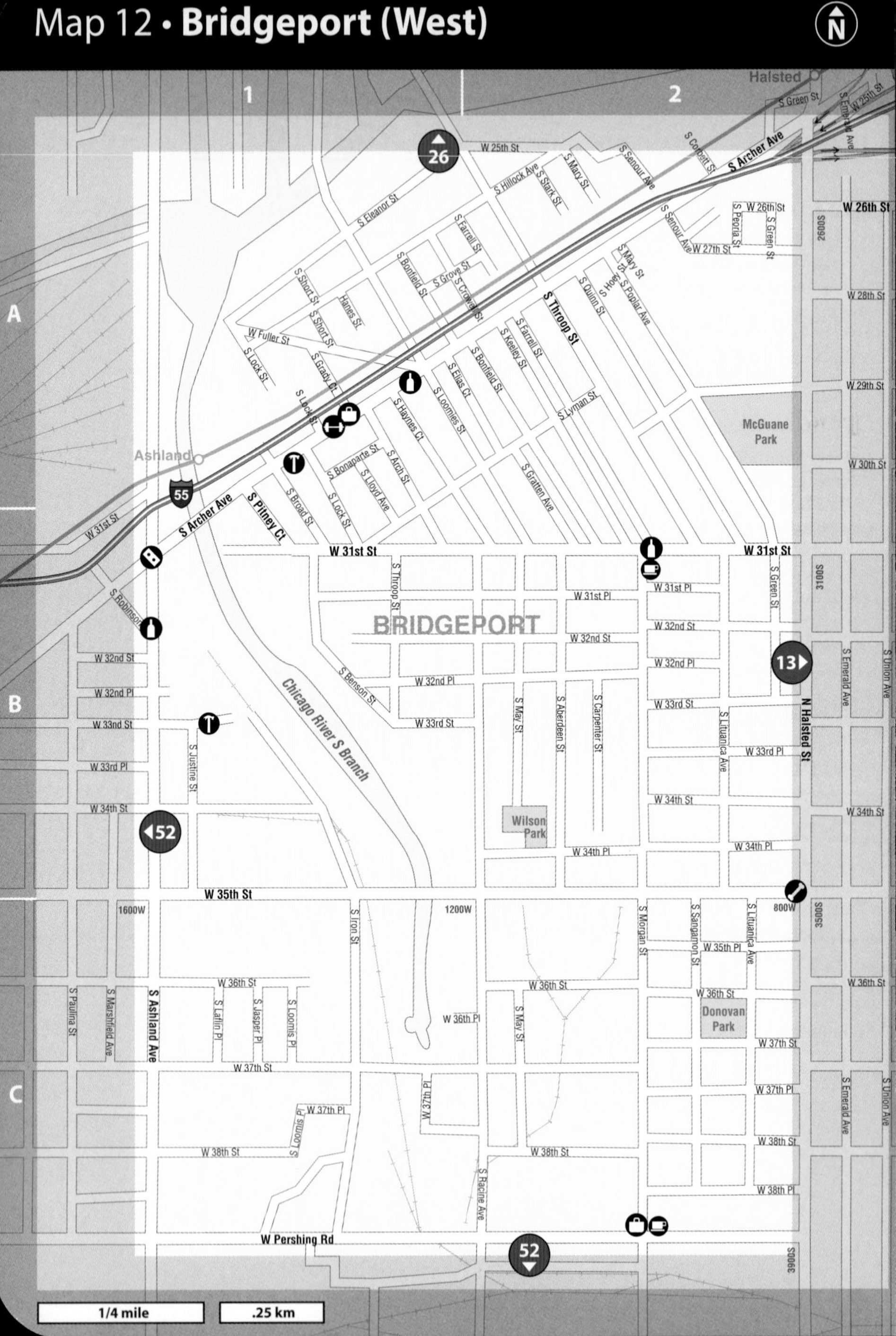

N
Halsted
1
2
26
W 25th St
S Archer Ave
BRIDGEPORT
Ashland
55
S Throop St
W 31st St
McGuane Park
Wilson Park
Donovan Park
Chicago River S Branch
13
52
W 35th St
S Ashland Ave
N Halsted St
W Pershing Rd
A
B
C
1/4 mile
.25 km

Never a destination spot, this area nonetheless has some offbeat institutions with old-school flavor. Bustling lunch stop Best's Kosher Outlet Store is a working-class favorite for made to order sandwiches and all-beef dogs.

Coffee

- **Bridgeport Coffeehouse** • 3101 S Morgan St
- **Dunkin' Donuts** • 970 W Pershing Rd

Gyms

- **Lance's Gym** • 2980 S Archer Ave

Hardware Stores

- **Cremieux Supply** • 3015 S Archer Ave
- **Elston Ace Hardware** • 1514 W 33rd St

Liquor Stores

- **All Star Food & Liquors** • 2911 S Archer Ave
- **Ashland S** • 3162 S Ashland Ave
- **J & Lee** • 960 W 31st St

Pet Shops

- **Bridgeport Pet Boutique** • 824 W 35th St

Shopping

- **Best's Kosher Outlet Store** • 1000 W Pershing Rd
- **Bridgeport Antiques** • 2963 S Archer Ave

Video Rental

- **Blockbuster** • 3145 S Ashland Ave

BRIDGEPORT
McGuane Park
Old Neighborhood Italian American Club
Richard J Daley House
Armour Square Park
US Cellular Field
Illinois Institute of Tech
Williams Park
Donovan Park
Stateway Gardens Park
Wentworth Gardens Park
35th-Bronzeville-IIT
Sox-35th
Dan Ryan Expy
W 26th St
W 31st St
W 35th St
W Pershing Rd
S Halsted St
S Wentworth Ave
S La Salle St
S State St
PAGE 248
PAGE 265
1/4 mile
.25 km

Bridgeport exemplifies how the "City That Works" actually works. The stomping grounds of the Daley family and de facto political center of the city, Bridgeport is also the quintessential Chicago neighborhood with its close-knit residents, legions of patronage workers, and distinctive "dese, dem, and dose" vernacular.

Banks

- **Charter One** • 600 W 37th St
- **Chase** • 757 W 35th St
- **Chase (ATM)** • 142 W 35th St
- **Chase (ATM)** • 3000 S Halsted St
- **Chase (ATM)** • 3241 S Federal St
- **Citibank** • 3430 S Halsted St
- **LaSalle (ATM)** • 333 W 35th St
- **Marquette** • 615 W 31st St
- **Marquette (ATM)** • 501 W 31st St
- **South Central** • 3032 S Halsted St
- **TCF (ATM)** • Jewel • 3033 S Halsted St
- **TCF (ATM)** • Osco • 741 W 31st St

Car Washes

- **J&J Full Service Car Wash** • 349 W 31st St
- **Looking Good Hand Car Wash** • 3540 S Halsted St

Gas Stations

- **BP/Amoco** • 3047 S Halsted St
- **Citgo** • 501 W 31st St
- **Clark Oil** • 444 W 26th St
- **Marathon** • 659 W 31st St ㉔
- **Mobil** • 243 W Pershing Rd ㉔
- **Shell** • 215 W 31st St

Landmarks

- **McGuane Park** • W 29th St & S Halsted St
- **Old Neighborhood Italian American Club** • 3031 S Shields Ave
- **Richard J Daley House** • 3536 S Lowe Ave

Libraries

- **Daley Public Library** • 3400 S Halsted St

Pharmacies

- **Osco Drug** • 741 W 31st St
- **Walgreens** • 3000 S Halsted St

Pizza

- **Fratellini Pizza** • 3258 S Wells St
- **Freddie's Pizza & Pasta Parlor** • 701 W 31st St
- **Little Caesar's Pizza** • 3010 S Halsted St
- **Phil's Pizza** • 3551 S Halsted St
- **Punky's Pizza & Pasta** • 2600 S Wallace St
- **Ricobene's Pizzeria** • 252 W 26th St

Police

- **9th District (Deering)** • 3501 S Lowe Ave

Schools

- **Big Picture Company High** • 2710 S Dearborn St
- **Bridgeport Catholic Academy** • 3700 S Lowe Ave
- **Bridgeport Catholic Academy North** • 512 W 28th Pl
- **Crispus Attucks Elementary** • 3813 S Dearborn St
- **George B McClellan Elementary** • 3527 S Wallace St
- **Illinois Institute of Technology** • 3300 S Federal St
- **James Ward Elementary** • 2701 S Shields Ave
- **KIPP Chicago Youth Village Academy** • 2710 S Dearborn St
- **Mark Sheridan Math & Science Academy** • 533 W 27th St
- **Robert Healy Annex** • 3040 S Parnell Ave
- **Robert Healy Elementary** • 3010 S Parnell Ave
- **Robert S Abbott Elementary** • 3630 S Wells St
- **Santa Lucia** • 3017 S Wells St
- **St Jerome** • 2805 S Princeton Ave
- **Vandercook College of Music** • 3140 S Federal St
- **Williams Elementary** • 2710 S Dearborn St
- **Williams Middle** • 2710 S Dearborn St

Supermarkets

- **Chinese Fresh Food Market** • 3001 S Halsted St
- **Jewel** • 3033 S Halsted St

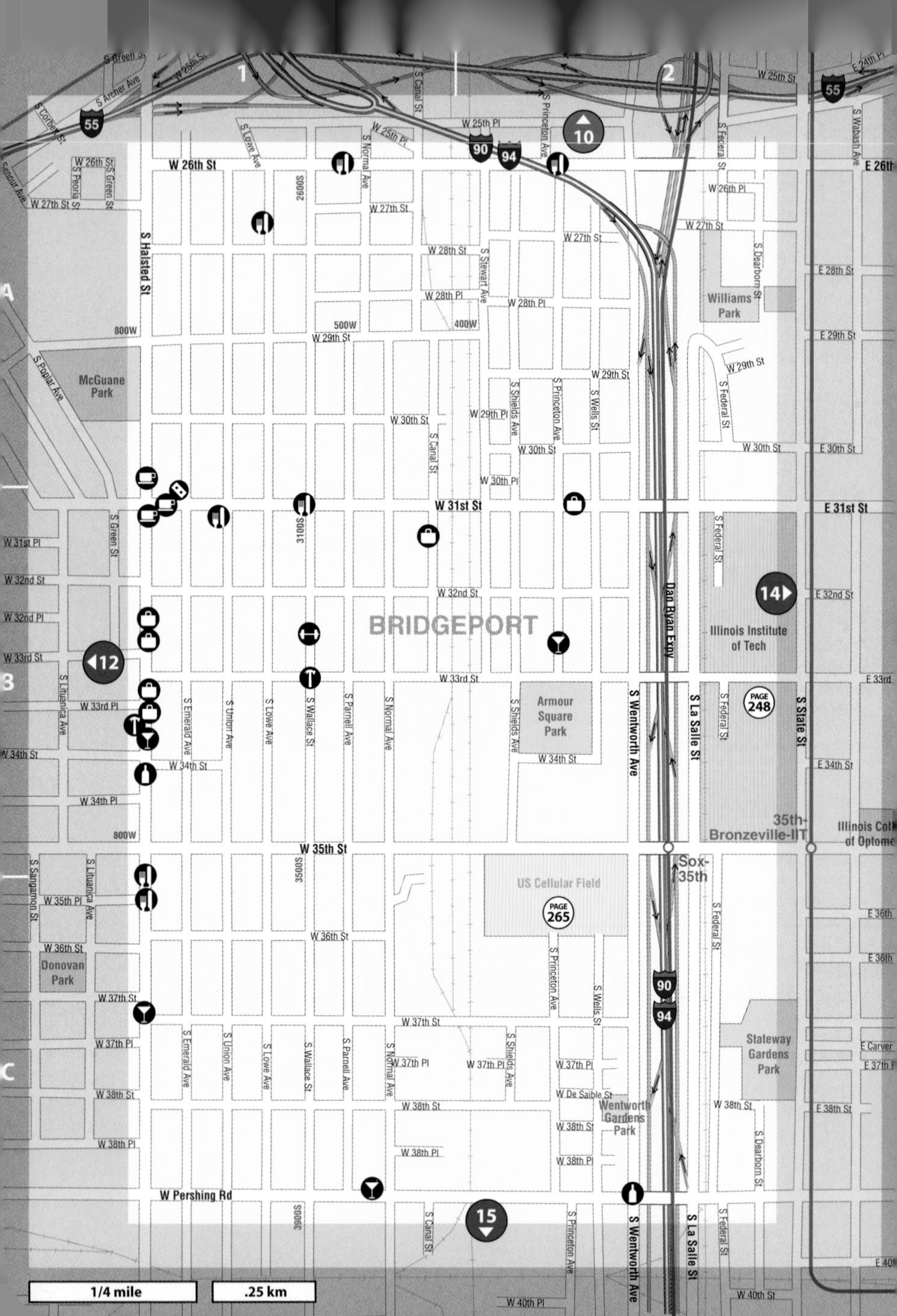

BRIDGEPORT
W 26th St
W 31st St
W 35th St
W Pershing Rd
S Halsted St
S Wentworth Ave
S La Salle St
S State St
Dan Ryan Expy
McGuane Park
Williams Park
Illinois Institute of Tech
Armour Square Park
US Cellular Field
Donovan Park
Wentworth Gardens Park
Stateway Gardens Park
35th-Bronzeville-IIT
Sox-35th
PAGE 248
PAGE 265
10
12
14
15
1/4 mile
.25 km

Sundries / Entertainment

Once second in city hearts after crosstown rivals the Cubs, the World Champion White Sox proved true the South Side mantra: you don't have to be glitzy to get the job done. Ditto for the much-maligned U.S. Cellular Field, where pure baseball trumps drunken revelry, and hey, what's not to like about Mullet Night? For a changeup from ballpark fare, try family-owned Franco's for Old World Italian or Ricobene's Pizzeria for their breaded steak sandwich.

Coffee

- **Dunkin' Donuts** • 749 W 31st St

Gyms

- **Curves (women only)** • 3252 S Wallace St

Hardware Stores

- **Joe Harris Paint & Hardware** • 3301 S Wallace St
- **Windy City Hardware** • 3364 S Halsted St

Liquor Stores

- **Bridgeport Liquors** • 3411 S Halsted St
- **Express Food & Liquor** • 3904 S Wentworth Ave

Nightlife

- **Cobblestone's Bar and Grill** • 514 W Pershing Rd
- **Jimbo's Lounge** • 3258 S Princeton Ave
- **Puffer's Bar** • 3356 S Halsted St
- **Schaller's** • 3714 S Halsted St

Restaurants

- **Franco's Ristorante** • 300 W 31st St
- **Freddie's Pizza & Pasta Parlor** • 701 W 31st St
- **Gio's** • 2724 S Lowe Ave
- **Kevin's Hamburger Heaven** • 554 W 39th St
- **Metropolis Rotisseria** • 924 W Armitage Ave
- **Phil's Pizza** • 3551 S Halsted St
- **Ramova Grill** • 3510 S Halsted St
- **Wing Yip Chop Suey** • 537 W 26th St

Shopping

- **Ace Bakery** • 3241 S Halsted St
- **Augustine's Spiritual Goods** • 3327 S Halsted St
- **Bridgeport News Travel & Tours** • 3252 S Halsted St
- **Health King Enterprises Chinese Medicinals** • 238 W 31st St
- **Henry's Sports & Bait Shop** • 3130 S Canal St
- **Let's Boogie Records & Tapes** • 3321 S Halsted St

Video Rental

- **Bridgeport Video** • 742 W 31st St

N

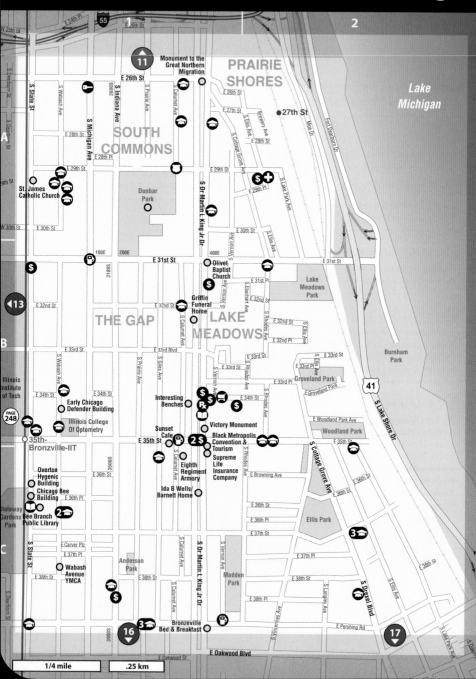

PRAIRIE SHORES
SOUTH COMMONS
THE GAP
LAKE MEADOWS
Lake Michigan
Monument to the Great Northern Migration
27th St
St. James Catholic Church
Dunbar Park
Olivet Baptist Church
Griffin Funeral Home
Lake Meadows Park
Illinois Institute of Tech
Early Chicago Defender Building
Illinois College Of Optometry
Interesting Benches
Victory Monument
Sunset Cafe
Black Metropolis Convention & Tourism
Supreme Life Insurance Company
Eighth Regiment Armory
Ida B Wells/ Barnett Home
35th-Bronzville-IIT
Overton Hygenic Building
Chicago Bee Building
Bee Branch Public Library
Stateway Gardens Park
Wabash Avenue YMCA
Anderson Park
Madden Park
Bronzeville Bed & Breakfast
Groveland Park
Woodland Park
Ellis Park
Burnham Park
S Lake Shore Dr
S Cottage Grove Ave
S Dr Martin L King Jr Dr
S Michigan Ave
S Indiana Ave
S State St
S Wabash Ave
S Prairie Ave
S Calumet Ave
S Giles Ave
S Vernon Ave
S Rhodes Ave
S Ellis Ave
S Eberhart Ave
S Lake Park Ave
S Drexel Blvd
S Langley Ave
S Vincennes Ave
S Dearborn St
Fort Dearborn Dr
Moe Dr
Brewery Ave
E 25th St
E 26th St
E 27th St
E 28th St
E 28th Pl
E 29th St
E 29th Pl
E 30th St
E 31st St
E 31st Pl
E 32nd St
E 32nd Pl
E 33rd Blvd
E 33rd St
E 33rd Pl
E 34th St
E 35th St
E 36th St
E 36th Pl
E 37th St
E 37th Pl
E 38th St
E 38th Pl
E Carver Plz
E Browning Ave
E Groveland Park
E Woodland Park Ave
E Pershing Rd
E Oakwood Blvd
E Oakwood St
E 24th Pl
W 25th St
W 30th St
100E
200E
400E
2600S
3100S
3500S
3900S
55
41
11
13
16
17
PAGE 248
1
2
A
B
C
1/4 mile
.25 km

Essentials

Named after two rather imposing urban renewal-era apartment complexes, this area also includes the spiritual heart of Chicago's African-American community, Bronzeville. Walking through the community will reveal spots of sparkling new townhouses interspersed with the occasional dowdy walk-up building and such notable landmark districts as the Calumet/Giles/Prairie District, which stretches through the 3100 to 3500 blocks of S Calumet, Giles and Prairie Avenues. Given the recent reinvestment in Burnham Park, a jaunt to consider the thriving skate park and other amenities is a fine idea.

Banks

- **Chase** • 3500 S King Dr
- **Chase (ATM)** • 3405 S King Dr
- **Harris Trust & Savings (ATM)** • 3201 S State St
- **Lakeside (ATM)** • 2900 S Ellis Ave
- **Northern Trust (ATM)** • The Rib House• 3851 S Michigan Ave
- **Shore** • 3401 S Dr Martin L King Jr Dr
- **TCF (ATM)** • 7-Eleven• 3201 S State St
- **TCF (ATM)** • Jewel • 443 E 34th St
- **Washington Mutual** • 3501 S King Dr

Car Rental

- **Enterprise** • 2640 S Michigan Ave • 312-808-1228

Gas Stations

- **BP** • 343 E 35th St
- **BP/Amoco** • 3101 S Michigan Ave
- **Citgo** • 437 E Pershing Rd

Emergency Rooms

- **Michael Reese** • 2929 S Ellis Ave ㉔

Landmarks

- **Bee Branch Public Library** • 3647 S State St
- **Black Metropolis Convention & Tourism Council** • 3501 S King Dr, Ste 1E
- **Bronzeville Bed & Breakfast** • 3911 S King Dr
- **Chicago Bee Building** • 3647 S State St
- **Douglas Tomb** • E 35th St & Lake Park Ave
- **Dunbar Park** • S Indiana Ave & E 31st St
- **Early Chicago Defender Building** • 3435 S Indiana Ave
- **Eighth Regiment Armory** • 3533 S Giles Ave
- **Griffin Funeral Home** • 3232 S King Dr
- **Ida B Wells / Barnett Home** • 3624 S King Dr
- **Interesting Benches** • S Dr Martin L King Jr Dr b/w E 33rd St & E 35th St
- **Monument to the Great Northern Migration** • S Dr Martin L King Jr Dr & E 26th St
- **Olivet Baptist Church** • 3101 S King Dr
- **Overton Hygenic Building** • 3619 S State St
- **St James Catholic Church** • 2929 S Wabash Ave
- **Sunset Café** • 315 E 35th St
- **Supreme Life Insurance Company Head Office** • 3501 S King Dr
- **Victory Monument** • 35th St & King Dr
- **Wabash Avenue YMCA** • 3763 S Wabash Ave

Libraries

- **Chicago Bee Public Library** • 3647 S State St
- **King Public Library** • 3436 S Dr Martin L King Jr Dr

Pharmacies

- **Walgreens** • 3405 S Dr Martin L King Jr Dr ㉔

Police

- **21st District (Prairie)** • 300 E 29th St

Schools

- **Albert Einstein Parent/Com Train Academy** • 3663 S Wabash Ave
- **Benjamin W Raymond Elementary** • 3663 S Wabash Ave
- **Chicago Military Academy** • 3519 S Giles Ave
- **Christ the King Lutheran** • 3701 S Lake Park Ave
- **Dawson Technical Institute** • 3901 S State St
- **De la Salle Institute** • 3455 S Wabash Ave
- **Donoghue Elementary** • 707 E 37th St
- **Doolittle Middle** • 535 E 35th St
- **Doolittle West Primary** • 521 E 35th St
- **Douglas Community Academy** • 3200 S Calumet Ave
- **Drake Elementary** • 2722 S Dr Martin L King Jr Dr
- **Dunbar Vocational Career Academy** • 3000 S Dr Martin L King Jr Dr
- **Illinois College of Optometry** • 3241 S Michigan Ave
- **Indust Skill Ctr** • 244 E Pershing Rd
- **JJ Pershing School for Humanities** • 3113 S Rhodes Ave
- **Lindblom College Preparatory High** • 707 E 37th St
- **McKinley Lakeside High** • 2929 S Wabash Ave
- **Phillips Academy** • 244 E Pershing Rd
- **Range Memorial Day** • 3806 S Indiana Ave
- **Sengstacke Academic Preparation** • 2641 S Calumet Ave
- **St James Elementary** • 2920 S Wabash Ave
- **St Joseph's Carondelet Child Center** • 739 E 35 St
- **University of Chicago-Donoghue** • 707 E 37 St
- **Wells Elementary** • 244 E Pershing Rd
- **William J & Charles H Mayo Elementary** • 249 E 37th St
- **Young Women's Leadership High** • 2641 S Calumet Ave
- **Youth Connection Charter—YCCS** • 3424 S State St
- **Youth Connection High** • 10 W 35th St

Supermarkets

- **Jewel-Osco** • 443 E 34th St

Map 14 • Prairie Shores / Lake Meadows

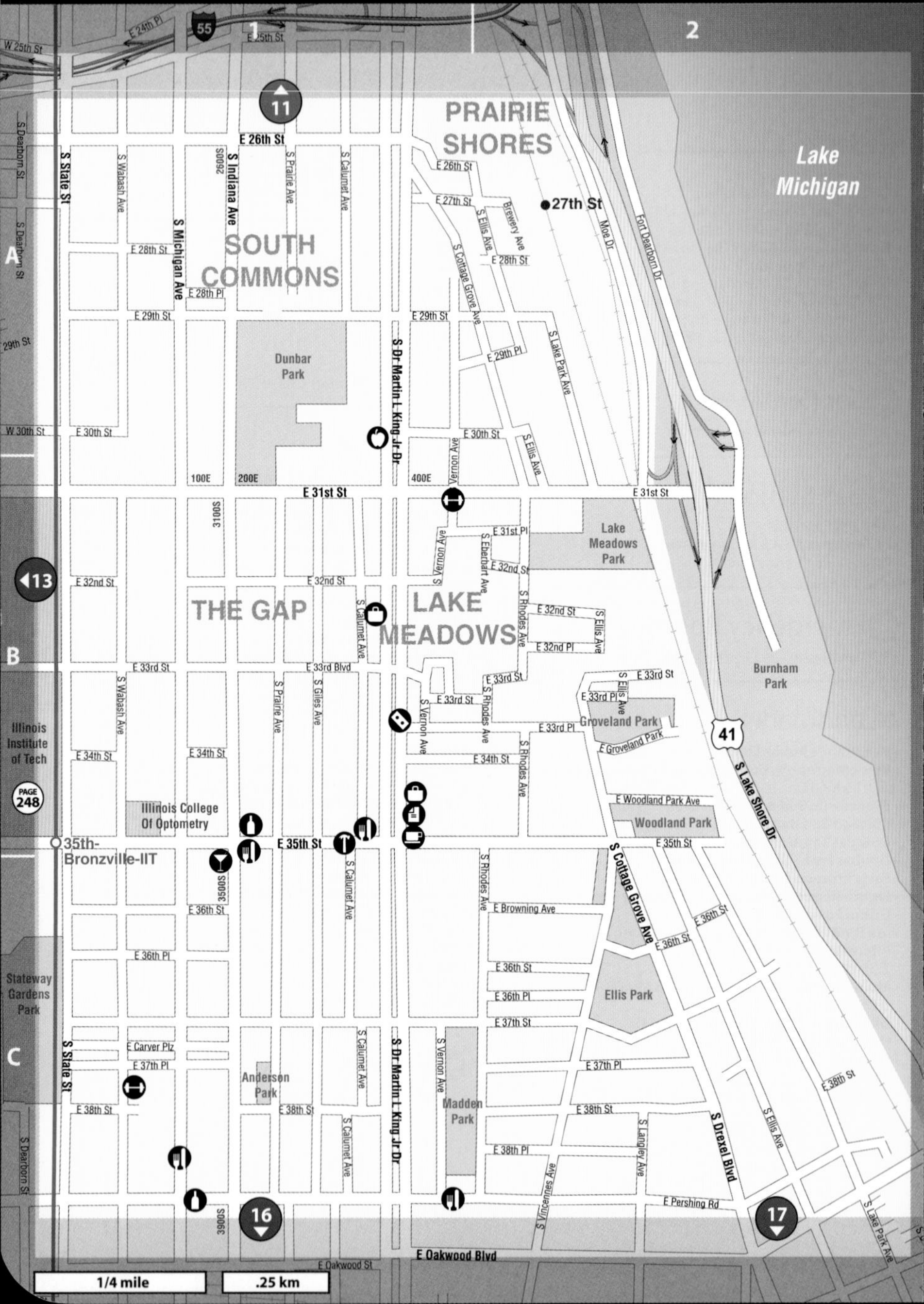

PRAIRIE SHORES
SOUTH COMMONS
THE GAP
LAKE MEADOWS
Lake Michigan
Dunbar Park
Lake Meadows Park
Groveland Park
Woodland Park
Ellis Park
Burnham Park
Anderson Park
Madden Park
Illinois Institute of Tech
Illinois College Of Optometry
Stateway Gardens Park
35th-Bronzville-IIT
27th St
S State St
S Wabash Ave
S Michigan Ave
S Indiana Ave
S Prairie Ave
S Calumet Ave
S Giles Ave
S Dr Martin L King Jr Dr
S Vernon Ave
S Cottage Grove Ave
S Ellis Ave
Brewery Ave
S Lake Park Ave
Moe Dr
Fort Dearborn Dr
S Lake Shore Dr
S Rhodes Ave
S Eberhart Ave
S Vincennes Ave
S Langley Ave
S Drexel Blvd
S Dearborn St
E 25th St
E 26th St
E 27th St
E 28th St
E 28th Pl
E 29th St
E 29th Pl
E 30th St
W 30th St
E 31st St
E 31st Pl
E 32nd St
E 32nd Pl
E 33rd St
E 33rd Blvd
E 33rd Pl
E 34th St
E Groveland Park
E Woodland Park Ave
E 35th St
E 36th St
E Browning Ave
E 36th Pl
E 37th St
E Carver Plz
E 37th Pl
E 38th St
E 38th Pl
E Pershing Rd
E Oakwood Blvd
E Oakwood St
W 25th St
E 24th Pl
29th St
100E
200E
400E
2600S
3100S
3500S
3900S
55
41
1
2
A
B
C
11
13
16
17
PAGE 248
1/4 mile
.25 km

This area of the city is fairly abuzz with neat–o buildings that reflect the city's influential African–American community, past and present. For starters, there's the Ida B. Wells/Barnett House and the former headquarters of the *Chicago Bee*. As curious suburbanites and newcomers return to rehab somewhat forlorn structures throughout the community, the area has begun to experience a 21st–century version of "urban renewal."

Coffee

- **Dunkin' Donuts** • 3481 S Dr Martin L King Jr Dr

Copy Shops

- **The UPS Store** • 3473 S Dr Martin L King Jr Dr

Farmer's Markets

- **Bronzeville (Jun–Oct; Sat, 7 am–2 pm)** • 3000 S Dr Martin L King Jr Dr

Gyms

- **Curves (women only)** • 439 E 31st St
- **Wabash YMCA** • 3763 S Wabash Ave

Hardware Stores

- **Meyers Ace Hardware** • 315 E 35th St

Liquor Stores

- **Poorwood Food & Liquors** • 200 E 35th St
- **Rothchild Liquor Marts** • 124 E Pershing Rd

Nightlife

- **Bossman Blues Center** • 3528 S Indiana Ave

Restaurants

- **Blue Sea Drive Inn** • 427 E Pershing Rd
- **Chicago Rib House** • 3851 S Michigan Ave
- **Hong Kong Delight** • 327 E 35th St
- **McDonald's** • 207 E 35th St

Shopping

- **Ashley Stewart** • 3455 S Dr Martin L King Jr Dr
- **Avenue** • 3429 S Dr Martin L King Jr Dr

Video Rental

- **Blockbuster** • 3349 S Dr Martin L King Jr Dr

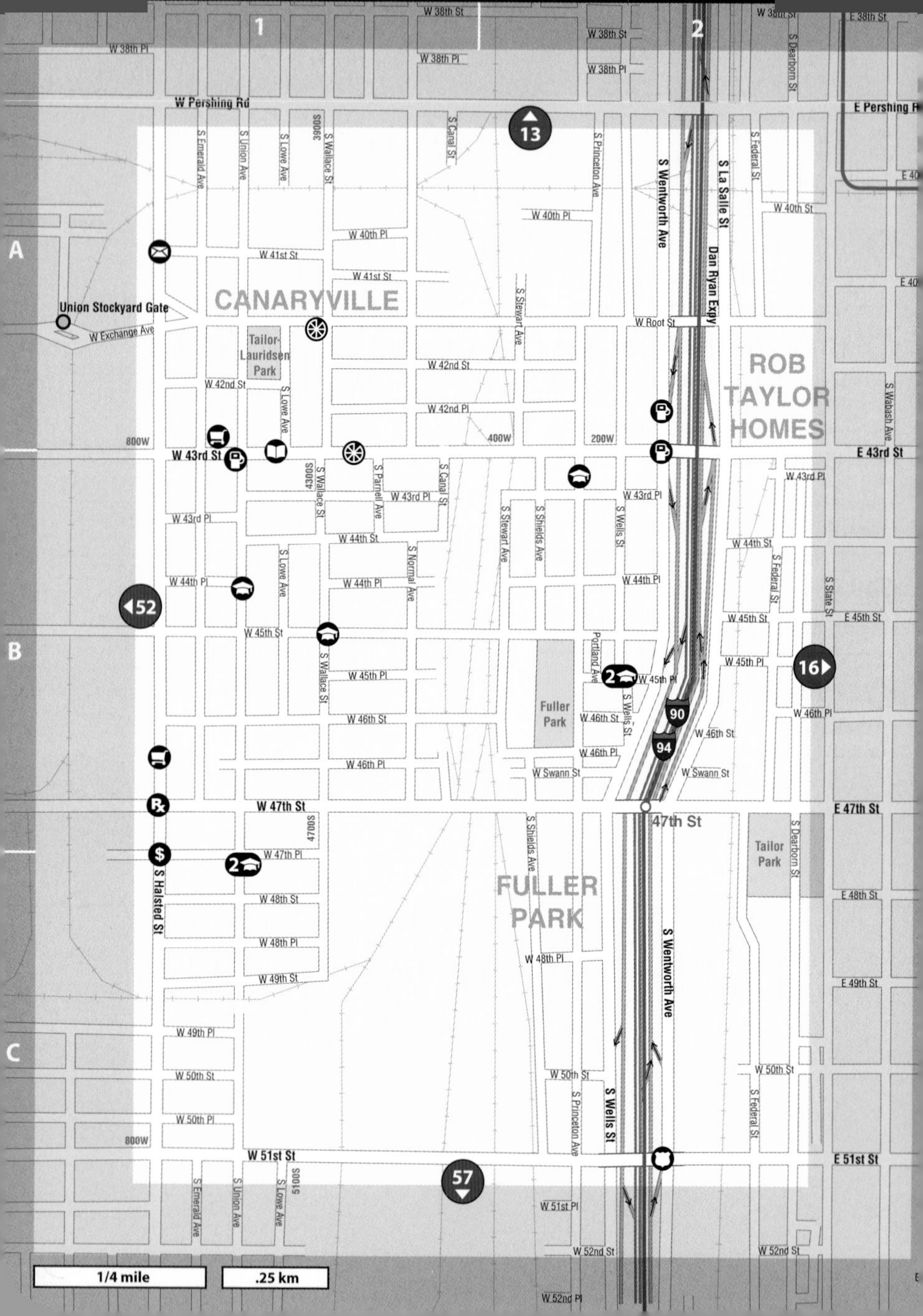

1
2
A
B
C

W 38th St
W 38th St
E 38th St
W 38th Pl
W 38th St
W 38th Pl
W 38th Pl
S Dearborn St
W Pershing Rd
E Pershing Rd
13
S Emerald Ave
S Union Ave
S Lowe Ave
3900S
S Wallace St
S Canal St
S Princeton Ave
S Wentworth Ave
S La Salle St
S Federal St
Dan Ryan Expy
W 40th Pl
W 40th St
W 40th Pl
W 41st St
W 41st St
S Stewart Ave
Union Stockyard Gate
W Exchange Ave
CANARYVILLE
Tailor-Lauridsen Park
W Root St
ROB TAYLOR HOMES
W 42nd St
W 42nd St
W 42nd Pl
S Lowe Ave
S Wabash Ave
800W
400W
200W
W 43rd St
E 43rd St
4300S
S Wallace St
S Parnell Ave
S Canal St
W 43rd Pl
W 43rd Pl
W 43rd Pl
W 43rd Pl
S Stewart Ave
S Shields Ave
S Wells St
W 44th St
W 44th St
S Lowe Ave
S Normal Ave
S Federal St
S State St
W 44th Pl
W 44th Pl
W 44th Pl
52
W 45th St
W 45th St
E 45th St
S Wallace St
Portland Ave
W 45th Pl
W 45th Pl
W 45th Pl
16
Fuller Park
S Wells St
W 46th St
W 46th St
W 46th St
W 46th Pl
90
94
W 46th Pl
W 46th Pl
W Swann St
W Swann St
W 47th St
47th St
E 47th St
4700S
S Shields Ave
Tailor Park
S Dearborn St
W 47th Pl
S Halsted St
W 48th St
E 48th St
FULLER PARK
W 48th Pl
W 48th Pl
S Wentworth Ave
W 49th St
E 49th St
W 49th Pl
W 50th St
W 50th St
W 50th St
S Princeton Ave
S Wells St
S Federal St
W 50th Pl
800W
W 51st St
E 51st St
5100S
57
S Emerald Ave
S Union Ave
S Lowe Ave
W 51st Pl
W 52nd St
W 52nd St
1/4 mile
.25 km
W 52nd Pl

Christmas Day 1865 was a pretty bad day for livestock, as the sprawling Union Stock Yards opened in the area, putting all beasts on the lookout. All that's left these days of the Stock Yards is the imposing limestone gate, which is certainly worth a quick glance, and perhaps a moment of silence. While cattle around the country breathed a collective sigh when the Stock Yards closed, this area quickly headed south afterward and is still in the process of recovery on all fronts.

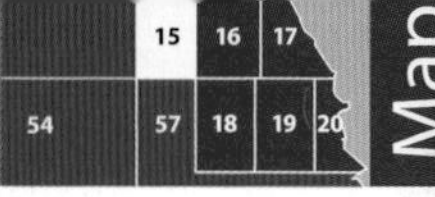

Banks

- **Chase (ATM)** • 4701 S Halsted St

Gas Stations

- **Citgo** • 4300 S Wentworth Ave
- **Econo–Gas** • 4248 S Wentworth Ave
- **Tuxedo Junction** • 4300 S Union Ave

Landmarks

- **Union Stockyard Gate** • Exchange Ave & Peoria St

Libraries

- **Canaryville Public Library** • 642 W 43rd St

Pharmacies

- **Walgreens** • 4700 S Halsted St

Pizza

- **Pizza Nova** • 558 W 43rd St
- **TNT Pizza & Beef** • 601 W Root St

Police

- **2nd District (Wentworth)** • 5101 S Wentworth Ave

Post Offices

- **US Post Office** • 4101 S Halsted St

Schools

- **Alexander Graham Elementary** • 4436 S Union Ave
- **Bronzeville Blue Gargoyle High** • 220 W 45th Pl
- **Francis Parkman Elementary** • 245 W 51st St
- **Garfield Alternative High** • 220 W 45th Pl
- **John H Sengstacke Achievement Academy** • 4747 S Union Ave
- **St Gabriel Elementary** • 4500 S Wallace St
- **Thomas A Hendricks Community Academy** • 4316 S Princeton Ave
- **Tilden High** • 4747 S Union Ave

Supermarkets

- **Fairplay Finer Foods** • 4640 S Halsted St
- **Save A Lot** • 710 W 43rd St

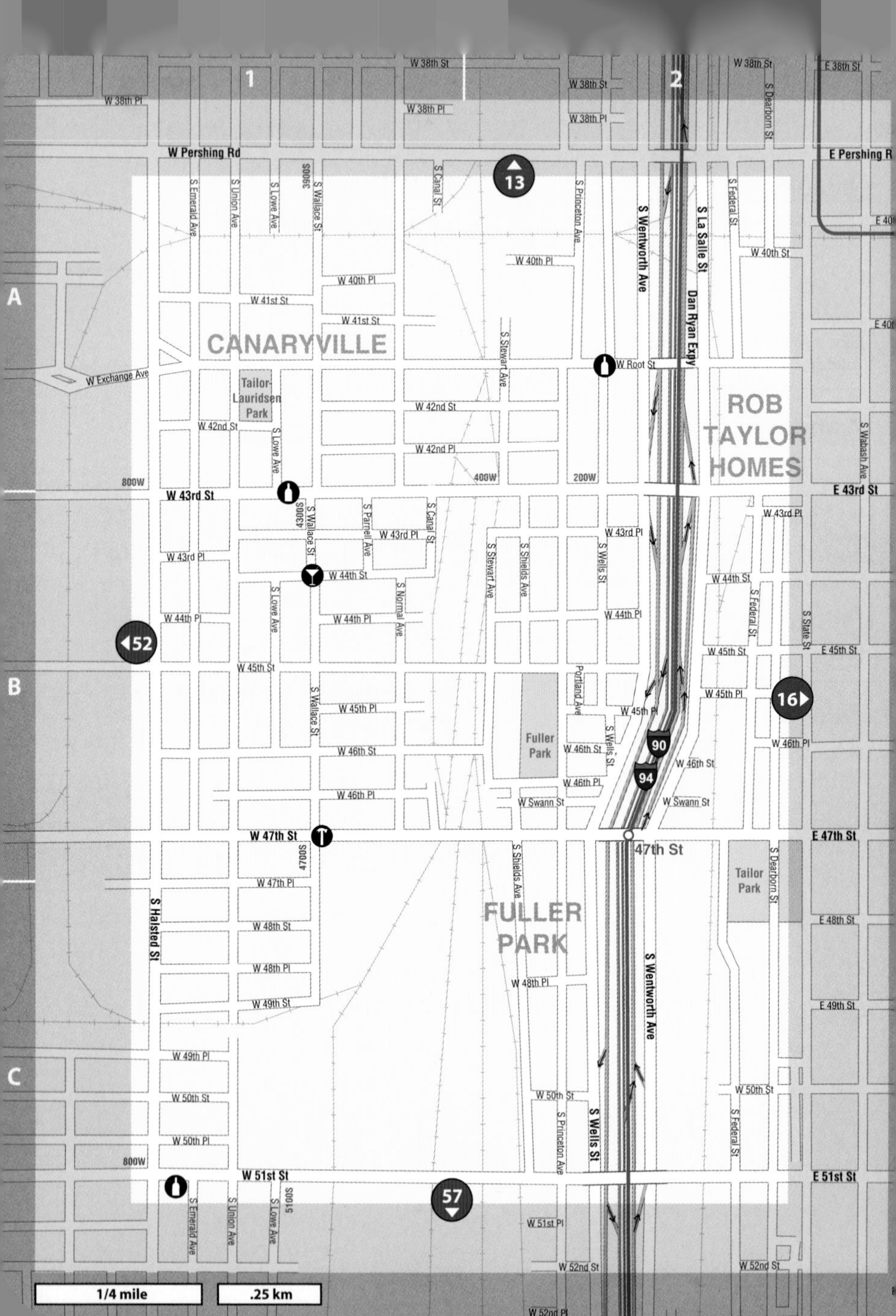

1
2
A
B
C
CANARYVILLE
ROB TAYLOR HOMES
FULLER PARK
Tailor-Lauridsen Park
Fuller Park
Tailor Park
W 38th St
W 38th Pl
E 38th St
W Pershing Rd
E Pershing Rd
W 40th Pl
W 40th St
W 41st St
W Exchange Ave
W Root St
W 42nd St
W 42nd Pl
W 43rd St
E 43rd St
W 43rd Pl
W 44th St
W 44th Pl
W 45th St
E 45th St
W 45th Pl
W 46th St
W 46th Pl
W Swann St
W 47th St
E 47th St
47th St
W 47th Pl
W 48th St
E 48th St
W 48th Pl
W 49th St
E 49th St
W 49th Pl
W 50th St
W 50th Pl
W 51st St
E 51st St
W 51st Pl
W 52nd St
W 52nd Pl
S Halsted St
S Emerald Ave
S Union Ave
S Lowe Ave
S Wallace St
S Parnell Ave
S Canal St
S Normal Ave
S Stewart Ave
S Shields Ave
S Princeton Ave
S Wells St
Portland Ave
S Wentworth Ave
S La Salle St
Dan Ryan Expy
S Federal St
S Dearborn St
S State St
S Wabash Ave
800W
400W
200W
300S
4300S
4700S
5100S
90
94
13
52
16
57
1/4 mile
.25 km

Urban enclaves can change quickly, sometimes in a matter of months, but Canaryville and Fuller Park have retained a scrappy and salt-of-the-earth sensibility for over a century. The closing of the massive Union Stock Yards in 1971 hit the community hard, and until recently the neighborhood was a stone's throw away from the largest public housing complex in the city. Even the most experienced urbanologists may be hard pressed to find much to do here on a casual visit.

Hardware Stores

- **Discount Hardware** • 601 W 47th St

Liquor Stores

- **Bravo Liquors** • 619 W 43rd St
- **Root Inn** • 234 W Root St
- **Shamsan Food & Liquor** • 737 W 51st St

Nightlife

- **Kelley's Tavern** • 4403 S Wallace St

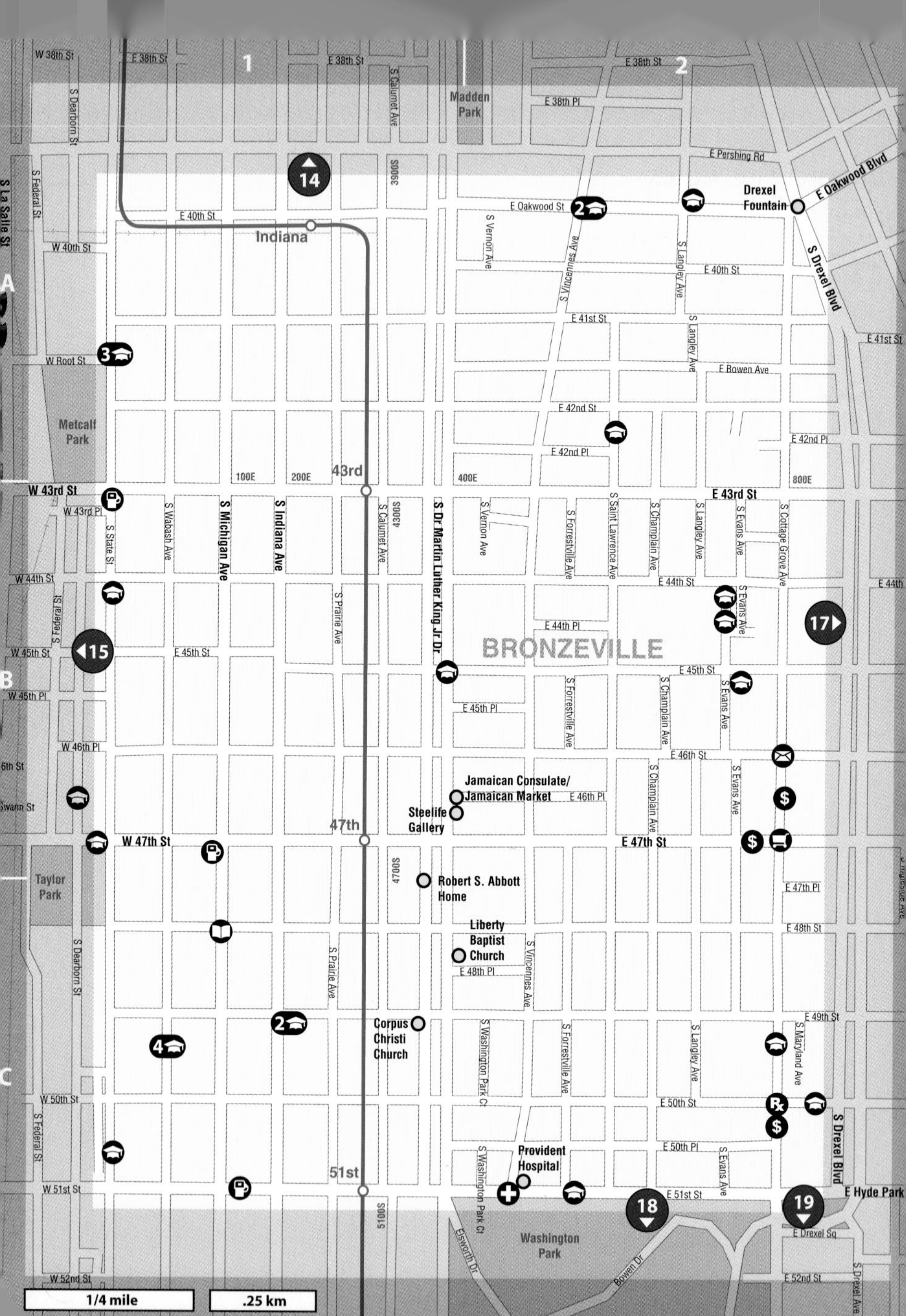

1
2
A
B
C
W 38th St
E 38th St
E 38th St
E 38th St
S Dearborn St
S Calumet Ave
Madden Park
E 38th Pl
E Pershing Rd
S Federal St
S La Salle St
14
3900S
E Oakwood St
2
Drexel Fountain
E Oakwood Blvd
E 40th St
Indiana
W 40th St
S Vernon Ave
S Vincennes Ave
S Langley Ave
E 40th St
S Drexel Blvd
E 41st St
S Langley Ave
E 41st St
3
W Root St
E Bowen Ave
Metcalf Park
E 42nd St
E 42nd Pl
E 42nd Pl
100E
200E
43rd
400E
800E
W 43rd St
E 43rd St
W 43rd Pl
S State St
S Wabash Ave
S Michigan Ave
S Indiana Ave
S Calumet Ave
4300S
S Dr Martin Luther King Jr Dr
S Vernon Ave
S Forrestville Ave
S Saint Lawrence Ave
S Champlain Ave
S Langley Ave
S Evans Ave
S Cottage Grove Ave
W 44th St
S Federal St
S Prairie Ave
E 44th St
E 44th
S Evans Ave
E 44th Pl
17
15
W 45th St
E 45th St
BRONZEVILLE
E 45th St
W 45th Pl
E 45th Pl
S Forrestville Ave
S Champlain Ave
S Evans Ave
W 46th Pl
E 46th St
6th St
Jamaican Consulate/
Jamaican Market
E 46th Pl
S Champlain Ave
S Evans Ave
Swann St
Steelife Gallery
47th
W 47th St
E 47th St
Taylor Park
4700S
Robert S. Abbott Home
E 47th Pl
Liberty Baptist Church
E 48th St
S Dearborn St
S Prairie Ave
S Vincennes Ave
E 48th Pl
2
E 49th St
Corpus Christi Church
4
S Washington Park Ct
S Forrestville Ave
S Langley Ave
S Maryland Ave
W 50th St
E 50th St
S Federal St
E 50th Pl
S Evans Ave
S Drexel Blvd
Provident Hospital
S Washington Park Ct
51st
W 51st St
E 51st St
5100S
18
19
E Hyde Park
Ellsworth Dr
Washington Park
E Drexel Sq
Bowen Dr
W 52nd St
E 52nd St
S Drexel Ave
1/4 mile
.25 km

Essentials

Bronzeville derived its name from a Mayor of Bronzeville promotion that orginated at the *Chicago Bee*, published by black comestic king Anthony Overton. It was later carried over to the *Chicago Defender* as an answer to the mainstream media's portrayal of the district as a "black ghetto," and among the notable "chief executives" was chirp Dinah Washington. From the 1920s to the 1970s Bronzeville paralleled Harlem's black arts movement and economic vitality and was one of the major black communities across the nation.

Banks

- **Chase (ATM)** • 5036 S Cottage Grove Ave
- **Northern Trust (ATM)** • McDonald's• 740 E 47th St
- **Shore** • 4659 S Cottage Grove Ave

Gas Stations

- **Amoco** • 4300 S State St
- **Citgo** • 123 E 51st St
- **Marathon** • 4700 S Michigan Ave

Emergency Rooms

- **Provident** • 500 E 51st St

Landmarks

- **Corpus Christi Church** • 4920 S King Dr
- **Drexel Fountain** • S Drexel Blvd & E Oakwood Blvd
- **Jamaican Consulate/Jamaican Market Place** • 4655 S King Dr, Ste 104
- **Liberty Baptist Church** • 4849 S King Dr
- **Provident Hospital** • 500 E 51st St
- **Robert S Abbott Home** • 4742 S King Dr
- **Steelife Gallery** • 4655 S King Dr

Libraries

- **Hall Public Library** • 4801 S Michigan Ave

Pharmacies

- **Walgreens** • 5036 S Cottage Grove Ave

Post Offices

- **US Post Office** • 4601 S Cottage Grove Ave

Schools

- **Anthony Overton, CPC** • 4935 S Indiana Ave
- **Anthony Overton Elementary** • 221 E 49th St
- **Bartholeme De Las Casas High** • 8 W Root St
- **Bronzeville Scholastic Institute** • 4934 S Wabash Ave
- **Carruthers Center for Inner City Studies, Northeastern Illinois University** • 700 E Oakwood Blvd
- **Colman Elementary** • 4655 S Dearborn St
- **DuSable Leadership Academy of B Shabazz** • 4934 S Wabash Ave
- **Dyett Academy Center** • 555 E 51st St
- **Hales Franciscan High** • 4930 S Cottage Grove Ave
- **Hartigan Campus** • 8 W Root St
- **Helen J McCorkle Elementary** • 4421 S State St
- **Holy Angel's** • 750 E 40th St
- **Irvin C Mollison Elementary** • 4415 S Dr Martin L King Jr Dr
- **Jean Baptiste Du Sable High** • 4934 S Wabash Ave
- **John Farren Elementary** • 5055 S State St
- **Ludwig Von Beethoven Elementary** • 25 W 47th St
- **Melville W Fuller Elementary** • 4214 S St Lawrence Ave
- **St Elizabeth Elementary** • 4052 S Wabash Ave
- **William Reavis Elementary** • 834 E 50th St
- **Williams Preparatory School of Medicine** • 4934 S Wabash Ave
- **Woodson North Middle** • 4414 S Evans Ave
- **Woodson South CPC** • 4511 S Evans Ave
- **Woodson South Elementary** • 4444 S Evans Ave

Supermarkets

- **Save A Lot** • 4701 S Cottage Grove Ave

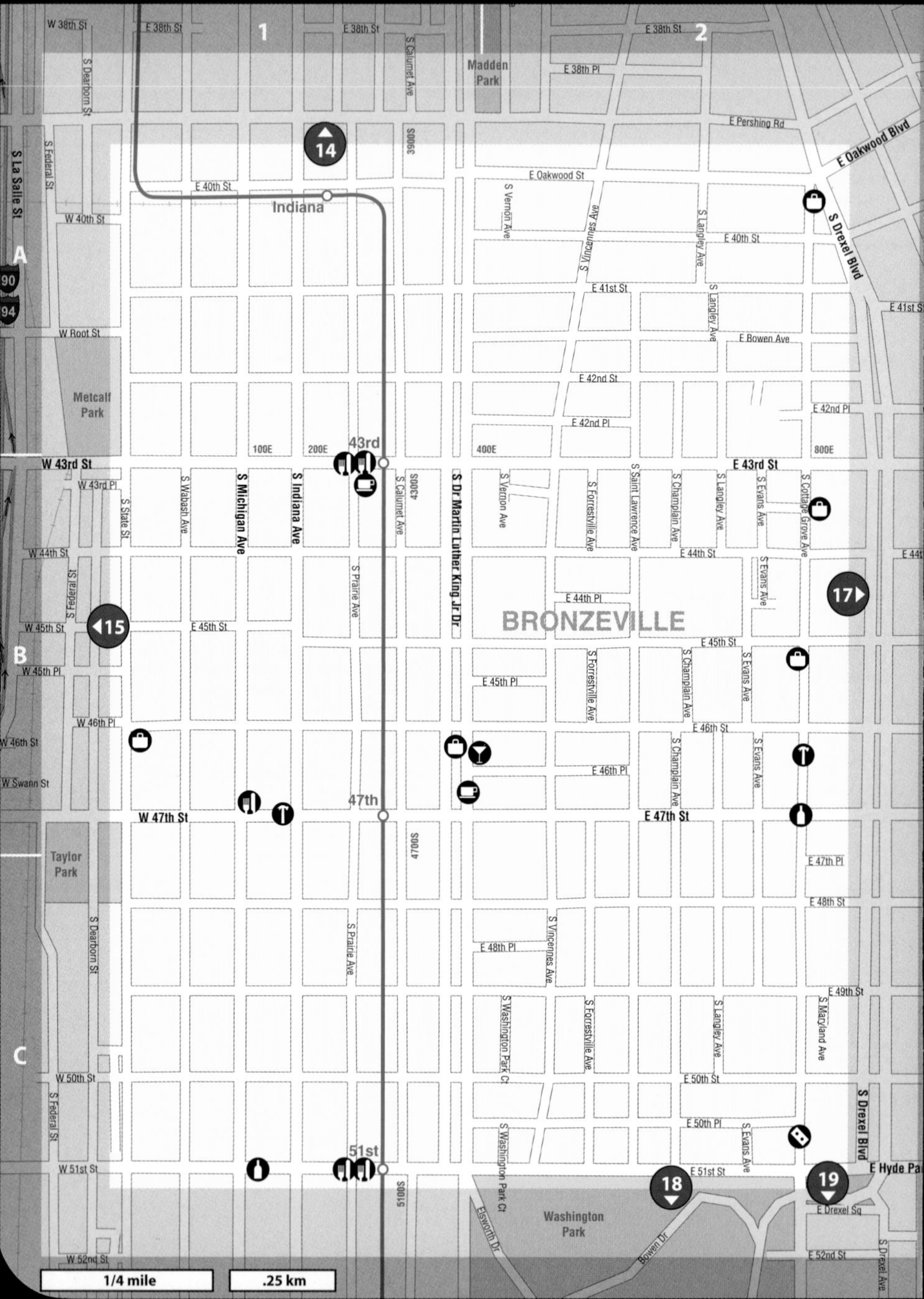

Map 16 • Bronzeville

1
2
A
B
C
W 38th St
E 38th St
E 38th St
E 38th St
S Dearborn St
S Calumet Ave
Madden Park
E 38th Pl
E Pershing Rd
E Oakwood Blvd
S La Salle St
S Federal St
14
3900S
E Oakwood St
E 40th St
Indiana
W 40th St
S Vernon Ave
S Vincennes Ave
S Langley Ave
E 40th St
S Drexel Blvd
90
94
E 41st St
E 41st St
S Langley Ave
W Root St
E Bowen Ave
Metcalf Park
E 42nd St
E 42nd Pl
E 42nd Pl
43rd
100E
200E
400E
800E
W 43rd St
E 43rd St
W 43rd Pl
S State St
S Wabash Ave
S Michigan Ave
S Indiana Ave
4300S
S Calumet Ave
S Dr Martin Luther King Jr Dr
S Vernon Ave
S Forrestville Ave
S Saint Lawrence Ave
S Champlain Ave
S Langley Ave
S Evans Ave
S Cottage Grove Ave
W 44th St
E 44th St
S Prairie Ave
S Evans Ave
E 44th Pl
17
BRONZEVILLE
S Federal St
15
W 45th St
E 45th St
E 45th St
W 45th Pl
S Forrestville Ave
S Champlain Ave
S Evans Ave
E 45th Pl
W 46th Pl
E 46th St
W 46th St
S Champlain Ave
S Evans Ave
E 46th Pl
W Swann St
47th
W 47th St
E 47th St
4700S
Taylor Park
E 47th Pl
E 48th St
S Dearborn St
S Prairie Ave
S Vincennes Ave
E 48th Pl
E 49th St
S Washington Park Ct
S Forrestville Ave
S Langley Ave
S Maryland Ave
W 50th St
E 50th St
S Drexel Blvd
S Federal St
E 50th Pl
S Washington Park Ct
S Evans Ave
51st
W 51st St
E 51st St
5100S
18
19
E Hyde Park
Washington Park
E Drexel Sq
Ellsworth Dr
Bowen Dr
W 52nd St
E 52nd St
S Drexel Ave
1/4 mile
.25 km

Spoken Word Café and the Harold Washington Cultural Center have replaced the jazz clubs that peppered Bronzeville and the Regal Theater, where the Jackson Five made their Chicago debut. They were among the talent film actor Carl Wright introduced as an emcee on the "chittlin circuit" that once catered to black audiences. Afrocentric Bookstore is the headquarters for black literati and filmmakers, and The Negro League Café offers a film series.

Coffee

- **Spoken Word Café** • 4655 S King Dr
- **The Negro League Café** • 301 E 43rd St

Hardware Stores

- **Brooks Hardware** • 103 E 47th St
- **Hyde Park Building Materials** • 4630 S Cottage Grove Ave

Liquor Stores

- **Calumet Food & Liquor** • 315 E 43rd St
- **Pappy's Liquors** • 4700 S Cottage Grove Ave
- **Petra** • 128 E 51st St

Nightlife

- **Jokes & Notes** • 4641 S King Dr

Restaurants

- **Barbara's** • 353 E 51st St
- **Harold's Chicken Shack** • 108 E 47th St
- **Harold's Chicken Shack** • 307 E 51st St
- **Negro League Café** • 301 E 43rd St

Shopping

- **Afrocentric Bookstore** • 4655 S King Dr
- **Issues Barber & Beauty Salon** • 3958 S Cottage Grove Ave
- **Leaders 1354** • 4351 S Cottage Grove Ave
- **Parker House Sausage Co** • 4605 S State St
- **Sensual Steps** • 4518 S Cottage Grove Ave

Video Rental

- **Blockbuster** • 5052 S Cottage Grove Ave

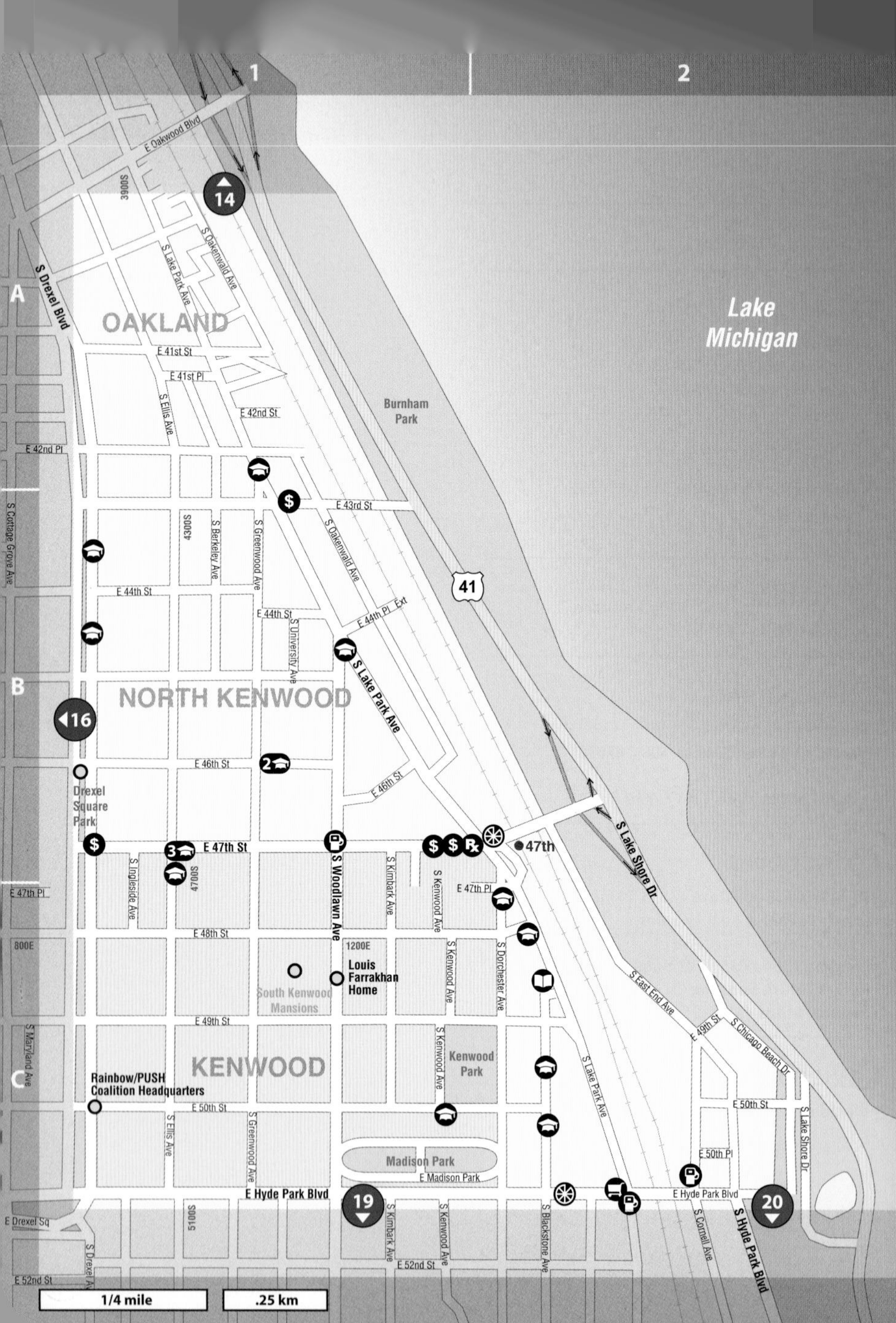
1
2
A
B
C
Lake Michigan
OAKLAND
NORTH KENWOOD
KENWOOD
Burnham Park
Drexel Square Park
South Kenwood Mansions
Louis Farrakhan Home
Rainbow/PUSH Coalition Headquarters
Kenwood Park
Madison Park
E Oakwood Blvd
S Drexel Blvd
S Cottage Grove Ave
S Oakenwald Ave
S Lake Park Ave
S Ellis Ave
E 41st St
E 41st Pl
E 42nd St
E 42nd Pl
E 43rd St
S Berkeley Ave
S Greenwood Ave
E 44th St
E 44th Pl Ext
S University Ave
E 46th St
E 47th St
E 47th Pl
S Ingleside Ave
S Woodlawn Ave
S Kimbark Ave
S Kenwood Ave
S Dorchester Ave
S Lake Shore Dr
47th
E 48th St
E 49th St
E 50th St
E 50th Pl
S East End Ave
E 49th St
S Chicago Beach Dr
S Maryland Ave
S Blackstone Ave
E Madison Park
E Hyde Park Blvd
S Hyde Park Blvd
S Cornell Ave
E Drexel Sq
S Drexel Ave
E 52nd St
3900S
4300S
4700S
5100S
800E
1200E
41
14
16
19
20
1/4 mile
.25 km

Many a 19th-century suburb prided itself on wide lawns and bucolic settings, and Kenwood was no exception. Though it was politely annexed to Chicago over one hundred years ago, the bucolic feeling lingers. These days, the neighborhood contains everything from the residence of Louis Farrakhan to the oldest Jewish congregation in the city, KAM Isaiah Israel. With few eateries in the area, visitors may want to take a lunch and wander over to Lake Michigan for a quiet respite.

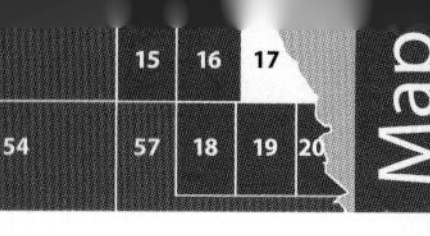

Banks

- **Chase (ATM)** • 1320 E 47th St
- **Citibank** • 1320 E 47th St
- **Harris Trust & Savings** • 901 E 47th St
- **Hyde Park (ATM)** • 4301 S Lake Park Ave

Gas Stations

- **Amoco** • 1158 E 47th St
- **Amoco** • 5048 S Cornell Ave
- **BP** • 5130 S Lake Park Ave

Landmarks

- **Drexel Square Park** • Drexel Blvd, from 51st St to 39th St
- **Louis Farrakhan Home** • 4855 S Woodlawn Ave
- **Rainbow/PUSH Coalition Headquarters** • 930 E 50th St
- **South Kenwood Mansions** • b/w S Dorchester Ave (east), S Ellis Ave (west), E Hyde Park Blvd (south), & E 47th St (north)

Libraries

- **Blackstone Public Library** • 4904 S Lake Park Ave

Pharmacies

- **Walgreens** • 1320 E 47th St

Pizza

- **Domino's** • 1453 E Hyde Park Blvd
- **Italian Fiesta Pizzeria** • 1400 E 47th St

Schools

- **Ancona Montessori** • 4770 S Dorchester Ave
- **Ariel Community** • 4434 S Lake Park Ave
- **Ariel Community Academy** • 1119 E 46th St
- **Childrens House at Harper Square** • 4800 S Lake Park Ave
- **Creative Mansion Childrens Academy** • 4745 S Ellis Ave
- **Dr Martin Luther King Jr High** • 4445 S Drexel Blvd
- **Florence B Price Elementary** • 4351 S Drexel Ave
- **Kenwood High** • 5015 S Blackstone Ave
- **Miriam Canter Middle** • 4959 S Blackstone Ave
- **North Kenwood/Oakland Elementary** • 1119 E 46th St
- **North Kenwood/Oakland Middle** • 1014 E 47th St
- **Robinson Elementary** • 4225 S Lake Park Ave
- **Shoesmith Elementary** • 1330 E 50th St
- **St Ambrose Elementary** • 1014 E 47th St
- **The Harvard School** • 4731 S Ellis Ave

Supermarkets

- **Village Foods** • 1521 E Hyde Park Blvd

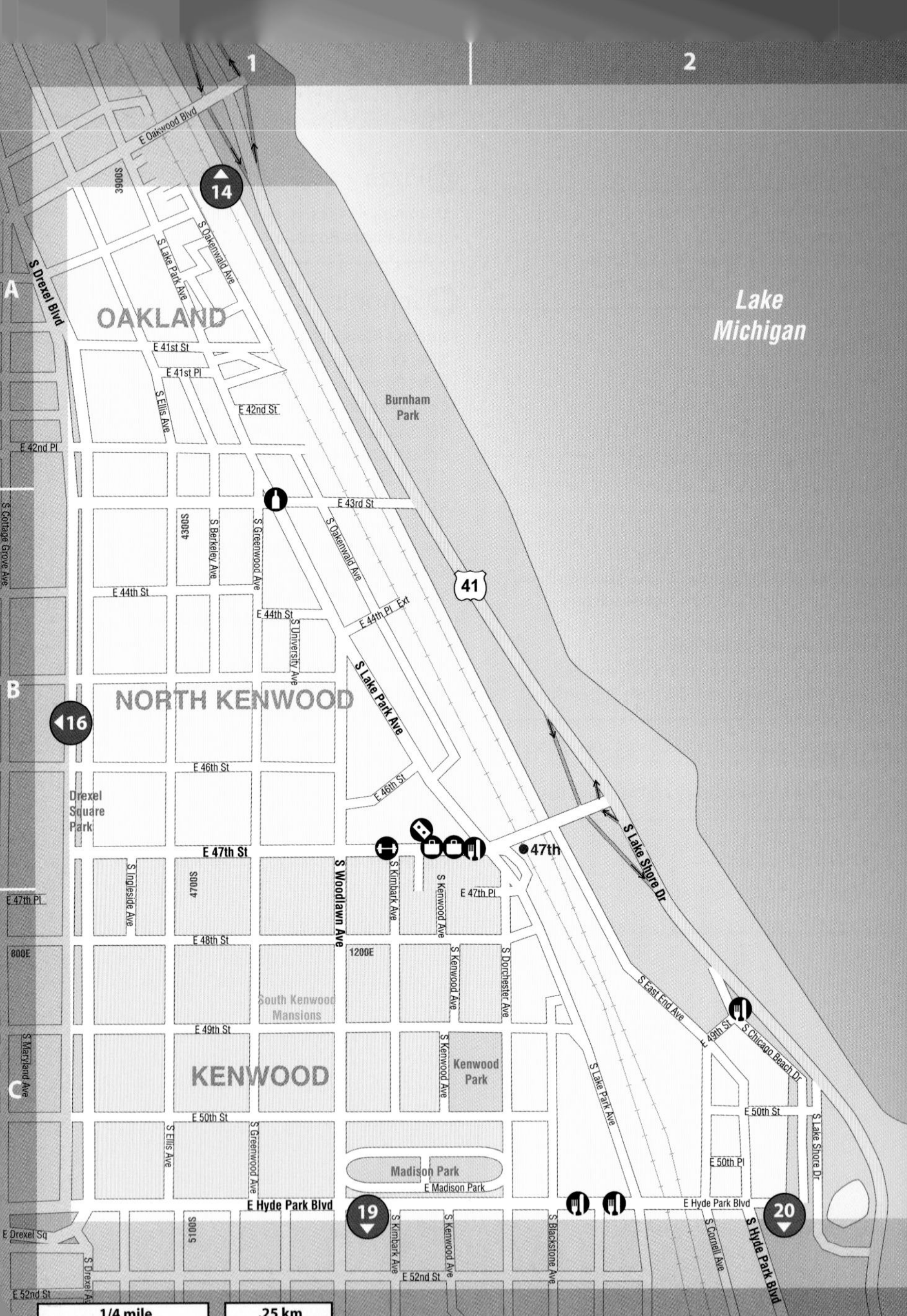

1
2
A
B
C
Lake Michigan
OAKLAND
NORTH KENWOOD
KENWOOD
Burnham Park
Drexel Square Park
South Kenwood Mansions
Kenwood Park
Madison Park
14
16
19
20
41
47th
S Drexel Blvd
E Oakwood Blvd
S Oakenwald Ave
S Lake Park Ave
E 41st St
E 41st Pl
E 42nd St
E 42nd Pl
S Ellis Ave
E 43rd St
S Cottage Grove Ave
S Berkeley Ave
S Greenwood Ave
E 44th St
E 44th Pl Ext
S University Ave
E 46th St
E 47th St
E 47th Pl
S Woodlawn Ave
S Kimbark Ave
S Kenwood Ave
S Ingleside Ave
E 48th St
S Dorchester Ave
E 49th St
S Maryland Ave
E 50th St
E 50th Pl
E Madison Park
E Hyde Park Blvd
S Lake Shore Dr
S East End Ave
S Chicago Beach Dr
S Blackstone Ave
S Cornell Ave
S Hyde Park Blvd
E Drexel Sq
E 52nd St
S Drexel Av
3900S
4300S
4700S
5100S
800E
1200E
1/4 mile
.25 km

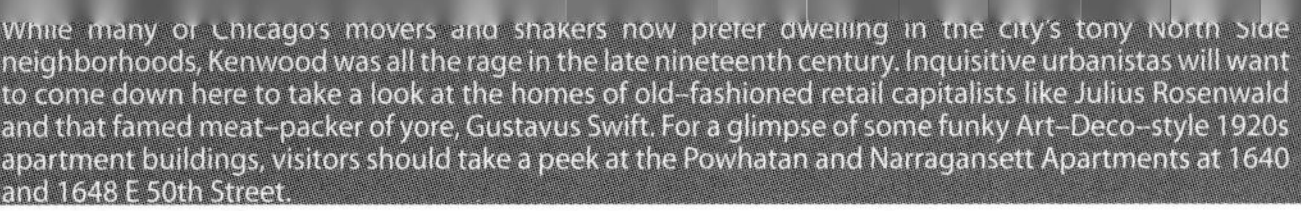
While many of Chicago's movers and shakers now prefer dwelling in the city's tony North Side neighborhoods, Kenwood was all the rage in the late nineteenth century. Inquisitive urbanistas will want to come down here to take a look at the homes of old-fashioned retail capitalists like Julius Rosenwald and that famed meat-packer of yore, Gustavus Swift. For a glimpse of some funky Art-Deco-style 1920s apartment buildings, visitors should take a peek at the Powhatan and Narragansett Apartments at 1640 and 1648 E 50th Street.

Gyms

- **Bally Total Fitness** • 1301 E 47th St

Liquor Stores

- **One Stop Food & Liquors** • 4301 S Lake Park Ave

Restaurants

- **Fung's Chop Suey** • 1400 E 47th St
- **Kenny's Ribs & Chicken** • 1461 E Hyde Park Blvd
- **Lake Shore Café** • 4900 S Lake Shore Dr
- **The Original Pancake House** • 1517 E Hyde Park Blvd

Shopping

- **Coop's Records** • 1350 E 47th St
- **South Shore Decor** • 1328 E 47th St

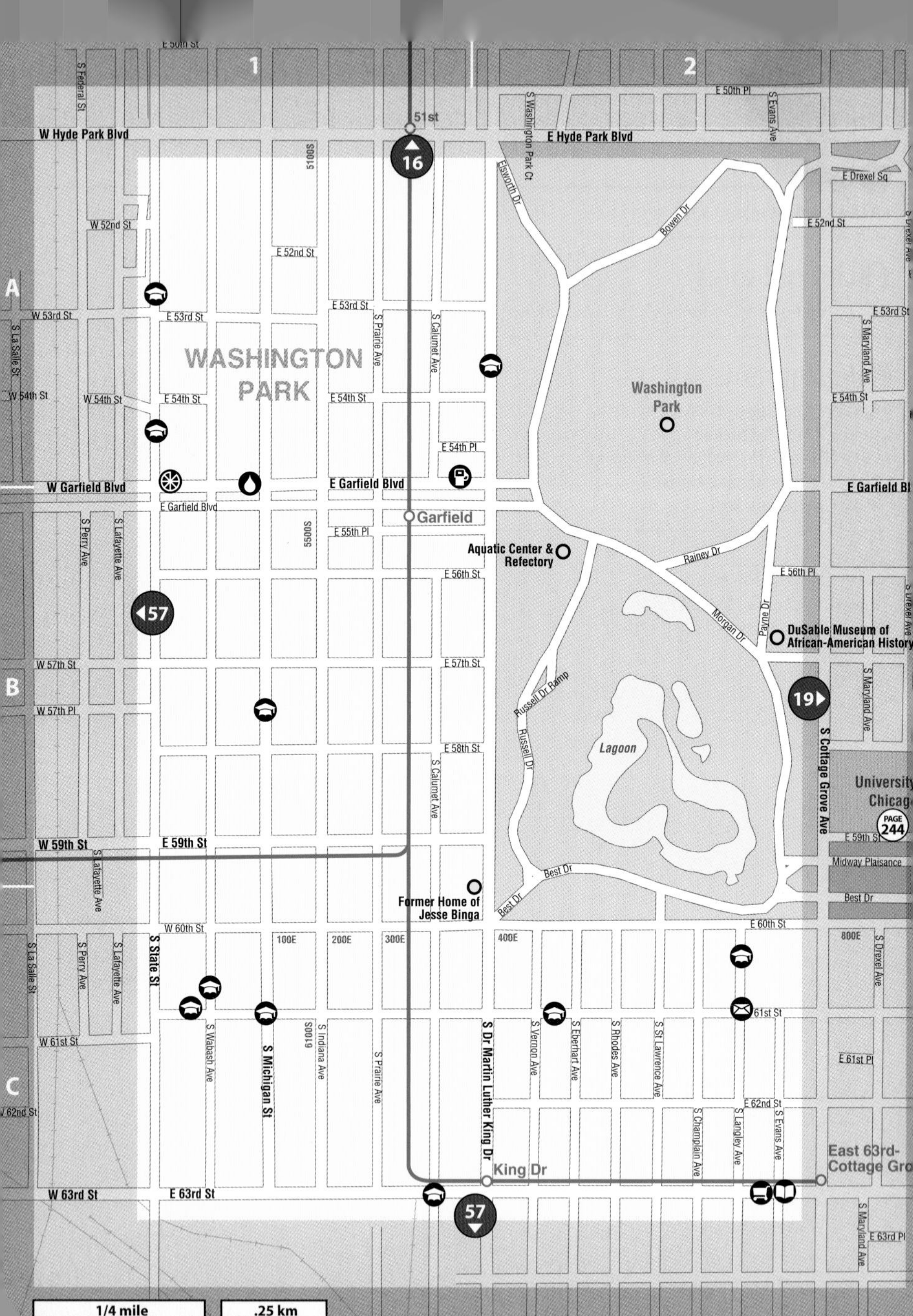

1
2
A
B
C
WASHINGTON PARK
Washington Park
Lagoon
51st
Garfield
King Dr
East 63rd-Cottage Grove
16
57
19
Aquatic Center & Refectory
DuSable Museum of African-American History
Former Home of Jesse Binga
University of Chicago
PAGE 244
E 50th St
E 50th Pl
W Hyde Park Blvd
E Hyde Park Blvd
E Drexel Sq
W 52nd St
E 52nd St
W 53rd St
E 53rd St
W 54th St
E 54th St
E 54th Pl
W Garfield Blvd
E Garfield Blvd
E 55th Pl
E 56th St
E 56th Pl
W 57th St
W 57th Pl
E 57th St
E 58th St
W 59th St
E 59th St
Midway Plaisance
Best Dr
W 60th St
E 60th St
W 61st St
61st St
E 61st Pl
W 62nd St
E 62nd St
W 63rd St
E 63rd St
E 63rd Pl
S Federal St
S La Salle St
S Perry Ave
S Lafayette Ave
S State St
S Wabash Ave
S Michigan St
S Indiana Ave
S Prairie Ave
S Calumet Ave
S Dr Martin Luther King Dr
S Vernon Ave
S Eberhart Ave
S Rhodes Ave
S St Lawrence Ave
S Champlain Ave
S Langley Ave
S Evans Ave
S Cottage Grove Ave
S Maryland Ave
S Drexel Ave
S Washington Park Ct
Elsworth Dr
Bowen Dr
Rainey Dr
Morgan Dr
Payne Dr
Russell Dr
Russell Dr Ramp
5100S
5500S
6000S
100E
200E
300E
400E
800E
1/4 mile
.25 km

For decades the western border of Washington Park was defined by the presence of the Robert Taylor public housing project, a good policy idea gone terribly wrong. In recent years, the projects have been torn down and the entire community has seen a mini-revival as new residential structures have popped up in long-vacant lots. The eastern half of Washington Park is dominated by the park itself, which contains the DuSable Museum of African-American History and a grand structure housing that all-important summer hangout: a swimming pool.

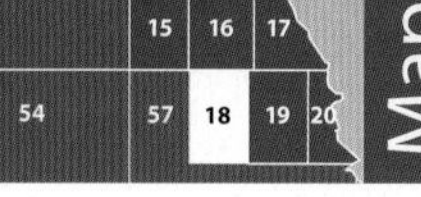

Car Washes

- **Adam's Car Wash** • 48 E Garfield Blvd

Gas Stations

- **Southtown Oil** • 368 E Garfield Blvd

Landmarks

- **Aquatic Center & Refectory** • 5531 S Martin Luther King Jr Dr
- **DuSable Museum of African-American History** • 740 E 56th Pl
- **Former Home of Jesse Binga** • 5922 S Dr Martin L King Jr Dr
- **Washington Park** • E 60th St thru E 51st St, from S Cottage Grove Ave to S Dr Martin L King Jr Dr

Libraries

- **Bessie Coleman Public Library** • 731 E 63rd St

Pizza

- **B&B Pizza King** • 4 W Garfield Blvd

Post Offices

- **US Post Office** • 700 E 61st St

Schools

- **ACE Technical High** • 5410 S State St
- **Austin O Sexton Elementary** • 6020 S Langley Ave
- **Beasley Academic Elementary** • 5255 S State St
- **Betsy Ross Elementary** • 6059 S Wabash Ave
- **Chicago International Elementary—Washington Park Campus** • 6105 S Michigan Ave
- **Edmund Burke Elementary** • 5356 S King Dr
- **John Foster Dulles High** • 6311 S Calumet Ave
- **Oneida Cockrell, CPC** • 30 E 61 St
- **William W Carter Elementary** • 5740 S Michigan Ave
- **Woodlawn Intergenerational High** • 448 E 61st St

Supermarkets

- **Brothers Food Market** • 723 E 63rd St

1
2
A
B
C
WASHINGTON PARK
Washington Park
Lagoon
University Chicag
PAGE 244
16
57
19
57
51st
Garfield
King Dr
East 63rd-Cottage Gro
W Hyde Park Blvd
E Hyde Park Blvd
E 50th Pl
W 52nd St
E 52nd St
E Drexel Sq
E 52nd St
W 53rd St
E 53rd St
E 53rd St
E 53rd St
W 54th St
W 54th St
E 54th St
E 54th St
E 54th St
E 54th Pl
W Garfield Blvd
E Garfield Blvd
E Garfield Blvd
E Garfield Bl
E 55th Pl
E 56th St
E 56th Pl
W 57th St
E 57th St
W 57th Pl
E 58th St
W 59th St
E 59th St
E 59th St
Midway Plaisance
Best Dr
W 60th St
E 60th St
E 61st St
W 61st St
E 61st Pl
E 62nd St
W 63rd St
E 63rd St
E 63rd Pl
S Federal St
S La Salle St
S Perry Ave
S Lafayette Ave
S State St
S Wabash Ave
S Michigan St
S Indiana Ave
S Prairie Ave
S Calumet Ave
S Dr Martin Luther King Dr
S Vernon Ave
S Eberhart Ave
S Rhodes Ave
S St Lawrence Ave
S Champlain Ave
S Langley Ave
S Evans Ave
S Cottage Grove Ave
S Maryland Ave
S Drexel Ave
S Washington Park Ct
Elsworth Dr
Bowen Dr
Rainey Dr
Morgan Dr
Payne Dr
Russell Dr Ramp
Russell Dr
Best Dr
5100S
5500S
6000S
100E
200E
300E
400E
800E
1/4 mile
.25 km

While family reunions, cricket tournaments, and pan-African festivals are the dominant leisure activities in Washington Park today, the park used to feature carriage rides, horse-racing, and other pursuits that loomed large in the social lives of Gilded Age dandies. Walking through the park, visitors should not miss the massive Fountain of Time sculpture at the western end of the Midway Plaisance, a moody interpretation of humanity offered up by the artist Lorado Taft.

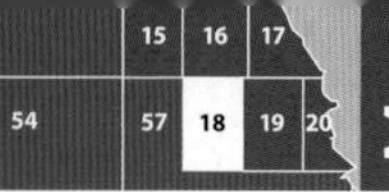

Copy Shops

- **JJC Creative Services** • 130 E Garfield Blvd

Hardware Stores

- **Boulevard Ace Hardware** • 227 E Garfield Blvd

Liquor Stores

- **Jordan Food & Liquor** • 315 E Garfield Blvd
- **Rothschild Liquor Marts** • 425 E 63rd St

Restaurants

- **Ms Lee's Good Food** • 205 E Garfield Blvd
- **Rose's BBQ Chicken** • 5426 S State St

HYDE PARK
WOODLAWN
Washington Park
Madison Park
Nichols Park
Spruce Park
Jackson Park
Midway Plaisance Park
Nuclear Energy Sculpture
University of Chicago
Frederick C Robie House
Rockefeller Memorial Chapel
Midway Plaisance Park & Skating Rink
East 63rd-Cottage Grove
53rd
55th
59th
63rd
E Hyde Park Blvd
E 55th St
E 56th St
E 63rd St
S Cottage Grove Ave
S Woodlawn Ave
S Lake Park Ave
S Stony Island Ave
S Park Shore East Ct
PAGE 244
PAGE 212
16
17
18
20
57
1/4 mile
.25 km

Neo-Gothic buildings and large-scale urban renewal come together in Hyde Park, one of the South Side's most diverse and eclectic communities. The presence of the University of Chicago draws an impressive band of intellectuals together, while there are still others who remain happily oblivious to their presence. As the area is quite well laid out for peripatetic walks, visitors will want to wander by the Robie House, Rockefeller Chapel, and the retail chaos along 53rd Street.

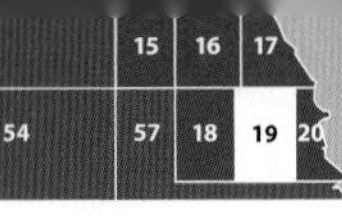

Banks

- **Chase** • 1204 E 53rd St
- **Chase (ATM)** • 1554 E 55th St
- **Chase (ATM)** • 5815 S Maryland Ave
- **Citibank** • 5812 S Ellis Ave
- **Citibank (ATM)** • 5807 S Woodlawn Ave
- **Cole Taylor** • 824 E 63rd St
- **Harris Trust & Savings (ATM)** • UC Hospital • 5758 S Maryland Ave
- **Hyde Park** • 1311 E 57th St
- **Hyde Park** • 1525 E 53rd St
- **Hyde Park (ATM)** • 1518 E 53rd St
- **Hyde Park (ATM)** • 1526 E 55th St
- **Northern Trust (ATM)** • McDonald's • 5220 S Lake Park Ave
- **TCF (ATM)** • 1214 E 53rd St
- **TCF (ATM)** • Osco • 1420 E 53rd St
- **TCF (ATM)** • 1455 E 57th St
- **University National** • 1354 E 55th St

Car Washes

- **Hyde Park Mobile Car Wash** • 1330 E 53rd St

Car Rental

- **Enterprise** • 5508 S Lake Park Ave • 773-288-0500

Gas Stations

- **BP** • 6011 S Cottage Grove Ave
- **Mobil** • 1330 E 53rd St

Emergency Rooms

- **University of Chicago** • 858 E 58th St
- **University of Chicago Children's** • 5721 S Maryland Ave

Landmarks

- **Frederick C Robie House** • 5757 S Woodlawn Ave
- **Midway Plaisance Park & Skating Rink** • S Ellis Ave & S University Ave, from E 59th St to E 60th St
- **Nichols Park** • 1300 E 55th St
- **Nuclear Energy Sculpture** • 5600 S Ellis Ave
- **Rockefeller Memorial Chapel** • 5850 S Woodlawn Ave

Libraries

- **University of Chicago Harper Memorial Library** • 1116 E 59th St

Pharmacies

- **CVS Pharmacy** • 1228 E 53rd St
- **Osco Drug** • 1420 E 53rd St
- **Walgreens** • 1554 E 55th St

Pizza

- **Caffe Florian** • 1450 E 57th St
- **Edwardo's Natural Pizza** • 1321 E 57th St
- **Giordano's** • 5309 S Blackstone Ave
- **Medici on 57th** • 1327 E 57th St
- **Pizza Capri** • 1501 E 53rd St
- **Pizza Hut** • 1406 E 53rd St

Post Offices

- **US Post Office** • 1526 E 55th St
- **US Post Office** • 956 E 58th St

Schools

- **Andrew Carnegie Elementary** • 1414 E 61st Pl
- **Bret Harte Elementary** • 1556 E 56th St
- **Charles Kozminski Elementary** • 936 E 54th St
- **Chicago Theological Seminary** • 5757 S University Ave
- **Donoghue Charter** • 1313 E 60 St
- **Hyde Park Day** • 1375 E 60th St
- **John Fiske Elementary** • 6145 S Ingleside Ave
- **Lutheran School of Theology at Chicago** • 1100 E 55th St
- **McCormick Seminary** • 5460 S University Ave
- **Meadville Lombard Theological** • 5701 S Woodlawn Ave
- **Phillip Murray Language Academy** • 5335 S Kenwood Ave
- **Sonia Sahnkman Orthogenic** • 1365 E 60th St
- **St Thomas the Apostle Elementary** • 5467 S Woodlawn Ave
- **Toyota Technological Institute at Chicago** • 1427 E 60th St
- **University of Chicago** • 5801 S Ellis Ave
- **University of Chicago Laboratory** • 1362 E 59th St
- **William H Ray Elementary** • 5631 S Kimbark Ave

Supermarkets

- **Bonne Sante Health Food** • 1512 E 53rd St
- **Co-op Market** • 1526 E 55th St
- **Co-op Market Express** • 1226 E 53rd St
- **Hyde Park Produce** • 1312 E 53rd St
- **University Market** • 1323 E 57th St

Parking

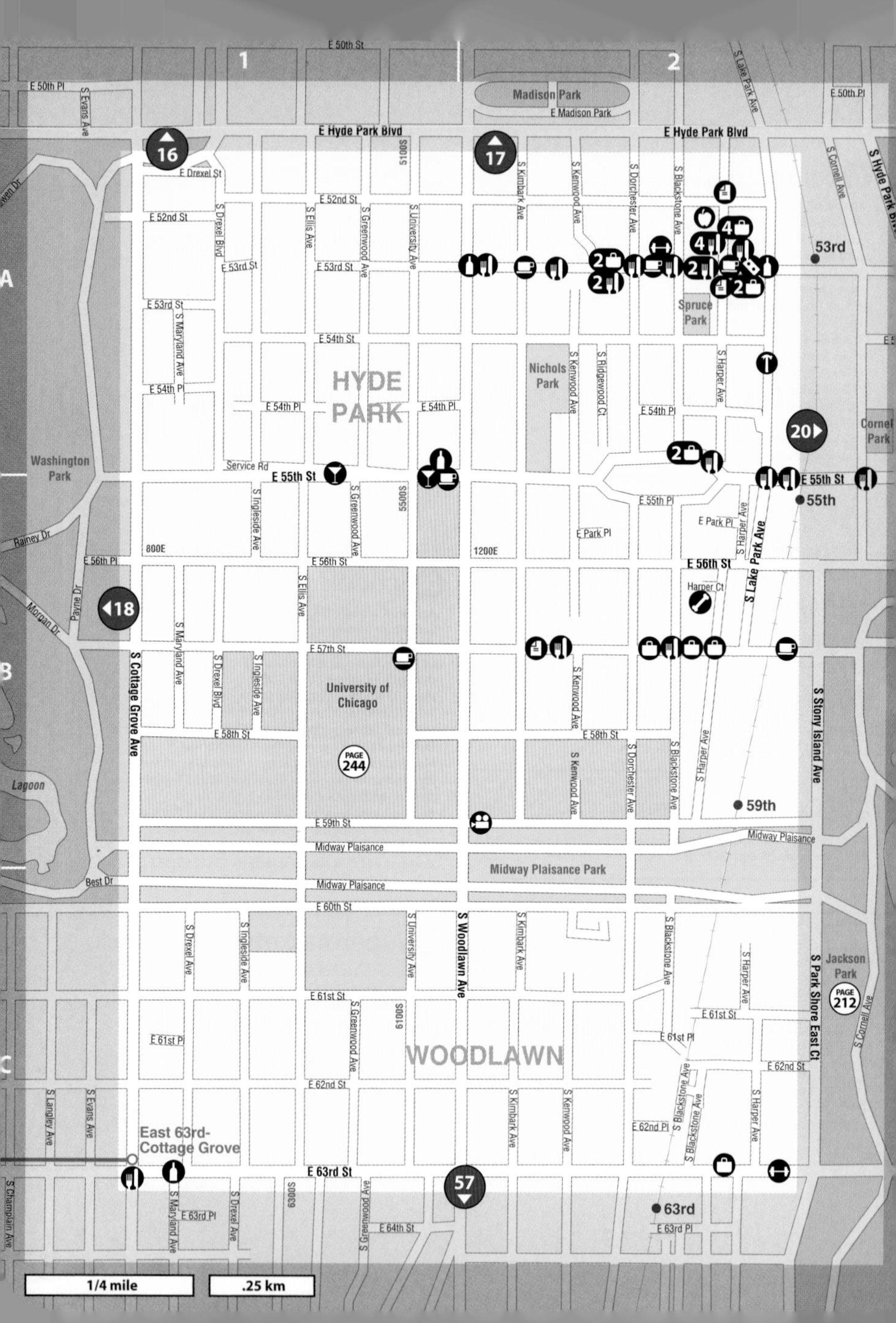

E 50th St
1
2
E 50th Pl
Madison Park
E Madison Park
E Hyde Park Blvd
16
17
E Drexel St
E 52nd St
E 53rd St
53rd
Spruce Park
HYDE PARK
Nichols Park
E 54th Pl
20
Washington Park
Service Rd
E 55th St
55th
E 55th Pl
E Park Pl
E 56th Pl
E 56th St
Harper Ct
18
E 57th St
University of Chicago
PAGE 244
E 58th St
S Cottage Grove Ave
S Lake Park Ave
S Stony Island Ave
Lagoon
59th
E 59th St
Midway Plaisance
Midway Plaisance Park
Best Dr
E 60th St
S Woodlawn Ave
Jackson Park
S Park Shore East Ct
PAGE 212
E 61st St
E 61st Pl
WOODLAWN
E 62nd St
E 62nd Pl
East 63rd-Cottage Grove
E 63rd St
57
63rd
E 63rd Pl
E 64th St
1/4 mile
.25 km

Hyde Park is dominated by the University of Chicago and those drawn close to soak up Kant and quantum physics. While Hyde Park struggles to identify a "nightlife," Woodlawn Tap is consistently there for the college crowd and neighborhood regulars. Bookstore Row on 57th Street provides a literary surge to the neighborhood. Restaurants range from the delivery-and-counter-seating-only Ribs 'n' Bibs, to the upscale La Petite Folie, to the ever-necessary Noodles Etc.

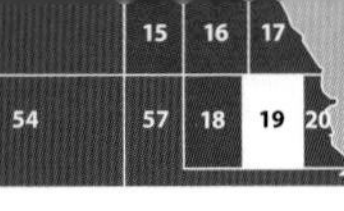

Coffee

- **Dunkin' Donuts** • 1411 E 53rd St
- **Einstein Bros Bagels** • University of Chicago • 5706 S University Ave
- **Istria Café** • 1520 E 57th St
- **Starbucks** • 1174 E 55th St
- **Starbucks** • 1500 E 53rd St
- **Third World Café** • 1301 E 53rd St

Copy Shops

- **Copy Works** • 5210 S Harper Ave
- **Fedex Kinko's** • 1315 E 57th St
- **The UPS Store** • 1507 E 53rd St

Farmer's Markets

- **Hyde Park (Jun–Oct; Thurs, 7 am–2 pm)** • E 52nd Pl & Harper Ave

Gyms

- **Curves (women only)** • 1424 E 53rd St
- **Curves (women only)** • 1514 E 63rd St

Hardware Stores

- **Elston Ace Hardware** • 5420 S Lake Park Ave

Liquor Stores

- **Binny's Beverage Depot** • 1531 E 53rd St
- **Fair Discount** • 801 E 63rd St
- **Kimbark Liquors & Wine Shop** • 1214 E 53rd St
- **Woodlawn Tap & Liquor Store** • 1172 E 55th St

Movie Theaters

- **University of Chicago Doc Films** • 1212 E 59th St

Nightlife

- **Seven Ten Lanes** • 1055 E 55th St
- **Woodlawn Tap** • 1172 E 55th St

Pet Shops

- **Hyde Park Pet** • 5210 S Harper Ave

Restaurants

- **Bonjour Café Bakery** • 1550 E 55th St
- **C'Est Si Bon** • 5225 S Harper Ave
- **Calypso Café** • Harper Ctr • 5211 S Harper Ave
- **Cedars Mediterranean Kitchen** • 1206 E 53rd St
- **Daley's Restaurant** • 809 E 63rd St
- **Dixie Kitchen and Bait Shop** • 5225 S Harper Ave
- **Hyde Park Gyros** • 1368 E 53rd St
- **Kikuya Japanese Restaurant** • 1601 E 55th St
- **La Petite Folie** • Hyde Park Shopping Ctr • 1504 E 55th St
- **Maravilla's Mexican Restaurant** • 5211 S Harper Ave
- **Medici on 57th** • 1327 E 57th St
- **Mellow Yellow** • 1508 E 53rd St
- **Nathan's** • 1372 E 53rd St
- **Noodles Etc** • 1333 E 53rd St
- **Rajun Cajun** • 1459 E 53rd St
- **Ribs 'n' Bibs** • 5300 S Dorchester Ave
- **Salonica** • 1440 E 57th St
- **Thai 55 Restaurant** • 1607 E 55th St
- **Valois** • 1518 E 53rd St

Shopping

- **57th Street Books** • 1301 E 57th St
- **The Baby PhD Store** • 5225 S Harper Ave
- **Border's** • 1539 E 53rd St
- **Coconuts** • 1506 E 53rd St
- **Cohn & Stern for Men** • 1500 E 55th St
- **Dr Wax Records and Tapes** • 5225 S Harper Ave
- **Futons N More** • 1370 E 53rd St
- **House of Africa** • 1510 E 63rd St
- **Hyde Park Records** • 1377 E 53rd St
- **O'Gara and Wilson** • 1448 E 57th St
- **Powell's Bookstore** • 1501 E 57th St
- **Toys Et Cetera** • 5211 S Harper Ave
- **Wesley's Shoe Corral** • 1506 E 55th St
- **Wheels and Things** • 5210 S Harper Ave

Video Rental

- **Hollywood Video** • 1530 E 53rd St

1
2
A
B
C
Lake Michigan
HYDE PARK
E 50th St
E 50th Pl
E Hyde Park Blvd
S Dorchester Ave
S Blackstone Ave
S Lake Park Ave
S Lake Shore Dr
Model Yacht Basin
17
S Hyde Park Blvd
53rd
E 53rd St
S Everett Ave
E 54th St
S Harper Ave
S Cornell Ave
Cornell Park
S Shore Dr
S South Shore Dr
E 54th Pl
Promontory Point Park
E 55th St
55th
E 55th Pl
E Park Pl
E 56th St
E 56th St
S Stony Island Ave
Harper Ct
57th Street Beach
E 57th St
E Museum Dr
E 57th Dr
Columbia Dr
Museum of Science and Industry
E Columbia Dr Cutoff
E 58th St
19
University of Chicago
PAGE 244
59th
E 59th St
Midway Plaisance
Plaisance Park
41
Wooded Island
West Lagoon
East Lagoon
Osaka Garden
Jackson Park Beach
E 61st St
E 61st Pl
S Park Shore East Ct
E 62nd Pl
PAGE 212
Jackson Park
E 63rd St
Coast Gd Dr Cut Off
58
E Hayes Dr
63rd
E 63rd Pl
South Lagoon
Yacht Harbor
1/4 mile
.25 km

This slice of Hyde Park is well-known for its luxury apartment buildings, a piece of Burnham Park known locally as "The Point," and, of course, the Museum of Science and Industry. After wandering along the relatively quiet beachfront at 57th Street, visitors should stumble in for an afternoon at the Museum. After all, it isn't everyday that you can find a demonstration coal mine, preserved cross-sections of humans (willing participants, of course), and a fairy castle all in one place.

Banks

- **Harris Trust & Savings** • 5493 S Cornell Ave

Landmarks

- **Osaka Garden/Wooded Island** • just south of the Museum of Science and Industry, b/w the West and East Lagoons
- **Promontory Point Park** • 5491 S Shore Dr

Pizza

- **Cholie's Pizza** • 1601 E 53rd St

Schools

- **Akiba–Schechter Jewish Day** • 5235 S Cornell Ave
- **Catholic Theological Union** • 5401 S Cornell Ave
- **Hyde Park Academy** • 6220 S Stony Island Ave

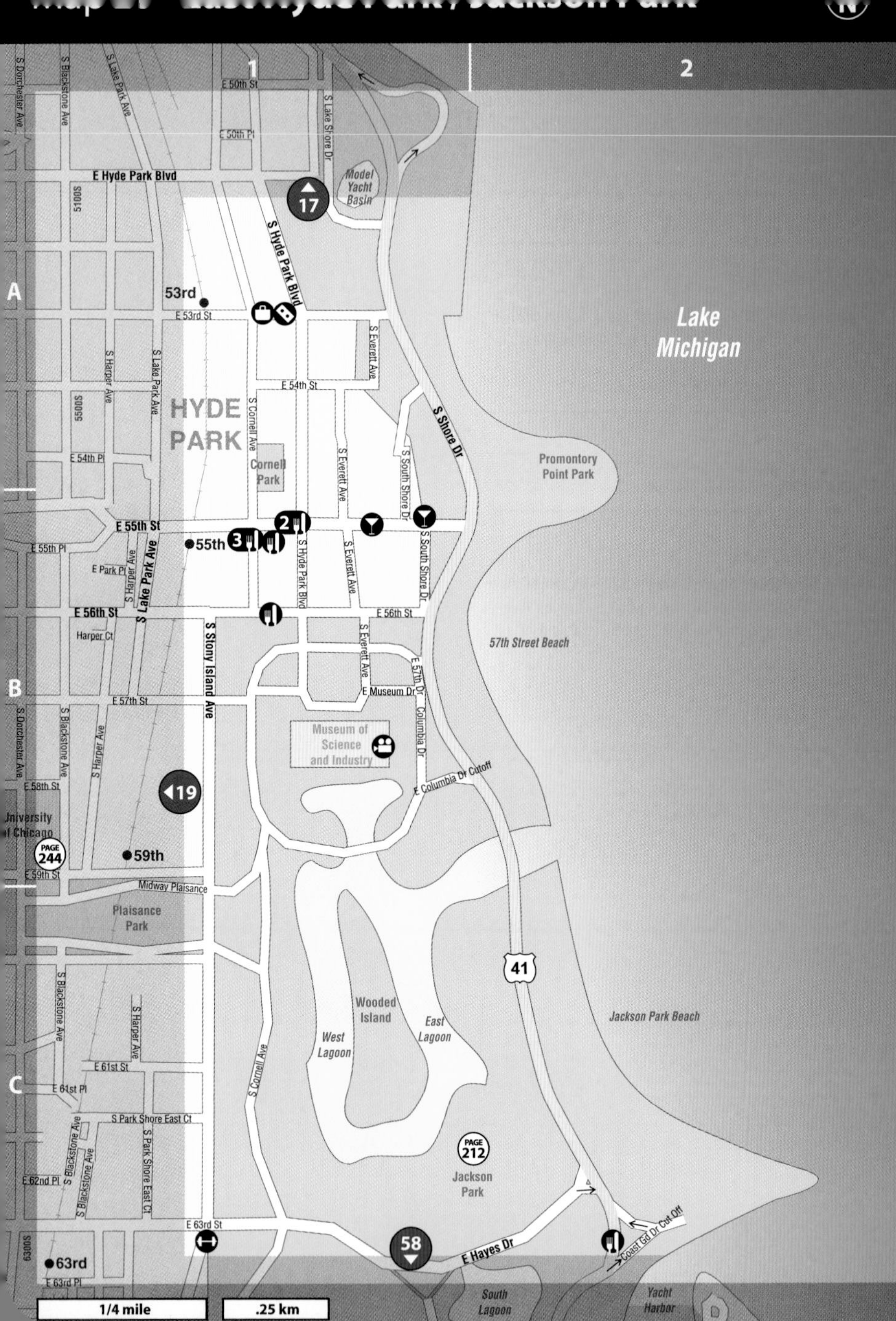
1
2
A
B
C
E 50th St
E 50th Pl
S Lake Shore Dr
S Dorchester Ave
S Blackstone Ave
S Lake Park Ave
E Hyde Park Blvd
5100S
Model Yacht Basin
17
S Hyde Park Blvd
53rd
E 53rd St
Lake Michigan
S Everett Ave
S Harper Ave
E 54th St
HYDE PARK
5500S
S Cornell Ave
S Shore Dr
S South Shore Dr
Cornell Park
E 54th Pl
Promontory Point Park
E 55th St
2
3
55th
E 55th Pl
E Park Pl
E 56th St
Harper Ct
S Stony Island Ave
57th Street Beach
E 57th St
E Museum Dr
E 57th Dr
Columbia Dr
Museum of Science and Industry
E Columbia Dr Cutoff
E 58th St
19
University of Chicago
PAGE 244
59th
E 59th St
Midway Plaisance
Plaisance Park
41
Wooded Island
East Lagoon
West Lagoon
Jackson Park Beach
E 61st St
E 61st Pl
S Park Shore East Ct
PAGE 212
Jackson Park
E 62nd Pl
E 63rd St
58
E Hayes Dr
Coast Gd Dr Cut Off
6300S
63rd
E 63rd Pl
South Lagoon
Yacht Harbor
1/4 mile
.25 km

Eschewing the buzz of Hyde Park, East Hyde Park is a bit more tranquil, though don't count out the thousands who flock to the Museum of Science and Industry and the rather popular beaches in the area. Walking over to Promontory Point is a good idea for those who like to people-watch, and the canopy of trees along South Hyde Park Boulevard during the spring and summer are a most welcome pause from the less-than-polite Chicago humidity.

Copy Shops

• **Post Link** • 1634 E 53rd St

Gyms

• **Southside YMCA** • 6330 S Stony Island Ave

Movie Theaters

• **Henry Crown MSI Omnimax** • Museum of Science & Industry • 5700 S Lake Shore Dr

Nightlife

• **Bar Louie** • 5500 S South Shore Dr
• **The Cove** • 1750 E 55th St

Restaurants

• **Café Corea** • 1603 E 55th St
• **Marina Café** • 6401 S Coast Guard Dr
• **Morry's Deli** • 5500 S Cornell Ave
• **Nile Restaurant** • 1611 E 55th St
• **Orly's Café** • 1660 E 55th St
• **Piccolo Mondo** • 1642 E 56th St
• **Siam Thai Cuisine** • 1639 E 55th St
• **Snail's Thai Cuisine** • 1649 E 55th St

Shopping

• **Art's Cycle Sales & Service** • 1652 E 53rd St

Video Rental

• **Blockbuster** • 1644 E 53rd St

Western
Eller Park
1
2
W Cortland St
Clybourn
N Wilmot Ave
N Winnebago Ave
W Moffat St
W Moffat St
W Moffat St
W Churchill St
Churchill Park
Dan Ryan Expy
W Bloomingdale Ave
W Bloomingdale Ave
W Willow St
Churchill
W Saint Paul Ave
W Saint Paul Ave
90
94
W Wabansia Ave
W Wabansia Ave
W Wabansia Ave
N Milwaukee Ave
A
W Caton St
W Concord Pl
W Concord Pl
N Oakley Ave
N Bell Ave
N Leavitt St
N Honore St
N Wood St
N Hermitage Ave
N Paulina St
N Marshfield Ave
2400W
28
Damen
Coyote Building
W North Ave
Crumbling Bucktown
Flat Iron Building
N Maplewood Ave
N Campbell Ave
N Artesian Ave
W Pierce Ave
W Pierce Ave
N Elk Grove Ave
W Le Moyne St
W Le Moyne St
W Le Moyne St
W Le Moyne St
W Julian St
WICKER PARK
Wicker Park
N Wicker Park Ave
N Bosworth Ave
N Greenview Ave
W Beach Ave
W Schiller St
N Dean St
W Hirsch St
W Blackhawk St
N Western Ave
N Claremont Ave
N Oakley Ave
N Bell Ave
N Leavitt St
W Evergreen Ave
W Evergreen Ave
N Bauwans St
W Ellen St
W Potomac Ave
W Potomac Ave
N Marion Ct
N Honore St
N Hermitage Ave
N Moorman St
Clemente Park
W Crystal St
W Crystal St
N Paulina St
N Mautene Ct
Division
B
W Division St
Division Street Russian Bath
2400W
2000W
22
50
W Haddon Ave
W Haddon Ave
W Haddon Ave
W Haddon Ave
1600W
Holy Trinity Orthodox Cathedral and Rectory
W Thomas St
W Thomas St
N Hoyne Ave
N Damen Ave
N Winchester Ave
N Wolcott Ave
N Honore St
N Wood St
N Hermitage Ave
N Marshfield Ave
N Ashland Ave
UKRAINIAN VILLAGE
W Cortez St
W Cortez St
W Cortez St
W Augusta Blvd
EAST UKRAINIAN VILLAGE
W Walton St
W Walton St
W Walton St
N Greenview Ave
W Iowa St
W Pearson St
W Pearson St
N Oakley Blvd
W Rice St
W Rice St
W Fry St
800N
23
W Chicago Ave
C
W Lee Pl
N Armour St
W Superior St
Superior Park
W Superior St
W Huron St
W Erie St
600N
W Ontario St
W Ohio St
N Artesian Ave
W Race Ave
W Race Ave
N Harland Ct
N Hermitage Ave
N Paulina St
N Marshfield Ave
1/4 mile
.25 km
W Ferdinand St

While yuppies rehab Victorians and developers strike gold, the young arty community that paved the way is finding it harder and harder to stomach rising rents in this former ethnic enclave. Proximity to downtown and the expressway, as well as the hotbed of commercial growth–from dive bars to edgy boutiques and nightclubs–still make this a desirable place to live, even if traffic and parking now rival Lincoln Park.

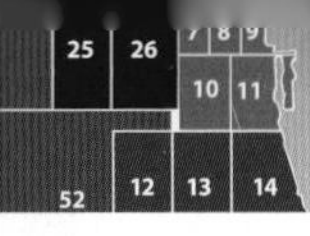

Banks

- **Chase** • 1849 W North Ave
- **Chase** • 1959 W Division St
- **MB Financial** • 936 N Western Ave
- **Midwest Bank & Trust Company** • 1601 Milwaukee Ave
- **North Community** • 1555 N Damen Ave
- **North Community** • 2000 W Division St
- **TCF** • Jewel • 1341 N Paulina St
- **TCF (ATM)** • 7-Eleven • 1400 N Milwaukee Ave
- **Washington Mutual** • 1811 W North Ave

Car Washes

- **Elite Car Wash** • 823 N Western Ave
- **Full Line Hand Car Wash** • 2123 W Division St

Gas Stations

- **BP** • 2405 W Augusta Blvd
- **Citgo** • 1720 W North Ave
- **Citgo** • 823 N Western Ave
- **Clark Oil** • 1949 W Augusta Blvd
- **Shell** • 1600 N Western Ave
- **Shell** • 1950 W Division St

Emergency Rooms

- **St Elizabeth's** • 1431 N Claremont Ave
- **St Mary of Nazareth** • 2233 W Division St

Landmarks

- **Coyote Building** • 1600 N Milwaukee Ave
- **Crumbling Bucktown** • 1579 N Milwaukee Ave
- **Division Street Russian Bath** • 1916 W Division St
- **Flat Iron Building** • 1579 N Milwaukee Ave
- **Holy Trinity Orthodox Cathedral and Rectory** • 1121 N Leavitt St
- **Wicker Park** • Pierce St & Hoyne St

Pharmacies

- **Jewel-Osco** • 1341 N Paulina St
- **Osco Drug** • 2418 W Division St
- **Walgreens** • 1372 N Milwaukee Ave
- **Walgreens** • 2440 W North Ave

Pizza

- **Leona's** • 1936 W Augusta Blvd
- **Piece** • 1927 W North Ave
- **Pizza Hut** • 1601 N Western Ave
- **Pizza Metro** • 1707 W Division St

Police

- **13th District (Wood)** • 937 N Wood St

Schools

- **A N Pritzker Elementary** • 2009 W Schiller St
- **Albert R Sabin** • 2216 W Hirsch St
- **Association House High** • 2150 W North Ave
- **Christopher Columbus Elementary** • 1003 N Leavitt St
- **De Diego Elementary** • 1313 N Claremont Ave
- **Frederic Chopin Elementary** • 2450 W Rice St
- **Hans Christian Andersen Elementary** • 1148 N Honore St
- **Josephinum High** • 1501 N Oakley Blvd
- **Richard Milburn High** • 1279 N Milwaukee Ave
- **Roberto Clemente Community High** • 1147 N Western Ave
- **St Helen Elementary** • 2347 W Augusta Blvd
- **St Nicholas** • 2200 W Rice St

Supermarkets

- **Jewel-Osco** • 1341 N Paulina St

Western
Eller Park
1
2
W Cortland St
Clybourn
N Wilmot Ave
W Moffat St
N Winnebago Ave
W Moffat St
W Moffat St
W Churchill St
Churchill Park
Dan Ryan Expy
W Bloomingdale Ave
W Bloomingdale Ave
W Willow St
Churchill
W Saint Paul Ave
W Saint Paul Ave
90
94
W Wabansia Ave
W Wabansia Ave
W Wabansia Ave
N Milwaukee Ave
A
W Caton St
W Concord Pl
W Concord Pl
N Oakley Ave
N Bell Ave
N Leavitt St
N Honore St
N Wood St
N Hermitage Ave
N Paulina St
N Marshfield Ave
1900N
Damen
28
W North Ave
N Maplewood Ave
N Campbell Ave
N Artesian Ave
W Pierce Ave
W Pierce Ave
N Elk Grove Ave
W Le Moyne St
W Le Moyne St
W Le Moyne St
W Le Moyne St
W Julian St
N Honore St
WICKER PARK
Wicker Park
N Wicker Park Ave
W Beach Ave
N Bosworth Ave
N Greenview Ave
W Schiller St
N Dean St
W Blackhawk St
W Hirsch St
N Western Ave
N Claremont Ave
N Oakley Ave
N Bell Ave
N Leavitt St
W Evergreen Ave
N Wicker Park Ave
W Evergreen Ave
N Bauwans St
W Ellen St
W Potomac Ave
N Marion Ct
N Honore St
W Potomac Ave
N Hermitage Ave
N Mooreman St
W Pot
Clemente Park
W Crystal St
W Crystal St
N Paulina St
N Mautene Ct
Division
B
W Division St
N Milwaukee Ave
2400W
2000W
22
50
W Haddon Ave
W Haddon Ave
W Haddon Ave
W Haddon Ave
1600W
N Hoyne Ave
N Damen Ave
N Winchester Ave
N Wolcott Ave
N Honore St
N Wood St
N Hermitage Ave
N Marshfield Ave
N Ashland Ave
W Thomas St
W Thomas St
UKRAINIAN VILLAGE
W Cortez St
W Cortez St
W Cortez St
W Augusta Blvd
EAST UKRAINIAN VILLAGE
W Walton St
W Walton St
W Walton St
N Greenview Ave
W Iowa St
W Pearson St
W Pearson St
N Oakley Blvd
800N
W Rice St
W Rice St
W Fry St
23
W Chicago Ave
C
N Armour St
W Lee Pl
W Superior St
Superior Park
W Superior St
W Huron St
W Erie St
600N
W Ontario St
W Ohio St
N Artesian Ave
W Race Ave
N Hartland Ct
N Hermitage Ave
N Paulina St
N Marshfield Ave
W Race Ave
1/4 mile
.25 km
W Ferdinand St

Described by some as 'Lincoln Park West,' this formerly rough-and-tough neighborhood has fallen prey to commercial giants Urban Outfitters and American Apparel. Nonetheless it remains one of the hippest parts of town for young artist-types, densely packed with faux-hawks, scooters, and wearable art. Fashion-forward boutiques, veggie-friendly eats, and cool cafes abound. Indie bands and avant-garde jazz wail through the night from Empty Bottle while brainy hipsters haunt the aisles at Quimby's and Myopic books.

Coffee

- **Alliance Bakery** • 1736 W Division St
- **Barista Café** • 852 N Damen Ave
- **Café Ballou** • 939 N Western Ave
- **Filter** • 1585 N Milwaukee Ave
- **Half & Half** • 1560 N Damen Ave
- **Letizia's Natural Bakery** • 2144 W Division St
- **Starbucks** • 1588 N Milwaukee Ave
- **Starbucks** • 1701 W Division St
- **Sweet Thang** • 1921 W North Ave
- **Windy City Cyber Café** • 1921 W North Ave

Copy Shops

- **Copymax** • 1573 N Milwaukee Ave
- **Fedex Kinko's** • 1800 W North Ave ㉔

Farmer's Markets

- **Wicker Park/Bucktown (Jun–Oct; Sun, 7 am–2 pm)** • W Schiller St & N Damen Ave

Gyms

- **Bucktown Fitness Club** • 2100 W North Ave
- **Cheetah Gym** • 1934 W North Ave
- **Curves (women only)** • 2010 W Pierce Ave

Liquor Stores

- **Carlos Food & Liquor** • 1401 N Western Ave
- **Ola's Liquor** • 947 N Damen Ave
- **Sahar Food & Liquor** • 1761 W Division St
- **Wicker Park Liquor** • 2006 W Division St

Nightlife

- **Borderline** • 1954 W North Ave
- **Club Foot** • 1824 W Augusta Blvd
- **D'Vine** • 1950 W North Ave
- **Davenport's** • 1383 N Milwaukee Ave
- **Double Door** • 1572 N Milwaukee Ave
- **Empty Bottle** • 1035 N Western Ave
- **Estelle's Café & Lounge** • 2013 W North Ave
- **Gold Star Bar** • 1755 W Division St
- **Iggy's** • 1840 W North Ave
- **Inner Town Pub** • 1935 W Thomas St
- **Innjoy** • 2051 W Division St
- **Lava Lounge** • 859 N Damen Ave
- **Marshall McGearty Tobacco Lounge** • 1553 N Milwaukee Ave
- **The Note** • 1565 N Milwaukee Ave
- **Phyllis' Musical Inn** • 1800 W Division St
- **Pint** • 1547 N Milwaukee Ave
- **Pontiac Café** • 1531 N Damen Ave
- **Rainbo Club** • 1151 N Damen Ave
- **Rodan** • 1530 N Milwaukee Ave
- **Salud Tequila Lounge** • 1471 N Milwaukee Ave
- **Small Bar** • 2049 W Division St
- **Subterranean Cabaret & Lounge** • 2011 W North Ave
- **Vintage Wine Bar** • 1942 W Division St

Pet Shops

- **Wicker Pet** • 2029 W North Ave

Restaurants

- **Adobo Grill** • 2005 W Division St
- **Bin Wine Café** • 1559 N Milwaukee Ave
- **Blue Line Club Car** • 1548 N Damen Ave
- **Bluefin** • 1952 W North Ave
- **Bob San** • 1805 W Division St
- **The Bongo Room** • 1470 N Milwaukee Ave
- **Café Ballou** • 939 N Western Ave
- **Cleo's** • 1935 W Chicago Ave
- **Cold Comfort Café & Deli** • 2211 W North Ave
- **Cooking Fools** • 1916 W North Ave
- **D'Vine Restaurant & Wine Bar** • 1950 W North Ave
- **Del Toro** • 1520 N Damen Ave
- **Dodo** • 935 N Damen Ave
- **Earwax** • 1561 N Milwaukee Ave
- **Enoteca Roma Winebar & Bruschetteria** • 2144 W Division St
- **Feast** • 1616 N Damen Ave
- **Flash Taco** • 1570 N Damen Ave
- **Francesca's Forno** • 1576 N Milwaukee Ave
- **Green Ginger** • 2050 W Division St
- **Half & Half** • 1560 N Damen Ave
- **Handlebar** • 2311 W North Ave
- **Hilary's Urban Eatery** • 1630 W Division St
- **Iggy's** • 1840 W North Ave
- **Las Palmas** • 1835 W North Ave
- **Leona's** • 1936 W Augusta Blvd
- **Mas** • 1670 W Division St
- **Milk & Honey** • 1920 W Division St
- **Mirai Sushi** • 2020 W Division St
- **Moonshine** • 1824 W Division St
- **Oberweis Ice Cream and Dairy Store** • 1293 N Milwaukee Ave
- **Pacific Café** • 1619 N Damen Ave
- **Paje** • 1332 N Milwaukee Ave
- **Papajin Chinese & Sushi Bar** • 1551 N Milwaukee Ave
- **Parlor** • 1745 W North Ave
- **Penny's Noodle Shop** • 1542 N Damen Ave
- **People Lounge** • 1560 N Milwaukee Ave
- **Picante** • 2016 W Division St
- **Piece** • 1927 W North Ave
- **Pot Pan Thai** • 1750 W North Ave
- **Sigara Hookah Café & Lounge** • 2013 W Division St
- **Smoke Daddy** • 1804 W Division St
- **Spring** • 2039 W North Ave
- **Sultan's Market** • 2057 W North Ave
- **Thai Lagoon** • 2322 W North Ave
- **Thai Village** • 2053 W Division St
- **Tre Via** • 1575 N Milwaukee Ave

Shopping

- **American Apparel** • 1563 N Milwaukee Ave
- **Asrai Garden** • 1935 W North Ave
- **The Brown Elephant** • 1459 N Milwaukee Ave
- **Casa de Soul** • 1919 W Division St
- **Cattails** • 1935 W Division St
- **City Soles** • 2001 W North Ave
- **DeciBel Audio** • 1407 N Milwaukee Ave
- **Habit** • 1951 W Division St
- **hejfina** • 1529 N Milwaukee Ave
- **Jade** • 1557 N Milwaukee Ave
- **Lille** • 1923 W North Ave
- **Lilly Vallente** • 1746 W Division St
- **Modern Times** • 1538 N Milwaukee Ave
- **Myopic Bookstore** • 1564 N Milwaukee Ave
- **Nina** • 1655 W Division St
- **Paper Doll** • 1747 W Division St
- **Penelope's** • 1913 W Division St
- **Plein Aire** • 2036 W Division St
- **Porte Rouge** • 1911 W Division St
- **Quimby's Bookstore** • 1854 W North Ave
- **Ragstock** • 1433 N Milwaukee Ave
- **Reckless Records** • 1532 N Milwaukee Ave
- **Ruby Room** • 1743 W Division St
- **Symmetry** • 1925 W Division St
- **Tatine** • 1742 W Division St
- **Silver Moon** • 1755 W North Ave
- **The Silver Room** • 1442 N Milwaukee Ave
- **Una Mae's Freak Boutique** • 1422 N Milwaukee Ave
- **Untitled** • 1941 W North Ave
- **Wag Artworks** • 2121 W Division St

Video Rental

- **Blockbuster** • 1303 N Milwaukee Ave
- **Brainstorm** • 1648 W North Ave
- **Earwax** • 1561 N Milwaukee Ave
- **Mass Video** • 2014 W Division St

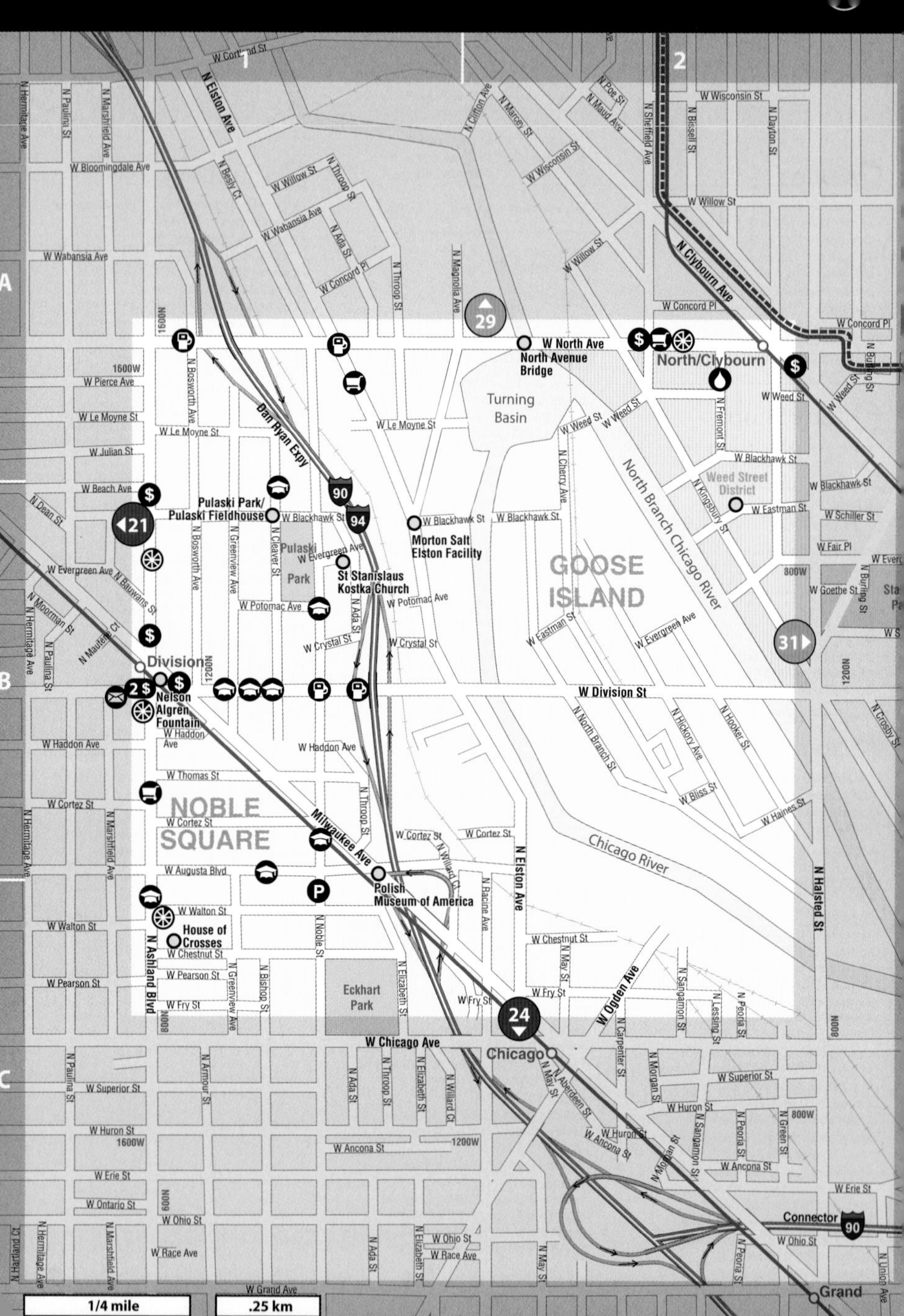

A
B
C
1
2
29
21
31
24
Division
Chicago
North/Clybourn
Grand
W North Ave
North Avenue Bridge
Turning Basin
Weed Street District
Pulaski Park/
Pulaski Fieldhouse
Pulaski Park
St Stanislaus Kostka Church
Morton Salt Elston Facility
GOOSE ISLAND
North Branch Chicago River
Chicago River
Nelson Algren Fountain
NOBLE SQUARE
Polish Museum of America
House of Crosses
Eckhart Park
Dan Ryan Expy
Milwaukee Ave
N Elston Ave
N Clybourn Ave
W Division St
W Chicago Ave
W Ogden Ave
N Ashland Blvd
N Halsted St
Connector
90
94
W Cortland St
W Wisconsin St
W Bloomingdale Ave
W Willow St
W Wabansia Ave
W Concord Pl
W Pierce Ave
W Le Moyne St
W Julian St
W Beach Ave
W Blackhawk St
W Evergreen Ave
W Potomac Ave
W Crystal St
W Haddon Ave
W Thomas St
W Cortez St
W Augusta Blvd
W Walton St
W Chestnut St
W Pearson St
W Fry St
W Superior St
W Huron St
W Ancona St
W Erie St
W Ontario St
W Ohio St
W Race Ave
W Grand Ave
W Weed St
W Eastman St
W Schiller St
W Fair Pl
W Goethe St
W Bliss St
W Haines St
N Hermitage Ave
N Paulina St
N Marshfield Ave
N Bosworth Ave
N Greenview Ave
N Cleaver St
N Ada St
N Throop St
N Noble St
N Bishop St
N Elizabeth St
N Willard Ct
N Racine Ave
N Magnolia Ave
N Clifton Ave
N Marcey St
N Sheffield Ave
N Bissell St
N Dayton St
N Fremont St
N Kingsbury St
N Cherry Ave
N North Branch St
N Hickory Ave
N Hooker St
N Crosby St
N Burling St
N May St
N Carpenter St
N Aberdeen St
N Morgan St
N Sangamon St
N Peoria St
N Green St
N Lessing St
N Union Ave
N Armour St
N Hartland Ct
N Dean St
N Moorman St
N Mautene Ct
N Bauwans St
N Besly Ct
N Poe St
N Maud Ave
1600W
1200W
800W
1/4 mile
.25 km

Essentials

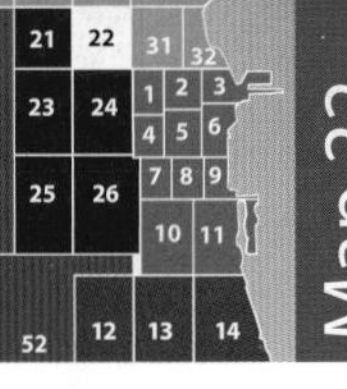

Gritty Goose Island industry crosses paths with the arty fringes of East Ukrainian Village. In the middle are a number of lovely historical churches, seemingly always buried under scaffolding. Elston Avenue is a popular route to crisscross the city from downtown to the northwest. Wave to the Morton Salt Girl on the roof of the salt factory as you pass her by.

Banks

- **Bank of America** • 1590 N Clybourn Ave
- **Bank of America (ATM)** • 1000 W North Ave
- **Chase** • 1230 N Milwaukee Ave
- **Fifth Third** • 1209 N Milwaukee Ave
- **Harris Trust & Savings** • 1242 N Ashland Blvd
- **MB Financial** • 1200 N Ashland Ave
- **New Century** • 1414 N Ashland Ave

Car Washes

- **Turtle Wax Car Wash** • 1550 N Fremont St

Gas Stations

- **Amoco** • 1600 N Elston Ave
- **BP** • 1334 W Division St
- **Gas Depot** • 1551 W North Ave
- **Shell** • 1400 W Division St

Landmarks

- **House of Crosses** • 1544 W Chestnut St
- **Morton Salt Elston Facility** • Elston Ave & Blackhawk St
- **Nelson Algren Fountain** • Division St & Ashland Blvd
- **North Avenue Bridge** • W North Ave
- **Polish Museum of America** • 984 N Milwaukee Ave
- **Pulaski Park/Pulaski Fieldhouse** • Blackhawk St & Cleaver St
- **St Stanislaus Kostka Church** • 1351 W Evergreen Ave
- **Weed Street District** • b/w Chicago River & Halsted St

Pizza

- **California Pizza Kitchen** • 939 W North Ave
- **Little Caesar's Pizza** • Kmart• 1360 N Ashland Ave
- **Pizza Hut** • 1601 W Division St
- **Pizza Metro II** • 925 N Ashland Ave

Post Offices

- **US Post Office** • 1635 W Division St

Schools

- **College of Office Technology** • 1520 W Division St
- **Elizabeth Peabody Elementary** • 1444 W Augusta Blvd
- **Holy Trinity High** • 1443 W Division St
- **Montessori–Near North** • 1434 W Division St
- **Noble Street High** • 1010 N Nobel St
- **Rudy Lozano Elementary** • 1424 N Cleaver St
- **St Stanislaus Kosta Elementary** • 1255 N Noble St
- **William H Wells High** • 936 N Ashland Ave

Supermarkets

- **Laura's Grocery** • 1051 N Ashland Ave
- **Stanley's Fresh Fruit & Vegetables** • 1558 N Elston Ave
- **Whole Foods Market** • 1000 W North Ave

Parking

Map 22 • Noble Square / Goose Island

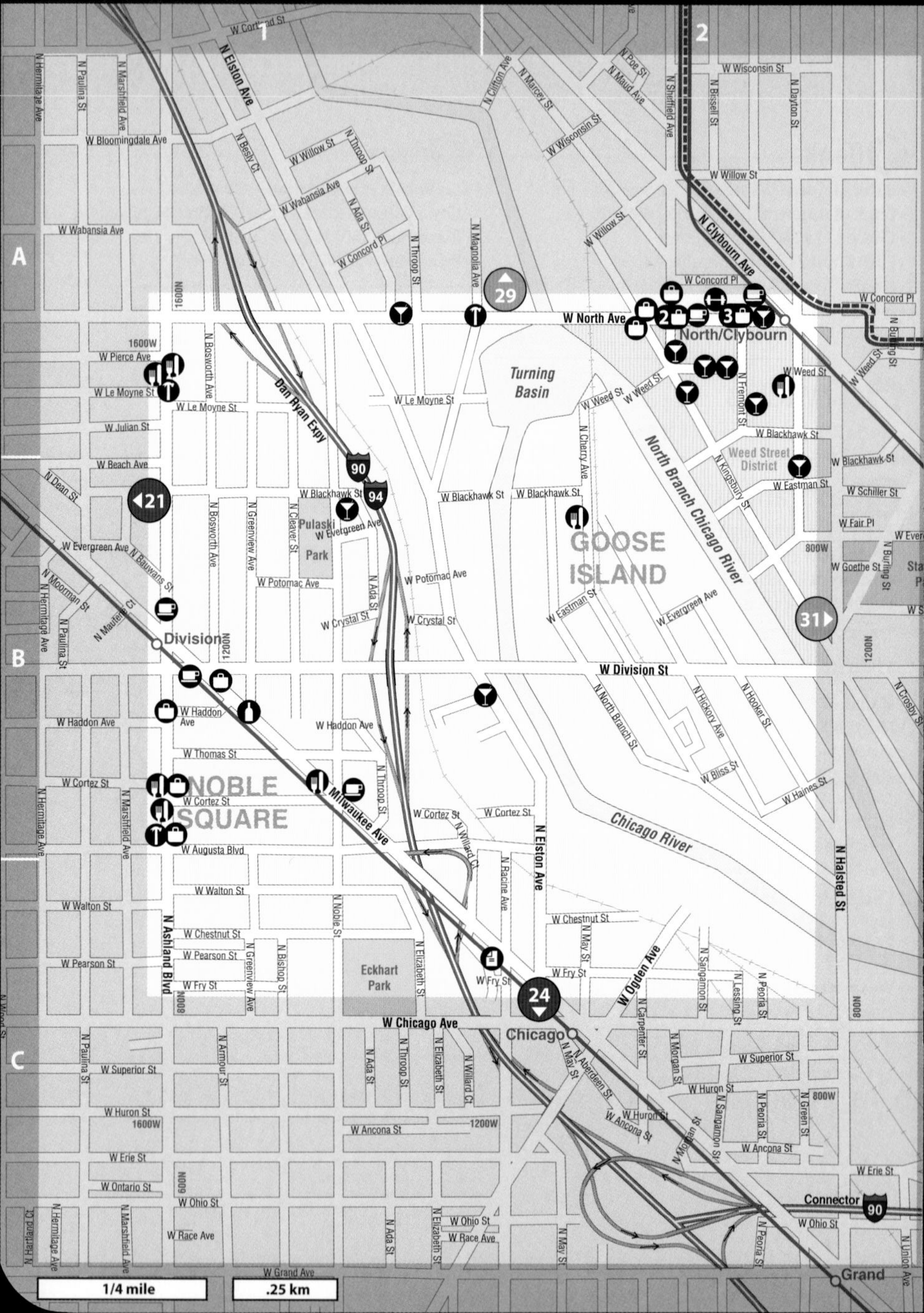

Funky shops and design studios cluster around Milwaukee, Division and Ashland, bleeding over from Wicker Park and Ukrainian Village. The clubby Weed Street district is a breeding laboratory for scene-conscious young unmarrieds. Further west at Exit, the pierced and leather-clad pretend there still is a punk scene in Chicago.

Coffee

- **Coffee on Milwaukee** • 1046 N Milwaukee Ave
- **Dunkin' Donuts** • 1200 N Milwaukee Ave
- **Dunkin' Donuts** • 1244 N Ashland Ave
- **Peet's Coffee and Tea** • 1000 W North Ave
- **Starbucks** • 1001 W North Ave

Copy Shops

- **Carnegie Printers** • 868 N Milwaukee Ave

Gyms

- **Crunch Fitness** • 939 W North Ave

Hardware Stores

- **Ace Hardware** • 1013 N Ashland Ave
- **Home Depot** • 1232 W North Ave
- **Paragon Hardware & Mill Supply** • 1512 N Ashland Ave

Liquor Stores

- **Crater Food & Liquor** • 1144 N Milwaukee Ave

Nightlife

- **Biology Bar** • 1520 N Fremont St
- **Crobar** • 1543 N Kingsbury St
- **Exit** • 1315 W North Ave
- **Four** • 1551 W Division St
- **Hot Shots** • 1440 N Dayton St
- **Jet Vodka Lounge** • 1555 N Sheffield Ave
- **Joe's** • 940 W Weed St
- **Slow Down, Life's Too Short** • 1177 N Elston Ave
- **Zentra** • 923 W Weed St

Restaurants

- **Corosh** • 1072 N Milwaukee Ave
- **El Barco Mariscos Seafood** • 1035 N Ashland Blvd
- **Luc Thang** • 1524 N Ashland Blvd
- **NYC Bagel** • 1001 W North Ave
- **Rudy's Taste** • 1024 N Ashland Ave
- **Sangria Restaurant and Tapas Bar** • 901 W Weed St
- **Schwa** • 1466 N Ashland Ave

Shopping

- **Banana Republic** • 917 W North Ave
- **Best Buy** • 1000 W North Ave
- **Cost Plus World Market** • 1623 N Sheffield Ave
- **Dusty Groove Records** • 1120 N Ashland Ave
- **Irv's Luggage Warehouse** • 820 W North Ave
- **J Crew** • 929 W North Ave
- **Old Navy** • 1596 N Kingsbury St
- **Olga's Flower Shop** • 1041 N Ashland Ave
- **Restoration Hardware** • 938 W North Ave
- **Right-On Futon** • 1184 N Milwaukee Ave
- **Transitions Bookplace** • 1000 W North Ave
- **Wax Addict Records** • 1014 N Ashland Ave

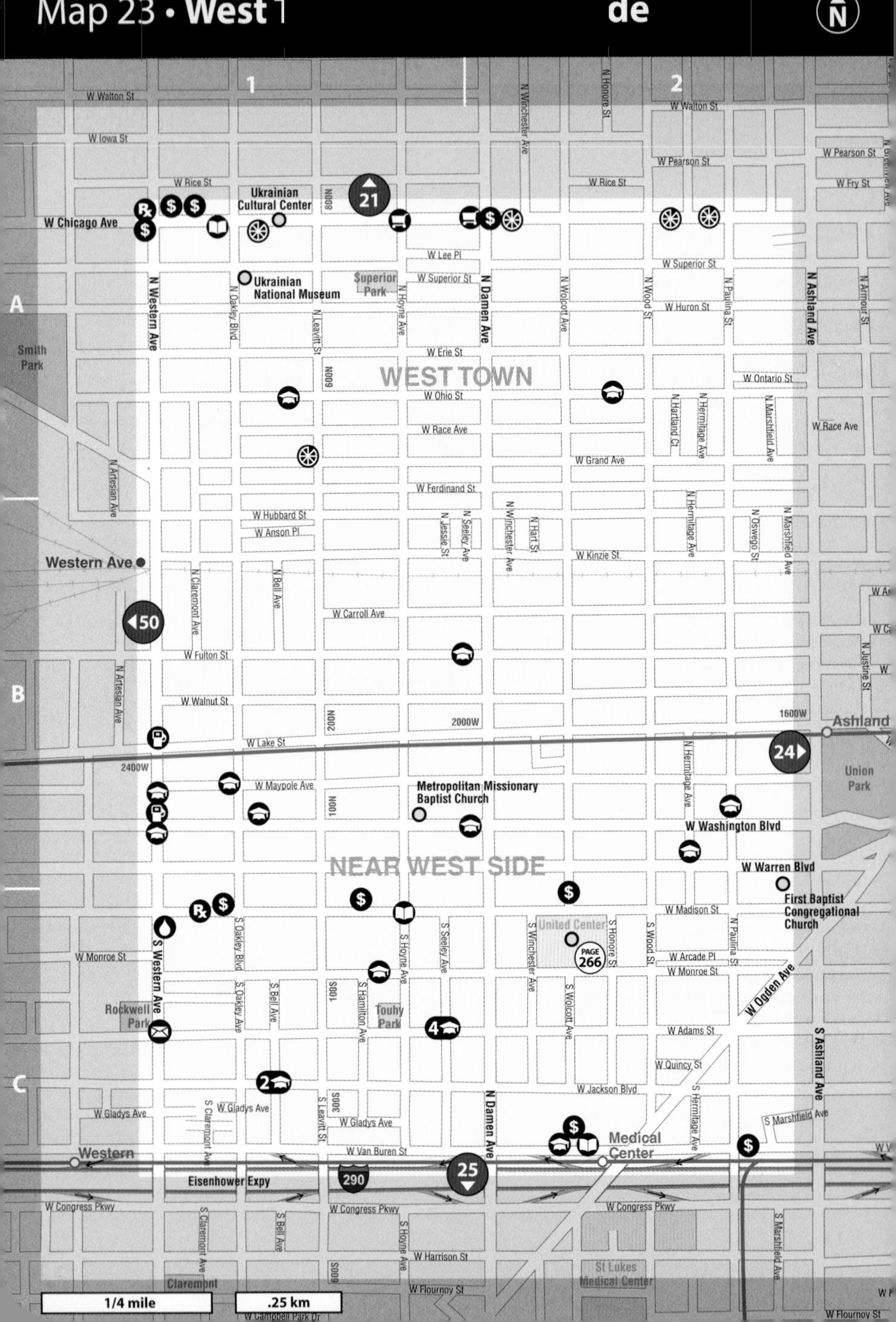

Map 23 • West 1
de
N
1
2
A
B
C
W Walton St
W Iowa St
W Rice St
W Pearson St
W Fry St
W Chicago Ave
Ukrainian Cultural Center
800N
21
W Lee Pl
W Superior St
Ukrainian National Museum
Superior Park
N Western Ave
N Oakley Blvd
N Leavitt St
N Hoyne Ave
N Damen Ave
N Wolcott Ave
N Wood St
N Paulina St
N Ashland Ave
N Armour St
W Huron St
Smith Park
W Erie St
600N
WEST TOWN
W Ohio St
W Ontario St
W Race Ave
N Hartland Ct
N Hermitage Ave
N Marshfield Ave
W Grand Ave
N Artesian Ave
W Ferdinand St
W Hubbard St
W Anson Pl
N Jessie St
N Seeley Ave
N Winchester Ave
N Hart St
N Oswego St
W Kinzie St.
Western Ave
N Claremont Ave
N Bell Ave
W Carroll Ave
50
W Fulton St
N Justine St
W Walnut St
200N
2000W
1600W
Ashland
W Lake St
24
2400W
Union Park
W Maypole Ave
Metropolitan Missionary Baptist Church
100N
W Washington Blvd
NEAR WEST SIDE
W Warren Blvd
First Baptist Congregational Church
W Madison St
United Center
S Oakley Blvd
S Hoyne Ave
S Seeley Ave
S Winchester Ave
S Honore St
S Wood St
N Paulina St
W Monroe St
S Western Ave
PAGE 266
W Arcade Pl
W Ogden Ave
S Bell Ave
100S
S Hamilton Ave
S Wolcott Ave
Rockwell Park
Touhy Park
4
W Adams St
S Ashland Ave
W Quincy St
W Jackson Blvd
2
S Hermitage Ave
W Gladys Ave
S Claremont Ave
S Leavitt St
300S
S Marshfield Ave
Medical Center
Western
W Van Buren St
290
25
Eisenhower Expy
W Congress Pkwy
S Claremont Ave
W Harrison St
600S
St Lukes Medical Center
Claremont
W Flournoy St
1/4 mile
.25 km
W Campbell Park Dr

This neighborhood was once the heart of the city's produce and meat markets. United Center, aka The House That Mike Built, infused energy into the area. A few food supplier warehouses still exist, mixing in with new loft conversions. And by the way, after some patchy years, the new Bulls seem to be on the verge of giving loyal hoops fans something to be excited about again.

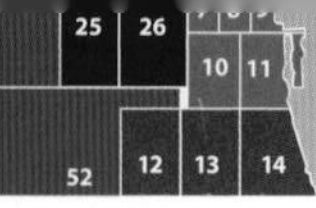

Banks

- **Chase (ATM)** • 1700 W Van Buren St
- **Chase (ATM)** • 2316 W Madison St
- **Citibank (ATM)** • 2005 W Chicago Ave
- **Fifth Third (ATM)** • 1901 W Madison St
- **LaSalle (ATM)** • 1900 W Van Buren St
- **MB Financial** • 820 N Western Ave
- **MidAmerica** • 2100 W Chicago Ave
- **MidAmerica** • 2154 W Madison St
- **Self Reliance Ukrainian American Federal Credit Union** • 2332 W Chicago Ave
- **TCF (ATM)** • Osco • 2427 W Chicago Ave

Car Washes

- **Boss Hand Car Wash** • 25 S Western Ave

Gas Stations

- **Marathon** • 101 N Western Ave
- **Shell** • 45 N Western Ave

Landmarks

- **First Baptist Congregational Church** • 1613 W Washington Blvd
- **Metropolitan Missionary Baptist Church** • 2151 W Washington Blvd
- **Ukrainian Cultural Center** • 2247 W Chicago Ave
- **Ukrainian National Museum** • 721 N Oakley Blvd
- **United Center** • 1901 W Madison St

Libraries

- **Mabel Manning Public Library** • 6 S Hoyne Ave
- **Malcolm X College Library** • 1900 W Van Buren St
- **Midwest Public Library** • 2335 W Chicago Ave

Pharmacies

- **Osco Drug** • 2427 W Chicago Ave
- **Walgreens** • 2340 W Madison St

Pizza

- **Angie's Restaurant** • 1715 W Chicago Ave
- **Bacci Pizzeria** • 2356 W Chicago Ave
- **Bella's Pizza & Restaurant** • 1952 W Chicago Ave
- **Martellito's Pizza No 1** • 2218 W Grand Ave
- **Naty's Pizza 2** • 1757 W Chicago Ave

Post Offices

- **US Post Office** • 116 S Western Ave

Schools

- **Best Practice High** • 2040 W Adams St
- **Ceregier Tech Prep** • 2040 W Adams St
- **Crane Achievement Academy** • 2245 W Jackson Blvd
- **Dett R Nathaniel Elementary** • 2306 W Maypole Ave
- **Ellen Mitchell Branch** • 2315 W Erie St
- **Ellen Mitchell Elementary** • 2233 W Ohio St
- **Foundations Elementary** • 2040 W Adams St
- **Healy High** • 100 N Western Ave
- **Henry Suder Elementary** • 2022 W Washington Blvd
- **Irene C Hernandez Achievement Center** • 2245 W Jackson Blvd
- **Iyc Chicago** • 136 N Western Ave
- **Malcolm X College** • 1900 W Van Buren St
- **Mancel Talcott Elementary** • 1840 W Ohio St
- **Nia Middle** • 2040 W Adams St
- **St Malachy Elementary** • 2252 W Washington Blvd
- **Ulysses S Grant Community Academy** • 145 S Campbell Ave
- **Victor Herbert Elementary** • 2131 W Monroe St
- **West Town High** • 2021 W Fulton St
- **William H Brown Elementary** • 54 N Hermitage Ave
- **Wilma Rudolph Learning Center** • 110 N Paulina St

Supermarkets

- **Edmar Foods** • 2019 W Chicago Ave
- **Ukrainian Village Grocery** • 2204 W Chicago Ave

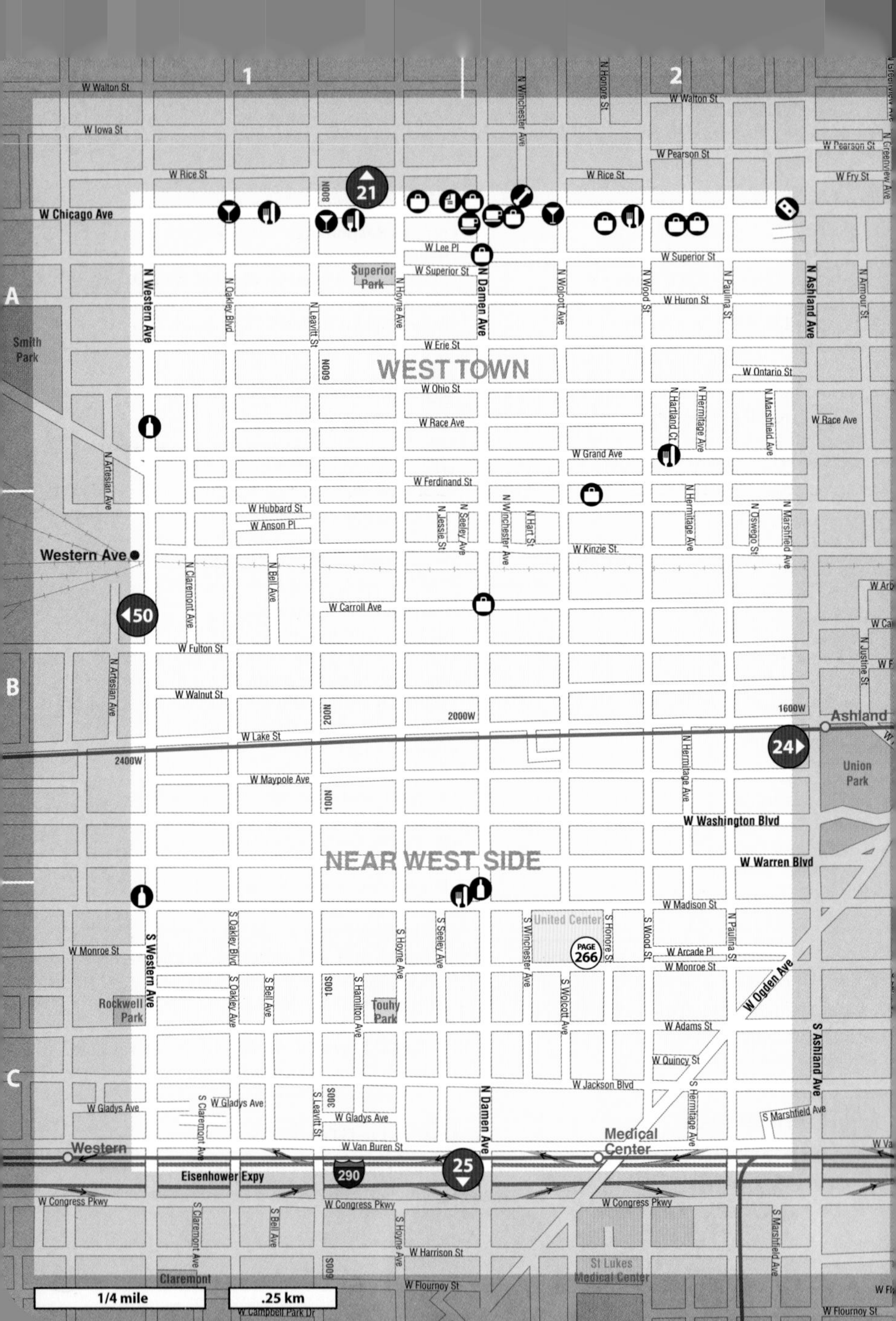

1
2
A
B
C
W Walton St
W Iowa St
W Pearson St
W Rice St
W Fry St
W Chicago Ave
W Lee Pl
W Superior St
Superior Park
W Huron St
Smith Park
N Western Ave
N Oakley Blvd
N Leavitt St
N Hoyne Ave
N Damen Ave
N Wolcott Ave
N Wood St
N Paulina St
N Ashland Ave
N Armour St
N Winchester Ave
N Honore St
800N
21
W Erie St
WEST TOWN
600N
W Ontario St
W Ohio St
W Race Ave
N Harland Ct
N Hermitage Ave
N Marshfield Ave
N Artesian Ave
W Grand Ave
W Ferdinand St
W Hubbard St
W Anson Pl
N Jessie St
N Seeley Ave
N Hart St
N Oswego St
Western Ave
W Kinzie St
N Claremont Ave
N Bell Ave
W Carroll Ave
50
W Fulton St
N Justine St
W Walnut St
200N
2000W
1600W
Ashland
W Lake St
2400W
24
Union Park
W Maypole Ave
100N
W Washington Blvd
NEAR WEST SIDE
W Warren Blvd
W Madison St
United Center
S Oakley Blvd
S Seeley Ave
S Hoyne Ave
S Winchester Ave
S Honore St
S Wood St
S Paulina St
PAGE 266
W Monroe St
S Western Ave
W Arcade Pl
S Bell Ave
100S
S Hamilton Ave
S Wolcott Ave
W Ogden Ave
Rockwell Park
Touhy Park
W Adams St
S Ashland Ave
W Quincy St
W Jackson Blvd
N Damen Ave
S Hermitage Ave
W Gladys Ave
S Claremont Ave
300S
S Leavitt St
S Marshfield Ave
Medical Center
Western
W Van Buren St
Eisenhower Expy
290
25
W Congress Pkwy
W Harrison St
600S
St Lukes Medical Center
Claremont
W Flournoy St
1/4 mile
.25 km
W Campbell Park Dr

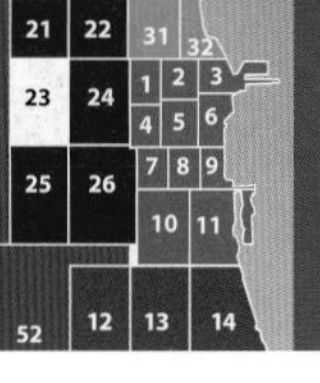

Between the architectural haven Salvage One, cowboy costumer Alcala's, designer toy store Rotofugi, and gardening boutique Sprout Home, the shopping is anything but ordinary in this neck of the woods. Get your coffee with a side of hipster at Atomix. Thank goodness for Edmar Foods, home to fresh, exotic and reasonably-priced produce.

Coffee

- **Atomix** • 1957 W Chicago Ave
- **Bleeding Heart Bakery** • 2018 W Chicago Ave

Copy Shops

- **Postnet** • 2038 W Chicago Ave

Liquor Stores

- **Campbell Food & Liquor** • 2459 W Madison St
- **DiCarlo's Armanetti Liquors** • 515 N Western Ave
- **Main St Liquors** • 2000 W Madison St

Nightlife

- **Darkroom** • 2210 W Chicago Ave
- **Sak's Ukrainian Village Restaurant** • 2301 W Chicago Ave
- **Tuman's** • 2159 W Chicago Ave

Pet Shops

- **Liz's Bird Shop** • 1931 W Chicago Ave

Restaurants

- **A Tavola** • 2148 W Chicago Ave
- **China Dragon Restaurant** • 2008 W Madison St
- **Il Jack's Italian Restaurant** • 1758 W Grand Ave
- **Old Lviv** • 2228 W Chicago Ave
- **Tecalitlan Restaurant** • 1814 W Chicago Ave

Shopping

- **Alcala's** • 1733 W Chicago Ave
- **Bleeding Heart Bakery** • 2018 W Chicago Ave
- **Decoro Studio** • 2000 W Carroll St
- **Donofrio's Double Corona Cigars** • 2058 W Chicago Ave
- **H&R Sports** • 1739 W Chicago Ave
- **Rotofugi** • 1953 W Chicago Ave
- **Salvage One Architectural Elements** • 1840 W Hubbard St
- **Sprout Home** • 745 N Damen Ave
- **Tomato Tattoo** • 1855 W Chicago Ave

Video Rental

- **Fredie's Video** • 1618 W Chicago Ave

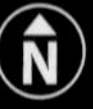

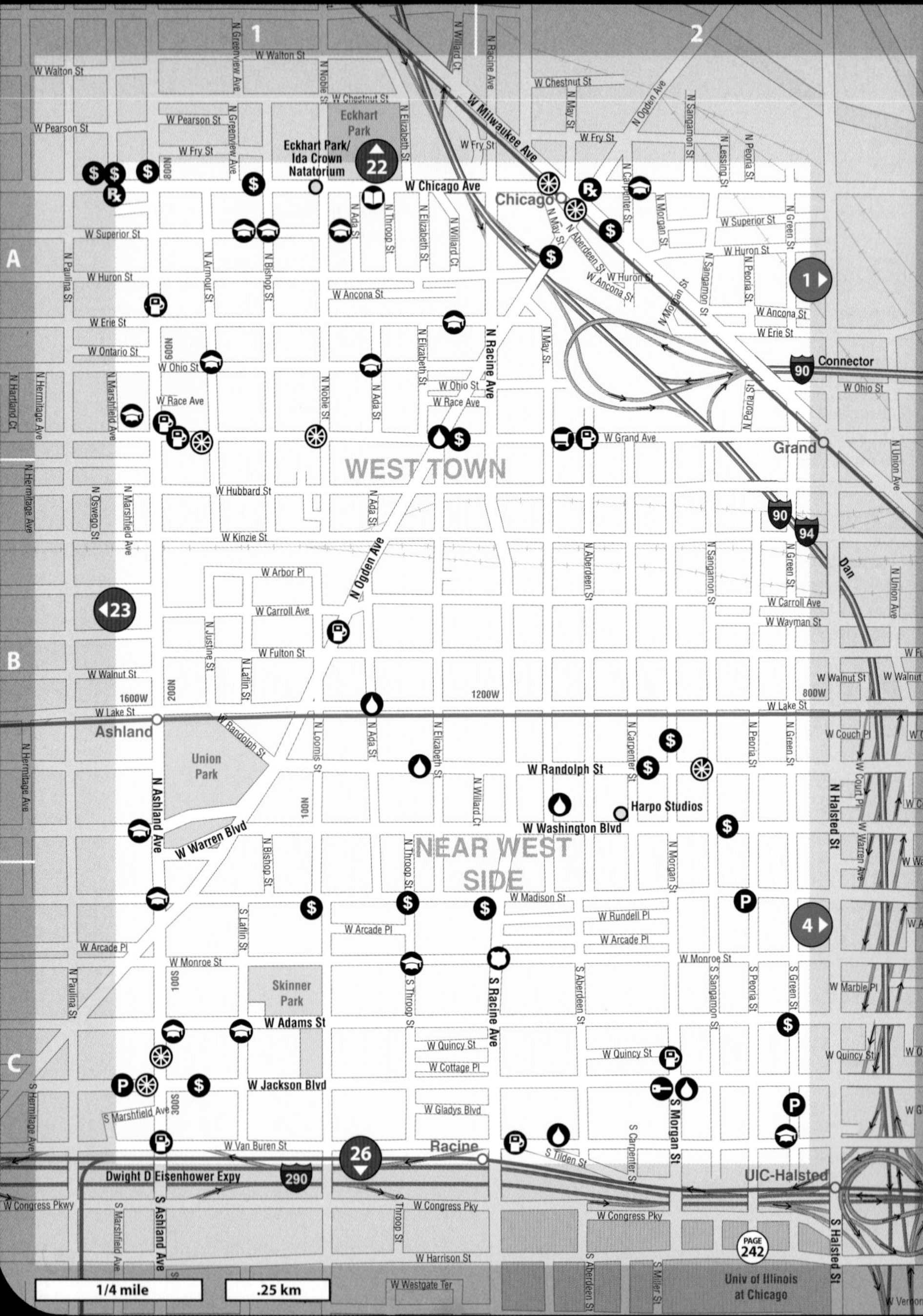

N
1
2
A
B
C
W Walton St
W Chestnut St
W Pearson St
W Fry St
Eckhart Park
Eckhart Park/
Ida Crown
Natatorium
22
W Chicago Ave
Chicago
W Milwaukee Ave
N Ogden Ave
W Superior St
W Huron St
W Ancona St
W Erie St
W Ontario St
W Ohio St
W Race Ave
W Grand Ave
Connector
90
94
Grand
WEST TOWN
W Hubbard St
W Kinzie St
W Arbor Pl
W Carroll Ave
W Wayman St
W Fulton St
W Walnut St
W Lake St
1600W
1200W
800W
Ashland
Union Park
W Randolph St
Harpo Studios
W Washington Blvd
W Warren Blvd
NEAR WEST SIDE
W Madison St
W Rundell Pl
W Arcade Pl
W Monroe St
Skinner Park
W Marble Pl
W Adams St
W Quincy St
W Cottage Pl
W Jackson Blvd
W Gladys Blvd
S Marshfield Ave
W Van Buren St
Racine
S Tilden St
26
Dwight D Eisenhower Expy
290
UIC-Halsted
W Congress Pkwy
W Congress Pky
W Harrison St
W Westgate Ter
Univ of Illinois at Chicago
PAGE 242
23
1
4
Dan
N Ashland Ave
S Ashland Ave
N Racine Ave
S Racine Ave
N Halsted St
S Halsted St
N Morgan St
S Morgan St
N Paulina St
N Marshfield Ave
N Hermitage Ave
N Armour St
N Bishop St
N Noble St
N Ada St
N Throop St
N Elizabeth St
N Willard Ct
N May St
N Aberdeen St
N Carpenter St
N Sangamon St
N Peoria St
N Green St
N Union Ave
N Loomis St
N Laflin St
N Justine St
N Oswego St
N Greenview Ave
N Lessing St
W Court Pl
W Couch Pl
S Throop St
S Laflin St
S Aberdeen St
S Sangamon St
S Peoria St
S Green St
S Carpenter St
S Miller St
S Hermitage Ave
1/4 mile
.25 km

Food distribution centers and wholesalers, warehouses, and loading docks rub shoulders with an alternative gallery scene, trendy restaurants, and hot clubs in this transitional 'hood where condo and loft development is king and Oprah Winfrey is queen. Young Cusack–wannabes take classes at the Chicago Academy for the Arts. Break a leg.

Banks

- **American Chartered (ATM)** • 1020 W Randolph St
- **Banco Popular** • 1445 W Chicago Ave
- **Broadway** • 900 W Van Buren St
- **Chase** • 923 W Washington Blvd
- **Chase (ATM)** • 1650 W Chicago Ave
- **First Eagle National** • 1201 W Madison St
- **La Salle** • 850 W Jackson Blvd
- **MB Financial** • 1420 W Madison St
- **MB Financial (ATM)** • 843 W Randolph St
- **MB Financial (ATM)** • 9 S Green St
- **North Community** • 1244 W Grand Ave
- **North Community** • 1600 W Chicago Ave
- **South Central** • 160 N Morgan St
- **TCF (ATM)** • 1645 W Jackson Blvd
- **TCF (ATM)** • Osco • 771 N Ogden Ave
- **US** • 745 N Milwaukee Ave
- **Washington Mutual** • 1301 W Madison St
- **Washington Mutual** • 1656 W Chicago Ave

Car Washes

- **A&A Automobile Service** • 1352 W Lake St
- **Bert's Car Wash** • 1231 W Grand Ave
- **May St Car Wash** • 27 N May St
- **Randolph St Auto Spa** • 1308 W Randolph St
- **Shell** • 1001 W Jackson Blvd
- **Strictly by Hand II** • 1125 W Van Buren St

Car Rental

- **Enterprise** • 318 S Morgan St • 312-432-9780

Gas Stations

- **BP** • 1600 W Van Buren St
- **Citgo** • 1535 W Grand Ave
- **Marathon** • 1100 W Grand Ave
- **Marathon** • 335 N Ogden Ave
- **Marathon** • 649 N Ashland Ave
- **Shell** • 1001 W Jackson Blvd
- **Shell** • 1160 W Van Buren St
- **Shell** • 505 N Ashland Ave

Landmarks

- **Eckhart Park/Ida Crown Natatorium** • Noble St & Chicago Ave
- **Harpo Studios** • 1058 W Washington Blvd

Libraries

- **Eckhart Park Branch** • 1330 W Chicago Ave

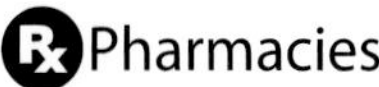

Pharmacies

- **Osco Drug** • 771 N Ogden Ave
- **Walgreens** • 1650 W Chicago Ave

Pizza

- **D'Agostino's Pizza and Pub** • 752 N Ogden Ave
- **Di's Best** • 1521 W Grand Ave
- **Moretti's** • 1645 W Jackson Blvd
- **Penny's Pizza** • 230 S Ashland Ave
- **Pie-Eyed Pizza** • 1111 W Chicago Ave
- **Salerno's Restaurant** • 1201 W Grand Ave
- **Tomato Head Pizza Kitchen** • 945 W Randolph St

Police

- **12th District (Monroe)** • 100 S Racine Ave

Schools

- **American Quality** • 850 W Jackson Blvd
- **Chicago Academy for the Arts** • 1010 W Chicago Ave
- **Esperanza Community Services** • 520 N Marshfield St
- **Holy Innocents** • 1448 W Superior St
- **James Otis Elementary** • 525 N Armour St
- **Jesse Spaulding** • 1628 W Washington Blvd
- **Mark Skinner Classical** • 111 S Throop St
- **Midwest Apostolic Bible College** • 14 S Ashland Ave
- **Milburn High** • 1448 W Superior St
- **Near North Special Ed Center** • 739 N Ada St
- **Philo Carpenter Elementary** • 1250 W Erie St
- **Santa Maria Addolorata** • 1337 W Ohio St
- **St Gregory Episcopal** • 201 S Ashland Ave
- **Whitney Young High** • 211 S Laflin St

Supermarkets

- **Bari Foods** • 1120 W Grand Ave

Parking

1
2
A
B
C
W Walton St
W Chestnut St
W Pearson St
W Fry St
W Chicago Ave
W Milwaukee Ave
Eckhart Park
22
Chicago
W Superior St
W Huron St
W Ancona St
W Erie St
W Ontario St
W Ohio St
W Race Ave
W Grand Ave
Connector
90
94
Grand
WEST TOWN
W Hubbard St
W Kinzie St
W Arbor Pl
W Carroll Ave
W Wayman St
W Fulton St
W Walnut St
W Lake St
1600W
1200W
800W
Ashland
Union Park
W Randolph St
W Warren Blvd
W Washington Blvd
NEAR WEST SIDE
W Madison St
W Rundell Pl
W Arcade Pl
W Monroe St
Skinner Park
W Adams St
W Quincy St
W Cottage Pl
W Jackson Blvd
W Gladys Blvd
W Van Buren St
Racine
Dwight D Eisenhower Expy
290
26
W Congress Pkwy
W Congress Pky
S Tilden St
UIC-Halsted
W Harrison St
W Westgate Ter
Univ of Illinois at Chicago
PAGE 242
23
4
N Ogden Ave
N Racine Ave
S Racine Ave
N Ashland Ave
S Ashland Ave
N Halsted St
S Halsted St
S Morgan St
1/4 mile
.25 km

Dining options in River West are plentiful to say the least. Of all the choices, we like DeCero for their contemporary pan-Latin spin and Green Zebra for innovative vegetarian choices. La Sardine packs 'em in like, well, sardines, for their Tuesday evening three-course fixed price special. Later on, go sip at Tasting Room on Randolph Street. On Tuesdays all of their wines by the glass are half price.

25 26 7 8 9 10 11 52 12 13 14

Coffee

- **Bialy's Café** • 1421 W Chicago Ave
- **Corduroy's Espresso Spot** • 1650 W Ogden Ave
- **Dunkin' Donuts** • 901 W Washington Blvd
- **Muse Café** • 817 N Milwaukee Ave
- **Sip Coffee House** • 1223 W Grand Ave
- **Starbucks** • 1001A W Madison St
- **Starbucks** • 520 N Ogden Ave
- **Swim Café** • 1357 W Chicago Ave
- **West Gate Coffeehouse** • 924 W Madison St

Copy Shops

- **AlphaGraphics** • 1017 W Washington Blvd
- **The UPS Store** • 516 N Ogden Ave
- **The UPS Store** • 910 W Van Buren St

Gyms

- **Cardinal Fitness of Madison Ave** • 1301 W Madison St
- **Curves (women only)** • 1151 W Madison St
- **Slim and Tone (women only)** • 1142 W Grand Ave
- **West Loop Gym** • 1024 W Kinzie St

Hardware Stores

- **AAA Saw & Tool Service & Supply** • 1401 W Washington Blvd
- **Imperial Hardware** • 1208 W Grand Ave

Liquor Stores

- **Randolph Wine Cellars** • 1415 W Randolph St
- **Rothchild Liquor Marts** • 1532 W Chicago Ave
- **Tasting Room (wine only)** • 1415 W Randolph St

Nightlife

- **Babalu** • 1645 W Jackson Blvd
- **Betty's Blue Star Lounge** • 1600 W Grand Ave
- **Café Fresco** • 1202 W Grand Ave
- **Chromium** • 817 W Lake St
- **Fulton Lounge** • 955 W Fulton Market
- **J Patricks** • 1367 W Erie St
- **Jack's Tap** • 901 W Jackson Blvd
- **Matchbox** • 770 N Milwaukee Ave
- **Players Bar & Grill** • 551 N Odgen Ave
- **Rhythm** • 1108 W Randolph St
- **Sonotheque** • 1444 W Chicago Ave
- **Tasting Room** • 1415 W Randolph St
- **Transit** • 1431 W Lake St
- **Twisted Spoke** • 501 N Ogden Ave
- **West Town Tavern** • 1329 W Chicago Ave

Restaurants

- **160 Blue** • 1400 W Randolph St
- **Amelia's Mexican Grille** • 1235 W Grand Ave
- **Amore Ristorante** • 1330 W Madison St
- **Aroma** • 941 W Randolph St
- **Avenue M** • 695 N Milwaukee Ave
- **Bella Notte** • 1374 W Grand Ave
- **Billy Goat Tavern** • 1535 W Madison St
- **Bombon Café** • 38 S Ashland Ave
- **Breakfast Club** • 1381 W Hubbard St
- **Buongiorno Café** • 1123 W Grand Ave
- **Burger Baron** • 1381 W Grand Ave
- **Butterfly Sushi Bar and Thai Cuisine** • 1156 W Grand Ave
- **Cannella's on Grand** • 1132 W Grand Ave
- **Carmichael's Chicago Steak House** • 1052 W Monroe St
- **Chicago Chocolate Café** • 847 W Randolph St
- **D'Agostino's Pizzeria** • 752 N Ogden Ave
- **D'Amotos Italian Bakery** • 1124 W Grand Ave
- **De Cero** • 814 W Randolph St
- **Dragonfly Mandarin Restaurants** • 832 W Randolph St
- **Fan Si Pan** • 1618 W Chicago Ave
- **Flo** • 1434 W Chicago Ave
- **Follia** • 953 W Fulton St
- **Green Zebra** • 1460 W Chicago Ave
- **Hacienda Tecalitlan** • 820 N Ashland Blvd
- **Ina's** • 1235 W Randolph St
- **Jak's Tap** • 901 W Jackson Blvd
- **Jerry's Sandwiches** • 1045 W Madison St
- **La Sardine** • 111 N Carpenter St
- **Le Peep Grill** • 1000 W Washington Blvd
- **Marche** • 833 W Randolph St
- **May Street Market** • 1132 W Grand Ave
- **Misto** • 1118 W Grand Ave
- **Moretti's** • 1645 W Jackson Blvd
- **Moto** • 945 W Fulton Market
- **Oggi Trattoria Café** • 1378 W Grand Ave
- **Rushmore** • 1023 W Lake St
- **Salerno's Pizza and Pasta** • 1201 W Grand Ave
- **Saultaus** • 1350 W Randolph St
- **Silver Palm** • 768 N Milwaukee Ave
- **Sushi X** • 1136 W Chicago Ave
- **Swim Café** • 1357 W Chicago Ave
- **Twisted Spoke** • 501 N Ogden Ave
- **Union Park** • 228 S Racine Ave
- **Vinnie's Sandwich Shop** • 1204 W Grand Ave
- **Vivo** • 838 W Randolph St
- **West Town Tavern** • 1329 W Chicago Ave
- **Windy City Café** • 1062 W Chicago Ave
- **Wishbone** • 1001 W Washington Blvd

Shopping

- **3 Design Three** • 1431 W Chicago Ave
- **Aesthetic Eye** • 1520 W Chicago Ave
- **Casati** • 949 W Fulton Market
- **Chicago Avenue Discount** • 1637 W Chicago Ave
- **Design Inc** • 1359 W Grand Ave
- **Douglas Dawson Gallery** • 400 N Morgan St
- **MK Brody** • 1101 W Randolph St
- **Jan's Antiques** • 225 N Racine Ave
- **PakMail** • 1461 W Chicago Ave
- **Pet Care Plus** • 1212 W Grand Ave
- **The Realm** • 1430 W Chicago Ave
- **Roots** • 1140 W Grand Ave
- **RR#1 Chicago Apothecary** • 814 N Ashland Blvd
- **Snap** • 470 N Ogden Ave
- **Upgrade Cycle Works** • 1130 W Chicago Ave
- **Xyloform** • 1423 W Chicago Ave

Video Rental

- **Blockbuster** • 1015 W Madison St
- **Grand Slam Video** • 1369 W Grand Ave

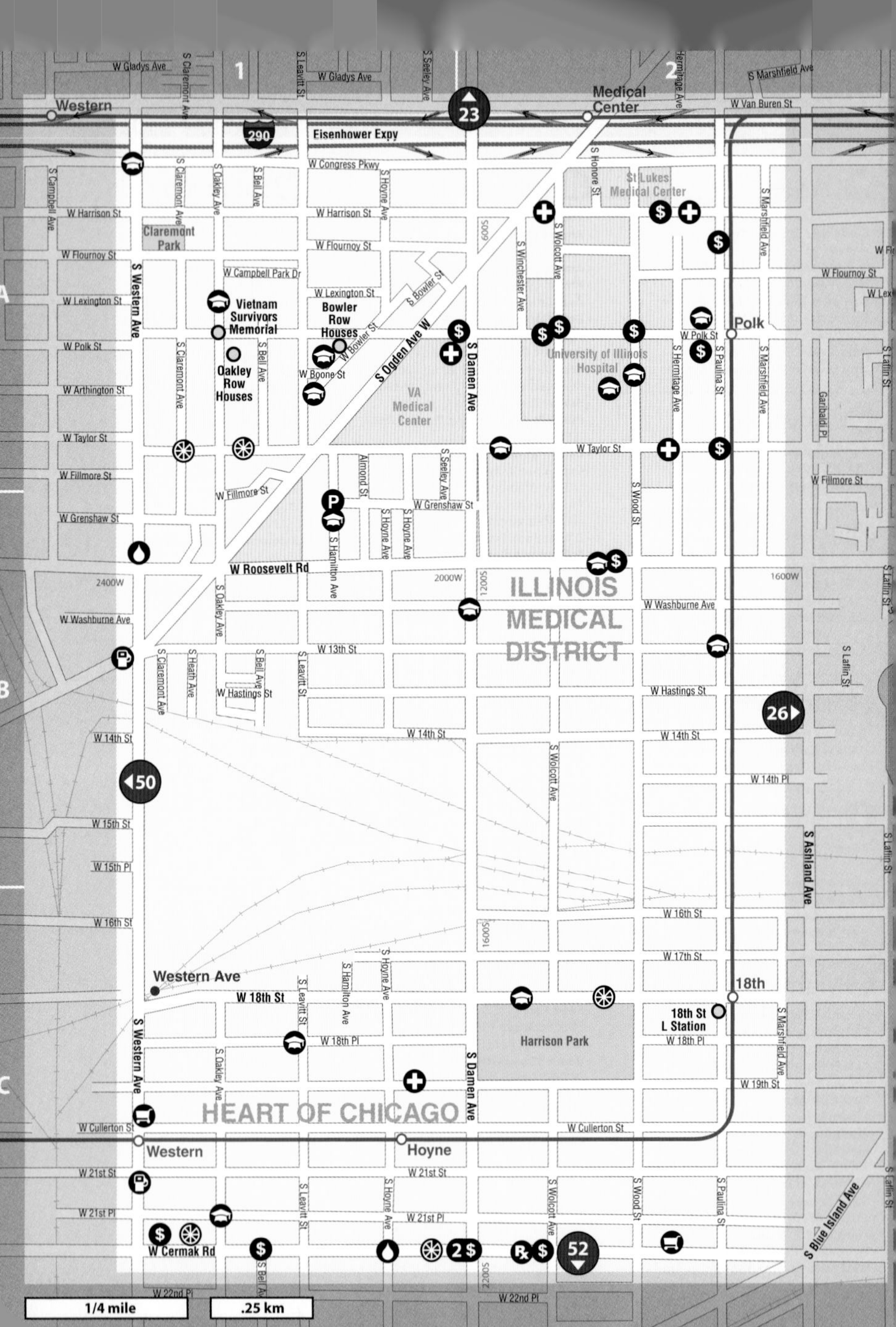

Western
Medical Center
Eisenhower Expy
290
23
St Lukes Medical Center
Claremont Park
Vietnam Survivors Memorial
Oakley Row Houses
Bowler Row Houses
VA Medical Center
University of Illinois Hospital
Polk
ILLINOIS MEDICAL DISTRICT
W Roosevelt Rd
26
50
Western Ave
W 18th St
18th
18th St L Station
Harrison Park
HEART OF CHICAGO
Western
Hoyne
52
S Western Ave
S Damen Ave
S Ogden Ave W
S Ashland Ave
S Blue Island Ave
W Cermak Rd
1/4 mile
.25 km

The conglomeration of facilities that make up the Illinois Medical District make it the second-largest such district in the country. Cook County Hospital, now Stroger Hospital, broke ground back in 1874. Made famous by the television series *ER*, its trauma center is first rate. You'd be well-advised to go elsewhere for non-emergency care – long waits are a chronic pain. A building boom in the Tri-Taylor area houses newly minted MDs.

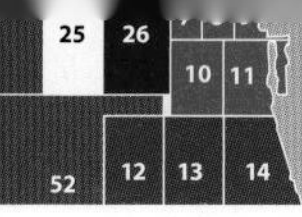

Banks

- **Bank of America** • 2332 W Cermak Rd
- **Bank of America (ATM)** • 1717 W Polk St
- **Bank of America (ATM)** • 1801 W Taylor St
- **Bank of America (ATM)** • 818 S Wolcott Ave
- **Chase** • 2000 W Cermak Rd
- **Chase (ATM)** • 1750 W Harrison St
- **Chase (ATM)** • 1850 W Roosevelt Rd
- **Chase (ATM)** • 1931 W Cermak Rd
- **Chase (ATM)** • 600 S Paulina St
- **Chase (ATM)** • 820 S Damen Ave
- **LaSalle (ATM)** • 1701 W Taylor St
- **LaSalle (ATM)** • 818 S Wolcott Ave
- **Metropolitan** • 2201 W Cermak Rd

Car Washes

- **Hot Spot Hand Car Wash & Detailing** • 2116 W Cermak Rd

Gas Stations

- **Citgo** • 2107 S Western Ave
- **Mobil** • 2401 W Ogden Ave
- **Shell** • 2401 W Roosevelt Rd

Emergency Rooms

- **John H Stroger** • 1901 W Harrison St
- **Rush-Presbyterian St Luke's** • 1750 W Harrison St
- **St Anthony's** • 2875 W 19th St
- **University of Illinois at Chicago** • 1740 W Taylor St
- **VA Medical Center** • 820 S Damen Ave

Landmarks

- **18th St L station** • W 18th St & S Paulina St
- **Bowler Row Houses** • 2148 W Bowler St
- **Oakley Row Houses** • 801 S Oakley Ave
- **Vietnam Survivors Memorial** • 815 S Oakley Ave

Pharmacies

- **Walgreens** • 1931 W Cermak Rd

Pizza

- **Bacci Pizzeria** • 2248 W Taylor St
- **Damenzo's Pizza** • 2324 W Taylor St
- **Pisa Pizza** • 2050 W Cermak Rd
- **Pizza Hut** • 2337 W Cermak Rd
- **Pizza Nova** • 1842 W 18th St

Schools

- **Chicago Hope Academy** • 2189 W Bowler St
- **Chicago Lighthouse Development** • 1850 W Roosevelt Rd
- **Children of Peace St Callistus** • 2187 W Bowler St
- **Josiah L Pickard Elementary** • 2301 W 21st Pl
- **Nancy Jefferson** • 1100 S Hamilton Ave
- **Octavio Paz Middle** • 2401 W Congress Pkwy
- **Orozco Elementary** • 1940 W 18th St
- **Rush Day** • 1720 W Polk St
- **Rush University** • 600 S Paulina St
- **St Ann Grade** • 2211 W 18th Pl
- **University of Illinois at Chicago** • 840 S Wood St
- **University of Illinois College of Medicine** • 808 S Wood St
- **Washington Irving Elementary** • 749 S Oakley Blvd
- **William E Gladstone Elementary** • 1231 S Damen Ave

Supermarkets

- **Aldi** • 1739 W Cermak Rd
- **Fairplay Finer Foods** • 2200 S Western Ave

Parking

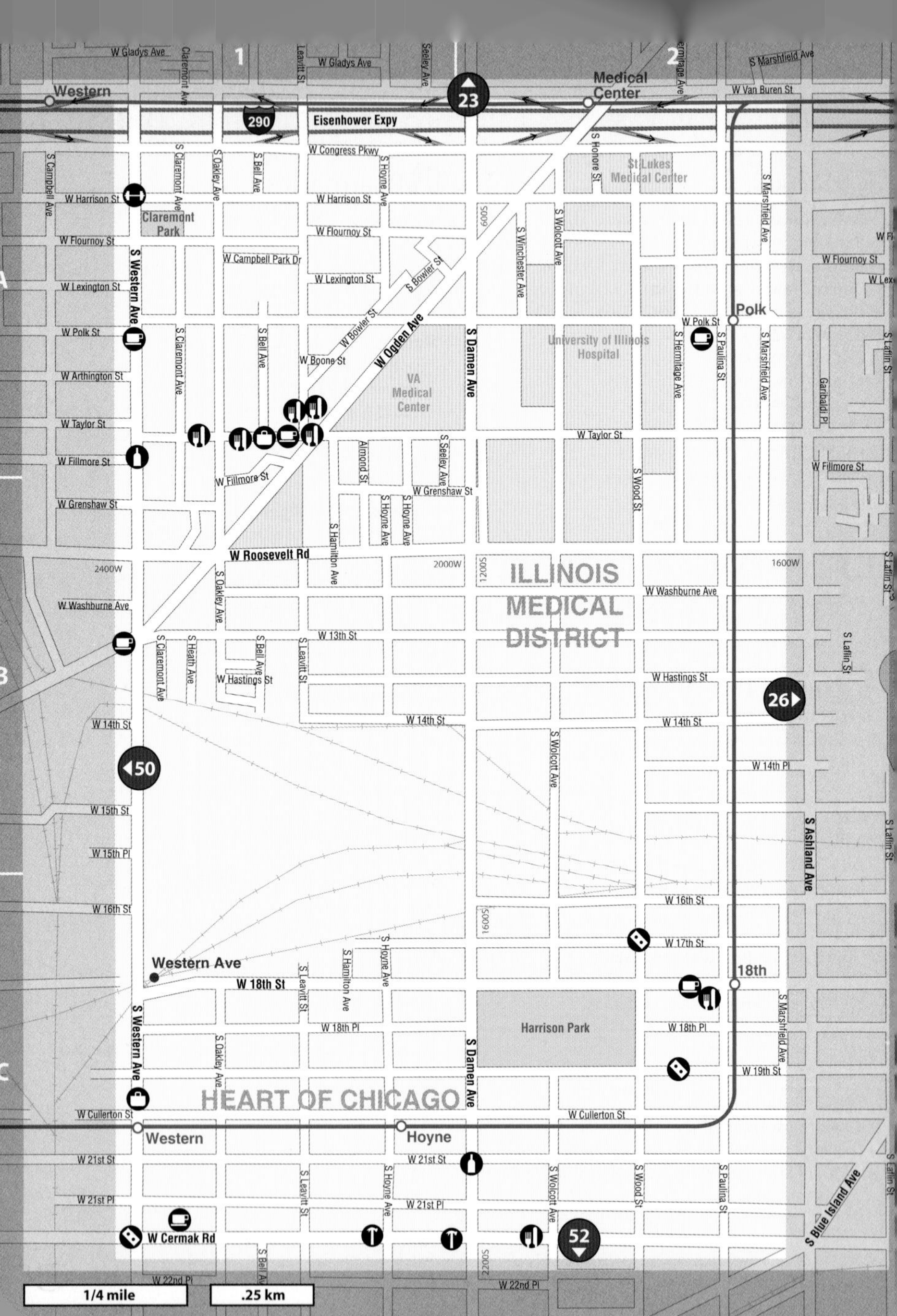

1
2
A
B
C
23
26
50
52
290
Western
Medical Center
Eisenhower Expy
W Van Buren St
W Gladys Ave
W Congress Pkwy
W Harrison St
Claremont Park
W Flournoy St
W Campbell Park Dr
W Lexington St
W Polk St
Polk
W Arthington St
W Boone St
W Bowler St
S Bowler St
W Ogden Ave
W Taylor St
W Fillmore St
W Grenshaw St
W Roosevelt Rd
W Washburne Ave
W 13th St
W Hastings St
W 14th St
W 14th Pl
W 15th St
W 15th Pl
W 16th St
W 17th St
Western Ave
W 18th St
18th
W 18th Pl
W 19th St
W Cullerton St
Western
Hoyne
W 21st St
W 21st Pl
W Cermak Rd
W 22nd Pl
S Western Ave
S Campbell Ave
S Claremont Ave
S Oakley Ave
S Bell Ave
S Leavitt St
S Hoyne Ave
S Seeley Ave
S Damen Ave
S Honore St
S Wolcott Ave
S Winchester Ave
S Hermitage Ave
S Paulina St
S Marshfield Ave
S Laflin St
S Ashland Ave
S Wood St
S Hamilton Ave
S Heath Ave
Almond St
Garibaldi Pl
S Blue Island Ave
St Lukes Medical Center
University of Illinois Hospital
VA Medical Center
Harrison Park
ILLINOIS MEDICAL DISTRICT
HEART OF CHICAGO
2400W
2000W
1600W
600S
1200S
1600S
2200S
1/4 mile
.25 km

Residents of the Tri-Taylor building boom head a few blocks east to Little Italy and north to River West for nightlife and fine dining. Local options include Lu-Lu's for a quick lunch and the Ferrara bakery, a bakery and sweet shop that offers carry-out as well as limited eat-in options. Further south, Pilsen bleeds into the Heart of Chicago 'hood, and there's no shortage of low-priced, authentic Mexican grub.

Coffee

- **Café Frida** • 739 S Western Ave
- **Dunkin' Donuts** • 1710 W 18th St
- **Dunkin' Donuts** • 1713 W Polk St
- **Dunkin' Donuts** • 2356 W Cermak Rd
- **Dunkin' Donuts** • 2401 W Ogden Ave
- **Netccino** • 2234 W Taylor St

Gyms

- **Curves (women only)** • 600 S Western Ave

Hardware Stores

- **Duran Hardware** • 2047 W Cermak Rd
- **Mitchell Hardware & Paints** • 2141 W Cermak Rd

Liquor Stores

- **Helen's Grocery & Liquors** • 2300 W 21st St

Restaurants

- **Carnitas Uruapan Restaurant** • 1725 W 18th St
- **Damenzo's** • 2324 W Taylor St
- **El Charco Verde** • 2255 W Taylor St
- **Ferrara Bakery** • 2210 W Taylor St
- **Lu-Lu's Hot Dogs** • 1000 S Leavitt St
- **TJ's Family Restaurant** • 1928 W Cermak Rd

Shopping

- **Accents Flowers and Gifts** • 2246 W Taylor St
- **Salvation Army Thrift Store** • 2024 S Western Ave

Video Rental

- **Blockbuster** • 2425 W Cermak Rd
- **Jacob Video** • 1801 W 17th St
- **Pedraza Video** • 1758 W 19th St

Map 26 • University Village/Little Italy/Pilsen
N
1
2
24
4
7
25
10
12
290
90
94
W Gladys Blvd
W Gladys Ave
S Marshfield Ave
W Van Buren St
Racine
S Tilden St
UIC-Halsted
W Congress Pkwy
W Harrison St
W Westgate Ter
W Flournoy St
W Lexington St
W Polk St
W Cabrini St
W Arthington St
W Taylor St
W Fillmore St
W Grenshaw St
W Roosevelt Rd
W Washburne Ave
W 12th Pl
W O'Brien St
W 13th St
W Maxwell St
W Hastings St
W Liberty St
W 14th St
W Barber St
W 14th Pl
W South Water Market
W 15th St
W 15th Pl
W 16th St
W 17th St
W 17th Pl
W 18th St
W 18th Pl
W 19th St
W 19th Pl
W Cullerton St
W 20th Pl
W 21st St
W 21st Pl
W Cermak Rd
W 22nd Pl
W Vernon Park Pl
S Ashland Ave
S Racine Ave
S Morgan St
S Loomis St
S Ada St
S Lytle St
S May St
S Aberdeen St
S Carpenter St
S Miller St
S Laflin St
S Bishop St
S Laflin Cir
Garibaldi Pl
S Paulina St
S Throop St
S Blue Island Ave
S Allport St
S Sangamon St
S Peoria St
S Newbury Ave
S Shelby Ct
Halsted St
S Union Ave
S Ruble St
S Desplaines St
S Canalport Ave
S Ford Ave
Dan Ryan Expy
Polk
18th
Halsted
600S
1200S
1600S
2200S
1600W
1200W
800W
Arrigo Park
Sheridan Park
Plgd Park
Addams Park
Dvorak Park
University of Illinois at Chicago East Campus
PAGE 242
National Italian-American Sports Hall of Fame
UNIVERSITY VILLAGE / LITTLE ITALY
PILSEN
1/4 mile
.25 km

Jane Addams, noted defender of the poor and social activist, wouldn't recognize her old 'hood today, but it still retains a bit of her feisty spirit. From the Mexican Fine Arts Museum in Pilsen to the newly relocated National Italian-American Sports Hall of Fame, there are institutions that pay homage to the diverse groups that call the area home. The University of Illinois at Chicago definitely holds sway around here, as the area fairly bustles with the textbook-toting set from sunup to sundown.

Banks

- **Bank of America (ATM)** • 700 S Halsted St
- **Bank of America (ATM)** • 750 S Halsted St
- **Chase** • 1130 W Taylor St
- **Chicago Community** • 1800 S Halsted St
- **Citibank (ATM)** • 1152 W Taylor St
- **Lakeside** • 1055 W Roosevelt Rd
- **LaSalle** • 1212 S Ashland Ave
- **LaSalle (ATM)** • 1200 W Harrison St
- **LaSalle (ATM)** • 750 S Halsted St
- **MB Financial** • 1618 W 18th St
- **MidAmerica** • 1314 S Halsted St
- **Midwest Bank & Trust Company (ATM)** • 1810 S Blue Island Ave
- **TCF** • Jewel • 1220 S Ashland Ave
- **TCF (ATM)** • 7-Eleven • 1350 S Halsted St
- **Washington Federal** • 1410 W Taylor St

Car Washes

- **G Express Hand Car Wash** • 1313 W 18th St
- **Pilsen Car Wash** • 2042 S Halsted St
- **Speed Hand Car Wash** • 1700 S Ashland Ave

Gas Stations

- **BP Amoco** • 1602 W Cermak Rd
- **Marathon** • 1549 W Roosevelt Rd

Landmarks

- **National Italian-American Sports Hall of Fame** • 1431 W Taylor St

Libraries

- **Lozano Public Library** • 1805 S Loomis St
- **Roosevelt Public Library** • 1101 W Taylor St
- **University of Illinois at Chicago Library** • 801 S Morgan St

Pharmacies

- **Jewel-Osco** • 1220 S Ashland Ave
- **Osco Drug** • 1713 S Ashland Ave

Pizza

- **Benny's Pizza II** • 1244 W 18th St
- **Caire's Pizza** • 1166 W 18th St
- **Chubby's Pizza** • 1429 W 18th St
- **Leona's** • 1419 W Taylor St
- **Pizza Tango** • 1013 W 18th St
- **Pompeii Bakery** • 1531 W Taylor St
- **Reggio's Pizza** • 1339 S Halsted St

Post Offices

- **US Post Office** • 1859 S Ashland Ave

Schools

- **Andrew Jackson Language Academy** • 1340 W Harrison St
- **Benito Juarez High** • 2150 S Laflin St
- **Bernice F Joyner CPC** • 1315 S Blue Island Ave
- **City as Classroom High** • 1814 S Union Ave
- **Galileo Scholastic Academy** • 820 S Carpenter St
- **John A Walsh Elementary** • 2015 S Peoria St
- **John M Smyth Elementary** • 1059 W 13th St
- **Joseph Jungman Elementary** • 1746 S Miller St
- **Joseph Medill Elementary** • 1301 W 14th St
- **Laurance Armour Day School RPS** • 630 S Ashland Ave
- **Manuel Perez Elementary** • 1241 W 19th St
- **McKinley Evgc** • 1326 W 14 Pl
- **Montefiore High** • 1310 S Ashland Ave
- **Moses Montefiore Middle** • 1310 S Ashland Ave
- **Perez Annex** • 2001 S Throop St
- **Peter Cooper Dual Language Academy** • 1624 W 19th St
- **Pilsen Academy** • 1420 W 17th St
- **Simpson Academy for Young Women** • 1321 S Paulina St
- **St Ignatius College Prep** • 1076 W Roosevelt Rd
- **St Pius V Elementary** • 1919 S Ashland Ave
- **St Procopius** • 1625 S Allport St
- **Thomas Jefferson Elementary** • 1522 W Fillmore St
- **Walsh Elementary** • 2015 S Peoria St

Supermarkets

- **Conte Di Savoia** • 1438 W Taylor St
- **Jewel-Osco** • 1220 S Ashland Ave

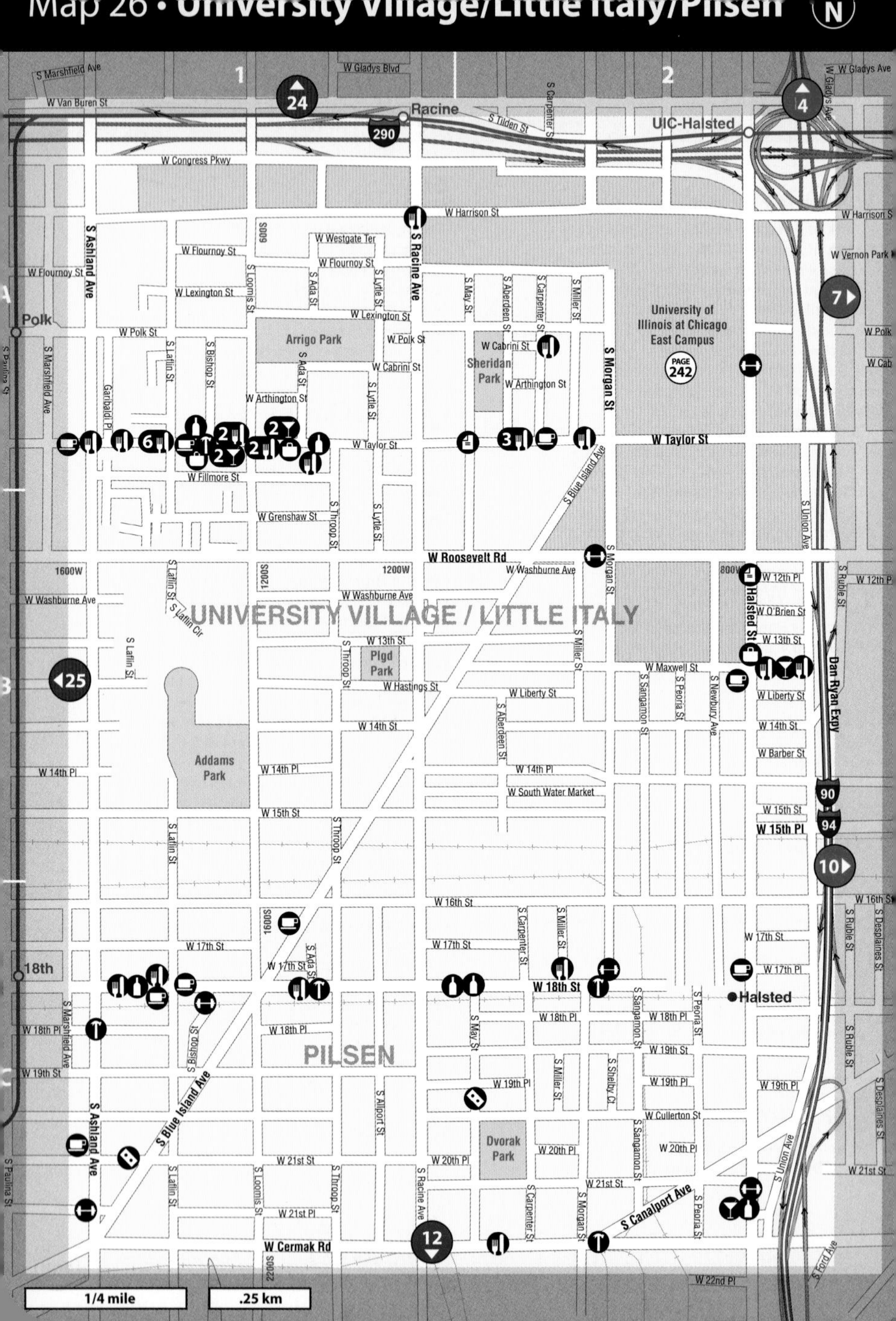

UNIVERSITY VILLAGE / LITTLE ITALY
PILSEN
University of Illinois at Chicago East Campus
PAGE 242
Arrigo Park
Sheridan Park
Addams Park
Plgd Park
Dvorak Park
Racine
UIC-Halsted
Polk
18th
Halsted
W Van Buren St
W Congress Pkwy
W Harrison St
W Taylor St
W Roosevelt Rd
W 18th St
W Cermak Rd
S Ashland Ave
S Racine Ave
S Morgan St
S Halsted St
S Blue Island Ave
S Canalport Ave
Dan Ryan Expy
1/4 mile
.25 km

Sprawling over the city's Near West Side is the University of Illinois at Chicago. Little Italy is close at hand, and if you look closely, you will note the presence of a number of thriving Italian neighborhood clubs here. Buy Scafuri Bakery's cannoli by the dozen. No summer trip to the area is complete without a stop at Mario's Lemonade on W Taylor Street or a pilgrimage to the Jane Addams Hull-House Museum.

Coffee

- **Café Jumping Bean** • 1439 W 18th St
- **Café Mestizo** • 2123 S Ashland Ave
- **Caribou Coffee** • 1328 S Halsted St
- **Dunkin' Donuts** • 1651 W Roosevelt Rd
- **Efebo's Internet Café** • 1640 S Blue Island Ave
- **Jamoch's Caffe** • 1066 W Taylor St
- **Kristoffer's Café & Bakery** • 1733 S Halsted St
- **Mi Cafetal** • 1519 W 18th St
- **Starbucks** • 1430 W Taylor St

Copy Shops

- **Postnet** • 1258 S Halsted St
- **The UPS Store** • 1137 W Taylor St

Gyms

- **Curves (Women only)** • 960 W 18th St
- **Duncan YMCA** • 1001 W Roosevelt Rd
- **Group Fitness** • 750 S Halsted St
- **Pilsen YMCA** • 1608 W 21st Pl
- **Temoc's Gym Fitness Center** • 2118 S Halsted St
- **World Gym** • 1822 S Bishop St

Hardware Stores

- **Alvarez Hardware** • 1323 W 18th St
- **Chiarugi Hardware** • 1449 W Taylor St
- **La Brocha Gorda** • 974 W 18th St
- **Seigle's Lumber (Lumber only)** • 977 W Cermak Rd
- **Torres Hardware** • 1836 S Ashland Ave

Liquor Stores

- **Amador Liquors** • 1167 W 18th St
- **Conte Di Savoia (Wine only)** • 1438 W Taylor St
- **El Trebol Liquors** • 1135 W 18th St
- **F&R Liquor** • 2129 S Halsted St
- **Guadalajara Food & Liquors** • 1527 W 18th St
- **Three Sons Food & Liquor** • 1311 W Taylor St

Nightlife

- **Bar Louie** • 1321 W Taylor St
- **Bevi Amo Wine Bar** • 1358 W Taylor St
- **Hawkeye's Bar & Grill** • 1458 W Taylor St
- **The Illinois Bar & Grill** • 1421 W Taylor St
- **Junior's Sports Lounge** • 724 W Maxwell St
- **Skylark** • 2149 S Halsted St

Restaurants

- **Al's Number 1 Italian Beef** • 1079 W Taylor St
- **Birreria Reyes de Ocotlan** • 1322 W 18th St
- **Caffe La Scala** • 626 S Racine Ave
- **Carm's Beef and Snack Shop** • 1057 W Polk St
- **Chez Joel** • 1119 W Taylor St
- **Couscous** • 1445 W Taylor St
- **De Pasada** • 1519 W Taylor St
- **Demitasse** • 1066 W Taylor St
- **Francesca's** • 1400 W Taylor St
- **Golden Thai** • 1509 W Taylor St
- **Japonica** • 1422 W Taylor St
- **Kohan Japanese Restaurant** • 730 W Maxwell St
- **La Cebollita** • 1723 S Ashland Ave
- **La Vita** • 1359 W Taylor St
- **Mario's Italian Lemonade** • 1068 W Taylor St
- **May Street Café** • 1136 W Cermak Rd
- **New Rosebud Café** • 1500 W Taylor St
- **Nuevo Leon** • 1515 W 18th St
- **Pizza Tango** • 1013 W 18th St
- **Playa Azul** • 1514 W 18th St
- **Sweet Maple Café** • 1339 W Taylor St
- **Taj Mahal** • 1512 W Taylor St
- **Taqueria Los Comales** • 1544 W 18th St
- **Taylor Street Taco Grill** • 1412 W Taylor St
- **Tuscany** • 1014 W Taylor St
- **WOW Café & Wingery** • 717 W Maxwell St

Shopping

- **Conte Di Savoia** • 1438 W Taylor St
- **Lush Wine and Spirits** • 1306 S Halsted St
- **Scafuri Bakery** • 1337 W Taylor St

Video Rental

- **Manny's Video II** • 1943 S May St

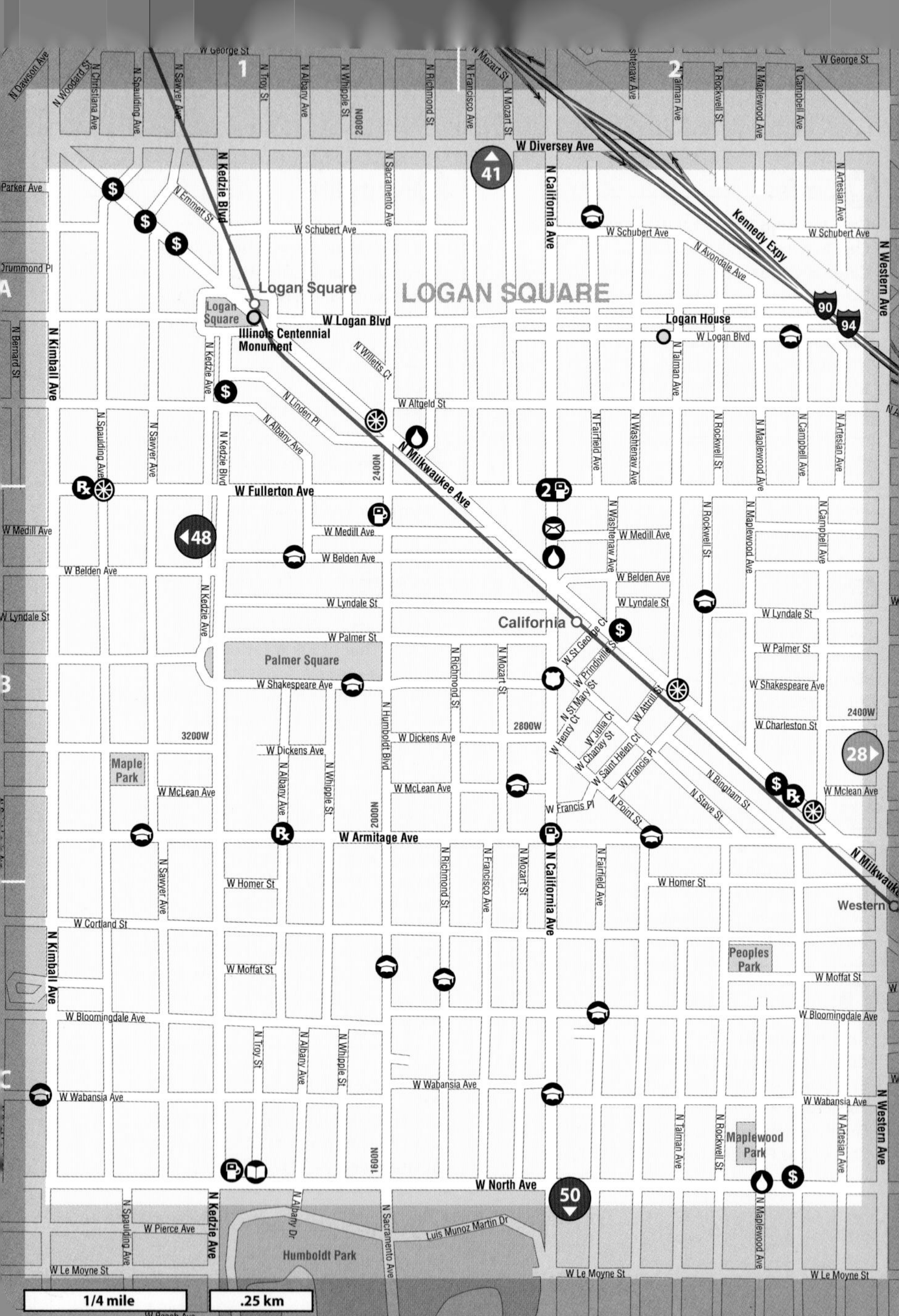

1
2
A
B
C
LOGAN SQUARE
Logan Square
Logan Square
Illinois Centennial Monument
Logan House
California
Western
Palmer Square
Maple Park
Peoples Park
Maplewood Park
Humboldt Park
41
48
28
50
2
90
94
W George St
W Diversey Ave
W Schubert Ave
W Logan Blvd
W Altgeld St
W Fullerton Ave
W Medill Ave
W Belden Ave
W Lyndale St
W Palmer St
W Shakespeare Ave
W Charleston St
W Dickens Ave
W McLean Ave
W Francis Pl
W Armitage Ave
W Homer St
W Cortland St
W Moffat St
W Bloomingdale Ave
W Wabansia Ave
W North Ave
W Pierce Ave
W Le Moyne St
W Beach Ave
Parker Ave
Drummond Pl
N Dawson Ave
N Woodard St
N Christiana Ave
N Spaulding Ave
N Sawyer Ave
N Kedzie Blvd
N Kedzie Ave
N Troy St
N Albany Ave
N Whipple St
N Richmond St
N Francisco Ave
N Mozart St
N California Ave
N Washtenaw Ave
N Talman Ave
N Rockwell St
N Maplewood Ave
N Campbell Ave
N Artesian Ave
N Western Ave
N Kimball Ave
N Bernard St
N Emmett St
N Linden Pl
N Willetts Ct
N Sacramento Ave
N Humboldt Blvd
N Milwaukee Ave
N Fairfield Ave
N Avondale Ave
Kennedy Expy
W St George Ct
W Prindiville St
W St Mary St
W Henry Ct
W Julia Ct
W Chaney St
W Saint Helen Ct
W Francis Pl
W Attrill St
N Bingham St
N Stave St
N Point St
N Albany Dr
Luis Munoz Martin Dr
3200W
2800W
2400W
2400N
2000N
1600N
1/4 mile
.25 km

With Bucktown and Wicker Park out of reach for today's struggling artists, Logan Square is the next best thing. With low rents—for now, historic Greystones, ethnic vibe—habla español?, dingy bars, and cheap eateries, it's a natural fit.

Banks

- **Banco Popular** • 2525 N Kedzie Blvd
- **Charter One** • 2500 W North Ave
- **Chase** • 2235 N Milwaukee Ave
- **Chase** • 2639 N Milwaukee Ave
- **Citibank (ATM)** • 2707 N Milwaukee Ave
- **Northern Trust** • 2814 W Fullerton Ave
- **TCF (ATM)** • Osco• 2053 N Milwaukee Ave
- **Washington Mutual** • 2741 N Milwaukee Ave

Car Washes

- **California Car Wash** • 2340 N California Ave
- **Dreamwash** • 2524 W North Ave
- **Logan Square Car Wash** • 2436 N Milwaukee Ave

Gas Stations

- **Amoco** • 2800 W Fullerton Ave
- **BP/Amoco** • 2801 W Armitage Ave
- **Citgo** • 2338 N Sacramento Ave
- **Citgo** • 3142 W North Ave
- **Shell** • 2801 W Fullerton Ave

Landmarks

- **Illinois Centennial Monument** • 3100 W Logan Blvd
- **Logan House** • 2656 W Logan Blvd

Libraries

- **Humboldt Park Public Library** • 1605 N Troy St

Pharmacies

- **Osco Drug** • 2053 N Milwaukee Ave
- **Walgreens** • 3110 W Armitage Ave
- **Walgreens** • 3320 W Fullerton Ave

Pizza

- **Big Tony's Pizza** • 3276 W Fullerton Ave
- **Congress Pizzeria** • 2033 N Milwaukee Ave
- **Domino's** • 2455 W Fullerton Ave
- **Father & Son Pizza** • 2475 N Milwaukee Ave
- **Lucky Vito's Pizzeria** • 2171 N Milwaukee Ave

Police

- **14th District (Shakespeare)** • 2150 N California Ave

Post Offices

- **US Post Office** • 2339 N California Ave

Schools

- **Bernhard Moos Elementary** • 1711 N California Ave
- **Charles R Darwin Elementary** • 3116 W Belden Ave
- **Harriet Beecher Stowe Elementary** • 3444 W Wabansia Ave
- **Humboldt Community Christian** • 1847 N Humboldt Blvd
- **J W Von Goethe Elementary** • 2236 N Rockwell St
- **Lorenz Brentano Math & Science Academy** • 2723 N Fairfield Ave
- **The Lutheran Day Nursery** • 1802 N Fairfield Ave
- **Richard Yates Elementary** • 1839 N Richmond St
- **Salem Christian** • 2845 W McLean Ave
- **Salomon P Chase Elementary** • 2021 N Point St
- **St Augustine College West** • 3255 W Armitage Ave
- **St John Berchman's** • 2511 W Logan Blvd
- **St Sylvester's** • 3027 W Palmer Blvd

Supermarkets

- **Provenance Food and Wine** • 2528 N California Ave

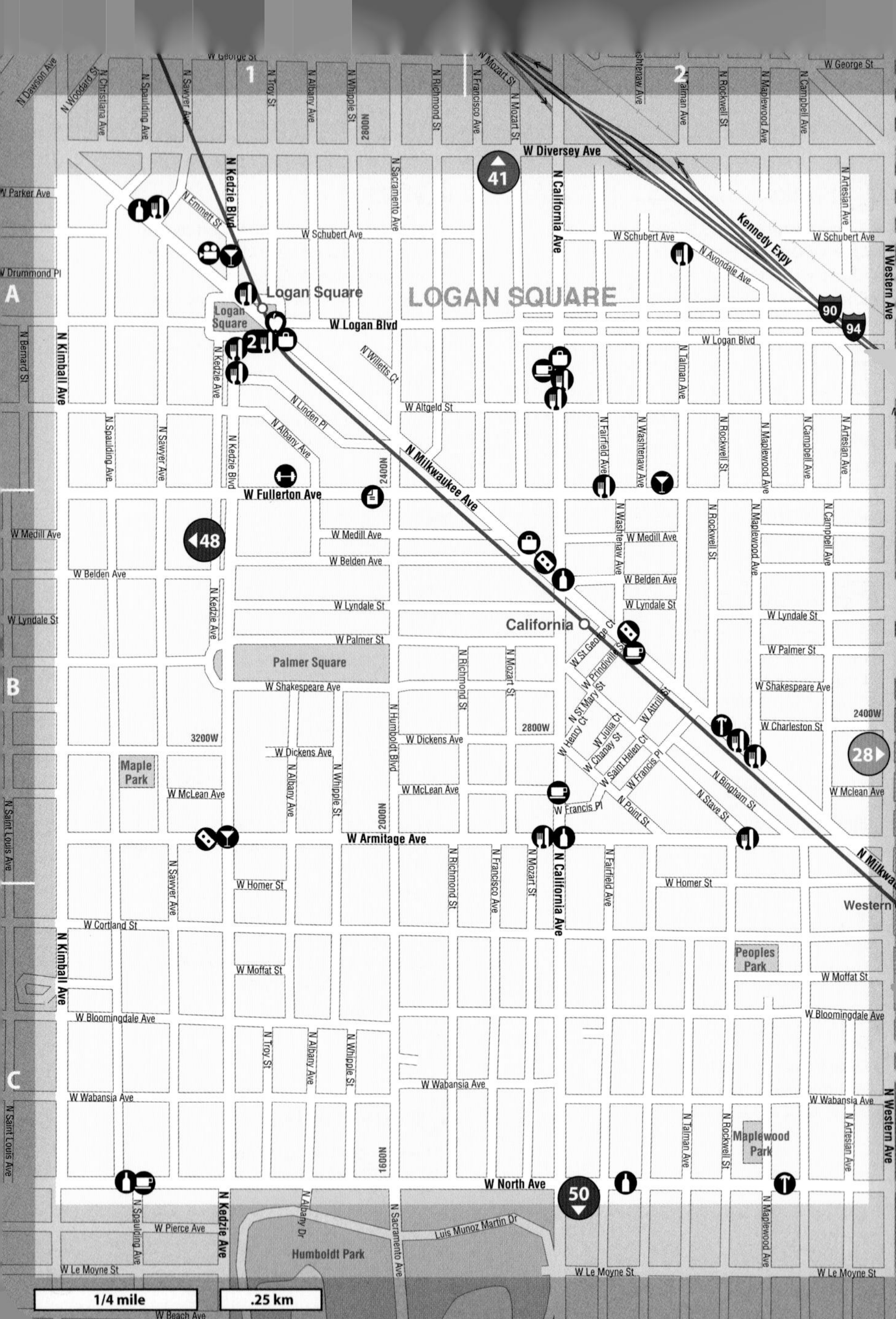

LOGAN SQUARE
Logan Square
California
Western
Palmer Square
Maple Park
Peoples Park
Maplewood Park
Humboldt Park
W Diversey Ave
W Schubert Ave
W Logan Blvd
W Altgeld St
W Fullerton Ave
W Medill Ave
W Belden Ave
W Lyndale St
W Palmer St
W Shakespeare Ave
W Charleston St
W Dickens Ave
W McLean Ave
W Armitage Ave
W Homer St
W Cortland St
W Moffat St
W Bloomingdale Ave
W Wabansia Ave
W North Ave
W Pierce Ave
W Le Moyne St
W Beach Ave
W George St
W Parker Ave
W Drummond Pl
N Milkwaukee Ave
N Kedzie Blvd
N Kedzie Ave
N Kimball Ave
N California Ave
N Western Ave
N Humboldt Blvd
N Sacramento Ave
N Richmond St
N Francisco Ave
N Mozart St
N Fairfield Ave
N Washtenaw Ave
N Talman Ave
N Rockwell St
N Maplewood Ave
N Campbell Ave
N Artesian Ave
N Spaulding Ave
N Sawyer Ave
N Albany Ave
N Troy St
N Whipple St
N Christiana Ave
N Woodard St
N Dawson Ave
N Bernard St
N Saint Louis Ave
N Emmett St
N Willetts Ct
N Linden Pl
N Avondale Ave
N St George Ct
W Prindiville St
W St Mary St
W Henry Ct
W Julia Ct
W Chanay St
W Saint Helen Ct
W Francis Pl
W Attrill St
N Bingham St
N Stave St
N Point St
Luis Munoz Martin Dr
N Albany Dr
Kennedy Expy
90
94
2400N
2000N
1600N
2800N
3200W
2800W
2400W
41
48
28
50
2
1
2
A
B
C
1/4 mile
.25 km

Sundries / Entertainment

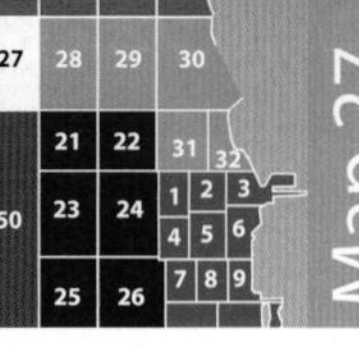

Quit your whining. Just because Starbucks moved in, that doesn't mean the 'hood's lost its indie status. Logan Squarers and beyond swear by Lula Café's eclectic cuisine and its easy-on-the-wallet prices. Fleur still features handmade goods from locals. And Provenance Food and Wine, a new gourmet grocery store, negates any there-goes-the-neighborhood kind of thinking.

Coffee

- **Dunkin' Donuts** • 2247 N Milwaukee Ave
- **Dunkin' Donuts** • 3309 W North Ave
- **No Friction Café** • 2023 N California Ave
- **Starbucks** • 2543 N California Ave

Copy Shops

- **Klein Printing Co** • 3035 W Fullerton Ave

Farmer's Markets

- **Logan Square (Jun–Oct; every other Tues, 1 pm-4 pm)** • W Logan Blvd & N Kedzie Blvd

Gyms

- **Curves (women only)** • 3143 W Fullerton Ave

Hardware Stores

- **Gillman's Hardware** • 2118 N Milwaukee Ave
- **Monroy's Hardware Store** • 2511 W North Ave

Liquor Stores

- **Foremost Liquor Store** • 2300 N Milwaukee Ave
- **Foremost Liquor Store** • 3301 W North Ave
- **International Liquor Store** • 2001 N California Ave
- **Red Star Liquors** • 2719 N Milwaukee Ave
- **Yafai Liquors** • 2700 W North Ave

Movie Theaters

- **Logan Theater** • 2646 N Milwaukee Ave

Nightlife

- **Fireside Bowl** • 2648 W Fullerton Ave
- **Streetside Café** • 3201 W Armitage Ave
- **The Winds Café** • 2657 N Kedzie Blvd

Pet Shops

- **... and Feathers Bird Studio** • 2406 W Fullerton Ave

Restaurants

- **Buona Terra Ristorante** • 2535 N California Ave
- **Café Bolero** • 2252 N Western Ave
- **Calvin's BBQ** • 2540 W Armitage Ave
- **Choi's Chinese Restaurant** • 2638 N Milwaukee Ave
- **Dunlay's on the Square** • 3137 W Logan Blvd
- **El Cid** • 2115 N Milwaukee Ave
- **El Nandu** • 2731 N Fullerton Ave
- **El Pollo Loco** • 2715 N Milwaukee Ave
- **Hachi's Kitchen** • 2521 N California Ave
- **Hot Spot** • 2824 W Armitage Ave
- **Johnny's Grill** • 2545 N Kedzie Blvd
- **Lula Café** • 2537 N Kedzie Blvd
- **Mama's Apple** • 2139 N Milwaukee Ave

Shopping

- **Fleur** • 3149 W Logan Blvd
- **Provenance Food and Wine** • 2528 N California Ave
- **Threads, Etc** • 2327 N Milwaukee Ave

Video Rental

- **Blockbuster** • 2251 N Milwaukee Ave
- **Hi-Fi Video** • 3129 W Armitage Ave
- **Morelia Video** • 2381 N Milwaukee Ave

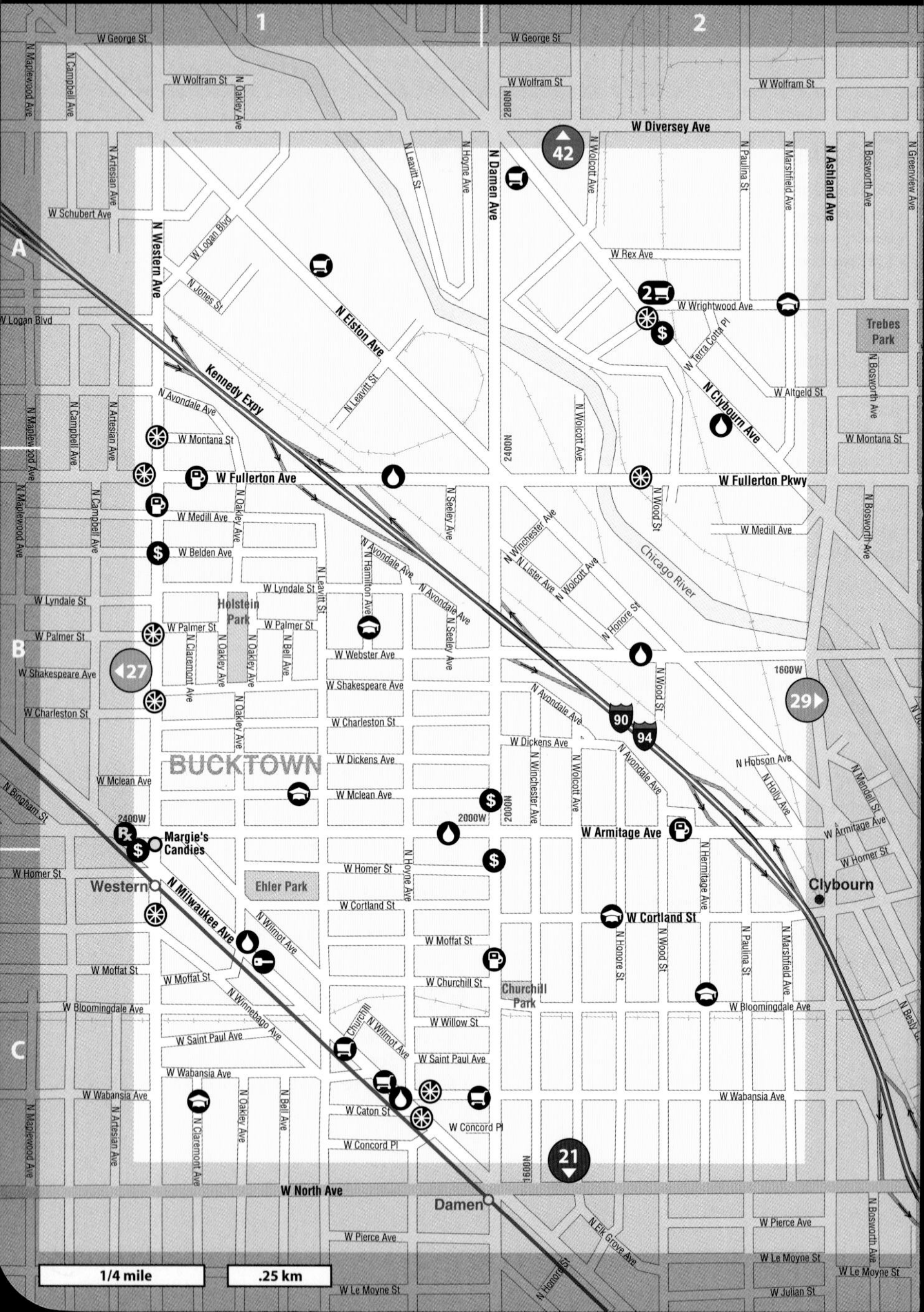

1
2
A
B
C
W George St
W Wolfram St
N Oakley Ave
N Maplewood Ave
N Campbell Ave
2800N
W Diversey Ave
42
N Leavitt St
N Hoyne Ave
N Damen Ave
N Wolcott Ave
N Paulina St
N Marshfield Ave
N Ashland Ave
N Bosworth Ave
N Greenview Ave
N Artesian Ave
W Schubert Ave
N Western Ave
W Logan Blvd
N Jones St
N Elston Ave
W Rex Ave
W Wrightwood Ave
W Terra Cotta Pl
Trebes Park
N Clybourn Ave
W Altgeld St
Kennedy Expy
N Avondale Ave
W Montana St
2400N
W Fullerton Ave
W Fullerton Pkwy
N Wood St
N Winchester Ave
N Seeley Ave
W Medill Ave
N Lister Ave
W Belden Ave
Chicago River
N Hamilton Ave
W Lyndale St
Holstein Park
W Palmer St
N Claremont Ave
N Bell Ave
N Honore St
W Webster Ave
W Shakespeare Ave
27
1600W
29
W Charleston St
90
94
W Dickens Ave
BUCKTOWN
N Hobson Ave
N Holly Ave
W Mclean Ave
N Mendell St
2400W
2000W
2000N
W Armitage Ave
Margie's Candies
N Hermitage Ave
W Homer St
Western
N Milwaukee Ave
Ehler Park
Clybourn
W Cortland St
N Wilmot Ave
W Moffat St
W Churchill St
Churchill Park
W Bloomingdale Ave
N Winnebago Ave
W Willow St
N Besly Ct
Churchill
W Saint Paul Ave
W Wabansia Ave
W Caton St
W Concord Pl
21
1600N
W North Ave
Damen
W Pierce Ave
N Elk Grove Ave
W Le Moyne St
N Honore St
W Julian St
1/4 mile
.25 km

As Bucktown's once-thriving art scene fades further into oblivion, real estate becomes out of reach for all but the young executives who are attracted to the area's upscale boutiques, restaurants, and arty-urban reputation.

Banks

- **Charter One** • 2550 N Clybourn Ave
- **Chase** • 1757 W Fullerton Ave
- **Citibank (ATM)** • 1951 N Western Ave
- **Cole Taylor** • 1965 N Milwaukee Ave
- **MidAmerica** • 1830 W Fullerton Ave
- **MidAmerica** • 1955 N Damen Ave
- **MidAmerica** • 2300 N Western Ave
- **Northern Trust (ATM)** • 2346 N Western Ave
- **TCF** • 2627 Elston Ave
- **TCF (ATM)** • 7-Eleven • 2010 N Damen Ave
- **Washington Mutual** • 2790 N Clybourn Ave

Car Washes

- **Bucktown Hand Car Wash** • 2036 W Armitage Ave
- **Clybourn Express & Car Wash** • 2452 N Clybourn Ave
- **Express Car Wash** • 2111 W Fullerton Ave
- **Fast Eddie's Hand Car Wash** • 1828 W Webster Ave
- **Prestige Hand Wash** • 1843 N Milwaukee Ave
- **Wash Express** • 1657 N Milwaukee Ave

Car Rental

- **Enterprise** • 1842 N Milwaukee Ave • 773-862-4700

Gas Stations

- **BP** • 2357 W Fullerton Ave
- **Citgo** • 1768 W Armitage Ave
- **Citgo** • 2501 N Western Ave
- **Marathon** • 2346 N Western Ave
- **Mobil** • 1750 N Western Ave

Landmarks

- **Margie's Candies** • 1960 N Western Ave

Pharmacies

- **Dominick's** • 2550 N Clybourn Ave
- **Walgreens** • 2001 N Milwaukee Ave

Pizza

- **Barcello's Pizzeria** • 1647 N Milwaukee Ave
- **Chuck E Cheese's** • 1830 W Fullerton Ave
- **Dominick's Finer Foods** • 2550 N Clybourn Ave
- **Homemade Pizza Co** • 1953 W Wabansia Ave
- **John's Restaurant & Lounge** • 2104 N Western Ave
- **LA Bonita** • 2165 N Western Ave
- **Li'l Guys/My Pie** • 2010 N Damen Ave
- **Plazzio's Pizza** • 1901 N Western Ave
- **Sonny's Pizza** • 2431 N Western Ave

Schools

- **Antonia Pantoja High** • 2435 N Western Ave
- **Casimir Pulaski Fine Arts Academy** • 2230 W McLean Ave
- **Chicago International Elementary - Bucktown Campus** • 2235 N Hamilton Ave
- **St Mary of the Angels** • 1810 N Hermitage Ave
- **Thomas Drummond Elementary** • 1845 W Cortland St
- **William H Prescott Elementary** • 1632 W Wrightwood Ave

Supermarkets

- **Aldi** • 1767 N Milwaukee Ave
- **Aldi** • 2600 N Clybourn Ave
- **Always Open** • 1704 N Milwaukee Ave
- **Costco** • 2746 N Clybourn Ave
- **Cub Foods** • 2627 N Elston Ave
- **Dominick's** • 2550 N Clybourn Ave
- **Olivia's Market** • 2014 W Wabansia Ave

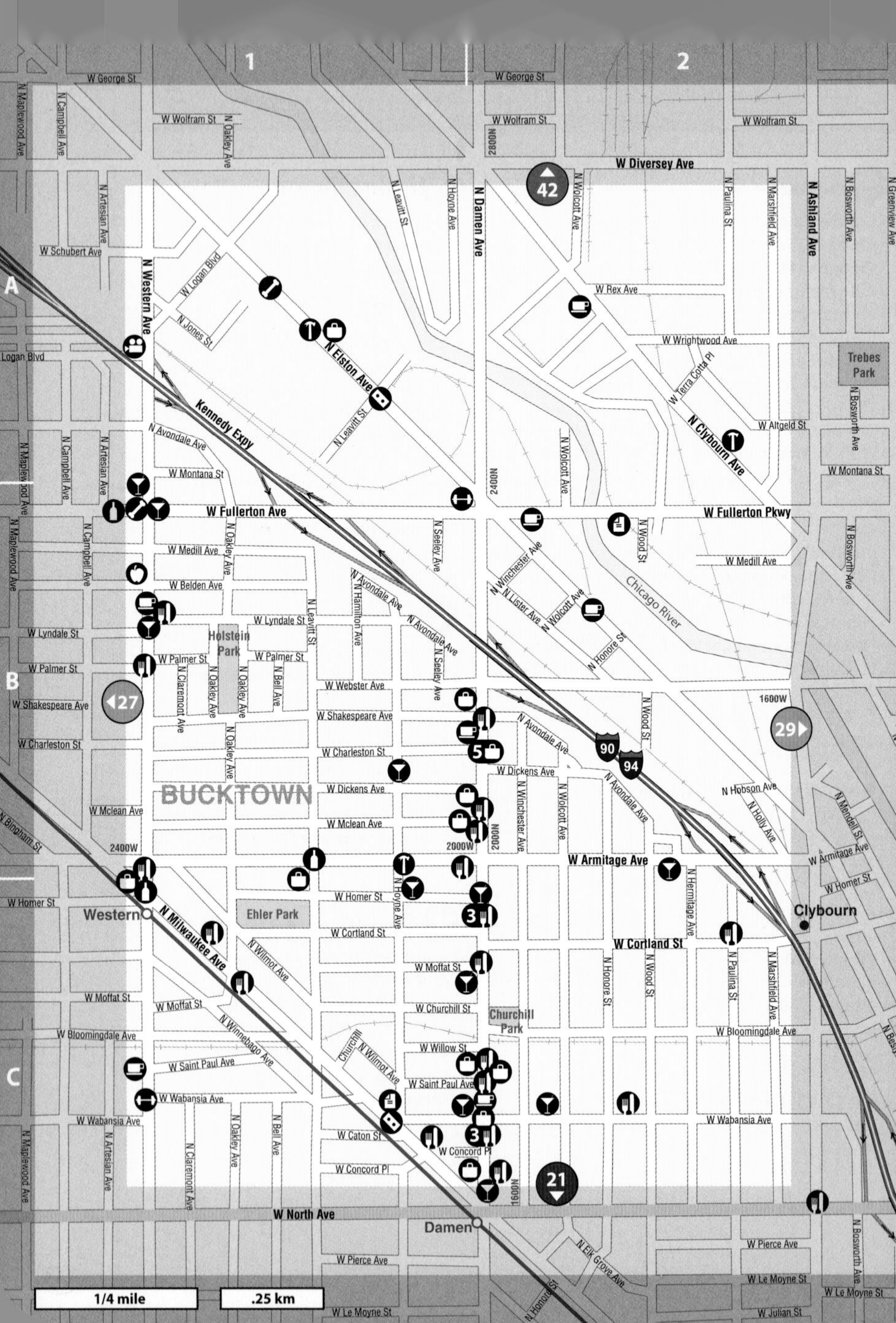

BUCKTOWN
W Diversey Ave
W Fullerton Ave
W Fullerton Pkwy
W Armitage Ave
W Cortland St
W North Ave
N Western Ave
N Damen Ave
N Ashland Ave
N Milwaukee Ave
N Elston Ave
N Clybourn Ave
Kennedy Expy
Chicago River
Holstein Park
Ehler Park
Churchill Park
Trebes Park
Western
Damen
Clybourn
1/4 mile
.25 km

Between the sweet shoppe of legends, Margie's Candies, and the sleek, sophisticated American eatery, Jane's, Bucktown maintains a palatable mix of young and old businesses. Ward off winter woes with Silver Cloud's mac and cheese; on a summer's day, not even nearby Cold Stone Creamery's ice cream beats a frosty cup of Miko's homemade Italian ice.

Coffee

- **Art Gallery Kafe** • 1907 N Milwaukee Ave
- **Caffe De Luca** • 1721 N Damen Ave
- **Coffee Beanery** • 2158 N Damen Ave
- **Dunkin' Donuts** • 1746 N Western Ave
- **Dunkin' Donuts** • 1909 N Western Ave
- **Dunkin' Donuts** • 1927 W Fullerton Ave
- **Red Hen Bread** • 1623 N Milwaukee Ave
- **Sara Lee Coffee** • 2278 N Elston Ave
- **Starbucks** • Dominick's• 2550 N Clybourn Ave
- **Starbucks** • Target• 2656 N Elston Ave

Copy Shops

- **Office Max** • 1829 W Fullerton Ave
- **The UPS Store** • 1658 Milwaukee Ave

Farmer's Markets

- **Bucktown (Jun–Oct; every other Sun, 7 am–2 pm)** • W Belden Ave & N Western Ave

Gyms

- **Ladies Workout Express (women only)** • 1722 N Western Ave

Hardware Stores

- **Ametric Supply** • 2461 N Clybourn Ave
- **Home Depot** • 2570 N Elston Ave

Liquor Stores

- **Bon Song Liquors** • 2000 N Leavitt St
- **Bucktown Food & Liquor** • 2422 W Fullerton Ave
- **Danny's Buy Low** • 2222 N Western Ave
- **MW Food & Liquor** • 1950 N Milwaukee Ave

Movie Theaters

- **AMC** • 2600 N Western Ave

Nightlife

- **Bar Louie** • 1704 N Damen Ave
- **Cans** • 1640 N Damen Ave
- **Charleston Tavern** • 2076 N Hoyne Ave
- **Danny's** • 2222 N Western Ave
- **Darwin's** • 1935 N Damen Ave
- **Gallery Cabaret** • 2020 N Oakley Ave
- **Lemmings** • 1850 N Damen Ave
- **The Liar's Club** • 1665 W Fullerton Ave
- **Lincoln Tavern** • 1858 W Wabansia Ave
- **The Map Room** • 1949 N Hoyne Ave
- **Marie's Rip Tide Lounge** • 1745 W Armitage Ave
- **The Mutiny** • 2428 N Western Ave
- **Northside Café** • 1635 N Damen Ave
- **Quenchers Saloon** • 2401 N Western Ave

Pet Shops

- **Petsmart** • 2665 N Elston Ave

Restaurants

- **Café De Luca** • 1721 N Damen Ave
- **Café Laguardia** • 2111 W Armitage Ave
- **Café Matou** • 1846 N Milwaukee Ave
- **Club Lucky** • 1824 W Wabansia Ave
- **Coast Sushi Bar** • 2045 N Damen Ave
- **Darwin's** • 1935 N Damen Ave
- **Hollywood Grill** • 1601 W North Ave ㉓
- **Honey 1 BBQ** • 2241 N Western Ave
- **Hot Chocolate** • 1747 N Damen Ave
- **Il Covo** • 2152 N Damen Ave
- **Irazu** • 1865 N Milwaukee Ave
- **Ixcapuzalco** • 2165 N Western Ave
- **Jane's** • 1655 W Cortland St
- **Le Bouchon** • 1958 N Damen Ave
- **Margie's Candies** • 1960 N Western Ave
- **Meritage Café & Wine Bar** • 2118 N Damen Ave
- **Miko's Italian Ice** • 1846 N Damen Ave
- **My Pie Pizza** • 2010 N Damen Ave
- **Northside Bar & Grill** • 1635 N Damen Ave
- **Rinconcito Sudamericano** • 1954 W Armitage Ave
- **Roong Thai Restaurant** • 1633 N Milwaukee Ave
- **Scylla** • 1952 N Damen Ave
- **Silver Cloud Club & Grill** • 1700 N Damen Ave
- **Think Café** • 2235 N Western Ave
- **Toast** • 2046 N Damen Ave

Shopping

- **Bleeker Street Antiques** • 1946 N Leavitt St
- **G Boutique** • 2131 N Damen Ave
- **Goddess and the Grocer** • 1646 N Damen Ave
- **Jean Alan** • 2134 N Damen Ave
- **Jolie Joli** • 1623 N Damen Ave
- **Mark Shale Outlet** • 2593 N Elston Ave
- **p.45** • 1643 N Damen Ave
- **Pagoda Red** • 1714 N Damen Ave
- **Pavilion Antiques** • 2055 N Damen Ave
- **Red Balloon Company** • 2060 N Damen Ave
- **Robin Richman** • 2108 N Damen Ave
- **T-Shirt Deli** • 1739 N Damen Ave
- **Tangerine** • 1719 N Damen Ave
- **Village Discount Outlet** • 2032 N Milwaukee Ave
- **Vienna Beef Factory Store** • 2501 N Damen Ave
- **Vive La Femme** • 2115 N Damen Ave

Video Rental

- **Blockbuster** • 1704 N Milwaukee Ave

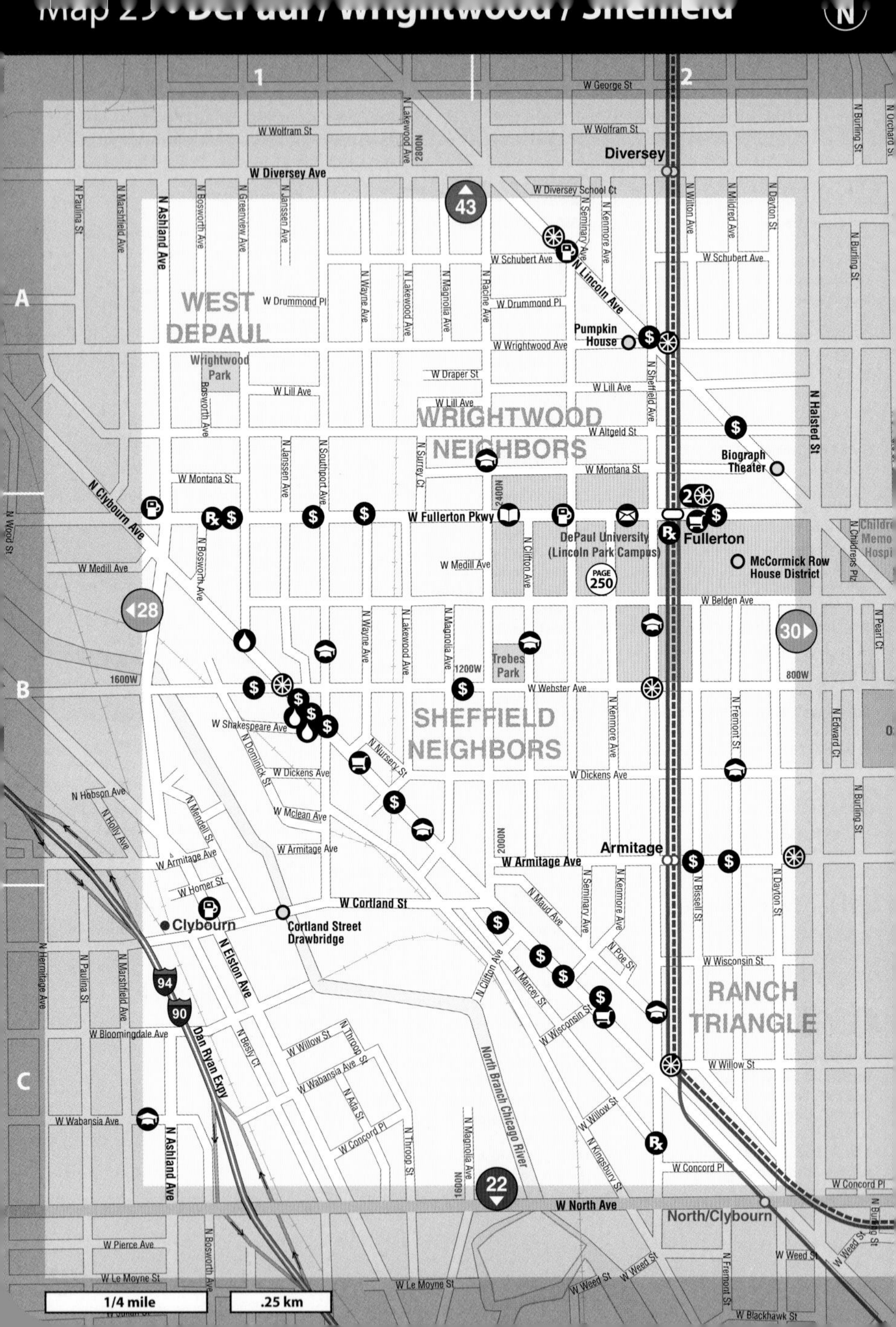
N
1
2
A
B
C
W George St
W Wolfram St
W Wolfram St
N Lakewood Ave
2800N
Diversey
W Diversey Ave
43
W Diversey School Ct
N Paulina St
N Marshfield Ave
N Ashland Ave
N Bosworth Ave
N Greenview Ave
N Janssen Ave
N Seminary Ave
N Kenmore Ave
N Wilton Ave
N Mildred Ave
N Dayton St
N Burling St
N Orchard St
W Schubert Ave
W Schubert Ave
N Lincoln Ave
WEST DEPAUL
W Drummond Pl
N Wayne Ave
N Magnolia Ave
N Racine Ave
W Drummond Pl
Pumpkin House
W Wrightwood Ave
Wrightwood Park
W Draper St
N Sheffield Ave
W Lill Ave
W Lill Ave
W Lill Ave
N Halsted St
WRIGHTWOOD NEIGHBORS
W Altgeld St
N Southport Ave
N Surrey Ct
Biograph Theater
W Montana St
W Montana St
2400N
N Clybourn Ave
W Fullerton Pkwy
DePaul University (Lincoln Park Campus)
Fullerton
N Wood St
W Medill Ave
W Medill Ave
N Clifton Ave
McCormick Row House District
PAGE 250
N Childrens Plz
28
W Belden Ave
N Pearl Ct
30
Trebes Park
1600W
1200W
800W
W Webster Ave
SHEFFIELD NEIGHBORS
W Shakespeare Ave
N Dominick St
N Nursery St
N Fremont St
N Edward Ct
W Dickens Ave
W Dickens Ave
N Hobson Ave
N Holly Ave
N Mendell St
W Mclean Ave
W Armitage Ave
2000N
Armitage
W Armitage Ave
W Armitage Ave
W Homer St
N Maud Ave
N Bissell St
W Cortland St
Clybourn
Cortland Street Drawbridge
N Elston Ave
N Poe St
W Wisconsin St
N Hermitage Ave
94
90
N Clifton Ave
N Marcey St
RANCH TRIANGLE
W Wisconsin St
W Bloomingdale Ave
Dan Ryan Expy
N Besly Ct
W Willow St
N Throop St
North Branch Chicago River
W Willow St
W Wabansia Ave
N Ada St
W Wabansia Ave
W Willow St
W Concord Pl
N Kingsbury St
1600N
W Concord Pl
W Concord Pl
22
W North Ave
North/Clybourn
W Pierce Ave
W Weed St
W Le Moyne St
W Le Moyne St
W Weed St
W Weed St
W Weed St
N Fremont St
W Blackhawk St
1/4 mile
.25 km

There's the good—neighborhood parks and quiet, tree-lined streets with elegant homes—the bad—an overabundance of frat boys and traffic jams—and the ugly—watch out for the occasional weekend puke puddle (DePaul University is right in the middle, you know). But it's this variety, we think, that gives this neighborhood its charm.

Banks

- **Associated (ATM)** • 1224 W Webster Ave
- **Bank of America** • 2163 N Clybourn Ave
- **Bank of America (ATM)** • 1471 W Webster Ave
- **Bank of America (ATM)** • 1845 N Clybourn Ave
- **Chase** • 2170 N Clybourn Ave
- **Chase** • 935 W Armitage Ave
- **Chase (ATM)** • 1340 W Fullerton Ave
- **Chase (ATM)** • 1520 W Fullerton Ave
- **Fifth Third** • 900 W Armitage Ave
- **New Century (ATM)** • 2475 N Lincoln Ave
- **TCF** • 1400 W Fullerton Ave
- **TCF (ATM)** • 7-Eleven • 2181 N Clybourn Ave
- **TCF (ATM)** • 7-Eleven • 2600 N Lincoln Ave
- **TCF (ATM)** • 7-Eleven • 957 W Armitage Ave
- **US** • 1953 N Clybourn Ave
- **Washington Mutual** • 2053 N Clybourn Ave
- **Washington Mutual** • 2662 N Lincoln Ave

Car Washes

- **Simon's** • 1439 W Shakespeare Ave
- **We'll Clean** • 2261 N Clybourn Ave
- **White Glove Car Wash** • 1415 W Shakespeare Ave

Gas Stations

- **BP** • 1607 W Fullerton Ave
- **Mobil** • 1106 W Fullerton Ave
- **Mobil** • 1901 N Elston Ave
- **Mobil** • 2670 N Lincoln Ave

Landmarks

- **Biograph Theater** • 2433 N Lincoln Ave
- **Cortland Street Drawbridge** • 1440 W Cortland St
- **McCormick Row House District** • W Chalmers Pl, W Belden Ave, & W Fullerton Pkwy
- **Pumpkin House** • 1052 W Wrightwood Ave

Libraries

- **Lincoln Park Public Library** • 1150 W Fullerton Ave

Pharmacies

- **CVS Pharmacy** • 1714 N Sheffield Ave
- **Dominick's** • 959 W Fullerton Ave
- **Walgreens** • 1520 W Fullerton Ave

Pizza

- **Amato's Pizza** • 953 W Willow St
- **Dominick's Finer Foods** • 959 W Fullerton Ave
- **Homemade Pizza** • 850 W Armitage Ave
- **Lou Malnati's Pizzeria** • 958 W Wrightwood Ave
- **Pat's Pizzeria** • 2679 N Lincoln Ave
- **Pequod's Pizzeria** • 2207 N Clybourn Ave
- **Tomato Head Pizza Kitchen** • 1001 W Webster Ave
- **Via-Carducci's Italian Eatery** • 1419 W Fullerton Ave

Post Offices

- **US Post Office** • 2405 N Sheffield Ave

Schools

- **Arts of Living** • 1855 N Sheffield Ave
- **DePaul University (Lincoln Park Campus)** • 2250 N Sheffield Ave
- **Jefferson Center/Factory Branch** • 2032 N Clybourn Ave
- **Jonathan Burr Elementary** • 1621 W Wabansia Ave
- **Oscar F Mayer Elementary** • 2250 N Clifton Ave
- **St James Lutheran** • 2101 N Fremont St
- **St Josephat** • 2245 N Southport Ave

Supermarkets

- **Dominick's** • 959 W Fullerton Ave
- **Trader Joe's** • 1840 N Clybourn Ave
- **Treasure Island** • 2121 N Clybourn Ave

WEST DEPAUL
WRIGHTWOOD NEIGHBORS
SHEFFIELD NEIGHBORS
RANCH TRIANGLE
Wrightwood Park
Trebes Park
DePaul University (Lincoln Park Campus)
PAGE 250
Diversey
Fullerton
Armitage
Clybourn
North/Clybourn
W Diversey Ave
W Fullerton Pkwy
W Armitage Ave
W Cortland St
W North Ave
N Ashland Ave
N Clybourn Ave
N Lincoln Ave
N Halsted St
N Elston Ave
Dan Ryan Expy
North Branch Chicago River
W George St
W Wolfram St
W Diversey School Ct
W Schubert Ave
W Drummond Pl
W Wrightwood Ave
W Draper St
W Lill Ave
W Altgeld St
W Montana St
W Medill Ave
W Belden Ave
W Webster Ave
W Shakespeare Ave
W Dickens Ave
W Mclean Ave
W Homer St
W Wisconsin St
W Willow St
W Wabansia Ave
W Concord Pl
W Bloomingdale Ave
W Pierce Ave
W Le Moyne St
W Weed St
W Blackhawk St
N Hobson Ave
N Holly Ave
N Paulina St
N Marshfield Ave
N Bosworth Ave
N Greenview Ave
N Janssen Ave
N Lakewood Ave
N Wayne Ave
N Magnolia Ave
N Racine Ave
N Seminary Ave
N Kenmore Ave
N Sheffield Ave
N Wilton Ave
N Mildred Ave
N Dayton St
N Burling St
N Orchard St
N Southport Ave
N Surrey Ct
N Clifton Ave
N Dominick St
N Mendell St
N Nursery St
N Maud Ave
N Poe St
N Marcey St
N Kingsbury St
N Bissell St
N Fremont St
N Edward Ct
N Childrens Plz
N Pearl Ct
N Hermitage Ave
N Besly Ct
N Throop St
N Ada St
N Wood St
2800N
2400N
2000N
1600N
1600W
1200W
800W
43
28
30
22
94
90
1/4 mile
.25 km

For years, Uncle Dan's has been outfitting hardcore campers and survivalists with clothes and gear, while Sam's Wine and Spirits does the trick for hardcore imbibers, with their great selection of intoxicating brews. Facets Multimedia runs a regular schedule of obscure arthouse cinema, and you can rent the videos here too. For music, The Hideout is a second home for Bloodshot Records fans, while aging punk rockers pay their rent in whiskey at Delilah's.

Coffee

- **Ambrosia Café** • 1963 N Sheffield Ave
- **Argo Tea** • 958 W Armitage Ave
- **Bean Café** • DePaul University • 2235 N Sheffield Ave
- **Dunkin' Donuts** • 1982 N Clybourn Ave
- **Einstein Bros Bagels** • 2212 N Clybourn Ave
- **Savor the Flavor** • 2545 N Sheffield Ave
- **Starbucks** • 1001 W Armitage Ave
- **Starbucks** • 1157 W Wrightwood Ave
- **Starbucks** • 2200 N Clybourn Ave
- **Starbucks** • 2454 N Ashland Ave
- **Starbucks** • 2475 N Lincoln Ave
- **Starbucks** • Dominick's • 959 W Fullerton Ave

Copy Shops

- **Fedex Kinko's** • 2300 N Clybourn Ave
- **Sir Speedy** • 1711 N Clybourn Ave
- **The UPS Store** • 1341 W Fullerton Ave
- **The UPS Store** • 858 W Armitage Ave

Gyms

- **Bally Total Fitness** • 1455 W Webster Ave
- **Crunch Fitness** • 2727 N Lincoln Ave
- **Lakeshore Athletic Club** • 1320 W Fullerton Ave
- **Webster Fitness Club** • 957 W Webster Ave

Hardware Stores

- **Armitage Hardware & Building Supply** • 925 W Armitage Ave
- **Hollywood Industrial Supply** • 1524 W Fullerton Ave

Liquor Stores

- **J&R Liquor & Foods** • 2401 N Ashland Ave
- **Kegs to Go** • 2581 N Lincoln Ave
- **Sam's Wine and Liquor Warehouse** • 1720 N Marcey St
- **Wine Discount Center** • 1826 N Elston Ave

Movie Theaters

- **Facets Multimedia Theatre** • 1517 W Fullerton Ave
- **Loews** • 1471 W Webster Ave

Nightlife

- **Big House** • 2354 N Clybourn Ave
- **Charlie's Ale House** • 1224 W Webster Ave
- **Delilah's** • 2771 N Lincoln Ave
- **Gin Mill** • 2462 N Lincoln Ave
- **Green Dolphin Street** • 2200 N Ashland Ave
- **Hideout** • 1354 W Wabansia Ave
- **Hog Head McDunna's** • 1505 W Fullerton Ave
- **Irish Eyes** • 2519 N Lincoln Ave
- **Kincade's** • 950 W Armitage Ave
- **Local Option** • 1102 W Webster Ave
- **Nic and Dino's Tripoli Tavern** • 1147 W Armitage Ave
- **The (Prop) House** • 1675 N Elston Ave
- **Red Lion Pub** • 2446 N Lincoln Ave
- **Webster Wine Bar** • 1480 Webster Ave
- **Wrightwood Tap** • 1059 W Wrightwood Ave
- **Zella** • 1983 N Clybourn Ave

Pet Shops

- **Barker & Meowsky** • 1003 W Armitage Ave
- **Galloping Gourmutts** • 2736 N Lincoln Ave
- **Petco** • 2000 N Clybourn Ave

Restaurants

- **Ambrosia Café** • 1963 N Sheffield Ave
- **Buffalo Wild Wings** • 2464 N Lincoln Ave
- **Clarke's Pancake House & Restaurant** • 2441 N Lincoln Ave
- **Goose Island Brewing Company** • 1800 N Clybourn Ave
- **Green Dolphin Street** • 2200 N Ashland Ave
- **John's Place** • 1200 W Webster Ave
- **Minnies** • 1969 N Halsted St
- **Red Lion Pub** • 2446 N Lincoln Ave
- **Sai Café** • 2010 N Sheffield Ave
- **Salt & Pepper Diner** • 2575 N Lincoln Ave
- **Shine & Morida** • 901 W Armitage Ave
- **State** • 935 W Webster Ave
- **Sweet Mandy B's** • 1207 W Webster Ave
- **Taco & Burrito House** • 1548 W Fullerton Ave
- **Tsuki** • 1441 W Fullerton Ave
- **Twisted Lizard** • 1964 N Sheffield Ave
- **Vosges** • 951 W Armitage Ave

Shopping

- **Active Endeavors** • 853 W Armitage Ave
- **Dirk's Fish** • 2070 N Clybourn Ave
- **Eskell** • 953 W Webster Ave
- **Isabella Fine Lingerie** • 1101 W Webster Ave
- **Jayson Home & Garden** • 1885 N Clybourn Ave
- **Left Bank** • 1155 W Webster Ave
- **Lush Cosmetics** • 859 W Armitage Ave
- **Sam's Wine and Liquor Warehouse** • 1720 N Marcey St
- **Tabula Tua** • 1015 W Armitage Ave
- **Uncle Dan's** • 2440 N Lincoln Ave
- **Vosges Haut Chocolat** • 951 W Armitage Ave
- **Wine Discount Center** • 1826 N Elston Ave

Video Rental

- **Blockbuster** • 2037 N Clybourn Ave
- **Blockbuster** • 2400 N Sheffield Ave
- **Facets Multimedia** • 1517 W Fullerton Ave

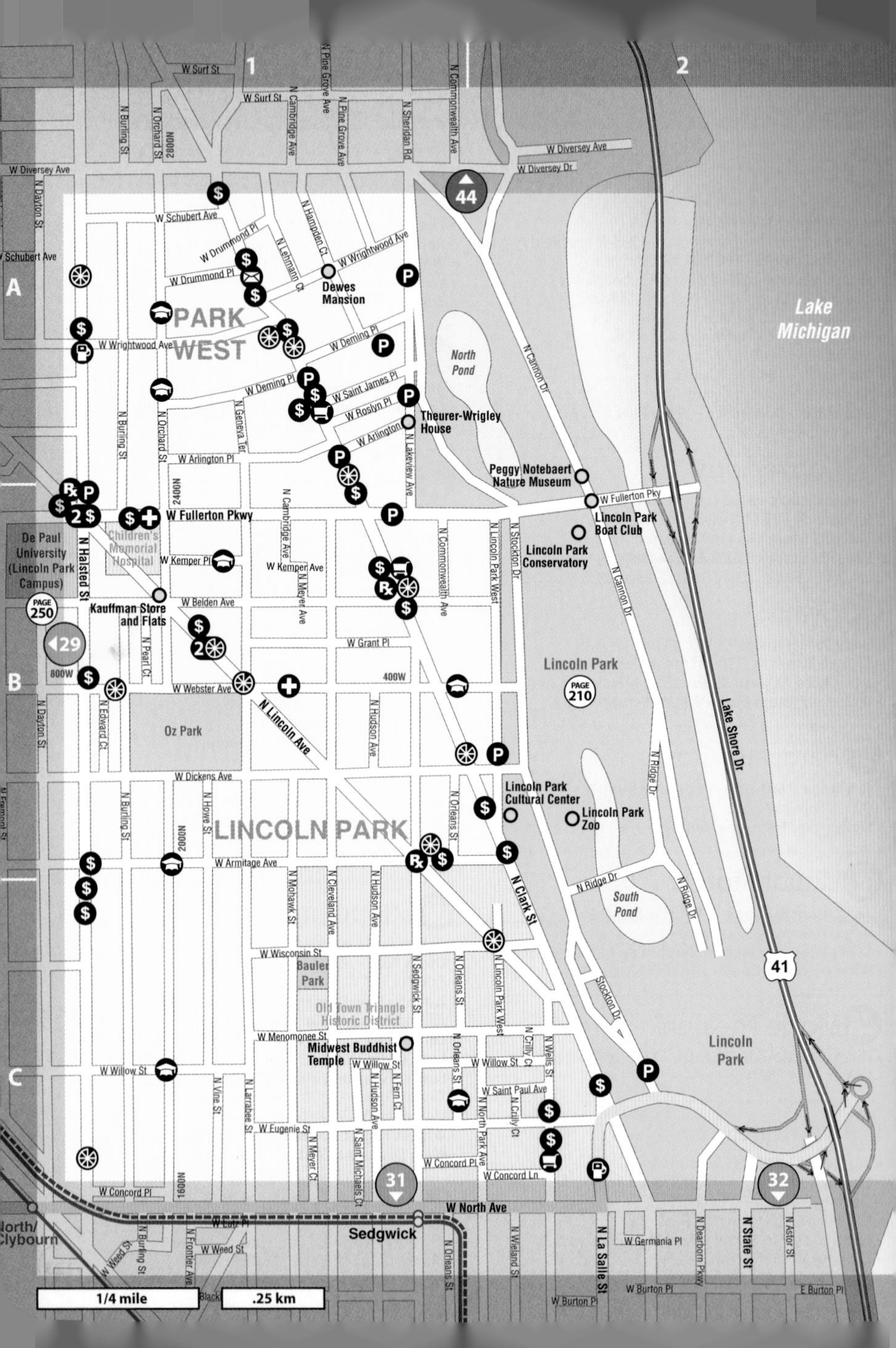

1
2
A
B
C
PARK WEST
LINCOLN PARK
Lake Michigan
North Pond
South Pond
Lincoln Park
Lincoln Park
Oz Park
Bauler Park
Old Town Triangle Historic District
Dewes Mansion
Theurer-Wrigley House
Peggy Notebaert Nature Museum
Lincoln Park Boat Club
Lincoln Park Conservatory
Children's Memorial Hospital
De Paul University (Lincoln Park Campus)
Kauffman Store and Flats
Lincoln Park Cultural Center
Lincoln Park Zoo
Midwest Buddhist Temple
Sedgwick
North/ Clybourn
PAGE 250
PAGE 210
44
29
31
32
41
W Fullerton Pkwy
W Fullerton Pky
W Diversey Ave
W Diversey Dr
W Surf St
W Schubert Ave
W Drummond Pl
W Wrightwood Ave
W Deming Pl
W Saint James Pl
W Roslyn Pl
W Arlington Pl
W Kemper Pl
W Belden Ave
W Grant Pl
W Webster Ave
W Dickens Ave
W Armitage Ave
W Wisconsin St
W Menomonee St
W Willow St
W Saint Paul Ave
W Eugenie St
W Concord Pl
W Concord Ln
W North Ave
W Lutz Pl
W Weed St
W Germania Pl
W Burton Pl
E Burton Pl
N Halsted St
N Clark St
N Lincoln Ave
N Cannon Dr
N Stockton Dr
Lake Shore Dr
N Ridge Dr
N Lakeview Ave
N Lincoln Park West
N Commonwealth Ave
N Sheridan Rd
N Pine Grove Ave
N Cambridge Ave
N Hampden Ct
N Lehmann Ct
N Geneva Ter
N Orchard St
N Burling St
N Dayton St
N Edward Ct
N Pearl Ct
N Howe St
N Mohawk St
N Cleveland Ave
N Hudson Ave
N Orleans St
N Sedgwick St
N Larrabee St
N Vine St
N Fern Ct
N North Park Ave
N Crilly Ct
N Wells St
N Meyer Ave
N Meyer Ct
N Saint Michaels Ct
N La Salle St
N Dearborn Pkwy
N State St
N Astor St
N Wieland St
N Frontier Ave
2800N
2400N
2000N
1600N
800W
400W
1/4 mile
.25 km

You'd be hard-pressed finding anyone that considers Lincoln Park anything other than extemely cushy, with its beautiful Greystone mansions and tree-lined streets. Lincoln Park is either heaven or hell, depending on your tolerance for Trixies and Chads (as Chicagoans refer to the 'hood's vapid, label-conscious denizens), and horrendous traffic congestion. Finding a parking spot is fleeting fantasy, leave your Beemer behind and hop on that Schwinn (or the bus) if you're planning to get anywhere.

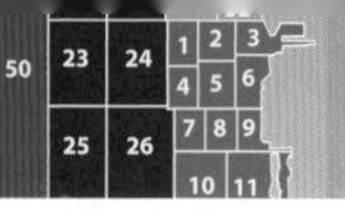

Map

Banks

- **Bank of America** • 2401 N Clark St
- **Bank of America (ATM)** • 2240 N Lincoln Ave
- **Bridgeview** • 1970 N Halsted St
- **Charter One** • 1640 N Wells St
- **Chase** • 1700 N Wells St
- **Chase** • 2501 N Clark St
- **Chase** • 2603 N Halsted St
- **Chase (ATM)** • 2300 N Childrens Plz
- **Citibank** • 2001 N Halsted St
- **Citibank** • 2555 N Clark St
- **Citibank (ATM)** • 2400 N Lincoln Ave
- **Citibank (ATM)** • 2635 N Clark St
- **Corus** • 2401 N Halsted St
- **Fifth Third (ATM)** • 2060 N Clark St
- **First American** • 356 W Armitage Ave
- **MidAmerica** • 2021 N Clark St
- **North Community** • 2000 N Halsted St
- **North Community** • 2201 N Halsted St
- **North Community** • 2335 N Clark St
- **North Community** • 2500 N Clark St
- **TCF (ATM)** • 1730 N Clark St
- **TCF (ATM)** • 7-Eleven • 2264 N Clark St
- **TCF (ATM)** • Osco • 2414 Lincoln Ave
- **TCF (ATM)** • 7-Eleven • 2619 N Clark St
- **Washington Mutual** • 2744 N Clark St

Gas Stations

- **BP** • 1647 N La Salle Dr
- **Shell** • 2600 N Halsted St

Emergency Rooms

- **Children's Memorial** • 2300 Children's Plz
- **Lincoln Park** • 550 W Webster Ave

Landmarks

- **Dewes Mansion** • 503 N Wrightwood Ave
- **Kauffman Store and Flats** • 2312 N Lincoln Ave
- **Lincoln Park Boat Club** • N Cannon Dr & Fullerton Pkwy
- **Lincoln Park Conservatory** • 2391 N Stockton Dr
- **Lincoln Park Cultural Center** • 2045 N Lincoln Park W
- **Lincoln Park Zoo** • N Cannon Dr, south of W Fullerton Pkwy
- **Midwest Buddhist Temple** • 435 W Menomonee St
- **Peggy Notebaert Nature Museum** • 2430 N Cannon Dr
- **Theurer-Wrigley House** • 2466 N Lakeview Ave

Pharmacies

- **CVS Pharmacy** • 401 W Armitage Ave
- **Osco Drug** • 2414 N Lincoln Ave
- **Walgreens** • 2317 N Clark St

Pizza

- **Bacino's** • 2204 N Lincoln Ave
- **Bricks** • 1909 N Lincoln Ave
- **Café Luigi** • 2548 N Clark St
- **Chicago's Pizza & Oven Grinder Co** • 2121 N Clark St
- **Domino's** • 2231 N Lincoln Ave
- **Edwardo's Natural Pizza** • 2622 N Halsted St
- **Gioio's Beef Stand Pizzeria** • 2572 N Clark St
- **Lincoln Park Pizza** • 2245 N Lincoln Ave
- **My Pie Pizzeria** • 2417 N Clark St
- **O' Fame** • 750 W Webster Ave
- **Pizza Capri** • 1733 N Halsted St
- **Ranalli's** • 2301 N Clark St
- **Red Moon Café** • 350 W Armitage Ave

Post Offices

- **US Post Office** • 2643 N Clark St

Schools

- **Abraham Lincoln Elementary** • 615 W Kemper Pl
- **Francis W Parker High** • 330 W Webster Ave
- **La Salle Language Academy** • 1734 N Orleans St
- **Lincoln Park High** • 2001 N Orchard St
- **Louisa May Alcott Elementary** • 2625 N Orchard St
- **St Clement** • 2524 N Orchard St
- **Walter L Newberry Math & Science Academy** • 700 W Willow St

Supermarkets

- **Big Apple Finer Foods** • 2345 N Clark St
- **Lincoln Park Market** • 2500 N Clark St
- **Treasure Island** • 1639 N Wells St

Parking

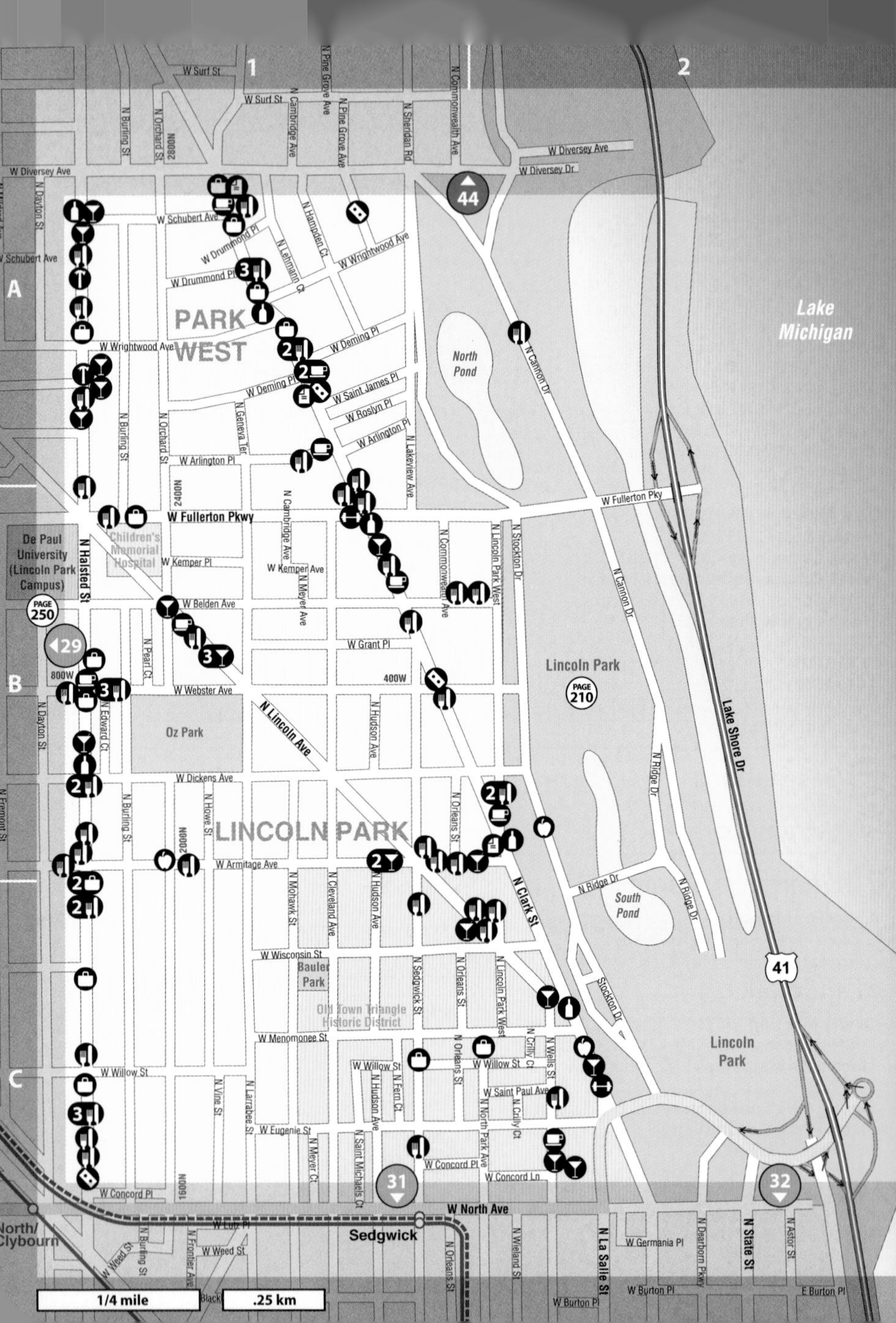

1
2
A
B
C
PARK WEST
LINCOLN PARK
Lake Michigan
North Pond
South Pond
Lincoln Park
PAGE 210
Lincoln Park
De Paul University (Lincoln Park Campus)
PAGE 250
Children's Memorial Hospital
Oz Park
Bauler Park
Old Town Triangle Historic District
44
29
31
32
41
W Surf St
W Diversey Ave
W Diversey Dr
W Schubert Ave
W Drummond Pl
W Wrightwood Ave
W Deming Pl
W Saint James Pl
W Roslyn Pl
W Arlington Pl
W Fullerton Pkwy
W Fullerton Pky
W Kemper Pl
W Belden Ave
W Grant Pl
W Webster Ave
W Dickens Ave
W Armitage Ave
W Wisconsin St
W Menomonee St
W Willow St
W Saint Paul Ave
W Eugenie St
W Concord Pl
W Concord Ln
W North Ave
W Lutz Pl
W Weed St
W Germania Pl
W Burton Pl
E Burton Pl
N Ridge Dr
N Dayton St
N Halsted St
N Burling St
N Orchard St
2800N
2400N
2000N
1600N
800W
400W
N Cambridge Ave
N Pine Grove Ave
N Sheridan Rd
N Commonwealth Ave
N Hampden Ct
N Lehmann Ct
N Geneva Ter
N Lakeview Ave
N Cannon Dr
N Stockton Dr
Stockton Dr
N Lincoln Park West
N Meyer Ave
N Pearl Ct
N Edward Ct
N Lincoln Ave
N Hudson Ave
N Fremont St
N Howe St
N Mohawk St
N Cleveland Ave
N Orleans St
N Clark St
N Sedgwick St
N Crilly Ct
N Wells St
N North Park Ave
N Vine St
N Larrabee St
N Fern Ct
N Meyer Ct
N Saint Michaels Ct
N Frontier Ave
N Wieland St
N La Salle St
N Dearborn Pkwy
N State St
N Astor St
Lake Shore Dr
North/Clybourn
Sedgwick
1/4 mile
.25 km

Sundries / Entertainment

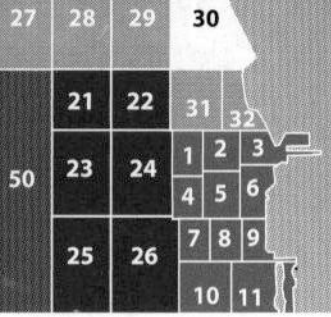

Right on the lake, with the zoo in its backyard, Lincoln Park is perfectly picturesque, especially when the sun is shining and the Green City Farmer's Market is basking in all its organic glory. Beyond the bevy of frat bars and Irish pubs, there's awesome, cheap Indian fare to be had at Hema's Kitchen and a laid-back vibe for bookish folk at the Bourgeois Pig coffee shop.

Coffee

- **Bourgeois Pig Café** • 738 W Fullerton Ave
- **Caribou Coffee** • 2453 N Clark St
- **Einstein Bros Bagels** • 2530 N Clark St
- **Monterotondo** • 612 W Wrightwood Ave
- **Savories** • 1651 N Wells St
- **Screenz Digital Universe** • 2717 N Clark St
- **Siena Coffee** • 2308 N Clark St
- **Starbucks** • 2063 N Clark St
- **Starbucks** • 2200 N Halsted St
- **Starbucks** • 2275 N Lincoln Ave
- **Starbucks** • 2525 1/2 N Clark St

Copy Shops

- **Screenz** • 2717 N Clark St
- **The UPS Store** • 2038 N Clark St
- **The UPS Store** • 2506 N Clark St

Farmer's Markets

- **Chicago's Green City Market (May–Oct; Wed & Sat, 7 am–1:30 pm)** • 1750 N Clark St
- **Lincoln Park (Jun–Oct; Sat, 7 am–2 pm)** • W Armitage Ave & N Orchard St
- **Lincoln Park Zoo (Jun–Sept; 4th Sun of month, 9 am–4 pm)** • 2001 N Stockton Dr

Gyms

- **Equinox** • 1750 N Clark St
- **Lincoln Park Fitness Center** • 444 W Fullerton Pkwy

Hardware Stores

- **Home Depot** • 2665 N Halsted St
- **Wahler Brothers True Value** • 2551 N Halsted St

Liquor Stores

- **Chalet Wine & Cheese Shop** • 2000 N Clark St
- **Country Fresh Finer Foods** • 2583 N Clark St
- **Dynamic Liquors** • 2132 N Halsted St
- **Miska's Liquor** • 2353 N Clark St
- **Old Town Sundries Liquors** • 1820 N Clark St

Movie Theaters

- **Three Penny Cinema** • 2424 N Lincoln Ave

Nightlife

- **B.L.U.E.S.** • 2519 N Halsted St
- **Bacchus** • 2242 N Lincoln Ave
- **Bar Louie** • 1800 N Lincoln Ave
- **Blu** • 2247 N Lincoln Ave
- **Corner Pocket** • 2610 N Halsted St
- **Gamekeepers** • 345 W Armitage Ave
- **Glascott's** • 2158 N Halsted St
- **GoodBar** • 2512 N Halsted St
- **Griffin's Public House** • 2710 N Halsted St
- **Hidden Shamrock** • 2723 N Halsted St
- **Katacomb** • 1909 N Lincoln Ave
- **Kingston Mines** • 2548 N Halsted St
- **Lion Head Pub & The Apartment** • 2251 N Lincoln Ave
- **Neo** • 2350 N Clark St
- **Park West** • 322 W Armitage Ave
- **Sauce** • 1750 N Clark St
- **Second City** • 1616 N Wells St
- **Tequila Roadhouse** • 1653 N Wells St
- **Wise Fools Pub** • 2270 N Lincoln Ave

Restaurants

- **Aladdin Café** • 2269 N Lincoln Ave
- **Alinea** • 1723 N Halsted St
- **Ambria** • 2300 N Lincoln Park W
- **Athenian Room** • 807 W Webster Ave
- **Austrian Bakery & Deli** • 2523 N Clark St
- **Ben & Jerry's** • 338 W Armitage Ave
- **Boka** • 1729 N Halsted St
- **Brick's Chicago** • 1909 N Lincoln Ave
- **Café Ba-Ba-Reeba!** • 2024 N Halsted St
- **Café Bernard** • 2100 N Halsted St
- **Charlie Trotter's** • 816 W Armitage Ave
- **Deli Boutique** • 2318 N Clark St
- **Duke's Bar and Grill** • 2616 N Clark St
- **Dunlay's** • 2600 N Clark St
- **Emilio's Tapas** • 444 Fullerton Pkwy
- **Ethel's Chocolate Lounge** • 819 W Armitage Ave
- **Fattoush** • 2652 N Halsted St
- **Frances' Deli** • 2552 N Clark St
- **Geja's Café** • 340 W Armitage Ave
- **Hema's Kitchen II** • 2411 N Clark St
- **Hey Sushi** • 2630 N Clark St
- **Itto Sushi** • 2616 N Halsted St
- **Karyn's** • 1901 N Halsted Ave
- **King Crab** • 1816 N Halsted St
- **Landmark** • 1633 N Halsted St
- **Mon Ami Gabi** • 2300 N Lincoln Park W
- **My Pie Pizza** • 2417 N Clark St
- **Nookies** • 1746 N Wells St
- **Nookies, Too** • 2114 N Halsted St
- **North Pond** • 2610 N Cannon Dr
- **O' Fame** • 750 W Webster Ave
- **Original Pancake House** • 2020 N Lincoln Park W
- **Piattini** • 934 W Webster Ave
- **PS Bangkok** • 2521 N Halsted St
- **Ranalli's** • 1925 N Lincoln Ave
- **Ranalli's** • 2301 N Clark St
- **Ritter's Breakfast Delivery** • 2665 N Clark St
- **RJ Grunt's** • 2056 N Lincoln Park W
- **Robinson's No 1 Ribs** • 655 W Armitage Ave
- **Salvatore's Ristorante** • 525 W Arlington Pl
- **Sedgwick's Bar & Grill** • 1935 N Sedgwick St
- **Sushi O Sushi** • 346 W Armitage Ave
- **Sushi Para II** • 2256 N Clark St
- **Taco Burrito Palace #2** • 2441 N Halsted St
- **Tilli's** • 1952 N Halsted St
- **Toast** • 746 W Webster Ave
- **Treats Frozen Desserts** • 2200 N Clark St
- **Twin Anchors** • 1655 N Sedgwick St
- **Vinci** • 1732 N Halsted St
- **Wiener's Circle** • 2622 N Clark St

Shopping

- **Art & Science** • 1971 N Halsted St
- **Barneys New York Co-Op** • 2209 N Halsted St
- **Buy Popular Demand** • 2629 N Halsted St
- **Cynthia Rowley** • 808 W Armitage Ave
- **Dave's Records** • 2604 N Clark St
- **Ethan Allen** • 1700 N Halsted St
- **Gallery 1756** • 1756 N Sedgwick St
- **GNC** • 2740 N Clark St
- **Hi Fi Records** • 2568 N Clark St
- **Lori's Designer Shoes** • 824 W Armitage Ave
- **Sally Beauty Supply** • 2727 N Clark St
- **Triangle Gallery of Old Town** • 1763 N North Park Ave
- **White Elephant** • 2300 Children's Plz

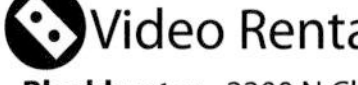

Video Rental

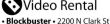

- **Blockbuster** • 2200 N Clark St
- **Blockbuster** • 2577 N Clark St
- **Odd Obsession Movies** • 1659 N Halsted St
- **Tokyo Video of Chicago (Japanese)** • 2755 N Pine Grove Ave

1
2
A
B
C
South Pond
Lincoln Park
PAGE 210
W Wisconsin St
N Bissell St
N Dayton St
N Mohawk St
N Cleveland Ave
N Hudson Ave
N Sedgwick St
N Orleans St
N Lincoln Park W
Stockton Dr
W Menomonee St
N Crilly Ct
W Willow St
N Fern Ct
W Saint Paul Ave
N Halsted St
N Burling St
W Eugenie St
N Vine St
N Meyer Ct
N Saint Michaels Ct
W Concord Pl
W Concord Ln
N State Pkwy
30
W North Ave
E North
N Kingsbury St
North/ Clybourn
W Luz Pl
Sedgwick
N Sandburg Ter
W Germania Pl
W Weed St
N Fremont St
N Frontier Ave
N Ogden Ave
W Blackhawk St
N North Park Ave
N Wieland St
W Burton Pl
N Dearborn Pkwy
OLD TOWN
W Eastman St
W Schiller St
N Clybourn Ave
N La Salle St
N Clark St
N State St
N Sutton Pl
W Fair Pl
W Evergreen Ave
Chicago River
W Goethe St
Stanton Schiller Park
W Sullivan St
22
W Scott St
N Schick Pl
32
Clark/ Division
N Hooker St
N Orchard St
N Howe St
W Division St
800W
200W
100W
N Hickory Ave
N Crosby St
N Cambridge Ave
W Elm St
N Larrabee St
N Felton Ct
Seward Park
W Hill St
W Bliss St
W Haines St
CABRINI GREEN
W Hobbie St
W Maple St
W Wendell St
N Rush St
W Oak St
N Franklin St
N North Branch St
W Walton St
NEAR NORTH
N Wells St
Washington Square Park
W Delaware Pl
W Locust St
W Iowa St
W Chestnut St
Moody Bible Institute
N Sangamon St
N Lessing St
N Peoria St
W Pearson St
W Institute Pl
N Carpenter St
W Chicago Ave
Chicago
Loyola U (Water Tower C)
N Morgan St
W Superior St
W Huron St
N Green St
W Ancona St
W Erie St
W Ontario St
Connector
90
W Ohio St
N Union Ave
N Desplaines St
W Grand Ave
Grand
W Illinois St
1/4 mile
.25 km

One of the oldest areas in Chicago, Old Town lives up to its name. And that's a good thing. Often compared to New York's Greenwich Village for its narrow cobble-stoned streets, Queen Anne–style homes, and independent shops and restaurants, this former bohemian spot has been tamed, but it still knows how to have a good time.

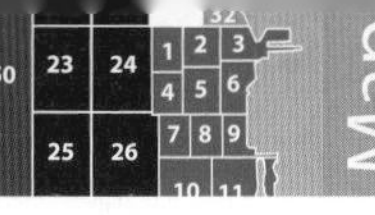

Banks

- **Bank of America (ATM)** • 1608 N Wells St
- **Chase** • 1350 N Wells St
- **Chase** • 424 W Division St
- **Chase (ATM)** • 1601 N Wells St
- **Fifth Third** • 837 W North Ave
- **LaSalle** • 1565 N Clybourn Ave
- **North Community** • 1561 N Wells St
- **Washington Mutual** • 1565 N La Salle Blvd
- **Washington Mutual** • 609 W North Ave

Car Washes

- **Gold Coast Car Wash** • 875 N Orleans St
- **We'll Clean** • 1520 N Halsted St

Car Rental

- **Enterprise** • 523 W North Ave • 312-482-8322

Gas Stations

- **Amoco** • 1560 N Halsted St
- **Mobil** • 1234 N Halsted Ave

Libraries

- **Near North Public Library** • 310 W Division St

Pharmacies

- **Dominick's** • 424 W Division St
- **Walgreens** • 1601 N Wells St

Pizza

- **Corlioni Pizzeria** • 349 W Oak St
- **Dominick's Finer Foods** • 424 W Division St
- **Domino's** • 143 W Division St
- **Father & Son Restaurant** • 645 W North Ave
- **Mangia Roma Pizzeria & Roman Eatery** • 1623 N Halsted St
- **Old Towne Pizza Pub** • 1339 N Wells St

Police

- **18th District (Near North)** • 1160 N Larrabee St

Schools

- **Catherine Cook Elementary** • 226 W Schiller St
- **Catherine Ferguson CPC** • 1420 N Hudson Ave
- **Cornerstone Academy** • 1111 N Wells St, 4th Fl
- **Edward Jenner Academy of the Arts** • 1119 N Cleveland Ave
- **Franklin Fine Arts Center** • 225 W Evergreen Ave
- **Friedrick Von Schiller Middle** • 640 W Scott St
- **George Manierre Elementary** • 1420 N Hudson Ave
- **Immaculate Conception** • 1431 N North Park Ave
- **Lake Shore Preparatory** • 300 W Hill St
- **Moody Bible Institute** • 820 N La Salle Blvd
- **Richard E Byrd Elementary** • 363 W Hill St
- **Ruben Salazar Bilingual Education Center** • 160 W Wendell St
- **St Joseph Elementary** • 1065 N Orleans St
- **Walter Payton Preparatory** • 1034 N Wells St

Supermarkets

- **Dominick's** • 424 W Division St

Parking

1
2
A
B
C
South Pond
Lincoln Park
PAGE 210
W Wisconsin St
N Bissell St
N Dayton St
N Mohawk St
N Cleveland Ave
N Hudson Ave
N Sedgwick St
N Orleans St
N Lincoln Park W
Stockton Dr
W Menomonee St
W Willow St
N Crilly Ct
N Fern Ct
W Saint Paul Ave
N Halsted St
N Burling St
W Eugenie St
N Vine St
N Meyer Ct
N Saint Michaels Ct
N State Pkwy
W Concord Pl
W Concord Ln
30
W North Ave
E North
North/ Clybourn
Sedgwick
W Weed St
N Frontier Ave
N North Park Ave
N Wieland St
Sandburg Ter
W Germania Pl
N Fremont St
N Ogden Ave
W Blackhawk St
W Burton Pl
N Dearborn Pkwy
N Clybourn Ave
OLD TOWN
W Eastman St
W Schiller St
N La Salle St
N Clark St
N Sutton Pl
N State St
W Fair Pl
W Evergreen Ave
Chicago River
W Goethe St
Stanton Schiller Park
W Sullivan St
N Schick Pl
W Scott St
22
32
Clark/ Division
N Hooker St
N Orchard St
N Howe St
W Division St
800W
400W
200W
100W
N Hickory Ave
N Kingsbury St
N Crosby St
W Elm St
N Cambridge Ave
N Larrabee St
N Felton Ct
W Hill St
W Maple St
N Rush St
W Bliss St
W Haines St
W Hobbie St
Seward Park
W Wendell St
CABRINI GREEN
W Oak St
N North Branch St
W Walton St
N Franklin St
NEAR NORTH
N Wells St
Washington Square Park
W Delaware Pl
W Locust St
W Iowa St
W Chestnut St
Moody Bible Institute
N Dearborn St
N Sangamon St
N Lessing St
N Peoria St
W Pearson St
W Institute Pl
Loyola Un (Water Tower C
N Carpenter St
W Chicago Ave
Chicago
N Morgan St
W Superior St
W Huron St
N Green St
N Orleans St
W Ancona St
W Erie St
Connector
90
W Ontario St
W Ohio St
N Union Ave
N Desplaines
Grand
W Grand Ave
W Illinois St
1/4 mile
.25 km

There's nothing fishy about Dinotto Ristorante's calamari—it tastes even better on their patio. The bar at Etre serves top names in designer denim. Smokers rejoice at Up Down Tobacco. Discover why spice is the variety of life at The Spice House, and contemplate life and your purchases at the Midwest Buddhist Temple (Map 36). Later, find comic relief at the legendary Second City improv theater (Map 30).

Coffee

- **Dunkin' Donuts** • 1234 N Halsted St
- **Dunkin' Donuts** • 333 W North Ave
- **Einstein Bros Bagels** • 1549 N Wells St
- **Starbucks** • 1229 N Clybourn Ave
- **Starbucks** • 200 W North Ave

Copy Shops

- **The UPS Store** • 1235 N Clybourn Ave
- **The UPS Store** • 333 W North Ave

Gyms

- **A Women's Gym (Women only)** • 1248 N Wells St
- **Crunch Fitness** • 820 N Orleans St
- **Energy Training Center** • 900 N North Branch St
- **Fitplex** • 1235 N La Salle Dr
- **New City YMCA** • 1515 N Halsted St
- **Wells St Athletic Club** • 1513 N Wells St
- **XSport Fitness** • 230 W North Ave

Hardware Stores

- **Tipre Hardware** • 229 W North Ave

Liquor Stores

- **Galleria Liquor** • 1559 N Wells St
- **Green Oak Food & Liquor** • 956 N Larrabee St
- **House of Glunz** • 1206 N Wells St
- **Old Town Liquors** • 1200 N Wells St

Movie Theaters

- **Lowes Piper Alley Theater** • 1608 N Wells St

Nightlife

- **Burton Place** • 1447 N Wells St
- **Dragon Room** • 809 W Evergreen Ave
- **North Park Tap** • 313 W North Ave
- **Old Town Ale House** • 219 W North Ave
- **Spoon** • 1240 N Wells St
- **Weeds** • 1555 N Dayton St
- **Zanies Comedy Club** • 1548 N Wells St

Pet Shops

- **Collar & Leash** • 1435 N Wells St
- **Furry Beastro** • 1500 N Wells St
- **Old Town Aquarium (Fish only)** • 1538 N Wells St

Restaurants

- **Bistrot Margot** • 1437 N Wells St
- **Chic Café** • Cooking and Hospitality Institute• 361 W Chestnut St
- **Cucina Bella Osteria & Wine Bar** • 1612 N Sedgwick St
- **Dinotto Ristorante** • 215 W North Ave
- **Fireplace Inn** • 1448 N Wells St
- **Flat Top Grill** • 319 W North Ave
- **Fresh Choice** • 1534 N Wells St
- **Kamehachi** • 1400 N Wells St
- **Kiki's Bistro** • 900 N Franklin St
- **Las Pinatas** • 1552 N Wells St
- **Mangia Rome** • 1623 N Halstead St
- **Michael's** • 101 W North Ave
- **Mizu** • 315 W North Ave
- **MK** • 868 N Franklin St
- **O'Brien's** • 1528 N Wells St
- **Old Jerusalem** • 1411 N Wells St
- **Salpicon** • 1252 N Wells St
- **Topo Gigio Ristorante** • 1516 N Wells St
- **Wells on Wells** • 1617 N Wells St

Shopping

- **Crate & Barrel Outlet Store** • 1864 N Clybourn Ave
- **Etre** • 1361 N Wells St
- **Fleet Feet Sports** • 210 W North Ave
- **Fudge Pot** • 1532 N Wells St
- **Jumbalia** • 1429 N Wells St
- **Old Town Gardens** • 1555 N Wells St
- **The Spice House** • 1512 N Wells St
- **Up Down Tabacco** • 1550 N Wells St
- **Village Cycle** • 1337 N Wells St

Video Rental

- **Blockbuster** • 400 W Division St
- **Video Shmideo** • 345 W North Ave
- **Video Shmideo** • 166 W Division St

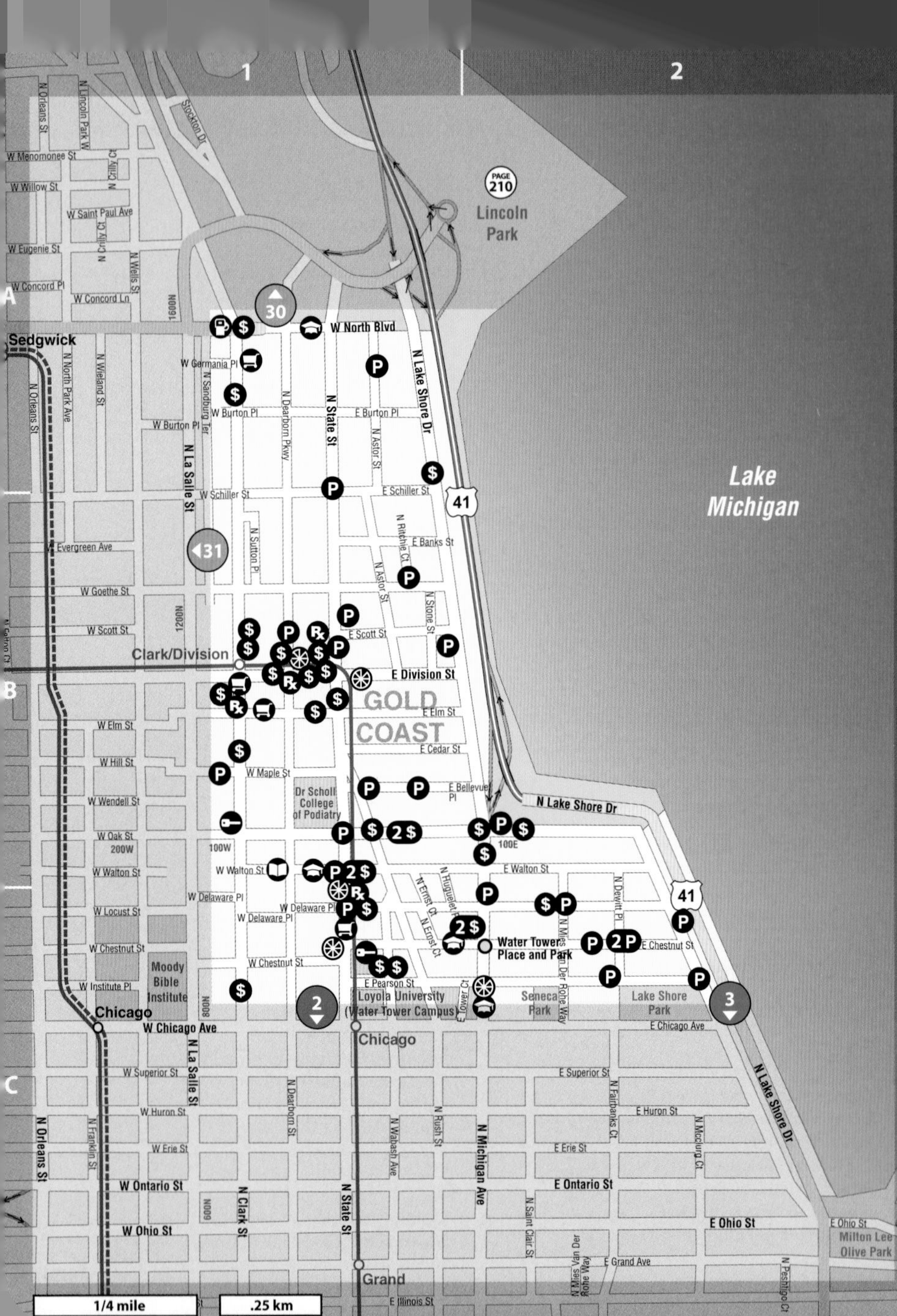

1
2
A
B
C
Lincoln Park
PAGE 210
Lake Michigan
GOLD COAST
Sedgwick
Clark/Division
Chicago
Grand
W North Blvd
W Germania Pl
W Burton Pl
E Burton Pl
W Schiller St
E Schiller St
E Banks St
W Evergreen Ave
W Goethe St
W Scott St
E Scott St
E Division St
E Elm St
W Elm St
E Cedar St
W Hill St
W Maple St
E Bellevue Pl
W Wendell St
W Oak St
W Walton St
E Walton St
W Delaware Pl
W Locust St
W Chestnut St
E Chestnut St
W Institute Pl
E Pearson St
W Chicago Ave
E Chicago Ave
W Superior St
E Superior St
W Huron St
E Huron St
W Erie St
E Erie St
W Ontario St
E Ontario St
W Ohio St
E Ohio St
E Grand Ave
E Illinois St
W Menomonee St
W Willow St
W Saint Paul Ave
W Eugenie St
W Concord Pl
W Concord Ln
N Lake Shore Dr
N State St
N Dearborn Pkwy
N Astor St
N Ritchie Ct
N Stone St
N Sutton Pl
N La Salle St
N Sandburg Ter
N Wieland St
N North Park Ave
N Orleans St
N Lincoln Park W
N Crilly Ct
N Wells St
Stockton Dr
N Clark St
N Dearborn St
N Wabash Ave
N Rush St
N Michigan Ave
N Saint Clair St
N Mies Van Der Rohe Way
N Fairbanks Ct
N Mcclurg Ct
N Peshtigo Ct
N Franklin St
N Huguelet Pl
N Ernst Ct
N Dewitt Pl
N Tower Ct
1600N
1200N
800N
600N
100W
200W
100E
41
30
31
2
3
Dr Scholl College of Podiatry
Moody Bible Institute
Water Tower Place and Park
Loyola University (Water Tower Campus)
Seneca Park
Lake Shore Park
Milton Lee Olive Park
1/4 mile
.25 km

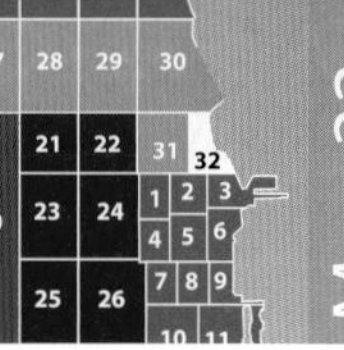

Between the tourist traps like Navy Pier and American Girl Place (Map 2), goofy bars on Division Street, and pick-up joints on Rush (that's the Viagra Triangle to you and me), it's easy for locals to make fun of this ritzy area. But the Gold Coast/Mag Mile (actually only three-quarters of a mile, but who's counting?) is also home to some of Chicago's most impressive architecture, museums (including LUMA, the new museum at Loyola University), and beautiful beaches. And admit it: You've marveled at the view from atop the Hancock's Signature Room, too.

Banks

- **Bank of America** • 1167 N State St
- **Bank of America (ATM)** • 45 W Division St
- **Bank of America (ATM)** • 58 E Oak St
- **Charter One** • 1201 N Clark St
- **Chase** • 1122 N Clark St
- **Chase** • John Hancock Ctr • 875 N Michigan Ave
- **Chase (ATM)** • 1200 N Clark St
- **Chase (ATM)** • 1200 N Dearborn St
- **Chase (ATM)** • 25 E Pearson St
- **Chase (ATM)** • 933 N State St
- **Citibank** • 68 E Oak St
- **Citibank (ATM)** • 1 E Delaware Pl
- **Delaware Place** • 190 E Delaware Pl
- **Diamond** • 100 W North Ave
- **Fifth Third** • 29 W Division St
- **Harris Trust & Savings** • 1000 N Lakeshore Dr
- **Harris Trust & Savings (ATM)** • Loyola University • 25 E Pearson St
- **LaSalle** • 940 N Michigan Ave
- **LaSalle (ATM)** • 1201 N State St
- **North Community** • 2 W Elm St
- **Northern Trust** • 120 E Oak St
- **Oak** • 1000 N Rush St
- **Park National** • 801 N Clark St
- **TCF** • Jewel• 1210 N Clark St
- **TCF (ATM)** • 1165 N Clark St
- **TCF (ATM)** • 1400 N Lakeshore Dr
- **TCF (ATM)** • 1525 N Clark St
- **TCF (ATM)** • 7-Eleven • 921 N State St
- **Washington Mutual** • 1200 N State Pkwy

Car Rental

- **Enterprise** • 850 N State St • 312-951-6262
- **Hertz** • 1025 N Clark St • 312-951-2930

Gas Stations

- **Shell** • 130 W North Ave

Landmarks

- **Water Tower Place and Park** • 845 N Michigan Ave

Libraries

- **Newberry Library** • 60 W Walton St

Pharmacies

- **CVS Pharmacy** • 1201 N State Pkwy
- **Osco Drug** • 1165 N Clark St
- **Walgreens** • 1200 N Dearborn St
- **Walgreens** • 933 N State St

Pizza

- **California Pizza Kitchen** • 835 N Michigan Ave
- **Chi-Town Pizza** • 11 E Division St
- **Edwardo's Natural Pizza** • 1212 N Dearborn St
- **Papa Milano** • 951 N State St
- **Pizano's Pizza & Pasta** • 864 N State St

Schools

- **Archbishop Quigley Prep Seminary** • 103 E Chestnut St
- **Latin School of Chicago** • 59 W North Blvd
- **Loyola University (Downtown Campus)** • 820 N Michigan Ave
- **William B Ogden Elementary** • 24 W Walton St

Supermarkets

- **Jewel-Osco** • 1210 N Clark St
- **Potash Brothers** • 1525 N Clark St
- **Potash Brothers** • 875 N State St
- **Treasure Island** • 75 W Elm St

Parking

Map 32 • Gold Coast / Mag Mile

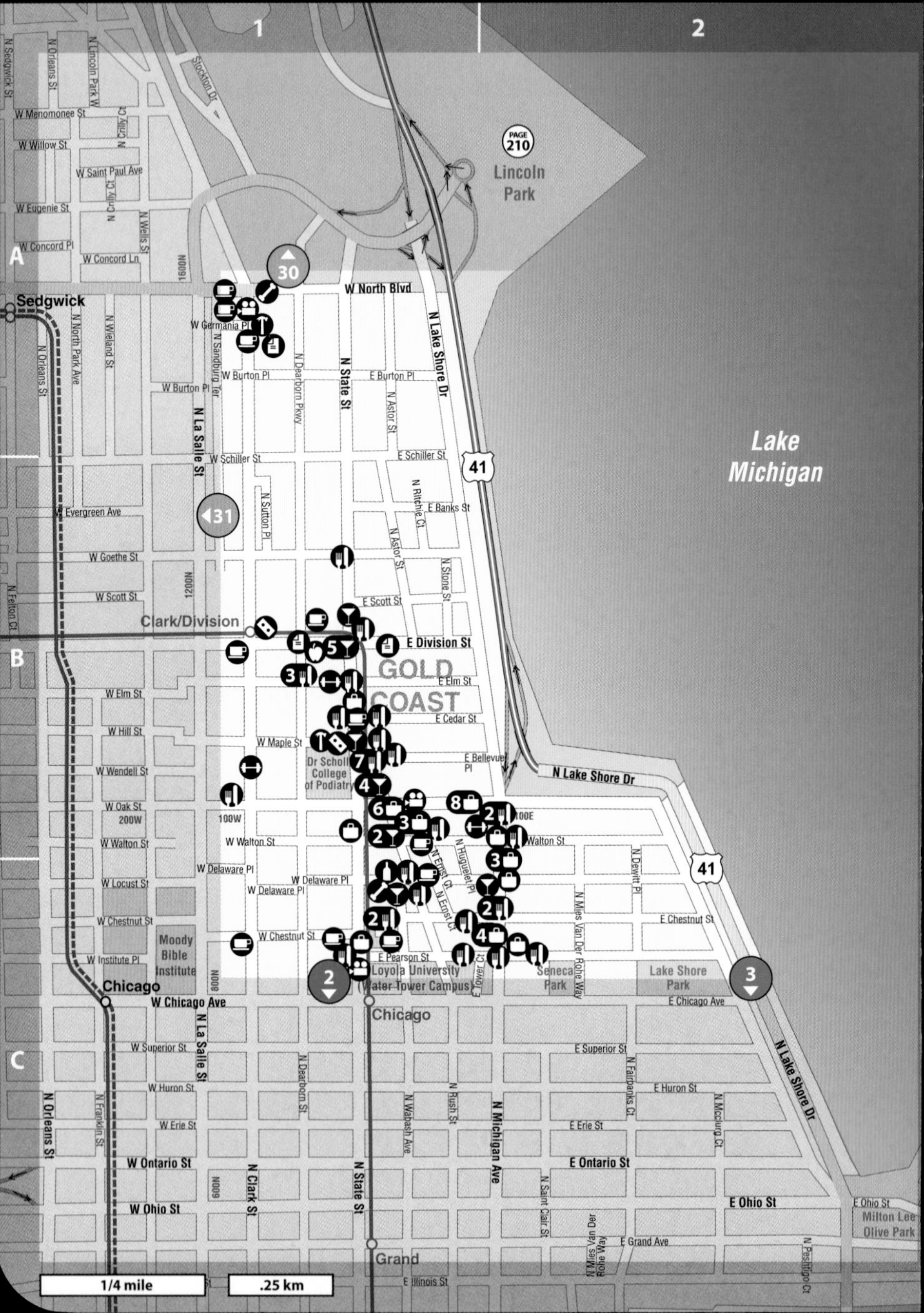

N

1
2
A
B
C

Lincoln Park
PAGE 210

Lake Michigan

GOLD COAST

Sedgwick
Clark/Division
Chicago
Grand

W North Blvd
W Menomonee St
W Willow St
W Saint Paul Ave
W Eugenie St
W Concord Pl
W Concord Ln
W Germania Pl
W Burton Pl
E Burton Pl
W Schiller St
E Schiller St
E Banks St
W Evergreen Ave
W Goethe St
W Scott St
E Scott St
E Division St
E Elm St
W Elm St
E Cedar St
W Hill St
W Maple St
E Bellevue Pl
W Wendell St
W Oak St
W Walton St
Walton St
W Delaware Pl
W Locust St
W Chestnut St
E Chestnut St
E Pearson St
W Institute Pl
W Chicago Ave
E Chicago Ave
W Superior St
E Superior St
W Huron St
E Huron St
W Erie St
E Erie St
W Ontario St
E Ontario St
W Ohio St
E Ohio St
E Grand Ave
E Illinois St

N Sedgwick St
N Orleans St
N Lincoln Park W
N Crilly Ct
N Wells St
Stockton Dr
N North Park Ave
N Wieland St
N Sandburg Ter
N La Salle St
N Dearborn Pkwy
N State St
N Astor St
N Lake Shore Dr
N Ritchie Ct
N Sutton Pl
N Stone St
N Felton Ct
N Huguelet Pl
N Ernst Ct
N Tower Ct
N Mies Van Der Rohe Way
N Dewitt Pl
N Franklin St
N Clark St
N Dearborn St
N Wabash Ave
N Rush St
N Michigan Ave
N Fairbanks Ct
N Mcclurg Ct
N Saint Clair St
N Peshtigo Ct

1600N
1200N
800N
600N
100W
200W
100E

Dr Scholl College of Podiatry
Moody Bible Institute
Loyola University (Water Tower Campus)
Seneca Park
Lake Shore Park
Milton Lee Olive Park

41
30
31
2
3

1/4 mile
.25 km

Gucci, Tiffany & Co. (Map 3), The Ritz-Carlton, Chanel, Ralph Lauren (Map 3), Barney's, Prada. They don't call it the Gold Coast for nothing. But with representation from top chain stores, there's plenty for us regular folk to buy here, too. Splurge on the creative Italian cuisine at Spiaggia and pop the question like so many others have. Save some dough by checking your email for free at the Apple Store (Map 3).

Coffee

- **Cyber Café** • 25 E Pearson St
- **Dunkin' Donuts** • 101 W Division St
- **Einstein Bros Bagels** • 44 E Walton St
- **Gloria Jean's Gourmet Coffee** • 1031 N State St
- **Starbucks** • 106 W Germania Pl
- **Starbucks** • 111 E Chestnut St
- **Starbucks** • 1538 N Clark St
- **Starbucks** • 39 W Division St
- **Starbucks** • 828 N State St
- **Starbucks** • 932 N Rush St

Copy Shops

- **Fedex Kinko's** • 1201 N Dearborn St
- **The UPS Store** • 47 W Division St

Farmer's Markets

- **Near North (Jun–Oct; Sat, 7 am–2 pm)** • 15 W Division St

Gyms

- **Curves (women only)** • 21 W Elm St
- **Equinox** • 900 N Michigan Ave
- **Gold Coast Multiplex** • 1030 N Clark St

Hardware Stores

- **Gordon's Ace Hardware** • 24 W Maple St
- **Potash Bros Ace Hardware** • 110 W Germania Pl

Liquor Stores

- **Chalet Wine & Cheese Shop** • 40 E Delaware Pl

Movie Theaters

- **The Alliance Francaise** • 810 N Dearborn St
- **Lowes Esquire** • 58 E Oak St
- **Village Theater** • 1548 N Clark St

Nightlife

- **Backroom** • 1007 N Rush St
- **Bar Chicago** • 9 W Division St
- **Butch McGuire's** • 20 W Division St
- **Cru Wine Bar** • 888 N Wabash Ave
- **Dublin's** • 1050 N State St
- **The Hunt Club** • 1100 N State St
- **Jilly's Retro Club** • 1007 N Rush St
- **Le Passage** • 937 N Rush St
- **Leg Room** • 7 W Division St
- **Mothers** • 26 W Division St
- **She-nanigans** • 16 W Division St
- **Signature Lounge** • John Hancock Ctr • 875 N Michigan Ave
- **Underground Wonder Bar** • 10 E Walton St
- **The Whisky** • 1015 N Rush St
- **Zebra Lounge** • 1220 N State St

Pet Shops

- **Paws-a-Tively** • 109 W North Ave
- **Tails in the City** • 1 E Delaware Pl

Restaurants

- **Ashkenaz** • 12 E Cedar St
- **Bistro 110** • 110 E Pearson St
- **Bistrot Zinc** • 1131 N State St
- **Café des Architectes** • Sofitel Chicago Water Tower• 20 E Chestnut St
- **Café Spiaggia** • 980 N Michigan Ave
- **Cape Cod Room** • Drake Hotel • 140 E Walton Pl
- **Carmine's** • 1043 N Rush St
- **Cheesecake Factory** • John Hancock Ctr • 875 N Michigan Ave
- **Cru Wine Bar & Café** • 888 N Wabash Ave
- **Dave & Buster's** • 1030 N Clark St
- **Foodlife** • 835 N Michigan Ave
- **Gibson's Steakhouse** • 1028 N Rush St
- **Hugo's Frog Bar & Fish House** • 1024 N Rush St
- **Il Mulino New York** • 1150 N Dearborn St
- **Johnny Rockets** • 901 N Rush St
- **Le Colonial** • 937 N Rush St
- **McCormick & Schmick's** • 41 E Chestnut St
- **Mike Ditka's** • 100 E Chestnut St
- **Morton's of Chicago** • 1050 N State St
- **Mr. J's Dawg & Burger** • 822 N State St
- **Original Pancake House** • 22 E Bellevue Pl
- **Pane Caldo** • 72 E Walton St
- **PJ Clarke's** • 1204 N State Pkwy
- **Pump Room** • Omni Ambassador East Hotel • 1301 N State Pkwy
- **Ra Sushi** • 1139 N State St
- **Ritz-Carlton Dining Room** • 160 E Pearson St
- **Signature Room** • John Hancock Ctr• 875 N Michigan Ave
- **Spiaggia** • 980 N Michigan Ave
- **Tavern on Rush** • 1031 N Rush St
- **Tempo** • 6 E Chestnut St
- **Tsunami** • 1160 N Dearborn St
- **Whiskey Bar and Grill** • 1015 N Rush St

Shopping

- **Anthropologie** • 1120 N State St
- **Barney's New York** • 25 E Oak St
- **BCBG** • 55 E Oak St
- **Bloomingdale's** • 900 N Michigan Ave
- **Bravco Beauty Center** • 43 E Oak St
- **Chanel at the Drake Hotel** • 935 N Michigan Ave
- **Club Monaco** • 900 N Michigan Ave
- **Elements** • 102 E Oak St
- **Europa Books** • 832 N State St
- **Fitigues Surplus** • 50 E Oak St
- **Frette** • 41 E Oak St
- **G'bani** • 949 N State St
- **Gucci** • 900 N Michigan Ave
- **H&M** • 840 N Michigan Ave
- **Hermes** • 110 E Oak St
- **Hershey's Chicago** • 822 N Michigan Ave
- **Lord & Taylor** • 835 N Michigan Ave
- **Lush Cosmetics** • 835 N Michigan Ave
- **MAC** • 40 E Oak St
- **Nicole Miller** • 63 E Oak St
- **Paul Stuart X/S** • John Hancock Ctr• 875 N Michigan Ave
- **Prada** • 30 E Oak St
- **Pratesi** • 67 E Oak St
- **Tod's** • 121 E Oak St
- **Ultimate Bride** • 106 E Oak St
- **Ultimo** • 114 E Oak St
- **Urban Outfitters** • 935 N Rush St
- **Water Tower** • 845 N Michigan Ave

Video Rental

- **Blockbuster** • 1201 N Clark St
- **Video Shmideo** • 6 W Maple St

1
2
A
B
C
WEST ROGERS PARK
Dobson St
W Howard St
W Jerome St
W Birchwood Ave
W Fargo Ave
W Jarvis Ave
W Sherwin Ave
W Chase Ave
W Jarlath St
W Touhy Ave
W Fitch Ave
W Estes Ave
W Greenleaf Ave
W Lunt Ave
W Coyle Ave
W Morse Ave
W Farwell Ave
W Pratt Ave
W North Shore Ave
W Albion Ave
W Arthur Ave
W Devon Ave
W Highland Ave
W Rosemont Ave
W Birch
W Far
W Ja
N Kedzie Ave
N Francisco Ave
N California Ave
N Fairfield Ave
N Talman Ave
N Maplewood Ave
N Artesian Ave
N Western Ave
N Oakley Ave
N Bell Ave
N Ridge Blvd
N Albany Ave
N Sacramento Ave
N Campbell Ave
N Claremont Ave
N Hamilton Ave
N Washtenaw Ave
N Rockwell St
N Richmond St
N Mozart St
N Troy Ave
N Whipple St
N Leavitt St
7600N
7200N
6800N
6400N
2800W
2400W
Rogers Park/
West Ridge
Historical Society
Rogers Park
High Ridge
YMCA
Bernard
Horwich JCC
Indian Boundary
Park
Lerner
Park
Chippewa
Park
Warren Park
Thillen's
Stadium
Croatian
Cultural Center
India
Town
46
34
35
36
3
1/4 mile
.25 km

Devon Avenue is known throughout India as the place to be in the United States. The international marketplace feel is supported with the smell of spices and various dialects of language. Every shop sells saris (in frameable fabrics), hookahs (with all flavors of tobacco), or Bollywood movies (with the fun dance sequences). On Devon Avenue west of California Avenue, there are Islamic, Russian, and Jewish bookstores and bakeries.

Banks

- **Chase** • 7015 N Western Ave
- **Chase (ATM)** • 7510 N Western Ave
- **Citibank** • 2801 W Devon Ave
- **Devon** • 6445 N Western Ave
- **First Commercial** • 2201 W Howard St
- **First Commercial** • 7050 N Western Ave
- **Greater Chicago** • 7555 N California Ave
- **LaSalle** • 2545 W Devon Ave
- **LaSalle** • 2855 W Touhy Ave
- **TCF (ATM)** • 7-Eleven• 2200 W Devon Ave

Car Washes

- **Fast Carwash** • 7130 N Western Ave

Gas Stations

- **Marathon** • 7130 N Western Ave

Landmarks

- **Bernard Horwich JCC** • 3003 W Touhy Ave
- **Croatian Cultural Center** • 2845 W Devon Ave
- **High Ridge YMCA** • 2424 W Touhy Ave
- **India Town** • W Devon Ave, near Washtenaw Ave
- **Indian Boundary Park** • 2500 W Lunt Ave
- **Rogers Park/West Ridge Historical Society** • 7344 N Western Ave
- **Thillen's Stadium** • Devon & Kedzie Ave
- **Warren Park** • 6601 N Western Ave

Libraries

- **Northtown Public Library** • 6435 N California Ave

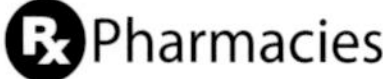

Pharmacies

- **Osco Drug** • 2825 W Devon Ave
- **Walgreens** • 7510 N Western Ave

Pizza

- **Domino's** • 3144 W Devon Ave
- **Eastern Style Pizza** • 2911 W Touhy Ave
- **Gulliver's Pizzeria & Restaurant** • 2727 W Howard St
- **Pizza Hut** • 951 Howard St
- **Villa Palermo Pizza** • 2154 W Devon Ave

Schools

- **ABC Academy Inc** • 2714 W Pratt Bl
- **ATT Ptach Special Education Program** • 2828 W Pratt Blvd
- **Bethesda Lutheran Elementary** • 6803 N Campbell Ave
- **Brisk Academy - Yeshivas Brisk** • 3000 W Devon Ave
- **Consolidated Hebrew High** • 2828 W Pratt Blvd
- **Daniel Boone Elementary** • 6710 N Washtenaw Ave
- **Decatur Classical** • 7030 N Sacramento Ave
- **George Armstrong Elementary** • 2110 W Greenleaf Ave
- **Hanna Sacks Girls' High** • 3021 W Devon Ave
- **Ida Crown Jewish Academy** • 2828 W Pratt Blvd
- **Lubavitch Boy's High** • 2756 W Morse Ave
- **Rogers Elementary** • 7345 N Washtenaw Ave
- **St Margaret Mary Elementary** • 7318 N Oakley Ave
- **St Scholastica High** • 7416 N Ridge Blvd
- **Virginia Frank Child Dev Center** • 3033 W Touhy Ave
- **Yeshiva Shearis Yisroel** • 2620 W Touhy Ave

Supermarkets

- **Jewel** • 2485 W Howard St
- **New York Kosher** • 2900 W Devon Ave
- **North Water Market** • 2626 W Devon Ave
- **Save A Lot** • 2151 W Devon Ave

1
2
A
B
C
Dobson St
W Howard St
W Jerome St
W Birchwood Ave
W Fargo Ave
W Jarvis Ave
W Sherwin Ave
W Chase Ave
N Kedzie Ave
N Francisco Ave
N California Ave
N Fairfield Ave
N Talman Ave
N Maplewood Ave
N Artesian Ave
N Western Ave
N Oakley Ave
N Bell Ave
N Ridge Blvd
W Birchw
W Farg
W Ja
W C
7600N
Rogers Park
N Campbell Ave
N Claremont Ave
N Hamilton Ave
N Albany Ave
N Sacramento Ave
W Jarlath St
7200N
W Touhy Ave
W Fitch Ave
WEST ROGERS PARK
W Estes Ave
W Greenleaf Ave
46
N Washtenaw Ave
Indian Boundary Park
W Lunt Ave
2800W
2400W
34
Lerner Park
W Coyle Ave
N Rockwell St
W Morse Ave
W Farwell Ave
6800N
W Pratt Ave
Chippewa Park
N Richmond St
N Mozart St
W North Shore Ave
Warren Park
W Albion Ave
N Troy Ave
N Whipple St
W Arthur Ave
N Leavitt St
6400N
W Devon Ave
35
36
W Highland Ave
W Rosemont Ave
1/4 mile
.25 km

Cultures mix fluidly in West Rogers Park. Between the Hebrew schools, the Russian shops, and the Indian markets are residential streets and five different parks with batting cages, sledding hills, baseball diamonds, tennis courts, and jogging paths. The Rogers Park/West Ridge Historical Society honors living on the far north side.

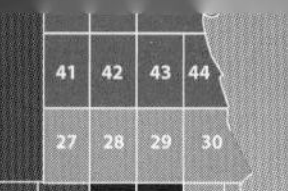

Map

Coffee

- **Dunkin' Donuts** • 3132 W Devon Ave
- **Dunkin' Donuts** • 7578 N Western Ave

Copy Shops

- **Progress Press** • 7315 N Western Ave

Gyms

- **Curves (women only)** • 7300 N Western Ave
- **High Ridge YMCA** • 2424 W Touhy Ave

Hardware Stores

- **Basco Plumbing & True Value** • 2953 W Devon Ave
- **Coast to Coast Store** • 6942 N Western Ave

Liquor Stores

- **Adelphi Liquors** • 2351 W Devon Ave
- **Beatrice Liquor** • 2901 W Devon Ave
- **M&Y Liquor & Grocery Store** • 2252 W Devon Ave

Nightlife

- **Cary's Lounge** • 2251 W Devon Ave
- **McKellin's** • 2800 W Touhy Ave
- **Mullen's Sports Bar and Grill** • 7301 N Western Ave

Pet Shops

- **Mickey's Pet Salon** • 2805 W Touhy Ave

Restaurants

- **Afghan Restaurant** • 2818 W Devon Ave
- **Annapurna** • 2608 W Devon Ave
- **Arya Bhavan** • 2508 W Devon Ave
- **Café Montenegro** • 6954 N Western Ave
- **Candlelite** • 7452 N Western Ave
- **Ghandi India Restaurant** • 2601 W Devon Ave
- **Good Morgan Kosher Fish Market** • 2948 W Devon Ave
- **Hashalom** • 2905 W Devon Ave
- **Hema's Kitchen** • 6406 N Oakley Ave
- **Indian Garden** • 2546 W Devon Ave
- **Mysore Woodland's** • 2548 W Devon Ave
- **Sher a Punjab** • 2525 W Devon Ave
- **Sukhadia's** • 2559 W Devon Ave
- **Tiffin** • 2536 W Devon Ave
- **U Lucky Dawg** • 6821 N Western Ave
- **Udupi Palace** • 2543 W Devon Ave
- **Viceroy of India** • 2520 W Devon Ave

Shopping

- **Argo Georgian Bakery** • 2812 W Devon Ave
- **AutoZone** • 2555 W Touhy Ave
- **Cheesecakes by JR** • 2841 W Howard St
- **Chicago Harley Davidson** • 6868 N Western Ave
- **Levinson's Bakery** • 2856 W Devon Ave
- **Office Mart** • 2801 W Touhy Ave
- **Raj Jewels** • 2652 W Devon Ave
- **Resham's** • 2540 W Devon Ave
- **Taj Sari Palace** • 2553 W Devon Ave
- **Tel-Aviv Kosher Bakery** • 2944 W Devon Ave
- **Three Sisters Deli** • 2854 W Devon Ave

Video Rental

- **Atlantic Video Rentals (Indian)** • 2541 W Devon Ave
- **Blockbuster** • 7572 N Western Ave
- **Elita Video (Russian)** • 2753 W Devon Ave
- **Golden Video** • 2761 W Devon Ave
- **New Devon Video** • 2304 W Devon Ave
- **Super Star Video (Indian and Pakistani)** • 2538 W Devon Ave
- **Sur Sangeet Video (Indian)** • 2521 W Devon Ave
- **Video Vision** • 2524 W Devon Ave
- **Western Video** • 7424 N Western Ave

1
2
A
B
C
Rogers Ave Park & Beach
Howard St Park & Beach
Fargo Ave Park & Beach
Jarvis Ave Park & Beach
Sherwin Ave Park & Beach
Chase Ave Park & Beach
Leone Park & Beach
Loyola Beach
Loyola Park
Pratt Blvd Park & Beach
Columbia Ave Park & Beach
North Shore Ave Park & Beach
Hartigan Park & Beach
Loyola University (Lake Shore Campus)
PAGE 254
ROGERS PARK
Howard
Jarvis
Morse
Loyola
Pottawattomie Park
Touhy Park
Paschen Park
Rogers Park
Robert A Black Golf Course
Warren Park
Angel Guardian Croatian Catholic Church
33
36
37
2
3
W Howard St
W Birchwood Ave
W Fargo Ave
W Jarvis Ave
W Sherwin Ave
W Chase Ave
W Touhy Ave
W Estes Ave
W Greenleaf Ave
W Lunt Ave
W Morse Ave
W Farwell Ave
W Pratt Blvd
W Columbia Ave
W North Shore Ave
W Wallen Ave
W Albion Ave
W Loyola Ave
W Arthur Ave
W Schreiber Ave
W Devon Ave
W Highland Ave
W Rosemont Ave
W Thorne Ave
W Sheridan
N Rogers Ave
N Ashland Ave
N Clark St
N Sheridan Rd
N Ravenswood Ave
N Paulina St
N Hermitage Ave
N Marshfield Ave
N Greenview Ave
N Glenwood Ave
N Wayne Ave
N Lakewood Ave
N Magnolia Ave
N Bosworth Ave
N Newgard Ave
N Broadway St
N Winthrop Ave
N Damen Ave
N Seeley Ave
N Hoyne Ave
N Winchester Ave
N Wolcott Ave
N Honore St
N Ridge Blvd
Elmwood Ave
Callan Ave
Clyde Ave
7600N
7200N
6800N
6400N
2000W
1600W
1200W
1/4 mile
.25 km

Loyola students, Caribbean and African immigrants, and old hippies populate this dense and lively 'hood. East Rogers Park is a "pocket" neighborhood—pockets of rehabbed vintage two-flat condos and well-tended grassy lawns compete with pockets of run-down courtyard buildings owned by slumlords. The mix keeps living here affordable, and the lakefront and Loyola Campus make it pleasant, although break-ins and gang activity continue to be a problem.

Banks

- **Bank of America (ATM)** • 6359 N Broadway St
- **Chase** • 1763 W Howard St
- **Chase** • 6415 N Sheridan Rd
- **Chase** • 6623 N Damen Ave
- **Chase (ATM)** • 1523 W Jarvis Ave
- **Chase (ATM)** • 7410 N Clark St
- **First Commercial** • 6930 N Clark St
- **First Commercial** • 6945 N Clark St
- **Harris Trust & Savings** • 6538 N Sheridan Rd
- **Harris Trust & Savings (ATM)** • Loyola University • 6525 N Sheridan Rd
- **Harris Trust & Savings (ATM)** • Loyola University • 6633 N Winthrop Ave
- **LaSalle** • 7516 N Clark St
- **MB Financial** • 6443 N Sheridan Rd
- **TCF (ATM)** • 7-Eleven• 1404 W Pratt Blvd
- **Washington Mutual** • 1425 W Morse Ave

Car Washes

- **Rogers Park Auto Body Shop** • 6828 N Clark St

Gas Stations

- **Citgo** • 1500 W Devon Ave
- **Citgo** • 7138 N Sheridan Rd
- **Marathon** • 7550 N Sheridan Rd
- **Mobil** • 7201 N Clark St
- **Shell** • 6346 N Clark St
- **Shell** • 6401 N Ridge Blvd

Landmarks

- **Angel Guardian Croatian Catholic Church** • 6346 N Ridge Ave
- **Robert A Black Golf Course** • 2045 W Pratt Blvd

Libraries

- **Rogers Park Public Library** • 6907 N Clark St

Pizza

- **Carmen's of Loyola Pizzeria** • 6568 N Sheridan Rd
- **Giordano's** • 6836 N Sheridan Rd
- **Hamilton's Pizza & Pub** • 6341 N Broadway St
- **JB Alberto's** • 1324 W Morse Ave
- **Leona's** • 6935 N Sheridan Rd
- **Vince's Pizzeria** • 1527 W Devon Ave

Police

- **24th District (Rogers Park)** • 6464 N Clark St

Post Offices

- **US Post Office** • 1723 W Devon Ave
- **US Post Office** • 7056 N Clark St
- **US Post Office** • 7617 N Paulina St

Schools

- **Chicago Math & Science Academy** • 1709 W Lunt Ave
- **Chicago Waldorf** • 1300 W Loyola Ave
- **Eugene Field Elementary** • 7019 N Ashland Blvd
- **Jordan Elementary** • 7414 N Wolcott Ave
- **Joyce Kilmer Elementary** • 6700 N Greenview Ave
- **Loyola University of Chicago** • 6525 N Sheridan Rd
- **New Field Primary** • 1707 W Morse Ave
- **North Shore Academy for Children** • 6711 N Sheridan Rd
- **North Shore Elementary** • 1217 W Chase Ave
- **Pactt Learning Center** • 7101 N Greenview Ave
- **Paideia Academy** • 6631 N Bosworth Ave
- **Peace Academy** • 6631 N Bosworth Ave
- **Roger C Sullivan High** • 6631 N Bosworth Ave

Supermarkets

- **Dominick's** • 1763 W Howard St
- **Dominick's** • 6623 N Damen Ave
- **New Leaf Natural Grocery** • 1261 W Loyola Ave
- **Rogers Park Fruit Market** • 7401 N Clark St

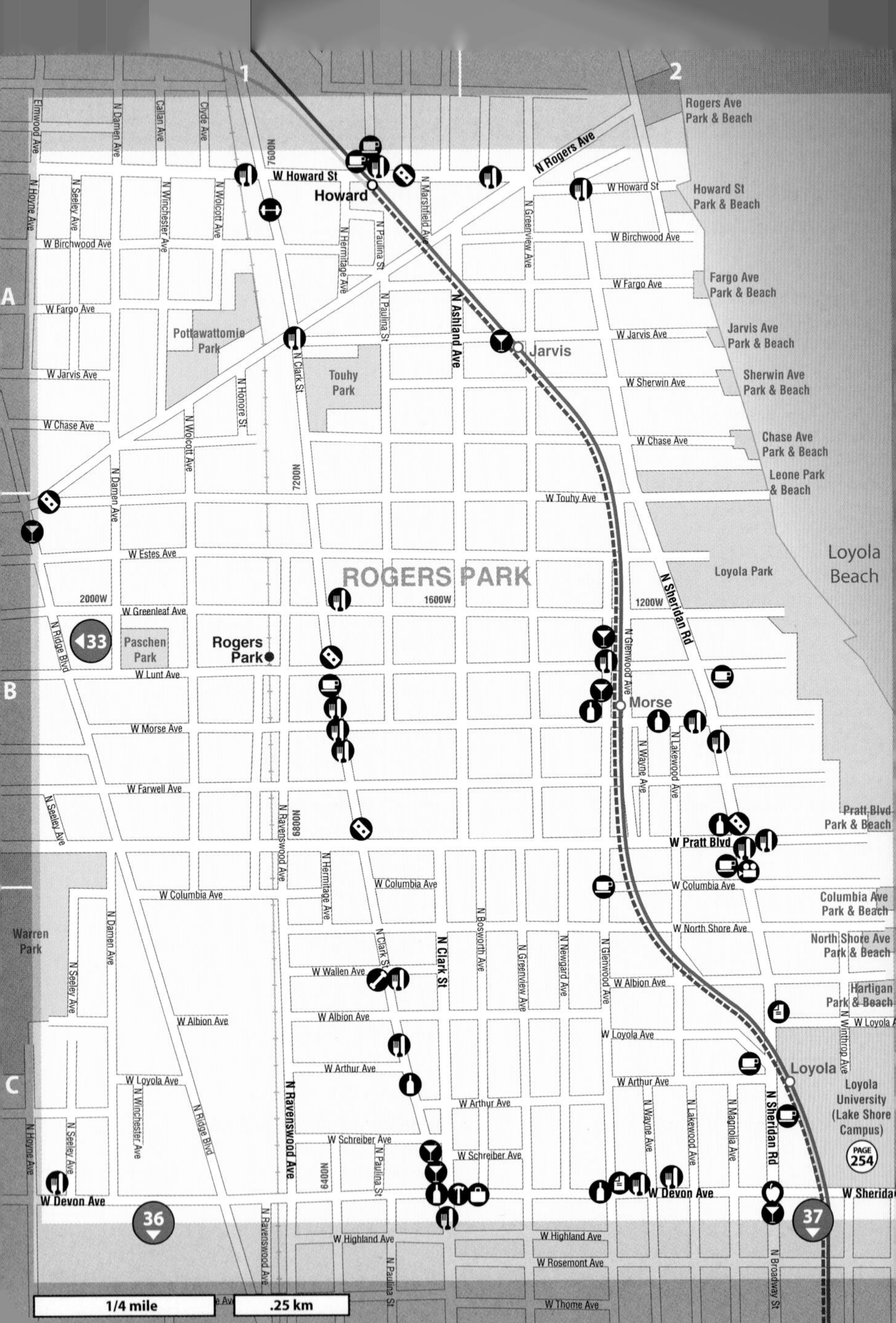

1
2
A
B
C
Rogers Ave Park & Beach
Howard St Park & Beach
Fargo Ave Park & Beach
Jarvis Ave Park & Beach
Sherwin Ave Park & Beach
Chase Ave Park & Beach
Leone Park & Beach
Loyola Beach
Loyola Park
Pratt Blvd Park & Beach
Columbia Ave Park & Beach
North Shore Ave Park & Beach
Hartigan Park & Beach
Loyola University (Lake Shore Campus)
PAGE 254
Pottawattomie Park
Touhy Park
Paschen Park
Warren Park
ROGERS PARK
Rogers Park
Howard
Jarvis
Morse
Loyola
33
36
37
N Rogers Ave
W Howard St
N Ashland Ave
N Sheridan Rd
N Clark St
N Ravenswood Ave
N Ridge Blvd
N Damen Ave
W Devon Ave
W Pratt Blvd
W Birchwood Ave
W Fargo Ave
W Jarvis Ave
W Sherwin Ave
W Chase Ave
W Touhy Ave
W Estes Ave
W Greenleaf Ave
W Lunt Ave
W Morse Ave
W Farwell Ave
W Columbia Ave
W North Shore Ave
W Wallen Ave
W Albion Ave
W Loyola Ave
W Arthur Ave
W Schreiber Ave
W Highland Ave
W Rosemont Ave
W Thome Ave
N Paulina St
N Hermitage Ave
N Marshfield Ave
N Greenview Ave
N Glenwood Ave
N Wayne Ave
N Lakewood Ave
N Magnolia Ave
N Winthrop Ave
N Broadway St
N Bosworth Ave
N Newgard Ave
N Wolcott Ave
N Winchester Ave
N Seeley Ave
N Hoyne Ave
N Honore St
Elmwood Ave
Callan Ave
Clyde Ave
2000W
1600W
1200W
7600N
7200N
6800N
6400N
1/4 mile
.25 km

Glenwood Avenue and the Loyola campus are abundant with crunchy cafés. The grandpapi of them all is the Heartland Café, featuring health-nut fare, a lefty gift shop, and live folk music. North Clark Street is dotted with Mexican spots that don't look like much but offer authentic food at low prices. The gay bar Jackhammer features the queer talent showcase, The Flesh Hungry Dog show, which attracts straights as well as gays.

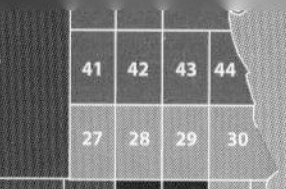

Coffee

- **Dunkin' Donuts** • 1200 W Loyola Ave
- **Dunkin' Donuts** • 6970 N Clark St
- **Ennui** • 6981 N Sheridan Rd
- **Kaffeccino** • 6441 N Sheridan Rd
- **Starbuck's** • 6738 N Sheridan Rd
- **Starbucks** • Dominick's• 1763 W Howard St
- **Worlds Fair Coffee** • 7603 N Paulina St

Copy Shops

- **Asos Copies & More** • 6604 N Sheridan Rd
- **The UPS Store** • 1400 W Devon Ave

Farmer's Markets

- **Loyola/Rogers Park (Jul-Oct, some sundays, 7 am-2 pm)** • W Devon Ave & N Broadway St

Gyms

- **Bally Total Fitness** • 7529 N Clark St

Hardware Stores

- **Clark-Devon Hardware** • 6401 N Clark St

Liquor Stores

- **Dino's Liquors** • 6400 N Clark St
- **Hahn Liquors** • 1410 W Devon Ave
- **Isam's Food & Liquor** • 6816 N Sheridan Rd
- **Lian's Liquor & Grocery** • 6507 N Clark St
- **Morse Liquors** • 1400 W Morse Ave
- **Soo Liquors** • 1420 W Morse Ave

Movie Theaters

- **Village North Theaters** • 6746 N Sheridan Rd

Nightlife

- **Hamilton's Pub** • 6341 N Broadway St
- **Jackhammer** • 6406 N Clark St
- **Lamp Post** • 7126 N Ridge Blvd
- **No Exit** • 6970 N Glenwood Ave
- **Poitin Stil** • 1502 W Jarvis Ave
- **Touche** • 6412 N Clark St

Pet Shops

- **Aquarium Gem** • 6623 N Clark St

Restaurants

- **A&T Restaurant** • 7026 N Clark St
- **Buffalo Joe's** • 1841 W Howard St
- **Café Suron** • 1146 W Pratt Blvd
- **Capt'n Nemos** • 7363 N Clark St
- **Caribbean American Bakery** • 1539 W Howard St
- **Deluxe Diner** • 6349 N Clark St 24
- **El Famous Burrito** • 7047 N Clark St
- **Ennui Café** • 6981 N Sheridan Rd
- **Ghareeb Nawaz** • 2032 W Devon Ave
- **Grande Noodles and Sushi Bar** • 6632 N Clark St
- **Heartland Café** • 7000 N Glenwood Ave
- **La Cazuela Mariscos** • 6922 N Clark St
- **Lake Side Café** • 1418 W Howard St
- **Morseland** • 1218 W Morse Ave
- **Panini Panini** • 6764 N Sheridan Rd
- **Quesadillas y Mariscos Dona Lolis** • 6924 N Clark St
- **Speakeasy Supperclub** • 1401 W Devon Ave
- **Taste of Peru** • 6545 N Clark St
- **Thai Spice** • 1320 W Devon Ave
- **Tickie's Belizean Cuisine** • 7605 N Paulina St

Shopping

- **Mar-Jen Discount Furniture** • 1536 W Devon Ave

Video Rental

- **Blockbuster** • 7007 N Clark St
- **Hollywood Video** • 1751 W Howard St
- **Pratt Video** • 6810 N Sheridan Rd
- **Syed Video** • 6808 N Clark St

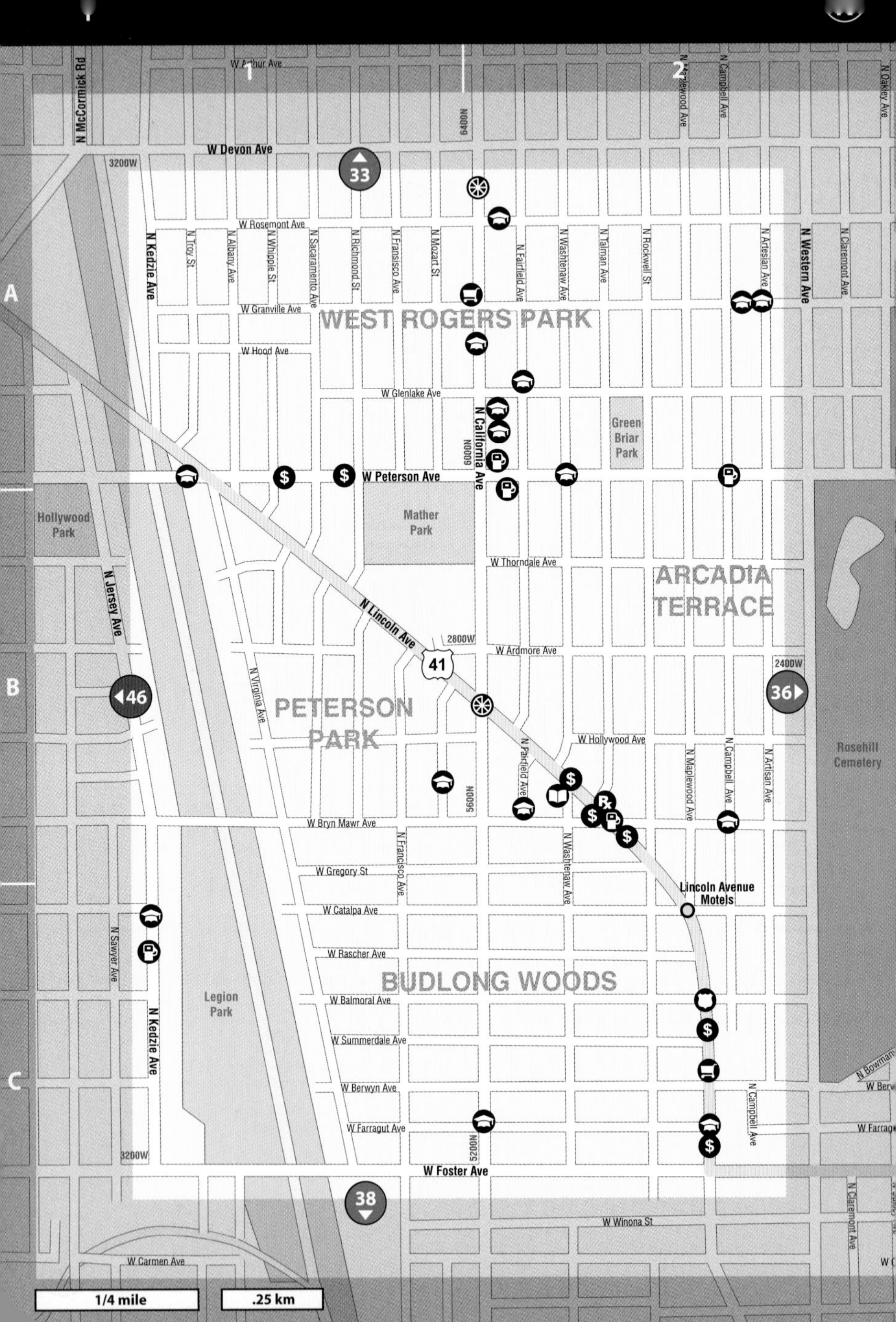

1
2
A
B
C
W Arthur Ave
N McCormick Rd
6400N
N Maplewood Ave
N Campbell Ave
N Oakley Ave
W Devon Ave
3200W
33
W Rosemont Ave
N Kedzie Ave
N Troy St
N Albany Ave
N Whipple St
N Sacramento Ave
N Richmond St
N Fransisco Ave
N Mozart St
N Fairfield Ave
N Washtenaw Ave
N Talman Ave
N Rockwell St
N Artesian Ave
N Western Ave
N Claremont Ave
W Granville Ave
WEST ROGERS PARK
W Hood Ave
W Glenlake Ave
N California Ave
6000N
Green Briar Park
W Peterson Ave
Hollywood Park
Mather Park
W Thorndale Ave
ARCADIA TERRACE
N Jersey Ave
N Lincoln Ave
2800W
W Ardmore Ave
41
2400W
46
36
N Virginia Ave
PETERSON PARK
W Hollywood Ave
Rosehill Cemetery
N Maplewood Ave
N Campbell Ave
N Artisan Ave
5600N
N Fairfield Ave
W Bryn Mawr Ave
N Francisco Ave
N Washtenaw Ave
W Gregory St
Lincoln Avenue Motels
W Catalpa Ave
N Sawyer Ave
W Rascher Ave
BUDLONG WOODS
Legion Park
W Balmoral Ave
N Kedzie Ave
W Summerdale Ave
N Bowmanville
W Berwyn Ave
N Campbell Ave
W Farragut Ave
5200N
3200W
W Foster Ave
38
W Winona St
N Claremont Ave
W Carmen Ave
1/4 mile
.25 km

This quiet enclave snuggled between the Chicago River and Rosehill Cemetery is home to many Koreans, Middle Easterners, and Eastern Europeans. The seedy hotels on Lincoln Avenue, once reputable but known more recently as prostitution and drug pits, are one by one succumbing to eminent domain and falling prey to the wrecking ball. Hence, the neighborhood is becoming more desirable for young families priced out of Ravenswood and Andersonville.

Banks

- **Charter One** • 5650 N Lincoln Ave
- **Chase** • 5224 N Lincoln Ave
- **Chase (ATM)** • 3019 W Peterson Ave
- **Chase (ATM)** • 5627 N Lincoln Ave
- **First Commercial** • 2935 W Peterson Ave
- **TCF (ATM)** • 7-Eleven • 5562 N Lincoln Ave
- **Washington Mutual** • 5341 N Lincoln Ave

Gas Stations

- **BP** • 2751 W Peterson Ave
- **Citgo** • 5447 N Kedzie Ave
- **Citgo** • 5601 N Lincoln Ave
- **Marathon** • 2500 W Peterson Ave
- **Mobil** • 2758 W Peterson Ave

Landmarks

- **Lincoln Avenue Motels** • N Lincoln Ave b/w W Foster Ave & W Devon Ave

Libraries

- **Budlong Woods Public Library** • 5630 N Lincoln Ave

Pharmacies

- **Walgreens** • 5627 N Lincoln Ave

Pizza

- **T's Grand Slam Pizza** • 5701 N California Ave
- **Tel Aviv Kosher Pizza** • 6349 N California Ave

Police

- **20th District (Foster)** • 5400 N Lincoln Ave

Schools

- **Budlong Elementary** • 2701 W Foster Ave
- **DeWitt Clinton Elementary** • 6110 N Fairfield Ave
- **Eagles Wings Urban Academy** • 2447 W Granville Ave
- **Jewish Childrens Bureau** • 6014 N California Ave
- **Joan Dachs Bais Yaakov Elementary** • 3200 W Peterson Ave
- **Kiddie Kollege** • 6025 N California Ave
- **Little Harvard Academy** • 2708 W Peterson Ave
- **Lubavitch Girls High** • 2754 W Rosemont Ave
- **Minnie Mars Jamieson Elementary** • 5650 N Mozart St
- **NAES College** • 2838 W Paterson Ave
- **North Shore SDA Junior Academy** • 5220 N California Ave
- **Northside College Preparatory** • 5501 N Kedzie Ave
- **St Hilary Elementary** • 5614 N Fairfield Ave
- **St Philip Lutheran** • 2500 W Bryn Mawr Ave
- **Telshe Yeshiva Chicago** • 3535 W Foster Ave
- **Victor V Neumann Alternative** • 2447 W Granville Ave
- **Yeshivas Tiferes Tzvi** • 6122 N California Ave

Supermarkets

- **Aldi** • 6220 N California Ave
- **Dominick's** • 5233 N Lincoln Ave

W Arthur Ave
1
2
N McCormick Rd
6400N
N Maplewood Ave
N Campbell Ave
N Oakley Ave
W Devon Ave
3200W
33
W Rosemont Ave
N Kedzie Ave
N Troy St
N Albany Ave
N Whipple St
N Sacaramento Ave
N Richmond St
N Fransisco Ave
N Mozart St
N Fairfield Ave
N Washtenaw Ave
N Talman Ave
N Rockwell St
N Artesian Ave
N Western Ave
N Claremont Ave
A
W Granville Ave
WEST ROGERS PARK
W Hood Ave
W Glenlake Ave
N California Ave
6000N
Green Briar Park
W Peterson Ave
Hollywood Park
Mather Park
W Thorndale Ave
ARCADIA TERRACE
N Jersey Ave
N Lincoln Ave
2800W
W Ardmore Ave
41
2400W
B
46
36
N Virginia Ave
PETERSON PARK
W Hollywood Ave
N Fairfield Ave
N Maplewood Ave
N Campbell Ave
N Artisan Ave
Rosehill Cemetery
5600N
W Bryn Mawr Ave
N Francisco Ave
N Washtenaw Ave
W Gregory St
W Catalpa Ave
N Sawyer Ave
W Rascher Ave
BUDLONG WOODS
Legion Park
W Balmoral Ave
N Kedzie Ave
W Summerdale Ave
C
N Bowmanville
W Berwyn Ave
N Campbell Ave
W Farragut Ave
3200W
5200N
W Foster Ave
38
W Winona St
N Claremont Ave
W Carmen Ave
1/4 mile
.25 km

Of the bazillion tiny unassuming Korean, Japanese, and Middle Eastern storefront restaurants peppering Peterson and Lincoln Avenues, Fondue Stube and Katsu stand out, as does Café Orange for its tentative nod at hipness—an unspeakable pretension in these parts. Local couples drink at Hidden Cove or Emerald Isle. Charcoal Delights is rumored to have the best gyros this side of Greektown.

Coffee

- **Café Utjeha** • 5350 N Lincoln Ave
- **Dunkin' Donuts** • 5200 N Lincoln Ave
- **Dunkin' Donuts** • 5723 N California Ave
- **Starbucks** • 6075 N Lincoln Ave

Gyms

- **Curves (Women only)** • 5360 N Lincoln Ave

Liquor Stores

- **Buy Low Liquors** • 6015 N Lincoln Ave
- **Eden Liquor Store & Foods** • 5359 N Lincoln Ave
- **K&B Food & Liquor** • 6343 N California Ave

Nightlife

- **Emerald Isle** • 2537 W Peterson Ave
- **Hidden Cove** • 5338 N Lincoln Ave

Restaurants

- **Aztecas Mexican Taqueria** • 5421 N Lincoln Ave
- **Café Orange** • 5639 N Lincoln Ave
- **Charcoal Delights** • 3139 W Foster Ave
- **Fondue Stube** • 2717 W Peterson Ave
- **Garden Buffet** • 5347 N Lincoln Ave
- **IHOP** • 5929 N Lincoln Ave
- **Katsu** • 2651 W Peterson Ave
- **Pueblito Viejo** • 5429 N Lincoln Ave
- **Solga** • 5828 N Lincoln Ave
- **Tom Yum Thai & Japanese** • 3232 W Foster Ave
- **Wolfy's** • 2734 W Peterson Ave
- **Woo Chon** • 5744 N California Ave

Shopping

- **Grazer's Gourmet** • 5333 N Lincoln Ave

Video Rental

- **New York Video (Korean only)** • 5340 N Lincoln Ave
- **Tom Video** • 5806 N Lincoln Ave

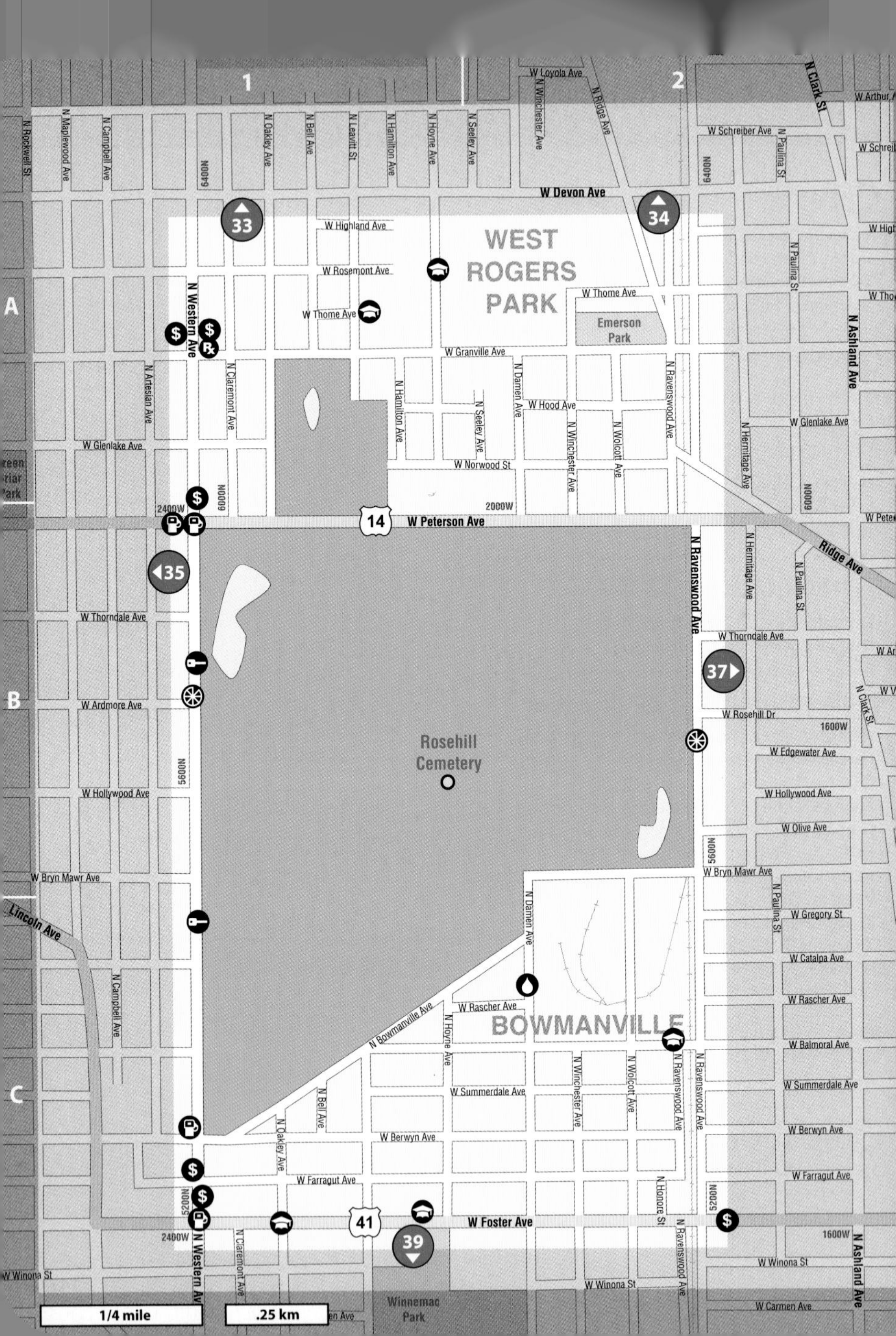

1
2
A
B
C
WEST ROGERS PARK
BOWMANVILLE
Rosehill Cemetery
Emerson Park
Winnemac Park
33
34
35
37
39
14
41
W Loyola Ave
W Devon Ave
W Highland Ave
W Rosemont Ave
W Thome Ave
W Granville Ave
W Hood Ave
W Glenlake Ave
W Norwood St
W Peterson Ave
W Thorndale Ave
W Ardmore Ave
W Rosehill Dr
W Edgewater Ave
W Hollywood Ave
W Olive Ave
W Bryn Mawr Ave
W Gregory St
W Catalpa Ave
W Rascher Ave
W Balmoral Ave
W Summerdale Ave
W Berwyn Ave
W Farragut Ave
W Foster Ave
W Winona St
W Carmen Ave
W Schreiber Ave
W Arthur Ave
N Rockwell St
N Maplewood Ave
N Campbell Ave
N Western Ave
N Artesian Ave
N Claremont Ave
N Oakley Ave
N Bell Ave
N Leavitt St
N Hamilton Ave
N Hoyne Ave
N Seeley Ave
N Winchester Ave
N Damen Ave
N Wolcott Ave
N Ravenswood Ave
N Honore St
N Hermitage Ave
N Paulina St
N Ashland Ave
N Clark St
N Ridge Ave
Ridge Ave
Lincoln Ave
N Bowmanville Ave
2400W
2000W
1600W
6400N
6000N
5900N
5600N
5200N
1/4 mile
.25 km

Montgomery Ward, Richard Sears, Oscar Mayer, several Chicago mayors, and one Vice President (Charles Gates Dawes) are interred in Rosehill, Chicago's largest cemetery. At 350 acres, it barely leaves room in the neighborhood for the car dealerships along Western Avenue or the burgeoning artistic vibe of Damen Avenue.

Banks

- **Chase** • 6210 N Western Ave
- **Chase (ATM)** • 6236 N Western Ave
- **North Community** • 5241 N Western Ave
- **TCF (ATM)** • 7-Eleven • 1750 W Foster Ave
- **TCF (ATM)** • 7-Eleven • 5206 N Western Ave
- **TCF (ATM)** • 7-Eleven • 6001 N Western Ave

Car Washes

- **Norwood 2 Hand Carwash** • 5462 N Damen Ave

Car Rental

- **Enterprise** • 5844 N Western Ave • 773-989-3390
- **Hertz** • 5534 N Western Ave • 773-506-2125

Gas Stations

- **Citgo** • 1840 W Peterson Ave
- **Citgo** • 5300 N Western Ave
- **Shell** • 5201 N Western Ave
- **Shell** • 6000 N Western Ave

Landmarks

- **Rosehill Cemetery and Mausoleum** • 5800 N Ravenswood Ave

Pharmacies

- **Walgreens** • 6236 N Western Ave

Pizza

- **Delisi's Pizzeria** • 5806 N Western Ave
- **Fireside Restaurant & Lounge** • 5739 N Ravenswood Ave

Schools

- **Eliza Chappell Elementary** • 2135 W Foster Ave
- **Northside Catholic Academy** • 6325 N Hoyne Ave
- **Pedia Learning Center** • 2300 W Foster Ave
- **Rogers Park Montessori** • 1800 W Balmoral Ave
- **Stone Scholastic Academy** • 6239 N Leavitt St

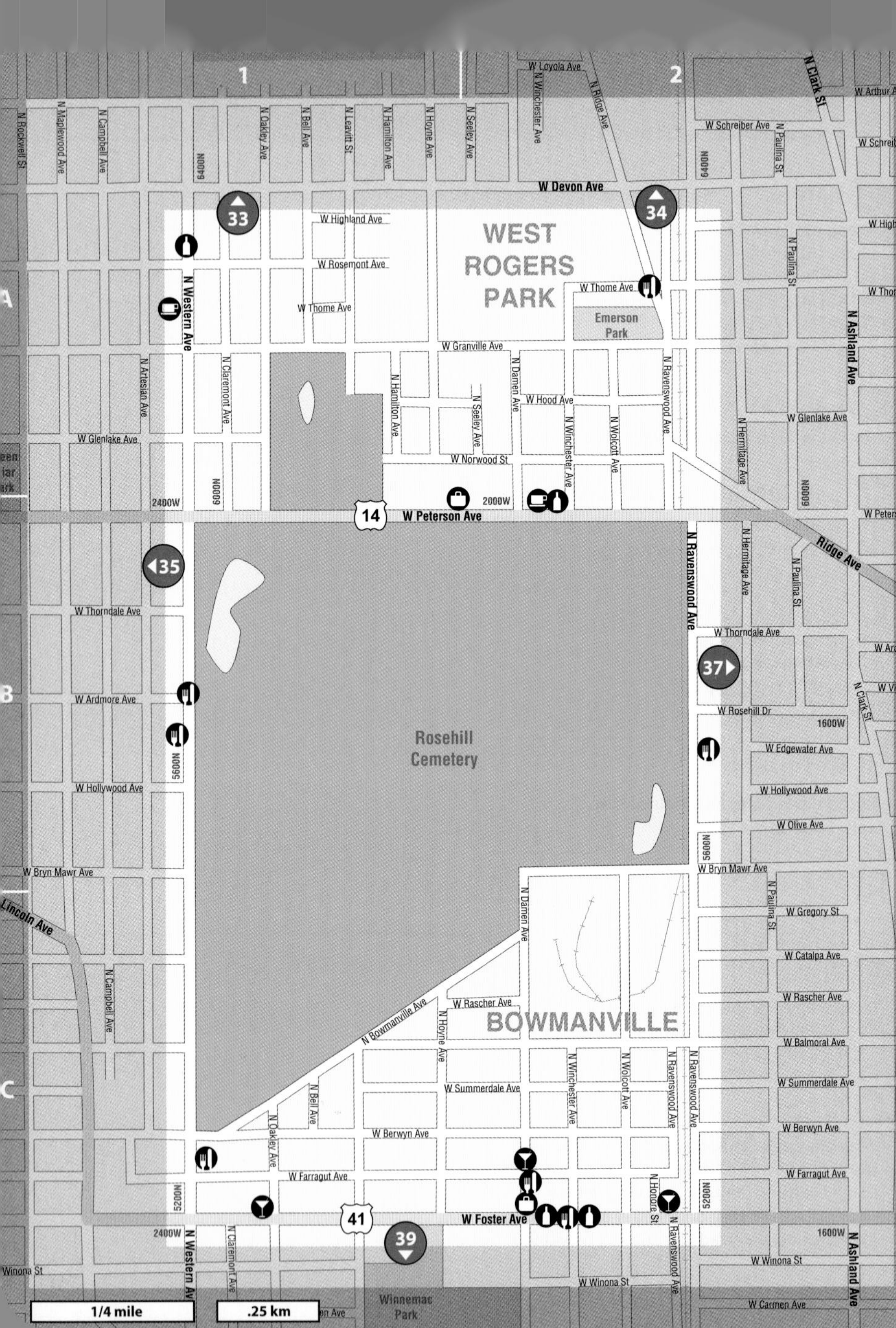

1
2
W Loyola Ave
N Winchester Ave
N Ridge Ave
N Clark St
W Arthur Ave
W Schreiber Ave
N Paulina St
N Rockwell St
N Maplewood Ave
N Campbell Ave
6400N
N Oakley Ave
N Bell Ave
N Leavitt St
N Hamilton Ave
N Hoyne Ave
N Seeley Ave
W Devon Ave
33
34
W Highland Ave
WEST
ROGERS
PARK
W Rosemont Ave
W Thome Ave
N Western Ave
Emerson
Park
W Granville Ave
N Artesian Ave
N Claremont Ave
N Damen Ave
N Ravenswood Ave
N Ashland Ave
W Hood Ave
N Wolcott Ave
W Glenlake Ave
N Hermitage Ave
W Norwood St
6000N
2400W
2000W
14
W Peterson Ave
Ridge Ave
35
W Thorndale Ave
37
W Ardmore Ave
W Rosehill Dr
1600W
Rosehill
Cemetery
W Edgewater Ave
5600N
W Hollywood Ave
W Olive Ave
W Bryn Mawr Ave
Lincoln Ave
W Gregory St
W Catalpa Ave
W Rascher Ave
N Bowmanville Ave
BOWMANVILLE
W Balmoral Ave
W Summerdale Ave
W Berwyn Ave
W Farragut Ave
5200N
41
W Foster Ave
N Honore St
39
W Winona St
Winona St
Winnemac
Park
W Carmen Ave
1/4 mile
.25 km

The area that circles Rosehill Cemetery is largely residential with a sprinkling of great restaurants and dive bars. While Fireside is a favorite for pizza, catfish and ribs, when craving Korean barbecue, San Soo Gab San is the place. Keep an eye on Leadway—it seems to be leading the pack in terms of interesting nightspots in the neighborhood.

Coffee

- **Dunkin' Donuts** • 1954 W Peterson Ave
- **Dunkin' Donuts** • 6254 N Western Ave

Liquor Stores

- **A&B Grocery & Liquors** • 6320 N Western Ave
- **Diala Grocery & Liquor** • 1935 W Foster Ave
- **Foster Food & Liquor** • 1900 W Foster Ave
- **L&M Food & Liquor** • 1968 W Peterson Ave

Nightlife

- **Big Joe's 2 & 6 Pub** • 1818 W Foster Ave
- **Claddagh Ring** • 2306 W Foster Ave
- **K's Dugout** • 1930 W Foster Ave
- **Leadway Bar & Café** • 5233 N Damen Ave

Restaurants

- **Delisi's Pizzeria** • 5806 N Western Ave
- **Fireside Restaurant & Lounge** • 5739 N Ravenswood Ave
- **Greenhouse Inn** • 6300 N Ridge Ave
- **Max's Italian Beef** • 5754 N Western Ave
- **San Soo Gab San** • 5247 N Western Ave
- **Yes Thai** • 5211 N Damen Ave

Shopping

- **Easy Street** • 5206 N Damen Ave
- **Target** • 2036 W Peterson Ave

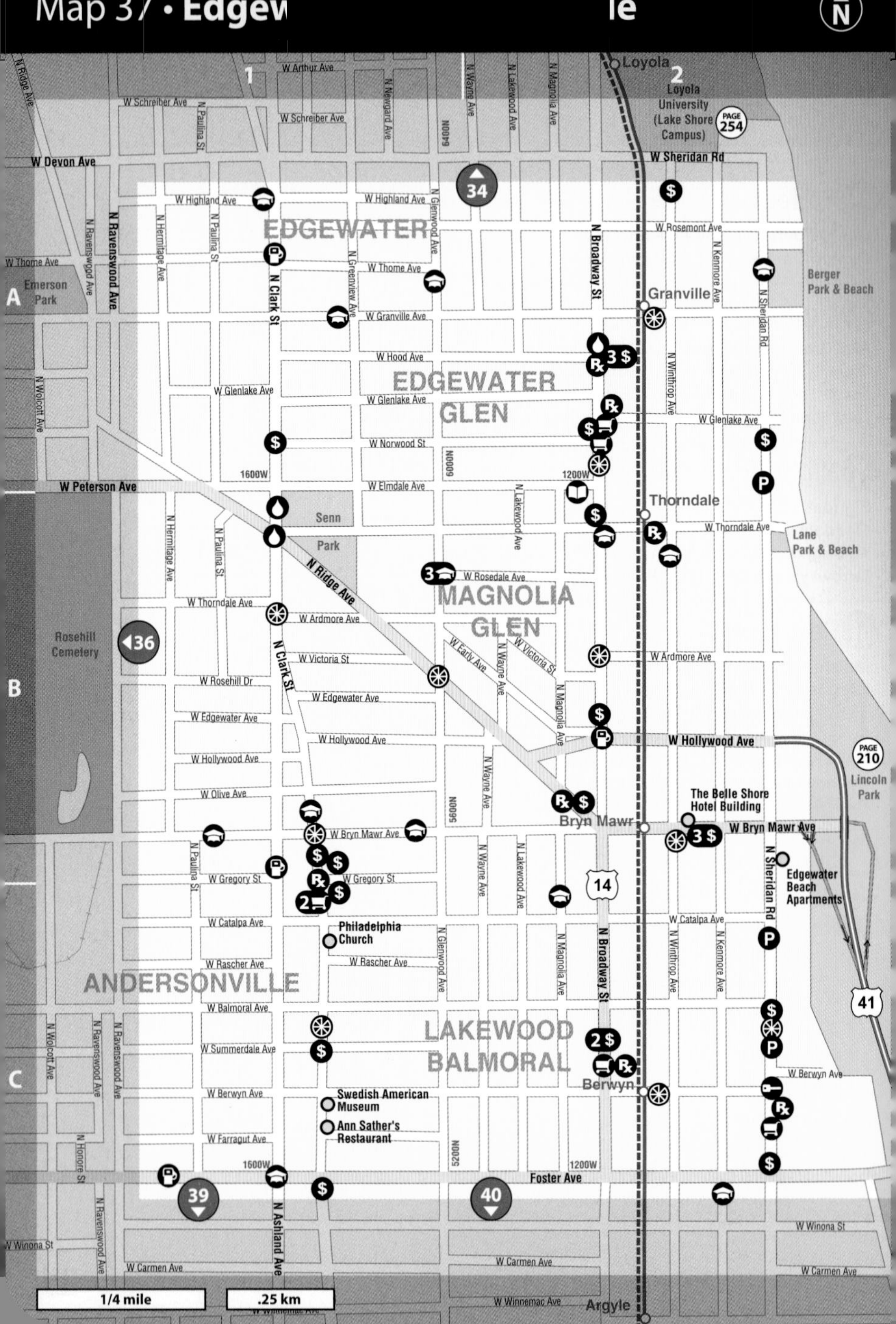
Loyola University (Lake Shore Campus)
PAGE 254
Berger Park & Beach
Emerson Park
EDGEWATER
EDGEWATER GLEN
Senn Park
Lane Park & Beach
MAGNOLIA GLEN
Rosehill Cemetery
The Belle Shore Hotel Building
PAGE 210
Lincoln Park
Edgewater Beach Apartments
Philadelphia Church
ANDERSONVILLE
LAKEWOOD BALMORAL
Swedish American Museum
Ann Sather's Restaurant
Loyola
Granville
Thorndale
Bryn Mawr
Berwyn
Argyle
W Devon Ave
W Sheridan Rd
W Peterson Ave
W Hollywood Ave
W Bryn Mawr Ave
Foster Ave
N Clark St
N Broadway St
N Sheridan Rd
N Ridge Ave
N Ashland Ave
N Ravenswood Ave
1/4 mile
.25 km

A range of housing types and small businesses (neighborhood groups start grumbling whenever the chains come knocking), along with cultural diversity, make Andersonville and Edgewater bastions for so-called "lakefront liberals." Besides beautiful residential areas and stroll-friendly commercial districts, Edgewater boasts the city's gay beach at Hollywood and the lakefront, not to mention the "lesbian Jewel."

Banks

- **Bridgeview** • 1058 W Bryn Mawr Ave
- **Bridgeview** • 5345 N Sheridan Rd
- **Bridgeview** • 6041 N Clark St
- **Broadway** • 5960 N Broadway St
- **Chase** • 1055 W Bryn Mawr Ave
- **Chase** • 6009 N Broadway St
- **Chase (ATM)** • 1036 W Bryn Mawr Ave
- **Chase (ATM)** • 5625 N Ridge Ave
- **Chase (ATM)** • 6125 N Broadway St
- **Chase (ATM)** • 6333 N Winthrop Ave
- **First Commercial** • 6033 N Sheridan Rd
- **Harris Trust & Savings (ATM)** • 6125 N Broadway St
- **North Community** • 5342 N Broadway St
- **North Side Federal Savings** • 5159 N Clark St
- **TCF** • 5343 N Broadway St
- **TCF** • 5516 N Clark St
- **TCF (ATM)** • 7-Eleven• 5623 N Clark St
- **TCF (ATM)** • Osco• 6150 N Broadway St
- **US** • 5340 N Clark St
- **Washington Mutual** • 5200 N Sheridan Rd
- **Washington Mutual** • 5531 N Clark St
- **Washington Mutual** • 5725 N Broadway St

Car Washes

- **Snappy Hand Car Wash** • 5961 N Ridge Ave
- **Super Spray Car Wash** • 5970 N Clark St
- **Superior Hand Car Wash** • 6147 N Broadway St

Car Rental

- **Enterprise** • 5313 N Sheridan Rd • 773-271-4500

Gas Stations

- **Clark Oil** • 1745 W Foster Ave
- **Marathon** • 5550 N Ashland Ave
- **Marathon** • 6262 N Clark St
- **Shell** • 5701 N Broadway St

Landmarks

- **Ann Sather's Restaurant** • 5207 N Clark St
- **The Belle Shore Hotel Building** • 1062 W Bryn Mawr Ave
- **Edgewater Beach Apartments** • 5555 N Sheridan Rd
- **Philadelphia Church** • 5437 N Clark St
- **Swedish American Museum** • 5211 N Clark St

Libraries

- **Edgewater Public Library** • 1210 W Elmdale Ave

Pharmacies

- **Dominick's** • 5235 N Sheridan Rd
- **Jewel-Osco** • 5345 N Broadway St
- **Jewel-Osco** • 5516 N Clark St
- **Osco Drug** • 6150 N Broadway St
- **Walgreens** • 5625 N Ridge Ave
- **Walgreens** • 6125 N Broadway St

Pizza

- **Barry's Spot Pizza** • 5759 N Broadway St
- **Calo Pizzeria Restaurant** • 5343 N Clark St
- **Dominick's Finer Foods** • 6009 N Broadway St
- **Domino's** • 5912 N Clark St
- **Franko's Pizza Express** • 1109 W Bryn Mawr Ave
- **Gino's North Pizzeria** • 1111 W Granville Ave
- **Pizza Mania** • 5777 N Ridge Ave
- **Pizzeria Aroma** • 1125 W Berwyn Ave
- **Primo Pizza** • 5600 N Clark St
- **Tedino's** • 5335 N Sheridan Rd

Schools

- **Helen C Peirce School of International Studies** • 1423 W Bryn Mawr Ave
- **Hyman G Rickover Navy Academy** • 5900 N Glenwood Ave
- **Jose J Marti Elementary** • 5126 N Kenmore Ave
- **Lake Shore** • 5611 N Clark St
- **Northside Catholic Academy** • 5525 N Magnolia Ave
- **Northside Catholic Academy (St Gertrude Campus)** • 6214 N Glenwood Ave
- **Rogers Park Montessori (Thorndale)** • 1244 W Thorndale Ave
- **Sacred Heart** • 6250 N Sheridan Rd
- **Senn High** • 5900 N Glenwood Ave
- **St Gregory High** • 1677 W Bryn Mawr Ave
- **Stephen K Hayt Elementary** • 1518 W Granville Ave
- **Swift Elementary** • 5900 N Winthrop Ave
- **Trumbull Elementary** • 5200 N Ashland Ave
- **William E Rodriguez Academic Preparatory** • 5900 N Glenwood Ave

Supermarkets

- **DelRay Farms** • 5205 N Broadway St
- **Dominick's** • 5235 N Sheridan Rd
- **Dominick's** • 6009 N Broadway St
- **Edgewater Produce** • 5515 N Clark St
- **Jewel-Osco** • 5343 N Broadway St
- **Jewel-Osco** • 5516 N Clark St
- **True Nature Foods Community Market** • 6034 N Broadway St

Parking

1
2
EDGEWATER
EDGEWATER GLEN
MAGNOLIA GLEN
ANDERSONVILLE
LAKEWOOD BALMORAL
Loyola
Loyola University (Lake Shore Campus)
PAGE 254
Granville
Thorndale
Bryn Mawr
Berwyn
Argyle
Berger Park & Beach
Lane Park & Beach
PAGE 210
Lincoln Park
Emerson Park
Senn Park
Rosehill Cemetery
34
36
39
40
14
41
W Arthur Ave
W Schreiber Ave
W Devon Ave
W Sheridan Rd
W Highland Ave
W Rosemont Ave
W Thome Ave
W Granville Ave
W Hood Ave
W Glenlake Ave
W Norwood St
W Peterson Ave
W Elmdale Ave
W Thorndale Ave
W Rosedale Ave
W Ardmore Ave
W Victoria St
W Early Ave
W Rosehill Dr
W Edgewater Ave
W Hollywood Ave
W Olive Ave
W Bryn Mawr Ave
W Gregory St
W Catalpa Ave
W Rascher Ave
W Balmoral Ave
W Summerdale Ave
W Berwyn Ave
W Farragut Ave
Foster Ave
W Winona St
W Carmen Ave
W Winnemac Ave
N Ridge Ave
N Ravenswood Ave
N Hermitage Ave
N Paulina St
N Clark St
N Greenview Ave
N Newgard Ave
N Glenwood Ave
N Wayne Ave
N Lakewood Ave
N Magnolia Ave
N Broadway St
N Winthrop Ave
N Kenmore Ave
N Sheridan Rd
N Wolcott Ave
N Honore St
N Ashland Ave
6400N
6000N
5600N
5200N
1600W
1200W
1/4 mile
.25 km

Andersonville is arguably the most pleasant neighborhood in Chicago to pass a weekend afternoon. Bruncher's gobble up amazing chilaquiles at Angel's, or gorge on 5-egg omelets at Pauline's, followed by casual shopping at the many independently-owned shops lining Clark Street. Refuel at Kopi, a crunchy café with a laidback vibe, before catching a film at arty/indie Chicago Filmmakers. La Tache, Andie's, Ras Dashen, and Jin Ju are some among the many notable neighborhood dining options.

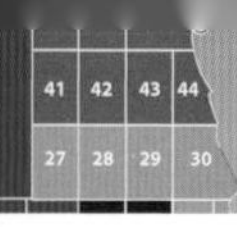

Coffee

- **A Taste of Heaven** • 5401 N Clark St
- **Café Du Monde** • 1147 W Granville Ave
- **Coffee Chicago** • 5256 N Broadway St
- **Dunkin' Donuts** • 1127 W Bryn Mawr Ave
- **Dunkin' Donuts** • 6250 N Clark St
- **Dunkin' Donuts** • 6332 N Broadway St
- **Einstein Bros Bagels** • 5318 N Clark St
- **Kopi, A Traveler's Café** • 5317 N Clark St
- **Metropolis Coffee Co** • 1039 W Granville Ave
- **Pause** • 1107 W Berwyn Ave
- **Peacock Café** • 6014 N Broadway St
- **Starbucks** • 1070 W Bryn Mawr Ave
- **Starbucks** • 5300 N Clark St
- **Starbucks** • Dominick's • 6009 N Broadway St

Copy Shops

- **The UPS Store** • 1055 W Bryn Mawr Ave
- **The UPS Store** • 5315 N Clark St

Farmer's Markets

- **Edgewater (Jun–Oct; Sat, 7 am–2 pm)** • N Broadway St & W Thorndale Ave

Gyms

- **Cheetah Gym** • 5248 N Clark St
- **Cheetah Gym** • 5838 N Broadway St
- **Curves (women only)** • 5339 N Sheridan Rd
- **Curves (women only)** • 6118 N Broadway St

Hardware Stores

- **Cas Hardware Store** • 5305 N Clark St
- **Clarendon Electric & Hardware** • 6050 N Broadway St
- **Marx Ace Hardware** • 5820 N Clark St

Liquor Stores

- **Buy Low Liquors** • 5201 N Clark St
- **Castle Wines & Spirits** • 1128 W Thorndale Ave
- **Granville Liquors** • 1100 W Granville Ave
- **In Fine Spirits** • 5418 N Clark St
- **M&D Food Liquors** • 5652 N Clark St
- **Sun Liquors** • 1101 W Granville Ave

Movie Theaters

- **Chicago Filmmakers** • 5243 N Clark St

Nightlife

- **@tmosphere** • 5355 N Clark St
- **Charlie's Ale House** • 5308 N Clark St
- **Edgewater Lounge** • 5600 N Ashland Ave
- **Farraguts Tavern** • 5240 N Clark St
- **Granville Anvil** • 1137 Granville Ave
- **Joie de Vine** • 1744 W Balmoral Ave
- **Madrigals** • 5316 N Clark St
- **Marty's Wine and Martini Bar** • 1511 W Balmoral Ave
- **Moody's Pub** • 5910 N Broadway St
- **Ole St Andrew's Inn** • 5938 N Broadway St
- **Ollie's** • 1064 W Berwyn Ave
- **Simon's** • 5210 N Clark St
- **StarGaze** • 5419 N Clark St

Pet Shops

- **FIDO Food Fair** • 5416 N Clark St
- **Parkview Pet Supplies** • 5358 N Broadway St
- **Ruff N'Stuff Dog Obedience** • 5430 N Clark St
- **Scrub-A-Dub Dub** • 1478 W Summerdale Ave

Restaurants

- **Adria Mare** • 5401 N Broadway St
- **Alice and Friends Vegetarian Café** • 5812 N Broadway St
- **Andie's** • 5253 N Clark St
- **Angel's** • 5403 N Clark St
- **Ann Sather** • 5207 N Clark St
- **Col-Ubas Steak House** • 5665 N Clark St
- **Corner Grille** • 5200 N Clark St
- **Ethiopian Diamond** • 6120 N Broadway St
- **Francesca's Bryn Mawr** • 1039 W Bryn Mawr Ave
- **Huey's Hot Dogs** • 1507 W Balmoral Ave
- **Indie Café** • 5951 N Broadway St
- **Jin Ju** • 5203 N Clark St
- **La Fonda Latino** • 5350 N Broadway St
- **La Tache** • 1475 W Balmoral Ave
- **M Henry** • 5707 N Clark St
- **Moody's Pub** • 5910 N Broadway St
- **Pasteur** • 5525 N Broadway St
- **Patio Beef** • 6022 N Broadway St
- **Pauline's** • 1754 W Balmoral Ave
- **Reza's** • 5255 N Clark St
- **RAS Dashen Ethiopian Restaurant** • 5846 N Broadway St
- **Standee's** • 1133 W Granville Ave
- **Sushi Luxe** • 5204 N Clark St
- **Svea** • 5236 N Clark St
- **Swedish Bakery** • 5348 N Clark St
- **Sweet Occasions and more** • 5306 N Clark St
- **Tanoshii** • 5547 N Clark St
- **Taste of Lebanon** • 1509 W Foster Ave
- **Tomboy** • 5402 N Clark St
- **Wickstrom's Swedish Deli** • 5247 N Clark St

Shopping

- **Alamo Shoes** • 5321 N Clark St
- **Alchemy Arts** • 1203 W Bryn Mawr Ave
- **Blue Hydrangea** • 1113 W Berwyn Ave
- **Bon Bon** • 5410 N Clark St
- **Broadway Antique Market** • 6130 N Broadway St
- **Brown Elephant** • 5404 N Clark St
- **Cassona** • 5241 N Clark St
- **Early to Bed** • 5232 N Sheridan Rd
- **Edgewater Antique Mall** • 6314 N Broadway St
- **Elda de la Rosa** • 5555 N Sheridan Rd
- **Erickson Jewelers** • 5304 N Clark St
- **Gethsemane Garden Center** • 5739 N Clark St
- **Johnny Sprocket's** • 1052 W Bryn Mawr Ave
- **Kate the Great Bookstore** • 5550 N Broadway St
- **Middle East Bakery** • 1512 W Foster Ave
- **Paper Trail** • 5309 N Clark St
- **Presence** • 5216 N Clark St
- **Scout** • 5221 N Clark St
- **Soothe Your Senses Day Spa** • 6260 N Broadway St
- **Surrender** • 5225 N Clark St
- **Toys & Treasures** • 5311 N Clark St
- **Tulip Toy Gallery** • 1480 W Berwyn Ave
- **White Attic** • 5408 N Clark St
- **Wikstrom's Scandinavian Foods and Gifts** • 5247 N Clark St
- **Women & Children First** • 5233 N Clark St

Video Rental

- **6206 Video** • 6206 N Broadway St
- **BJ Video** • 5552 N Broadway St
- **Blockbuster** • 5300 N Broadway St
- **Diamond Grocery & Video (Indian)** • 6322 N Broadway St
- **Hollywood Video** • 6201 N Clark St
- **Lion Video** • 5218 N Sheridan Rd
- **Mina's TV and Video** • 6137 N Clark St
- **National Video** • 1108 W Granville Ave
- **Select Video** • 5358 N Clark St
- **Specialty Video** • 5307 N Clark St
- **Video Town** • 1127 W Thorndale Ave

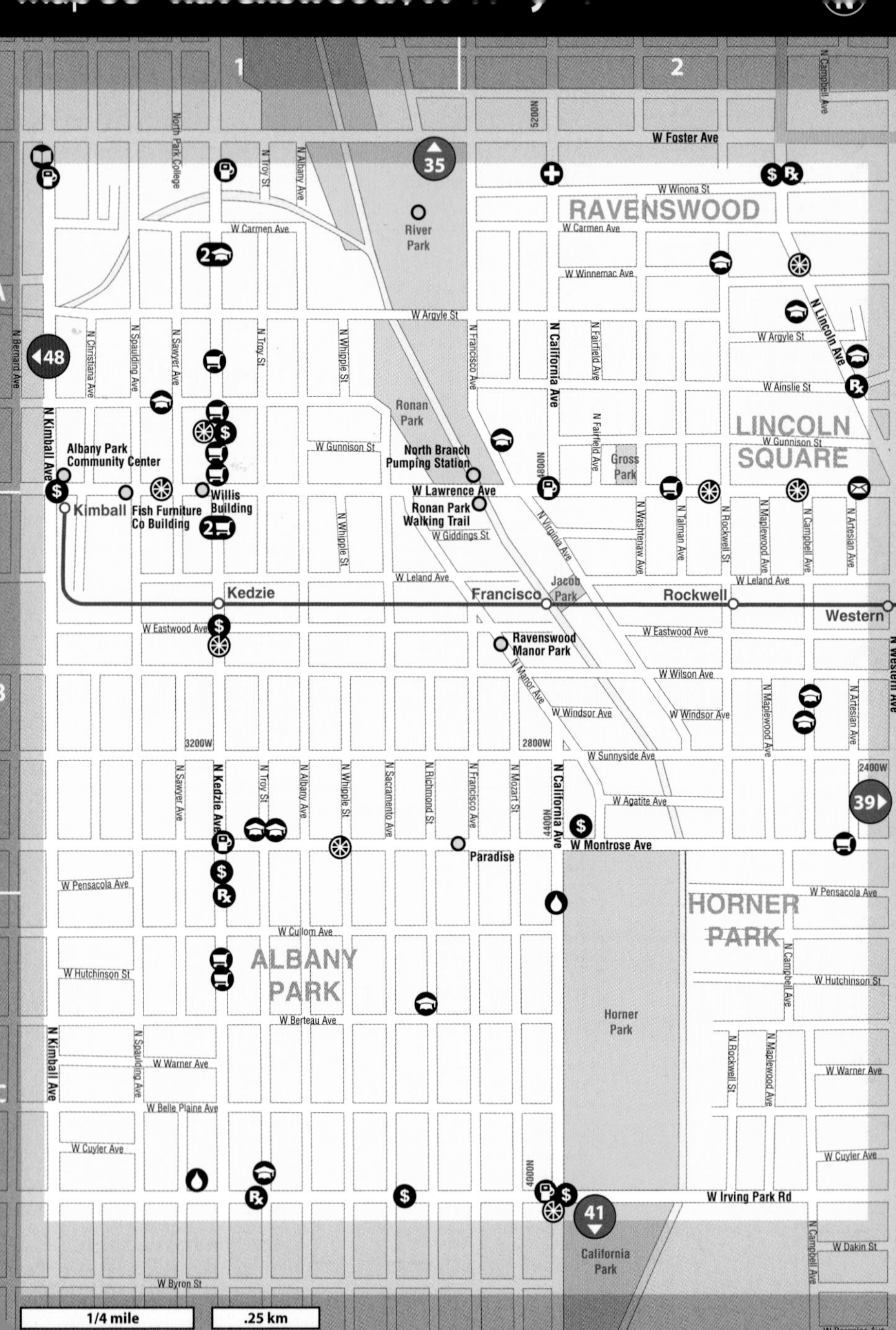
1
2
A
B
C
35
48
39
41
RAVENSWOOD
LINCOLN SQUARE
HORNER PARK
ALBANY PARK
W Foster Ave
W Winona St
W Carmen Ave
W Winnemac Ave
W Argyle St
W Ainslie St
W Gunnison St
W Lawrence Ave
W Giddings St
W Leland Ave
W Eastwood Ave
W Wilson Ave
W Windsor Ave
W Sunnyside Ave
W Agatite Ave
W Montrose Ave
W Pensacola Ave
W Cullom Ave
W Hutchinson St
W Berteau Ave
W Warner Ave
W Belle Plaine Ave
W Cuyler Ave
W Irving Park Rd
W Dakin St
W Byron St
W Berenice Ave
N Campbell Ave
N Bernard Ave
N Kimball Ave
N Christiana Ave
N Spaulding Ave
N Sawyer Ave
N Troy St
N Albany Ave
N Whipple St
N Francisco Ave
N California Ave
N Fairfield Ave
N Lincoln Ave
N Virginia Ave
N Washtenaw Ave
N Talman Ave
N Rockwell St
N Maplewood Ave
N Artesian Ave
N Western Ave
N Manor Ave
N Kedzie Ave
N Sacramento Ave
N Richmond St
N Mozart St
North Park College
5200N
4800N
4400N
4000N
3200W
2800W
2400W
River Park
Ronan Park
Gross Park
Jacob Park
Horner Park
California Park
Albany Park Community Center
Kimball
Fish Furniture Co Building
Willis Building
North Branch Pumping Station
Ronan Park Walking Trail
Ravenswood Manor Park
Paradise
Kedzie
Francisco
Rockwell
Western
1/4 mile
.25 km

Within the Ravenswood neighborhood is The Manor, a small area of about a quarter of a mile that packs a lot of power and wealth. Generations of Chicago's elite live in this haven next to the river, where owls nest in trees and boat owners have private docks. Further west, Albany Park is one of the hottest spots for new condo conversions in the city. Urban pioneers enjoy lots of space and a plethora of excellent ethnic shops and restaurants.

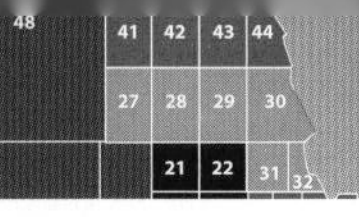

Banks

- **Albany** • 3400 W Lawrence Ave
- **Charter One** • 2752 W Montrose Ave
- **Chase** • 2959 W Irving Park Rd
- **Chase** • 4843 N Kedzie Ave
- **Chase (ATM)** • 4343 N Kedzie Ave
- **Citibank (ATM)** • 4635 N Kedzie Ave
- **TCF (ATM)** • 7-Eleven• 2800A W Irving Park Rd
- **TCF (ATM)** • Osco• 5158 N Lincoln Ave

Car Washes

- **Minute Man Car Wash** • 3218 W Irving Park Rd
- **Ruby Hand Car Wash** • 4334 N California Ave

Gas Stations

- **BP** • 2800 W Lawrence Ave
- **BP** • 3201 W Montrose Ave
- **Citgo** • 2816 W Irving Park Rd
- **Shell** • 5155 N Kimball Ave

Emergency Rooms

- **Swedish Covenant** • 5145 N California Ave

Landmarks

- **Albany Park Community Center** • 3401 W Ainslie St
- **Fish Furniture Co Building** • 3322 W Lawrence Ave
- **North Branch Pumping Station** • Lawrence Ave & the Chicago River
- **Paradise** • 2916 W Montrose Ave
- **Ravenswood Manor Park** • 4626 N Manor Ave
- **River Park** • 5100 N Francisco Ave
- **Ronan Park Walking Trail** • 3000 W Argyle St
- **Willis Building** • 3221 W Lawrence Ave

Libraries

- **Albany Park Public Library** • 5150 N Kimball Ave

Pharmacies

- **Osco Drug** • 5158 N Lincoln Ave
- **Walgreens** • 3153 W Irving Park Rd
- **Walgreens** • 4343 N Kedzie Ave
- **Walgreens** • 4801 N Lincoln Ave

Pizza

- **Angelo's Pizza & Restaurant** • 3026 W Montrose Ave
- **Boomer's** • 5035 N Lincoln Ave
- **Bravo International Pizzaria** • 3256 W Lawrence Ave
- **Golden Crust Pizzeria** • 4620 N Kedzie Ave
- **Little Caesars Pizza** • 2501 W Lawrence Ave
- **Noli's Pizza** • 4839 N Kedzie Ave
- **Papa Giorgio's** • 2604 W Lawrence Ave
- **Shamino's Pizza** • 2800 W Irving Park Rd

Post Offices

- **US Post Office** • 2522 W Lawrence Ave

Schools

- **Albany Park Multicultural Academy** • 5039 N Kimball Ave
- **Gateway to Learning** • 4925 N Lincoln Ave
- **Lawrence Hall Youth Services** • 4833 N Francisco Ave
- **Little Fox Day** • 5014 N Lincoln Ave
- **Newton Bateman Elementary** • 4220 N Richmond St
- **North Park University** • 3225 W Foster Ave
- **North River Elementary** • 4416 N Troy St
- **Our Lady of Mercy** • 4416 N Troy St
- **Thomas J Waters Fine Arts Elementary** • 4540 N Campbell Ave
- **Transfiguration** • 5044 N Rockwell St
- **Von Steuben Metropolitan Science Center** • 5039 N Kimball Ave
- **William G Hibbard Elementary** • 3244 W Ainslie St

Supermarkets

- **Al-Khayyam Bakery and Market** • 4738 N Kedzie Ave
- **Aldi** • 2431 W Montrose Ave
- **Andy's Fruit Ranch** • 4733 N Kedzie Ave
- **Cermak Produce** • 4234 N Kedzie Ave
- **Clark Market** • 4853 N Kedzie Ave
- **Harvestime Foods** • 2632 W Lawrence Ave
- **Holy Land Grocery** • 4806 N Kedzie Ave
- **Peter Grocery** • 4947 N Kedzie Ave
- **Sahar Meat Market** • Albany Plz Mall• 4829 N Kedzie Ave

RAVENSWOOD
LINCOLN SQUARE
HORNER PARK
ALBANY PARK
River Park
Ronan Park
Gross Park
Jacob Park
Horner Park
California Park
Kimball
Kedzie
Francisco
Rockwell
Western
W Foster Ave
W Winona St
W Carmen Ave
W Winnemac Ave
W Argyle St
W Ainslie St
W Gunnison St
W Lawrence Ave
W Giddings St
W Leland Ave
W Eastwood Ave
W Wilson Ave
W Windsor Ave
W Sunnyside Ave
W Agatite Ave
W Montrose Ave
W Pensacola Ave
W Cullom Ave
W Hutchinson St
W Berteau Ave
W Warner Ave
W Belle Plaine Ave
W Cuyler Ave
W Irving Park Rd
W Dakin St
W Byron St
W Berenice Ave
N Kimball Ave
N Bernard Ave
N Christiana Ave
N Spaulding Ave
N Sawyer Ave
N Kedzie Ave
N Troy St
N Albany Ave
N Whipple St
N Sacramento Ave
N Richmond St
N Francisco Ave
N Mozart St
N California Ave
N Fairfield Ave
N Washtenaw Ave
N Talman Ave
N Rockwell St
N Maplewood Ave
N Campbell Ave
N Artesian Ave
N Western Ave
N Lincoln Ave
N Virginia Ave
N Manor Ave
North Park College
5200N
4800N
4400N
4000N
3200W
2800W
2400W
1/4 mile
.25 km

The area around the Rockwell L stop is an arty outpost of friendly cafes and small businesses. Further west, North Kedzie around Lawrence Avenue is chockablock with Middle Eastern restaurants, groceries, and halal meat. Perhaps it's the Muslim influence: despite a lively dining scene, this area is in desperate need of a few friendly local watering holes.

Coffee

- **Beans & Bagels** • 2601 W Leland Ave
- **Chicago Espresso Co** • 4645 N Kedzie Ave
- **Coffee Liberte** • 4807 N Spaulding Ave
- **Donut Doctor** • 3342 W Lawrence Ave
- **Dunkin' Donuts** • 3101 W Irving Park Rd
- **Dunkin' Donuts** • 4821 N Kedzie Ave
- **Jaafer Sweets** • Albany Plz Mall • 4825 N Kedzie Ave
- **Merle's Coffee House** • 4642 N Francisco Ave
- **Olympic Club** • 2615 W Lawrence Ave
- **Starbucks** • 4558 N Kedzie Ave

Copy Shops

- **Shree Printing Corporation** • 3011 W Irving Park Rd

Farmer's Markets

- **Chicago World Market (Sun, 10 am–3 pm)** • 4540 N Campbell Ave

Gyms

- **Curves (women only)** • 4953 N Kedzie Ave
- **Women's Workout World (women only)** • 2540 W Lawrence Ave

Hardware Stores

- **Ace Hardware** • 4874 N Lincoln Ave
- **Jay's Hardware** • 4608 N Kedzie Ave

Liquor Stores

- **Buy Low Liquor Store** • 3360 W Montrose Ave
- **Cardinal Wine & Spirits** • 4905 N Lincoln Ave
- **Food & Liquors Express** • 2752 W Lawrence Ave
- **Foremost Liquor Store** • 4616 N Kedzie Ave
- **J&A Liquors** • 3213 W Lawrence Ave
- **Jerusalem Liquors** • 3133 W Lawrence Ave
- **Peacock Liquors** • 3056 W Montrose Ave
- **Prestige Liquors** • 3210 W Montrose Ave
- **Quick Stop** • 2901 W Irving Park Rd

Nightlife

- **Brisku's Bistro** • 4100 N Kedzie Ave
- **Lincoln Square Lanes** • 4874 N Lincoln Ave
- **Lost & Found** • 3058 W Irving Park Rd
- **Montrose Saloon** • 2933 W Montrose Ave
- **Peek Inn** • 2825 W Irving Park Rd
- **Skadarlija** • 4024 N Kedzie Ave

Pet Shops

- **Ruff Haus Pets** • 4652 N Rockwell St

Restaurants

- **Al-Khaymeih** • 4742 N Kedzie Ave
- **Arun's** • 4156 N Kedzie Ave
- **Brasa Roja** • 3125 W Montrose Ave
- **Café Restaurant Art** • 4658 N Rockwell St
- **City Noor Kebab** • 4714 N Kedzie Ave
- **Cousin's IV (Incredible Vitality)** • 3038 W Irving Park Rd
- **Dharma Garden Thai Restaurants** • 3111 W Irving Park Rd
- **Golden Crust Italian Pizzeria** • 4620 N Kedzie Ave
- **Great Sea Chinese Restaurants** • 3254 W Lawrence Ave
- **Han Bat** • 2723 W Lawrence Ave
- **Huddle House** • 4748 N Kimball Ave
- **Jimmy's Fast Food** • 4810 N Drake Ave
- **Kang Nam** • 4849 N Kedzie Ave
- **Kitchen Chicago** • 4664 N Manor Ave
- **Lutz Continental Café** • 2458 W Montrose Ave
- **Manzo's Ristorante** • 3210 W Irving Park Rd
- **Mi Rancho / Angelo's** • 3026 W Montrose Ave
- **Noon O Kabab** • 4661 N Kedzie Ave
- **Paradise Japanese** • 2916 W Montrose Ave
- **Penguin** • 2723 W Lawrence Ave
- **Rockwell's Neighborhood Grill** • 4632 N Rockwell St
- **Sahar Pita** • 4835 N Kedzie Ave
- **Salam** • 4636 N Kedzie Ave
- **Santa Rita Taqueria** • 2752 W Lawrence Ave
- **Semiramis** • 4639 N Kedzie Ave
- **Shelly's Freez** • 5119 N Lincoln Ave
- **Tagine** • 4749 N Rockwell St
- **Thai Little Home Café** • 4747 N Kedzie Ave
- **Thai Valley** • 4600 N Kedzie Ave

Shopping

- **Lincoln Antique Mall** • 3115 W Irving Park Rd
- **The Music Store** • 3121 W Irving Park Rd
- **Odin Tatu** • 3313 W Irving Park Rd
- **Rave Sports** • 3346 W Lawrence Ave
- **Sassy Boutique** • 3210 W Lawrence Ave
- **Scents & Sensibility** • 4654 N Rockwell St
- **Village Discount Outlet** • 3301 W Lawrence Ave
- **Village Discount Outlet** • 4027 N Kedzie Ave

Video Rental

- **AV Video Center** • 5153 N Lincoln Ave
- **Azteca Video** • 3308 W Montrose Ave
- **Bosna Video (Primarily Serbo-Croat)** • 2501 W Lawrence Ave
- **Hollywood Video** • 4246 N Kedzie Ave
- **V&K Video** • 4750 N Kedzie Ave

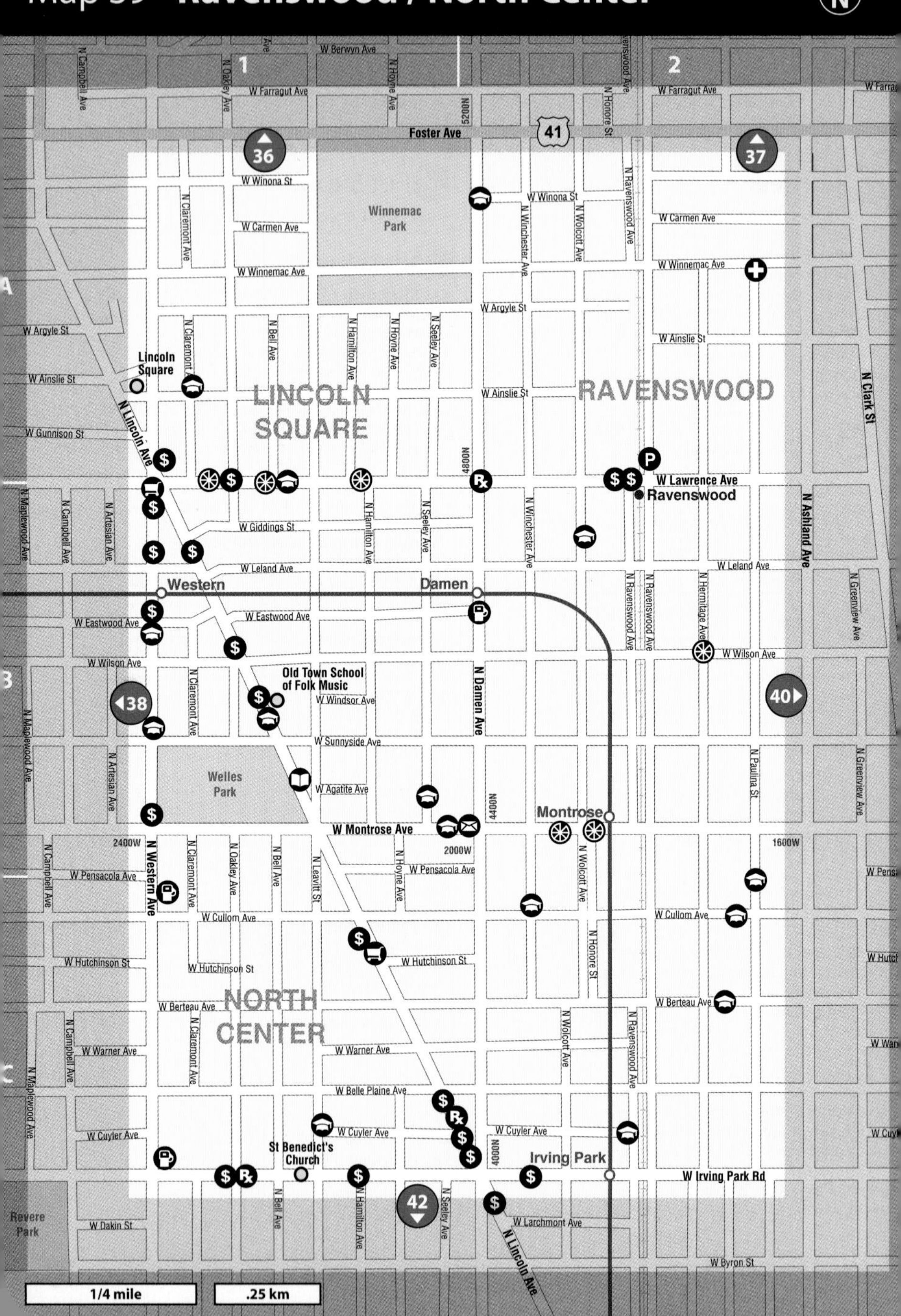
N
1
2
A
B
C
W Berwyn Ave
W Farragut Ave
Foster Ave
41
36
37
5200N
N Campbell Ave
N Oakley Ave
N Hoyne Ave
N Honore St
N Ravenswood Ave
W Winona St
Winnemac Park
W Carmen Ave
W Winnemac Ave
N Claremont Ave
N Winchester Ave
N Wolcott Ave
W Argyle St
W Ainslie St
N Bell Ave
N Hamilton Ave
N Seeley Ave
Lincoln Square
LINCOLN SQUARE
RAVENSWOOD
N Clark St
W Gunnison St
N Lincoln Ave
4800N
W Lawrence Ave
Ravenswood
N Maplewood Ave
N Artesian Ave
W Giddings St
N Ashland Ave
W Leland Ave
Western
Damen
W Eastwood Ave
N Hermitage Ave
N Greenview Ave
W Wilson Ave
Old Town School of Folk Music
W Windsor Ave
N Damen Ave
38
40
W Sunnyside Ave
Welles Park
W Agatite Ave
4400N
Montrose
N Paulina St
W Montrose Ave
2400W
2000W
1600W
N Western Ave
N Leavitt St
W Pensacola Ave
W Cullom Ave
W Hutchinson St
W Berteau Ave
NORTH CENTER
W Warner Ave
W Belle Plaine Ave
W Cuyler Ave
St Benedict's Church
4000N
Irving Park
W Irving Park Rd
42
Revere Park
W Dakin St
W Larchmont Ave
W Byron St
1/4 mile
.25 km

The Ravenswood area easily rivals Lincoln Park in price and with good reason. Older, family-style, neighborhood living has prompted realtors to rename North Center the "St. Ben's" area (after St. Benedict's Church) to up the ante. Further north, Lincoln Square serves as a hub for European culture. Almost by default, this has become known as Chicago's Germantown with its quaint, village-esque strip and big Oktoberfest fun.

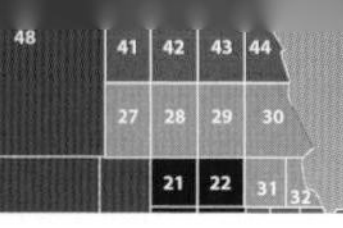

Banks

- **Albany** • 4400 N Western Ave
- **Bridgeview** • 4553 N Lincoln Ave
- **Charter One** • 4037 N Lincoln Ave
- **Charter One** • 4820 N Western Ave
- **Chase** • 1825 W Lawrence Ave
- **Chase** • 4711 N Lincoln Ave
- **Chase (ATM)** • 2301 W Irving Park Rd
- **Community Bank of Ravenswood** • 2300 W Lawrence Ave
- **Corus** • 3959 N Lincoln Ave
- **Corus** • 4800 N Western Ave
- **Great Bank of Lincoln Square** • 4725 N Western Ave
- **Lincoln Park Savings** • 1946 W Irving Park Rd
- **Lincoln Park Savings** • 2139 W Irving Park Rd
- **TCF** • Osco• 4051 N Lincoln Ave
- **TCF** • Jewel• 4250 N Lincoln Ave
- **TCF (ATM)** • 7-Eleven• 4631 N Western Ave
- **Washington Mutual** • 4000 N Lincoln Ave
- **Washington Mutual** • 4605 N Lincoln Ave

Gas Stations

- **Mobil** • 4000 N Western Ave
- **Mobil** • 4638 N Damen Ave
- **Shell** • 4346 N Western Ave

Emergency Rooms

- **Methodist Hospital of Chicago** • 5025 N Paulina St ㉔

Landmarks

- **Lincoln Square** • 4800 N Lincoln Ave
- **Old Town School of Folk Music** • 4544 N Lincoln Ave
- **St Benedict's Church** • 2215 W Irving Park Rd

Libraries

- **Sulzer Public Library** • 4455 N Lincoln Ave

Pharmacies

- **CVS Pharmacy** • 4800 N Damen Ave
- **Osco Drug** • 4051 N Lincoln Ave
- **Walgreens** • 2301 W Irving Park Rd

Pizza

- **Chicago's Pizza** • 1919 W Montrose Ave
- **Pizza DOC** • 2251 W Lawrence Ave
- **Pizza Hut** • 2309 W Lawrence Ave
- **Stefano's** • 2124 W Lawrence Ave
- **Villa May Delicious Pizza** • 1834 W Montrose Ave

Post Offices

- **US Post Office** • 2011 W Montrose Ave

Schools

- **Adler** • 2239 W Lawrence Ave
- **Infinity Chicago North Elementary** • 1713 W Cullom Ave
- **James B McPherson Elementary** • 4728 N Wolcott Ave
- **Jane Addams High** • 1800 W Cuyler Ave
- **John C Coonley Elementary** • 4046 N Leavitt St
- **Mary E Courtenay Language Arts Center** • 1726 W Berteau Ave
- **North Park Elementary** • 2017 W Montrose Ave
- **Old Town School of Folk Music** • 4544 N Lincoln Ave
- **Pilgrim Lutheran** • 4300 N Winchester Ave
- **Queen of Angels** • 4520 N Western Ave
- **Ravenswood Baptist Christian** • 4437 N Seeley Ave
- **Ravenswood Elementary** • 4332 N Paulina St
- **Roald Amundsen High** • 5110 N Damen Ave
- **St Matthias** • 4910 N Claremont Ave

Supermarkets

- **Deal$** • 4738 N Western Ave
- **Jewel** • 4250 N Lincoln Ave

Parking

1
2
A
B
C
36
37
38
40
42
41
W Berwyn Ave
W Farragut Ave
Foster Ave
W Winona St
W Carmen Ave
W Winnemac Ave
Winnemac Park
W Argyle St
W Ainslie St
W Gunnison St
W Lawrence Ave
W Giddings St
W Leland Ave
W Eastwood Ave
W Wilson Ave
W Windsor Ave
W Sunnyside Ave
W Agatite Ave
W Montrose Ave
W Pensacola Ave
W Cullom Ave
W Hutchinson St
W Berteau Ave
W Warner Ave
W Belle Plaine Ave
W Cuyler Ave
W Irving Park Rd
W Dakin St
W Larchmont Ave
W Byron St
LINCOLN SQUARE
RAVENSWOOD
NORTH CENTER
Welles Park
Revere Park
Western
Damen
Montrose
Irving Park
Ravenswood
N Lincoln Ave
N Western Ave
N Damen Ave
N Ashland Ave
N Clark St
N Campbell Ave
N Oakley Ave
N Hoyne Ave
N Claremont Ave
N Bell Ave
N Hamilton Ave
N Seeley Ave
N Winchester Ave
N Wolcott Ave
N Ravenswood Ave
N Honore St
N Hermitage Ave
N Greenview Ave
N Paulina St
N Maplewood Ave
N Artesian Ave
N Leavitt St
2400W
2000W
1600W
4400N
4800N
5200N
4000N
1/4 mile
.25 km

Ravenswood/North Center offers a smorgasbord to fit all culinary tastes. From the American, Cuban (Café 28) and Cantonese (Orange Garden) mix on Irving Park Road, to the German delis, meat markets and restaurants along Lincoln Avenue, visitors can literally eat their way through this diverse and entertaining area. The Old Town School of Folk Music, farmer's markets, and specialty boutiques round out one of Chicago's hottest upcoming areas.

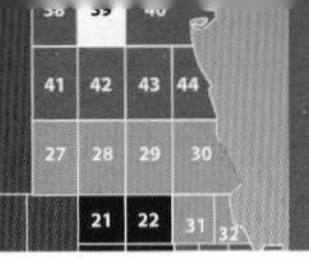

Coffee

- **Beans & Bagels** • 1812 W Montrose Ave
- **Bourbon** • 4768 N Lincoln Ave
- **Café Marrakech Expresso** • 4747 N Damen Ave
- **Dunkin' Donuts** • 1743 W Lawrence Ave
- **Dunkin' Donuts** • 4010 N Western Ave
- **Dunkin' Donuts** • 4645 N Western Ave
- **Katerina's** • 1920 W Irving Park Rd
- **Perfect Cup** • 4700 N Damen Ave
- **Red Eye Café** • 4164 N Lincoln Ave
- **So Addictive** • 4805 N Damen Ave
- **Starbucks** • 1900 W Montrose Ave
- **Starbucks** • 4015 N Lincoln Ave
- **Starbucks** • 4553 N Lincoln Ave

Copy Shops

- **The UPS Store** • 4064 N Lincoln Ave

Farmer's Markets

- **Lincoln Square (Jun–Oct; Tues, 7 am–3 pm)** • W Leland Ave & N Lincoln Ave
- **North Center (Jun–Oct; Sat, 7 am–2 pm)** • W Belle Plaine Ave & N Damen Ave

Gyms

- **Curves (women only)** • 4351 N Lincoln Ave

Hardware Stores

- **Sears** • 1900 W Lawrence Ave

Liquor Stores

- **Best Buy Food & Liquor** • 1832 W Montrose Ave
- **Bozic's Imports & Wholesale** • 4725 N Western Ave
- **Bright** • 1628 W Lawrence Ave
- **Cotler's Liquors** • 4959 N Damen Ave
- **Fine Wine Brokers (wine only)** • 4621 N Lincoln Ave
- **Fox Liquors** • 4707 N Damen Ave
- **George's Liquors** • 1964 W Lawrence Ave
- **Houston Liquor & Foods** • 1829 W Irving Park Rd
- **Leland Inn** • 4662 N Western Ave

Movie Theaters

- **Davis Theater** • 4614 N Lincoln Ave

Nightlife

- **Celtic Crown Public House** • 4301 N Western Ave
- **Chicago Brauhaus** • 4732 N Lincoln Ave
- **Daily Bar & Grill** • 4560 N Lincoln Ave
- **Foley's** • 1841 W Irving Park Rd
- **The Globe Pub** • 1934 W Irving Park Rd
- **Heuttenbar** • 4721 N Lincoln Ave
- **Katerina's** • 1920 W Irving Park Rd
- **Laschet's Inn** • 2119 W Irving Park Rd
- **The Long Room** • 1612 W Irving Park Rd
- **Margie's Pub** • 4145 N Lincoln Ave
- **O'Donovan's** • 2100 W Irving Park Rd
- **O'Lanagan's** • 2335 W Montrose Ave
- **The Rail** • 4709 N Damen Ave
- **Resi's Bierstube** • 2034 W Irving Park Rd
- **Wild Goose** • 4265 N Lincoln Ave
- **Windy City Inn** • 2257 W Irving Park Rd

Pet Shops

- **Barking Lot** • 2442 W Irving Park Rd
- **Off the Leash** • 4955 N Damen Ave
- **Sit!** • 2316 W Leland Ave
- **Vahle's Bird & Pet Shop** • 4710 N Damen Ave

Restaurants

- **Alps East Restaurant** • 2012 W Irving Park Rd
- **Bistro Campagne** • 4518 N Lincoln Ave
- **Block 44** • 4365 N Lincoln Ave
- **Brioso** • 4603 N Lincoln Ave
- **Café 28** • 1800 W Irving Park Rd
- **Café Selmarie** • 4729 N Lincoln Ave
- **Chicago Brauhaus** • 4732 N Lincoln Ave
- **Chicago Joe's** • 2256 W Irving Park Rd
- **Cy's Steak & Chop House** • 4138 N Lincoln Ave
- **Daily Bar & Grill** • 4560 N Lincoln Ave
- **Essence of India** • 4601 N Lincoln Ave
- **Feed the Beast**• 4300 N Lincoln Ave
- **First Slice Pie Café** • 4401 N Ravenswood Ave
- **Garcia's** • 4749 N Western Ave
- **Glenn's Diner** • 1820 W Montrose Ave
- **Glunz Bavarian Haus** • 4128 N Lincoln Ave
- **Golden Angel Restaurant** • 4340 N Lincoln Ave
- **Jury's Food & Drink** • 4337 N Lincoln Ave
- **La Boca della Verita** • 4618 N Lincoln Ave
- **Lincoln Restaurant** • 4008 N Lincoln Ave
- **Los Nopales** • 4544 N Western Ave
- **Margie's Candies** • 1813 W Montrose Ave
- **O'Donovan's** • 2100 W Irving Park Rd
- **Opart Thai House** • 4658 N Western Ave
- **Orange Garden** • 1942 W Irving Park Rd
- **Over Easy Café** • 4943 N Damen Ave
- **Pizza DOC** • 2251 W Lawrence Ave
- **Roong Petch** • 1828 W Montrose Ave
- **Royal Thai** • 2209 W Montrose Ave
- **Smokin' Woody's** • 4160 N Lincoln Ave
- **Soiree Bar and Restaurant** • 4539 N Lincoln Ave
- **Spacca Napoli** • 1769 W Sunnyside Ave
- **Spoon Thai** • 4608 N Western Ave
- **Tank Sushi** • 4514 N Lincoln Ave
- **Thai Oscar** • 4638 N Western Ave

Shopping

- **Angel Food Bakery** • 1636 W Montrose Ave
- **Architectural Artifacts** • 4325 N Ravenswood Ave
- **Book Cellar** • 4736 N Lincoln Ave
- **The Cheese Stands Alone** • 4547 N Western Ave
- **The Chopping Block** • 4747 N Lincoln Ave
- **Delicatessen Meyer** • 4750 N Lincoln Ave
- **Different Strummer** • 4544 N Lincoln Ave
- **East Meets West** • 2118 W Lawrence Ave
- **European Import Center** • 4752 N Lincoln Ave
- **Evil Clown Records** • 4314 N Lincoln Ave
- **Gallimaufry Gallery** • 4712 N Lincoln Ave
- **Glass Art & Decorative Studio** • 4507 N Lincoln Ave
- **Griffins & Gargoyles Antiques** • 2140 W Lawrence Ave
- **Hazel** • 1902 W Montrose Ave
- **Laurie's Planet of Sound** • 4639 N Lincoln Ave
- **Margie's Candies** • 1813 W Montrose Ave
- **Martin's Big & Tall Store for Men** • 4745 N Lincoln Ave
- **Merz Apothecary** • 4716 N Lincoln Ave
- **Quake Collectables** • 4628 N Lincoln Ave
- **Timeless Toys** • 4749 N Lincoln Ave

Video Rental

- **Blockbuster** • 1958 W Irving Park Rd
- **Blockbuster** • 2301 W Lawrence Ave
- **Darkstar Video** • 4355 N Lincoln Ave
- **Decade DVD** • 4612 N Lincoln Ave
- **Lincoln Square Video (Yugoslavian)** • 4725 N Lincoln Ave
- **Tom's Video** • 1830 W Wilson Ave

1
2
A
B
C
Berwyn
W Berwyn Ave
W Farragut Ave
W Foster Ave
41
37
5200N
W Winona St
W Carmen Ave
UPTOWN
W Winnemac Ave
Argyle
W Argyle St
St Augustine College
1200W
W Margate Ter
Lincoln Park
PAGE 210
N Lake Shore Dr
N Simonds Dr
N Marine Dr
W Ainslie St
St Boniface Cemetery
N Ashland Ave
N Clark St
N Janssen Ave
N Beacon St
N Broadway St
N Winthrop Ave
W Castlewood Ter
W Gunnison St
Uptown Theatre
Green Mill Pub
Aragon Ballroom
4800N
Lawrence
W Lawrence Ave
Lawrence Ave
N Magnolia Ave
N Sheridan Rd
W Lakeside Ave
N Clarendon Ave
Chase Park
W Leland Ave
SHERIDAN PARK
N Greenview Ave
W Eastwood Ave
N Clifton Ave
N Kenmore Ave
W Wilson Dr
W Wilson Av
Wilson
39
N Dover St
N Malden St
N Racine Ave
Truman College
W Windsor Ave
N Hazel St
N Marine Dr
W Sunnyside Ave
Clarendon Park
1600W
800W
W Agatite Ave
4400N
Tattoo Factory
W Montrose Ave
W Mo
W Pensacola Ave
N Dayton St
W Junior Ter
W Cullom Ave
BUENA PARK
Graceland Cemetery
W Hutchinson St
W Buena Ave
W Berteau Ave
W Gordon Ter
W Warner Ave
W Belle Plaine
W Belle Plaine Ave
W Cuyler Ave
W Bittersweet Pl
N Southport Ave
Wunder's Cemetery
4000N
W Irving Park Rd
Sheridan
43
44
N Wayne Ave
N Lakewood Ave
W Dakin St
N Fremont St
N Frontier Ave
W Byron St
W Sheridan Rd
1/4 mile
.25 km

Politically, Uptown is divided between development-minded pro-gentrification yuppies and grassroots, anti-gentrification hippies. The arrival of a Borders Books and three Starbucks are tilting the balance. Meanwhile, SOFO (the area defined by Argyle, Foster, Broadway, and Ashland) is where Andersonville's vibe bleeds southward toward somewhat more accessible rents and condo prices.

Banks

- **American Metro** • 4878 N Broadway St
- **Bridgeview** • 4753 N Broadway St
- **Bridgeview** • 5117 N Clark St
- **Chase** • 1101 W Lawrence Ave
- **Chase** • 3956 N Sheridan Rd
- **Chase** • 5134 N Clark St
- **Chase (ATM)** • 1500 W Wilson Ave
- **Citibank (ATM)** • 4015 N Sheridan Rd
- **Harris Trust & Savings** • 4531 N Broadway St
- **Harris Trust & Savings (ATM)** • 4750 N Sheridan Rd
- **International Bank of Chicago** • 5069 N Broadway St
- **New Asia** • 4929 N Broadway St
- **North Community** • 4701 N Clark St
- **TCF** • 1050 W Wilson Ave
- **TCF** • 4355 N Sheridan Rd
- **TCF (ATM)** • 7-Eleven • 1425 W Montrose Ave
- **Washington Mutual** • 4356 N Broadway St

Car Washes

- **Chicago's #1 Car Washes** • 4900 N Broadway St
- **Motor City Lube and Spa Detail** • 939 W Irving Park Rd

Gas Stations

- **Amoco** • 755 W Lawrence Ave
- **Citgo** • 1530 W Lawrence Ave
- **Citgo** • 4000 N Clark St
- **Gas City** • 4070 N Clark St
- **Marathon** • 5156 N Broadway St
- **Shell** • 4800 N Ashland Ave
- **Uptown Service Station** • 4900 N Broadway St

Emergency Rooms

- **Louis A Weiss Memorial** • 4646 N Marine Dr
- **Thorek** • 850 W Irving Park Rd

Landmarks

- **Aragon Ballroom** • 1106 W Lawrence Ave
- **Graceland Cemetery** • 4001 N Clark St
- **Green Mill Pub** • 4802 N Broadway St
- **St Augustine College** • 1333 W Argyle St
- **Tattoo Factory** • 4441 N Broadway St
- **Uptown Theatre** • 4816 N Broadway St

Libraries

- **Bezazian Public Library** • 1226 W Ainslie St
- **Uptown Public Library** • 929 W Buena Ave

Pharmacies

- **Jewel-Osco** • 4355 N Sheridan Rd
- **Osco Drug** • 845 W Wilson Ave
- **Walgreens** • 1500 W Wilson Ave
- **Walgreens** • 4025 N Sheridan Rd
- **Walgreens** • 4646 N Marine Dr

Pizza

- **Bo Jono's Pizzeria** • 4185 N Clarendon Ave
- **CW Napkin** • 4443 N Sheridan Rd
- **Domino's** • 1415 W Irving Park Rd
- **Gigio's Pizzeria** • 4643 N Broadway St
- **Laurie's Pizzeria & Liquors** • 5153 N Broadway St
- **Michael's Pizzeria & Sports Pub** • 4091 N Broadway St
- **O-Tomat-O** • 4429 N Broadway St
- **Papa Romeo's Pizza** • 1617 W Irving Park Rd
- **Pizza Factory** • 4443 N Sheridan Rd
- **Ranalli's Up North** • 1522 W Montrose Ave
- **Rosati's Pizza** • 4863 N Broadway St
- **Uptown Pizza** • 1031 W Wilson Ave

Post Offices

- **US Post Office** • 1343 W Irving Park Rd
- **US Post Office** • 4850 N Broadway St

Schools

- **Arai Campus** • 900 W Wilson Ave
- **Christopher House-Uptown DCC** • 4701 N Winthrop Ave
- **Day School** • 800 W Buena Ave
- **Joan F Arai Middle** • 900 W Wilson Ave
- **John T McCutcheon Branch** • 4850 N Kenmore Ave
- **Joseph Brennemann Elementary** • 4251 N Clarendon Ave
- **Lakeview High** • 4015 N Ashland Ave
- **Lycee Francais de Chicago** • 613 W Bittersweet Pl
- **Our Lady of Lourdes** • 4641 N Ashland Ave
- **Park View Montessori** • 640 W Irving Park Rd
- **Passages Elementary** • 1447 W Montrose Ave
- **Prologue Alternative High** • 1105 W Lawrence Ave
- **Prologue High** • 640 W Irving Park Rd
- **St Augustine College** • 1333 W Argyle St
- **St Mary of the Lake Elementary** • 1026 W Buena Ave
- **St Thomas of Canterbury** • 4827 N Kenmore Ave
- **A Step Ahead Learning Center** • 4208 N Broadway St
- **Stewart Elementary** • 4525 N Kenmore Ave
- **Stockton CPC** • 4425 N Magnolia Ave
- **Stockton Elementary** • 4420 N Beacon St
- **Truman College** • 1145 W Wilson Ave
- **Walt Disney Elementary** • 4140 N Marine Dr
- **William C Goudy Elementary** • 5120 N Winthrop Ave

Supermarkets

- **Aldi** • 4450 N Broadway St
- **Jewel-Osco** • 4355 N Sheridan Rd

Parking

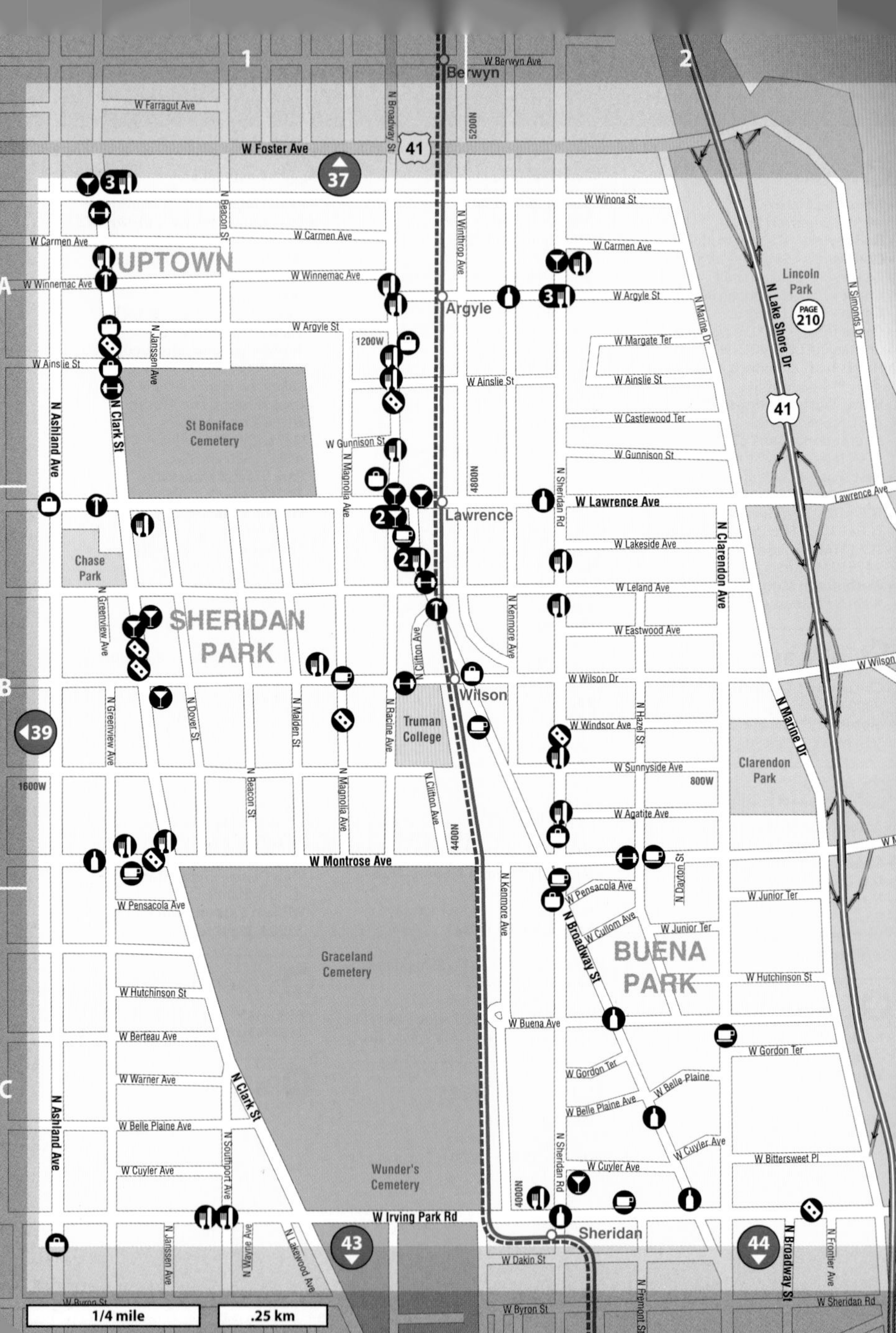

1
2
A
B
C
Berwyn
Argyle
Lawrence
Wilson
Sheridan
UPTOWN
SHERIDAN PARK
BUENA PARK
W Berwyn Ave
W Farragut Ave
W Foster Ave
W Winona St
W Carmen Ave
W Winnemac Ave
W Argyle St
W Margate Ter
W Ainslie St
W Castlewood Ter
W Gunnison St
W Lawrence Ave
Lawrence Ave
W Lakeside Ave
W Leland Ave
W Eastwood Ave
W Wilson Dr
W Wilson
W Windsor Ave
W Sunnyside Ave
W Agatite Ave
W Montrose Ave
W Pensacola Ave
W Cullom Ave
W Junior Ter
W Hutchinson St
W Berteau Ave
W Warner Ave
W Belle Plaine Ave
W Belle Plaine
W Buena Ave
W Gordon Ter
W Cuyler Ave
W Bittersweet Pl
W Irving Park Rd
W Dakin St
W Byron St
W Sheridan Rd
N Broadway St
N Winthrop Ave
N Beacon St
N Janssen Ave
N Clark St
N Ashland Ave
N Greenview Ave
N Magnolia Ave
N Dover St
N Malden St
N Racine Ave
N Clifton Ave
N Kenmore Ave
N Sheridan Rd
N Hazel St
N Marine Dr
N Clarendon Ave
N Lake Shore Dr
N Simonds Dr
N Dayton St
N Southport Ave
N Wayne Ave
N Lakewood Ave
N Fremont St
N Frontier Ave
5200N
4800N
4400N
4000N
1200W
1600W
800W
41
37
39
43
44
3
2
St Boniface Cemetery
Chase Park
Truman College
Graceland Cemetery
Wunder's Cemetery
Lincoln Park
PAGE 210
Clarendon Park
1/4 mile
.25 km

The nightlife of SOFO (South of Foster) is hopping. Standbys such as the Green Mill (famed for gangland connections and the Sunday night poetry slam) and Big Chicks (a favored gay neighborhood bar with superb art collection) have long drawn folks to uptown. Now diners flock to Tweet, Agami, and Hopleaf (which also serves up an impressive selection of Belgian beer). Hey—be careful walking around drunk and/or alone at night. Parts of this 'hood are still rather sketchy.

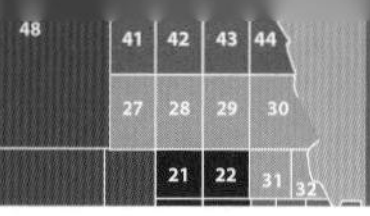

Coffee

- **Corona's Coffee Shop** • 909 W Irving Park Rd
- **Dollop Coffee Co** • 4181 N Clarendon Ave
- **Dunkin' Donuts** • 1441 W Montrose Ave
- **Dunkin' Donuts** • 4547 N Broadway St
- **Starbucks** • 4355 N Sheridan Rd
- **Starbucks** • 4600 N Magnolia Ave
- **Starbucks** • 4753 N Broadway St
- **Urban Tea Lounge** • 838 W Montrose Ave

Gyms

- **Bodyfit Athletic Club** • 4704 N Broadway St
- **Curves (Women only)** • 1144 W Wilson Ave
- **Know No Limits** • 5121 N Clark St
- **Man's World Health Club** • 4862 N Clark St
- **World Gym Fitness Center** • 909 W Montrose Ave

Hardware Stores

- **Andersonville Hardware** • 5036 N Clark St
- **Crafty Beaver Home Center** • 1522 W Lawrence Ave
- **Uptown Ace Hardware** • 4654 N Broadway St

Liquor Stores

- **GNS Food & Liquor** • 4092 N Broadway St
- **JJ Peppers Food Store** • 4800 N Sheridan Rd
- **Laurie's Pizzeria & Liquors** • 5153 N Broadway St
- **Manhattan Liquors** • 4200 N Broadway St
- **Rayan's Discount Liquors** • 1532 W Montrose Ave
- **Sheridan-Irving Liquor** • 3944 N Sheridan Rd
- **Wine Store** • 1040 W Argyle St

Nightlife

- **Big Chicks** • 5024 N Sheridan Rd
- **Carol's Pub** • 4659 N Clark St
- **Crew Bar & Grill** • 4804 N Broadway St
- **Green Mill Pub** • 4802 N Broadway St
- **Hopleaf** • 5148 N Clark St
- **Max's Place** • 4621 N Clark St
- **Nick's Uptown** • 4015 N Sheridan Rd
- **Riviera** • 4746 N Racine Ave
- **T's** • 5025 N Clark St
- **The Uptown Lounge** • 1136 W Lawrence Ave

Restaurants

- **Agami** • 4712 N Broadway St
- **Andie's** • 1467 W Montrose Ave
- **Anna Maria Pasteria** • 4400 N Clark St
- **Bale French Bakery** • 5018 N Broadway St
- **Café Too** • 4715 N Sheridan Rd
- **Deleece** • 4004 N Southport Ave
- **Don Quijote** • 4761 N Clark St
- **Furama** • 4936 N Broadway St
- **Golden House Restaurant** • 4744 N Broadway St
- **Hai Yen Restaurant** • 1055 W Argyle St
- **Hama Matsu** • 5143 N Clark St
- **Holiday Club** • 4000 N Sheridan Rd
- **JJ Fish & Chicken** • 4515 N Sheridan Rd
- **La Donna** • 5146 N Clark St
- **Magnolia Café** • 1224 W Wilson Ave
- **Nhu Hoa** • 1020 W Argyle St
- **Pho Xe Lua** • 1021 W Argyle St
- **Pho Xe Tang** • 4953 N Broadway St
- **Riques** • 5004 N Sheridan Rd
- **Siam Noodle & Rice** • 4654 N Sheridan Rd
- **Silver Seafood** • 4829 N Broadway St
- **Smoke Country House** • 1467 W Irving Park Rd
- **Thai Pastry** • 4925 N Broadway St
- **Tokyo Marina** • 5058 N Clark St
- **Tweet** • 5020 N Sheridan Rd

Shopping

- **Angel Food Bakery** • 1636 W Montrose Ave
- **Eagle Leathers** • 5005 N Clark St
- **Play It Again Sports** • 3939 N Ashland Ave
- **Salvation Army Thrift Store** • 4315 N Broadway St
- **Shake Rattle and Read Book Box** • 4812 N Broadway St
- **Tai Nam Market Center** • 4925 N Broadway St
- **Unique Thrift Store** • 4445 N Sheridan Rd
- **Village Discount Outlet** • 4898 N Clark St
- **Wilson Broadway Mall** • 1114 W Wilson Ave

Video Rental

- **Albert Video** • 1435 W Montrose Ave
- **Banana Video** • 4923 N Clark St
- **Bankok Video & Grocery** • 4617 N Clark St
- **Blockbuster** • 4620 N Clark St
- **Hollywood Video** • 4883 N Broadway St
- **Line Video** • 4554 N Magnolia Ave
- **Nationwide Video** • 736 W Irving Park Rd
- **United Video** • 4519 N Sheridan Rd

1
2
A
B
C
Horner Park
California Park
Revere Park
IRVING PARK
AVONDALE
W Cuyler Ave
W Irving Park Rd
W Byron St
W Dakin St
W Berenice Ave
W Grace St
W Bradley Pl
W Waveland Ave
W Addison St
W Eddy St
W Cornelia Ave
W Newport St
W Roscoe St
W Henderson St
W School St
W Melrose St
W Belmont Ave
W Fletcher St
W Barry Ave
W Nelson St
W Wellington Ave
W George St
W Diversey Ave
W Parker Ave
W Schubert Ave
N Kimball Ave
N Christiana Ave
N Spaulding Ave
N Sawyer Ave
N Kedzie Ave
N Troy St
N Albany St
N Whipple St
N Sacramento St
N Sacramento Ave
N Richmond St
N Francisco Ave
N Mozart St
N California Ave
N Fairfield Ave
N Washtenaw Ave
N Talman Ave
N Rockwell St
N Maplewood Ave
N Campbell Ave
N Artesian Ave
N Elston Ave
N Irene Ave
N Avondale Ave
N Milwaukee Ave
N Allen Ave
N Wisner Ave
N Dawson Ave
N Woodard St
N Emmett St
N Bernard St
Sacramento Park
Com-Ed Plant
Brands Park
Chicago River
DeVry Institute of Technology
Belmont
4000N
3600N
3200N
2800N
3200W
2800W
2400W
38
48
42
27
90
94
1/4 mile
.25 km

It's official: southern Avondale has now been designated "hot Avondale" by real estate developers. Certainly the sight of hipsters sipping coffee next to the blue collar regulars at Clara's are a clear indication that young artsy types have set their sights on the affordable spaces and ample parking to be found in this frontier neighborhood, as all points connected by the Blue Line are designated, eventually, for coolness.

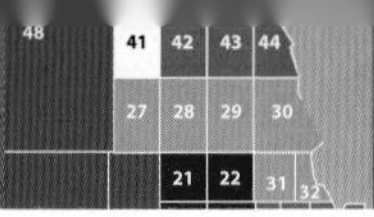

Banks

- **Chase** • 3227 W Addison St
- **Chase (ATM)** • 3302 W Belmont Ave
- **Harris Trust & Savings** • 2927 W Addison St
- **LaSalle** • 3350 W Diversey Ave
- **North Community** • 2758 W Belmont Ave
- **TCF** • Jewel• 3570 N Elston Ave
- **TCF (ATM)** • 7-Eleven • 3800 N Kedzie Ave
- **US** • 3611 N Kedzie Ave
- **Washington Mutual** • 3339 W Belmont Ave

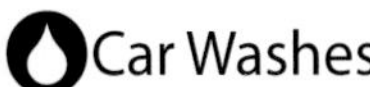

Car Washes

- **123 Hand Car Wash** • 3635 N Kedzie Ave

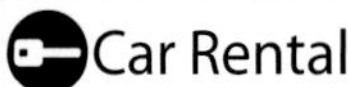

Car Rental

- **Enterprise** • 3029 N Kedzie Ave • 773-478-3310

Gas Stations

- **BP** • 3201 W Addison St
- **Citgo** • 2920 N California Ave
- **Citgo** • 3001 W Belmont Ave
- **Marathon** • 2811 N Sacramento Ave
- **Marathon** • 3057 N Kedzie Ave
- **Mobil** • 2801 W Diversey Ave
- **Shell** • 3159 W Addison St

Landmarks

- **Com-Ed Plant** • N California Ave & W Roscoe St

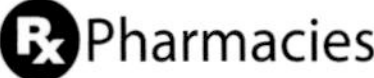

Pharmacies

- **CVS** • 3411 W Addison St
- **Dominick's** • 3300 W Belmont Ave
- **Jewel-Osco** • 3572 N Elston Ave
- **Walgreens** • 3302 W Belmont Ave

Pizza

- **Dominick's** • 3300 W Belmont Ave
- **Little Caesar's Pizza** • 3135 W Addison St
- **Pipo's Pizza** • 2550 W Addison St

Post Offices

- **US Post Office** • 3750 N Kedzie Ave

Schools

- **A-Karrasel** • 3030 N Kedzie Ave
- **Albert G Lane Tech** • 2501 W Addison St
- **Avondale Elementary** • 2945 N Sawyer Ave
- **Carl Von Linne Elementary** • 3221 N Sacramento Ave
- **DeVry Institute of Technology** • 3300 N Campbell Ave
- **Gordon Technical High** • 3633 N California Ave
- **Grover Cleveland Elementary** • 3121 W Byron St
- **Immaculate Heart of Mary** • 3820 N Spaulding Ave
- **Logandale Middle** • 3212 W George St
- **Resurrection Catholic Academy** • 2845 W Barry Ave

Supermarkets

- **Dominick's** • 3300 W Belmont Ave
- **Jewel-Osco** • 3570 N Elston Ave

Horner Park
W Irving Park Rd
California Park
Revere Park
IRVING PARK
W Addison St
Sacramento Park
Com-Ed Plant
Chicago River
DeVry Institute of Technology
Brands Park
N Elston Ave
W Belmont Ave
Belmont
AVONDALE
N Kimball Ave
N Kedzie Ave
N California Ave
N Western Ave
W Diversey Ave
N Milwaukee Ave
W Schubert Ave
W Wellington Ave
W George St
W Roscoe St
W Waveland Ave
W Grace St
W Cuyler Ave
38
48
42
27
90
94
1/4 mile
.25 km

When encased meat emporium Hot Doug's relocated here to a stretch of California, local foodies took note. During lunch hour and on Saturdays, lines extend well beyond the doors for Doug's dogs and fries. Meanwhile, nearby pub Chief O'Neill's remains popular for their better-than-average Irish fare, convivial bar, ample outdoor seating, and occasional live Celtic music.

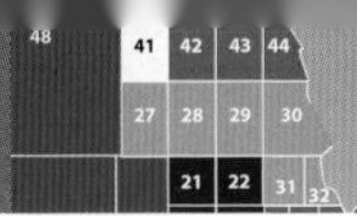

Coffee

- **Dunkin' Donuts** • 3214 N Kimball Ave
- **Dunkin' Donuts** • 3310 W Addison St
- **Dunkin' Donuts** • 3427 W Diversey Ave
- **MoJoes Hot House** • 2849 W Belmont Ave
- **Starbucks** • Target• 2939 W Addison St

Hardware Stores

- **Cobey True Value Hardware** • 3429 W Diversey Ave
- **Elston Ace Hardware** • 2825 W Belmont Ave
- **Home Depot** • 3500 N Kimball Ave
- **Kabbe True Value Hardware** • 2550 W Diversey Ave

Liquor Stores

- **Discount Store** • 3457 N Albany Ave
- **JJ Peppers** • 3201 W Diversey Ave

Nightlife

- **Chief O'Neill's** • 3471 N Elston Ave
- **Christina's Place** • 3759 N Kedzie Ave
- **N** • 2977 N Elston Ave
- **Nelly's Saloon** • 3256 N Elston Ave
- **Stadium West** • 3188 N Elston Ave

Pet Shops

- **Belmont Feed** • 3036 W Belmont Ave
- **Pet A Cure** • 2949 W Diversey Ave
- **Pet Supplies Plus** • 3640 N Elston Ave

Restaurants

- **Chief O'Neill's** • 3471 N Elston Ave
- **Clara's** • 3159 N California Ave
- **Eat First Chinese Restaurant** • 3337 W Belmont Ave
- **Fierro's Argentine Grill** • 2550 W Addison St
- **Hot Doug's** • 3324 N California Ave
- **IHOP** • 2818 W Diversey Ave
- **Kuma's Corner** • 2900 W Belmont Ave
- **La Finca** • 3361 N Elston Ave
- **Sunshine Restaurant** • 3521 N Kedzie Ave
- **Taqueria Trespazada** • 3144 N California Ave

Video Rental

- **Blockbuster** • 3233 W Addison St
- **Blockbuster** • 3951 N Kimball Ave

NORTH CENTER
ROSCOE VILLAGE
LAKEVIEW
Irving Park
Addison
Paulina
W Irving Park Rd
W Cuyler Ave
W Belle Plaine Ave
W Dakin St
W Larchmont Ave
W Byron St
W Berenice Ave
W Grace St
W Bradley Pl
W Waveland Ave
W Patterson Ave
W Addison St
W Eddy St
W Cornelia Ave
W Newport Ave
W Roscoe St
W Henderson St
W School St
W Melrose St
W Belmont Ave
W Fletcher St
W Barry Ave
W Nelson St
W Wellington Ave
W Oakdale Ave
W George St
W Wolfram St
W Diversey Ave
W Schubert Ave
W Rex Ave
N Western Ave
N Campbell Ave
N Maplewood Ave
N Rockwell St
N Artesian Ave
N Claremont Ave
N Oakley Ave
N Bell Ave
N Leavitt St
N Hamilton Ave
N Hoyne Ave
N Seeley Ave
N Damen Ave
N Lincoln Ave
N Wolcott Ave
N Ravenswood Ave
N Hermitage Ave
N Paulina St
N Marshfield Ave
N Ashland Ave
N Bosworth Ave
N Honore St
N Clybourn Ave
N Logan Blvd
Chicago River
Revere Park
DeVry Institute of Technology
19th District Police Headquarters
Gross Park
Hamlin Park
2400W
2000W
1600W
4000N
3600N
3200N
2800N
39
41
43
28
1/4 mile
.25 km

Roscoe Village still has a fun vibe although the arty residency is giving way to fit, tan, 30–40 something a**holes. The cop shop at Belmont and Western is the local district headquarters. You'll get hauled here for holding if you get into trouble on the north side. Due north, the area surrounding St. Benedict's church and parish school is a tree-lined residential enclave consisting of high-priced single-family homes.

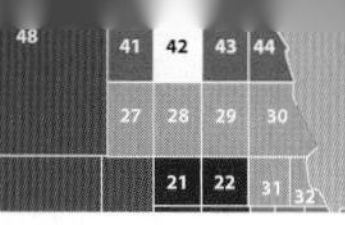

Banks

- **Chase** • 3531 N Western Ave
- **Chase** • 3868 N Lincoln Ave
- **Chase (ATM)** • 1649 W Belmont Ave
- **Chase (ATM)** • 3358 N Western Ave
- **Lincoln Park Savings** • 3234 N Damen Ave
- **North Community** • 2800 N Western Ave
- **North Community** • 3401 N Western Ave
- **TCF** • Jewel• 3400 N Western Ave
- **TCF (ATM)** • 7-Eleven • 3801 N Western Ave
- **Washington Mutual** • 3348 N Western Ave

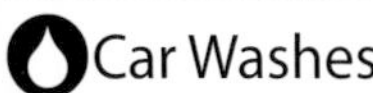

Car Washes

- **Ultra Sonic Car Wash** • 3650 N Western Ave

Car Rental

- **Enterprise** • 3844 N Western Ave • 773-539-5900
- **Rent-A-Wreck** • 3535 N Lincoln Ave • 773-281-1111

Gas Stations

- **BP/Amoco** • 3955 N Western Ave
- **Citgo** • 2401 W Diversey Ave
- **Gas for Less** • 2801 N Damen Ave
- **Marathon** • 3145 N Western Ave

Landmarks

- **19th District Police Headquarters** • 2452 W Belmont Ave

Libraries

- **Lincoln-Belmont Public Library** • 1659 W Melrose St

Pharmacies

- **CVS Pharmacy** • 2815 N Western Ave
- **CVS Pharmacy** • 3944 N Western Ave
- **Dominick's** • 3350 N Western Ave
- **Jewel-Osco** • 3400 N Western Ave
- **Walgreens** • 1649 W Belmont Ave
- **Walgreens** • 3358 N Western Ave

Pizza

- **Carreno's Pizzeria** • 1955 W Addison St
- **Dominick's Finer Foods** • 3350 N Western Ave
- **Pete's Pizza** • 3737 N Western Ave
- **Piazza Bella Trattoria** • 2116 W Roscoe St
- **Robey Pizza** • 1954 W Roscoe St

Police

- **19th District (Belmont)** • 2452 W Belmont Ave

Post Offices

- **US Post Office** • 3635 N Lincoln Ave

Schools

- **Alex Bell Elementary** • 3730 N Oakley Ave
- **Alexander Hamilton Elementary** • 1650 W Cornelia Ave
- **Cardinal Bernardin Early Child** • 1651 W Diversey Pkwy
- **Friedrich L Jahn Elementary** • 3149 N Wolcott Ave
- **George Schneider Elementary** • 2957 N Hoyne Ave
- **John L Audubon Elementary** • 3500 N Hoyne Ave
- **St Andrew Elementary** • 1710 W Addison St
- **St Benedict High** • 3900 N Leavitt St
- **St Benedict Middle** • 3920 N Leavitt St

Supermarkets

- **Dominick's** • 3350 N Western Ave
- **Jewel-Osco** • 3400 N Western Ave
- **Paulina Meat Market** • 3501 N Lincoln Ave
- **Trader Joe's** • 3745 N Lincoln Ave

NORTH CENTER
ROSCOE VILLAGE
LAKEVIEW
Irving Park
Addison
Paulina
Revere Park
DeVry Institute of Technology
Gross Park
Hamlin Park
Chicago River
W Irving Park Rd
W Addison St
W Roscoe St
W Belmont Ave
W Diversey Ave
N Western Ave
N Damen Ave
N Ashland Ave
N Lincoln Ave
N Clybourn Ave
1/4 mile
.25 km

Vintage and antique shopping on this stretch of Belmont is lots of fun. Roscoe Avenue between Damen and Western is full of restaurants. Try Victory's Banner for vegetarian brunch. It's run by sari-clad followers of Sri Chimnoy, whose videos play while you dine.

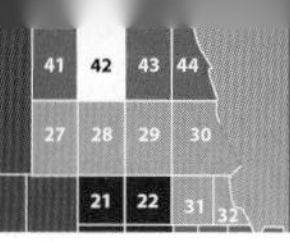

Coffee

- **Dinkel's Bakery** • 3329 N Lincoln Ave
- **Dunkin' Donuts** • 1755 W Addison St
- **Dunkin' Donuts** • 3535 N Western Ave
- **Lakeview Billiard Café** • 3449 N Lincoln Ave
- **Mojoe's Café Lounge** • 2256 W Roscoe St
- **Starbucks** • 1700 W Diversey Pkwy
- **Starbucks** • 2023 W Roscoe St
- **Starbucks** • 2159 W Belmont Ave
- **Starbucks** • 3356 N Lincoln Ave
- **Starbucks** • Albertsons • 3400 N Western Ave
- **Su Van's Café and Bake Shop** • 3351 N Lincoln Ave
- **Thai Linda Café** • 2022 W Roscoe St

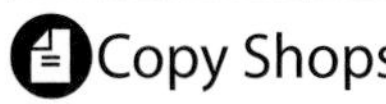

Copy Shops

- **Fedex Kinko's** • 3435 N Western Ave

Farmer's Markets

- **Roscoe Village (Jun–Oct; Sun, 7 am–2 pm)** • W Belmont Ave & N Wolcott Ave

Gyms

- **Curves (women only)** • 2037 W Roscoe St
- **Lakeview YMCA** • 3333 N Marshfield Ave
- **Slim and Tone (women only)** • 2044 W Belmont Ave

Hardware Stores

- **Community Home Supply** • 3924 N Lincoln Ave
- **Staubers Ace Hardware** • 3911 N Lincoln Ave

Liquor Stores

- **Armanetti Wine Shop** • 3530 N Lincoln Ave
- **Miller's Tap & Liquor Store** • 2204 W Roscoe St
- **Miska's Liquor** • 2156 W Belmont Ave
- **Pelly's Liquors** • 3444 N Lincoln Ave
- **R&S Liquor** • 2425 W Diversey Ave
- **West Lakeview Liquors** • 2156 W Addison St

Nightlife

- **Art of Sports** • 2444 W Diversey Ave
- **Beat Kitchen** • 2100 W Belmont Ave
- **Black Rock** • 3614 N Damen Ave
- **Cody's Public House** • 1658 W Barry Ave
- **Four Moon Tavern** • 1847 W Roscoe St
- **Four Treys** • 3333 N Damen Ave
- **G&L Fire Escape** • 2157 W Grace St
- **Martyrs'** • 3855 N Lincoln Ave
- **Mulligan's Public House** • 2000 W Roscoe St
- **Riverview Tavern & Restaurant** • 1958 W Roscoe St
- **Seanchai** • 2345 W Belmont Ave
- **The Village Tap** • 2055 W Roscoe St
- **Waterhouse** • 3407 N Paulina Ave
- **Xippo** • 3759 N Damen Ave

Pet Shops

- **Sam & Willy's** • 3405 N Paulina St

Restaurants

- **Brett's Café Americain** • 2011 W Roscoe St
- **Carreno's Pizzeria** • 1955 W Addison St
- **Costello Sandwich & Sides** • 2015 W Roscoe St
- **El Tinajon** • 2054 W Roscoe St
- **Four Moon Tavern** • 1847 W Roscoe St
- **Kaze Sushi** • 2032 W Roscoe St
- **Kitsch'n on Roscoe** • 2005 W Roscoe St
- **La Mora** • 2132 W Roscoe St
- **Lee's Chop Suey** • 2415 W Diversey Ave
- **Mrs Murphy and Sons** • 3905 N Lincoln Ave
- **Piazza Bella Trattoria** • 2116 W Roscoe St
- **Riverview Tavern & Grill** • 1958 W Roscoe St
- **Sola** • 3868 N Lincoln Ave
- **T-Spot Sushi** • 3925 N Lincoln Ave
- **Terragusto** • 1851 W Addison St
- **Thai Linda Café** • 2022 W Roscoe St
- **Turquoise Restaurant on Roscoe** • 2147 W Roscoe St
- **Victory's Banner** • 2100 W Roscoe St
- **The Village Tap** • 2055 W Roscoe St
- **Volo Restaurant and Wine Bar** • 2008 W Roscoe St
- **Wishbone** • 3300 N Lincoln Ave

Shopping

- **Antique Resources** • 1741 W Belmont Ave
- **Father Time Antiques** • 2108 W Belmont Ave
- **Glam to Go** • 2002 W Roscoe St
- **Good Old Days Antiques** • 2138 W Belmont Ave
- **Lynn's Hallmark** • 3353 N Lincoln Ave
- **My Closet** • 3350 N Paulina St
- **Village Discount Outlet** • 2043 W Roscoe St

Video Rental

- **Blockbuster** • 1645 W School St
- **Blockbuster** • 3322 N Western Ave
- **Hard Boiled Records and Video** • 2010 W Roscoe St

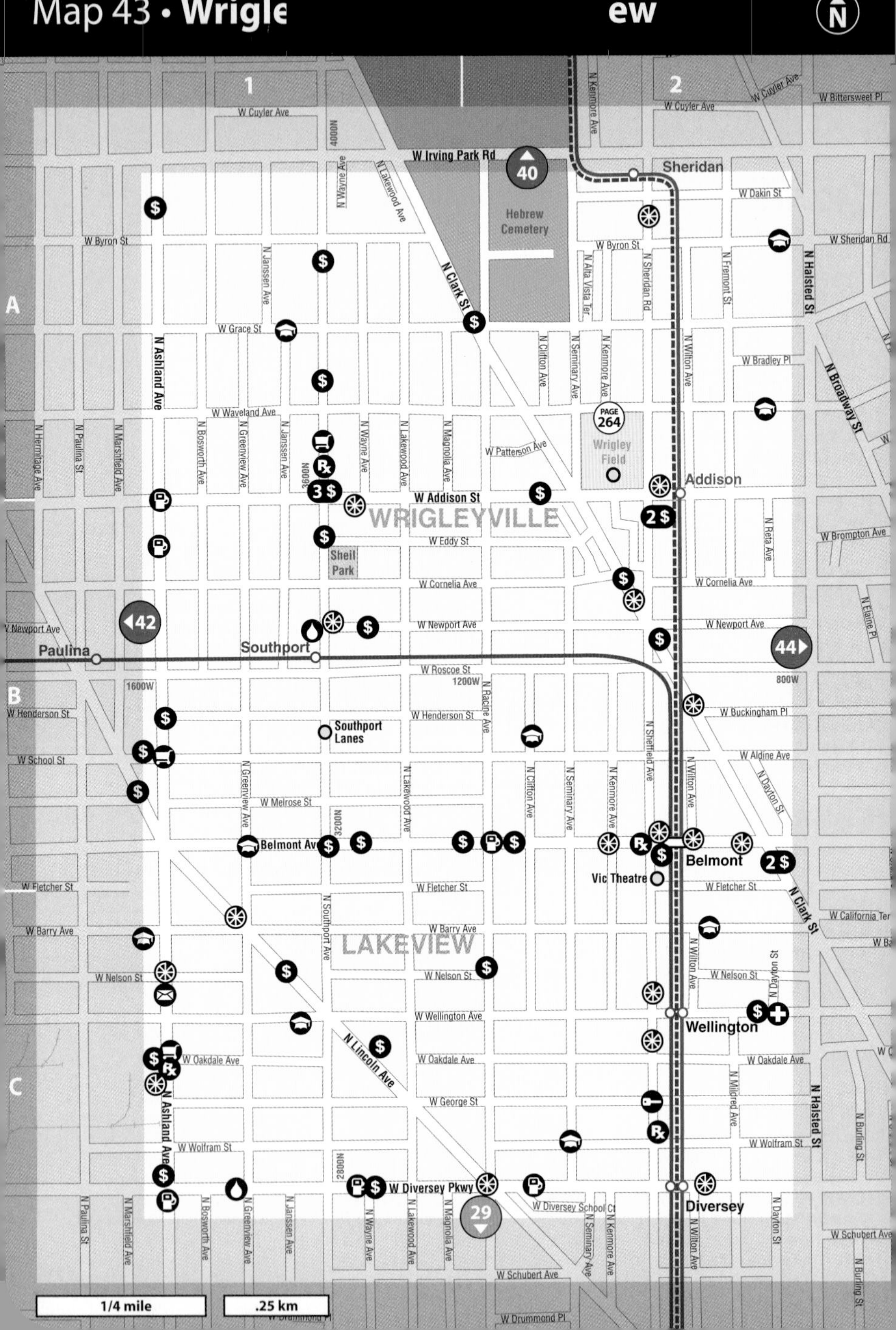

Map 43 • Wrigle
ew
1
2
A
B
C
W Cuyler Ave
W Bittersweet Pl
W Irving Park Rd
40
Sheridan
W Dakin St
Hebrew Cemetery
W Byron St
W Sheridan Rd
N Halsted St
N Clark St
W Grace St
N Ashland Ave
W Bradley Pl
N Broadway St
W Waveland Ave
PAGE 264
Wrigley Field
W Patterson Ave
Addison
W Addison St
WRIGLEYVILLE
W Eddy St
Sheil Park
W Brompton Ave
W Cornelia Ave
42
W Newport Ave
Paulina
Southport
44
W Roscoe St
1200W
800W
1600W
W Henderson St
W Buckingham Pl
Southport Lanes
W School St
W Aldine Ave
W Melrose St
Belmont Ave
Belmont
Vic Theatre
W Fletcher St
W Barry Ave
W California Ter
LAKEVIEW
W Nelson St
W Wellington Ave
Wellington
N Lincoln Ave
W Oakdale Ave
W George St
W Wolfram St
W Diversey Pkwy
29
W Diversey School Ct
Diversey
W Schubert Ave
W Drummond Pl
N Hermitage Ave
N Paulina St
N Marshfield Ave
N Bosworth Ave
N Greenview Ave
N Janssen Ave
N Wayne Ave
N Lakewood Ave
N Magnolia Ave
N Racine Ave
N Clifton Ave
N Seminary Ave
N Kenmore Ave
N Alta Vista Ter
N Sheridan Rd
N Sheffield Ave
N Wilton Ave
N Fremont St
N Reta Ave
N Elaine Pl
N Dayton St
N Mildred Ave
N Burling St
N Southport Ave
4000N
3600N
3200N
2800N
1/4 mile
.25 km

Pleasant, pretty streets belie atrocious traffic and parking, as well as the constant summertime disturbance of drunken Cubs fans roaming the streets and urinating in alleys and doorways. On the plus side, residents don't have to travel far for anything—tons of good restaurants, a variety of nightlife, the lakefront, and loads of services from groceries to video rentals cram into this youthful 'hood.

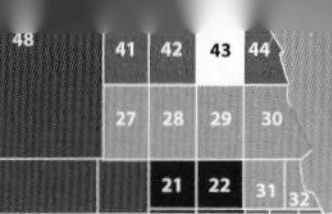

Banks

- **Bank of America** • 963 W Belmont Ave
- **Bank of America (ATM)** • 3182 N Clark St
- **Charter One** • 3066 N Lincoln Ave
- **Charter One** • 3948 N Ashland Ave
- **Chase** • 1240 W Belmont Ave
- **Chase** • 2968 N Lincoln Ave
- **Chase** • 3335 N Ashland Ave
- **Chase** • 3730 N Southport Ave
- **Chase (ATM)** • 940 W Addison St
- **Citibank (ATM)** • 3857 N Southport Ave
- **Corus** • 3179 N Clark St
- **Corus** • 3604 N Southport Ave
- **First American** • 1345 W Diversey Pkwy
- **Lakeside** • 2800 N Ashland Ave
- **LaSalle** • 3201 N Ashland Ave
- **LaSalle** • 3301 N Ashland Ave
- **North Community** • 1401 W Belmont Ave
- **North Community** • 3420 N Clark St
- **Northern Trust (ATM)** • Illinois Masonic Hospital• 836 W Wellington Ave
- **TCF** • Jewel• 2940 N Ashland Ave
- **TCF** • Jewel• 3630 N Southport Ave
- **TCF (ATM)** • Taco Bell• 1111 W Addison St
- **TCF (ATM)** • 7-Eleven• 1153 W Belmont Ave
- **TCF (ATM)** • 1344 W Newport Ave
- **TCF (ATM)** • 1362 W Belmont Ave
- **TCF (ATM)** • 3056 N Racine Ave
- **TCF (ATM)** • 7-Eleven• 3554 N Sheffield Ave
- **TCF (ATM)** • Osco• 3637 N Southport Ave
- **TCF (ATM)** • 3800 N Clark St
- **Washington Mutual** • 3252 N Lincoln Ave
- **Washington Mutual** • 3500 N Clark St
- **Washington Mutual** • 3556 N Southport Ave

Car Washes

- **Quiroga's Detail & Hand Car Wash** • 3448 N Southport Ave
- **We'll Clean** • 1515 W Diversey Pkwy

Car Rental

- **Enterprise** • 2900 N Sheffield Ave • 773-880-5001

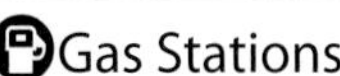

Gas Stations

- **Amoco** • 1200 W Belmont Ave
- **BP** • 1355 W Diversey Pkwy
- **Citgo** • 3600 N Ashland Ave
- **Shell** • 1160 W Diversey Pkwy
- **Shell** • 2801 N Ashland Ave
- **Shell** • 3552 N Ashland Ave

Emergency Rooms

- **Advocate Illinois Masonic Medical Center** • 836 W Wellington Ave

Landmarks

- **Southport Lanes** • 3325 N Southport Ave
- **Vic Theatre** • 3145 N Sheffield Ave
- **Wrigley Field** • 1060 W Addison St

Pharmacies

- **Jewel-Osco** • 2940 N Ashland Ave
- **Osco Drug** • 3637 N Southport Ave
- **Walgreens** • 1001 W Belmont Ave
- **Walgreens** • 2835 N Sheffield Ave, Ste 505

Pizza

- **Art of Pizza** • 3033 N Ashland Ave
- **Bacci Pizzeria** • 950 W Addison St
- **Chicago's Pizza** • 3006 N Sheffield Ave
- **Chicago's Pizza & Pasta** • 3114 N Lincoln Ave
- **D'Agostino Pizzeria & Restaurant** • 1351 W Addison St
- **Gino's East of Chicago** • 2801 N Lincoln Ave
- **Giordano's** • 1040 W Belmont Ave
- **Homemade Pizza Co** • 3430 N Southport Ave
- **La Gondola Pizzeria & Cucina Italiana** • 2914 N Ashland Ave
- **Leona's** • 3215 N Sheffield Ave
- **Papa Romeo's Pizza** • 926 W Diversey Pkwy
- **Philly's Best** • 907 W Belmont Ave
- **Pizano's Pizza & Pasta** • 3466 N Clark St
- **Pizza Capri** • 962 W Belmont Ave
- **Pizza Rustica** • 3913 N Sheridan Rd
- **Pompeii Bakery** • 2955 N Sheffield Ave

Post Offices

- **US Post Office** • 3024 N Ashland Ave

Schools

- **Augustus H Burley Elementary** • 1630 W Barry Ave
- **Hawthorne Scholastic Academy** • 3319 N Clifton Ave
- **Horace Greeley Elementary** • 832 W Sheridan Rd
- **Inter-American Elementary** • 919 W Barry Ave
- **James G Blaine Elementary** • 1420 W Grace St
- **John V LeMoyne Elementary** • 851 W Waveland Ave
- **Louis J Agassiz Elementary** • 2851 N Seminary Ave
- **St Alphonsus Academy** • 1439 W Wellington Ave
- **St Luke Academy** • 1500 W Belmont Ave

Supermarkets

- **Jewel** • 3630 N Southport Ave
- **Jewel-Osco** • 2940 N Ashland Ave
- **Whole Foods Market** • 3300 N Ashland Ave

WRIGLEYVILLE
LAKEVIEW
Hebrew Cemetery
Wrigley Field
PAGE 264
Sheil Park
Sheridan
Addison
Paulina
Southport
Belmont
Wellington
Diversey
40
42
44
29
1
2
A
B
C
W Cuyler Ave
W Irving Park Rd
W Byron St
W Grace St
W Waveland Ave
W Addison St
W Eddy St
W Cornelia Ave
W Newport Ave
W Roscoe St
W Henderson St
W School St
W Melrose St
W Belmont Ave
W Fletcher St
W Barry Ave
W Nelson St
W Wellington Ave
W Oakdale Ave
W George St
W Wolfram St
W Diversey Pkwy
W Diversey School Ct
W Schubert Ave
W Drummond Pl
W Dakin St
W Bittersweet Pl
W Sheridan Rd
W Bradley Pl
W Patterson Ave
W Brompton Ave
W Buckingham Pl
W Aldine Ave
W California Ter
N Ashland Ave
N Clark St
N Lincoln Ave
N Halsted St
N Broadway St
N Southport Ave
N Sheffield Ave
N Wilton Ave
N Kenmore Ave
N Seminary Ave
N Clifton Ave
N Racine Ave
N Magnolia Ave
N Lakewood Ave
N Wayne Ave
N Janssen Ave
N Greenview Ave
N Bosworth Ave
N Marshfield Ave
N Paulina St
N Hermitage Ave
N Alta Vista Ter
N Sheridan Rd
N Fremont St
N Reta Ave
N Elaine Pl
N Dayton St
N Mildred Ave
N Burling St
4000N
3600N
3200N
2800N
1600W
1200W
800W
1/4 mile
.25 km

Sur

Live music venue Metro has been rocking the area for 25+ years. The beautiful Music Box Theatre is the place to go for art house films—especially on weekends when they feature a live organist (their occasional sing-a-longs to musicals are also big hits). Spice lovers (and silverware haters) know to gnaw at Mama Desta's Red Sea Ethiopian restaurant. Touristy spots near the ballpark all cater to Cubs fans—caveat emptor. Further south at Clark and Belmont is the Punkin' Donuts—prime hang-out area for the city's pierced and pouty youth.

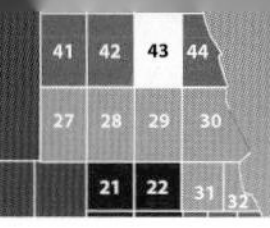

Coffee

- **Café Avanti** • 3714 N Southport Ave
- **Café Zam Zam** • 2960 N Lincoln Ave
- **Caribou Coffee** • 3240 N Ashland Ave
- **Dunkin' Donuts** • 3000 N Ashland Ave
- **Dunkin' Donuts** • 3200 N Clark St
- **Einstein Bros Bagels** • 3420 N Southport Ave
- **Einstein Bros Bagels** • 3455 N Clark St
- **The Julius Meinl Café** • 3601 N Southport Ave
- **Mellow Grounds Coffee Lounge** • 3807 N Ashland Ave
- **My Place for Tea** • 3210 N Sheffield Ave
- **Starbucks** • 1000 W Diversey Ave
- **Starbucks** • 1023 W Addison St
- **Starbucks** • 3045 N Greenview Ave
- **Starbucks** • 3184 N Clark St
- **Starbucks** • 3359 N Southport Ave

Copy Shops

- **FedEx Kinko's** • 3524 N Southport Ave ㉔
- **The UPS Store** • 3105 N Ashland Ave
- **The UPS Store** • 3540 N Southport Ave

Gyms

- **Chicago Fitness Center** • 3131 N Lincoln Ave ㉔
- **Curves (women only)** • 2825 N Sheffield Ave
- **Curves (women only)** • 3556 N Southport Ave
- **Lincoln Park Athletic Club** • 1019 W Diversey Pkwy
- **Number One Gym** • 3232 N Sheffield Ave
- **XSport Fitness** • 3240 N Ashland Ave ㉔

Hardware Stores

- **Ace Hardware** • 3921 N Sheridan Rd
- **Alhambra** • 3737 N Southport Ave
- **Tenenbaum Hardware & Paint** • 1138 W Belmont Ave

Liquor Stores

- **1000 Liquors** • 1000 W Belmont Ave
- **Bel-Port Food & Liquor** • 1362 W Belmont Ave
- **East Lake View Food & Liquor** • 3814 N Clark St
- **Foremost Liquor Store** • 3014 N Ashland Ave
- **Gilday Liquors** • 946 W Diversey Pkwy
- **Gold Crown Liquors Store** • 3425 N Clark St
- **Howards Wine Cellar (Wine only)** • 1244 W Belmont Ave
- **Que Syrah Fine Wines** • 3726 N Southport Ave

Movie Theaters

- **Music Box Theatre** • 3733 N Southport Ave
- **Vic Theatre Brew & View** • 3145 N Sheffield Ave

Nightlife

- **Bar Celona** • 3474 N Clark St
- **Berlin** • 954 W Belmont Ave
- **Bernie's** • 3664 N Clark St
- **Blarney Stone** • 3424 N Sheffield Ave
- **Bungalow Bar and Lounge** • 1622 W Belmont Ave
- **Cherry Red** • 2833 N Sheffield Ave
- **Cubby Bear** • 1059 W Addison St
- **Dark Horse** • 3443 N Sheffield Ave
- **Elbo Room** • 2871 N Lincoln Ave
- **Fizz Bar and Grill** • 3220 N Lincoln Ave
- **Fly Me to the Moon** • 3400 N Clark St
- **Ginger Man Tavern** • 3740 N Clark St
- **Goose Island Brewery** • 3535 N Clark St
- **Gunther Murphy's** • 1638 W Belmont Ave
- **Guthrie's Tavern** • 1300 W Addison St
- **Higgins' Tavern** • 3259 N Racine Ave
- **Improv Olympic** • 3541 N Clark St
- **Jack's Bar & Grill** • 2856 N Southport Ave
- **John Barleycorn** • 3524 N Clark St
- **Justin's** • 3358 N Southport Ave
- **Lincoln Tap Room** • 3010 N Lincoln Ave
- **Metro** • 3730 N Clark St
- **Moxie** • 3517 N Clark St
- **Murphy's Bleachers** • 3655 N Sheffield Ave
- **Raw Bar** • 3720 N Clark St
- **Schuba's** • 3159 N Southport Ave
- **Sheffield's** • 3258 N Sheffield Ave
- **Slugger's** • 3540 N Clark St
- **Smart Bar** • 3730 N Clark St
- **Ten Cat Tavern** • 3931 N Ashland Ave
- **Trace** • 3714 N Clark St
- **Trader Todd's** • 3216 N Sheffield Ave
- **Uncommon Ground Café** • 3800 N Clark St
- **Underground Lounge** • 952 W Newport Ave
- **Wild Hare** • 3530 N Clark St
- **Y*k-zies-Clark** • 3710 N Clark St

Pet Shops

- **4 Legs** • 3809 N Clark St
- **Abby's Let's Pet** • 3404 N Ashland Ave
- **Aquatic World (fish only)** • 3041 N Lincoln Ave
- **Olly's Kingdom** • 3525 N Southport Ave
- **Petco** • 3118 N Ashland Ave

Restaurants

- **A La Turka** • 3134 N Lincoln Ave
- **Ann Sather** • 3416 N Southport Ave
- **Ann Sather** • 929 W Belmont Ave
- **Art of Pizza** • 3033 N Ashland Ave
- **Blue Bayou** • 3734 N Southport Ave
- **Bolat** • 3346 N Clark St
- **Capt'n Nemos** • 3650 N Ashland Ave
- **Clarke's Diner** • 930 W Belmont Ave ㉔
- **Coobah** • 3423 N Southport Ave
- **Cy's Crab House** • 3819 N Ashland Ave
- **Duck Walk** • 919 W Belmont Ave
- **Frasca** • 3358 N Paulina St
- **Fundajo Grill** • 3140 N Lincoln Ave
- **Gino's** • 2801 Lincoln Ave
- **Golden Apple** • 2971 N Lincoln Ave ㉔
- **Heaven on Seven** • 3478 N Clark St
- **House of Sushi & Noodles** • 1610 W Belmont Ave
- **Julius Meinl** • 3601 N Southport Ave
- **Lucky's** • 3472 N Clark St
- **Mama Desta's Red Sea** • 3216 N Clark St
- **Matsu Yama** • 1059 W Belmont Ave
- **Matsuya** • 3469 N Clark St
- **Menagerie** • 1232 W Belmont Ave
- **Mia Francesca** • 3311 N Clark St
- **Moe's Cantina** • 3518 N Clark St
- **Orange** • 3231 N Clark St
- **Original Gino's East** • 2801 N Lincoln Ave
- **Panes** • 3002 N Sheffield Ave
- **Penny's Noodle Shop** • 3400 N Sheffield Ave
- **Penny's Noodle Shop** • 950 W Diversey Ave
- **Pepper Lounge** • 3441 N Sheffield Ave
- **Pick Me Up** • 3408 N Clark St
- **Pizza Rustica** • 3913 N Sheridan Rd
- **Platiyo** • 3313 N Clark St
- **PS Bangkok** • 3345 N Clark St
- **Rise** • 3401 N Southport Ave
- **S&G** • 3000 N Lincoln Ave
- **Salt & Pepper Diner** • 3537 N Clark St
- **Shiroi Hana** • 3242 N Clark St
- **Socca** • 3301 N Clark St
- **Standard India** • 917 W Belmont Ave
- **Strega Nona** • 3747 N Southport Ave
- **Tango Sur** • 3763 N Southport Ave
- **Taqueria El Milagro** • 1434 W Belmont Ave
- **Tombo Kitchen** • 3244 N Lincoln Ave
- **Twisted Spoke** • 3365 N Clark St
- **Vines on Clark** • 3554 N Clark St
- **Wrigleyville Dog** • 3737 N Clark St

Shopping

- **The Alley** • 3228 N Clark St
- **Belmont Army Surplus** • 855 W Belmont Ave
- **Bookworks** • 3444 N Clark St
- **Disgraceland** • 3338 N Clark St
- **Fashion Tomato** • 937 W Belmont Ave
- **Hollywood Mirror** • 812 W Belmont Ave
- **Krista K** • 3458 N Southport Ave
- **Midwest Stereo** • 1613 W Belmont Ave
- **Namaskar Boutique** • 3950 N Southport Ave
- **Never Mind** • 953 W Belmont Ave
- **Ragstock** • 812 W Belmont Ave
- **Shane** • 3657 N Southport Ave
- **Strange Cargo** • 3448 N Clark St
- **Uncle Fun** • 1338 W Belmont Ave

Video Rental

- **Blockbuster** • 2803 N Ashland Ave
- **Blockbuster** • 3753 N Clark St
- **Hollywood Video** • 3128 N Ashland Ave
- **Nationwide Video** • 843 1/2 W Belmont

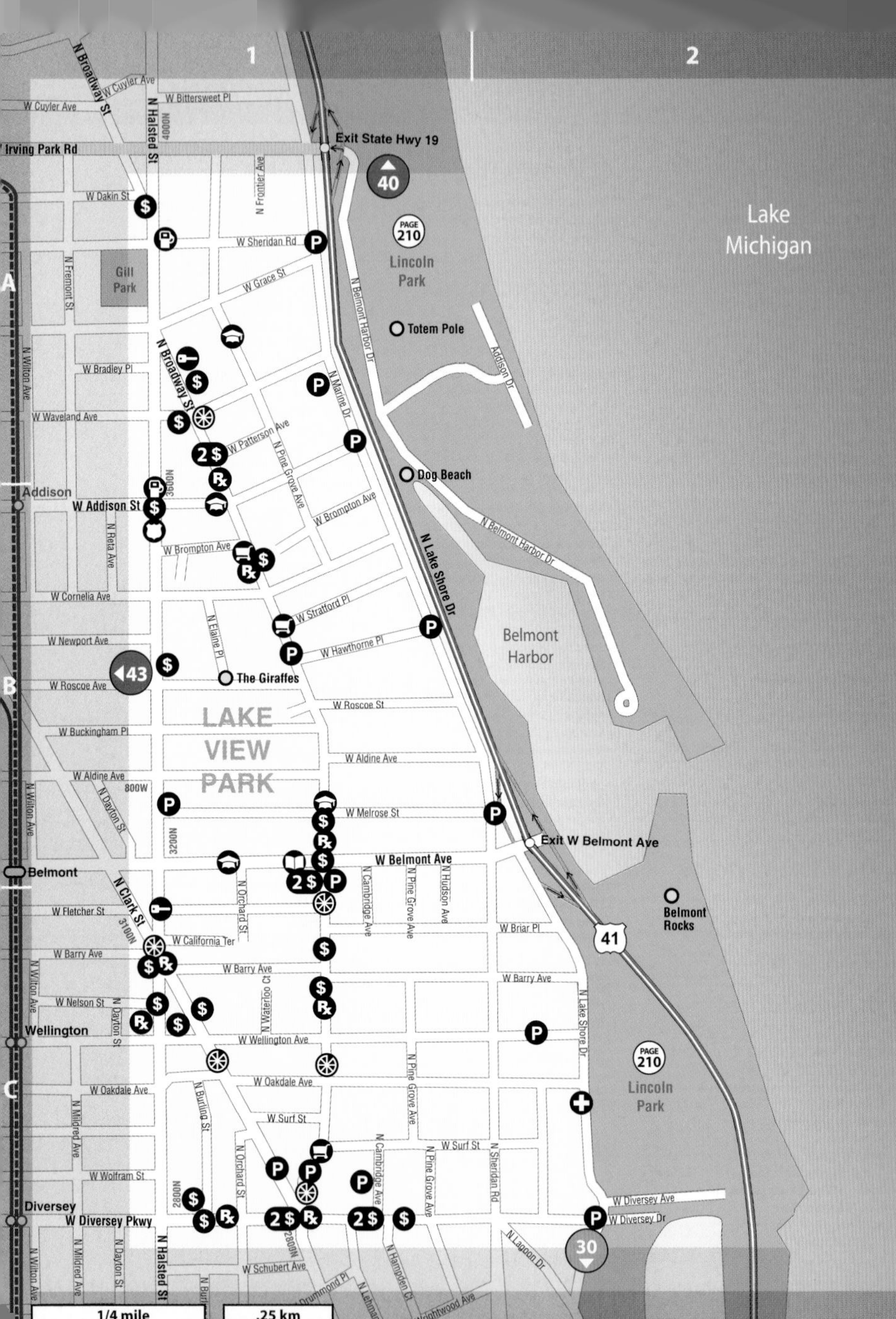

1
2
A
B
C
Lake Michigan
Lincoln Park
Totem Pole
Dog Beach
Belmont Harbor
Belmont Rocks
LAKE VIEW PARK
Gill Park
The Giraffes
Exit State Hwy 19
Exit W Belmont Ave
N Lake Shore Dr
Irving Park Rd
N Broadway St
N Halsted St
N Clark St
W Addison St
W Belmont Ave
W Diversey Pkwy
Addison
Belmont
Wellington
Diversey
PAGE 210
40
43
41
30
1/4 mile
.25 km

A.K.A. Boystown, due to its highly visable gay community, East Lakeview is home to Chicago's annual Pride Parade and the equally flamboyant Halsted Street Market Days. South of Belmont things tone down a bit, and brownstone and Graystone condos are just as likely occupied by young (straight) married couples as by gays. Great shopping and active nightlife make parking in East Lakeview absolutely awful.

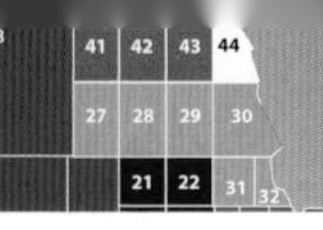

Banks

- **Central Federal Savings** • 2800 N Broadway St
- **Charter One** • 664 W Diversey Pkwy
- **Chase** • 3032 N Clark St
- **Chase** • 3714 N Broadway St
- **Chase (ATM)** • 2801 N Broadway St
- **Chase (ATM)** • 3046 N Halsted St
- **Chase (ATM)** • 3107 N Broadway St
- **Chase (ATM)** • 3201 N Broadway St
- **Chase (ATM)** • 3646 N Broadway St
- **Chase (ATM)** • 740 W Diversey Pkwy
- **Harris Trust & Savings** • 3601 N Halsted St
- **Harris Trust & Savings** • 558 W Diversey Pkwy
- **LaSalle** • 3051 N Clark St
- **LaSalle** • 538 W Diversey Pkwy
- **MidAmerica** • 3020 N Broadway St
- **North Community** • 3180 N Broadway St
- **North Community** • 3639 N Broadway St
- **North Community** • 742 W Diversey Pkwy
- **TCF** • Jewel• 3531 N Broadway St
- **TCF (ATM)** • Osco• 3101 N Clark St
- **TCF (ATM)** • 3158 N Broadway St
- **TCF (ATM)** • 3241 N Broadway St
- **TCF (ATM)** • 7-Eleven• 3407 N Halsted St
- **TCF (ATM)** • 7-Eleven• 3700 N Broadway St
- **TCF (ATM)** • 3932 N Broadway St

Car Rental

- **Budget** • 3721 N Broadway St • 773-528-1770
- **Hertz** • 3151 N Halsted St • 773-832-1912

Gas Stations

- **Mobil** • 3901 N Broadway St
- **Shell** • 801 W Addison St

Emergency Rooms

- **St Joseph's** • 2900 N Lake Shore Dr

Landmarks

- **Belmont Rocks** • W Briar Pl at the lake
- **Dog Beach** • Northern tip of Belmont Harbor
- **The Giraffes** • N Elaine Pl & W Roscoe Ave
- **Totem Pole** • W Waveland Ave & N Belmont Harbor Dr

Libraries

- **John Merlo Public Library** • 644 W Belmont Ave

Pharmacies

- **CVS Pharmacy** • 3033 N Broadway St
- **Jewel-Osco** • 3531 N Broadway St
- **Osco Drug** • 3101 N Clark St
- **Walgreens** • 2801 N Broadway St
- **Walgreens** • 3046 N Halsted St
- **Walgreens** • 3201 N Broadway St
- **Walgreens** • 3646 N Broadway St
- **Walgreens** • 740 W Diversey Pkwy

Pizza

- **Buca Di Beppo** • 2941 N Clark St
- **Chili Mac's Pizza** • 3152 N Broadway St
- **Domino's** • 3103 N Clark St
- **Nancy's Pizza** • 2930 N Broadway St
- **Pizza Paninos** • 3702 N Broadway St
- **Renaldi's Pizza Pub** • 2827 N Broadway St

Police

- **23rd District (Town Hall)** • 3600 N Halsted St

Schools

- **Bernard Zell Ansche Emet Day** • 3760 N Pine Grove Ave
- **Lake View Academy** • 716 W Addison St
- **Mt Carmel Academy** • 720 W Belmont Ave
- **Nettelhorst Elementary** • 3252 N Broadway St

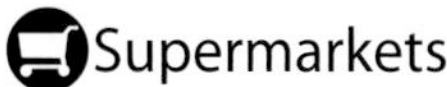

Supermarkets

- **Jewel-Osco** • 3531 N Broadway St
- **Treasure Island** • 3460 N Broadway St

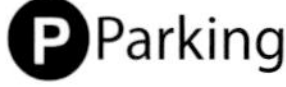

Parking

1
2
Lake Michigan
Exit State Hwy 19
40
PAGE 210
Lincoln Park
Gill Park
Belmont Harbor
LAKE VIEW PARK
43
Exit W Belmont Ave
41
30
N Broadway St
N Halsted St
W Cuyler Ave
W Bittersweet Pl
Irving Park Rd
N Frontier Ave
W Dakin St
W Sheridan Rd
W Grace St
N Fremont St
N Belmont Harbor Dr
Addison Dr
N Marine Dr
W Bradley Pl
W Waveland Ave
W Patterson Ave
N Pine Grove Ave
N Wilton Ave
Addison
W Addison St
W Brompton Ave
N Reta Ave
N Lake Shore Dr
W Cornelia Ave
W Stratford Pl
N Elaine Pl
W Newport Ave
W Hawthorne Pl
W Roscoe Ave
W Roscoe St
W Buckingham Pl
W Aldine Ave
N Dayton St
W Melrose St
W Belmont Ave
Belmont
N Clark St
N Orchard St
N Cambridge Ave
N Hudson Ave
W Fletcher St
W California Ter
W Briar Pl
W Barry Ave
W Nelson St
N Waterloo Ct
Wellington
W Wellington Ave
W Oakdale Ave
N Burling St
W Surf St
N Mildred Ave
N Sheridan Rd
W Wolfram St
W Diversey Ave
W Diversey Dr
Diversey
W Diversey Pkwy
N Lagoon Dr
W Schubert Ave
N Hampden Ct
W Drummond Pl
N Lehmann Ct
W Wrightwood Ave
4000N
3600N
800W
3200N
3100N
2800N
1/4 mile
.25 km

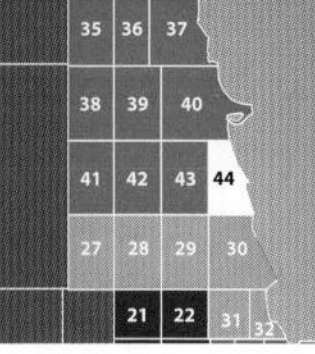

Numerous dining options and a hopping bar scene (gay bars north of Belmont, Irish pubs, south), make this area a hot destination for nightlife. Catch the latest arthouse film at the Century Cinema. Roscoe's and Sidetrack are two cavernous gay clubs that really pack 'em in. If you are coming to East Lakeview, do yourself a favor and cab it. Taxis are abundant in these parts and it's a cinch to hail one at any hour.

Coffee

- **Borders** • 2817 N Clark St
- **Caribou Coffee** • 3025 N Clark St
- **Caribou Coffee** • 3300 N Broadway St
- **Caribou Coffee** • 3500 N Halsted St
- **Coffee & Tea Exchange** • 3311 N Broadway St
- **Dunkin' Donuts** • 801 W Diversey Pkwy
- **House of Hookah** • 607 W Belmont Ave
- **Intelligentsia Coffee Roasters** • 3123 N Broadway St
- **Red Hen Bread** • 500 W Diversey Pkwy
- **Starbucks** • 3358 N Broadway St
- **Starbucks** • 3845 N Broadway St
- **Starbucks** • 617 W Diversey Pkwy

Copy Shops

- **FedEx Kinko's** • 3001 N Clark St
- **Sir Speedy** • 2818 N Halsted St
- **The UPS Store** • 3023 N Clark St
- **The UPS Store** • 3712 N Broadway St

Farmer's Markets

- **North Halsted Chicago Farmers Market (Jun–Oct; Sat, 7 am–2 pm)** • On Halsted St north of W Bradley Pl

Gyms

- **Bally Total Fitness** • 2828 N Clark St
- **Chicago Sweat Shop** • 3215 N Broadway St
- **East Lakeview Multiplex** • 3657 N Pine Grove Ave
- **Halsted Street Multiplex** • 3228 N Halsted St
- **Quads** • 3727 N Broadway St

Hardware Stores

- **Clark Street Ace Hardware** • 3011 N Clark St
- **Edwards True Value Hardware** • 2804 N Halsted St
- **Lehman's True Value Hardware** • 3473 N Broadway St
- **Midtown True Value Hardware** • 3130 N Broadway St

Liquor Stores

- **Broadway Food & Liquor** • 3158 N Broadway St
- **Eastgate Wine & Spirits** • 446 W Diversey Pkwy
- **Gold Medal Liquors** • 3823 N Broadway St
- **Kafka Wine (Wine only)** • 3325 N Halsted St
- **Paradise Liquors** • 2934 N Broadway St
- **Sysha Food and Liquor** • 702 W Diversey Pkwy

Movie Theaters

- **Landmark Century Centre Cinema** • 2828 N Clark St

Nightlife

- **Charlie's Chicago** • 3726 N Broadway St
- **Circuit** • 3641 N Halsted St
- **The Closet** • 3325 N Broadway St
- **Cocktail** • 3359 N Halsted St
- **Duke of Perth** • 2913 N Clark St
- **Gentry on Halsted** • 3320 N Halsted St
- **Hydrate** • 3458 N Halsted St
- **Jacquelines** • 3420 N Broadway St
- **Kit Kat Lounge** • 3700 N Halsted St
- **Little Jim's** • 3501 N Halsted St
- **minibar** • 3341 N Halsted St
- **Monsignor Murphy's** • 3019 N Broadway St
- **Roscoe's** • 3356 N Halsted St
- **Sidetrack** • 3349 N Halsted St
- **Spin** • 800 W Belmont Ave
- **Town Hall Pub** • 3340 N Halsted St

Pet Shops

- **Paradise Pet Salon** • 3920 N Broadway St
- **Petco** • 3046 N Halsted St
- **Petsmart - Store** • 2832 N Broadway St
- **Scrub Your Pup** • 2935 N Clark St
- **Wigglyville** • 3337 N Broadway St

Restaurants

- **Aladdin's Eatery** • 614 W Diversey Pkwy
- **Angelina Ristorante** • 3561 N Broadway St
- **Ann Sather** • 3411 N Broadway St
- **Arco de Cuchilleros** • 3445 N Halsted St
- **The Bagel** • 3107 N Broadway St
- **Café Blossom** • 608 W Barry Ave
- **Chicago Diner** • 3411 N Halsted St
- **Clark Street Dog** • 3040 N Clark St
- **Cornelia's Restaurant** • 750 W Cornelia Ave
- **Cousin's** • 2833 N Broadway St
- **Duke of Perth** • 2913 N Clark St
- **eatZi's** • Century Mall, 2828 N Clark St
- **Erwin, An American Café & Bar** • 2925 N Halsted St
- **Firefly** • 3335 N Halsted St
- **Half Shell** • 676 W Diversey Pkwy
- **Jack's on Halsted** • 3201 N Halsted St
- **Kit Kat Lounge & Supper Club** • 3700 N Halsted St
- **Koryo** • 2936 N Broadway St
- **La Creperie** • 2845 N Clark St
- **Las Mananitas** • 3523 N Halsted St
- **Mark's Chop Suey** • 3343 N Halsted St
- **Mars** • 3124 N Broadway St
- **Melrose** • 3233 N Broadway St
- **Nancy's Original Stuffed Pizza** • 2930 N Broadway St
- **Nookie's Tree** • 3334 N Halsted St
- **Renaldi's Pizza Pub** • 2827 N Broadway St
- **Wakamono** • 3317 N Broadway St
- **X/O** • 3441 N Halsted St
- **Yoshi's Café** • 3257 N Halsted St

Shopping

- **Borderline** • 3333 N Broadway St
- **Century Mall** • 2828 N Clark St
- **Cupcakes** • 613 W Briar Pl
- **Clothes Optional** • 2918 N Clark St
- **Equinox** • 3401 N Broadway St
- **GayMart** • 3459 N Halsted St
- **Onu Asian Market** • 3310 N Broadway St
- **Pastoral Artisan** • 2945 N Broadway St
- **The Pleasure Chest** • 3155 N Broadway St
- **Reckless Records** • 3161 N Broadway St
- **Spare Parts** • 2947 N Broadway St
- **Tulip Toy Gallery** • 3448 N Halsted St
- **Unabridged Bookstore** • 3251 N Broadway St
- **Windy City Sweets** • 3308 N Broadway St

Video Rental

- **Blockbuster** • 3120 N Clark St
- **Broadway Video** • 3916 N Broadway St
- **Golden Video** • 3619 N Broadway St
- **Hollywood Video** • 2868 N Broadway St
- **Nationwide Video** • 2827 N Broadway St
- **Nationwide Video** • 3936 N Clarendon Ave
- **RJ's Video** • 3452 N Halsted St
- **Specialty Video** • 3221 N Broadway St
- **West Coast Video** • 3114 N Broadway St
- **Windy City Video** • 3701 N Halsted St

MORTON GROVE
SKOKIE
NILES
LINCOLNWOOD
PARK RIDGE
EDISON PARK
WILDWOOD
EDGEBROOK
Forest Preserve
Bryn Mawr Country Club
SAUGANASH
PULASKI PARK
NORWOOD PARK
OLD NORWOOD PARK
HOLLYWOOD PARK
ORIOLE PARK
UNION RIDGE
La Bagh Woods
NORTH PARK
FOSTER
BIG OAKS
JEFFERSON PARK
NORTH MAYFAIR
HARWOOD HEIGHTS
NORRIDGE
MAYFAIR
ALBANY PARK
IRVING WOODS
DUNNING
PORTAGE PARK
IRVING PARK
KILBOURNE PARK
BELMONT TERRACE
BELMONT HEIGHTS
SCHORSCH VILLAGE
BELMONT CENTRAL
CRAGIN
KELVYN PARK
LOGAN SQUARE
MONTCLARE
HANSON PARK
ELMWOOD PARK
GALEWOOD
NORTH AUSTIN
HERMOSA
HUMBOLT PARK
Superdawg Drive-In
Harlem CTA Station
Harlem
Jefferson Park
Copernicus Center
Montrose
Gompers Park
Eugene Field Park
The Admiral Theater
Irving Park
Addison
Belmont
Logan Square Column
Logan Square
Walt Disney House
Hanson Park Fieldhouse
Church St
W Dempster St
Lincoln Ave
Edens Expy
Niles Center Rd
Skokie Blvd
Main St
Crawford Ave
Mc Cormick Rd
Milwaukee Ave
Oakton St
Central Carpenter Rd
W Howard St
Gross Point Rd
W Touhy Ave
N Lincoln Ave
W Pratt Ave
S Dee Rd
N Newark Ave
Lehigh Ave
Caldwell Ave
W Devon Ave
N Canfield Ave
W Talcott Ave
Northwest Hwy
Milwaukee Ave
W Peterson Ave
N Elston Ave
N Pulaski Rd
Foster Ave
Higgins Rd
W Foster Ave
Lawrence Ave
W Lawrence Ave
N Kedzie Ave
Montrose Ave
W Montrose Ave
Kennedy Expy
N Central Ave
W Irving Park Blvd
Forest Preserve Dr
N Harlem Ave
N Cumberland Ave
W Addison Ave
Milwaukee Ave
N Cicero Ave
N Narragansett Ave
N Oak Park
N Austin Ave
W Belmont Ave
Laramie Ave
W Diversey Ave
W Grand Ave
W Fullerton Ave
Thatcher Rd
W Armitage Ave
Humbolt Blvd
W North Ave
1 mile
1 km
14
21
54
41
94
90
43
19
171
50
64
45
46
33
35
38
41
47
48
27
49
1
2

Essentials

If there's one thing you can count on in Northwest Chicago, it's that you can count on just about everything. Compared to other sections of the city, the Northwest is a bastion of stability. Most of the people and businesses have been around forever, and even typically transitory ethnic enclaves are fairly entrenched. This includes a crazy quilt of Eastern European, Middle Eastern, Korean, and Italian quarters, blocks, and streets. Northwest Chicago is blessed with an abundance of small parks and field houses, as well as a large hunk of forest preserve, giving much of the area a bucolic, suburban feel.

Landmarks

- **Copernicus Center** • 5216 W Lawrence Ave
- **Eugene Field Park** • 5100 N Ridgeway Ave
- **Gompers Park** • 4222 W Foster Ave
- **Hanson Park Fieldhouse** • 5501 W Fullerton Ave
- **Harlem CTA Station** • N Harlem Ave & The Kennedy Expy
- **Logan Square Column** • 3100 W Logan Blvd
- **Superdawg Drive-In** • 6363 N Milwaukee Ave
- **The Admiral Theater** • 3940 W Lawrence Ave
- **Walt Disney House** • 2156 N Tripp Ave

Sundries / Entertainment

Northwest Chicago wears its blue-collar ethnic proclivities on its sleeve. Local shops and restaurants don't go out of their way to attract clientele outside of their own, and signs, menus, and even the staff at the area's abundant Korean and Eastern European businesses make little effort to communicate in English. (The same can be said for the clientele at many of the area's numerous ostensibly English-speaking corner taverns.) Adventuresome diners rise to the challenge—some of the city's best unsung gems are to be found here, including Hungarian Paprikash, Thai vegan spot Amitabul, and the Swedish Tre Kronor. Toss back authentic pints at the 5th Province Pub. Located in the Irish-American Heritage Center, it's only open on Friday and Saturday nights. Rosa's Lounge is a venerable, beloved Chicago jazz and blues venue.

Coffee

- **Cafeteria Marianao II** • 4825 W Armitage Ave
- **Caffe' Italia** • 2625 N Harlem Ave
- **Capitol Café** • 2550 N Pulaski Rd
- **Damato Bakery & Café** • 7326 W Lawrence Ave
- **Dunkin' Donuts** • 2337 N Cicero Ave
- **Dunkin' Donuts** • 2640 N Narragansett Ave
- **Dunkin' Donuts** • 3039 N Central Ave
- **Dunkin' Donuts** • 3359 N Harlem Ave
- **Dunkin' Donuts** • 3801 W Belmont Ave
- **Dunkin' Donuts** • 3843 N Cicero Ave
- **Dunkin' Donuts** • 3946 W Devon Ave
- **Dunkin' Donuts** • 4045 W Lawrence Ave
- **Dunkin' Donuts** • 4359 N Pulaski Rd
- **Dunkin' Donuts** • 4644 W Diversey Ave
- **Dunkin' Donuts** • 4867 N Milwaukee Ave
- **Dunkin' Donuts** • 5000 W Irving Park Rd
- **Dunkin' Donuts** • 5050 N Cicero Ave
- **Dunkin' Donuts** • 5205 N Nagle Ave
- **Dunkin' Donuts** • 5550 N Harlem Ave
- **Dunkin' Donuts** • 5650 W Fullerton Ave
- **Dunkin' Donuts** • 5959 W Diversey Ave
- **Dunkin' Donuts** • 6001 W Addison St
- **Dunkin' Donuts** • 6342 N Milwaukee Ave
- **Dunkin' Donuts** • 6408 W Irving Park Rd
- **Dunkin' Donuts** • 7156 N Harlem Ave
- **Dunkin' Donuts** • 7171 W Irving Park Rd
- **Dunkin' Donuts** • 7201 W Grand Ave
- **Dunkin' Donuts** • 7801 W Lawrence Ave
- **Edgebrook Coffee Shop** • 6322 N Central Ave
- **Euro Café** • 3435 N Harlem Ave
- **Gloria Jean's Coffee Bean** • 4202 N Harlem Ave
- **Hotti Biscotti** • 3545 W Fullerton Ave
- **J Bean Coffee & Café** • 7221 W Forest Preserve Ave
- **Java Thai** • 4272 W Irving Park Rd
- **Michael's Gourment Coffee** • 7714 W Belmont Ave
- **Neferetiti Café** • 3737 W Lawrence Ave
- **Open Hearth Coffee Shop** • 5207 N Kimball Ave
- **Schlegl's Bakery & Café** • 3334 W Foster Ave
- **Starbucks** • Target • 2901 S Cicero Ave
- **Starbucks** • Target • 4104 N Harlem Ave
- **Starbucks** • 4159 W Peterson Ave
- **Starbucks** • 4365 W Irving Park Rd
- **Starbucks** • 5406 W Devon Ave
- **Starbucks** • 6451 W Diversey Ave
- **Starbucks** • Target • 6525 W Diversey Ave
- **Sun Café** • 5259 W Montrose Ave
- **Tassili** • 4342 N Elston Ave

Movie Theaters

- **La Salle Bank Cinema** • 4901 W Irving Park Rd
- **Loews Norridge 10** • 4520 N Harlem Ave

Nightlife

- **5th Province Pub** • Irish-American Heritage Ctr• 4626 N Knox Ave
- **Abbey Pub** • 3420 W Grace St
- **Emerald Isle** • 6686 N Northwest Hwy
- **Fischman Liquors** • 4780 N Milwaukee Ave
- **Hollywood Lounge** • 3301 W Bryn Mawr Ave
- **Little Rascals** • 4356 W Belmont Ave
- **Moretti's** • 6727 N Olmstead Ave
- **New Polonia Club** • 6101 W Belmont Ave
- **Old Irving Park Sports Bar & Grill** • 4217 W Irving Park Blvd
- **Rosa's Lounge** • 3420 W Armitage Ave
- **Vaughan's Pub** • 5485 N Northwest Hwy

Restaurants

- **Amitabul** • 6207 N Milwaukee Ave
- **Birria Huentitan** • 4019 W North Ave
- **Blue Angel** • 5310 N Milwaukee Ave
- **Chiyo** • 3800 W Lawrence Ave
- **Don Juan** • 6730 N Northwest Hwy
- **Edgebrook Coffee Shop** • 6322 N Central Ave
- **Elephant** • 5348 W Devon Ave
- **Fonda Del Mar** • 3749 W Fullerton Ave
- **Fontana** • 3424 W Irving Park Rd
- **Gale Street Inn** • 4914 N Milwaukee Ave
- **Grota Smorgasborg** • 3112 N Central Ave
- **Halina's Polish Delights** • 5914 W Lawrence Ave
- **Hiromi's** • 3609 W Lawrence Ave
- **Joy Ribs** • 6320 N Lincoln Ave
- **Mario's Café** • 5241 N Harlem Ave
- **Mayan Sol** • 3830 W Lawrence Ave
- **Mirabell** • 3454 W Addison St
- **Montasero's Ristorante** • 3935 W Devon Ave
- **Noodles** • 5956 W Higgins Ave
- **Paprikash** • 5210 W Diversey Ave
- **Pollo Campero** • 2730 N Narragansett Ave
- **Red Apple** • 3121 N Milwaukee Ave
- **Ristorante Agostino** • 2817 N Harlem Ave
- **Sabatino's** • 4441 W Irving Park Rd
- **Seo Hae** • 3534 W Lawrence Ave
- **So Gong Dong Tofu House** • 3307 W Bryn Mawr Ave
- **Taqueria La Oaxaquena** • 6113 W Diversey Ave
- **Teresa II Polish Restaurants & Lounge** • 4751 N Milwaukee Ave
- **Trattoria Pasta D'Arte** • 6311 N Milwaukee Ave
- **Tre Kronor** • 3258 W Foster Ave

Shopping

- **Albany Office Supply** • 3419 W Lawrence Ave
- **American Science & Surplus** • 5316 N Milwaukee Ave
- **El Mundo Del Dulce (Candy World)** • 4806 N Drake Ave
- **Harlem Irving Plaza** • N Harlem Ave & W Irving Park Blvd
- **NY Shoes Imports** • 3546 W Lawrence Ave
- **Perfumes R' Us** • 3608 W Lawrence Ave
- **Rolling Stone Records** • 7300 W Irving Park Rd
- **Salvation Army Thrift Store** • 3837 W Fullerton Ave
- **Srpska Tradicija** • 3615 W Lawrence Ave
- **Sweden Shop** • 3304 W Foster Ave
- **Village Discount Outlet** • 4635 N Elston Ave

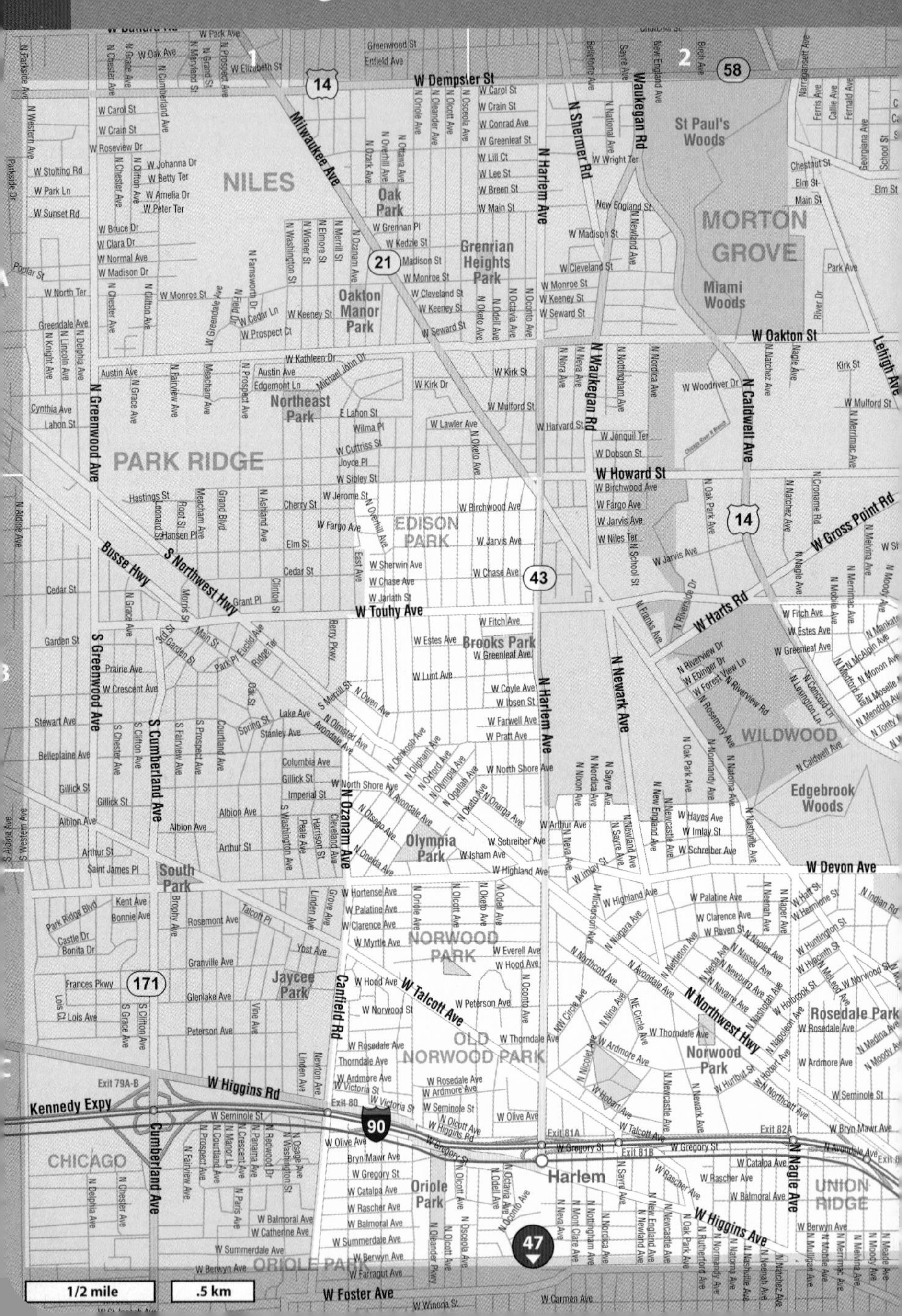
1
2
NILES
PARK RIDGE
MORTON GROVE
EDISON PARK
NORWOOD PARK
OLD NORWOOD PARK
WILDWOOD
CHICAGO
UNION RIDGE
ORIOLE PARK
Harlem
St Paul's Woods
Miami Woods
Oak Park
Grenrian Heights Park
Oakton Manor Park
Northeast Park
Brooks Park
Olympia Park
South Park
Jaycee Park
Norwood Park
Oriole Park
Edgebrook Woods
Rosedale Park
W Dempster St
W Oakton St
W Howard St
W Touhy Ave
W Devon Ave
W Higgins Rd
W Higgins Ave
W Foster Ave
W Talcott Ave
W Harts Rd
W Gross Point Rd
Milwaukee Ave
N Harlem Ave
N Waukegan Rd
Waukegan Rd
N Shermer Rd
N Caldwell Ave
N Greenwood Ave
S Greenwood Ave
S Cumberland Ave
Cumberland Ave
N Ozanam Ave
Canfield Rd
N Newark Ave
N Nagle Ave
N Northwest Hwy
S Northwest Hwy
Busse Hwy
Kennedy Expy
Lehigh Ave
14
21
43
58
171
90
Exit 79A-B
Exit 80
Exit 81A
Exit 81B
Exit 82A
47
1/2 mile
.5 km

SKOKIE
LINCOLNWOOD
EDGEBROOK
SAUGANASH
PULASKI PARK
HOLLYWOOD PARK
Oakton Park
Little League Park
Laramie Park
Coyle Park
Forest Glen Woods
Peterson Park
Nature Center
Legion Park
La Bagh Woods
Gompers Park
Field Park
Kiwanis Park
Dempster St
Main St
W Oakton St
Howard St
W Touhy Ave
W Pratt Ave
Devon Ave
W Peterson Ave
W Foster Ave
Niles Center Rd
Skokie Blvd
Lincoln Ave
W Gross Point Rd
Carpenter Rd
N Central Ave
Edens Expy
N Cicero Ave
N Crawford Ave
McCormick Blvd
N McCormick Rd
N Jersey Ave
N Kedzie Ave
N Lehigh Ave
Exit 37A-B
Exit 39A-B
Exit 41A-B
Exit 41C
Exit 42
Exit 83B
Exit N Elston Ave
94
41
50
54
14
33
35
48
3
4
A
B
C

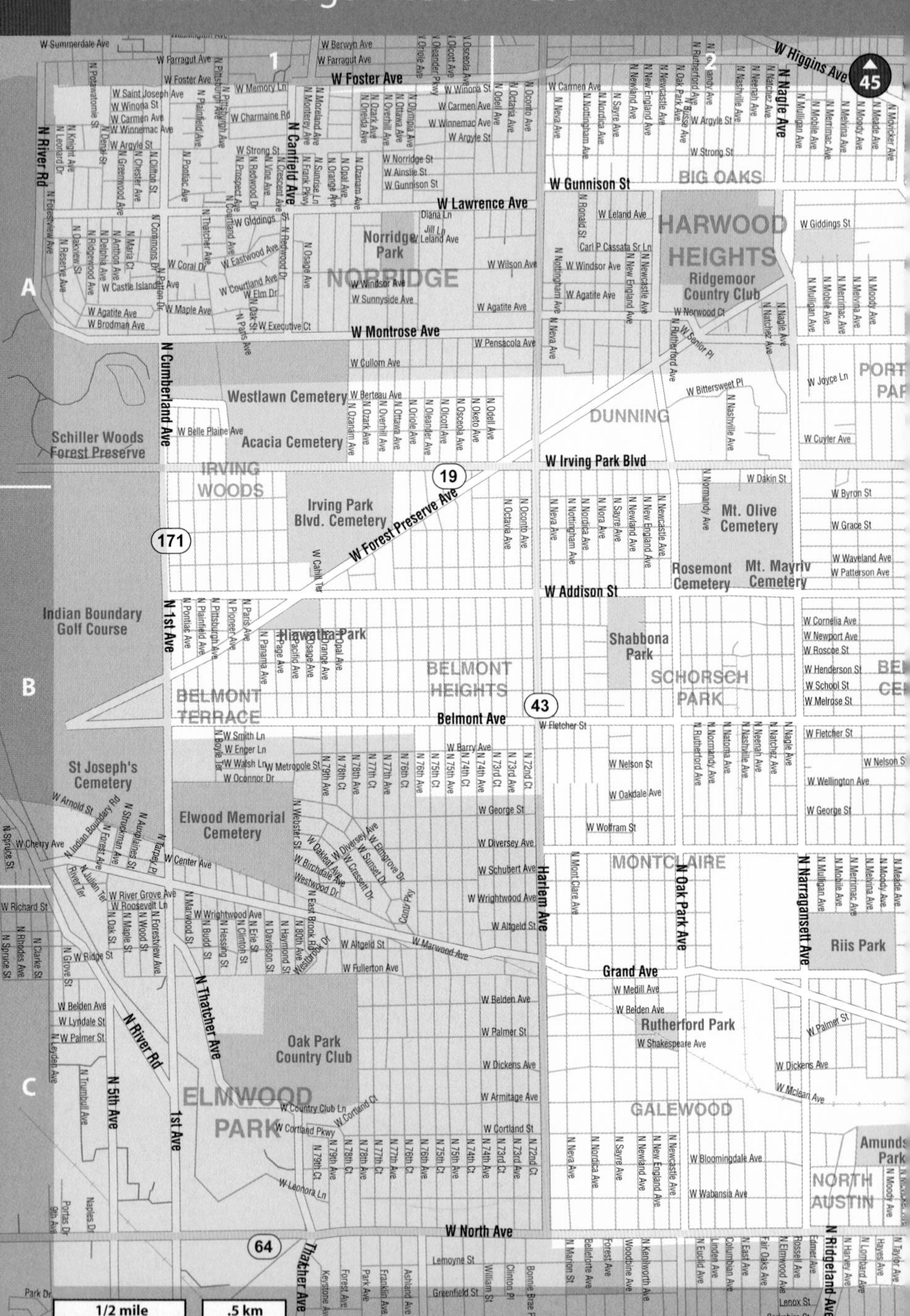
1
2
45
A
B
C
W Foster Ave
W Lawrence Ave
W Gunnison St
W Montrose Ave
W Irving Park Blvd
W Addison St
Belmont Ave
Grand Ave
W North Ave
W Higgins Ave
N Cumberland Ave
N Canfield Ave
N Nagle Ave
N River Rd
N 1st Ave
Harlem Ave
N Oak Park Ave
N Narragansett Ave
N Ridgeland Ave
N Thatcher Ave
Thatcher Ave
1st Ave
N 5th Ave
W Forest Preserve Ave
W Marwood Ave
19
171
43
64
NORRIDGE
Norridge Park
HARWOOD HEIGHTS
Ridgemoor Country Club
BIG OAKS
DUNNING
Westlawn Cemetery
Acacia Cemetery
Schiller Woods Forest Preserve
IRVING WOODS
Irving Park Blvd. Cemetery
Mt. Olive Cemetery
Rosemont Cemetery
Mt. Mayriv Cemetery
Indian Boundary Golf Course
Hiawatha Park
Shabbona Park
BELMONT HEIGHTS
SCHORSCH PARK
BELMONT TERRACE
St Joseph's Cemetery
Elwood Memorial Cemetery
MONTCLAIRE
Riis Park
Rutherford Park
Oak Park Country Club
ELMWOOD PARK
GALEWOOD
NORTH AUSTIN
1/2 mile
.5 km

La Bagh Woods
W Foster Ave
46
Gompers Park
38
NORTH MAYFAIR
Jefferson Park
Kennedy Expy
N Elston Ave
W Lawrence Ave
W Wilson Ave
Mayfair Park
MAYFAIR
Dickinson Park
Montrose
W Montrose Ave
N Milwaukee Ave
ALBANY PARK
N Keeler Ave
N Pulaski Rd
N Kedzie Ave
Portage Park
N Kostner Ave
OLD IRVING PARK
Irving Park
W Irving Park Blvd
N Central Ave
N Laramie Ave
N Cicero Ave
N Hamlin Ave
N Kimball Ave
41
Addison
W Addison St
Chopin Park
Kilbourn Park
KILBOURN PARK
Belmont
W Belmont Ave
CRAGIN
Kenwel Playground Park
W Diversey Ave
Kosciusz Park
Kelvyn Park
KELVYN PARK
Cragin Park
Logan Square
W Fullerton Ave
Hansen Park
Blackhawk Park
Hermosa Park
Palmer Square
W Grand Ave
Mozart Park
W Armitage Ave
HERMOSA
Henry Greenbaum Park
N Humbolt Ave
27
W North Ave
NORTH AUSTIN
49
Humbolt Park
La Follette Park

CRAGIN
HERMOSA
LOGAN SQUARE
BUCKTOWN
WEST HUMBOLDT PARK
Humboldt Park
WICKER PARK
HUMBOLDT PARK
UKRAINIAN VILLAGE
NOBLE SQUARE
NORTH AUSTIN
EAST GARFIELD PARK
Conservatory-Central Park Drive
WEST TOWN
Austin Town Hall
Bison Statues
Garfield Park Conservatory
Engine 44 Firehouse Mural
SOUTH AUSTIN
WEST GARFIELD PARK
Garfield Park
NEAR WEST SIDE
Delta Fish Market
Our Lady of Sorrows
Columbus Park
Columbus Park Refectory
Eisenhower Expy
LAWNDALE
TRI-TAYLOR
Medical Center
ILLINOIS MEDICAL DISTRICT
UNIVERSITY VILLAGE/ LITTLE ITALY
LITTLE VILLAGE
DOUGLAS PARK
Douglas Park
Central Park
CICERO
HEART OF CHICAGO
PILSEN
MCKINGLEY PARK
BRIDGEPORT
STICKNEY
BRIGHTON PARK
Chicago Sanitary and Ship Canal
Stevenson Expy
ARCHER HEIGHTS
SLEEPY HOLLOW
LE CLAIR COURTS
VITTUM PARK
GAGE PARK
BACK OF THE YARDS
Sherman Park
Chicago Midway
WEST ELSDON
Midway
ENGLEWOOD
W Grand Ave
W Armitage Ave
W North Ave
W Division St
W Chicago Ave
W Lake St
W Washington Blvd
W Jackson Blvd
W Roosevelt Rd
W Douglas Blvd
W 16th St
W 18th St
W Cermak Rd
W Ogden Ave
W 26th St
W 31st St
W 35th St
W Pershing Rd
W 40th St
S Archer Ave
W 43rd St
W 47th St
W Archer Ave
W 51st St
W 55th St
W Garfield Blvd
W 59th St
N Austin Blvd
N Central Ave
N Laramie Ave
Cicero Ave
N Pulaski Rd
N Homan Ave
N Kedzie Ave
N California Ave
N Western Ave
N Damen Ave
N Ashland Ave
N Racine A
N Clybourn Ave
Dan Ryan Expy
Randolph Pl
Washington Blvd
Adams Ave
W Ogden Ave
N Kostner Ave
S Kostner Ave
Hamlin Blvd
Central Park Ave
Independence Blvd
S Homan Ave
Sacramento Blvd
S California Ave
S Pulaski Rd
S Austin Blvd
S Central Ave
S Laramie Ave
Marshal Blvd
S Western Ave
S Oakley Ave
S Damen Ave
S Ashland Ave
S Blue Island Ave
S Racine Ave
S Morgan St
S Halsted St
S Canalport Av
S Throop St
S Kedzie Ave
Austin
Central
Laramie
Cicero
Pulaski
Kedzie
California
Ashland
Western
Racine
Kedzie-Homan
Polk
18th
54th/Cermak
Kildare
Hoyne
35th/Archer
Halsted
1
2
90
94
64
290
50
34
55
PAGE 216
48
27
21
49
50
23
25
4
12
51
52
15
53
54
1 mile
1 km

Essentials

Heart of Chicago houses a proud Italian immigrant community, mixing peacefully with West Pilsen's Latin vibe. Some of Chicago's roughest areas are encompassed by the westside territory, specifically from Douglas Park to Austin. Come for the parks—over 300 acres worth, with lakes, beaches, even a waterfall—but park nearby and skedaddle before dark. The Chicago Sanitary and Ship Canal boasts a couple of Chicago's oldest drawbridges, long out of commission.

o Landmarks

- **Austin Town Hall** • 5610 W Lake St
- **Bison Statues at Humboldt Park** • 1400 N Sacramento Ave
- **Columbus Park Refectory** • Columbus Park, 500 S Central Ave
- **Delta Fish Market** • 228 S Kedzie Ave
- **Engine 44 Firehouse Mural** • 412 N Kedzie Ave
- **Garfield Park Conservatory** • 300 N Central Park Ave
- **Our Lady of Sorrows School** • 3121 W Jackson Blvd

Sundries / Entertainment

There's no absence of take-out rib joints, chop suey, or taquerias on the west side. Finding a place where you can actually sit down to enjoy a meal presents more of a challenge. For those so inclined, Edna's serves up some of the city's best soul food—save room for dessert. Puerto Rican stews are the specialty at cafeteria-style La Palma. The 2400 block of South Oakley rivals Taylor Street for authentic Italian feasts. Hipsters nostalgic for their grandparents' era hang out at the retro-styled California Clipper.

Coffee

- **Coffee Break** • 4741 S Ashland Ave
- **Dunkin' Donuts** • 1345 N Pulaski Rd
- **Dunkin' Donuts** • 2477 S Archer Ave
- **Dunkin' Donuts** • 3910 S Archer Ave
- **Dunkin' Donuts** • 4302 S Ashland Ave
- **Dunkin' Donuts** • 4701 S Kedzie Ave
- **Dunkin' Donuts** • 4800 W Lake St
- **Dunkin' Donuts** • 6641 S Cicero Ave
- **Dunkin' Donuts** • 800 N Kedzie Ave
- **Humboldt Pie** • 1001 N California Ave
- **Starbucks** • Target • 4433 S Pulaski Rd
- **Starbucks** • 4701 S Cicero Ave

Movie Theaters

- **ICE Lawndale Cinemas** • 3330 W Roosevelt Rd

Nightlife

- **Black Beetle** • 2532 W Chicago Ave
- **California Clipper** • 1002 N California Ave
- **Freddie's Pepper Box** • 4501 W Madison St
- **La Justicia** • 3901 W 26th St
- **Ms Carol's Place** • 3858 W Madison St
- **Red's Lounge** • 3479 S Archer Ave

Restaurants

- **Amarind's** • 6822 W North Ave
- **Bacchanalia Ristorante** • 2413 S Oakley Ave
- **Bruna's** • 2424 S Oakley Ave
- **Coco** • 2723 W Division St
- **Coleman's Hickory House** • 5754 W Chicago Ave
- **Edna's Restaurant** • 3175 W Madison St
- **Falco's Pizza** • 2806 W 40th St
- **Feed** • 2803 W Chicago Ave
- **Flying Saucer** • 1123 N California Ave
- **Haro** • 2436 S Oakley Ave
- **Ignotz** • 2421 S Oakley Ave
- **La Palma** • 1340 N Homan Ave
- **Lalo's** • 3515 W 26th St
- **Lindy's and Gertie's** • 3685 S Archer Ave
- **MacArthur's** • 5412 W Madison Ave
- **Maiz** • 1041 N California Ave
- **New Submarine Pier** • 4048 S Archer Ave
- **Pico Rico** • 4107 W North Ave
- **Taqueria Puebla Mexico** • 3625 W North Ave
- **Taqueria Atotonilco** • 3916 W 26th St
- **Tassili Café** • 4342 N Elston Ave
- **Tommy's Rock-n-Roll Café** • 2548 W Chicago Ave

Shopping

- **Buyer's Flea Market** • 4545 W Division St
- **Family Dollar** • 5410 W Chicago Ave
- **Moo & Oink** • 4848 W Madison St
- **Village Discount Outlet** • 2514 W 47th St
- **Village Discount Outlet** • 4020 W 26th St

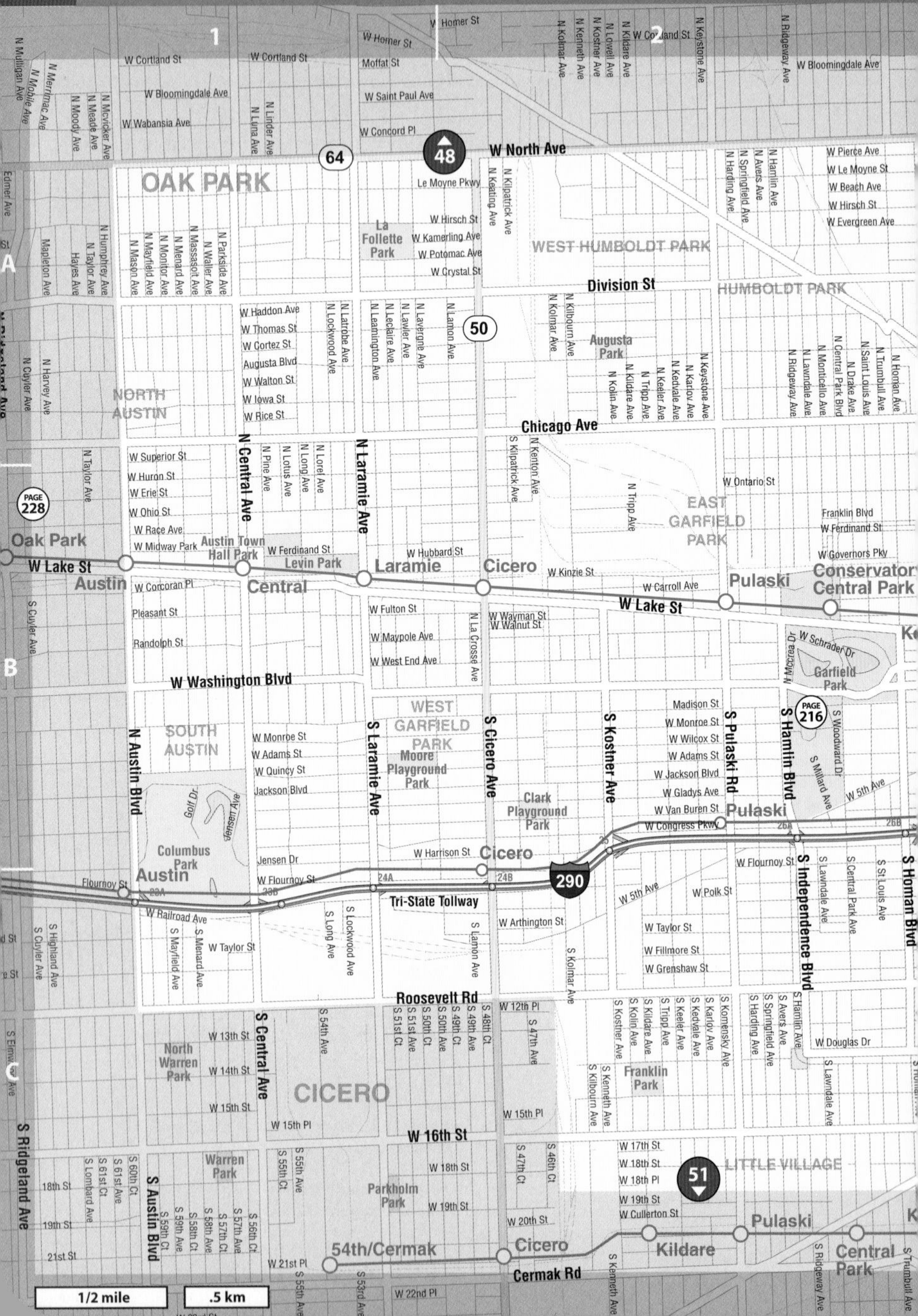
OAK PARK
NORTH AUSTIN
SOUTH AUSTIN
WEST HUMBOLDT PARK
HUMBOLDT PARK
EAST GARFIELD PARK
WEST GARFIELD PARK
CICERO
LITTLE VILLAGE
W North Ave
Division St
Chicago Ave
W Lake St
W Washington Blvd
Roosevelt Rd
W 16th St
Cermak Rd
N Central Ave
N Laramie Ave
S Cicero Ave
S Kostner Ave
S Pulaski Rd
S Hamlin Blvd
N Austin Blvd
S Laramie Ave
S Central Ave
S Austin Blvd
S Ridgeland Ave
S Independence Blvd
S Homan Blvd
Tri-State Tollway
Columbus Park
Augusta Park
La Follette Park
Levin Park
Austin Town Hall Park
Moore Playground Park
Clark Playground Park
Garfield Park
Franklin Park
North Warren Park
Warren Park
Parkholm Park
Austin
Central
Laramie
Cicero
Pulaski
Conservatory Central Park
Kildare
Central Park
54th/Cermak
Oak Park
PAGE 228
PAGE 216
48
51
64
50
290
1/2 mile
.5 km

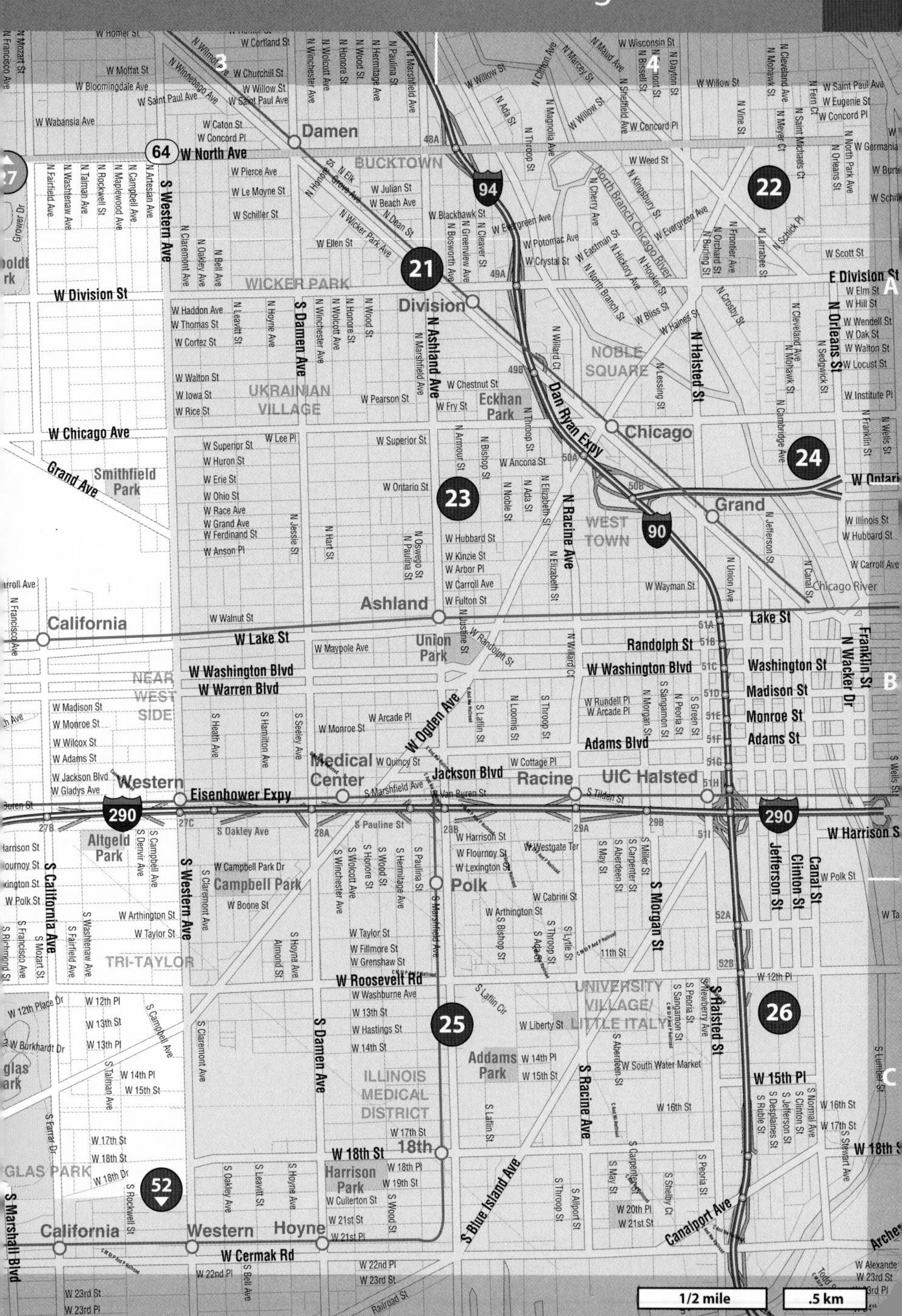
3
4
A
B
C
Damen
64
W North Ave
BUCKTOWN
94
22
21
WICKER PARK
W Division St
Division
E Division St
NOBLE SQUARE
N Halsted St
N Orleans St
UKRAINIAN VILLAGE
Eckhan Park
Dan Ryan Expy
Chicago
W Chicago Ave
Grand Ave
Smithfield Park
23
24
W Ontario St
Grand
WEST TOWN
90
N Racine Ave
N Ashland Ave
S Western Ave
S Damen Ave
Chicago River
Ashland
California
W Lake St
Lake St
Union Park
Randolph St
W Washington Blvd
Washington St
W Warren Blvd
NEAR WEST SIDE
Madison St
Monroe St
Adams Blvd
Adams St
Franklin St
N Wacker Dr
W Ogden Ave
Medical Center
Jackson Blvd
Racine
UIC Halsted
Western
Eisenhower Expy
290
Altgeld Park
Campbell Park
Polk
S California Ave
S Western Ave
S Morgan St
Jefferson St
Clinton St
Canal St
W Harrison St
TRI-TAYLOR
W Roosevelt Rd
UNIVERSITY VILLAGE/ LITTLE ITALY
S Halsted St
25
26
Addams Park
ILLINOIS MEDICAL DISTRICT
S Racine Ave
W 15th Pl
18th
W 18th St
Harrison Park
S Blue Island Ave
Canalport Ave
52
California
Western
Hoyne
W Cermak Rd
S Marshall Blvd
1/2 mile
.5 km

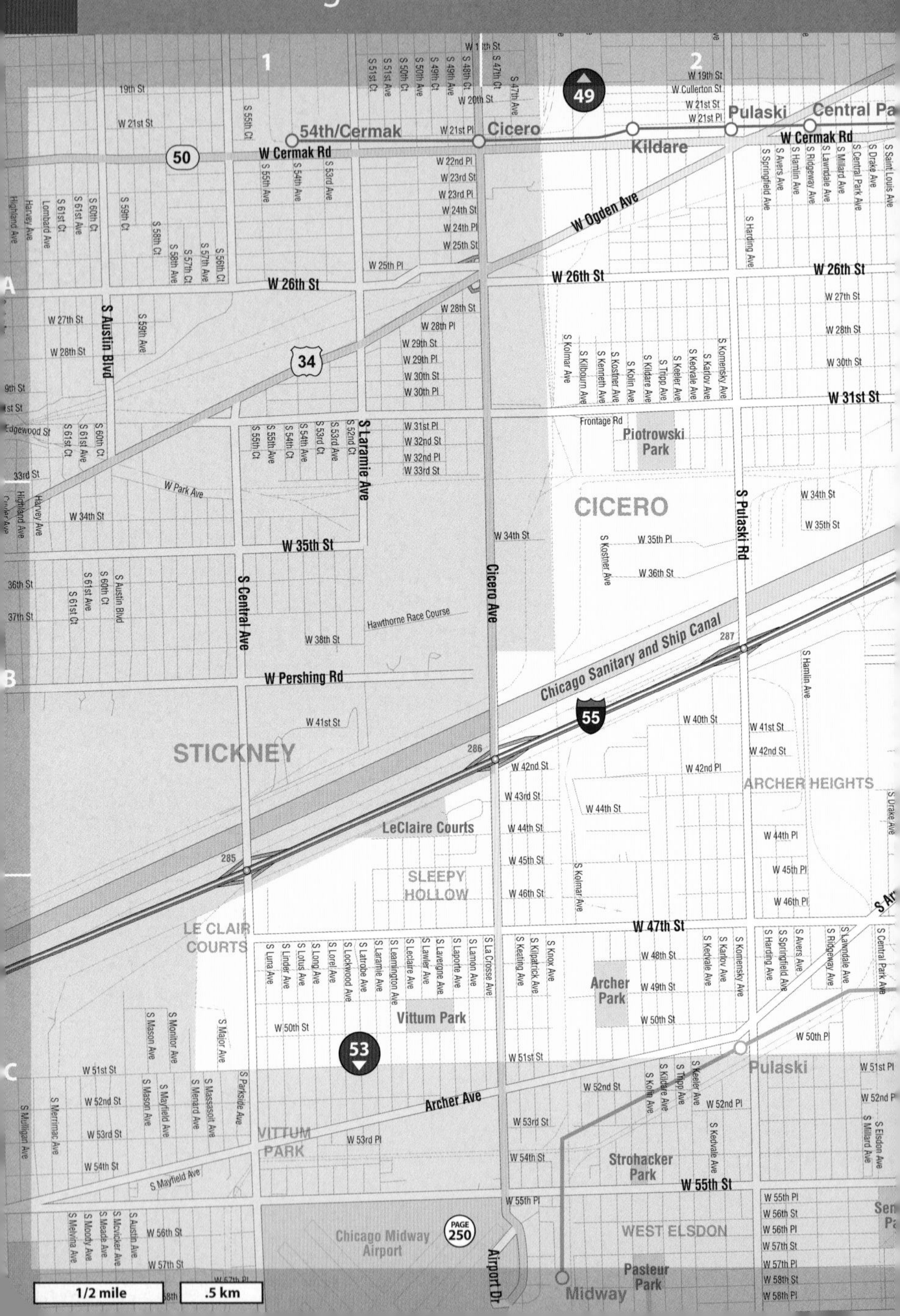
1
2
A
B
C
49
50
34
55
53
54th/Cermak
Cicero
Kildare
Pulaski
Central Pa
W Cermak Rd
W Ogden Ave
W 26th St
S Austin Blvd
S Laramie Ave
S Central Ave
Cicero Ave
S Pulaski Rd
W 31st St
W 35th St
W Pershing Rd
W Park Ave
Hawthorne Race Course
Piotrowski Park
CICERO
STICKNEY
Chicago Sanitary and Ship Canal
ARCHER HEIGHTS
LeClaire Courts
SLEEPY HOLLOW
LE CLAIR COURTS
W 47th St
Archer Park
Vittum Park
VITTUM PARK
Archer Ave
Strohacker Park
W 55th St
WEST ELSDON
Chicago Midway Airport
PAGE 250
Pasteur Park
Midway
Airport Dr
S Mayfield Ave
Frontage Rd
285
286
287
1/2 mile
.5 km

California
Hoyne
Western
W Cermak Rd
PILSON
HEART OF CHICAGO
S Blue Island Ave
Halsted
Ashland
MCKINGLEY PARK
McGuane Park
W 26th St
W 31st St
W 31st Blvd
S California Ave
S Damen Ave
S Pitney Ct
Chicago River S Branch
Wilson Park
W 35th St
35/Archer
BRIDGEPORT
Donovan Park
McKinley Park
S Archer Ave
W Pershing Rd
S Ashland Ave
S Western Ave
S Halsted St
Kelly Park
BRIGHTON PARK
W 43rd St
S Western Blvd
Davis Square Park
W 47th St
S Racine Ave
Western
Oakley Playground Park
Cornell Square Park
W 51st St
Sherman Park
W Garfield Blvd
Gage Park
W 59th St

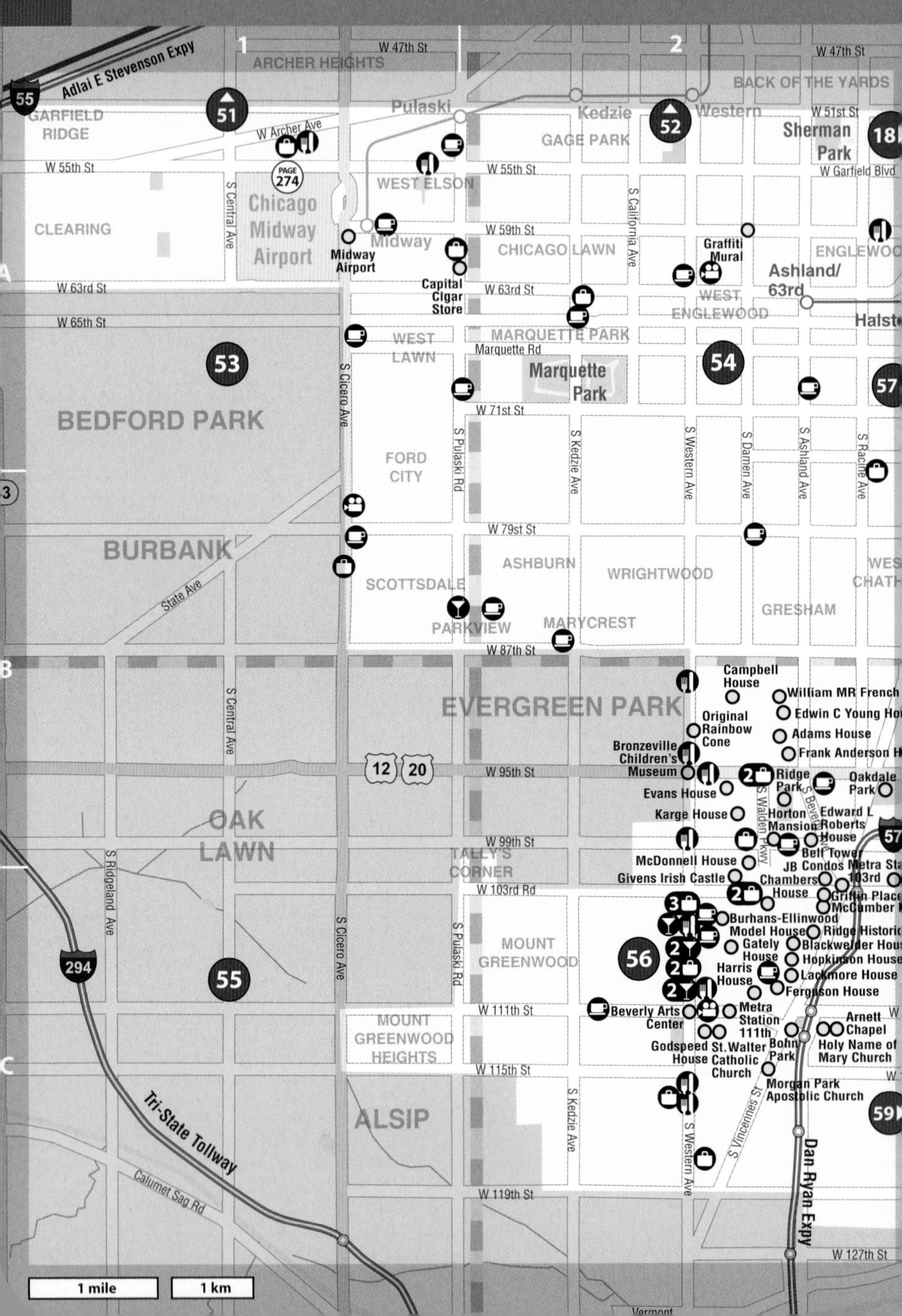
Adlai E Stevenson Expy
55
ARCHER HEIGHTS
W 47th St
BACK OF THE YARDS
GARFIELD RIDGE
51
W Archer Ave
Pulaski
Kedzie
52
Western
W 51st St
Sherman Park
18
GAGE PARK
W 55th St
PAGE 274
WEST ELSON
W Garfield Blvd
S Central Ave
Chicago Midway Airport
CLEARING
Midway
Midway Airport
W 59th St
CHICAGO LAWN
S California Ave
Graffiti Mural
ENGLEWOOD
Ashland/ 63rd
Capital Cigar Store
W 63rd St
WEST ENGLEWOOD
Halsted
W 65th St
WEST LAWN
MARQUETTE PARK
Marquette Rd
53
Marquette Park
54
57
BEDFORD PARK
W 71st St
S Cicero Ave
S Pulaski Rd
S Kedzie Ave
S Western Ave
S Damen Ave
S Ashland Ave
S Racine Ave
FORD CITY
W 79st St
BURBANK
ASHBURN
WRIGHTWOOD
SCOTTSDALE
State Ave
GRESHAM
PARKVIEW
MARYCREST
W 87th St
EVERGREEN PARK
Campbell House
William MR French
Edwin C Young House
Original Rainbow Cone
Adams House
Frank Anderson House
Bronzeville Children's Museum
12
20
W 95th St
Ridge Park
Oakdale Park
Evans House
S Walden Pkwy
Karge House
Horton Mansion
Edward L Roberts House
OAK LAWN
W 99th St
TALLY'S CORNER
Bell Tower
McDonnell House
JB Condos
Metra Station 103rd
Givens Irish Castle
Chambers House
W 103rd Rd
Griffin Place
McCumber House
Burhans-Ellinwood Model House
Ridge Historical
S Ridgeland Ave
Gately House
Blackwelder House
MOUNT GREENWOOD
56
Hopkinson House
294
55
Harris House
Lackmore House
Ferguson House
W 111th St
Beverly Arts Center
Metra Station 111th
Arnett Chapel
MOUNT GREENWOOD HEIGHTS
Godspeed House
St. Walter Catholic Church
Bohn Park
Holy Name of Mary Church
W 115th St
Morgan Park Apostolic Church
Tri-State Tollway
ALSIP
S Vincennes St
59
Calumet Sag Rd
W 119th St
Dan Ryan Expy
W 127th St
1 mile
1 km
Vermont

Essentials

Perhaps the most racially and ethnically diverse area in all of Chicagoland, the Southwest side, home to Midway Airport and the infamous Southside Irish Parade, is a cultural stew where shared blue-collar values override perceived differences. This is true in the rougher areas, such as Englewood and Gresham, as well as in the more prosperous (and historically significant) Beverly and Morgan Park 'hoods. Marquette Park is a popular hangout, for local gangs as well as golfers and fishermen. The area surrounding it has a strong Arab-American vibe. This is the place to go on the Southwest side for falafel and shwarma.

o Landmarks

- **Adams House** • 9326 S Longwood Dr
- **Arnett Chapel, African Methodist Episcopal Churh** • 11218 S Bishop St
- **Bell Tower Condos** • 10321 S Longwood Dr
- **Beverly Arts Center** • 2407 W 111th St
- **Blackwelder Summerling House** • 10910 S Prospect Ave
- **Bohn Park** • 111th St & Prospect Ave
- **Bronzeville Children's Museum** • 9600 S Western Ave
- **Burhans-Ellinwood Model House** • 10410 S Hoyne Ave
- **Campbell House** • 9250 S Damen Ave
- **Capital Cigar Store** • 6258 S Pulaski Rd
- **Edward L Roberts House** • 10134 S Longwood Dr
- **Edwin C Young House** • 9215 S Pleasant Ave
- **Evans House** • 9914 S Longwood Dr
- **Ferguson House** • 10954 S Prospect Ave
- **Frank Anderson House** • 10400 S Pleasant Ave
- **Gately House** • 10655 S Hoyne Ave
- **Givens Irish Castle** • 10244 S Longwood Dr
- **Godspeed House** • 11216 S Oakley Ave
- **Graffiti Mural** • W 59th St & S Damen Ave
- **Harris House** • 10856 S Longwood Dr
- **Holy Name of Mary Church** • 1423 W 112th St
- **Hopkinson House** • 10820 S Drew St
- **Horton Mansion** • 10200 S Longwood Dr
- **Howe House** • 10208 S Wood St
- **JB Chambers House** • 10330 S Seeley Ave
- **Karge House** • 2035 W 99th St
- **Lackmore House** • 10956 S Prospect Ave
- **McCumber House** • 10305 S Seeley Ave
- **Metra 103rd/Washington Heights Rock Island District Branch Line Station** • 103rd St & Vincennes Ave
- **Metra Rock Island Main Line 111th St/Monterey Ave Station** •
- **Midway Airport** • 5700 S Cicero Ave
- **Morgan Park Apostolic Penecostal Church** • 11401 S Vincennes Ave
- **Morgan Park United Methodist Church** • 11030 S Longwood Dr
- **Oakdale Park** • 956 W 95th St
- **Original Rainbow Cone** • 9233 S Western Ave
- **Ridge Historical Society** • 10621 S Seeley Ave
- **Ridge Park** • 9625 S Longwood Dr
- **St Walter Catholic Church** • 11722 S Oakley Ave
- **Walter Burley Griffin Place** • W 104th Pl, Wood St to Prospect Ave
- **William MR French House** • 9203 S Pleasant Ave

Sundries/Entertainment

Irish pubs lining the Western Avenue Irish Parade route are too numerous to list. Diners on the Southwest Side usually take it to go. Shoppers converge on the Ford City Shopping Center where the cinema features 16 screens, while juvenile comedians gear up with fake vomit and whoopee cushions at Izzy Rizzy's House of Tricks.

Coffee

- **Beverly Bakery** • 10528 S Western Ave
- **Beverly Bean** • 2734 W 111th St
- **Café Luna** • 1742 W 99th St
- **Dunkin' Donuts** • 10401 S Western Ave
- **Dunkin' Donuts** • 1431 W 95th St
- **Dunkin' Donuts** • 3210 W 87th St
- **Dunkin' Donuts** • 3977 W Columbus Ave
- **Dunkin' Donuts** • 4612 W 59th St
- **Dunkin' Donuts** • 5448 S Pulaski Rd
- **Dunkin' Donuts** • 6100 S Western Ave
- **Dunkin' Donuts** • 6500 S Kedzie Ave
- **Dunkin' Donuts** • 6925 S Pulaski Rd
- **Dunkin' Donuts** • 7059 S Ashland Ave
- **Dunkin' Donuts** • 7901 S Damen Ave
- **Dunkin' Donuts** • 7905 S Cicero Ave
- **Java Express** • 10701 S Hale Ave

Movie Theaters

- **AMC Ford City 14** • 7601 S Cicero Ave
- **Beverly Arts Center** • 2407 W 111th St
- **ICE 62nd St & Western** • 2258 W 62nd St

Nightlife

- **Cork & Kerry** • 10614 S Western Ave
- **Groucho's** • 8355 S Pulaski Rd
- **Jeremy Lanigan's Irish Pub** • 3119 W 111th St
- **Keegan's Pub** • 10618 S Western Ave
- **Mrs O'Leary's Dubliner** • 10910 S Western Ave
- **Sean's Rhino Bar** • 10330 S Western Ave

Restaurants

- **Beverly Woods Restaurant** • 11532 S Western Ave
- **Bobak's** • 5725 S Archer Ave
- **Franconello's Italian Restaurant** • 10222 S Western Ave
- **Hoe China Tea** • 4020 W 55th St
- **Jack's Java** • 9500 S Western Ave
- **Janson's Drive-In / Snyder's Red Hots** • 9900 S Western Ave
- **Leona's Restaurant** • 11015 S Western Ave
- **Lume's** • 11601 S Western Ave
- **Tatra Inn** • 6040 S Pulaski Rd
- **Top Notch Beefburger** • 2116 W 95th St
- **Uncle Joe's Jerk** • 10210 S Vincennes Ave

Shopping

- **African American Images Bookstore** • 1909 W 95th St
- **The Beverly Cigar Company** • 10513 S Western Ave
- **Beverly & Novelty Costume Shop** • 11626 S Western Ave
- **Beverly Records** • 11612 S Western Ave
- **Bobak's** • 5275 S Archer Ave
- **Borders Book, Music, Movies & Café** • 2210 W 95th St
- **Calabria Imports** • 1905 W 103rd St
- **County Fair** • 10800 S Western Ave
- **Ford City Shopping Center** • 7601 S Cicero Ave
- **Grich Antiques** • 10857 S Western Ave
- **Izzy Rizzy's House of Tricks** • 6356 S Pulaski Rd
- **Mr Peabody Records** • 11832 S Western Av
- **Ms Priss** • 9915 S Walden Pkwy
- **Optimo Hat** • 10215 S Western Ave
- **Reading on Walden** • 9913 S Walden Pkwy
- **Village Discount Outlet** • 6419 S Kedzie Av
- **Village Discount Outlet** • 7443 S Racine Av
- **World Folk Music** • 1808 W 103rd St

Adlai E Stevenson Expy
55
W 47th St
S Central Ave
Vittum Park
Archer Park
ARCHER HEIGHTS
Pulaski
51
W 51st St
W Archer Ave
GARFIELD RIDGE
W 55th St
Park Number 468
WEST ELSON
Wentworth Kinzie Park
Pasteur Park
Airport Dr
Midway
Valley Forge Park
Minuteman Park
Chicago Midway Airport
W 59th St
S Harlem Ave
S Pulaski Rd
50
PAGE 274
Nathan Hale Park
W 63rd St
WEST LAWN
Lawler Park
West Lawn Park
S Cicero Ave
BEDFORD PARK
Rainey Hancock Park
79th St
SCOTTSDALE
BURBANK
Scottsdale Park
Durkin Center Park
Harlem Ave
W 87th St
55
1/2 mile
.5 km

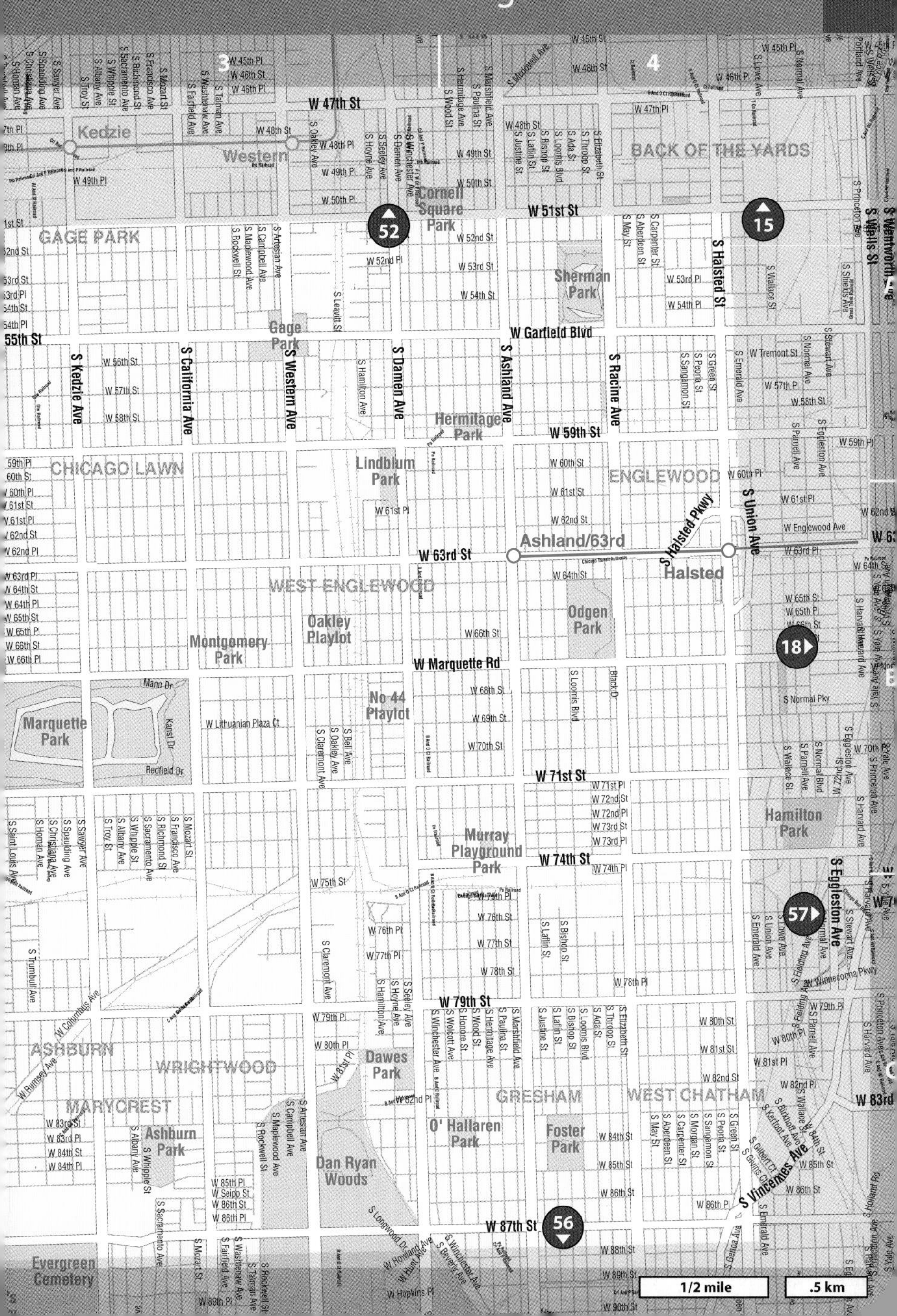

3
4
W 47th St
Kedzie
Western
BACK OF THE YARDS
Cornell Square Park
W 51st St
52
15
GAGE PARK
Sherman Park
S Halsted St
Gage Park
W Garfield Blvd
55th St
S Kedzie Ave
S California Ave
S Western Ave
S Damen Ave
S Ashland Ave
S Racine Ave
Hermitage Park
W 59th St
CHICAGO LAWN
Lindblum Park
ENGLEWOOD
S Union Ave
S Halsted Pkwy
Ashland/63rd
W 63rd St
Halsted
WEST ENGLEWOOD
Odgen Park
Oakley Playlot
Montgomery Park
18
W Marquette Rd
Marquette Park
No 44 Playlot
W 71st St
Hamilton Park
Murray Playground Park
W 74th St
S Eggleston Ave
57
W 79th St
ASHBURN
WRIGHTWOOD
Dawes Park
MARYCREST
GRESHAM
WEST CHATHAM
W 83rd
O' Hallaren Park
Foster Park
Ashburn Park
Dan Ryan Woods
S Vincennes Ave
W 87th St
56
Evergreen Cemetery
1/2 mile
.5 km

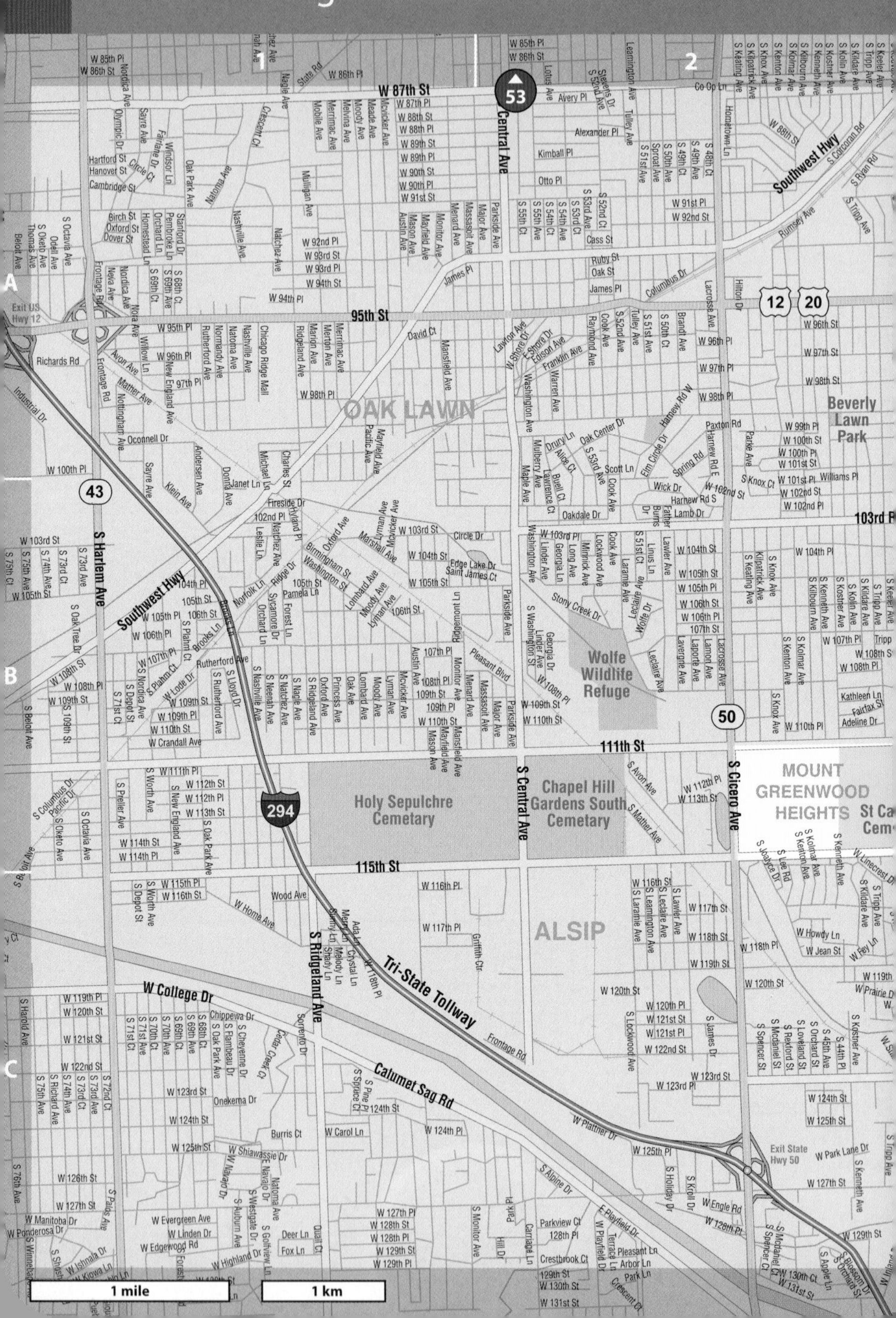
OAK LAWN
ALSIP
Beverly Lawn Park
Wolfe Wildlife Refuge
MOUNT GREENWOOD HEIGHTS
Holy Sepulchre Cemetery
Chapel Hill Gardens South Cemetery
95th St
111th St
115th St
W 87th St
S Harlem Ave
S Central Ave
S Cicero Ave
S Ridgeland Ave
Southwest Hwy
Tri-State Tollway
Calumet Sag Rd
W College Dr
1 mile
1 km

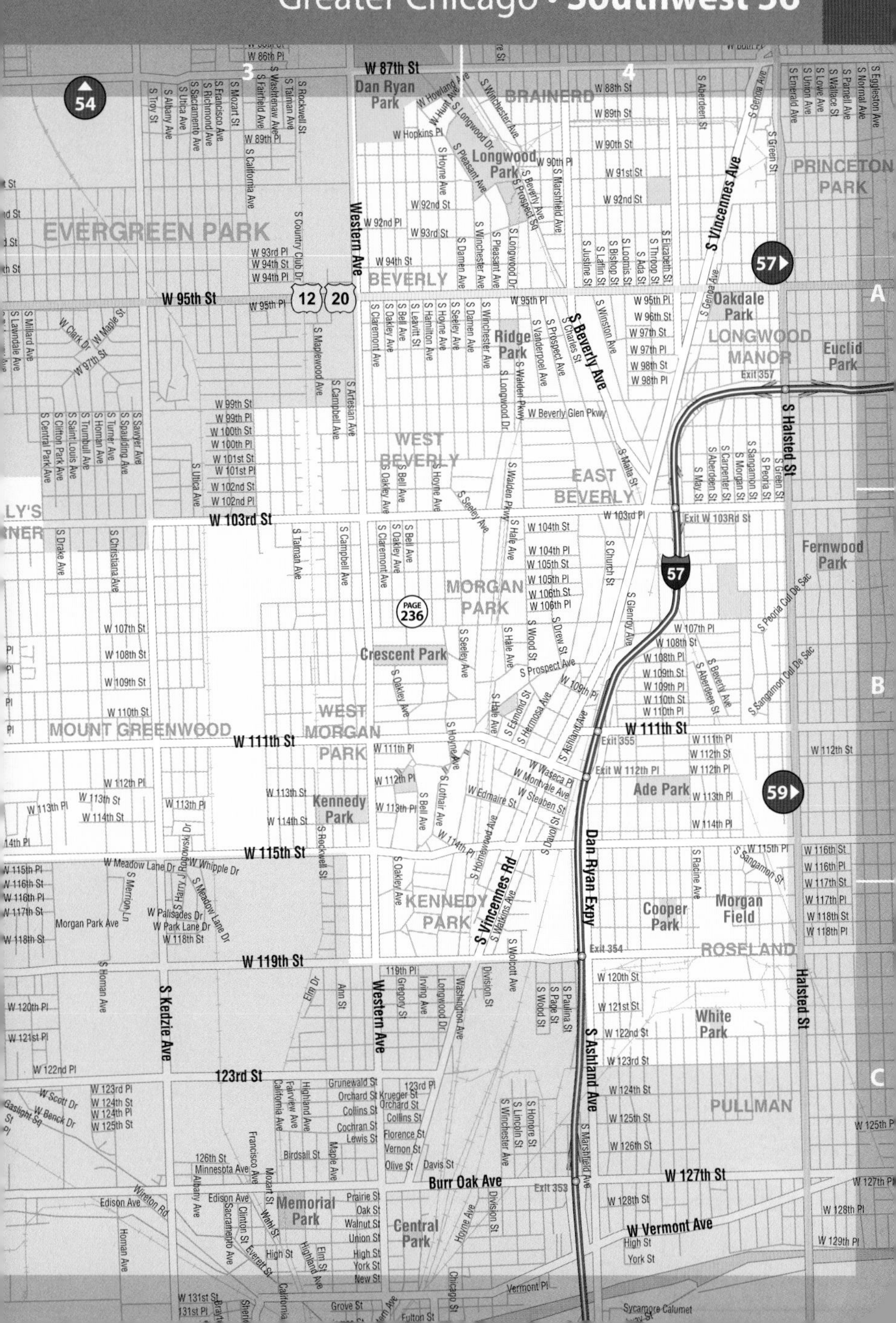

3
4
54
57
59
A
B
C
W 87th St
W 86th Pl
Dan Ryan Park
BRAINERD
W 88th St
W 89th St
W 89th Pl
W 90th St
W 90th Pl
W 91st St
W 92nd St
W 92nd Pl
W 93rd St
W 93rd Pl
W 94th St
W 94th Pl
W 95th St
W 95th Pl
12
20
Longwood Park
PRINCETON PARK
EVERGREEN PARK
BEVERLY
Western Ave
S Vincennes Ave
S Beverly Ave
Oakdale Park
LONGWOOD MANOR
Euclid Park
Ridge Park
Exit 357
S Halsted St
W 96th St
W 97th St
W 97th Pl
W 98th St
W 98th Pl
W 99th St
W 99th Pl
W 100th St
W 100th Pl
W 101st St
W 101st Pl
W 102nd St
W 102nd Pl
W 103rd St
W 103rd Pl
Exit W 103Rd St
W Beverly Glen Pkwy
WEST BEVERLY
EAST BEVERLY
W 104th St
W 104th Pl
W 105th St
W 105th Pl
W 106th St
W 106th Pl
W 107th St
W 107th Pl
W 108th St
W 108th Pl
W 109th St
W 109th Pl
W 110th St
W 110th Pl
Fernwood Park
MORGAN PARK
PAGE 236
Crescent Park
S Prospect Ave
WEST MORGAN PARK
MOUNT GREENWOOD
W 111th St
W 111th Pl
Exit 355
W 112th St
W 112th Pl
Exit W 112th Pl
Ade Park
W 113th St
W 113th Pl
W 114th St
W 114th Pl
Kennedy Park
W Edmaire St
W Steuben St
W Waseca Pl
W Montvale Ave
W 115th St
W 115th Pl
W 116th St
W 116th Pl
W 117th St
W 117th Pl
W 118th St
W 118th Pl
Dan Ryan Expy
S Vincennes Rd
KENNEDY PARK
Cooper Park
Morgan Field
ROSELAND
Exit 354
W 119th St
W 120th St
W 120th Pl
W 121st St
W 121st Pl
W 122nd St
W 122nd Pl
W 123rd St
123rd St
W 124th St
W 124th Pl
W 125th St
W 125th Pl
W 126th St
White Park
PULLMAN
S Kedzie Ave
S Ashland Ave
Halsted St
Morgan Park Ave
Burr Oak Ave
Exit 353
W 127th St
W 127th Pl
W 128th St
W 128th Pl
W 129th Pl
W Vermont Ave
Memorial Park
Central Park
Edison Ave
Wireton Rd
High St
York St
New St
Vermont Pl
Grove St
Fulton St
Sycamore Calumet
W 131st St
131st Pl

Greater Chicago • South

Essentials

The far Southside still lives in the shadows of the abandoned steel mills that built this area. With them went the regional economy. What remaining scraps that were left are now being tugged at by the pull of legalized casinos a few miles down the road in Indiana. Meanwhile, south central Chicago from Chatham southward comprises the comfortable middle-class area dubbed the "black bungalow belt". Here, strong community ties defy the Southside's rough-and-tumble reputation. Further afield, the white ethnic enclave of Hegewisch lives in a world of its own, fenced in by forest preserves and industrial wasteland.

oLandmarks

- **Carter G Woodson Regional Library** • 9525 S Halsted St
- **Cedar Park Cemetery & Funeral Home** • 12540 S Halsted St
- **Chicago Skyway** • 8801 S Anthony St
- **Chicago State University** • 9501 S King Dr
- **Lilydale First Baptist Church** • 649 W 113th St
- **Lilydale Progressive Missionary Baptist Church** • 10706 S Michigan Ave
- **Market Hall** • E 112th St & Champlain Ave
- **New Regal Theatre** • 1645 E 79th St
- **Oak Woods Cemetery** • 1035 E 67th St
- **Palmer Park** • 201 E 111th St
- **Pullman Clock Tower** • 11141 S Cottage Grove Ave
- **Robert S Abbott Park** • 49 E 95th St
- **South Shore Cultural Center** • 7059 South Shore Dr
- **Trinity United Church of Christ** • 400 W 95th St
- **West Pullman Elementary School** • 11941 S Parnell Ave
- **West Pullman Park** • 401 W 123rd St

Sundries / Entertainment

Many of the Southside's more upscale lounges are restricted to those 25 and over. Jeffrey Pub is a long-standing gay dance club. Jazz legend Von Freeman jams every Tuesday night at New Apartment Lounge. Most of the area's barbeque shacks serve their take-out through bulletproof glass. For excellent, authentic soul food, go no further than Army & Lou's on E 75th Street. Vegetarians flock down the street to the always-bustling Soul Vegetarian East.

Coffee

- **Dunkin' Donuts** • 11100 S Corliss Ave
- **Dunkin' Donuts** • 120 W 87th St
- **Dunkin' Donuts** • 14 W 95th St
- **Dunkin' Donuts** • 150 W 63rd St
- **Dunkin' Donuts** • 207 W 79th St
- **Dunkin' Donuts** • 250 E 103rd St
- **Dunkin' Donuts** • 814 E 87th St
- **Dunkin' Donuts** • 8255 S Halsted St
- **Dunkin' Donuts** • 8753 S Stony Island Ave
- **Dunkin' Donuts** • 9802 S Halsted St
- **Spoon's Coffee Boutique** • 712 E 75th St
- **Starbucks** • 7101 S Stony Island Ave

Movie Theaters

- **ICE Chatham 14** • 210 87th St

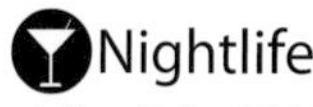

Nightlife

- **Jeffrey Pub** • 7041 S Jeffery Blvd
- **New Apartment Lounge** • 504 E 75th St
- **Pullman's Pub** • 611 E 113th St
- **Reds** • 6926 S Stony Island Ave

Restaurants

- **Army & Lou's** • 422 E 75th St
- **Atomic Sub** • 6353 S Cottage Grove Ave
- **Cal Harbor Restaurant** • 546 E 115th St
- **Captain Hard Times** • 436 E 79th St
- **Chatham Pancake House** • 700 E 87th St
- **Dat's Donuts** • 8251 S Cottage Grove Ave
- **Helen's Restaurant** • 1732 E 79th St
- **Leon's Bar-B-Que** • 8249 S Cottage Grove Ave
- **Phil's Kastle** • 3532 E 95th St
- **Seven Seas Submarine** • 11216 S Michigan Ave
- **Soul Queen** • 9031 S Stony Island Ave
- **Soul Vegetarian East** • 205 E 75th St
- **Tropic Island Jerk Chicken** • 1922 E 79th St

Shopping

- **Halsted Indoor Mall** • 11444 S Halsted St
- **Underground Afrocentric Bookstore** • 1727 E 87th St

1
2
Washington Park
Washington Park Lagoon
Midway Plaisance
Garfield
E Garfield Blvd
E 55th St
18
19
20
Jackson Park
East Lagoon
S Lake Shore Dr
S Park Shore East Ct
ENGLEWOOD
E 59th St
63rd
Halsted
King Dr
East 63rd - Cottage Grove
W 63rd St
WEST WOODLAWN
WOODLAWN
PAGE 212
South Lagoon
E Marquette Rd
E 67th St
69th
PARK MANOR
GRAND CROSSING
Exit I 90 Connector
Exit S St Lawrence Ave
90
E 71st St
S South Chicago Ave
SOUTH SHORE
S Stony Island Ave
54
MARYNOOK
W 74th St
E 75th St
Rosenblum Park
Grand Crossing Park
E 76th St
E 79th St
79th
CHATHAM
S Cottage Grove Ave
S State St
S Vincennes Ave
94
Dan Ryan Expy
W 83rd St
E 83rd St
Avalon Park
STONY ISLAND PARK
Chicago Skyway
Exit S Stony Island Ave
87th
E 87th St
WEST CHESTERFIELD
CALUMENT HEIGHTS
Owens Park
S Lafayette Ave
S King Dr
Tuley Park
BURNSIDE
PRINCETON PARK
S Halsted Ave
E 95th St
95th
59
12
20
1 mile
1 km

3 | 4

A

B

C

Lake Michigan

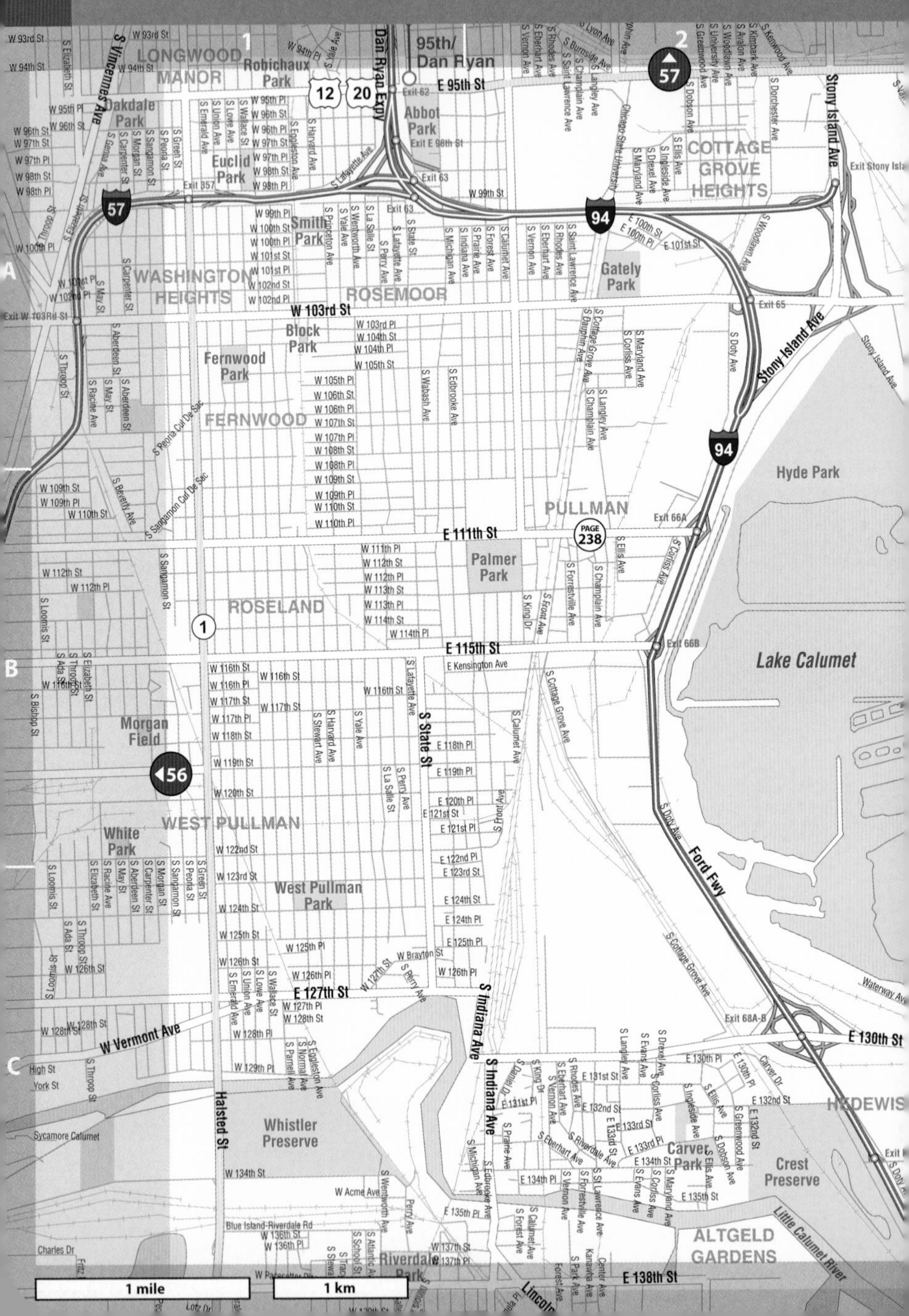

1
2
A
B
C
LONGWOOD MANOR
Robichaux Park
95th/ Dan Ryan
Dan Ryan Expy
12
20
E 95th St
57
Oakdale Park
Abbot Park
Euclid Park
COTTAGE GROVE HEIGHTS
S Vincennes Ave
Exit 357
Exit 62
Exit E 98th St
Exit 63
Exit Stony Island
Stony Island Ave
W 99th St
94
Smith Park
WASHINGTON HEIGHTS
ROSEMOOR
Gately Park
Exit W 103Rd St
W 103rd St
Exit 65
Block Park
Fernwood Park
FERNWOOD
Hyde Park
PULLMAN
Exit 66A
E 111th St
PAGE 238
Palmer Park
ROSELAND
1
E 115th St
Exit 66B
Lake Calumet
Morgan Field
56
S State St
WEST PULLMAN
White Park
West Pullman Park
Ford Fwy
E 127th St
S Indiana Ave
W Vermont Ave
Exit 68A-B
E 130th St
HEGEWISCH
Whistler Preserve
Carver Park
Crest Preserve
Halsted St
Blue Island-Riverdale Rd
Riverdale Park
ALTGELD GARDENS
Little Calumet River
E 138th St
1 mile
1 km

Lake Michigan
Chicago Skyway
E 95th St
E 100th St
E 103rd St
E 106th St
E 130th St
S Colfax Ave
S Torrence Ave
S Avenue L
S Ewing Ave
S Avenue O
S Saginaw Ave
S Brainard Ave
S Indianapolis Ave
Calumet Ave
Calumet Park
Veterans Memorial Park
Trumbull Park
Wolfe Plg Park
Rowen Park
Eggers Woods
Wolf Lake Park
Wolf Lake
Mann Park
Burnham Woods
Forsyth Park
JEFFERY MANOR
SOUTH DEERING
HEGEWISCH
Calumet River
INDIANA
ILLINOIS
1 mile
1 km
A
B
C
3
4

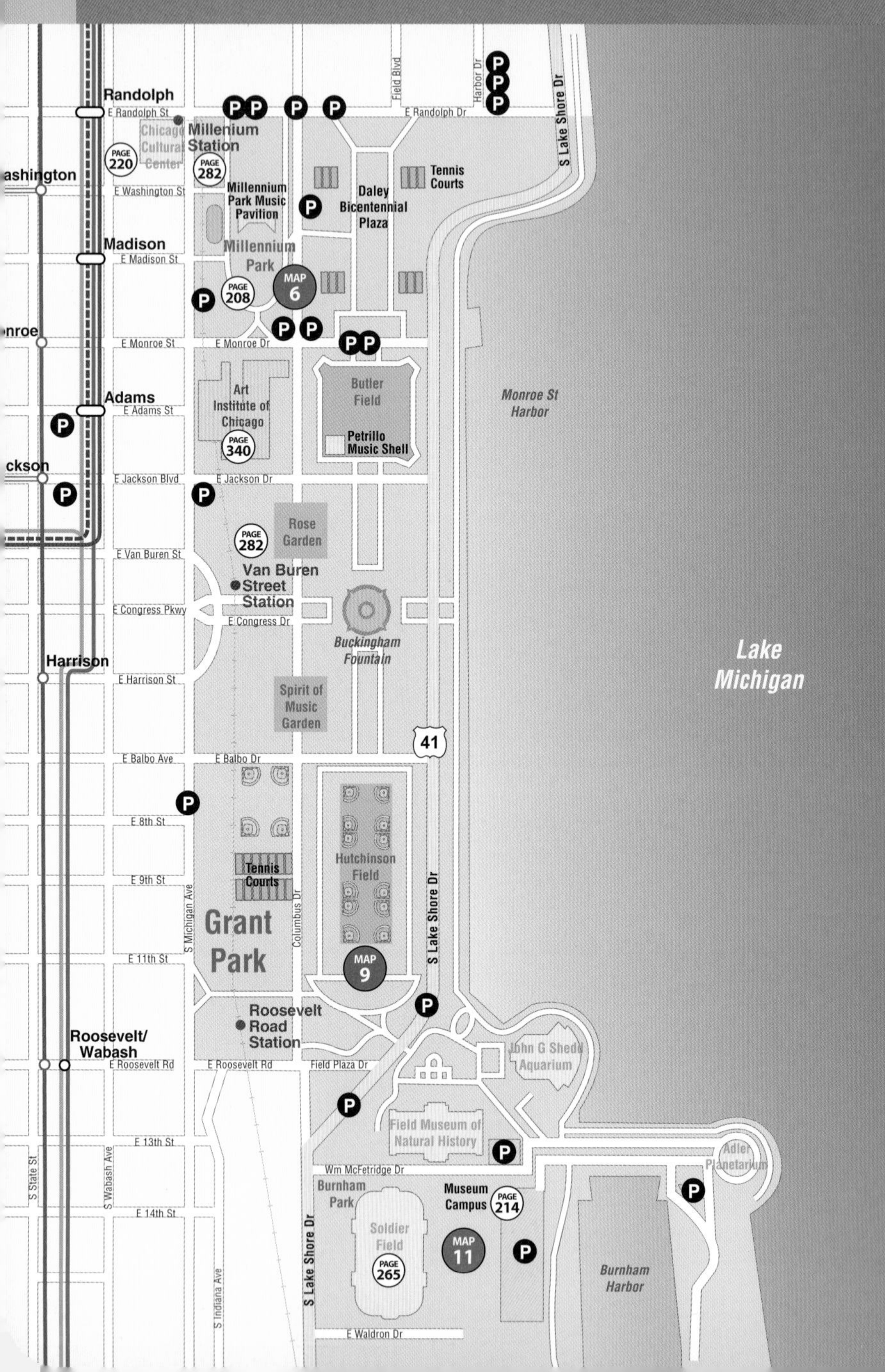

Randolph
E Randolph St
Chicago Cultural Center
Millenium Station
PAGE 220
PAGE 282
ashington
E Washington St
Millennium Park Music Pavilion
Daley Bicentennial Plaza
Tennis Courts
Field Blvd
Harbor Dr
E Randolph Dr
S Lake Shore Dr
Madison
E Madison St
Millennium Park
PAGE 208
MAP 6
nroe
E Monroe St
E Monroe Dr
Adams
E Adams St
Art Institute of Chicago
PAGE 340
Butler Field
Petrillo Music Shell
Monroe St Harbor
ckson
E Jackson Blvd
E Jackson Dr
PAGE 282
Rose Garden
E Van Buren St
Van Buren Street Station
E Congress Pkwy
E Congress Dr
Buckingham Fountain
Harrison
E Harrison St
Spirit of Music Garden
Lake Michigan
41
E Balbo Ave
E Balbo Dr
E 8th St
Tennis Courts
Hutchinson Field
E 9th St
S Michigan Ave
Columbus Dr
S Lake Shore Dr
Grant Park
E 11th St
MAP 9
Roosevelt Road Station
Roosevelt/ Wabash
E Roosevelt Rd
E Roosevelt Rd
Field Plaza Dr
John G Shedd Aquarium
Field Museum of Natural History
Adler Planetarium
E 13th St
Wm McFetridge Dr
Burnham Park
Museum Campus
PAGE 214
S State St
S Wabash Ave
E 14th St
Soldier Field
PAGE 265
MAP 11
Burnham Harbor
S Lake Shore Dr
S Indiana Ave
E Waldron Dr

Overview

Grant Park, where grass meets glass, is Chicago's venerable "front lawn." Spanning the Lake Michigan shoreline from N Randolph Street to S Roosevelt Road and west to Michigan Avenue, it's safe to say there's not a more trafficked park this side of New York City's Central Park. Grant Park is a study in contrasts: on the one side featuring massive summer festivals (such as the annual homage to obesity known as Taste of Chicago) that turn the park into Chicago's dirty doormat; but during the rest of the year, a quiet place to relax, play, and count the number of panhandlers who ask if you can " help them out with a quarter."

The park's history can be traced back to 1835 when concerned citizens lobbied to prevent development along their pristine waterfront. Little did they know that when the State of Illinois ruled to preserve the land as "public ground forever to remain vacant of buildings" this meant for everyone, including the wealthy elite who were literally perched on the lofty balconies of the tawny palaces that lined the downtown shores of Lake Michigan. Be careful what you wish for, yes? Architect and city planner Daniel Burnham laid the groundwork for the park and made plans to erect museums, civic buildings, and general park attractions along the waterfront. This plan got somewhat sidetracked by the Great Chicago Fire of 1871. Interestingly enough, remaining debris from the fire was pushed into the lake and now forms part of the foundation for much of Grant Park and Chicago's famous shoreline. Chicagoans can thank local land-lover and legendary mail-order magnate Aaron Montgomery Ward for pressuring the State of Illinois in 1911 to preserve the land as an undeveloped open space.

Nature

Grant Park's lawns, gardens, lakefront, and bench-lined paths attract a mixed crowd of lunching office workers, exercise fanatics, readers, gawking tourists, homeless and not-so-homeless panhandlers, and just your run-of-the-mill idiots. South and north of famous Buckingham Fountain are the formal Spirit of Music Garden and Rose Garden, respectively. Near Daley Bicentennial Plaza (located on the park's north side) is the riotously colorful Wildflower Garden which is not to be missed during the time of the year when one can expect to see flowers in bloom. There is also a multitude of sculptures, ranging in form and style and strewn with abandon throughout the park, so expect to see art appreciators and imitators alike milling about as well.

Sports

Daley Bicentennial Plaza (337 E Randolph St, 312-742-7648) is equipped with a fitness center, skating rink, and 12 outdoor tennis courts. The courts are open year-round from 7 am to 10 pm on weekdays and from 9 am to 5 pm on weekends. Court time costs $7 per hour and there's a two-hour limit. Reservations are recommend and should be made well in advance (312-742-7650). The skating rink is open daily from November to March for iceskating ($5 skate rental available) and open for free in-line skating the rest of the year. On the south end of the park, baseball diamonds and tennis courts are available on a first-come basis unless they are reserved for league play.

Buckingham Fountain

Buckingham Fountain is Grant Park's spouting centerpiece at the intersection of Congress Parkway and Columbus Drive. Designed by Edward Bennett, the fountain has been showering onlookers with wind-blown spray since 1927 and is notable for its role in the opening sequence of the sitcom *Married...with Children*. Today the water flows April through October from 10 am to 11 pm daily. For 20 minutes each hour the center basin jettisons water 150 feet into the air. Lights and music accompany the skyrocketing water display during evening hours. Food concessions and restrooms can be found nearby.

Festivals & Events

Chicagoans used to gather at the Petrillo Music Shell for free Grant Park Orchestra and Chorus concerts during the summer months. Now they go to the Millennium Park Music Pavilion, located between Michigan and Columbus Avenues that, in and of itself, is worth a visit. Concerts take place June through August (312-742-7638; www.grantparkmusicfestival.com). You can't always pass up a free headliner concert at Grant Park's monstrous Summer Festivals. If at all possible, avoid the gut-to-gut feeding frenzy that is the Taste of Chicago. But if you must go, hit it on a weekday afternoon. We'll accept your "thank you" now; if you go on the weekend, you'll understand why. For a complete event schedule, contact the Mayor's Office of Special Events at 312-744-3370, or check out www.cityofchicago.org/specialevents.

How to Get There

By Car: Exits off Lake Shore Drive west to Grant Park are Randolph Street, Monroe Drive, Jackson Drive, Balbo Drive, and Roosevelt Road. Also, enter the park from Michigan Avenue heading east on the same streets. The underground East Monroe Garage is off Monroe Drive. Columbus Drive runs through Grant Park's center and has metered parking.

By Train: From the Richard B. Ogilvie Transportation Center, travel east to Michigan Avenue and Grant Park on CTA buses 14, 56, and 20 ($1.75 one-way). From Union Station, board CTA buses 60, 157, 123, and 151.
Metra trains coming from the south stop at the Roosevelt Road station on the south end of Grant Park before terminating at the underground Randolph Street station below Millennium Park.

By L: Get off at any L stop in the Loop between Randolph Street and Van Buren Street ($1.75 one-way). Walk two blocks east to Grant Park.

By Bus: CTA buses 151, 145, 146, 147, 3, and 10 (weekends only) stop along Michigan Avenue in front of Grant Park ($1.75 one-way).

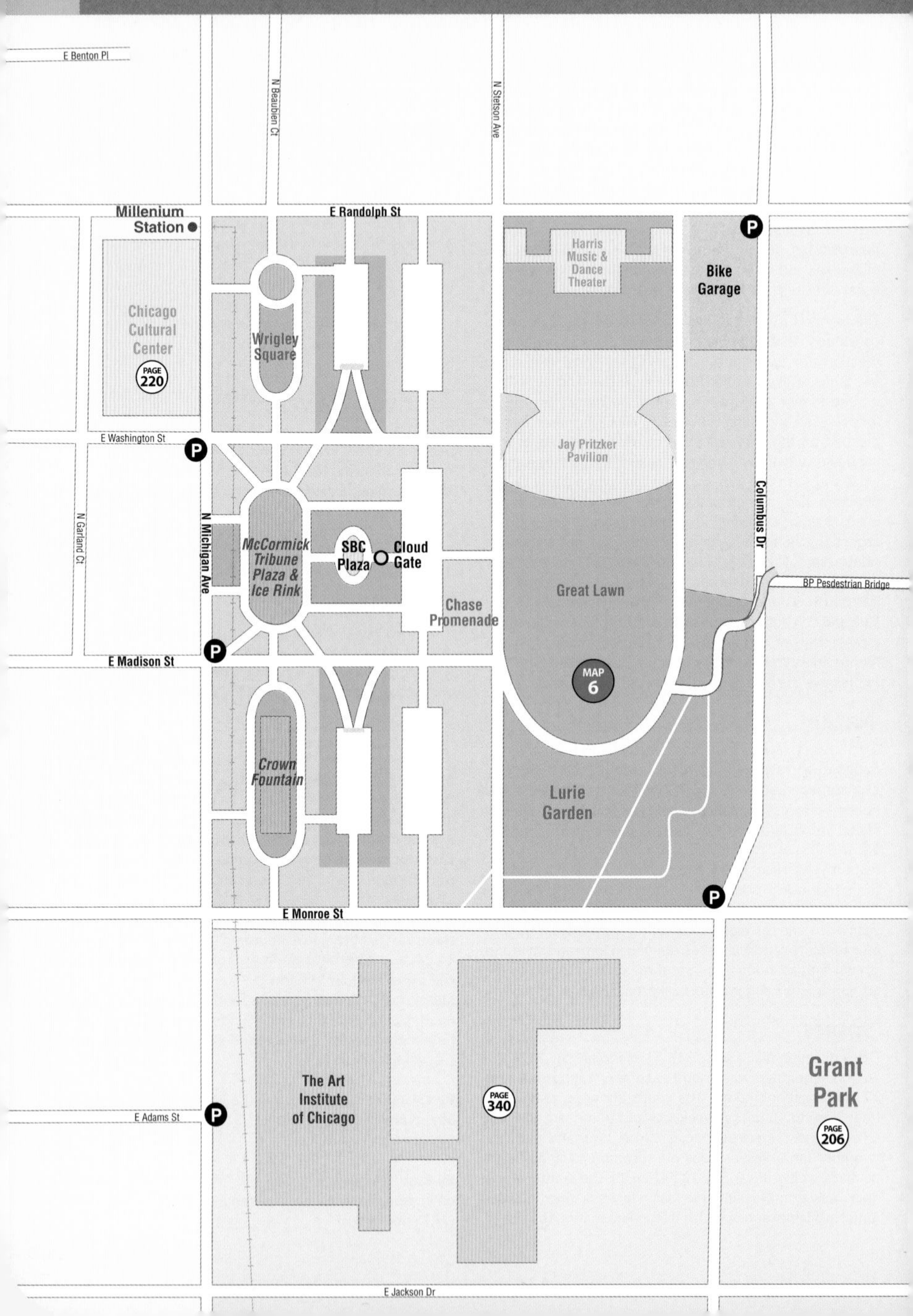
E Benton Pl
N Beaubien Ct
N Stetson Ave
Millenium Station
E Randolph St
Harris Music & Dance Theater
Bike Garage
Chicago Cultural Center
PAGE 220
Wrigley Square
E Washington St
Jay Pritzker Pavilion
Columbus Dr
N Garland Ct
N Michigan Ave
McCormick Tribune Plaza & Ice Rink
SBC Plaza
Cloud Gate
Great Lawn
BP Pesdestrian Bridge
Chase Promenade
E Madison St
MAP 6
Crown Fountain
Lurie Garden
E Monroe St
The Art Institute of Chicago
PAGE 340
Grant Park
PAGE 206
E Adams St
E Jackson Dr

Overview

Only four years behind schedule (who's counting?) and hundreds of millions of dollars over budget (okay, this we counted), Millennium Park finally launched itself in late 2001 as the cultural epicenter Mayor Daley promised us it would be back in 1997. Even if it did take myriad stopgap funding measures resembling yesteryear Al Capone strong-arm tactics to eternally endow us with the SBC Plaza, McCormick Tribune Plaza & Ice Rink, and the Chase Promenade, locals and tourists alike agree it was well worth it. Even staunch longtime local naysayers have come to acknowledge that, when is said and done, the end result really is an amazing addition to Grant Park's northpoint and is, without a doubt, one of downtown Chicago's crowning jewels. The only remaining piece needed to complete the vision of this massive puzzle is the Chicago Art Institute Expansion Project. Scheduled for tape cutting in 2007, the project will probably be finished around the spring of 2009. A delay on a Daley promise? Shocking.

Jay Pritzker Pavilion

The cornerstone of Millennium Park, without question, is the Pritzker Pavilion. It seems the whole park may have very well been conceived to give Frank Gehry's architectural masterpiece an appropriate setting. Spectacularly innovative, the pavilion's façade features immense stainless steel ribbons unfurling 40 feet into the sky. The pavilion's stage area is as big as Orchestra Hall across the street and can accommodate a 120-person orchestra and a 150-person choir. Seating for the free concert events includes a 4,000-seat terrace and an additional 95,000-square-foot lawn area that can accommodate 7,000 picnickers. A one-of-a-kind integrated sound system offers outdoor acoustics that rival the best in the world.

Harris Music & Dance Theater

Several dance and theatrical troupes share the 1,500-seat underground space behind Gehry's behemoth bandshell, including Hubbard Street Dance (not to be missed, but good luck getting tickets!), the Chicago Children's Choir, and the Jazz Institute of Chicago. Two underground parking garages flank the theater, and as with all parking in this area, it's first come/first served and a bit of a mess on the weekends.

Tickets and schedule available at www.madtchi.com.

Nature & Sculpture

The park has several different defined spaces: Wrigley Square, with its neoclassical epistyle; the Chase Promenade, gearing up to house art fairs and ethnic festivals; and the SBC Plaza (between the skating rink and promenade), which is home to Anish Kapoor's 100-ton stainless steel jelly-bean sculpture, *Cloud Gate*. Flanking the skating rink to the south is the modernist Crown Fountain, which features two glass brick towers, 50-feet in height, with projected video images of the faces of actual Chicago residents. The Lurie Garden, a ridiculously conceptual assemblage of seasonal foliage, offers a beautiful public gathering space as well as more contemplative environments. The BP Bridge, a 925-foot-long winding bridge—Frank Gehry's first—connects Millennium Park to Daley Bicentennial Plaza just east of the park. Clad in brushed stainless steel panels, the BP Bridge complements the Pritzker Pavilion in function as well as design by creating an acoustic barrier for traffic noise. It's well worth the walk.

Sports

The 15,910-square-foot McCormick Tribune ice skating rink opens annually in November. Admission is free and skates are available for rental. The park also houses a state-of-the-art bicycle garage. The heated space provides parking for 300 bikes, showers, a repair facility, and a café.

Dining

The 300-seat Park Grill (voted "Top 5 Best Burger in Chicago") overlooking the skating rink offers burgers, steaks, and salads year round. In the summer, carry-away grub is available from a variety of kiosks throughout the park.

How to Get There

No matter your mode of travel, approach the area around Millennium Park with patience and allow extra time. For train, L, and bus transportation recommendations, see NFT's Grant Park or Art Institute sections. Metra's Randolph Street train station, servicing only south-bound trains, is located under Millennium Park.

If you choose to drive, underground parking is available. Access the Grant Park North Garage from Michigan Avenue. Enter Millennium Park Garage from the lower levels of Randolph Street and mid-level of Columbus Drive.

Overview

The largest of Chicago's 552 parks, Lincoln Park stretches 1,208 acres along the lakefront from the breeder cruising scene at the North Avenue Beach to the gay cruising scene at Hollywood Beach. The park boasts one of the world's longest bike trails, but thanks to an ever-increasing abundance of stroller-pushers, leashless dogs, and headphone-wearing rollerbladers, the path proves treacherous for cyclists and pedestrians alike. Nonetheless, sporty types and summertime cruisers still find satisfaction indoors and out at Lincoln Park. Take a break from winter inside the Lincoln Park Conservatory, a tropical paradise full o' flush green plants no matter what the thermometer reads. Public buildings, including animal houses at the Lincoln Park Zoo, Café Brauer, Peggy Notebaert Nature Museum, and vintage beach bath houses, make the park as architecturally attractive as it is naturally beautiful.

Nature

Much of southern Lincoln Park is open green space popular for football, soccer, dog play, and barbeques. Paths shaded by mature trees lead to stoic statues. Until the 1860s, Lincoln Park was nothing more than a municipal cemetery filled with the shallow graves of cholera and smallpox victims, and it was concern about a public health threat that instigated the creation of the park. Although the city attempted to relocate all the bodies in the cemetery-to-park conversion of 1869, digging doggies may unearth more than picnickers' chicken bones.

In spring, bird watchers flock to Lincoln Park's ponds and nature trails. Addison Bird Sanctuary Viewing Platform north of Belmont Harbor overlooks five fenced-in acres of wetlands and woods. Birding programs around North Pond are run by the Lincoln Park Conservancy and the Chicago Ornithological Society (773-883-7275; www.friendslp.org). More than 160 species of birds have been identified at the 10-acre pond. Free guided walks are held on Wednesdays starting at 7 am. Bring binoculars and plenty of coffee. The Fort Dearborn Chapter of the Illinois Audubon Society hosts free park and zoo bird walks (847-675-3622, www.illinoisaudubon.org). Migratory birds gather around the revamped 1889 Alfred Caldwell Lily Pool at Fullerton Parkway and North Cannon Drive. Next to the Conservatory, Grandmother's Garden and the more formal French-style garden across the street are favorites for both wedding party photos and the homeless during the warmer months.

Sports

Baseball diamonds on the park's south end are bordered by La Salle Drive and Lake Shore Drive, next to the newly renovated field house and NorthStar Eatery. Upgrades planned for the area include a running track, soccer field, and basketball and volleyball courts. Bicyclists and runners race along Lincoln Park Lagoon to the footbridge over Lake Shore Drive to North Avenue Beach, Chicago's volleyball mecca. To reserve courts and rent equipment, go to the south end of the landmark, boat-shaped bath house (312-742-3224). Just north of the bath house is a seasonal rollerblade rink and fitness club. North of Montrose Harbor on lakefront North Wilson Drive is a new, free skateboard park.

The nine-hole Sydney R. Marovitz Public Golf Course (3600 Recreation Dr, 312-742-7930) hosts hackers year-round. Snail-slow play allows plenty of time to enjoy skyline views from this lakefront cow pasture, which is always crowded. Greens fees are $19.75 weekdays, $22.75 on weekends, and you can rent clubs for $10. Reserve tee times by calling 312-245-0909, or show up at sunrise. The starter sits in the northeast corner of the clock tower field house. For those who want to take it even more leisurely, check out the Diversey Miniature Golf Course (312-742-7929), which offers an 18-hole course complete with waterfalls and footbridges.

Four clay tennis courts, the last ones left in Chicago, are open 7 am–8 pm and cost $16 per hour (the 7 am-9 am early bird special costs $24); tennis shoes are required. For reservations and further information, call 312-742-7821. (Also nearby is the Diversey Golf Range (141 W Diversey Ave, 312-742-7929), open year-round (100 balls for $11, 50 balls for $8). The free courts at Montrose are preferred by budget-conscious folks in the know.)

Members of the Lincoln Park Boat Club row in Lincoln Park Lagoon. Rowing classes for the public are offered May through September (www.lpbc.net).

Whimsical, swan-shaped paddleboats at South Pond next to Café Brauer are as boring to paddle as you'd guess, but just try telling a kid that. Located at 2021 N Stockton Drive, this restored Prairie School national landmark houses seasonal restaurants and an upstairs ballroom and is a popular venue for weddings and other private functions. Fishermen frequent South Pond and the lagoon. Belmont, Montrose, and Diversey Harbors also allow shore fishing.

Lincoln Park Zoo

Address: *220 N Cannon Dr*
Chicago, IL 60614
Phone: *312-742-2000*
Website: *www.lpzoo.com*
Hours: *Daily, 9 am–6 pm; animal buildings, 10 am–5 pm (call for special summer and weekend hours)*
Admission: *FREE*

Lions and tigers and bears and kids, oh my! We're not sure which scares us most. Established in 1868, Lincoln Park Zoo is the country's oldest free zoo, and while questions were raised in regards to nine animal deaths last year, it still is a leader in wildlife conservation. National TV shows *Zoo Parade* and Ray Rayner's show *Ark in the Park* were filmed here. Look for some family (or, at least, in-law) resemblance at the cushy Regenstein Center for African Apes which opened in 2004, cost $26 million to build, and covers 29,000 square feet of living space. (Don't worry, it's supported by corporate sponsorships and private funds, not your tax dollars.) Come early and hear the white-cheek gibbons, the smallest of the ape family, mimic car alarms in their morning song to mark their territory. Flanking the zoo's northwest side is the free Lincoln Park Conservatory, a fantastic source of oxygen renewal recommended for hangover sufferers.

Peggy Notebaert Nature Museum

Address: *2430 N Cannon Dr*
Chicago, IL 60614
Phone: *773-755-5100*
Website: *www.naturemuseum.org*
Hours: *Mon–Fri 9 am–4:30 pm; Sat–Sun 10 am–5 pm*
Admission: *$7 adults, $5 seniors & students, $4 children ages 3–12, Thursdays free*

The Peggy Notebaert Nature Museum succeeds in making Illinois' level landscape interesting. The contemporary version of the 1857 Chicago Academy of Sciences, this hands-on museum depicts the close connection between urban and natural environments and represents global environmental issues through a local lens. A flowing water lab and flitting butterfly haven invite return visits. A must-see for anyone with a passion for taxidermy and/or *Silence of the Lambs*.

Chicago Historical Society

Address: *Clark St & North Ave*
Chicago, IL 60614
Phone: *312-642-4600*
Website: *www.chicagohistory.org*
Hours: *Mon–Sat 9:30 am–4:30 pm; Sun, closed*
Admission: *$5 adults, $3 seniors & students, $1 children ages 6–12, Mondays free*

The Chicago Historical Society holds over 20 million primary documents relating to the history of the Chicago area. Exhibits about the city's pioneer roots, architecture, music, fashion, neighborhoods, windy politics, and oral histories breathe life into an otherwise dry history. Locals can access the excellent free research center (open Tuesday through Saturday) for genealogical information and housing history. Big Shoulders Café (312-587-7766) is an affordable, light lunch spot nearby.

Performances

Lincoln Park Cultural Center (2045 N Lincoln Park W, 312-742-7726) stages plays, theater workshops, and family-friendly performances year-round. Theater on the Lake (Fullerton Ave & Lake Shore Dr, 312-742-7529) performs nine weeks of alternative drama in summer. The newly renovated theater now hosts events throughout the calendar year, thanks to much-needed climate control improvements. Lincoln Park Zoo hosts outdoor summer concerts as well. Call the events hotline at 312-742-2283.

How to Get There

By Car: Lake Shore Drive exits to Lincoln Park are Bryn Mawr Avenue, Foster Avenue, Lawrence Avenue, Wilson Drive, Montrose Drive, Irving Park Parkway, Belmont Avenue, Fullerton Avenue, and North Avenue.

Free parking lots are at Recreational Drive near Belmont Harbor and Simonds Drive near Montrose Harbor. Paid lots are at North Avenue Beach, Chicago Historical Society, Lincoln Park Zoo, and Grant Hospital Garage. Stockton Drive and Cannon Drive have free street parking. A metered lot is on Diversey Parkway, next to the golf range.

By Bus: CTA buses 151, 156, 77, 146, and 147 travel through Lincoln Park ($1.75 one-way). For schedules and fares, contact the RTA Information Center (312-836-7000; www.rtachicago.com).

By L: Get off the Red Line at any stop between Fullerton and Bryn Mawr avenues ($1.75 one-way), then head one mile east.

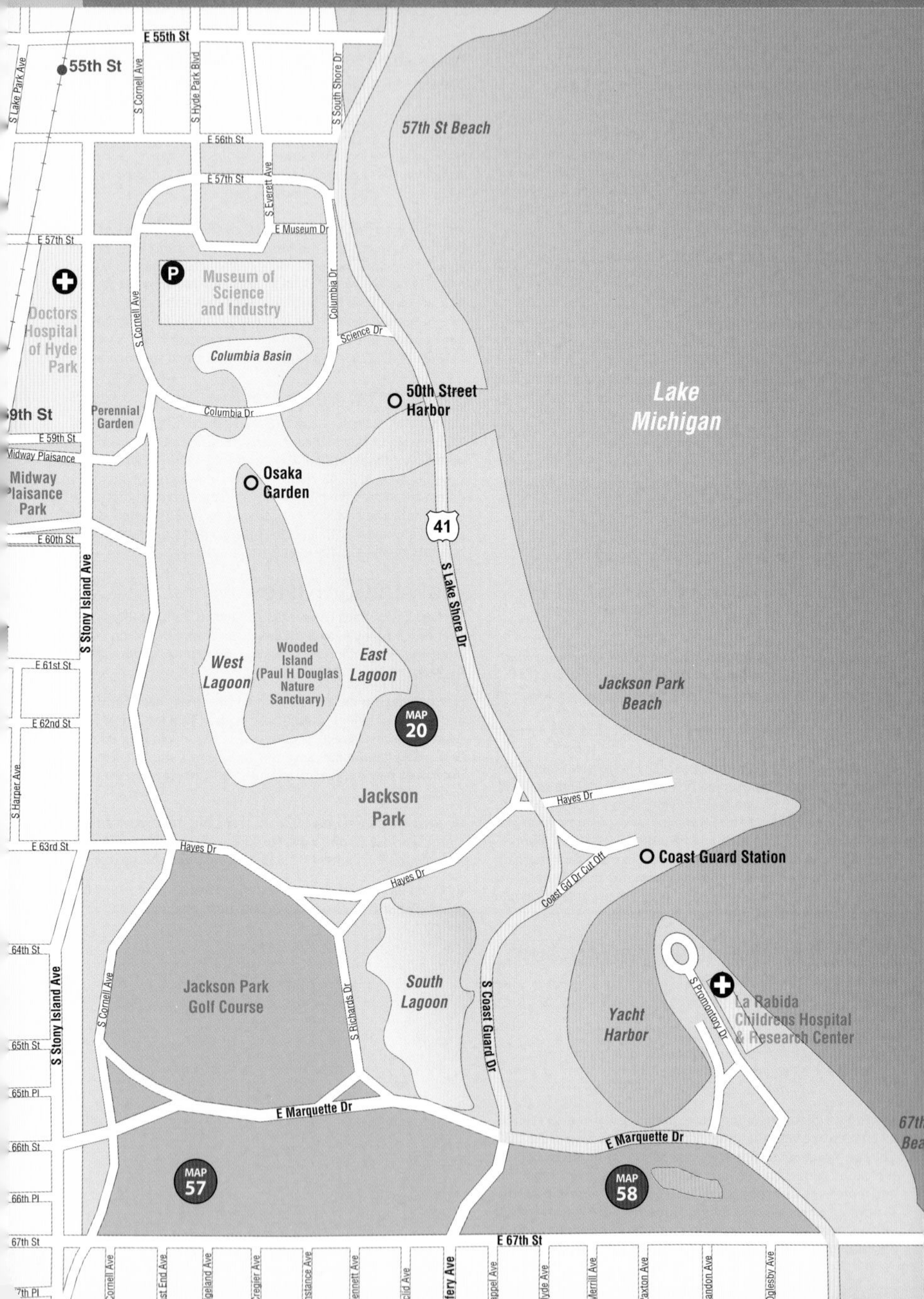
E 55th St
55th St
S Lake Park Ave
S Cornell Ave
S Hyde Park Blvd
S South Shore Dr
57th St Beach
E 56th St
E 57th St
S Everett Ave
E Museum Dr
E 57th St
Museum of Science and Industry
Doctors Hospital of Hyde Park
Columbia Dr
Science Dr
S Cornell Ave
Columbia Basin
50th Street Harbor
Lake Michigan
59th St
Perennial Garden
Columbia Dr
E 59th St
Midway Plaisance
Midway Plaisance Park
Osaka Garden
41
E 60th St
S Lake Shore Dr
S Stony Island Ave
Wooded Island (Paul H Douglas Nature Sanctuary)
West Lagoon
East Lagoon
Jackson Park Beach
E 61st St
E 62nd St
MAP 20
S Harper Ave
Jackson Park
Hayes Dr
E 63rd St
Hayes Dr
Hayes Dr
Coast Guard Station
Coast Gd Dr Cut Off
64th St
S Stony Island Ave
S Cornell Ave
Jackson Park Golf Course
S Richards Dr
South Lagoon
S Coast Guard Dr
S Promontory Dr
La Rabida Childrens Hospital & Research Center
Yacht Harbor
65th St
65th Pl
E Marquette Dr
E Marquette Dr
66th St
MAP 57
MAP 58
66th Pl
67th St
E 67th St
S Cornell Ave
S East End Ave
S Ridgeland Ave
S Cregier Ave
S Constance Ave
S Bennett Ave
S Euclid Ave
Jeffery Ave
S Chappel Ave
S Clyde Ave
S Merrill Ave
S Paxton Ave
S Crandon Ave
S Oglesby Ave

Overview

Historic Jackson Park, which borders Lake Michigan, Hyde Park, and Woodlawn, was, for a long time, an unused tract of fallow land. The 500-acre parcel was eventually transformed into a real city park in the 1870s thanks to Frederick Law Olmsted of Central Park fame. The Midway Plaisance connects Jackson to its sister, Washington Park. Jackson Park experienced its 15 minutes of worldwide fame in 1893 when it played host to the World's Fair Columbian Exposition. Today, the Museum of Science and Industry and La Rabida Children's Hospital and Research Center occupy two of the former fair structures.

Until recently Jackson Park had gone to seed. But thanks to Mayor Daley's green thumb, the government has been pumping money into park-rehabilitation projects and Jackson Park is reaping the benefits. Major improvements to the area's lakefront, bike path, athletic centers, and beaches have Jackson Park shimmering again.

Museum of Science and Industry

Address:	*57th St & Lake Shore Dr Chicago, IL 60637*
Phone:	*773-684-1414*
Website:	*www.msichicago.org*
Hours:	*Mon–Sat 9:30 am–4 pm; Sun 11 am–4 pm*
Admission:	*$11 adults, ($10 for Chicagoans); $7 children ages 3–11, ($6.25 for Chicagoans); $9.50 seniors, ($8.75 for Chicagoans)*

(Note: The Museum offers free admission on what would seem to be arbitrary days and hours vary month to month, so check the website regularly.)

The 1893 World's Fair Arts Palace is now home to the Museum of Science and Industry. The mammoth 350,000 square-foot palace is one of the largest science museums in the world. Generations of Chicagoans and visitors have been wowed by hatching baby chicks, *U-505* (the only World War II German submarine captured), and the Walk-Through Heart. The model railroad, another favorite exhibit, has been expanded to the now 3,500-square-foot *Great Train Journey*, which depicts the route from Chicago to Seattle. Other popular attractions include the fast-food toy exhibit, the coal mine, and the Fairy Castle.

Nature

Two lagoons surround Wooded Island, aka Paul H. Douglas Nature Sanctuary. Osaka Garden, a serene Japanese garden with an authentic tea house and entrance gate, sits at the island's northern tip. The ceremonial garden, like the golden replica of Statue of the Republic on Hayes Avenue, recalls the park's 1893 Exposition origins. The Chicago Audubon Society (773-539-6793; www.chicagoaudubon.org) conducts bird walks in the park. These sites and the Perennial Garden at 59th Street and Cornell Drive are also butterfly havens.

Sports

Back in the very beginning of the 20th century, the Jackson Park Golf Course was the only public course in the Midwest. Today, the historic 18-hole course is certified by the Audubon Cooperative Sanctuary and has beautiful wilderness habitats. (Or are those scruffy fairways?) Greens fees are $23.50 during the week and $25 on weekends (all rates are discounted for residents). A driving range is adjacent to the course (312-245-0909).

In the past six years, the city has spent over $10 million to improve fitness facilities in its parks, and the Jackson Park field house was the happy recipient of a much-needed facelift. The swanky new weight room and gymnasium are open to adults weekdays from 9:30 am to 2 pm and from 6 pm to 9 pm, and weekends from 9:30 am to 4:30 pm. The facilities are open to teens from 2 pm to 6 pm. Adult membership passes cost $50 for ten weeks and teens work out for free. From Hayes Drive north along Cornell Avenue are outdoor tennis courts, baseball diamonds, and a running track. Tennis courts are on the west side of Lakeshore Drive at 63rd Street. Jackson Park's beaches are at 57th Street and 63rd Street (water playground, too). Inner and Outer Harbors allow shore fishing (6401 S Stony Island Ave, 773-256-0903).

Neighboring Parks

North of Jackson Park at 55th Street and Lake Shore Drive is Promontory Point, a scenic lakeside picnic spot. Harold Washington Park, 51st Street and Lake Shore Drive, has a model yacht basin and eight tennis courts on 53rd Street.

To the west, 460-acre Washington Park (5531 S Martin Luther King Dr, 773-256-1248) has an outdoor swimming pool, playing fields, and nature areas. It's also worth stopping by to see Lorado Taft's 1922 Fountain of Time sculpture and the DuSable Museum of African-American History (740 E 56th Pl, 773-947-0600; www.dusablemuseum.org).

At 71st Street and South Shore Drive are South Shore Beach, with a harbor, bird sanctuary, and South Shore Cultural Center (7059 South Shore Dr, 773-256-0149). South Shore Golf Course is a nine-hole public course. Greens fees are $13.60 weekdays and $15 on weekends (312-245-0909).

How to Get There

By Car: From the Loop, drive south on Lake Shore Drive, exit west on 57th Street. From the south, take I-94 W. Exit on Stony Island Avenue heading north to 57th Drive. The museum's parking garage entrance is on 57th Drive. The Music Court lot is behind the museum. A free parking lot is on Hayes Drive.

By Bus: From the Loop, CTA buses 6 and 10 (weekends and daily in summer) stop by the museum.

By L: (the quickest way to get to Jackson Park)**:** Take the Green Line to the Garfield Boulevard (55th Street) stop ($1.75 one-way); transfer to the eastbound 55 bus.

By Train: Sporadic service. From the Loop's Randolph Street and Van Buren Street stations, take Metra Electric service ($2.05 one-way). Trains stop at the 55th, 56th, and 57th Street Station platform (may be under construction). Walk two blocks east. From the Richard B. Ogilvie Transportation Center, walk two blocks south to Union Station on Canal Street and catch CTA bus 1.

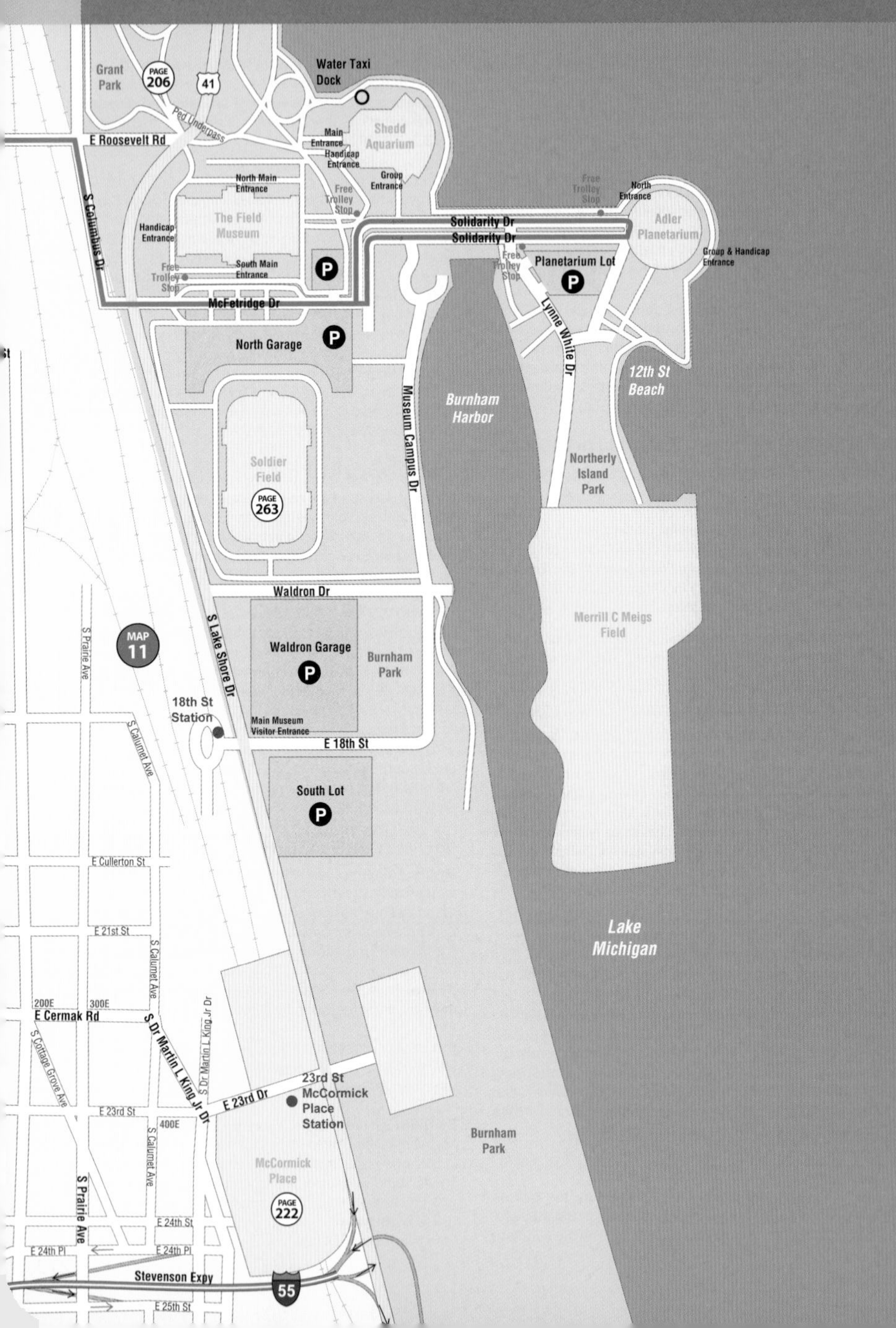

Grant Park
PAGE 206
41
Water Taxi Dock
Ped Underpass
E Roosevelt Rd
Shedd Aquarium
Main Entrance
Handicap Entrance
Group Entrance
North Main Entrance
Free Trolley Stop
The Field Museum
Handicap Entrance
South Main Entrance
Free Trolley Stop
S Columbus Dr
Solidarity Dr
Solidarity Dr
Free Trolley Stop
North Entrance
Adler Planetarium
Group & Handicap Entrance
Free Trolley Stop
Planetarium Lot
McFetridge Dr
North Garage
Lynne White Dr
12th St Beach
Museum Campus Dr
Burnham Harbor
Soldier Field
PAGE 263
Northerly Island Park
Waldron Dr
S Lake Shore Dr
Waldron Garage
Burnham Park
Merrill C Meigs Field
MAP 11
S Prairie Ave
18th St Station
Main Museum Visitor Entrance
E 18th St
S Calumet Ave
South Lot
E Cullerton St
E 21st St
S Calumet Ave
Lake Michigan
200E
300E
E Cermak Rd
S Dr Martin L King Jr Dr
S Dr Martin L King Jr Dr
S Cottage Grove Ave
E 23rd Dr
23rd St McCormick Place Station
E 23rd St
400E
S Calumet Ave
Burnham Park
McCormick Place
PAGE 222
S Prairie Ave
E 24th St
E 24th Pl
E 24th Pl
Stevenson Expy
55
E 25th St

Overview

Museum Campus is the ultimate destination for educational field trips. South of Grant Park at the intersection of Roosevelt Road and Lake Shore Drive, Museum Campus' 57 acres of uninterrupted lakefront parkland connect three world-renowned Chicago institutions: The Field Museum, Shedd Aquarium, and Adler Planetarium & Astronomy Museum. You've got Mayor Daley to thank for all of this beautiful space; it was the bossman himself who championed the rerouting of Lake Shore Drive to create the Museum Campus, which opened in 1998. Chicagoans, take note: Although none of the museums that make up the museum campus are shouting from rooftops about it, all three offer reduced admission rates to locals. Be sure to ask for it.

The Field Museum

Address: *1400 S Lake Shore Dr*
Chicago, IL 60605
Phone: *312-922-9410*
Website: *www.fieldmuseum.org*
Hours: *Open daily 9 am–5 pm, except Christmas*
Admission: *$19 adults, $14 students & seniors, $9 children ages 4–11, discount for Chicagoans*

The massive, classical Greek architectural-style museum constructed in 1921 houses over 20 million artifacts. From dinosaurs, diamonds, and earthworms to man-eating lions, totem poles, and mummies, there is just too much to savor in a single visit. In 2006, the museum introduced a new permanent exhibit called The Evolving Planet. Its an interactive stroll through 4 billion years of evolution, from single-celled organisms through dinosaurs, hominids, and finally to human beings. Science: 1, Intelligent Design: 0. As with most museums, some temporary exhibits cost additional bucks on top of normal museum fees. Free museum tours are held weekdays at 11 am and 2 pm.

John G. Shedd Aquarium

Address: *1200 S Lake Shore Dr*
Chicago, IL 60605
Phone: *312-939-2426*
Website: *www.shedd.org*
Hours: *Memorial Day–Labor Day: Daily, 9 am–6 pm (Jun–Aug open 'til 10 pm on Thurs)*
Labor Day–Memorial Day: Mon–Fri: 9 am–5 pm; Sat–Sun: 9 am–6 pm. Closed Christmas
Admission: *$23 adults ($17 Chicagoans), $16 seniors over 65 and children under 11 ($12 Chicagoans)*

Opened in 1929, the Beaux Arts architectural-style aquarium's six wings radiate from a giant, circular coral reef tank. The museum features revolving exhibits with a special focus on marine ecology and preservation. Popular favorties include Wild Reef, where you can get up close and personal with the sharks. On Thursday evenings from mid-June through August, the Shedd hosts Jazzin at the Shedd from 5 to 10 pm, featuring live jazz, a light sit-down dinner with cocktails overlooking the downtown skyline, and full access to the aquarium until 10 pm.

Burnham Park

Burnham Park, the site of the 1933 Century of Progress exhibition, encompasses McCormick Place, Burnham Harbor, the former Merrill C. Meigs Airport (closed in a political coup by Mayor Daley in 2003), and Soldier Field. A free skateboard park is located at Lake Shore Drive and 31st Street. The 12th Street Beach is on Northerly Island. Other beaches are at 31st Street and 49th Street. Outdoor basketball courts are east of Lake Shore Drive around 35th Street and 47th Street. Along Solidarity Drive and Burnham Harbor shore, fishing is welcome. The wilderness Nature Area at 47th Street attracts butterflies and birds.

Adler Planetarium

Address: *1300 S Lake Shore Dr*
Chicago, IL 60605
Phone: *312-922-7827*
Website: *www.adlerplanetarium.org*
Hours: *9:30 am-4:30 pm daily; First Friday of every month: 9:30 am-10 pm; Closed Thanksgiving and Christmas.*
Admission: *$16 for adults ($11 Chicagoans), $14 kids ages 4–17 ($10 Chicagoans), $15 seniors over 65 ($10 Chicagoans)*

The Adler Planetarium & Astronomy Museum has interactive exhibits explaining space phenomena and intergalactic events. The museum's 2,000 historic astronomical and navigational instruments form the western hemisphere's largest collection. On the first Friday of every month, weather permitting, amateur astronomers young and old are invited to bring out their telescopes to the Planetarium lawns. Roving scientists offer tips and instructions on how to use them and what to look for. On any day of the week, Chicago skyline views from the planetarium grounds are out of this world.

How to Get There

By Car: From the Loop, take Columbus Drive south; turn east on McFetridge Drive. From the south, take Lake Shore Drive to McFetridge Drive. Area parking lots are near Soldier Field, Field Museum, Adler Planetarium, and McCormick Place. All parking on Museum Campus costs $16 per day. Metered parking is available on Solidarity Drive.

By Bus: CTA buses 2, 6, 10, 12, 14, 127, 130, and 146 serve the area ($2.00 one-way, $1.75 with Chicago Card). For schedules and fares, contact the RTA Information Center at 312-913-3110; www.rtachicago.com.

By L: Ride the Orange, Red, or Green Lines to the Roosevelt Road stop ($2.00 one-way, $1.75 with Chicago Card). Walk east through the pedestrian underpass at Roosevelt Road.

By Train: From Richard B. Ogilvie Transportation Center, travel east on CTA bus 20 to State Street; transfer to the 146 ($2.00 one-way, $1.75 with Chicago Card). From Union Station take CTA bus 1, 151, or 126; transfer at State Street to the 146 or 10. From La Salle Street station, take the 146 ($2.00 one-way, $1.75 with Chicago Card). South Shore and Metra trains stop at the Roosevelt Road station.

By Trolley: Free trolleys travel to the Museum Campus from public transportation stations and some parking lots during the warmer months. See www.cityofchicago.org/transportation or call 1-877-CHICAGO for more details.

On Foot: Walk south through Grant Park past bobbing boats and the gushing Buckingham Fountain to the Museum Campus.

Water Taxis: Seasonally, water taxis operate between Navy Pier and Museum Campus (312-222-9328; www.shorelinesightseeing.com).

W Kinzie St
Carroll Dr
W Carroll Ave
W Fulton St
Garfield Park Conservatory
N Central Park Ave
N St Louis Ave
N Homan Ave
W Fulton Blvd
N Avers Ave
Pulaski
Conservatory Dr
Gold Dome Building
Conservatory Central Park Drive
W Walnut St
W Lake St
N Pulaski Rd
N Harding Ave
N Hamilton Ave
W Maypole Ave
W West End St
N McCrea Dr
Lagoon
Garfield
W Washington Blvd
W Warren Ave
Warren Dr
MAP 49
Park
W Madison St
S Woodward Dr
S Central Park Ave
S St Louis Ave
S Homan Ave
S Spaulding Ave
S Pulaski Rd
S Springfield Ave
S Hamilton Blvd
W Monroe St
Music Court Dr
W Wilcox Ave
W Adams Ave
W Adams St
Tennis Courts
W Jackson Blvd
Independence Blvd
S Christiana Ave
S Trumbull Ave
W Gladys Ave
W Fifth Ave
W Van Buren St
S Millard Ave
W Congress Pkwy
290
Dwight D Eisenhower Expy
W Harrison St

Overview

Until recently, the slowly gentrifying (read: sketchy) West Side was the home of the city's best kept secret garden—Garfield Park Conservatory. But the secret has been unveiled since the Chicago Park District invested over $12 million to restore this national landmark. The 185-acre park boasts fishing lagoons, a swimming pool, an ice rink, baseball diamonds, and basketball and tennis courts. Garfield Park's landmark Gold Dome Building houses a fitness center, a basketball court, and the Peace Museum.

Garfield and its sister parks—Humboldt Park (1400 N Sacramento Ave, 312-742-7549) and Douglas Park (1401 S Sacramento Ave, 773-762-2842)—constitute a grand system of sprawling green spaces linked by broad boulevards designed in 1869 by William Le Baron Jenney (better known as the "father of the skyscraper"). However, Jenney's plan didn't bear fruit until almost 40 years later (after the uprooting of corrupt park officials), when Danish immigrant and former park laborer Jens Jensen became chief landscape architect. In 1908, Jensen completed the parks and consolidated their three small conservatories under the 1.8-acre Garfield Park Conservatory's curvaceous glass dome, designed to resemble a "great Midwestern haystack."

Garfield Park Conservatory

Address:	*300 N Central Park Ave* *Chicago, IL 60624*
Phone:	*773-746-5100*
Website:	*www.garfield-conservatory.org*
Hours:	*9 am–5 pm daily; Thurs: 9 am–8 pm*
Admission:	*FREE*

One of the nation's largest conservatories, Garfield Park has six thematic plant houses with 1,000 species and more than 10,000 individual plants from around the world. Plants Alive!, a 5,000-square-foot children's garden, has touchable plants, a soil pool for digging, a Jurassic Park–sized bumble bee, and a two-story, twisting flower stem that doubles as a slide. School groups often book the garden for field trips, so call first to determine public access hours. Annual Conservatory events include the Spring Flower Show, Azalea/Camellia Show, Chocolate Festival, Summer Tropical Show, Chrysanthemum (Chicago's city flower) Show, and Holiday Garden Show. Every weekend, seasonally, visitors can browse the open air Garfield Market featuring crafts, plants, and produce. There is a farmer's market at the park on Saturday mornings from June through October.

The Peace Museum

Address:	*100 N Central Park Ave* *Chicago, IL 60624*
Phone:	*773-638-6450*
Website:	*www.peacemuseum.org*
Hours:	*Thurs–Fri 1 pm–6 pm, Sat–Sun 1 pm–4 pm*
Admission:	*$5*

Located on the top floor of the landmark Garfield Park Gold Dome Building is the Peace Museum. The tiny museum's collection of 10,000 artworks, photographs, and artifacts promoting non-violence are displayed through rotating, thematic exhibits. Special exhibits include a John Lennon guitar, an original U2 song sheet, and moving drawings by Nagasaki and Hiroshima survivors. Call for information on current and traveling exhibits.

Fishing

Garfield Park's two lagoons at Washington Boulevard and Central Park Avenue and those at Douglas and Humboldt Parks are favorite West Side fishing holes. Seasonally, they are stocked with bluegill, crappie, channel catfish, and largemouth bass, along with an occasional unfortunate gang member. Review your health insurance plan before eating what you hook. Kids can take free fishing classes at the park lagoons during the summer through the Chicago Park District (312-747-6067). Groups of ten kids or more fish every day of the week at a new location. You'll have to call in advance, as groups are organized by appointment only. The program runs June 20-August 12, Mon-Fri, between 10 am and 4 pm.

Nature

The Chicago Park District leads free nature walks and has created marked trails with information plaques at the city's bigger parks, Garfield, Douglas, and Humboldt Parks included. Seasonally, visitors can view as many as 100 species of colorful butterflies at the formal gardens of the three parks. The parks' lagoons are officially designated Chicago "birding parks," so take binoculars. Picnics for 50 people or more and tent set-up require party-throwers to obtain permits issued by the Chicago Park District.

How to Get There

By Car: Garfield Park is ten minutes from the Loop. Take I-290 W; exit on Independence Boulevard and drive north. Turn east on Washington Boulevard to Central Park Avenue. Go north on Central Park Avenue two blocks past the Golden Dome field house and Lake Street to the Conservatory. A free parking lot is on the building's south side, just after Lake Street. Street parking is available on Central Park Avenue, Madison Street, and Washington Boulevard.

By L: From the Loop, take the Green Line west ($1.75 one-way) to the new Conservatory-Central Park Drive stop, a renovated Victorian train station at Lake Street and Central Park Avenue.

By Bus: From the Loop, board CTA 20 Madison Street bus westbound ($1.75 one-way). Get off at Madison Street and Central Park Avenue. Walk four blocks north to the Conservatory.

Additional Information

Chicago Park District, 312-742-7529; www.chicagoparkdistrict.com

Nature Chicago Program—City of Chicago and Department of the Environment, 312-744-7606; www.cityofchicago.org

Chicago Ornithological Society, 312-409-9678; www.chicagobirder.org

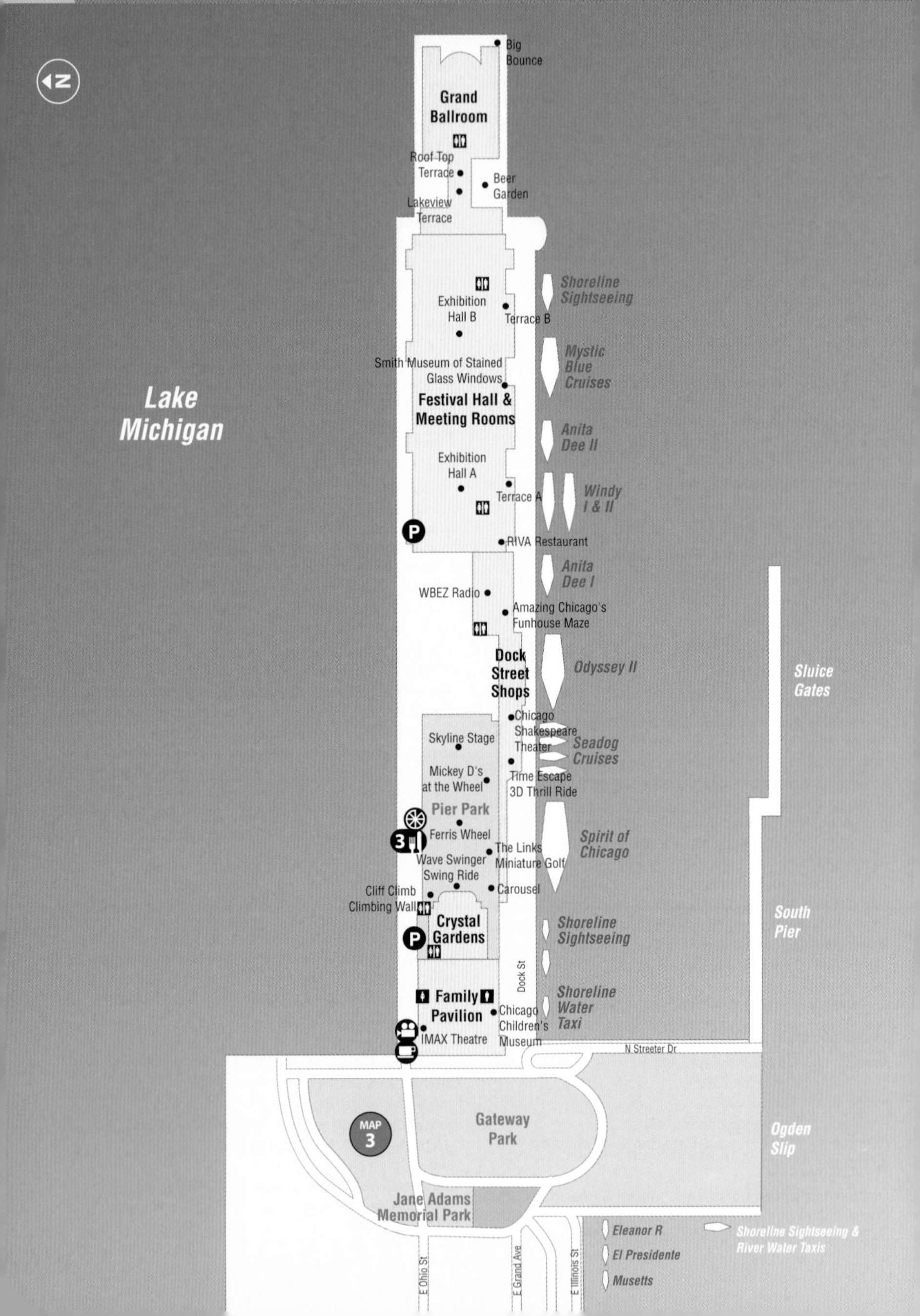

Big Bounce

Grand Ballroom

Roof Top Terrace

Beer Garden

Lakeview Terrace

Exhibition Hall B

Terrace B

Shoreline Sightseeing

Mystic Blue Cruises

Smith Museum of Stained Glass Windows

Festival Hall & Meeting Rooms

Lake Michigan

Anita Dee II

Exhibition Hall A

Terrace A

Windy I & II

RIVA Restaurant

Anita Dee I

WBEZ Radio

Amazing Chicago's Funhouse Maze

Dock Street Shops

Odyssey II

Sluice Gates

Chicago Shakespeare Theater

Skyline Stage

Seadog Cruises

Mickey D's at the Wheel

Time Escape 3D Thrill Ride

Pier Park

Ferris Wheel

3

The Links Miniature Golf

Spirit of Chicago

Wave Swinger Swing Ride

Cliff Climb Climbing Wall

Carousel

Crystal Gardens

Shoreline Sightseeing

South Pier

Dock St

Family Pavilion

Shoreline Water Taxi

Chicago Children's Museum

IMAX Theatre

N Streeter Dr

Gateway Park

MAP 3

Ogden Slip

Jane Adams Memorial Park

Eleanor R

Shoreline Sightseeing & River Water Taxis

El Presidente

Musetts

E Ohio St

E Grand Ave

E Illinois St

General Information

NFT Map:	3
Address:	600 E Grand Ave Chicago, IL 60611
Phone:	312-595-7437
Website:	www.navypier.com
Pier Hours:	Opens 10 am daily. Closing times of restaurants, shops, and attractions vary by season, holiday, and public exhibitions/ events.
Skyline Stage:	1,500-seat outdoor performance pavilion in Pier Park; performances are May through September 312-595-5005
IMAX Theatre:	312-595-5629
Free Fireworks:	Memorial Day to Labor Day nights, Wednesdays (9:30 pm) & Saturdays (10:15 pm) Free to the public.
WBEZ Radio:	National Public Radio's local station, 312-948-4600; www.wbez.org.
Exhibit Space:	Festival Hall, Lakeview Terrace, Ballroom Lobby, Grand Ballroom; 36 meeting rooms

Overview

A quintessential tourist trap, Navy Pier (a.k.a. the mall on the lake) is often avoided by real Chicagoans, who scoff at its self-consciously inoffensive blandness. Save for an occasional Skyline Stage concert or high-end nosh at Riva, a trek to the pier is best reserved for those times when you have Grandma and a bevy of nieces and nephews in town. Not to mention plenty of spending cash.

Opened to the public in 1916 as a municipal wharf, the pier has also done time as a) the University of Illinois at Chicago's campus, b) a hospital, c) a military training facility, d) a concert venue, and e) a white elephant. In 1989, the Metropolitan Pier and Exposition Authority invested $150 million to transform the crumbling pier into a peninsular entertainment-exhibition complex that attracts 8 million uninspired people a year. In addition to convention space, Navy Pier also houses two museums, the Shakespeare Theater, the Crystal Gardens, outdoor concert pavilion, vintage grand ballroom, 15-story Ferris wheel, IMAX Theatre, and, just for the hell of it, a radio station.

Chicago Shakespeare Theater

The professional Chicago Shakespeare Theater has a 510-seat, courtyard-style theater and a 180-seat studio theater that are Chicago's sole venues dedicated to performing wordsmith Willy's works. In addition to the season's plays, the theater produces Shakespeare "shorts" for younger patrons. A bookstore and teacher resource center are also on-site (312-595-5600; www.chicagoshakes.com).

Chicago Children's Museum

The Chicago Children's Museum features daily activities, a creative crafts studio, and 15 interactive exhibits ranging from dinosaur digs and waterworks to a toddler tree house, safety town, and construction zone. The museum is open Sunday-Wednesday and Friday 10 am to 5 pm, and Thursday and Saturday until 8 pm. Admission is $8 for adults and children, $7 for seniors, and Target First Free Mondays allow children 15 and under in free the first Monday of every month. Thursdays 5 pm–8 pm are Kraft Free Family Nights, which means free admission for all. Dates vary. (312-527-1000; www.chichildrensmuseum.org).

Smith Museum of Stained Glass Windows

This is the first stained-glass-only museum in the country. The 150 windows installed in the lower level of Festival Hall are mainly from Chicago-area buildings and the city's renowned stained glass studios. Windows representing over a century of artistic styles include works by Louis Comfort Tiffany, Frank Lloyd Wright, Louis Sullivan, and John LaFarge. The free museum is open during Pier hours (312-595-5024).

Getting There

By Car: From the north, exit Lake Shore Drive at Grand Avenue; proceed east. From the southeast, exit Lake Shore Drive at Illinois Street; go east. Three garages are on the Pier's north side, and plenty of parking lots are just west of Lake Shore Drive in Streeterville (Map 3).

By Bus: CTA buses 29, 56, 65, 66, 120, 121, and 124 serve Navy Pier.

By L: Take the Green or Red Line to Grand Avenue ($1.75 one-way). Board eastbound CTA Bus 29 (additional 25¢), or take the free trolley.

By Train: From Richard B. Ogilvie Transportation Center, take CTA buses 56 or 124. From Union Station, board bus 121.

By Trolley: Free, daily trolleys that typically run every 20 minutes travel between Navy Pier and State Street along Grand Avenue and Illinois Street. Pick-up points are indicated by "Navy Pier Trolley Stop" signs along the route. Go to: www.tylin.com/chicago/tma

By Boat: Seasonal water shuttles (one-way $12 adults, $6 kids) travel between Navy Pier and the Museum Campus and along the Chicago River to the Sears Tower (312-222-9328; www.shorelinesightseeing.com).

Pizza

- **Connie's Pizza** • 700 E Grand Ave

Coffee

- **Starbucks** • 600 E Grand Ave

Movie Theaters

- **Navy Pier IMAX Theatre** • 600 E Grand Ave

Restaurants

- **Bubba Gump Shrimp Co** • 700 E Grand Ave
- **Capi's Italian Kitchen** • 700 E Grand Ave
- **Riva** • 700 E Grand Ave

General Information

NFT Maps: 5, 6
Address: 78 E Washington St
Chicago, IL 60602
Phone: 312-744-6630
Website: www.cityofchicago.org/culturalcenter
Hours: November 1–March 31,
Mon–Thurs 10 am–7 pm; Fri 10 am–6 pm;
Sat 10 am–5 pm; Sun 11 am–5 pm
April 1–October 31, Mon–Thurs 8 am–7 pm, Fri 8 am–6 pm, Sat 9 am–6 pm,
Sun 10 am–6 pm,
and closed on holidays

Overview

The Chicago Cultural Center is the Loop's public arts center. Free—that's right, we said FREE—concerts, theatrical performances, films, lectures, and exhibits are offered daily. Admission to the Cultural Center and its art galleries are all free, too. Call 312-346-3278 for weekly event updates.

The building itself, constructed in 1897, is a neoclassical landmark featuring intricate glass and marble mosaics on its walls and grand stairways. Once the city's central public library, the Cultural Center boasts the world's largest Tiffany dome in Preston Bradley Hall and the Renaissance-style Grand Army of the Republic Exhibition Hall. Free (there's that lovely word again) 45-minute architectural tours are held on Wednesdays, Fridays, and Saturdays at 1:15 pm. If you're interested in a guided group tour highlighting the building's history, call 312-744-8032 for more information. The building is also home to the Chicago Greeter Program, which allows visitors the opportunity to take a 2-3 hour walking tour with a chatty and knowledgeable guide around one of any number of neighborhoods throughout the city. Interested parties must book in advance at www.chicagogreeter.com. Surprise, surprise: it's free, as well.

Performances

The Cultural Center's free Jazz, Blues, and Beyond "LunchBreak" series provides downtown working stiffs with a welcome midday respite. The jazz concerts are held at 12:15 pm in the Randolph Café every Tuesday, while the classical concerts and opera are performed Mondays at 12:15 pm in Preston Bradley Hall. Call 312-744-6630 for information on frequently scheduled special programs.

Off-Loop theater productions appear regularly in the Center's Studio Theater, including the seasonal ShawChicago series featuring plays by Bernard Shaw on Saturdays, Sundays, and Mondays. Performances are free, but reservations are required (312-409-5605; www.shawchicago.org).

Art Galleries

A permanent exhibit in the Landmark Gallery, Chicago Landmarks Before the Lens is a stunning black-and-white photographic survey of Chicago architecture. Five additional galleries regularly rotate exhibits, showcasing work in many media by renowned and local artists. Tours of current exhibits are ongoing.

How to Get There

By Car: Travel down Michigan Avenue to Randolph Street. From Lake Shore Drive, exit at Randolph Street. For parking garages in the area, see Map 6.

By Train: From the Richard B. Ogilvie Transportation Center, travel east to Michigan Avenue on CTA buses 157, 20, 56, and 127. From Union Station, take CTA buses 60, 157, and 151. From the Randolph Street station below Millennium Park, walk west across Michigan Avenue. For schedules and fares, contact the RTA Information Center (312-836-7000; www.rtachicago.com).

By L: Take the Green Line to the Randolph stop. Walk east one block.

By Bus: CTA buses 151, 145, 147, and 3 stop on Michigan Avenue in front of the Cultural Center.

General Information

NFT Map: 5
Address: 400 S State St
Chicago, IL 60605
Phone: 312-747-4300
Website: www.chipublib.org

Overview

Harold Washington Library Center is the world's largest public library. Named after Chicago's first African-American mayor, the 756,640-square-foot neoclassical architectural monstrosity has over 70 miles of shelves storing more than 9 million books, microforms, serials, and government documents. Over 50 works of notable sculpture, painting, and mosaic adorn the free library visited by over 6,000 patrons daily.

The library's collection begins on the ground floor with the **popular library**, containing current general titles and bestsellers, from thrillers to travel books to biography. The library's **audio-visual collection** (including an impressive collection of books on tape as well as videos, DVDs, and popular music CDs) is also housed here. The second floor is home to the **children's library**, and the **general reference library** begins on the third floor where the **circulation desks** are located. Among the notable features of the library is the eighth floor **Music Information Center** housing sheet music and printed scores, 150,000 recordings, the **Chicago Blues Archives**, eight individual piano practice rooms, and a chamber music rehearsal room. The ninth floor **Winter Garden**, with its olive trees and soaring 100-foot high ceilings is a popular site for special events. If you have your sights set on getting hitched here, leave your priest or rabbi at home—HWL's status as a civic building precludes religious services on its premises.

Frequent free public programs are held in the lower level's 385-seat auditorium, video theater, exhibit hall, and meeting rooms. Call 312-747-4649 for information on scheduled events. Additionally, the website houses a bbs for those participating in Chicago's "One City, One Book" reading club who want to discuss the latest selection.

Library hours are Monday through Thursday 9 am to 7 pm, Friday and Saturday 9 am to 5 pm, and Sunday 1 pm to 5 pm. Free library tours can be arranged for groups by calling 312-747-4136.

Research Services

To check the availability or location of an item, call Catalog Information at 312-747-4340 or search the library's Online Catalog on www.chipublib.org. Their Email Reference Service responds to information requests within two days. For faster answers to common research questions, check out the website's handy Virtual Library Service under Selected Internet Resources, then click on "Reference Shelf."

Computer Services

The library's 96 computers with Internet access and 37 more with word processing, desktop publishing, graphic presentation, and spreadsheet applications are located on the third floor in the Computer Commons. Computer use is free and available on a first-come-first-served basis. You can reserve computers for up to one hour per day based on walk-in availability. Limited time slots are also available via phone reservation at 312-747-4450. For downloads, bring your own formatted disk or purchase one at the library for $2. Free laser printing is also provided. Operating hours are Monday through Thursday 9 am–7 pm, Friday and Saturday 9 am–5 pm, and Sunday 1 pm–5 pm.

Thomas Hughes Children's Library

The 18,000-square-foot Thomas Hughes Children's Library on the second floor serves children through age 14. Thomas Hughes was a British man who, upon hearing of the tragedy of the Chicago Fire, started a book collection resulting in the 8,000 titles that composed the first Chicago Public Library. In addition to more than 120,000 children's books representing 40 foreign languages, there is a reference collection on children's literature for adults. Twenty free computers, twelve with Internet connections, are also available. Children's programs are hosted weekly (312-747-4200).

Special Collections

The library's Special Collections & Preservation Division's highlights include: Harold Washington Collection, Civil War & American History Research Collection, Chicago Authors & Publishing Collection, Chicago Blues Archives, Chicago Theater Collection, World's Columbian Exposition Collection, and Neighborhood History Research Collection. The collections' reading room is closed Sunday.

How to Get There

By Car: The library is at the intersection of State Street and Congress Parkway in South Loop. Take I-290 E into the Loop. See Map 5 for area parking garages.

By L: The Brown Line, Purple Line, and Orange Line stop at the Library Station. Exit the Red Line and O'Hare Airport Blue Line at Van Buren Station; walk one block south. Change from the Harlem/Lake Street Green Line to the northbound Orange Line at Roosevelt Road station; get off at Library Station.

By Bus: CTA buses that stop on State Street in front of the library are the 2, 6, 29, 36, 62, 151, 145, 146, and 147.

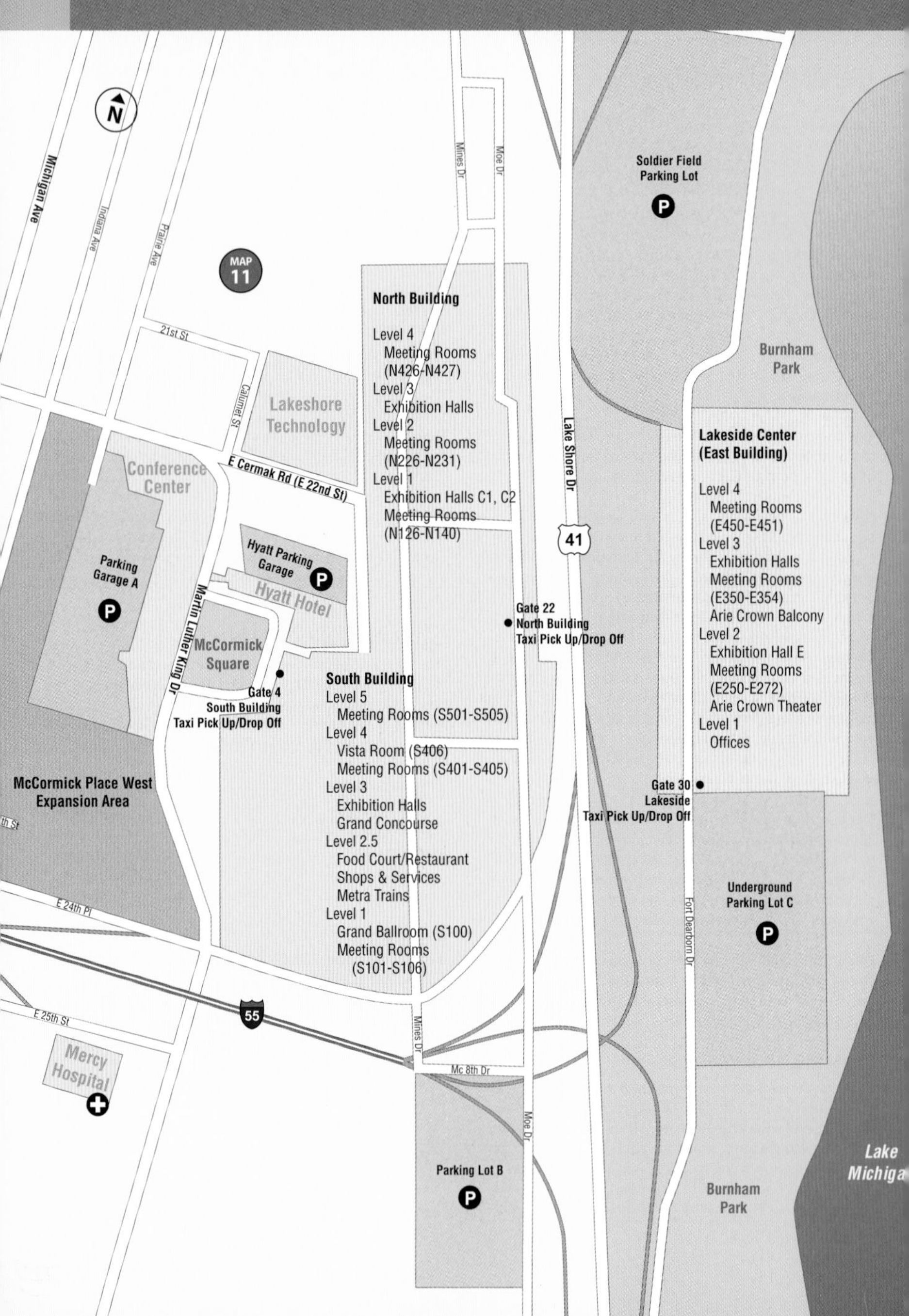
N
Michigan Ave
Indiana Ave
Prairie Ave
MAP 11
21st St
Calumet St
Lakeshore Technology
Conference Center
E Cermak Rd (E 22nd St)
Parking Garage A
Hyatt Parking Garage
Hyatt Hotel
Martin Luther King Dr
McCormick Square
Gate 4
South Building
Taxi Pick Up/Drop Off
McCormick Place West Expansion Area
E 24th Pl
E 25th St
Mercy Hospital
55
Mines Dr
Moe Dr
North Building
Level 4
Meeting Rooms
(N426-N427)
Level 3
Exhibition Halls
Level 2
Meeting Rooms
(N226-N231)
Level 1
Exhibition Halls C1, C2
Meeting Rooms
(N126-N140)
Gate 22
North Building
Taxi Pick Up/Drop Off
South Building
Level 5
Meeting Rooms (S501-S505)
Level 4
Vista Room (S406)
Meeting Rooms (S401-S405)
Level 3
Exhibition Halls
Grand Concourse
Level 2.5
Food Court/Restaurant
Shops & Services
Metra Trains
Level 1
Grand Ballroom (S100)
Meeting Rooms
(S101-S106)
Mc 8th Dr
Parking Lot B
Lake Shore Dr
41
Soldier Field
Parking Lot
Burnham Park
Lakeside Center
(East Building)
Level 4
Meeting Rooms
(E450-E451)
Level 3
Exhibition Halls
Meeting Rooms
(E350-E354)
Arie Crown Balcony
Level 2
Exhibition Hall E
Meeting Rooms
(E250-E272)
Arie Crown Theater
Level 1
Offices
Gate 30
Lakeside
Taxi Pick Up/Drop Off
Fort Dearborn Dr
Underground
Parking Lot C
Burnham Park
Lake Michiga

General Information

NFT Map:	11
Mailing Address:	2301 S Lake Shore Dr Chicago, IL 60616
Phone:	312-791-7000
Website:	www.mccormickplace.com
South Building:	Exhibit Hall A; charter bus stop
North Building:	Exhibit Halls B and C; Metra train station
Lakeside Center:	Exhibit Halls D and E; 4,249-seat Arie Crown Theater (Level 2); underground parking garage

Overview

When it comes to the convention business, size matters. With 2.2 million square feet of exhibit space spread among three buildings, McCormick Place is the largest convention center in the country. The center sees more than three million visitors a year attending its trade shows and public exhibitions in the South Building, North Building, and Lakeside Center (East Building). The city's colossal cash cow is about to get even bigger with the addition of a new $850 million West Building. Originally intended for completion in 2008, new outlooks have it ready by the end of 2007—AND it's on budget. A City of Chicago project ahead of time and on budget? Surely another sign that the apocolypse will be occuring soon. End times notwithstanding, the expansion will add 470,000 square feet of exhibit space and 250,000 square feet of meeting rooms to the already gargantuan center.

McCormick Place's growth continues to bolster the rapid gentrification of South Loop, and with each expansion the complex's overall aesthetic appeal steadily improves. But despite major renovations, Chicagoans still refer to the complex as "the mistake on the lake." Mayor Daley called the black boxy behemoth the "Berlin Wall" that separates Chicagoans from their beloved lakefront.

Finding Your Way Around

Getting to McCormick Place is the easy part. Then you have to navigate the inside. The main entrance is off Martin Luther King Drive, next to the Hyatt Hotel. Here's how to crack the code names for meeting rooms and exhibit halls:

All meeting room locations start with E (Lakeside Center/East Building), N (North Building), or S (South Building). The first numeral represents the floor level, and the last two digits specify which room. Room numbers are never duplicated among the complex's three buildings.

Exhibit halls are named by consecutive letters starting with the South Building where Hall A (Level 3) is located. North Building houses Halls B (Level 3) and C (Level 1). Exhibit Halls D (Level 3) and E (Level 2) are in Lakeside Center.

Restaurants & Services

Connie's Pizza and McDonald's Express are in the North Building (Level 2). The Plate Room Food Court is in the Grand Concourse (Level 2.5 and 3), where Starbucks, shops, a shoe shine, and massage services are also located. (Aren't convention centers just *great?*) Business centers and ATMs are in the Grand Concourse (Level 2.5), North Building (Level 2), and Lakeside Center (Level 2). Although it's not yet completed as we write, the new West Building expansion will have a large food court on the second floor. If you're totally lost, there are Visitor Information Centers in each building. Good luck finding them.

How to Get There

By Car: From the Loop, take Lake Shore Drive south; from the southeast, travel north on Lake Shore Drive. Signage to McCormick Place on Lake Shore Drive is frequent and clear. Parking garages are in Lakeside Center and the Hyatt. Lots are at 31st Street and Lake Shore Drive and at Martin Luther King Drive across from the South Building. Additional lots are north of McCormick Place at Burnham Harbor and Soldier Field.

By Bus: From the Loop, CTA buses 3 and 4 stop in front of the South Building. From Richard B. Ogilvie Transportation Center, take buses 124, 125, or 157 to Michigan Avenue; transfer to a southbound 3 or 4 ($1.75 with transfer one-way). From Union Station, board eastbound bus 1 to Michigan Avenue; transfer to a southbound 3 or 4.

During major shows, countless charter buses circle downtown hotels, transporting conventioneers to McCormick Place for free. With the new express busway, charter buses travel from Randolph Street to the South Building in less than ten minutes. For schedules, check with the hotels and at McCormick Place information desks.

By Train: A Metra train ride from the Loop's Randolph Street and Van Buren Street stations to the McCormick Place Station takes nine minutes ($1.85 one-way). Escalators to the train platform are on the west side of the Grand Concourse (Level 2.5).

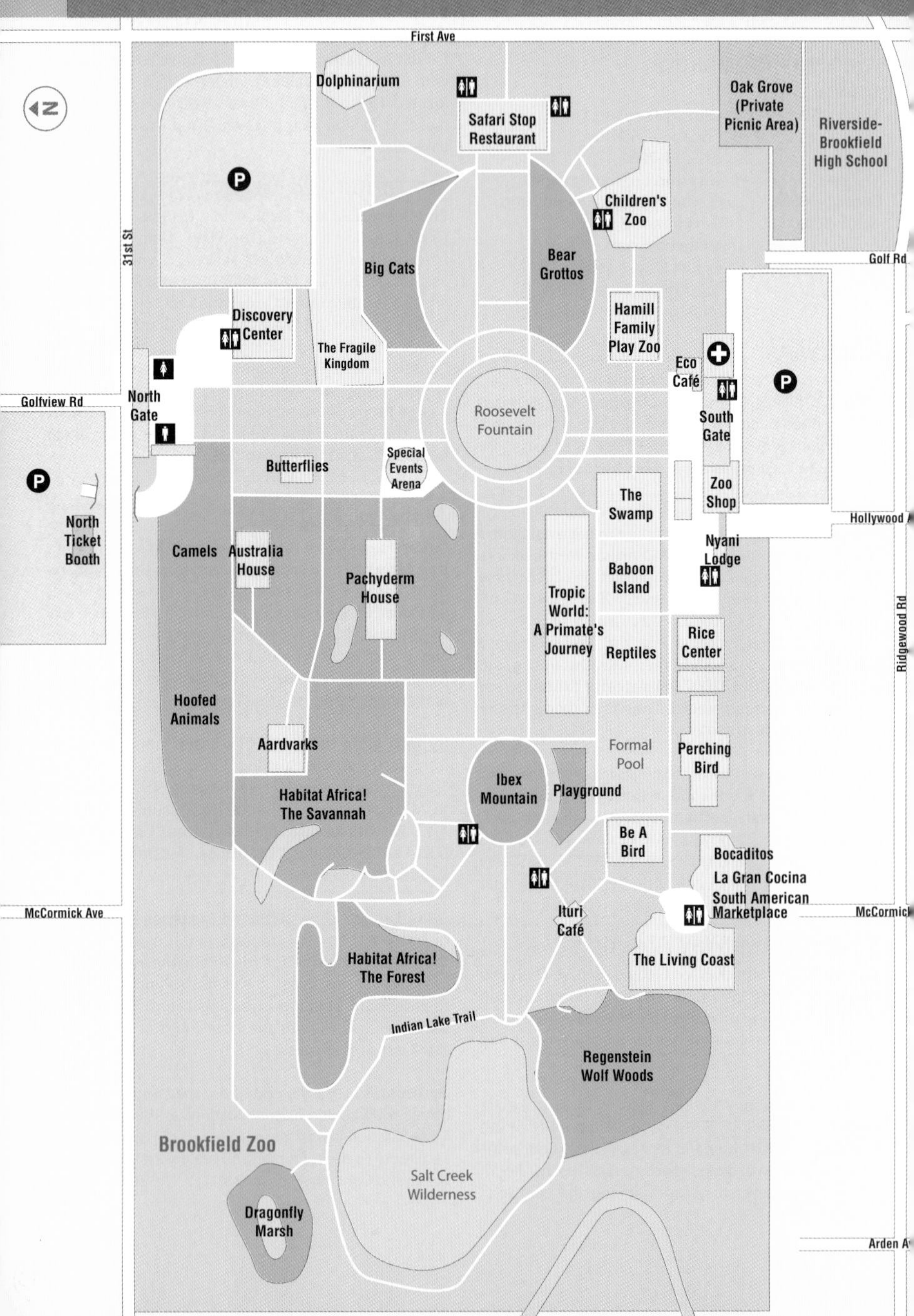

First Ave
Dolphinarium
Safari Stop Restaurant
Oak Grove (Private Picnic Area)
Riverside-Brookfield High School
Children's Zoo
Big Cats
Bear Grottos
31st St
Golf Rd
Discovery Center
The Fragile Kingdom
Hamill Family Play Zoo
Eco Café
North Gate
Golfview Rd
Roosevelt Fountain
South Gate
Butterflies
Special Events Arena
Zoo Shop
The Swamp
Hollywood A
North Ticket Booth
Camels
Australia House
Pachyderm House
Nyani Lodge
Baboon Island
Tropic World: A Primate's Journey
Reptiles
Rice Center
Ridgewood Rd
Hoofed Animals
Aardvarks
Formal Pool
Perching Bird
Ibex Mountain
Playground
Habitat Africa! The Savannah
Be A Bird
Bocaditos
La Gran Cocina
South American Marketplace
McCormick Ave
McCormic
Ituri Café
Habitat Africa! The Forest
The Living Coast
Indian Lake Trail
Regenstein Wolf Woods
Brookfield Zoo
Salt Creek Wilderness
Dragonfly Marsh
Arden A

General Information

Address:	31st St & First Ave Brookfield, IL 60513
Phone:	708-485-0263
Website:	www.brookfieldzoo.org
Hours:	Open daily from 10 am–5 pm, and until 7:30 on Sundays from Labor Day to Memorial Day
Admission:	$10 adults, $6 children 3–11 & seniors, free children two and under

Overview

While Lincoln Park Zoo is the city's free zoo, Brookfield Zoo offers a far more comprehensive wild animal experience with a strong emphasis on conservation education. 216 acres of creepy critters make for a memorable day trip. We'll skip the analogy with the Joliet Riverboat Casino.

Hamill Family Play Zoo

This interactive play area is part of a program to create a huge new wing of the zoo dedicated solely to kids. Great—just what a zoo needs: more kids. Children get to interact in a variety of ways, including donning costumes to play "zoo keeper" or "ring-tailed lemur," creating and frolicking in their own simulated habitats, planting seeds in the greenhouse, or spotting creepy insects in the outdoor bug path. Think a grownup would look silly dressed like a lemur? We want to play!

Regenstein Wolf Woods

The zoo's impressive wolf exhibit allows visitors to follow the progress of a small pack of endangered male wolves as they do the wolfy things wolves do. One-way glass allows spectators to get up close and personal with the wolves without freaking them out. So far, the mirrors have been 100% unsuccessful in detecting any wolf shoplifting.

Other Exhibits

Of course the zoo is full of exhibits, some more fascinating than others. Among them are the seasonal butterfly exhibit and the dragonfly march. Here are some other worthwhile sights:

- **Habitat Africa**: This is broken up into two sections: The Rainforest, with its zebras and African millipedes (heebie-jeebies), and The Savannah, with our favorite, the giraffes.
- **Dolphinarium**: Dolphin shows are scheduled at regular intervals two or three times a day (sometimes more during peak seasons and on weekends).
- **Tropic World**: Visit Kamba, the baby gorilla born in front of a captivated, slightly disgusted crowd of zoo visitors (mother Koola now knows how Marie Antoinette felt when she shared the delivery of her offspring with the French peasantry) and Bakari, the newest addition to the Gorilla family, who was born to mother Binto in May '05.

Eating at the Zoo

- **La Gran Cocina**: At the South American Marketplace. Walk-up stir-fry, chicken, pizza, and fruit.
- **Eco Café**: Near the Hamill Family Play Zoo. Brookfield Zoo teamed up with Whole Foods to create the Eco Café, offering yogurt, organic chips, and other healthy snacks. The green theme goes far beyond the menu, too. Much of the café's structure and function are of the tree-hugging sort.
- **Bocaditos**: Table service dining on the second floor of the South American Marketplace. Peruvian fare with a "familiar" twist (read: blanded down for white-bread palates).
- **Ituri Café**: Near the Habitat Africa playground. Walk-up food vendor with picnic tables.

How to Get There

By Car: From the Eisenhower or Stevens Expressway, exit at First Avenue. From there, signs will direct you the short distance to the zoo. Lot parking is $8.

By Train: From downtown Chicago, take the Burlington Northern Metra line to Zoo Stop/ Hollywood Station.

By Bus: Pace buses 304 and 331 stop right at the zoo's gates.

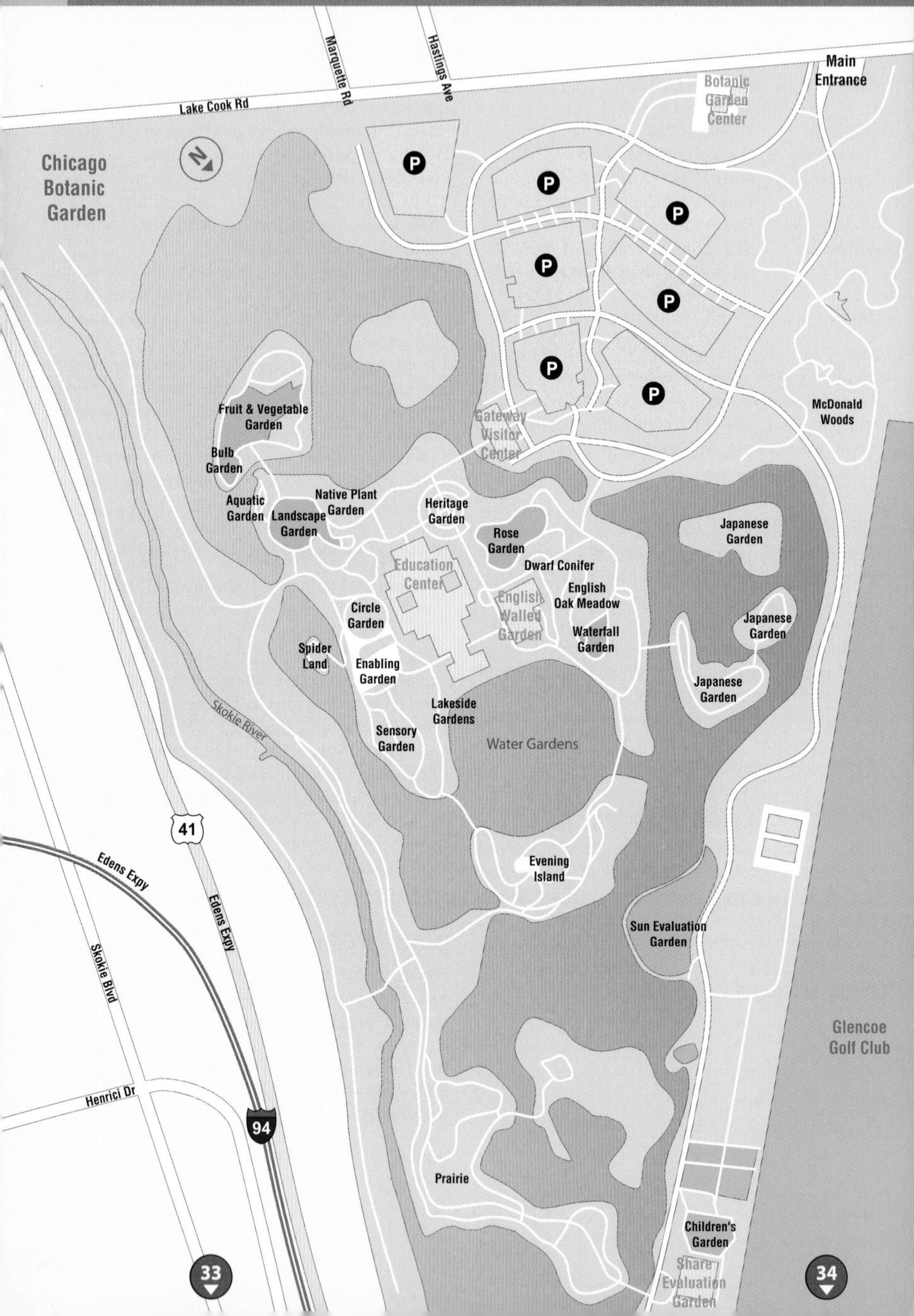

Lake Cook Rd
Marquette Rd
Hastings Ave
Main Entrance
Botanic Garden Center
Chicago Botanic Garden
Fruit & Vegetable Garden
Bulb Garden
Gateway Visitor Center
McDonald Woods
Aquatic Garden
Native Plant Garden
Landscape Garden
Heritage Garden
Rose Garden
Japanese Garden
Education Center
Dwarf Conifer
English Walled Garden
English Oak Meadow
Circle Garden
Waterfall Garden
Japanese Garden
Spider Land
Enabling Garden
Japanese Garden
Lakeside Gardens
Skokie River
Sensory Garden
Water Gardens
41
Evening Island
Edens Expy
Edens Expy
Sun Evaluation Garden
Skokie Blvd
Glencoe Golf Club
Henrici Dr
94
Prairie
Children's Garden
Shrub Evaluation Garden

General Information

Address: 1000 Lake Cook Rd, Glencoe, IL 60022
Phone: 847-835-5440
Website: www.chicagobotanic.org
Hours: Open 364 days, 8 am to sunset; closed December 25
Admission: Free

Overview

Spanning 385 acres, the serene and lovely Chicago Botanic Garden has been the backdrop for many a chi-chi wedding since they opened the gates in 1972.

Nature

Twenty-three gardens and two prairie habitats make up the Botanic Garden. Among them are a specialized Japanese garden, a rose garden, a bulb garden, a greenhouse full of tropical vegetation, and several beds solely dedicated to indigenous plants and flowers.

Where to Eat

• **Garden Café:** Serves breakfast and café fare—salads, sandwiches, beer, and wine. Open November to March: 8 am-4 pm; April to October: 8 am-5 pm weekdays, 8 am-5:30 pm weekends, and open to 7 pm on Carillion Concert Mondays.
• **Garden Grill:** Grill being the operative word, serves burgers, dogs, and the like. Open June to October 31 for lunch Friday to Sunday 11:30 am-2:30 pm, weather permitting. Open for dinner from late May to late September, 5:30 pm-8 pm, featuring a barbeque buffet and beer garden.

Note: Picnicking allowed in designated areas only.

How to Get to There

By Car: Take I-90/94 W (The Kennedy) to I-94 (The Edens) and US 41. Exit on Lake Cook Road, then go a half-mile east to the garden.

By Train: Take the Union Pacific North Line to Central (in Evanston), and catch the Pace bus 213 to Lake Cook and Nyoda, or take the same Metra train to Highland Park, and catch the Pace 473 to Lake Cook and Skokie. Easy Pace connections are also available from the Metra Glencoe stop.

By Bicycle: The Chicago Bikeway System winds through the forest preserves all the way up to the garden. Join it near the Billy Caldwell Golf Club at 6200 N Caldwell. A bicycle map is available on the Botanic Garden website.

Where to Stay

You can make an excursion of your visit to Ravinia and/or the Botanic Garden by booking a room at:

Renaissance Chicago North Shore (933 Skokie Blvd, Northbrook, 847-498-6500); **Residence Inn Chicago** (530 Lake Cook Rd, Deerfield, 847-940-4644); **Hyatt Deerfield** (1750 Lake Cook Rd, 800-233-1234); **Highland Park Courtyard** (1505 Lake Cook Rd, 847-831-3338).

Ravinia Festival

Address: 200 Ravinia Park Rd, Highland Park, IL 60035
Phone: 847-266-5100
Website: www.ravinia.org
Hours: June through mid-September, gates open at 5 pm

Overview

Not to be outdone, the adjoining Ravinia Festival, the nation's oldest outdoor concert venue, has been hosting classical music concerts since 1904. The summer home of the CSO, Ravinia eventually added pop and jazz to their bill, including such notables as Janis Joplin, Aretha Franklin (a Ravinia regular), k.d. lang, Tony Bennet (also a regular), as well as top names from opera and world music.

The Pavilion—Those who are serious about the music experience pay a premium for one of the 3,200 seats in this covered, open-air pavilion, affording them a view of the stage and better acoustics.

The Lawn—Although you can't see the stage, great outdoor acoustics bring the concert to you on the lawn, where blanket rights come cheap—typically $10 a pop. Just add picnic.

The Martin Theatre—The only remaining building original to the Festival, the 1904 Martin Theatre now hosts Martinis at the Martin, a cabaret series celebrating the Great American Songbook.

Eating at Ravinia

Ravinia is well known for lawn picnickers who compete to outdo each other with elaborate spreads, including roll-up tables, table linens, candelabras, champagne, and caviar. For those less ambitious, Ravinia offers take-out sandwiches and picnic fare at The Gatehouse, burgers and dogs at Le Café, ice cream and other sweet treats at Carousel Market, or you can make reservations to eat in at their fine-dining restaurant, Mirabelle. Wine, beer, and soft drinks are also available at concession stands throughout the park.

How to Get There

By Car: I-94 and I-294 have marked exits for Ravinia. Skip traffic back-ups on Lake Cook Road by exiting at Deerfield, Central, or Clavey Roads, and following directions to Park and Ride lots, which offer free parking and shuttle buses to Ravinia. The West Lot, Ravinia's closest parking spot, costs $7-$10 for parking and fills up early for the most popular concerts.

By Train: During festival season, the Union Pacific North Line offers the "Ravinia Special." For $5 round-trip, the train departs Madison and Canal at 5:50 pm, with stops at Clybourn, Ravenswood, Rogers Park, and Evanston, arriving at the Ravinia gates at 6:30 pm, and departing for the city 15 minutes after the concert's end.

Grand Ave
132
83
W Big Hollow Rd
Six Flags
Great America
W Belvidere Rd
W Belvidere Rd
21
94
Skokie Hwy
83
137
W Peterson Rd
60
45
176
21
60
60
Skokie Hwy
22
W Half Day Rd
W Half Day Rd
83
N Rand Rd
53
W Lake Cook Rd
Northwest Hwy
E Dundee Rd
E Dundee Rd
45
68
53
Elmhurst Rd
Edens Expy
Palatine Rd
Willow Rd
Algonquin Rd
294
Rand Rd
Golf Rd
58
Higgins Rd
Algonquin Rd
Elmhurst Rd
290
Elgin Ohare Expy
83
N York Rd
180
Kennedy Expy

General Information

Address: 542 N Rte 21
Gurnee, IL 60031
Phone: 847-249-4636
Website: www.sixflags.com/parks/greatamerica
Hours: Open May to October. Hours are generally 10 am–10 pm, but vary by season. See website for specific hours and dates.
Entry: $54.99 adult fare, $34.99 for kids under 54", includes admission to both Six Flags and Hurricane Harbor.

Overview

Long lines, crappy food, hokey entertainment, and sun poisoning…if that isn't the stuff dreams are made of, then baby, we don't know what is.

Tickets

Reduced rates are available for advanced purchase through the website and via promotions throughout the season—look for discounted deals at Dominick's as well as on specially marked Coke cans. For die-hard thrill seekers, season passes offer the best deal at $94.99 apiece or $84.99 each for a family of four or more. Individual tickets and season passes can be purchased online at www.sixflagsticketing.com.

For the Kiddies

Camp Cartoon Network and Looney Tunes National Park offer easy-going rides and games for tykes 54 inches and under, while Bugs, Yosemite Sam, and the rest amble around for photo ops. The double-decker classic kiddie ride Columbia Carousel, located just past the park's main entrance, may be too tame for young 'uns hopped up on funnel cake and Tweety-pops.

Thrill Rides

Every few years, Six Flags tries to outdo itself with a new, even more death-defying and harrowing ride. Most recently, this magnificent feat was accomplished with the opening of the Superman-Ultimate Flight ride. Passengers soar through the air head-first as though they were flying, nearly brushing the ground below them on the giant loop-de-loop. Other thrills include the Raging Bull "hyper-twister," where you drop at incredible degrees and speeds into subterranean depths. Batman The Ride allows your feet to dangle free, while riders remain standing during the Iron Wolf. We had serious misgivings about the decision to ride the Déjà Vu as we sat suspended, face-down, 120-something feet above the ground, secured only by a shoulder harness before dropping down at a 90-degree angle. (We survived unscathed.) Meanwhile, the classic wooden American Eagle coaster offers vintage, but no-less-worrisome, rickety thrills.

Hurricane Harbor Water Park

Opened in 2005, Great America's adjoining Hurricane Harbor water park introduced attractions such as "Skull Island," which press materials dub the thrill-evoking "world's largest interactive water play structure." How's that for screaming "fun?" There are also miles of water rides and a splashing park for wee tots ("Mommy, why is the water yellow?"). The park also features a 1,000+ gallon water drop that dumps itself upon unsuspecting visitors every ten minutes. Leave the Prada at home.

Fright Fest

Avoid the heat and long lines of the summer season and creep into the park during the month of October (mostly on weekends) among the Halloween-themed décor and scary music playing over the P.A. This is, by far, our favorite time to go and worth the price of a season pass for the convenience of just dropping by for a few thrills whenever the hell you feel like it (the park is open until Midnight on most Saturday nights during Fright Fest).

Areas are marked according to levels of scariness, so those with young children or weak hearts can plan accordingly. In the spookiest parts of the park, actors in ghoulish costumes sneak around startling visitors (hope we didn't ruin the surprise). There are also two haunted houses that charge separate admission fees.

Also in the 'hood

Gurnee Mills Outlet Mall
Address: 6170 W Grand Ave, Gurnee, IL 60031
Phone: 847-263-7500
Hours: Open Mon–Fri 10 am–9 pm, Sat 10 am–9:30 pm, Sun 11 am–7 pm

Gurnee Mills is a theme park for the avid shopper. Included among the usual chain grub and garb are outlet stores for fashion and housewares such as Abercrombie & Fitch, Athlete's Foot, Banana Republic, Levi's, Saks Fifth Avenue, and more. We'll refrain from saying that going to an outlet mall makes you even more of a jackass than going to a regular mall.

Make a Night of It

Where to stay in Gurnee:
• **Baymont Inn & Suites**, 5688 N Ridge Rd, 847-662-7600
• **Country Inn & Suites**, 5420 Grand Ave, 847-625-9700
• **Fairfield Inn**, 6090 Gurnee Mills Cir East, 847-855-8868
• **Grand Hotel & Suites**, 5520 Grand Ave, 847-249-7777
• **Hampton Inn**, 5550 Grand Ave, 847-662-1100

How to Get There

By Car: Take I-94 or I-294 west, exit at Grand Avenue. Be aware that traffic is very congested in July and August! Arrive extra early or extra late to beat the crowds.

By Train & Bus: Take the Metra Union Pacific North Line to Waukegan, where you can catch the Pace bus 565 to Great America. Note: Public transportation to Great America from the Ogilvie Transportation Center and Madison and Canal takes just over two hours each way.

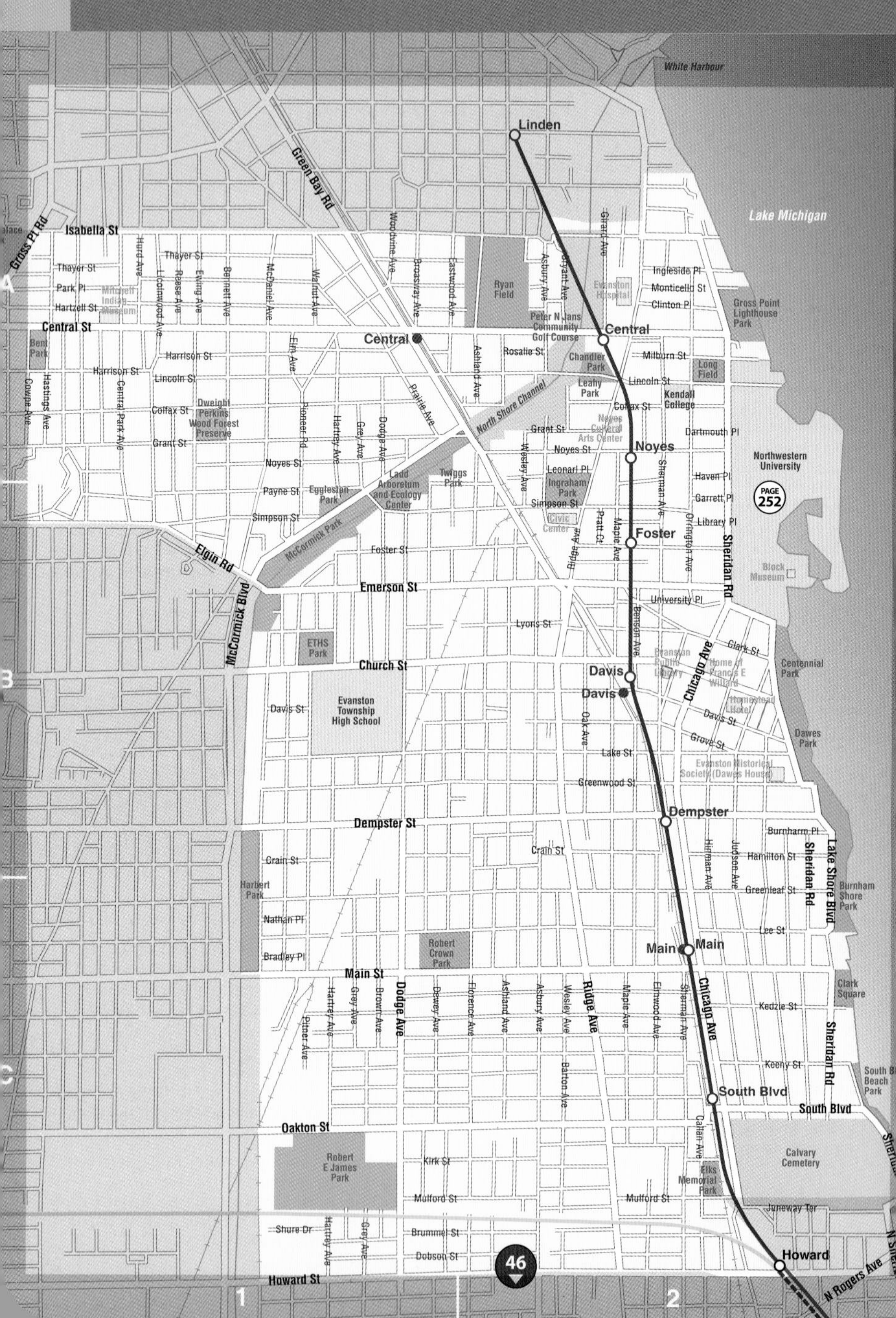
White Harbour
Linden
Lake Michigan
Green Bay Rd
Gross Pt Rd
Isabella St
Thayer St
Park Pl
Hartzell St
Mitchell Indian Museum
Central St
Bent Park
Hurd Ave
Lincolnwood Ave
Reese Ave
Ewing Ave
Bennett Ave
McDaniel Ave
Walnut Ave
Woodbine Ave
Broadway Ave
Eastwood Ave
Ryan Field
Asbury Ave
Bryant Ave
Girard Ave
Evanston Hospital
Ingleside Pl
Monticello St
Clinton Pl
Gross Point Lighthouse Park
Peter N Jans Community Golf Course
Central
Rosalie St
Chandler Park
Milburn St
Long Field
Harrison St
Lincoln St
Leahy Park
Kendall College
Hastings Ave
Cowper Ave
Central Park Ave
Colfax St
Dwight Perkins Wood Forest Preserve
Grant St
Elm Ave
Prairie Ave
Ashland Ave
North Shore Channel
Pioneer Rd
Hartrey Ave
Grey Ave
Dodge Ave
Wesley Ave
Noyes Cultural Arts Center
Dartmouth Pl
Noyes
Noyes St
Leonard Pl
Northwestern University
Ladd Arboretum and Ecology Center
Twiggs Park
Ingraham Park
Sherman Ave
Haven Pl
Payne St
Eggleston Park
Simpson St
Garrett Pl
PAGE 252
Civic Center
Library Pl
McCormick Park
Foster
Elgin Rd
Foster St
Ridge Ave
Pratt Ct
Maple Ave
Orrington Ave
Sheridan Rd
Block Museum
McCormick Blvd
Emerson St
University Pl
Benson Ave
Lyons St
ETHS Park
Evanston Public Library
Chicago Ave
Home of Francis E Willard
Clark St
Centennial Park
Church St
Davis
Homestead Hotel
Davis St
Evanston Township High School
Oak Ave
Grove St
Dawes Park
Lake St
Evanston Historical Society (Dawes House)
Greenwood St
Dempster
Dempster St
Burnham Pl
Crain St
Hinman Ave
Judson Ave
Hamilton St
Lake Shore Blvd
Harbert Park
Greenleaf St
Burnham Shore Park
Nathan Pl
Lee St
Robert Crown Park
Main
Bradley Pl
Main St
Brown Ave
Dewey Ave
Florence Ave
Elmwood Ave
Clark Square
Pitner Ave
Kedzie St
Keeny St
Barton Ave
South Blvd
South Boulevard Beach Park
Oakton St
Callan Ave
Calvary Cemetery
Robert E James Park
Kirk St
Elks Memorial Park
Mulford St
Juneway Ter
Shure Dr
Brummel St
Dobson St
Howard
46
Howard St
N Rogers Ave
1
2
A
B
C

Overview

Although the suburb is a short 12 miles from Chicago's bustling Loop, Evanston seems a world away. Spacious Victorian and Prairie Style homes with mini-vans and Mercedes parked on tree-lined streets overlook Lake Michigan and surround the quaint college town's downtown. Unlike other development-minded and sub-divided suburbs, Evanston still maintains a Chicago-esque feel and remains as one of its most attractive bordering neighbors.

Once home to Potawatami Indians, Evanston was actually founded after the establishment of the town's most well-known landmark, Northwestern University. Plans for the school began in 1851, and after the university opened for business four years later, its founder John Evans (along with a bunch of other Methodist dudes) proposed the establishment of the city, and so the town was incorporated as the village of Evanston in 1863. Today, residents are as devoted to cultural and intellectual pursuits as the morally minded patriarchs were to enforcing prohibition. The sophisticated, racially diverse suburb of over 74,000 packs a lot of business and entertainment into its 8.5 square miles. Superb museums, many national historic landmarks, parks, artistic events, eclectic shops, and theaters make up for the poor sports performances by Northwestern University's Wildcats in recent Big Ten football and basketball seasons.

Culture

Evanston has several museums and some interesting festivals that warrant investigation. Besides Northwestern's Block Museum of Art, the impressive Mitchell Museum of the American Indian showcases life of the Midwest's Native Americans (2600 Central Park Ave, 847-475-1030). The 1865 home of Frances E. Willard, founder of the Women's Christian Temperance Union and a women's suffrage leader, is located at 1730 Chicago Avenue (847-328-7500). Tours of the historic home are offered on the afternoons of every first and third Sunday of each month except January and February. Admission costs $5 for adults and $3 for children 12 and under.

Festivals & Events

- **May**: Evanston goes Baroque during Bach Week, 847-236-0452, www.bachweek.org.
- **June**: Fountain Square Arts Festival, 847-328-1500, and free Starlight Concerts hosted in many of the city's 80 parks through August, 847-448-8058
- **July**: Ethnic Arts Festival, 847-448-8058
- **September**: Town architectural walking tour, 312-922-3432, www.architecture.org.
- **December**: First Night, a city-wide arts celebration, rings in the New Year, 866-475-6483, www.firstnightevanston.org

Nature

Evanston is blessed with six public beaches open June 10th through Labor Day. For hours, fees, and boating information, contact the City of Evanston's Recreation Division (847-866-2910; www.cityofevanston.org). The town's most popular parks (and there are nearly 90 of them) encircle its beaches: Grosse Point Lighthouse Park, Centennial Park, Burnham Shores Park, Dawes Park, and South Boulevard Beach Park. All are connected by a bike path and fitness trail. On clear days, Chicago's skyline is visible from Northwestern's campus. West of downtown, McCormick, Twiggs, and Herbert Parks flank the North Shore Channel. Bicycle trails thread along the shore from Green Bay Road south to Main Street. North of Green Bay Road is Peter N Jans Community Golf Course, a short 18-hole, par 60 public links at 1031 Central Street (847-475-9173) and the Ladd Memorial Arboretum and Ecology Center, located at 2024 McCormick Boulevard (847-864-5181).

How to Get There

By Car: Lake Shore Drive to Sheridan Road is the most direct and scenic route from Chicago to Evanston. Drive north on LSD, which ends at Hollywood; then drive west to Sheridan and continue north. Near downtown, Sheridan becomes Burnham Place briefly, then Forest Avenue. Go north on Forest, which turns into Sheridan again by lakefront Centennial Park.

By Train: Metra's Union Pacific North Line departing from the Richard B. Ogilvie Transportation Center in West Loop stops at the downtown Davis Street CTA Center station, 25 minutes from the Loop ($3.05 one-way). This station is the town transportation hub, where Metra and L trains and buses interconnect. For all Metra, L, and CTA bus schedules, call 312-836-7000; www.rtachicago.com.

By L: The CTA Purple Line Express L train travels direct to and from the Loop during rush hours ($1.75 one-way). Other hours, ride the Howard-Dan Ryan Red Line to Howard Street, and transfer to the Puple Line for free.

By Bus: From Chicago's Howard Street Station, CTA and Pace Suburban buses service Evanston ($1.50 rush hours one-way; other, $1.25).

Additional Information

Evanston Convention & Visitors' Bureau, 847-328-1500
Chicago's North Shore Convention & Visitors Bureau 847-763-0011; www.visitchicagonorthshore.com
Evanston Public Library, 1703 Orrington Ave, 847-866-0300; www.epl.org

Rosalie St
Chandler Park
Milburn St
Long Field
Leahy Park
Lincoln St
North Shore Channel
Kendall College
Colfax St
McCormick Park
Bryant Ave
Colfax St
Noyes Ct
Grant St
Dartmouth Pl
Light Opera Works
Noyes
Noyes St
Northwestern University
PAGE 252
Wesley Ave
Maple Ave
Leonard Pl
Haven Pl
Gaffield Pl
Ingraham Park
Ridge Ave
Philbrick Park
Garrett Pl
Simpson St
Fireman's Park
Green Bay Rd
Hamlin St
Pratt Ct
Leon Pl
Library Pl
Foster
Foster St
Sheridan Rd
Garnett Pl
Sherman Ave
Orrington Ave
Mary-Leah Block Gallery
Emerson St
University Pl
University Pl
Elgin Rd
Railroad Ave
Lake Michigan
Lyons St
Benson Ave
Chicago Ave
Clark St
Church St
Home of Francis E Willard
Hinman Ave
Centennial Park
Evanston Public Library
Judson Ave
Davis
Orrington Ave
Church St
Davis St
Davis
Alexander Park
Homestead Hotel
Davis St
Grove St
Forest Pl
Dawes Park
Wesley Ave
Ashbury Ave
Ridge Ave
Oak Ave
Maple Ave
Grove St
Raymond Park
Lake St
Elmwood Ave
Evanston Historical Society (Dawes House)
Evanston Historical Society
Greenwood St
Forest Ave
Dempster
Dempster St
Burnharm Pl

Landmarks

- **Evanston Historical Society** • 225 Greenwood St
- **Light Opera Works** • 927 Noyles St

Nightlife

- **1800 Club** • 1800 Sherman Ave
- **Bill's Blues Bar** • 1029 Davis St
- **Keg of Evanston** • 810 Grove St
- **Prairie Moon** • 1502 Sherman Ave
- **Tommy Nevin's Pub** • 1450 Sherman Ave
- **The Stained Glass Wine Bar** • 1735 Benson Ave

Restaurants

- **Asada Brazilian Grill** • 1012 Church St
- **Blind Faith Café** • 525 Dempster St
- **Buffalo Joe's** • 812 Clark St
- **Café Mozart** • 600 Davis St
- **Cajun Charlie's New Orleans Grill** • 1601 Simpson St
- **Clarke's** • 720 Clark St
- **Dixie Kitchen** • 825 Church St
- **Dozika** • 601 Dempster St
- **Hecky's Barbeque** • 1902 Green Bay Rd
- **Jamaica Gates** • 618 1/2 Church St
- **Joy Yee Noodle Shop** • 521 Davis St
- **Kafein Café** • 1621 Chicago Ave
- **Las Palmas** • 817 University Pl
- **Lulu's Dim Sum and Then Sum** • 804 Davis St
- **Mt Everest** • 630 Church St
- **Narra** • 1710 Orrington Ave
- **Noodles & Company** • 930 Church St
- **Olive Mountain** • 610 Davis St
- **Pete Miller's Original Steakhouse** • 1557 Sherman Ave
- **Tapas Barcelona** • 1615 Chicago Ave
- **Trattoria Demi** • 1571 Sherman Ave
- **Unicorn Café** • 1723 Sherman Ave
- **Va Pensiero** • Margarita Inn • 1566 Oak Ave

Shopping

- **Active Endeavors** • 901 Church St
- **Art & Science Hair Salon** • 811 Church St
- **Asinamali Women's Boutique** • 1722 Sherman Ave
- **Bookman's Alley** • 1712 Sherman Ave
- **Campus Gear** • 1717 Sherman Ave
- **Reckless Records** • 606 Davis St
- **Something Wicked Mystery Bookstore** • 816 Church St
- **Uncle Dan's Great Outdoors** • 700 Church St
- **William's Shoes** • 710 Church St

North Ave
Le Moyne St
Greenfield St
Berkshire St
Division St
Thomas St
Augusta St
Iowa St
Chicago St
Superior St
Erie St
Ontario St
W Lake St
Common Blvd
Pleasant St
Randolph St
Washington Blvd
W Washington Blvd
Madison St
Monroe St
Adams St
Jackson Blvd
Van Muren St
Harrison St
Garfield St
Lexington St
Havard St
Filmore St
Roosevelt Rd
Eisenhower Expy
290
N Ridgeland Ave
S Ridgeland Ave
N Oak Park Ave
S Oak Park Ave
N Austin Blvd
S Austin Blvd
S Austin Ave
S Harlem Ave
Harvey Ave
Lombard Ave
Hayes Ave
Taylor Ave
Humphrey Ave
Mapleton Ave
Marion Ave
Belleforte Ave
Forest Ave
Grove Ave
Euclid Ave
Wesley Ave
East Ave
Scoville Ave
Elmwood Ave
Cuyler Ave
Clinton Ave
Kenilworth Ave
Carpenter Ave
Lyman Ave
Mason Ave
Mayfield Ave
Menard Ave
Waller Ave
Parkside Ave
Maple Ave
Wisconsin Ave
Wenonah Ave
Home Ave
Hirsch St
Potomac St
Walton St
Rice St
Huron St
Ohio St
Race St
Midway St
Fulton St
West End St
Lindberg Park
Field Park
Taylor Park
Anderson Park
Concordia University
Frank Lloyd Wright Home & Studio
Ernest Hemingway Museum
West Suburban Hospital
Austin Gardens
Oak Park Visitor's Center
Unity Temple
Scoville Park
Harlem/ Lake
Oak Park
Ridgeland
Austin
Stevenson Park
Austin Park
Historic Pleasant Home
Mills Park
Oak Park Hospital
Fox Park
Longfellow Park
Harlem
Forest Park
Oak Park Conservatory
Rehm Park
Barrie Pig Park
Columbus Park
Maple Park
Carroll Park

General Information

Oak Park Visitors Bureau: 708-524-7800; www.visitoakpark.com
Oak Park Tourist: www.oprf.com

Overview

You can thank Oak Park for Prairie Style architecture, *A Moveable Feast*, McDonald's, and, yes, *Tarzan*. The creators of each called this charming suburb their home: Ernest Hemingway, Frank Lloyd Wright, Ray Kroc, and Edgar Rice Burroughs, respectively.

Best known for its architectural gems and strong public schools, Oak Park (pop. 52,500) is a happy hunting ground for homebuyers seeking upscale, integrated living 10 miles from the Loop. Less impressed than most with his picture-perfect hometown, Hemingway famously described Oak Park as "a village of wide lawns and narrow minds."

Village trustees must still be smarting from Hemingway's crack because they publicize an official policy on maintaining diversity. The "diversity statement" sounds like some sort of disclaimer or a zealot's vision for heaven on Earth: "Ours is a community that encourages contributions of all citizens regardless of race, gender, ethnicity, sexual orientation, disability, religion . . ."—and indeed, Oak Park has quite a reputation as the place all the hip GLBT kids go when it's time to become hip GLBT parents.

Architecture

Oak Park harbors the nation's largest concentration of Frank Lloyd Wright buildings, 25 in the village and another 6 in neighboring River Forest. The village's must-see sites are located in a compact area bordered by Division Street, Lake Street, Forest Avenue, and Ridgeland Avenue. Designs by Wright, William Drummond, George W. Maher, John Van Bergen, and E. E. Roberts are represented throughout.

You can ground yourself in Prairie Style architectural principles at the brilliant Frank Lloyd Wright Home and Studio. Maintained by the Frank Lloyd Wright Preservation Trust, guided tours of the designer's personal space are offered weekdays at 11 am, 1 pm, and 3 pm and weekends at 11:20 am, 1:20 pm, and 3:20 pm (951 Chicago Ave, 708-848-1976; www.wrightplus.org). Only 15 people are allowed per tour, and tickets can be purchased on the foundation's website or on-site (early arrival recommended) at a cost of $12 for adults and $10 for children 7-18 and seniors. Worthwhile walking tours of the surrounding streets are also offered, though a combined $20 ticket ($16 for children 7-18 and seniors) covers both the home-studio site and walking tour at a discount.

Completed in 1908, Unity Temple (875 Lake St, 708-383-8873; www.unitytemple-utrf.org) was Wright's first commissioned public building; today it houses Oak Park's Unitarian-Universalist congregation. Unity Temple is open daily for self-directed tours and on weekends for guided visits ($7 for adults, $5 for students and seniors). Designed by George W. Maher, Historic Pleasant Home (217 S Home Ave, 708-383-2654; www.pleasanthome.org) aptly illustrates the architectural evolution from Victorian design to early Prairie Style with tours held Thursday through Sunday at 12:30 pm, 1:30 pm, and 2:30 pm ($5 adults, $3 children; Fridays free).

The Oak Park Visitors Center offers maps and a PDA walking tour of the Ridgeland Historic District highlighting 15 of the area's Victorian "Painted Ladies" ($9 for adults, $6 for students and seniors) 10 am-3:30 pm daily. Call 708-524-7800, or visit www.visitoakpark.com for more information.

Culture & Events

Once a year in May, the public gets to snoop inside Wright-designed private residences during the popular Wright Plus Housewalk ($85). His home-studio and Robie House in Hyde Park (shuttle provided) are also included in the tour (708-848-9518; www.wrightplus.org).

Get your fill of he-man author Hemingway at the Ernest Hemingway Museum (200 N Oak Park Ave, 708-848-2222; www.hemingway.org), open Sunday through Friday 1 pm-5 pm, and Saturday 10 am-5 pm ($7 adults, $5.50 students and seniors). His birthplace, also included with the price of admission, is located just up the street at 339 N Oak Park Avenue. For a one-stop confab with both of Oak Park's favorite sons, stroll three blocks north and two west to the 600 block of N. Kenilworth Ave, where Wright's Balch House (611) stands across the street from the Prairie Style home (600) to which Hemingway's family moved when he was 5 years old.

Summer evenings, catch Shakespeare's works performed outdoors in Austin Gardens by the Oak Park Festival Theatre company (708-445-4440; www.oakparkfestival.com). The lush Oak Park Conservatory, originally built in 1929 to provide a place for all of the exotic plants Oak Park residents collected on their travels abroad, is located at 615 Garfield Street (708-386-4700; www.oprf.com/conservatory; suggested $1 donation) and definitely worth a visit.

Nightlife

• **Avenue Ale House** • 825 S Oak Park Ave

Restaurants

• **Buzz Café** • 905 S Lombard Ave
• **Café Le Coq** • 734 Lake St
• **Cucina Paradiso** • 814 North Blvd
• **Jeruselum Café** • 1030 Lake St
• **Khyber Pass** • 1031 Lake St
• **Mama Thai** • 1112 W Madison St
• **Marion Street Grill** • 189 N Marion St
• **New Rebozo** • 1116 Madison St
• **Oak Park Abbey** • 728 Lake St
• **Pete's Red Hots** • 6346 W Roosevelt Rd
• **Petersen Ice Cream** • 1100 Chicago Ave
• **Philander's Oak Park** • Carlton Hotel • 1120 Pleasant St

Shopping

• **Alphabet Soup** • 1107 W Lake St
• **Antiques, Etc** • 125 N Marion St
• **Fly Bird** • 719 Lake St
• **Magic Tree Bookstore** • 141 N Oak Park Ave
• **Pumpkin Moon** • 1028 North Blvd

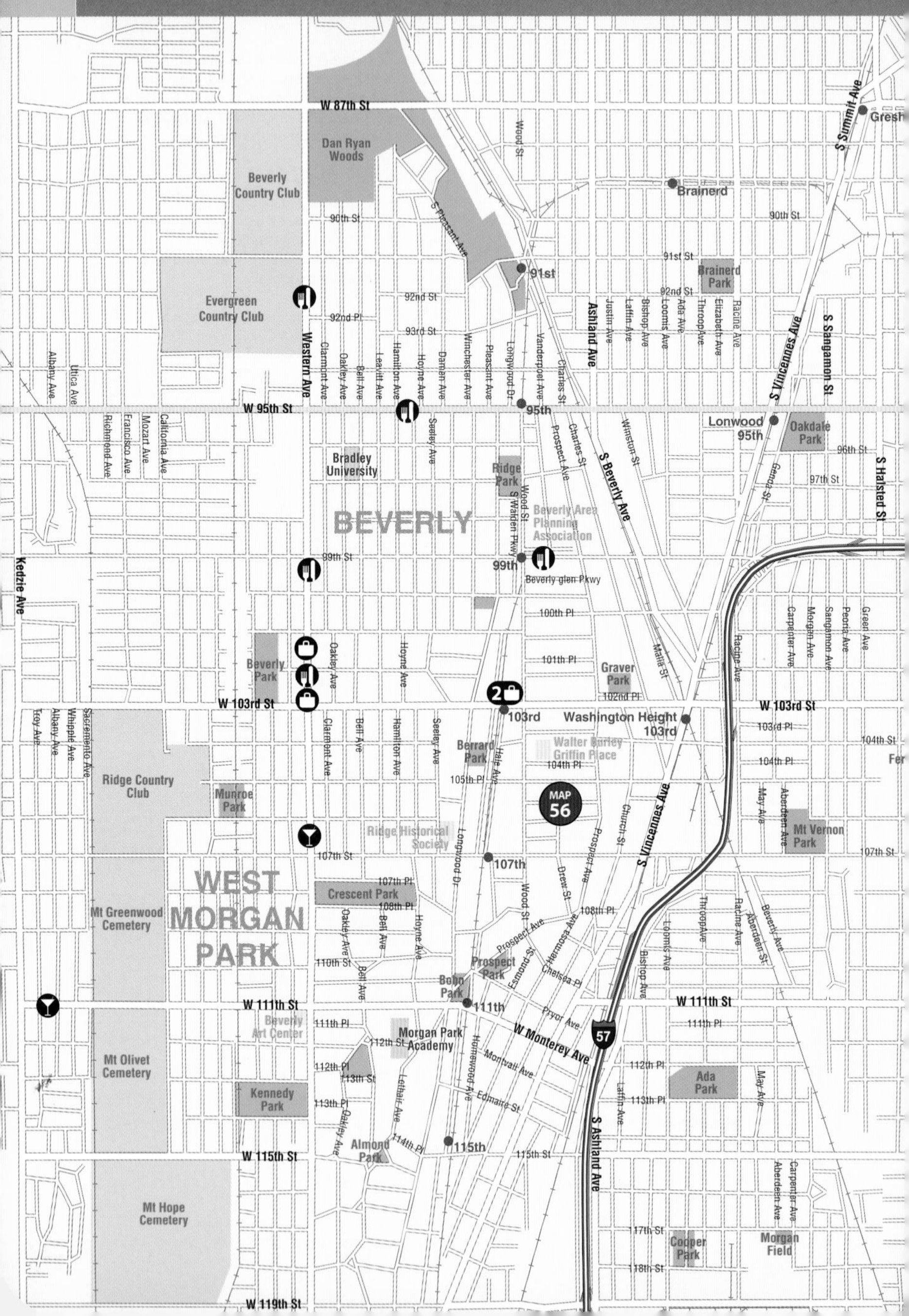
W 87th St
Dan Ryan Woods
Beverly Country Club
Evergreen Country Club
Brainerd
Brainerd Park
91st
Bradley University
BEVERLY
Ridge Park
Beverly Area Planning Association
99th
Beverly Park
Graver Park
103rd
Washington Height 103rd
Berrard Park
Walter Burley Griffin Place
Ridge Country Club
Munroe Park
Ridge Historical Society
107th
Lonwood 95th
Oakdale Park
Mt Vernon Park
WEST MORGAN PARK
Mt Greenwood Cemetery
Crescent Park
Prospect Park
Bohn Park
111th
Beverly Art Center
Morgan Park Academy
Mt Olivet Cemetery
Kennedy Park
Almond Park
115th
Ada Park
Mt Hope Cemetery
Cooper Park
Morgan Field
W 95th St
W 103rd St
W 111th St
W 115th St
W 119th St
Western Ave
Kedzie Ave
S Ashland Ave
S Vincennes Ave
S Beverly Ave
S Halsted St
W Monterey Ave
MAP 56
57

Overview

Beverly Hills, best known simply as Beverly, is the stronghold of Chicago's heralded "South Side Irish" community. An authentic medieval castle, baronial mansions, rolling hills, and plenty of pubs compose Chicago's Emerald Isle of 39,000 residents.

Once populated by Illinois and Potawatomi Indian tribes, Beverly is now home to clans of Irish-American families who moved here after the Great Chicago Fire. Famous residents include Andrew Greeley, Brian Piccolo, George Wendt, the Schwinn Bicycle family, and decades of loyal Chicago civil servants.

Proud and protective of their turf, these close-knit South Siders call Beverly and its sister community, Morgan Park, "the Ridge." The somewhat integrated neighborhood occupies the highest ground in Chicago, 30 to 60 feet above the rest of the city atop Blue Island Ridge.

Although the Ridge is just 15 miles from the Loop, most North Siders never venture south of Cermak Road except to invade Beverly on St. Patrick's Day weekend to see the parade and guzzle green beer at pubs lining Western Avenue. Chicago playwright Mike Houlihan called the strip the "South Side Irish Death March."

But there is more than a 6-pack of reasons to visit Beverly. The Ridge Historic District is one of the country's largest urban areas on the National Register of Historic Places. Surprised, huh?

Architecture

Sadly, many Chicagoans are unaware of the rich architectural legacy on the city's far South Side. Beverly and Morgan Park encompass four landmark districts including the Ridge Historic District, three Chicago Landmark Districts, and over 30 Prairie Style structures.

Within approximately a nine-mile radius, from 87th Street to 115th Street and Prospect Avenue to Hoyne Avenue, one can view a vast collection of homes and public buildings representing American architectural styles developed between 1844 and World War II.

The 109th block of Prospect Avenue, every inch of Longwood Drive, and Victorian train stations at 91st Street, 95th Street, 99th Street, 107th Street, 111th Street, and 115th Street are all great Chicago landmarks. Walter Burley Griffin Place on W 104th Street has Chicago's largest concentration of Prairie School houses built between 1909 and 1913 by Griffin, a student of Frank Lloyd Wright and designer of the city of Canberra in Australia.

Beverly Area Planning Association (BAPA) (10233 S Wood St, 773-233-3100; www.bapa.org) provides a good architectural site map, plus events and shopping information for the district. History buffs might want to visit the Ridge Historical Society and museum, open Tuesdays, Thursdays, and Sundays from 2 pm to 5 pm (10621 S Seeley Ave, 773-881-1675; www.ridgehistoricalsociety.org).

Culture & Events

The new Beverly Arts Center is the epicenter of Ridge culture. The $8 million facility provides visual and performance art classes for all ages and hosts Chicago's only contemporary Irish film festival during the first week of March (2407 W 111th St, 773-445-3838; www.beverlyartcenter.org).

Historic Ridge homes open their doors to the public on the third Sunday of May for the annual Home Tour, Chicago's oldest such tour. Sites are chosen for their diverse architectural styles and historical significance. Tour hours are from 11 am to 5 pm and tickets can be purchased through BAPA or the Beverly Arts Center for $25 in advance or $30 the day of the event. All tours depart from the Beverly Arts Center by 3 pm and homes close promptly at 5 pm. Guided trolley tours are also offered for an additional $3.

A Chicago must-see, the justly famous South Side Irish Parade marches down Western Avenue from 103rd to 115th Streets on the Sunday prior to St. Patrick's Day. Contact BAPA at 773-233-3100 for more details.

Where to Eat

- **Café Luna**, 1742 W 99th St, 773-239-8990. Eclectic. Sink your teeth into their heart-healthy sandwiches and sinful desserts.
- **Franconello's**, 10222 S Western Ave, 773-881-4100. Italian. Perhaps the only pure Italians in Beverly making pasta dishes at this authentic Roma restaurant.
- **Janson's Drive-In**, 9900 S Western Ave, 773-238-3612. No indoor seating at this classic drive-thru.
- **Rainbow Cone**, 9233 S Western Ave, 773-238-7075. Ice cream. On summer nights more than 50 folks line up for sweet treats at this 76-year-old soda fountain.
- **Top Notch Beefburger**, 2116 W 95th St, 773-445-7218. Burgers really are top notch at this '50s-style grill.

Where to Drink

- **Lanigan's Irish Pub**, 3119 W 111th St, 773-233-4004. Anyone know where you can find a pint in Beverly? I've got quite a mean thirst.
- **Dubliner**, 10910 S Western Ave, 773-238-0784. One of the many Irish pubs lining Western Avenue.

Where to Shop

- **Bev Art Brewer and Winemaker Supply**, 10033 S Western Ave, 773-233-7579. Everything you need to brew and bottle it yourself.
- **Calabria Imports**, 1905 W 103rd St, 773-396-5800. Imported Italian gourmet foodstuffs.
- **Optimo Hat Co**, 10215 S Western Ave, 773-238-2999. Custom made men's hats.
- **World Folk Music Company**, 1808 W 103rd St, 773-779-7059. Instruments, sheet music, and lessons for budding Guthries and Baezs.

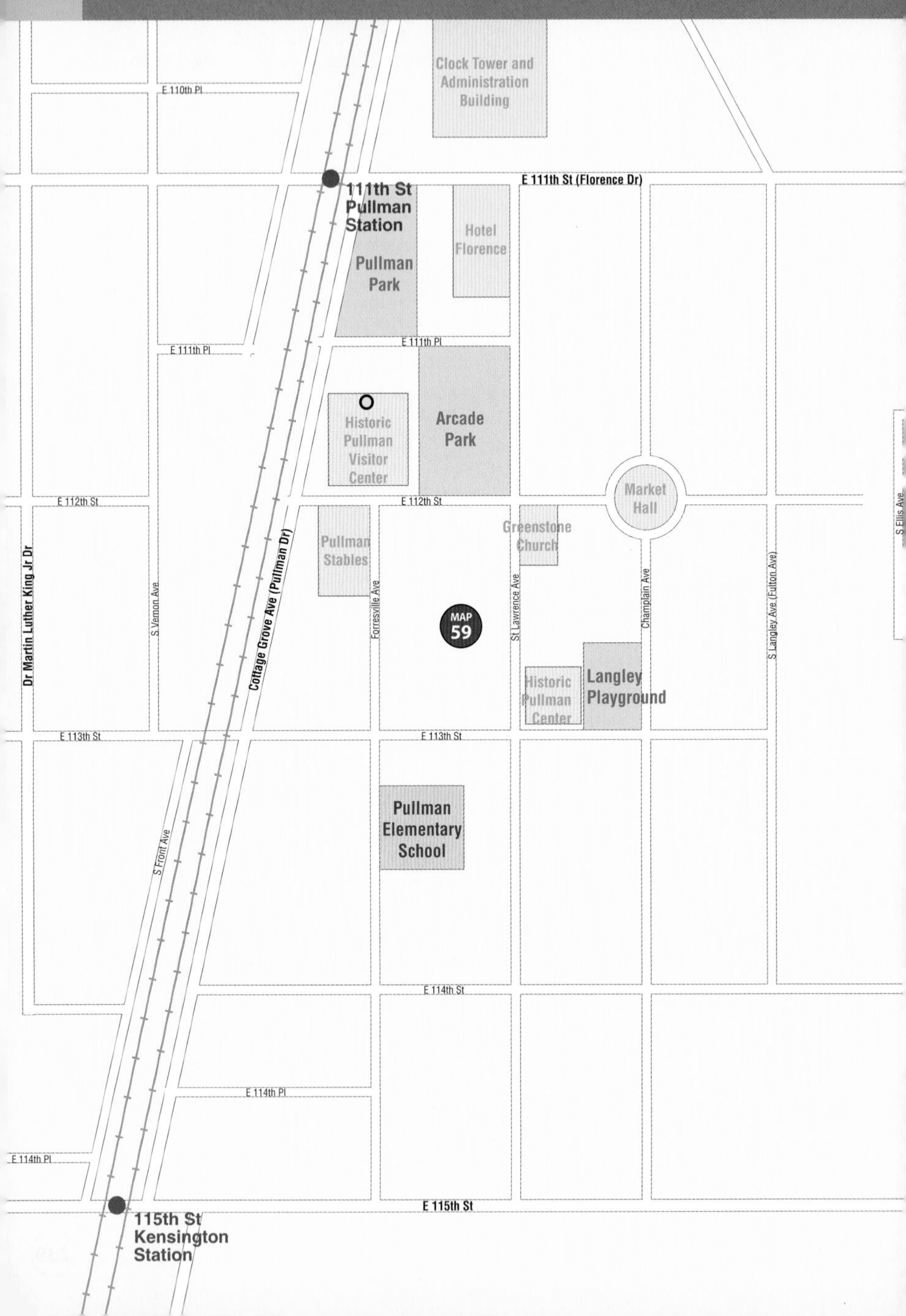

Clock Tower and Administration Building
E 110th Pl
E 111th St (Florence Dr)
111th St Pullman Station
Hotel Florence
Pullman Park
E 111th Pl
E 111th Pl
Historic Pullman Visitor Center
Arcade Park
E 112th St
E 112th St
Market Hall
Pullman Stables
Greenstone Church
Dr Martin Luther King Jr Dr
S Vernon Ave
Cottage Grove Ave (Pullman Dr)
Forresville Ave
MAP 59
St Lawrence Ave
Champlain Ave
S Langley Ave (Fulton Ave)
S Ellis Ave
Historic Pullman Center
Langley Playground
E 113th St
E 113th St
Pullman Elementary School
S Front Ave
E 114th St
E 114th Pl
E 114th Pl
E 115th St
115th St Kensington Station

Overview

Although railroad magnate George Pullman's utopian community went belly-up, the Town of Pullman he founded 14 miles south of the Loop survives as a National Landmark Historic District. Built between 1880 and 1885, Pullman is one of America's first planned model industrial communities.

The "workers' paradise" earned Pullman humanitarian hoorahs, as well as a 6% return on his investment. Pullman believed that if laborers and their families lived in comfortable housing with gas, plumbing, and ventilation—in other words, livable conditions—their productivity would increase, as would his profits. Pullman was voted "the world's most perfect town" at the Prague International Hygienic and Pharmaceutical Exposition of 1896.

All was perfect on the plantation until a depression incited workers to strike in 1894, and the idealistic industrialist refused to negotiate with his ungrateful workers. While George Pullman's dream of a model community of indentured servitude died with him in 1897, hatred for him lived on. Pullman's tomb at Graceland Cemetery is more like a bomb shelter. To protect his corpse from irate labor leaders, Pullman was buried under a forest of railroad ties and concrete.

Architecture & Events

Architect Solon Beman and landscape architect Nathan Barrett based Pullman's design on French urban plans. Way back when, Pullman was made up of mostly brick rowhouses (95% still in use), several parks, shops, schools, churches, and a library, as well as various health, recreational, and cultural facilities.

Today, the compact community's borders are 111th Street (Florence Drive), 115th Street, Cottage Grove Avenue (Pullman Drive), and S Langley Avenue (Fulton Avenue). If you're interested in sightseeing within the historic district, we suggest you start at the Pullman Visitor Center (11141 S Cottage Grove Ave, 773-785-8901; www.pullmanil.org). There you can pick up free, self-guided walking tour brochures and watch an informative 20-minute film on the town's history. Call the center for additional specialty tour information and lecture details.

The annual House Tour on the second weekend in October is a popular Pullman event where several private residences open their doors to the public from 11 am to 5 pm on Saturday and Sunday ($15 in advance, $18 on day of event). May through October, the center also offers a two-hour Guided Walking Tour every first Sunday of the month at 1:30 pm ($5). Key tour sites include Hotel Florence, Greenstone Church (interior), Market Square, the stables, and the fire station.

Where to Eat

• **Seven Seas Submarine**, 11216 S Michigan Ave, 773-785-0550. Dine in or take out at this tiny sandwich shop.

• **Cal Harbor Restaurant**, 546 E 115th St, 773-264-5435. Omelettes, burgers, etc. at family grill.

Where to Drink

• **Pullman's Pub**, 611 E 113th St, 773-568-0264. Suds in a pre-Prohibition watering hole.

How to Get There

By Car: Take I-94 S to the 111th Street exit. Go west to Cottage Grove Avenue and turn south, driving one block to 112th Street to the Visitor Center surrounded by a large, free parking lot.

By Train: Metra's Electric Main Line departs from Millennium Station (underground) at Michigan Avenue between S Water Street and Randolph Street. Ride 30 minutes to Pullman Station at 111th Street ($3.05 one-way). Walk east to Cottage Grove Avenue, and head south one block to 112th and the Visitor Center.

By L: From the Loop, take the Red Line to the 95th Street station. Board CTA 111 Pullman bus going south ($2 with transfer).

By Bus: CTA 4 bus from the Randolph Street Station travels south to the 95th Street and Cottage Grove stop. Transfer to 111 Pullman bus heading south ($2 with transfer).

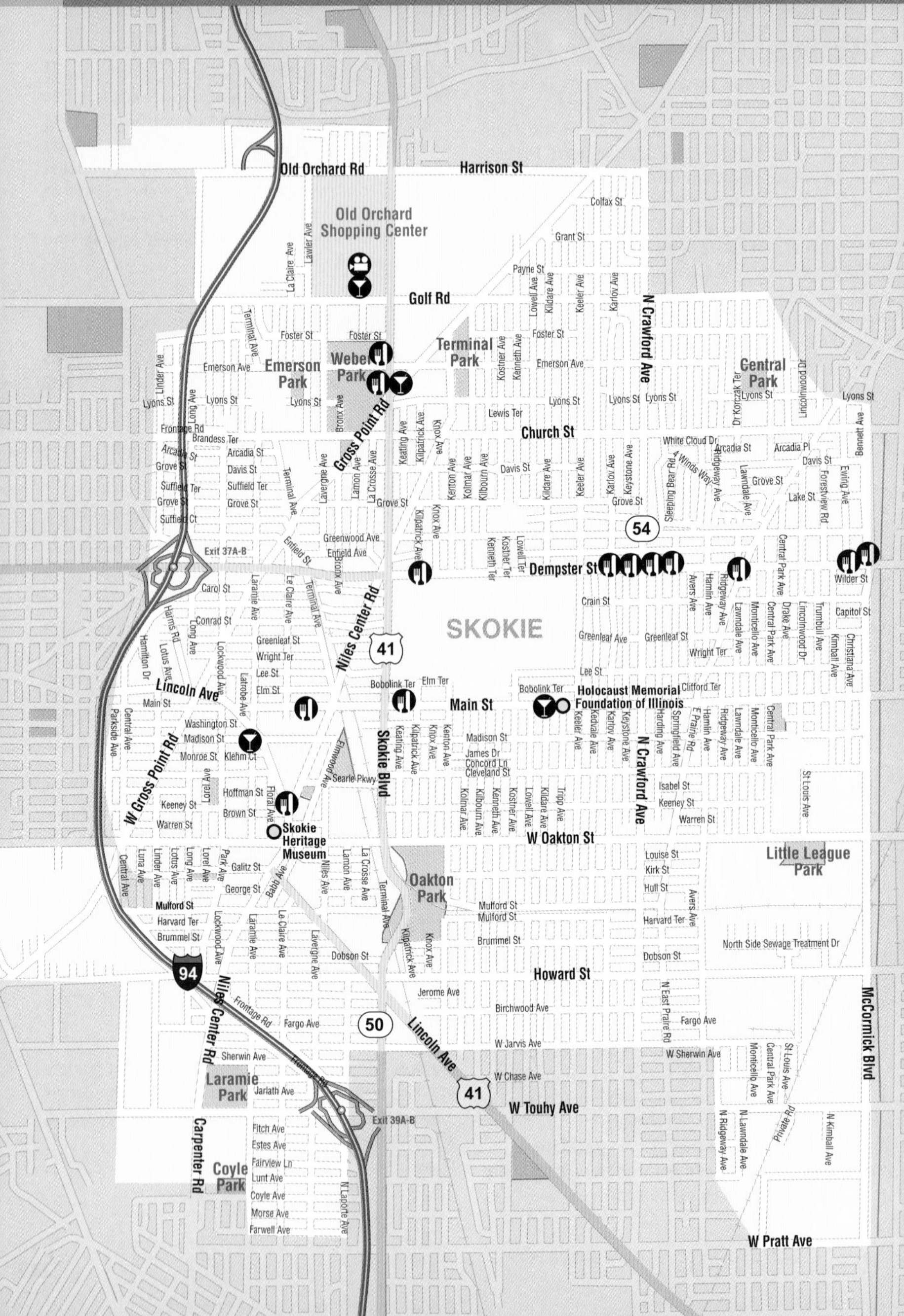
Old Orchard Rd
Harrison St
Old Orchard Shopping Center
Golf Rd
Emerson Park
Weber Park
Terminal Park
Central Park
Church St
N Crawford Ave
Dempster St
SKOKIE
Holocaust Memorial Foundation of Illinois
Main St
Lincoln Ave
Niles Center Rd
Gross Point Rd
W Gross Point Rd
Skokie Blvd
Skokie Heritage Museum
W Oakton St
Oakton Park
Little League Park
Howard St
Lincoln Ave
W Touhy Ave
Laramie Park
Coyle Park
Carpenter Rd
McCormick Blvd
W Pratt Ave
Exit 37A-B
Exit 39A-B
North Side Sewage Treatment Dr
54
41
50
94

General Information

www.skokie.org

Overview

When Skokie was first incorporated under the moniker Niles Center in 1888, it was considered to be the rowdy neighbor of temperate Evanston due to the large number of taverns within its borders. By 1940, residents were clamoring for a name change and a PR facelift. In November of that year, the village was renamed Skokie after the nearby Skokie River and canals, which themselves were named after an old Indian name for the area translating to "swampland." Personally, we'd be more attracted to a party town, but nonetheless, the facelift was a success. With the completion of the Edens Expressway in the 1950s, residential development in Skokie was booming.

Part of the boom consisted of Eastern European refugees from World War II, many of whom were Jewish. It is estimated that between 1945 and 1955, 3,000 Jewish families resettled in Skokie. Synagogues and Jewish services followed, and the village soon developed a self-perpetuating reputation as a thriving Jewish enclave.

Skokie made international headlines in 1977–78 when it contested plans by the National Socialist Party of America, a branch of the American Nazi Party, to march on the village square. The NSPA was defended by the ACLU in a divisive case that brought the contest between free expression and freedom against hate speech into the international fore. As far as the NSPA was concerned, the decision to march in Skokie was an act of political manipulation. Chicago had denied the Nazis' right to march in SW Chicago's Marquette Park, which was the NSPA's home turf. The group then threatened to relocate their planned assembly to Skokie. When the Village of Skokie lost their bid to ban the march, Chicago finally conceded, allowing the Nazis to gather at Marquette Park in June 1978. A handful of Nazis showed up, countered by thousands of anti-Nazi protestors.

As if being the head of a neo-Nazi movement and threatening to march on the front lawns of concentration camp survivors doesn't already make you the world's biggest jackass/creep, NSPA leader Frank Collin sealed the deal in 1979 when he was arrested and incarcerated on child molestation charges.

Culture & Events

In 1988, an urban renewal project to restore the north shore's decrepit Chicago River waterfront resulted in the two-mile Sculpture Park, an outdoor recreation area featuring walking paths, picnic areas, and more than 72 sculptures by artists of local, national, and international renown (although, rubes that we are, we confess we haven't heard of any of 'em). The park, sandwiched between McCormick Blvd and the north branch of the Chicago River, runs from Touhy to Dempster.

Time travel through history at the Skokie Heritage Museum—an assemblage of historical photos, papers, and artifacts painstakingly gathered by the Skokie Historical Society. The museum, housed in a restored 1919 firehouse, also features the history of Skokie's firefighters. Behind the museum, an authentic 1840s log cabin relocated to this location allows kids a glimpse into the town's pioneer past.

Skokie is also home to the Holocaust Memorial of Illinois. Each year up to 15,000 local school kids visit this small but stirring exhibit of Jewish life before, during, and after the Holocaust. Fundraising efforts are underway for a much larger, grander space, capable of serving upward of 100,000 visitors annually.

Every year in mid-May, The Skokie Festival of Cultures draws clog dancers, falafel hawkers, and accordion players from around the state for a weekend festival celebrating Skokie's diverse cultural heritage. The sulky loitering high schoolers and fat ladies in track suits, on the other hand, are 100% local.

North Shore Center for the Performing Arts

Home to the Skokie Valley Symphony Orchestra, The Centre East Theater, and, most notably, the highly acclaimed Northlight Theater, the North Shore Center for the Performing Arts is a state-of-the-art performance venue. Touring artists perform here, world class theater (sometimes featuring ensemble members from Steppenwolf) is mounted here, and it's also a north shore venue for exhibits and trade shows. Designed by architect Graham Gund in 1996, The North Shore Center for the Performing Arts has given northeast Illinois culture seekers a reason to come to Skokie besides bagels and lox.

Old Orchard Shopping Center

The idea of an outdoor mall anywhere in the Midwest seems like the epitome of bad planning. Nonetheless, Old Orchard pulls it off with aplomb and an attitude and vibe that's not too far away from the Disneyland of commerce—if Disneyland wasn't already the Disneyland of commerce. Curving pathways, benches, and gardens make this mall a pleasant place to shop in the summer, while in the winter annual holiday decorations, carolers, and such add to a festive feeling. The shopping consists of some big name department stores—Bloomingdales, Lord & Taylor, Nordstrom, and Marshall Fields—er—Macy's. Other shops are upscale boutiques and typical mall fare.

Old Orchard has a food court with all the usual suspects and a few adjacent dine-and-drink chains, like California Pizza Kitchen, Chammps, and Maggiano's. There's also a decent cinema, Loews/AMC Garden, with two theaters—Cinema West and Cinema East—for a combined total of 13 screens that show the latest first-run blockbusters.

Where to Drink

Ironic in light of its alcohol-fueled history, Skokie is not really known as a place to imbibe socially. Young residents head to youthful watering holes in the vicinity of the Northwestern campus in formerly teetotaling Evanston (will the ironies never end?). Meanwhile, local drunks hang out at anonymous corner taverns just like anywhere else. Retail workers, middle managers, and the secretarial set mingle and mate at the food and booze joints adjacent to Old Orchard.

Where to Eat

Old Orchard Shopping Center is filled with family-friendly chain options. Happily, Skokie still houses enough locally owned, independent restaurants to add interest and diversity to their dining scene. Folks travel from all over Chicagoland for local delis and kosher fare.

How to Get There

By L: The Skokie Swift Yellow Line runs non-stop between the Howard Street Red Line terminus and the Skokie Dempster station at 5001 Dempster St. Trains run approximately every 10-15 minutes between 5 am and 10 pm.

By Car: Take the Edens Expressway (I-94), and exit at Dempster.

Movie Theaters

- **Loews/AMC Garden Cinema** • 175 Old Orchard Ctr

Nightlife

- **Chammps** • 134 Old Orchard Ctr
- **Don's Tavern** • 9335 Skokie Blvd
- **Principal's Pub** • 4249 Main St
- **Rick's Place** • 8266 Lincoln Ave

Restaurants

- **Barnum and Bagel** • 4700 Dempster St
- **Don's Fishmarket** • 9335 Skokie Blvd
- **El Tipico** • 3341 Dempster St
- **Grecian Kitchen Delights** • 3938 Dempster St
- **Hub's Ribs** • 3727 Dempster St
- **Hy Life Bistro** • 4120 Dempster St
- **Kabul House** • 3320 Dempster St
- **Kaufman's Deli** • 4905 Dempster St
- **Papillon** • 5111 Brown St
- **Pita Inn** • 3910 Dempster
- **Ruby of Siam** • 9420 Skokie Blvd
- **Shallots Bistro** • 4741 Main St
- **Slice of Life** • 4120 W Dempster

University of Illinois at Chicago

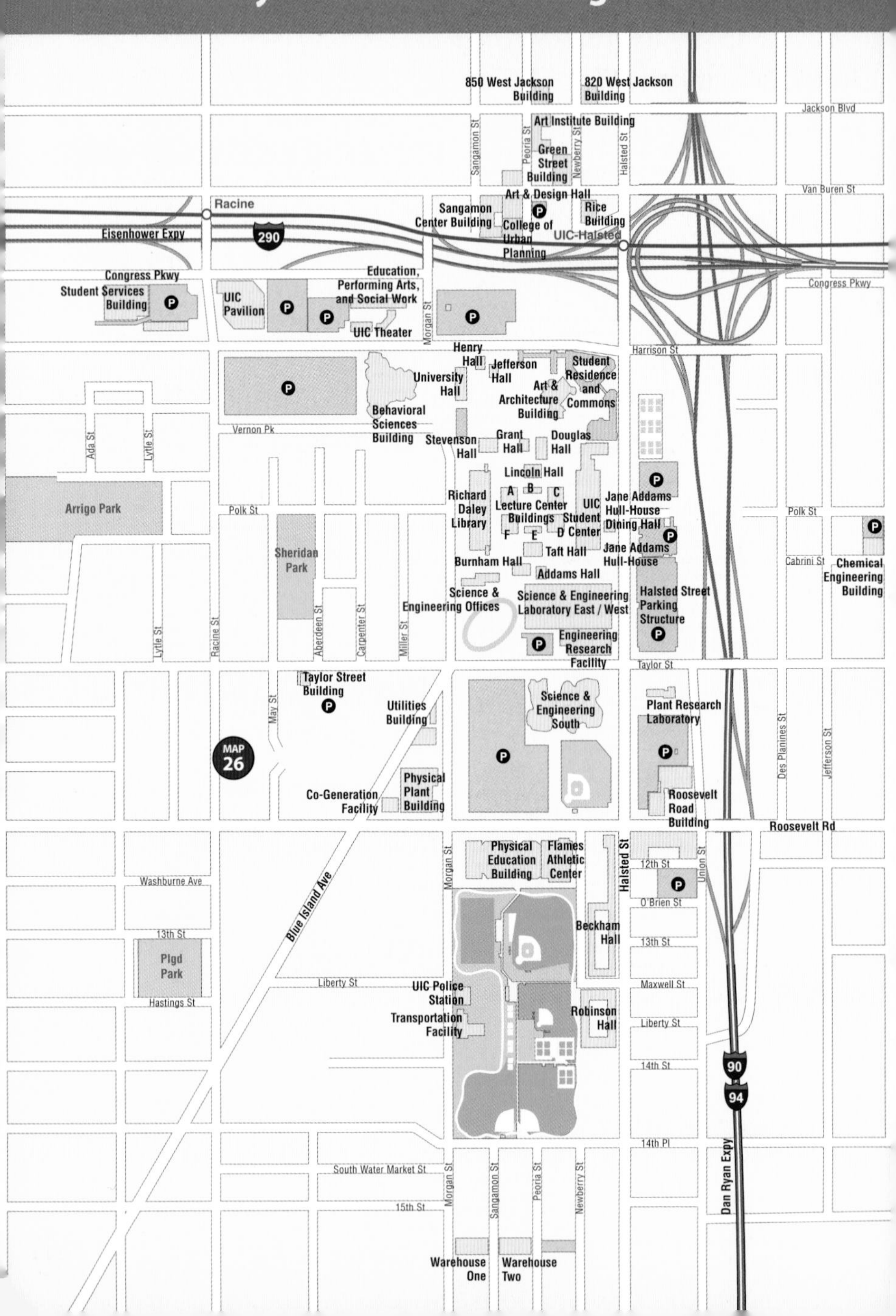

General Information

NFT Map: 26
Address: 1200 W Harrison St
Chicago, IL 60680
Phone: 312-996-7000
Website: www.uic.edu

Overview

With over 25,000 students, the University of Illinois at Chicago (UIC) is the largest university in the city. Located on the Near West Side, UIC is ethnically diverse and urban to the core. It is a leading public research university and home to the nation's largest medical school.

However, its legacy as a builder in Chicago is a bit spotty. In the mid-1960s, the school leveled most of what was left of a vibrant Italian-American neighborhood to build its campus next to the Eisenhower. During current development of the South Campus, UIC continues to consume city blocks south of Roosevelt Road. UIC's expansion all but erased the colorful, landmark Maxwell Street flea market area (this bustling mess of market now only takes place on Sundays along nearby S Canal Street). The saving grace of the school's construction craze is that many of the original, ugly, cement slab structures are kissing the wrecking ball and being replaced with more inspired buildings. But even with the multi-million-dollar improvements, the campus still doesn't ignite any desire to visit. Other than going to class or the doctor, a lone trip to UIC to see the Jane Addams Hull-House Museum is sufficient.

Tuition

For the 2005–2006 academic year, an Illinois resident undergraduate student's tuition and fees totaled $4,151; room and board cost between $5,058 and $8,942 depending on the meal plan and type of housing. These figures do not include books, supplies, lab fees, or personal expenses.

Sports

Lately, the Division I Flames have been hot. The men's basketball team's first appearance in the NCAA Tournament was in 1997. They returned in 2002 after winning their first-ever Horizon League Tournament and went on to win the title again in 2004. Additionally, the Flames women's gymnastics, tennis squad, and softball teams have all advanced to NCAA Tournament play in recent years.

Other Flames men's and women's teams are swimming & diving and cross-country/track & field. UIC also has men's tennis, gymnastics, baseball, and soccer, plus women's basketball and volleyball. Basketball games and women's volleyball matches are played at the recently renovated UIC Pavilion at the corner of S Racine Avenue and Harrison Street. For tickets, call 312-413-8421, or visit www.uicflames.com.

Too bad the NCAA doesn't have a bowling tournament because UIC would be a strong contender. The campus has its own alley located at 750 S Halsted Street (312-413-5170) where the public is welcome to sling balls and swig beers with students.

Culture on Campus

Jane Addams Hull-House (800 S Halsted St, 312-413-5353; www.uic.edu/jaddams/hull, America's first settlement house, opened in 1889. The free museum documents the pioneering organization's social welfare programs that supported the community's destitute immigrant workers. Museum hours are 10 am to 4 pm Tuesday through Friday and noon to 4 pm on Sunday, closed on Mondays and Saturdays.

Department Contact Information

All area codes are 312 unless otherwise noted.

Admissions and Records 996-4350
Graduate College 413-2550
College of Architecture & the Arts 996-5611
College of Applied Health Sciences 996-6695
College of Dentistry 996-1020
College of Business Administration 996-2671
College of Education 996-5641
College of Engineering 996-2400
College of Liberal Arts and Sciences 996-3366
College of Medicine 996-3500
College of Nursing 996-7800
College of Pharmacy 996-7240
School of Public Health 996-6620
College of Social Work 996-7096
College of Urban Planning and Public Affairs . 413-8088
Office of Continuing Education 996-8025
University of Illinois Medical Center 355-4000

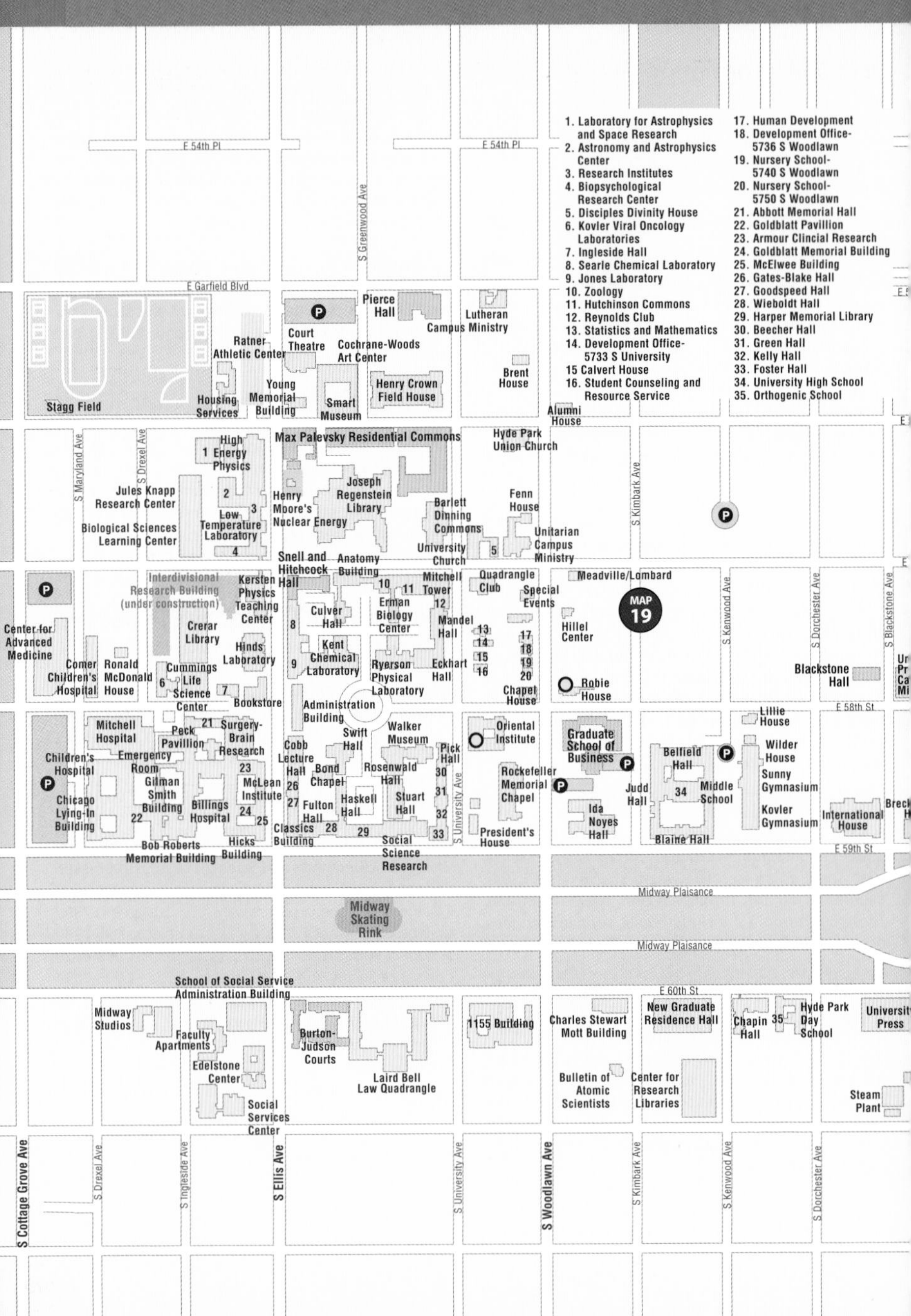

1. Laboratory for Astrophysics and Space Research
2. Astronomy and Astrophysics Center
3. Research Institutes
4. Biopsychological Research Center
5. Disciples Divinity House
6. Kovler Viral Oncology Laboratories
7. Ingleside Hall
8. Searle Chemical Laboratory
9. Jones Laboratory
10. Zoology
11. Hutchinson Commons
12. Reynolds Club
13. Statistics and Mathematics
14. Development Office-5733 S University
15 Calvert House
16. Student Counseling and Resource Service
17. Human Development
18. Development Office-5736 S Woodlawn
19. Nursery School-5740 S Woodlawn
20. Nursery School-5750 S Woodlawn
21. Abbott Memorial Hall
22. Goldblatt Pavillion
23. Armour Clincial Research
24. Goldblatt Memorial Building
25. McElwee Building
26. Gates-Blake Hall
27. Goodspeed Hall
28. Wieboldt Hall
29. Harper Memorial Library
30. Beecher Hall
31. Green Hall
32. Kelly Hall
33. Foster Hall
34. University High School
35. Orthogenic School
MAP 19
E 54th Pl
S Greenwood Ave
E Garfield Blvd
Stagg Field
Ratner Athletic Center
Housing Services
Young Memorial Building
Court Theatre
Pierce Hall
Cochrane-Woods Art Center
Smart Museum
Henry Crown Field House
Lutheran Campus Ministry
Brent House
Alumni House
Max Palevsky Residential Commons
Hyde Park Union Church
High Energy Physics
S Maryland Ave
S Drexel Ave
Jules Knapp Research Center
Biological Sciences Learning Center
Low Temperature Laboratory
Henry Moore's Nuclear Energy
Joseph Regenstein Library
Barlett Dinning Commons
Fenn House
Unitarian Campus Ministry
University Church
S Kimbark Ave
Snell and Hitchcock Hall
Anatomy Building
Interdivisional Research Building (under construction)
Kersten Physics Teaching Center
Mitchell Tower
Quadrangle Club
Special Events
Meadville/Lombard
Hillel Center
S Kenwood Ave
S Dorchester Ave
S Blackstone Ave
Center for Advanced Medicine
Crerar Library
Culver Hall
Erman Biology Center
Mandel Hall
Kent Chemical Laboratory
Hinds Laboratory
Comer Children's Hospital
Ronald McDonald House
Cummings Life Science Center
Ryerson Physical Laboratory
Eckhart Hall
Chapel House
Robie House
Blackstone Hall
Bookstore
Administration Building
E 58th St
Lillie House
Mitchell Hospital
Peck Pavillion
Surgery-Brain Research
Swift Hall
Walker Museum
Oriental Institute
Graduate School of Business
Wilder House
Children's Hospital
Emergency Room
Cobb Lecture Hall
Bond Chapel
Pick Hall
Belfield Hall
Sunny Gymnasium
Gilman Smith Building
McLean Institute
Rosenwald Hall
Rockefeller Memorial Chapel
Judd Hall
Middle School
Chicago Lying-In Building
Billings Hospital
Fulton Hall
Haskell Hall
Stuart Hall
S University Ave
Ida Noyes Hall
Kovler Gymnasium
International House
Classics Building
President's House
Blaine Hall
Bob Roberts Memorial Building
Hicks Building
Social Science Research
E 59th St
Midway Plaisance
Midway Skating Rink
Midway Plaisance
School of Social Service Administration Building
E 60th St
Midway Studios
Faculty Apartments
Burton-Judson Courts
1155 Building
Charles Stewart Mott Building
New Graduate Residence Hall
Chapin Hall
Hyde Park Day School
University Press
Edelstone Center
Laird Bell Law Quadrangle
Bulletin of Atomic Scientists
Center for Research Libraries
Steam Plant
Social Services Center
S Cottage Grove Ave
S Drexel Ave
S Ingleside Ave
S Ellis Ave
S University Ave
S Woodlawn Ave
S Kimbark Ave
S Kenwood Ave
S Dorchester Ave

General Information

NFT Map:	19
Mailing Address:	University of Chicago Administration Building 5801 S Ellis Ave Chicago, IL 60637
Phone:	773-702-1234
Website:	www.uchicago.edu
Visitor's Center:	Ida Noyes Hall, 1st Fl 1212 E 59th St
Phone:	773-702-9739
Guest Parking:	Lot located off Woodlawn Ave b/w 58th St and 59th St. Metered parking is available north of Ida Noyes Hall.

Overview

Located amidst the pleasant tree-lined streets of Hyde Park, the University of Chicago is a world-renowned research institution with a winning tradition in Nobel Prizes. Seventy-three Nobel laureates have been associated with the university as faculty, students, or researchers. (Seven of the laureates are current faculty members.) The university prides itself on the fact that, while it does have some professional schools (including top-ranked programs in law, medicine, and social work), it eschews such applied fields as journalism and the ever-popular field of animal husbandry. More importantly (for some people), the University of Chicago helped found the Big Ten Conference and created "the world's first controlled release of nuclear energy"—uh, for us regular folks, that's the atomic bomb.

Besides producing hordes of brainy gurus of economics, business, law, and medicine, University of Chicago graduates include artists, writers, politicians, film directors, and actors. To name a few: Studs Terkel, Sara Paretsky, Carol Mosely-Braun, Kurt Vonnegut, Susan Sontag, John Ashcroft (well, you can't win 'em all), Ed Asner, Saul Bellow, Katharine Graham, Philip Glass, Saul Alinsky, Paul Goodman, and co-creators of Chicago's Second City comedy troupe, Bernard Sahlins and Mike Nichols.

Established in 1890, the University of Chicago was founded and funded by John D. Rockefeller. Built on 200 acres donated by Marshall Field and designed by architect Henry Ives Cobb, the university's English Gothic buildings of ivy-clad limestone ooze old money and intellectual achievements. Rockefeller described the university as "the best investment I ever made." We just hope parents footing the bill for their kids' education feel the same.

Tuition

The University of Chicago operates on a trimester schedule rather than the more common two-semester academic year. In the 2005–2006 academic year, an undergraduate student paid approximately $31,629 for tuition and fees with an additional $10,104 for room and board. Most students spend another $2,686 on books, lab fees, and personal expenses, which all adds up to a grand total of over $45,080 per year! Costs for graduate students vary based on the school. Chicago has 13,000 students, 4,400 of them undergraduates. About 2,000 of the graduate students attend classes at the downtown riverfront campus Gleacher Center (450 N Cityfront Plaza Dr, 312-464-8787; www.gleachercenter.com), where the popular Graham School of General Studies holds most of its continuing education classes.

Sports

There was a time when the University of Chicago racked up football trophies as well as Nobel Prizes. In 1935, the first Heisman Trophy winner was senior Jay Berwanger. The Maroons won seven Big Ten football championships between 1899 and 1924 (led at this time by Amos Alonzo Stagg), followed by a steady losing streak. In 1946 the university, under the direction of the famed Robert Maynard Hutchins, threw in the proverbial towel, resigning from the Big Ten in favor of developing students' brains rather than their brawn.

But the school hasn't totally abandoned sports. A member of the University Athletic Association, Chicago has women's volleyball, softball, swimming, tennis, soccer, basketball, cross-country, and track & field teams and men's baseball, basketball, cross-country, soccer, swimming, tennis, football, track & field teams, and a wrestling squad.

Culture on Campus

Located at 5757 S Woodlawn Avenue is Frank Lloyd Wright's Prairie Style residential masterpiece, the Robie House (708-848-1976; www.wrightplus.org). The one-time private home is considered one of the most important buildings in the history of American architecture, and it will be even more impressive once the ten-year, $8-million-dollar renovation plans are complete. (Adults tickets cost $12, children 7-18 and seniors pay $10.) Two must-see but often overlooked free museums on campus are the Oriental Institute Museum (1155 E 58th St, 773-702-9514; www.oi.uchicago.edu) and the Smart Museum of Art (5550 S Greenwood Ave, 773-702-0200; www.smartmuseum.uchicago.edu). Showcasing archeological finds from university digs since the 1900s, the Oriental Institute has treasures from the ancient Near East dating from 9000 BC to 900 AD. The Smart Museum displays 8,000 fine arts items with strong collections in painting and sculpture spanning centuries and continents.

The university's professional Court Theatre, which recently celebrated its 50th anniversary, presents fresh interpretations of classic dramas (5535 S Ellis Ave, 773-753-4472; www.courttheatre.org). Previous seasons have included critically acclaimed productions of Albee's *Who's Afraid of Virginia Woolf?*, Wilde's *The Importance of Being Earnest*, Williams's *The Glass Menagerie*, and August Wilson's *Fences*.

Department Contact Information

Log on to www.uchicago.edu/uchi/directories for a university directory and links to division and department web pages.

Undergraduate Student Admissions	773-702-8650
Biological Sciences	773-702-2105
Humanities	773-702-8512
Physical Sciences	773-702-7950
Social Sciences	773-702-8799
Divinity School	773-702-8200
Graduate School of Business	773-702-7743
Graduate Affairs	773-702-7813
Graham School of General Studies	773-702-1722
Harris Graduate School of Public Policy Studies	773-702-8400
Law School	773-702-9494
Pritzker School of Medicine	773-702-1939
School of Social Service Administration	773-702-1250

Columbia College Chicago

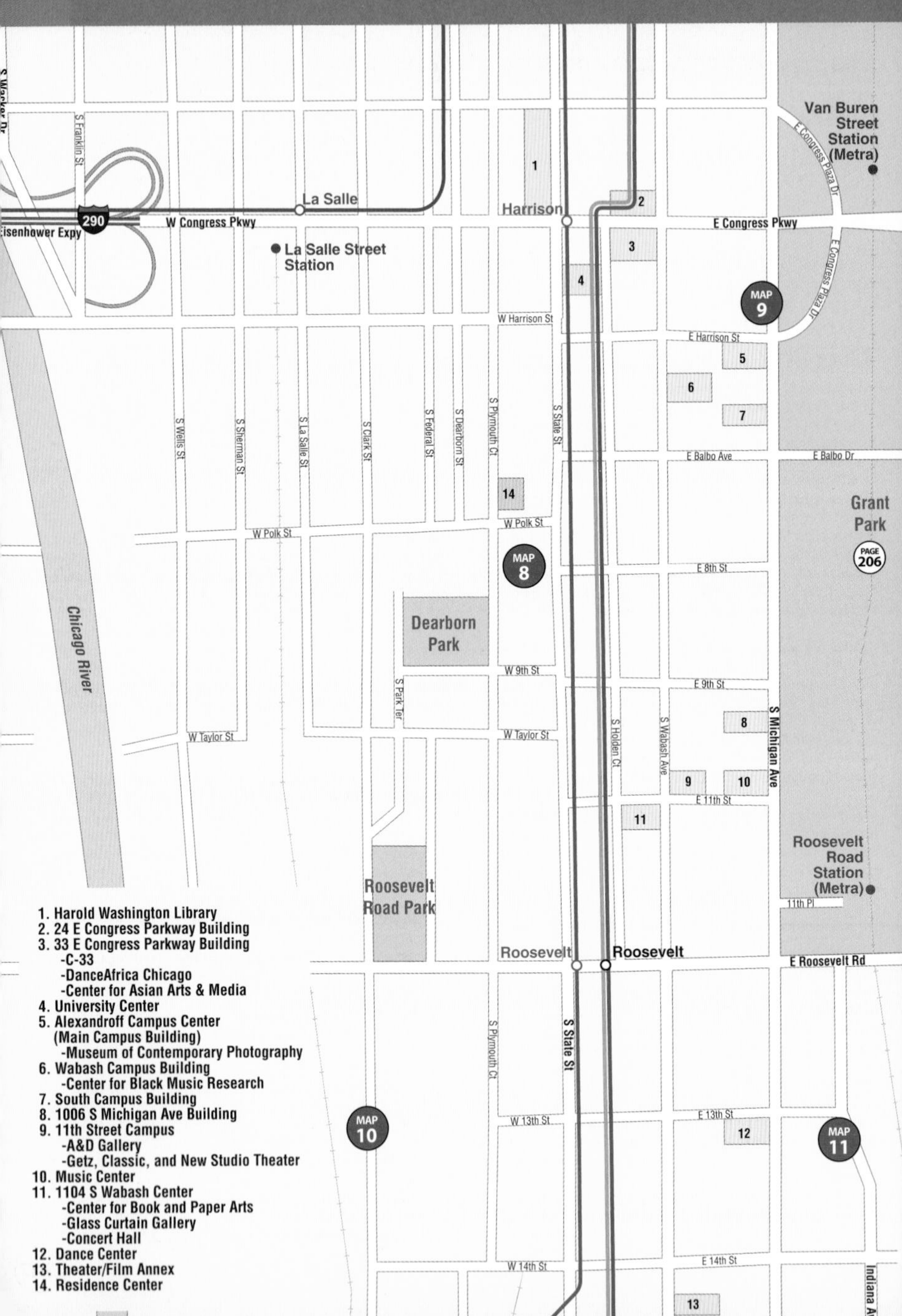

General Information

NFT Maps:	8, 9
Address:	600 S Michigan Ave Chicago, IL 60605
Phone:	312-663-1600
Website:	www.colum.edu
Event Information:	www.colum.edu/calendar

Overview

Named in honor of the World's Columbian Exposition, Columbia College Chicago first opened its doors in 1890 as a women's college of speech. Over the years, the college has evolved into the nation's largest and most diverse private arts and media school. Columbia has been gaining attention thanks to the successes of alumni from their highly regarded film, television, and fiction departments, which have sprouted a bountiful harvest of feature films (in which alums have had key writing and production roles— *Barbershop, Real Women Have Curves, Analyze This, Schindler's List, Leaving Las Vegas*), Emmy Awards (*Alias*, art direction; *Star Trek: Enterprise*, special effects; *Samurai Jack*, animation; *Carnivale*, cinematography), and critically acclaimed books (by alums Joe Meno, Don DeGrazia, and Sam Weller, all now faculty in the fiction writing department). A partial listing of other programs includes photography, dance, theater, music, art and design, journalism, fashion design, poetry, education, and management for the arts, entertainment, and media.

Tuition

The 2006–2007 school year has full-time undergraduate students paying $16,328 per year. While on-campus residency averages $8,000, those who choose the "Super Dorm" (University Center) will pay an average of $11,000. It is the largest dormitory in the United States and is shared with DePaul and Roosevelt Universities.

Culture

Columbia College is one of Chicago's premier cultural arts presenters with more than 300,000 visitors attending its events each year. The college brings the DanceAfrica Chicago Festival to the city every fall and a regular schedule of innovative dance performances throughout the year. The Museum of Contemporary Photography is one of only two fully accredited photography museums in the United States. Columbia is home to the Chicago Jazz Ensemble directed by trumpet virtuoso Jon Faddis. The Story Week Festival of Writers has become the literary event for the city each spring. The college brings in authors, editors, agents, and publishers for a week of readings, panels, and a read-like-a-rockstar night at the Metro. Spring also brings Fashion Columbia and the Manifest Urban Arts Festival celebrating the achievements of graduates. The college's galleries and theaters regularly feature the work of both students and notable artists.

- **Center for Book and Paper Arts**
  1104 S Wabash Ave, 2nd Fl
  312-344-6630
  www.colum.edu/centers/bpa

- **Museum of Contemporary Photography**
  600 S Michigan Ave
  312-663-5554
  www.mocp.org

- **A&D Gallery**
  619 S. Wabash Ave
  312-344-8687
  www.colum.edu/adgallery

- **Glass Curtain Gallery**
  1104 S Wabash Ave
  312-344-6650

- **C-33**
  33 E Congress Pkwy
  312-344-7696

- **Dance Center**
  1306 S Michigan Ave
  312-344-8300
  www.dancecenter.org

- **Getz, Classic, and New Studio Theaters**
  72 E 11th St
  312-344-6126
  www.colum.edu/undergraduate/theater/calendar

- **Concert Hall**
  1014 S Michigan Ave
  312-344- 6240

- **DanceAfrica Chicago**
  33 E Congress Pkwy
  312-344-7070
  www.danceafricachicago.com

- **Center for Asian Arts & Media**
  29 E Congress Pkwy, 1st Fl
  312-344-7870
  www.asianartsandmedia.org

- **Center for Black Music Research**
  623 S Wabash Ave
  312-344-7559
  www.cbmr.org

- **Chicago Jazz Ensemble**
  600 S Michigan Ave
  312-344-6270
  www.chijazz.com

Department Contact Information

Undergraduate Admissions 312-344-7131
Graduate Admissions 312-344-7260
School of Fine and Performing Arts 312-344-7298
School of Media Arts 312-344-8220
School of Liberal Arts and Sciences 312-344-8217

Illinois Institute of Technology

W 30th St
Stuart Field
Stuart Building
Permit Parking
Keating Sports Center
Baseball Field
E 31st St
Life Sciences
Permit Parking
Permit Parking
Bailey
Cunningham
Engineering 1 Building
Visitor Parking
Gunsaulus
VanderCook College of Music
MAP 13
S Dearborn St
S State St
S State St
S La Salle St
Dan Ryan Expy
Carman
Carr Memorial Chapel
Alumni Memorial Hall
The Commons
North
Fowler
South
East
Visitor Parking
Hermann Hall
Perlstein Hall
McCormick Tribune Campus Center
McCormick Student Village
Graduate
Wishnick Hall
Lewis
90
94
Machinery Hall
E 33rd St
Main Hall
Siegel Hall
S Wabash Ave
Farr
State Street Village
Visitor Parking
Permit Parking
PKP
KPD
Galvin Library
SPE
ASA
The Quad
Permit Parking
DTD
AEP
Crown Hall
ASP
PKS
TRI
E 34th St
S Federal St
Aspect Intensive English Institute
Visitor Parking
Visitor Parking
Permit Parking
IIT Research Institute
IIT Research Institute Tower
E 35th St
Sox-35th
35th-Bronzeville-IIT

General Information

NFT Map:	13
Main Campus:	3300 S Federal St Chicago, IL 60616
Phone:	312-567-3000
Website:	www.iit.edu

Overview

In the 19th century, when higher education was reserved for society's upper crust, meat magnate Philip Danforth Armour put his money to good use and funded an institution dedicated to students from lower financial brackets. The Armour Institute carried his name until a merger with the engineering school Lewis Institute in 1940 changed the name to Illinois Institute of Technology. Over the next 40 years, the college continued to merge with other small technical colleges, resulting in the IIT we know today. The school is as notable for its Mies Van Der Rohe–designed campus as for its groundbreaking work in aeronautics research. The new student center, designed by Dutch architect Rem Koolhaas, includes a space-aged metallic tube through which the local L train travels.

Chicago-Kent College of Law, Stuart School Graduate School of Business, and the Institute of Design are based in the Loop. The Rice campus, in west suburban Wheaton, offers undergraduate continuing education and degree programs to working professionals. Two of the many research organizations IIT has incorporated since 1936 to serve various needs of private industry and government are the National Center for Food Safety and Technology in the southwest suburbs and the IIT Research Institute on the main campus in Bronzeville, housed in IIT's tallest building.

IIT grants PhDs and other professional degrees in a vast array of areas including science, mathematics, engineering, architecture, psychology, design, business, and law. The interprofessional, technology-focused curriculum is designed to prepare the 6,400 students to become groundbreakers in an increasingly complex global workplace. IIT was recently named a "College of Distinction" by a new college guide honoring some of America's top educational institutions.

In June 2004, IIT's Research Institute Life Sciences Group was awarded $28 million in research funding. The prestigious award is among the largest ever received by IITRI for drug development.

Tuition

In the 2005–2006 academic year, undergraduate tuition cost $22,920. Room and board costs vary by residence but generally run between $7,000 and $10,000.

Sports

The IIT Scarlet Hawks are affiliated with the National Association of Intercollegiate Athletics Division I. Students can compete with other schools in baseball, basketball, cross-country, diving, soccer, swimming, and volleyball.

The 2004 swim season saw the Scarlet Hawks' third year head coach Rob Bond named NAIA Men's Swimming and Diving National Coach of the Year.

New Developments on Campus

The newest student residency, completed in 2003, is State Street Village. Located at State and 33rd Streets, the hall was designed by well-known Chicago-based architect Helmut Jahn. The German-born designer was named one of the Ten Most Influential Living American Architects by the American Institute of Architects (AIA) in 1991. Jahn, a graduate of IIT himself, created the six-building complex across the street from Van Der Rohe's masterful historical landmark, the S.R. Crown Hall. Jahn's new building brings student housing to a new level with poured-in-place concrete and glass-clad and corrugated stainless steel panels that reduce noise and vibrations from passing trains while simultaneously exhibiting a cutting-edge aesthetic. Currently underway is development of the $50 million University Technology Park on the main campus, to be built in phases over the next ten years.

Department Contact Information

Undergraduate Admissions	312-567-3025
Graduate Admissions	312-567-3020
Alumni Office	312-567-5040
Armour College of Engineering	312-567-3009
Center for Law and Financial Markets	312-906-6576
Center for Professional Development	630-682-6040
Chicago-Kent College of Law	312-906-5000
College of Architecture	312-567-3263
College of Science & Letters	312-567-3800
Keating Sports Center	312-567-3000
Institute of Business and Interprofessional Studies	312-567-3947
Institute of Design	312-595-4900
Institute of Psychology	312-567-3500
Stuart Graduate School of Business	312-906-6500
University Technology Park	312-567-3900

General Information

Lincoln Park Campus:	Schmitt Academic Center 2320 N Kenmore Ave Chicago, IL 60614-3298 Phone: 773-325-7000 x5700
Loop Campus:	1 E Jackson Blvd Chicago, IL 60604 Phone: 312-362-8000
Website:	www.depaul.edu
Suburban Campuses:	
University Center of Lake County (Grayslake)	847-665-4000
Naperville	312-476-4500/630-548-9378
Oak Forest	312-476-3000/708-633-9091
O'Hare	312-476-3600/847-296-5348
Rolling Meadows	312-476-4800/847-437-9522

Overview

Established in 1898 by the Vincentian Fathers as a school for immigrants, DePaul has become the country's largest Catholic university (with over 23,000 students) and the biggest private educational institution in Chicago. The university offers 150 undergraduate and graduate programs of study. According to The Princeton Review's recent survey of college students nationwide, DePaul students rated as some of the happiest college students in the country. It must be all the bars near campus on Halsted Street and Lincoln Avenue.

Of the university's seven campuses in the Chicago area, the Lincoln Park and Loop campuses serve as the core locations. The highly acclaimed Theatre School, College of Liberal Arts and Sciences, School of Music, and School of Education hold down the 36-acre Lincoln Park campus amidst renovated historic homes on tree-lined streets.

DePaul's Loop Campus at Jackson Boulevard and State Street is where you'll find the College of Commerce, College of Law, and School of Computer Science, Telecommunications, and Information Systems. Nationally respected Kellstadt Graduate School of Business and DePaul's thriving continuing education program, the "School of New Learning," can also be found on the Loop Campus. The heart of the Loop campus is DePaul Center, located in the old Goldblatt Brothers Department Store. Prominent DePaul alumni include Chicago father-son mayors Richard M. Daley and his dad, the late Richard J. Daley; McDonald's Corporation's former CEO Jack Greenberg; Pulitzer Prize-winning composer George Perle; and actress Gillian Anderson.

Tuition

Each college has its own tuition; room and board costs depend on the residence facility and meal plan chosen. In the 2006–2007 academic year, undergraduate tuition for the College of Arts & Sciences was $22,365. Tuition for the School of Music and for the Theatre School cost about $25,500. Room and board cost between $6,000 and $8,500. Add on the cost of books, lab fees, and personal expenses.

Sports

DePaul's Blue Demons men's basketball team teased Chicago with an NCAA Division I Championship in 2000, when the team appeared in its first tournament since 1992. Coach Dave Leitao, who took over in '02, planned to reinstate the Demons' winning record and almost succeeded in 2003. Almost. The team lost its chance at the title in the second round of the tournament and hasn't been making headlines since. The Blue Demons play at United Center (1901 W Madison St, 312-455-4500; www.unitedcenter.com) and Allstate Arena (6920 N Mannheim Rd in Rosemont, 847-635-6601; www.allstatearena.com). For tickets, call Ticketmaster at 312-559-1212, visit www.ticketmaster.com, go to the stadiums' box offices, or visit the DePaul Athletic Center box office (2323 N Sheffield Ave, 773-325-7526; www.depaulbluedemons.com).

Blue Demons' men's and women's teams include basketball, cross-country, soccer, tennis, and track & field. DePaul also has a men's golf team, as well as women's softball and volleyball squads. For stats and schedules, visit the Blue Demons' website.

Culture on Campus

DePaul's vibrant Theatre School is the oldest of its kind in the Midwest. Founded in 1925 as the Goodman School of Drama, the school stages over 200 performances during its Showcase, Chicago Playworks, New Directors Series, and School Workshop seasons. The Theatre School Showcase performs contemporary and classic plays at its 1,325-seat Merle Reskin Theatre, a French Renaissance–style theater built in 1910 and located at 60 E Balbo Drive in the South Loop. The Chicago Playworks for Families and Young Audiences and the School of Music's annual opera are also performed at the Merle Reskin Theatre. For tickets ($8–$12), directions, and parking garage locations, call 312-922-1999 or go to theatreschool.depaul.edu. Take the Red Line to the Harrison Street or Jackson Street stops just southwest of the theater. CTA buses 29, 36, 151, and 146 also stop nearby. Check the Theatre School website for New Directors Series and School Workshop productions, theater locations, and ticket prices.

DePaul University Art Gallery is located in the John T. Richardson Library at 2350 N Kenmore Avenue (773-325-7506). Permanent collections of sculpture and oil paintings from local and international artists adorn the free gallery. A pay parking lot is located one block east of the library on N Sheffield Avenue. DePaul's John T. Richardson Library and Loop campus library in DePaul Center are open to the public year-round. Take plenty of change for the copy machines as check-out privileges are reserved for students and faculty.

Department Contact Information

Lincoln Park Campus Admissions Office...... 773-325-7500
Loop Campus Admissions Office............. 312-362-8300
College of Commerce....................... 312-362-5358
College of Law............................ 312-325-7316
Undergraduate College of Arts & Sciences ... 773-325-7310
Graduate College of Arts & Sciences 773-325-7315
John T Richardson Library.................. 773-325-7506
Kellstadt Graduate School of Business 312-362-8810
Loop Campus Library 312-362-8432
School for New Learning 312-362-8001
School of Computer Science, Telecommunications and Information Systems.................. 312-362-8381
School of Music............................ 773-325-7260
Theatre School............................. 773-325-7917

Northwestern University (Evanston Campus)

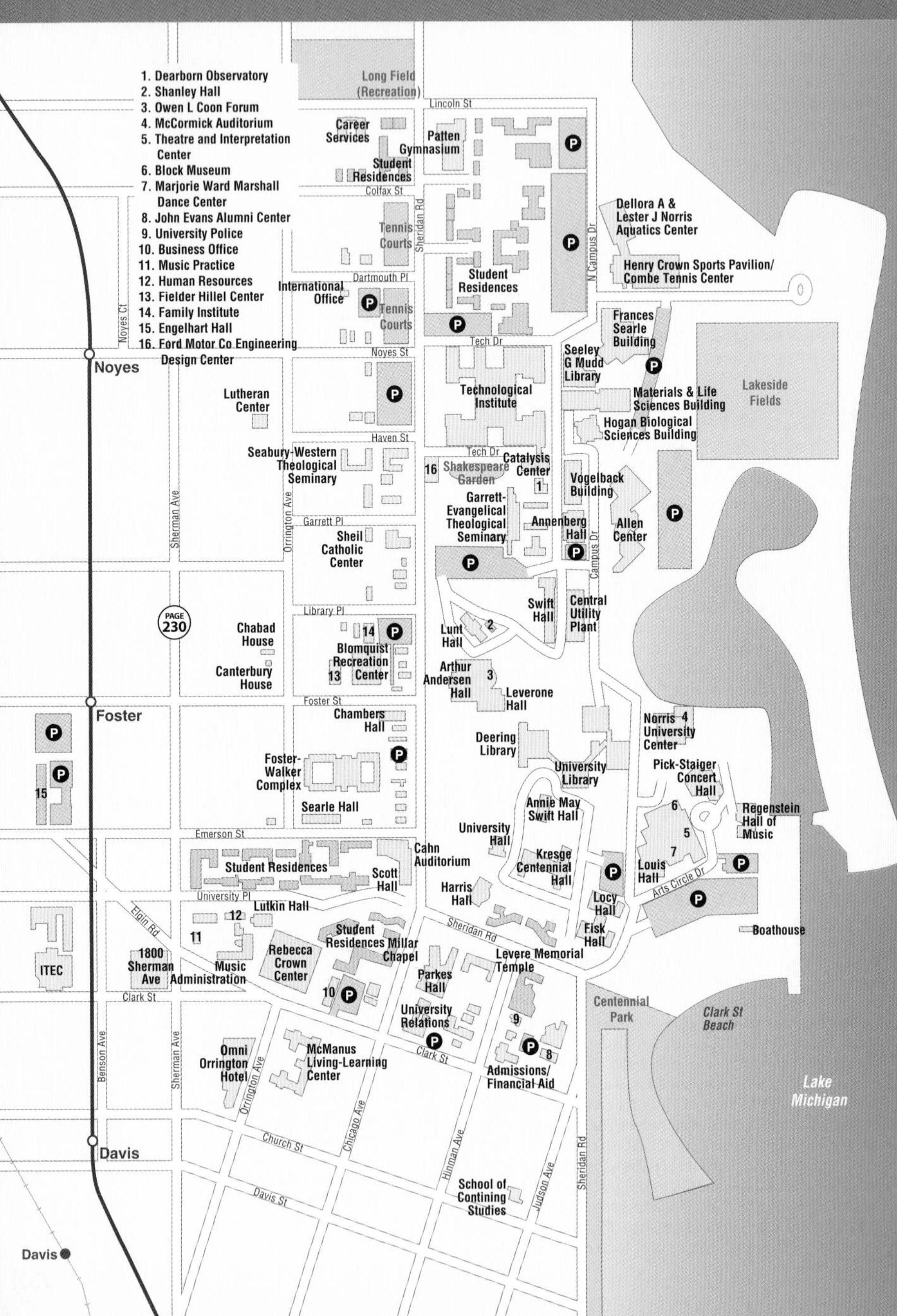

Northwestern University (Evanston Campus)

General Information

Evanston Campus: 633 Clark St
Evanston, IL 60208
Phone: 847-491-3741
Chicago Campus: Abbot Hall
710 N Lake Shore Dr
Chicago, IL 60611
Phone: 312-503-8649
Website: www.northwestern.edu

Overview

Northwestern University, along with the University of Chicago, likes to think of itself as part of the "Ivy League of the Midwest." Almost 18,000 full- and part-time students attend Northwestern's 11 schools, located in Evanston and downtown Chicago. This is a far cry from the two original faculty members and 10 students in attendance when the school opened in 1855. The University's name was derived from its founders' need to service the citizens of the former Northwest Territory.

Founded in 1851, Northwestern University was established in Evanston by many of the same Methodist founding fathers of the town itself. The 240-acre lakefront campus is bordered roughly by Lincoln Street to the north and Clark Street to the south and Sheridan Road to the west. The Evanston campus houses the Weinberg College of Arts and Sciences; McCormick School of Engineering and Applied Science; the Schools of Music, Communication, Education and Social Policy; the Graduate School; Medill School of Journalism; and J. L. Kellogg School of Management.

The university did a bit of branching out when it purchased land for the Chicago campus in 1920. Located on a 25-acre lot between the lake and Michigan Avenue in the Streeterville neighborhood, the Chicago campus houses the Schools of Law, Medicine, and Continuing Studies. Graduate school and Kellogg courses are also offered at the Chicago campus. Several excellent hospitals and medical research institutions affiliated with the university dominate the northern edge of Streeterville. The Robert H. Lurie Medical Research Center at Fairbanks Court and Superior Street, completed in 2004, has expanded the university's research abilities with nine floors of laboratory space. The new women's hospital across from it will be finished in 2007.

Tuition

In the 2005–2006 academic year, undergraduate tuition, books and fees cost $34,719 and room and board cost $9,873.

Sports

Like all Big Ten Conference schools, Northwestern has football and basketball teams—but that's all we can really say of the Wildcats lately. There was more to talk about in the 1990s with back-to-back bowl appearances in the 1996 Rose Bowl (their first bowl appearance since winning in 1949) and the 1997 Citrus Bowl. After Nebraska de-clawed, skinned, and gutted the Wildcats at the 2000 Alamo Bowl, it seems the team has been licking its wounds. They made an appearance in, and lost, the 2003 Motor City Bowl against Bowling Green. 2006 looks no better for Wildcat fans—they travel to Penn State, Wisconsin, and Michigan. At least they get Ohio State at home...

The Wildcats' home is Ryan Field at 1501 Central Avenue, about three blocks east of the Central Avenue stop on the elevated Purple Line. Basketball games are held at the Welsh-Ryan Arena behind the stadium. For tickets, call 847-491-2287. All sporting events are listed at www.nusports.com and you can also purchase tickets online. Northwestern students can obtain free tickets to any game by presenting their WILDCARD ID.

Northwestern also has men's wrestling and baseball teams, plus men's and women's basketball, golf, soccer, tênnis, and swimming and diving teams. Additionally, Wildcat women compete in cross-country, fencing, softball, field hockey, and volleyball, with a lacrosse team that's ranked number one in the country, and a tennis team ranked second.

Culture on Campus

The Mary and Leigh Block Museum of Art on the Evanston campus (40 Arts Circle Dr, 847-491-4000; www.blockmuseum.northwestern.edu) has 4,000 items in its permanent collection including Old Masters prints, architectural drawings, contemporary photographic images, and modern sculpture. The Block is also home to the state-of-the-art Pick-Laudati Auditorium that hosts film festivals and contemporary classics as well as different cinema series and lectures throughout the year. Hours: Tues: 10 am to 5 pm; Wed–Fri: 10 am to 8 pm; weekends: noon–5 pm. Admission is always free.

The Pick-Staiger Concert Hall (50 Arts Circle Dr, 847-491-5441; www.pickstaiger.com) is not only the stage for the university's musical performances, but it is also home to several professional performance organizations such as the Chicago Chamber Musicians, Symphony of the Shores, Chicago String Ensemble, Performing Arts Chicago, and others. Each year, Pick-Staiger Concert Hall also hosts the Segovia Classical Guitar Series and the Keyboard Conversations Series. Call 847-467-4000 to purchase tickets.

Northwestern University also runs a student newspaper, the *Daily Northwestern*, and a student radio station, WNUR.

Department Contact Information

Undergraduate Admissions........847-491-7271
Graduate School (Evanston)........847-491-7264
Graduate School (Chicago)........312-503-8900
Weinberg College of Arts and Sciences 847-491-7561
Feinberg School of Medicine........312-503-8649
Kellogg School of Management........847-491-3300
Medill School of Journalism........847-467-1882
School of Communication........847-491-7023
School of Continuing Studies (Evanston)........847-491-5611
School of Education and Social Policy........847-491-8193
McCormick School of Engineering
and Applied Science 847-491-7379
School of Law........312-503-6950
School of Music........847-491-7575

Loyola University (Lake Shore Campus)

Loyola University (Lake Shore Campus)

General Information

Lake Shore:	6525 N Sheridan Rd Chicago, IL 60626 Phone: 773-274-3000
Water Tower/Lewis Towers Campus:	820 N Michigan Ave Chicago, IL 60611 Phone: 312-915-6000
Medical Center:	2160 S First Ave Maywood, IL 60153 Phone: 708-216-9000
Website:	www.luc.edu

Overview

Loyola University, one of the largest Jesuit universities in the United States, is known throughout the Midwest for its first-rate schools of business and law as well as for its Medical Center (a well-respected research institution). Approximately 15,000 students attend the university.

Lake Shore campus, the largest of Loyola's four campuses, is on the lake in Rogers Park and houses the College of Arts & Sciences, the Graduate School, Niehoff School of Nursing, Mundelein College Adult Education Program, and Cudahy Library. The university's Water Tower campus downtown on Michigan Avenue is home to the Schools of Business, Education, Law, and Social Work and some College of Arts & Sciences courses. Loyola operates the Stritch School of Medicine and the master's degree programs through the Niehoff School of Nursing at its suburban Maywood campus. The university also has a campus in Rome, that is one of the largest American campuses in Western Europe.

Tuition

In the 2005–2006 academic year, undergraduate tuition cost $23,900. Room and board prices ranged from $5,974 to $9,924. Add on books, lab fees, and personal expenses. Graduate student tuition, fees, and expenses vary by college. It seems like a hefty sum, but Loyola University was ranked by *U.S. News & World Report* as one of the "best values" for a college education.

Sports

Loyola is the only school in Illinois to win a Division I National Championship basketball tournament, with the Loyola Ramblers taking the NCAA men's basketball championship in 1963. The Ramblers' most recent tournament appearance was in 1985. If they keep winning every 22 years, the Ramblers should be making headlines any year now. Catch them at the Joseph J. Gentile Center on the Lake Shore Campus. For tickets, visit the box office, call 773-508-2569, or go to loyolaramblers.cstv.com.

Loyola University has men's and women's basketball, cross-country, track, soccer, and volleyball teams. The women also have a softball squad. The men's volleyball team is ranked as one of the top ten in the nation.

Culture on Campus

Opened in October 2005, the Loyola University Museum of Art (LUMA) is the new home of the famous Martin D'Arcy collection of medieval, renaissance, and baroque art. Paintings by masters Tintoretto, Guercino, Bassano, and Stomer, plus sculpture, furniture, jewelry, decorative arts, and liturgical vessels are part of the over-500-piece collection dating from 1150 to 1750. The museum, located at 920 N Michigan Avenue, is free on Tuesdays. Suggested general admission is $6, $5 for seniors, and free if you can pass for 14 and under. Hours: Tues: 10 am–8 pm; Wed–Sun: 10 am–5 pm. For more information, call 312-915-7600. The university's Cudahy Library, Lewis Library at the Water Tower campus, Science Library, Health Sciences Library, and Graduate Business School Library are all open to the public. Checkout privileges, however, are reserved for the university's students and faculty.

The Loyola University Theatre performs four classic dramas per year at the Kathleen Mullady Theatre (1134 W Loyola Ave, 773-508-3847) in the Centennial Forum/ Mertz Hall building on the Lake Shore campus. Tickets cost $15 for the general public, $7 for seniors and students at other universities, and $5 for Loyola students. You can purchase tickets through the box office, open Monday through Friday from 3 pm to 7 pm.

Department Contact Information

Undergraduate Admissions	773-915-6500
Adult Education	312-915-6501
College of Arts & Sciences	773-508-3500
School of Business Administration	312-915-6112
School of Education	312-916-6800
School of Law	312-915-7120
Stritch School of Medicine	708-216-3229
Niehoff School of Nursing	773-508-3249
Rome Center of Liberal Arts	800-344-7662
School of Social Work	312-915-7005
Graduate School of Business	312-915-6124
The Graduate School	773-508-3396
University Libraries	773-508-2658

General Information

Chicago Park District: www.chicagoparkdistrict.com
312-742-PLAY (7528)
Chicagoland Bicycle Federation: www.chibikefed.org
312-427-3325
Chicago Area Runner's Association: www.cararuns.org
312-666-9836

Overview

Greater Chicago offers more than 250 recreational off-road paths that allow bikers, skaters, walkers, and joggers to exercise without worrying about vehicular traffic—now if only we could get dogs off the paths! In addition to recreational paths in the city's parks, designated off-street trails line the Lakefront, North Shore Channel, North Branch Trail along the Chicago River, Burnham Greenway, and Major Taylor Trail.

Lakefront Trail

Chicago has one of the prettiest and most accessible shorelines of any city in the US (if you survive the treacherous crossing of Lake Shore Drive to get there). Use one of Lake Shore Drive's over/underpasses and you'll discover 15 miles of bathing beaches and over 20 miles of bike paths—just don't anticipate being able to train for the Tour de France during summer weekends, when the sheer number of people makes it impossible to bike along the path at faster than a snail's pace. But thanks to Burnham and Bennett's 1909 "Plan for Chicago," at least we can count on the shoreline remaining non-commercial, with great cycling, jogging, blading, skating, and swimming opportunities for all.

Major Taylor Trail

If you've ever wanted to take in a slice of Chicago's southwestern-most corner (and let's face it, who hasn't?), try the six-mile bike route that begins at Dawes Park at 81st and Hamilton Streets near Western Avenue. The route incorporates an abandoned railroad right-of-way and runs to the southeast through Beverly and Morgan Park, ending up at the Cook County Forest Preserve near 130th and Halsted Streets. The trail was named in honor of cycling legend Marshall "Major" Taylor, one of the first African-American cyclists, who lived out the final years of his life in a YMCA in Chicago.

North Branch Trail

To access the northern end of the trail, take Lake Cook Road to the Chicago Botanic Garden, located east of I-94. You can also start from any of the forest preserves as the path winds southward. To access the southern end of the trail in Chicago, take Milwaukee Avenue to Devon Avenue and head a short way east to the Caldwell Woods Preserve. The North Branch winds along the Chicago River and the Skokie Lagoons, but unlike most of the other trails, this one crosses streets, so be careful and look out for cars as you approach.

Burnham Greenway

The following information was dug up from a Trust for Public Land report on the state of the proposed route of the Burnham Greenway Trail before it was paved:

> Site History: Five-mile Conrail right-of-way between Chicago and the south suburbs, running through both industrial and natural areas.
> Contamination: Phase II indicated pollution from adjacent uses, including fly dumping, railroad pollutants, and some unnatural coloration in adjacent water. Assessment determined no risk as long as the soil remains undisturbed.
> REMEDIATION: Corridor will be paved.

So as long as you stick to the paved trail and don't go digging around off the path, you should remain in good health! The path is suitable for riding, skating, rollerblading, and pedestrian activity.

North Shore Channel Trail

This trail follows North Shore Channel of the Chicago River from Lawrence Avenue through Lincolnwood, Skokie, and Evanston to Green Bay Road at McCormick Boulevard. Not all of the seven miles of the trail are paved bike paths and you'll have to switch back and forth between path and street. Skokie recently paved the trail segment between Oakton and Howard Streets, but there are still many missing links in the route, much to the chagrin of Friends of the Chicago River (FOCR), who are trying to extend and improve the Channel Trail.

Chicago Park District

Many of the parks under the jurisdiction of the Chicago Park District have paths dedicated to cycling, jogging, walking, rollerblading, and skating. The Chicago Area Runner's Association is so committed to lobbying for runners' rights that it successfully petitioned to have the Lincoln Park running paths plowed through the winter so they could continue their running activities. This calls into question the sanity of such masochistic dedication, but we can only assume that the entire year is needed to prepare for the Chicago Marathon, held annually in October. Check out the chart on the facing page to determine Chicago Parks that designate jogging/walking and cycling/skating paths.

Park District—North Region	*Address*	*Phone*	*Jog/Walk*	*Bike/Skate*	*Map*
Brooks Park	7100 N Harlem Ave	773-631-4401	■		45
Emerson Park	1820 W Granville Ave	773-761-0433	■		36
Eugene Field Park	5100 N Ridgeway Ave	773-478-9744		■	48
Oz Park	2021 N Burling St	312-742-7898	■		30
Peterson Park	5801 N Pulaski Ave	312-742-7584	■		46
Portage Park	4100 N Long Ave	773-685-7235	■		48
River Park	5100 N Francisco Ave	312-742-7516		■	38
Shabbona Park	6935 W Addison St	773-685-6205	■		47
Warren Park	6601 N Western Ave	773-262-6314	■	■	33
Frank J Wilson Park	4630 N Milwaukee Ave	773-685-6454	■		48
Winnemac Park	5100 N Leavitt St	312-742-5101	■		39

Park District—Central Region	*Address*	*Phone*	*Jog/Walk*	*Bike/Skate*	*Map*
Columbus Park	500 S Central Ave	312-746-5046	■	■	49
Douglas Park	1401 S Sacramento Ave	312-747-7670	■	■	50
Dvorak Park	1119 W Cullerton St	312-746-5083	■		26
Humboldt Park	1400 N Sacramento Ave	312-742-7549	■	■	50
Riis Park	6100 W Fullerton Ave	312-746-5363	■	■	47
Rutherford Sayre Park	6871 W Belden Ave	312-746-5368	■		47
Union Park	1501 W Randolph St	312-746-5494	■		24

Park District—Southwest Region	*Address*	*Phone*	*Jog/Walk*	*Bike/Skate*	*Map*
Bogan Park	3939 W 79th St	773-284-6456	■		53
Cornell Square Park	1809 W 50th St	312-747-6097	■		54
Hayes Park	2936 W 85th St	312-747-6177	■		54
LeClaire Courts/Hearst Community	5120 W 44th St	312-747-6438	■		53
Mt Greenwood Park	3724 W 111th St	312-747-6564	■		55
Rainey Park	4350 W 79th St	773-284-0696	■		53
Senka Park	5656 S St Louis Ave	312-747-7632	■		54
Sherman Park	1301 W 52nd St	312-747-6672	■		54
Avalon Park	1215 E 83rd St	312-747-6015	■		57
Bradley Park	9729 S Yates Ave	312-747-6022	■		60
Gately Park	810 E 103rd St	312-747-6155	■		59
Hamilton Park	513 W 72nd St	312-747-6174	■		57
Lake Meadows Park	3117 S Rhodes Ave	312-747-6287	■	■	14
Meyering Playground Park	7140 S Martin Luther King Dr	312-747-6545	■		57
Palmer Park	201 E 111th St	312-747-6576	■		59
Rosenblum Park	8050 S Chappel Ave	312-747-6649	■		60
Washington Park	5531 S Martin Luther King Dr	773-256-1248	■	■	57

Park District—Lakefront Region	*Address*	*Phone*	*Jog/Walk*	*Bike/Skate*	*Map*
Calumet Park	9801 S Ave G	312-747-6039	■		60
Jackson Park	6401 S Stony Island Ave	773-256-0903	■	■	58
Lincoln Park	2045 Lincoln Park West	312-742-7726	■	■	30
Loyola Park	1230 W Greenleaf Ave	773-262=8605	■	■	34
Rainbow Park & Beach	3111 E 77th St	312-745-1479		■	58

General Information

Chicagoland Bicycle Federation:	650 S Clark St, #300, 312-427-3325; www.biketraffic.org
Chicago Park District:	www.chicagoparkdistrict.com; 312-742-PLAY
Chicago Cycling Club:	www.chicagocyclingclub.org; 773-509-8093 (Organized weekend rides April through October)
Chicago Transit Authority:	www.transitchicago.com
DOT Bikes Website:	www.chicagobikes.org

Overview

Despite the environmental and physical benefits, and Mayor Daley's efforts to make Chicago streets more hospitable to pedallers, bike riders are still seen by most drivers as a road nuisance and the designated bike lanes on streets such as Milwaukee, King Drive, and Elston are a joke—illegal passing lanes are more like it. Furthermore, designated lakefront bike paths are more often than not crowded with headphone-wearing roller bladers, leashless dogs, and shoulder-to-shoulder stroller pushers. Nonetheless, every year thousands of Chicagoans choose to take their lives into their hands by taking it to the street in a demonstration of the type of urban perseverance by which great cities were built. Or is it simple foolhardiness?

If you are a cyclist in Chicago, bear in mind that bicycles, like other vehicles of the roads, are subject to the same laws and rights as drivers—but good luck enforcing them. This includes the right to take a lane and the obligation to hand signal for turns. Helmets are still optional, but you'd have to have a pretty thick head to tempt fate without one. The same goes for an adequate assortment of chains and u-locks. Bike thievery is rampant in every neighborhood in the city.

Bikes Onboard Mass Transit

Bicycles are permitted (free) on all L trains at all times except 7 am–9 am and 4 pm–6 pm on weekdays. Use the accessible turnstile or ask an attendant to open an access gate. Don't try to take your bike through the tall steel gates—it will get stuck! Only two bikes per carriage are allowed, so check for other bikes before you get on. Bikes are only permitted on CTA buses equipped with front exterior bike racks, such as the 63rd Street, 72 North Avenue, 75th Street, and 65 Grand buses. If your bike is the first to be loaded, lower the rack and place it in position with the front wheel facing the curb. If there is already a bike on the rack, place your bike's rear wheel toward the curb. If two bikes are already loaded, wait for the next bus. Plan on taking the Metra? Leave your bike at home! Items larger than a briefcase are not permitted on Metra trains.

Bike Shops	*Address*	*Phone*	*Map*
Kozy Cyclery	219 W Erie St	312-266-1700	2
Sport Mart	620 N La Salle Dr	312-337-6151	2
Bike Chicago	600 E Grand Ave	312-755-0488	3
Mission Bay Multi Sports	738 W Randolph St	312-466-9111	4
Kozy Cyclery	601 S La Salle St	312-360-0020	8
Cycle Bike Shop	1465 S Michigan Ave	312-987-1080	11
Wheels & Things	5210 S Harper Ave	773-493-4326	19
Art's Cycle	1646 E 55th St	773-363-7524	20
Rapid Transit Cycle Shop	1900 W North Ave	773-227-2288	21
Quick Release Bike Shop	1527 N Ashland Ave	773-871-3110	22
Working Bikes Cooperative	1125 S Western Ave	312-421-5048	23
Boulevard Bikes	2535 N Kedzie Blvd	773-235-9109	27
Upgrade Cycle Works	1130 W Chicago Ave	312-226-8650	24
Irv's Bike Shop	1725 S Racine Ave	312-226-6330	26
Oscar Wastyn Cycles	2634 W Fullerton Ave	773-384-8999	27
Kozy Cyclery	1451 W Webster Ave	773-528-2700	29
Cycle Smithy	2468 1/2 N Clark St	773-281-0444	30
Performance Bicycle Shop	2720 N Halsted St	773-248-0107	30
Village Cycle Center	1337 N Wells St	312-726-2453	31
Roberts Cycle	7054 N Clark St	773-274-9281	34
Uptown Bikes	4653 N Broadway St	773-728-5212	40
On The Route Bicycles	3146 N Lincoln Ave	773-477-5066	43
Johnny Sprocket's	3001 N Broadway	773-244-1079	44
Kozy Cyclery	3712 N Halstead St	773-281-2263	44
Sports Authority	3134 N Clark St	773-871-8500	44
Edgebrook Cycle & Sport	6450 N Central Ave	773-792-1669	46
Yojimbo's Garage	1310 N Clybourn Ave	312-587-0878	31

General Information

Chicago Park District: 312-742-PLAY (7529); www.chicagoparkdistrict.com

Overview

Due to the temperature extremes that Chicago experiences, its residents can enjoy both ice skating and inline skating at various times of the year. Ice skating can be a fun, free winter activity if you have your own skates, and if you don't many rinks rent them. Skateboarding is also a popular pastime and a number of parks throughout the city are equipped with skating facilities.

Inline Skating

Similar to bike riding, inline skating in Chicago serves dual purposes. If you plan on strapping on the blades to get from A to B, be super-careful navigating the streets. As it is, Chicago drivers tend to have difficulty seeing cyclers, and chances are they won't notice you until you've slammed into their open car door. Wear protective gear whenever possible, especially a helmet, and learn to shout loudly so that people can anticipate your approach. If recreational skating is more your speed, check out the Recreational Paths page for cool places to skate. If you'd like to join the hundreds of summer skaters out there, and you don't have your own gear, the following places offer skate rental: Londo Mondo, 1100 N Dearborn St at W Maple St, 312-751-2794; Bike Chicago at Navy Pier, 312-755-0488. Hourly rates range from $7 to $10, while daily rates are from $20 to $35.

Skate Parks

If what you're after is a phat jam session, grab your blades or board and a couple of buddies and head down to the magnificent Burnham Skate Park (east of Lake Shore Drive at 31st St). With amazing grinding walls and rails, vert walls, and banks, Burnham Park presents hours of fun and falls. Less intense but equally fun are the two skate parks with ramps, quarter pipes, and grind rails. One can be found at West Lawn Park (4233 W 65th St, 773-284-2803) the other at Oriole Park (5430 N Olcott Ave, 773-631-6197).

Ice Skating

The long-running and popular Skate on State was canceled due to the opening of two new ice rinks: the McCormick Tribune Ice Rink at Millennium Park and the Midway Plaisance ice rink.

The rink at Millennium Park is a beautiful place to skate during the day or evening, with Chicago's glorious skyline in the background. And after the ice melts, the area plays host to al fresco dining and entertainment in the summer months. Located at 55 N Michigan Ave, enter on the east side of Michigan Avenue between Monroe Drive and Randolph Street. Parking is available for $10 at the Grant Park North Garage. (Enter from Michigan Avenue median at Washington or Madison Streets.) Entry is free, skate rental is $7, and if you have your own and want them sharpened there's a $5 fee (312-742-5222; www.millenniumpark.org).

The Olympic-sized skating rink and warming house complex at Midway Plaisance is the alternative to Millennium Park. Located at 59th and Woodlawn Ave, entry is free and skate rentals cost $3. During the summer, the facility is used for rollerskating and other entertainment (312-745-2470).

Other ice skating rinks are located seasonally at:

McFetridge Sports Complex (year-round) • 3843 N California Ave, 773-478-2609 (admission is $4 for kids under 12 years, $5 for adults + $3 skate rental)

Daley Bicentennial Plaza Rink • 337 E Randolph St, 312-742-7648 (free admission + $4 rental)

McKinley Park • 2210 W Pershing Rd, 312-747-6527 ($3–$5 rental)

Mt. Greenwood Park • 3721 W 111th St, 312-747-6564 ($2–$3 rental)

Navy Pier Ice Rink • 600 E Grand Ave, 312-595-5100 ($12 admission + rental)

Riis Park • 6100 W Fullerton Ave, 312-746-5363 ($2–$3 rental)

The Rink (roller skating) • 1122 E 87th St, 773-221-2600 ($1)

Rowan Park • 11546 S Avenue L, 773-646-1967 ($2–$3 rental)

Warren Park • 6601 N Western Ave, 773-262-6314 ($4 admission + $4 rental)

West Lawn Park • 4233 W 65th St, 773-284-2803 (free admission + $5 rental)

Gear

If you're after skateboard gear, check out Air Time Skate Boards at 3317 N Clark St, 773-248-4970 and Uprise Skateboard Shop at 1820 N Milwaukee Ave, 773-342-7763.

For skating equipment, Air Time (above) also does inline skates, as does Londo Mondo which has two locations: 1100 N Dearborn Street at W Maple St, 312-751-2794 and 2148 N Halstead St, 773-327-2218.

For all your ice skating needs, try the Skater's Edge store in the McFetridge Sports Complex (3843 N California Ave, 773-463-1505). They deal in hockey skates and other equipment as well as inline skates and accessories such as sequined dresses!

There are a number of golf courses and driving ranges within the city limits, so you can spend a day on the green or hit a few balls before the shops and museums open. Jackson Park is the Chicago Park District's premiere 18-hole facility, and the scenery alone will make you forget the bustle of the city. Sydney R. Marovitz Golf Course is usually busy, but it has great views of the lake. Harborside International is the place to go if you're looking for a challenging Scottish-links experience; visit Family Golf Center for a lunchtime 9.

Golf Courses	*Address*	*Phone*	*Map*	*weekdays*	*weekends*
Riverside Golf Club	2320 Desplaines Ave	708-447-1049	10	$65	$75
Robert A Black Golf Course	2045 W Pratt Blvd	312-742-7931	34	$16	$17.50
Sydney R Marovitz Golf Course	3600 N Recreation Dr	312-742-7930	43	$19.75	$22.75
Edgebrook Golf Course	6100 N Central Ave	773-763-8320	NW	$24–44	$28–49
Indian Boundary Golf Course	8600 W Forest Preserve Ave	773-625-9630	NW	$25–44	$28–49
Columbus Park Golf Course	5701 W Jackson Blvd	312-746-5573	W	$12	$13.50
Marquette Park Golf Course	6700 S Kedzie Ave	312-245-0909	SW	$15	$16.25
Harborside International Golf Center	11001 S Doty Ave	312-782-7837	S	$80	$92
Jackson Park Golf Course	63rd St & Lake Shore Dr	773-667-0524	S	$22.50	$25.50
South Shore Country Club	7059 S South Shore Dr	312-245-0909	S	$14.25	$15.50
Peter N Jans Community Golf Course	1031 Central St	847-475-9173	Evanston	$17	$23
Glencoe Park District Course	621 Westley Rd, Glencoe	847-835-0250	n/a	$37	$45
The Glen Club	2901 W Lake Ave, Glenview	847-724-7272	n/a	$105–140	$117–155
Winnetka Park District Course	1300 Oak St, Winnetka	847-501-2050	n/a	$40	$46

Driving Ranges	*Address*	*Phone*	*Map*	*Fees*
Diversey Driving Range	141 W Diversey Dr	312-742-7929	3	$11/100 balls, $2 clubs
Jackson Park Golf Course	63rd St & Lake Shore Dr	773-667-0524	S	$6/50–65 balls, $2 clubs
Harborside International Golf Center	11001 S Doty Ave	312-782-7837	S	$10/100 balls, $3 clubs

Volleyball Courts

Hoops The Gym • 312-850-4667
Two locations: 1380 W Randolph St; 1001 W Washington Blvd
State-of-the-art court rentals. 24/7.

Lincoln Park/North Avenue Beach • 312-742-7529 (reservations and price information)
101 courts—12 are always open to the public. Much league play and reserved courts.
Office hours: Mon–Fri: 1 pm–9 pm; Weekends: 8 am–5 pm.

Lincoln Park/Montrose Beach • 312-742-5121
45 courts allotted on a first-come-first-served basis. League play in the evening.

Jackson Park/63rd Street Beach • 312-742-4838
Four free courts—first-come-first-served.

312-742-PLAY (general park info); 312-742-5121 (Department of Beaches and Pools).

All outdoor pools are free for the summer (Memorial Day-Labor Day). During the year, all lap swim fees for indoor pools are for 10-week sessions ($20 before 9 am; $10 after 9 am). Register for aquatic exercise, diving, lifeguard, underwater hockey, and water polo classes at chicagoparkdistrict.com.

Outdoor Pools	*Address*	*Phone*	*Map*
Wentworth Gardens Park	3770 S Wentworth Ave	312-747-6996	13
Taylor Park	41 W 47th St	312-747-6728	15
Washington Park	5531 S Martin Luther King Dr	773-256-1248	18
Pulaski Park	1419 W Blackhawk St	312-742-7559	22
Union Park	1501 W Randolph St	312-746-5494	24
Dvorak Park	1119 W Cullerton St	312-746-5083	26
Wrightwood Park	2534 N Greenview Ave	312-742-7816	29
River Park	5100 N Francisco Ave	312-742-7516	38
Chase Park	4701 N Ashland Ave	312-742-7518	40
McFetridge Sports Center (California Park)	3843 N California Ave	773-478-2609	41
Hamlin Park	3035 N Hoyne Ave	312-742-7785	42

Indoor Pools	*Address*	*Phone*	*Map*
McGuane Park	2901 S Poplar Ave	312-747-7463	12
Dyett Recreational Center	513 E 51st St	312-745-1211	16
Clemente Park	2334 W Division St	312-742-7466	21
Eckhart Park	1330 W Chicago Ave	312-746-5553	24
Harrison Park	1824 S Wood St	312-746-9490	25
Sheridan Park	910 S Aberdeen St	312-746-5370	26
Stanton Park	618 W Scott St	312-742-9553	31
Mather Park	5941 N Richmond St	773-534-2412	35
Welles Park	2333 W Sunnyside Ave	312-742-7515	39
Gill Park	833 W Sheridan Rd	312-742-5807	43

Bowling Alleys	*Address*	*Phone*	*Rate*	*Map*
10 Pin-Strike Bar Bowl & Grille	330 N State St	312-644-0300	$6.96 game, $5.95 shoes	2
Lucky Strike Lanes	322 E Illinois St	312-245-8331	$5.95 game, $3.95 shoes	3
7-10 Bowl	1055 E 55th St	773-347-2695	$16 per hour per lane, $2 shoes	19
Spare Time	2747 N Lincoln Ave	773-549-2695	$20/hr per lane, $2 shoes	29
Timber Lanes	1851 W Irving Park Rd	773-549-9770	$3 game, $2 shoes	39
Diversey-River Bowl	2211 W Diversey Pkwy	773-227-5800	Mon-Thurs: $19/hr per lane; Fri-Sat: $26/hr per lane, after 6 pm: $32/hr per lane; Sun $26/hr per lane, $3 shoes	42
Waveland Bowl	3700 N Western Ave	773-472-5900	$3 game before 4 pm, $4 game after 4 pm; $2 shoes	42
Southport Lanes & Billiards	3325 N Southport Ave	773-472-6600	Mon–Thurs: $15/hr per lane; Fri–Sat: $20/hr per lane; Sun: $10/hr per lane, $2 shoes	43
Habetler Bowl	5250 N Northwest Hwy	773-774-0500	$4 game for adults, $2.50 for kids; $1 game Tuesdays after 9:30 pm and Thursdays from 9 am–4 pm, $3.50 shoes	46
Fireside Bowling Alleys	2648 W Fullerton Ave	773-486-2700	$2.50 game or $15 per hour, $2 shoes	W

While we admit we're suckers for any sport that includes the word "love" in its scoring system, we try not to think of the significance that it means "zero" in tennis talk. Find love and more at these Chicago tennis courts.

All tennis courts (except Daley Bicentennial Plaza in Grant Park, Diversey Park, Chase Park, California Park, and Waveland Park) are free and open to the public on a first-come-first-served basis. Courts are open daily—check each park for individual hours. 312-742-7529 (general info); 773-256-0949 (Lake Front Region Office).

Tennis Courts	*Address*	*Phone*	*Fees*	*Map*
Daley Bicentennial Plaza	337 E Randolph St	312-742-7648	$7/hr; reservations required	6
Grant Park	331 E Randolph St	312-742-7648		6
Roosevelt Park	62 W Roosevelt Rd	312-742-7648		8
Mandrake Park	900 E Pershing Rd	312-747-7661		12
McGuane Park	2901 S Poplar Ave	312-747-6497		12
Armour Square Park	3309 S Shields Ave	312-747-6012		13
Ellis Park	707 E 37th St	312-746-5962		14
Fuller Park	331 W 45th St	312-747-6144		15
Taylor Park	41 W 47th St	312-747-6728		15
Metcalfé Park	4134 S State St	312-747-6728		16
Kenwood Community Park	1330 E 50th St	312-747-6286		17
Nichols Park	1355 E 53rd St	312-747-2703		19
Clemente Park	2334 W Division St	312-742-7538		21
Union Park	1501 W Randolph St	312-746-5494		24
Harrison Park	1824 S Wood St	312-746-5491		25
Sheridan Park	910 S Aberdeen St	312-746-5369		26
Jonquil Park	1023 W Wrightwood Ave	N/A		29
Oz Park	2021 N Burling St	312-742-7898		30
Lake Shore Park	808 N Lake Shore Dr	312-742-7891		32
Indian Boundary Park	2500 W Lunt Ave	773-764-0338		33
Lerner Park	7000 N Sacramento Ave	N/A		33
Rogers Park	7345 N Washtenaw Ave	773-262-1482		33
Warren Park	6601 N Western Ave	773-262-6314		33
Loyola Park	1230 W Greenleaf Ave	773-262-8605		34
Pottawattomie Park	7340 N Rogers Ave	773-262-5835		34
Touhy Park	7348 N Paulina St	773-262-6737		34
Green Briar Park	2650 W Peterson Ave	773-761-0582		35
Legion Park at the Chicago River	W Peterson Ave to W Foster Ave at the Chicago River	N/A		35
Mather Park	5941 N Richmond St	312-742-7501		35
Emmerson Playground Park	1820 W Granville Ave	773-761-0433		36
Senn Park	1550 W Thorndale Ave	N/A		37
Horner Park	2741 W Montrose Ave	773-478-3499		38
River Park	5100 N Francisco Ave	312-742-7516		38
Welles Park	2333 W Sunnyside Ave	312-742-7511		39
Chase Park	4701 N Ashland Ave	312-742-7518	$5/hr	40
Brands Park	3259 N Elston Ave	773-478-2414		41
California Park	3843 N California Ave	773-478-2609		41
Revere Park	2509 W Irving Park Rd	773-478-1220		41
McFetridge Sports Center (California Park)	3843 N California Ave	773-478-2609	$16-$24/hr	41
Hamlin Park	3035 N Hoyne Ave	312-742-7785		42
Lincoln Park-Diversey Tennis Center	2800 N Lake Shore Dr	312-742-7821	$16/hr; reservations must be made in person	44
Lincoln Park-Waveland Tennis Center	W Waveland Ave & N Lake Shore Dr	312-742-7674	$7/hr; reservations required	44

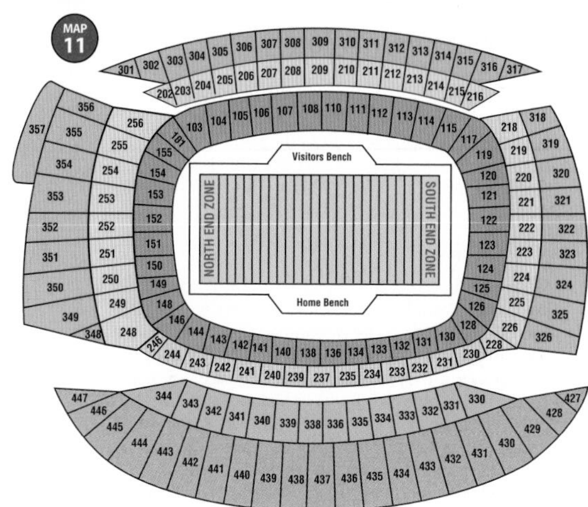

General Information

NFT Map:	11
Address:	1410 S Museum Campus Dr Chicago, IL 60605
Phone:	312-235-7000
Lost & Found:	312-235-7202
Website:	www.soldierfield.net
Box Office:	847-615-BEAR (2327)
Bears Website:	www.chicagobears.com
Ticketmaster:	312-559-1212; www.ticketmaster.com

Overview

The "new" Soldier Field is big, burly, and visually abrasive, *much like the pre-game tailgaters in the parking lots*. Plans began for its construction in 1919 as a memorial to American soldiers who died in the wars. It officially opened on October 9th, 1924 (the 53rd anniversary of the Chicago Fire) as Municipal Grant Park Stadium. Renamed and dedicated in 1925, Soldier Field eventually became a key installment in the multi-million-dollar Lakefront Improvement Plan for the Chicago shoreline between Navy Pier and McCormick Place. An estimated $365 million went toward the 63,000-seat stadium, which opened in time for the 2003–2004 NFL Season and debuted on ABC's *Monday Night Football*. Improved Solider Field amenities include 60% more seating on the sidelines, twice as many bathrooms (with 1,000 fixtures), three times as many concessions stands (400), several cozy meeting nooks throughout the stadium, two 82 x 23-foot video screens, and a 100,000-square-foot lounge/entertainment facility. Critics debate whether the expanded structure resembles a giant toilet-bowl or a flying saucer (Voters Decide: Toilet Bowl Wins in a Landslide!). Maybe 2006 will be the year of the "Toilet Bowl Shuffle!" But the fact remains that the Bears have yet to experience a winning season in the new facility. After the disappointing 2004–2005, all eyes are on Bears Head Coach Lovie Smith as he and his staff recruit, rework, and rebuild this historic franchise.

How to Get Tickets

Contact Ticketmaster to purchase individual game tickets. Season tickets should be easier to come by for the 2005–2006 season because it is a rebuilding year for the Bears. The best way to get great seats (other than by having them left to you in a will) is to work with a licensed ticket broker. Fans marked their territory early in 2004 by purchasing a one-time Permanent Seat License (PSL), and in exchange for paying big premiums to help cover construction expenses, PSL holders are promised first choice of ticket seating each year. Of the stadium's 63,000 seats, 27,500 are PSL zones and the remaining 33,500 are non-licensed seats in the stadium's higher altitudes. A $100 per-seat, non-refundable deposit is required to get on a season ticket waiting list. The deposit will be applied to the first year of non-PSL season tickets and you can find an application on the Bears website.

How to Get There

By Car: From the north or south, take Lake Shore Drive; follow the signs to Soldier Field. For parking lots, exit at E McFetridge, E Waldron, E 14th Boulevard, and E 18th Drive. From the west, take I-55 E to Lake Shore Drive, turn north, and follow the signs. Travel east on I-290, then south on I-90/94 to I-55; get on I-55 E to Lake Shore Drive.

Parking lots surrounding Soldier Field cost between $7 and $12, including the new underground North Parking Garage. Call the Standard Parking Customer Service Hotline with questions (312-583-9153). Two parking and game-day tailgating lots are located south of Waldron Drive. There are also lots on the Museum Campus off McFetridge Drive and near McCormick Place off 31st Street and E 18th Street.

By Train: On game days, CTA Soldier Field Express bus 128 runs non-stop between the Ogilvie Transportation Center and Union Station to Soldier Field. Service starts two hours before the game, runs up to 45 minutes before kickoff, and up to 45 minutes post-game.

By L: Take the Red, Orange, or Green Lines to the Roosevelt station stop. Either board eastbound CTA bus 12 or the free Green Trolley to the Museum Campus, and then walk south to Soldier Field.

By Bus: CTA buses 12, 127, and 146 stop on McFetridge Drive near Soldier Field. Contact the RTA Information Center for routes and schedules at 312-836-7000 or online at www.rtachicago.com.

By Trolley: The Green Trolley travels along Michigan Avenue, Washington Street, Canal Street, and Adams Street to the Museum Campus. From there, you can walk south to the field. For routes and schedules, visit www.cityofchicago.org/transportation.

General Information

NFT Map: 43
Address: 1060 W Addison St
Chicago, IL 60613
Cubs Box Office Phone: 773-404-2827
Tickets.com: 800-THE-CUBS (843-2827)
Lost & Found: 773-404-4185
Website: www.cubs.com

Overview

North-side baseball fans descend upon Wrigley Field like faithful Catholics to St. Peter's in Rome. Built in 1914 and originally known as Weeghman Park, the stadium was renamed Wrigley Field in 1926 to honor chewing gum mogul and former Cub owner William Wrigley, Jr. It is the second-oldest ball park in Major League Baseball (Boston's Fenway Park—1912) and is a refreshing throwback to simpler times. Ivy-strewn walls, classic grass field, and a manual scoreboard transcend both time and technology during this age of artificial playing surfaces and high-tech super stadiums. The glow from night-game lights warms the hearts of most North Chicago locals who aren't game attendees. On the other side of the fence, Wrigleyville activists have lobbied to limit the amount of time the lights are burning in an attempt to limit their neighborhood's party reputation, to stop drunks peeing in alleyways, and to protect their over-inflated property values.

Wrigley Field has been the site of some of baseball's most historic moments: Ernie Banks's 500th career home run in 1970, Kerry Wood's twenty strikeouts in 1998, and Sammy Sosa's sixty home runs in 1998, 1999, and 2001. The Cubs haven't won a World Series title since their back-to-back wins over Detroit in 1907 and 1908, yet this loveable losing team has one of the most impressive attendance records in Major League Baseball. Of course, most patrons pay no attention to the game as an outing to Wrigley has become an opportunity to drink beer and "be seen." Perhaps in 2007, the prayers of faithful fans will finally be answered. Regardless of whether the Cubs win or lose, they still get to call "The Friendly Confines" home. Nostalgia for the "old school" landmark ballpark has many fans challenging recent proposals to expand Wrigley Field.

How to Get Tickets

Individual game tickets can be purchased from the Cubs' website, by calling 800-843-2827, or in person at some Chicagoland Sears and Sports Authority stores. You can also buy tickets at the Wrigley Field Box Office, open weekdays from 8 am to 6 pm and weekends from 9 am to 4 pm. You can usually score discount tickets to afternoon games Monday through Thursday in April, May, and September. Children aged two and up require tickets.

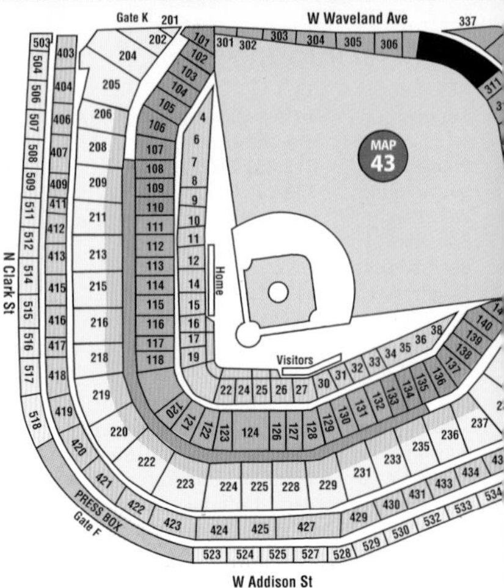

How to Get There

By Car: If you must… Remember the old days when Wrigleyville hillbillies used to let you park on their front lawns for five bucks? Well, today traffic on game days is horrendous and parking prices are sky-high. Post-game spill-out from local bars freezes traffic as police do their best to prevent drunken revelers from stumbling into the streets. From the Loop or south, take Lake Shore Drive north; exit at Irving Park Road, and head west to Clark Street; turn south on Clark Street to Wrigley Field. From the north, take Lake Shore Drive to Irving Park Road; head west to Clark Street, and turn south. From Chicago's West Side, take I-290 E or I-55 N to Lake Shore Drive, then follow directions above. From the northwest, take I-90 E and exit at Addison Street; travel east three miles. From the southwest side, take I-55 N to I-90/94 N. Exit at Addison Street; head east to the park.

Street parking around Wrigley Field is heavily restricted. The Cubs operate a garage at 1126 W Grace Street. Purchase parking passes through the mail or at the Wrigley Field Box Office. On game nights, tow trucks cruise Wrigleyville's streets nabbing cars without a resident permit sticker. Park smart at the DeVry Institute, and catch CTA bus 154/Wrigley Express to and from the park. ($6 covers parking and roundtrip shuttle per carload.)

By L: Riding the Howard/Dan Ryan Red Line is the fastest and easiest way to get to Wrigley Field ($1.75 one-way). Get off at the Addison Street stop one block east of the field.

By Bus: CTA buses 22, 8, and 152 stop closest to Wrigley Field ($1.75 one-way). For routes and schedules, visit www.rtachicago.com.

General Information

NFT Map:	13
Address:	333 W 35th St Chicago, IL 60616
General Info:	312-674-1000
Ticket Sales:	866-SOX-GAME
Website:	www.whitesox.com

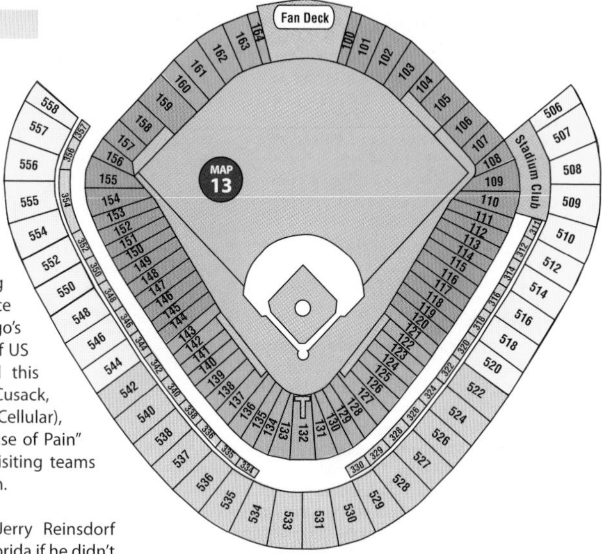

Overview

So when the phrase "new and improved" is used when speaking about the White Sox, they are talking about the team and not what was once the parking lot of South Side Chicago's iconic Comiskey Park, now the locale of US Cellular Field. Chicagoans nicknamed this monstrosity "The Joan" (after Joan Cusack, local resident and spokesperson for US Cellular), and it's now better known as the "House of Pain" because of the hurt the Sox put on visiting teams during their 2005 Championship Season.

In 1988 Chicago White Sox owner Jerry Reinsdorf threatened to move the White Sox to Florida if he didn't get a new stadium. Not only did the notoriously cheap Reinsdorf get his wish, he got taxpayers to pick up the tab for the $167 million US Cellular Field. The park opened in 1991 to mixed reviews and was renovated as recently as 2003 to accommodate the MLB All-Star Game. Where Wrigley Field is intimate, "The Joan" is boorish and somewhat whorish. This is the ballpark where rowdy fans rush the field to pummel umpires into submission and assault off-duty Chicago Police Officers (and their wives!) when asked to curtail their expletive-laden jeering. The oft-Bohemic White Sox fans shout creative strings of curse words (between beer guzzles and finger flip-offs) and no one is spared from their gritty offensiveness. But under all the crass commentary burns a fierce love for a tough ball club that has given its passionate fans plenty to cheer about…especially after bringing home the World Series Trophy in 2005. Manager Ozzie Guillen, who oddly enough is as rough, gruff, and outspoken as the ballpark itself, commands yet another tight squad in 2006 and looks to be in perfect position and form to repeat as World Champs.

How to Get Tickets

Purchase tickets through the team's website (www.whitesox.mlb.com) or at the US Cellular Field Box Office (weekdays: 10 am–6 pm, weekends: 10 am–4 pm). Children shorter than the park's turnstile arm (approximately 36 inches) are admitted free, but must share your seat. Ballpark bargains include Half-Price Mondays for all regular seats, Pepsi Two-for-One Tuesdays (an empty Pepsi product plus the purchase of one Upper Level ticket earns you another seat for free), and Willy Wonka's Kids Days on select Sundays when children 13 and under get in for $1. All discounted tickets must be purchased at park ticket windows on game day. Check the website for Value Days schedules.

How to Get There

By Car: US Cellular Field is located at the 35th Street exit off the Dan Ryan Expressway. Take I-90/94, stay in the local lanes, and exit at 35th Street. If you possess a prepaid green parking coupon or plan on paying cash for parking ($18), exit at 35th Street. Follow signs to "Sox Parking" at lots E, F, and L on the stadium's south side. Fans with red, prepaid season parking coupons exit at 31st Street, and follow signs for "Red Coupons" to lots A, B, and C just north of the stadium. If the 35th Street exit is closed due to heavy traffic, which is often the case on game days, proceed to the 39th Street exit; turn right for "Sox Parking" and left for "Red Coupons." The handicapped parking and stadium drop-off area is in Lot D, west of the field and accessible via 37th Street.

By Bus: CTA buses 24 and 35 stop closest to the park. Others stopping in the vicinity are the 29, 44, and 39. Armies of cops surround the venue on game days because the neighborhood is rough, especially at night.

By L: Ride the Red Line to the Sox-35th Street stop just west of the ballpark. Get off the Green Line at the 35th-Bronzeville-IIT Station.

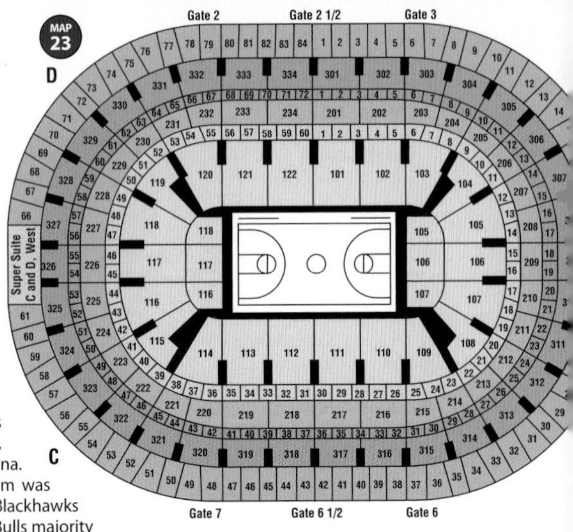

General Information

NFT Map: 23
Address: 1901 W Madison St
Chicago, IL 60612
Phone: 312-455-4500
Website: www.unitedcenter.com
Ticketmaster: 312-559-1212;
www.ticketmaster.com
Chicago Bulls: 312-455-4000
Bulls Website: www.bulls.com
Chicago Blackhawks: 312-455-7000
Blackhawks Website:
www.chicagoblackhawks.com

Overview

The commanding crown of Chicago's developing West Town District, the United Center is home to both the NHL's Blackhawks and the NBA's Bulls. This ultra-high-tech stadium is also a theater, convention hall, and premier concert arena. Opened in 1994, the $175 million stadium was privately funded by deep-pocketed Blackhawks owner William Wirtz and penny-pinching Bulls majority owner Jerry Reinsdorf (a privately funded and owned stadium—what a concept!) and built to replace the beloved but aging Chicago Stadium. The Bulls have had trouble recapturing both the winning record and popularity they experienced during the Michael Jordan era; however, they still manage to sell out most of their home games. Local hopes are placed squarely on the shoulders of head coach Scott Skiles, and with the Bulls gaining momentum in the standings with each passing season, Skiles's efforts seem to be paying off. And just in case you forget whose "house" this is, the impressive statue of Michael Jordan located in front of the main entrance to the United Center is there to remind you.

Although it's been some time since the Blackhawks won the Stanley Cup (1961), the team enjoys unwavering support from its boisterous fans who relish games against their long-standing rivals, the St. Louis Blues. The Blackhawks' prior trips to the playoffs (2001–2002 season) and the lack of a season at all in 2004–2005 resulted in record attendance (but unfortunately not a record performance) for the 2006 season. Coach Brian Sutter is still at the reins of this storied franchise and hopes to heat things up on the ice once again in 2007. Chicago Blackhawks fans are some of the more loyal in the NHL and will show up for 2007 in full battle gear. Suffice to say, nothing short of bringing home the Stanley Cup will do for this team and their devout fans.

How to Get Tickets

Book tickets over the phone or online with Ticketmaster, by United Center mail order, or visit the United Center box office at Gate 4. Box office hours are Monday to Saturday, 11 am to 6 pm. For Bulls and Blackhawks season tickets and group bookings call the phone numbers above.

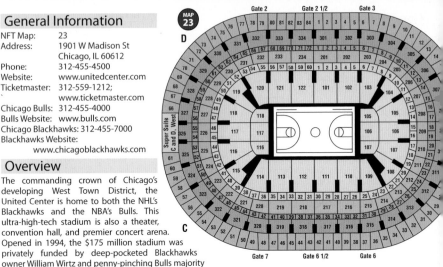

How to Get There

By Car: From the Loop, drive west on Madison Street to United Center. From the north, take I-90/94 and exit at Madison Street; head west to the stadium. From the southwest, take I-55 N to the Damen/Ashland exit; head north to Madison Street. From the west, take I-290 E to the Damen Avenue exit; go north to Madison Street.

Parking lots surround United Center, as do countless cops. General public parking is in Lot B on Warren Boulevard (cars, $15–31; limo, RV, and bus parking, $25). Lot H on Wood Street is closest to the stadium and is reserved for VIPs. Disabled parking is in Lots G and H on Damen Avenue.

By L: Take the Forest Park Branch of the Blue Line to the Medical Center-Damen Avenue Station. Walk two blocks north to United Center.

By Bus: CTA bus 19 United Center Express is the most intelligent and safest choice. In service only on event and game days, this express bus travels from Chicago Avenue south down Michigan Avenue, then west along Madison Street to the United Center. Michigan Avenue stops are at Chicago Avenue, Illinois Street, and Randolph Street. On Madison Street, stops are at State Street, Wells Street, and Clinton Street ($1.75 one-way). Service starts two hours before events and continues for 45 minutes after events. CTA bus 20 also travels Madison Street beginning at Wabash Avenue and has "owl service."

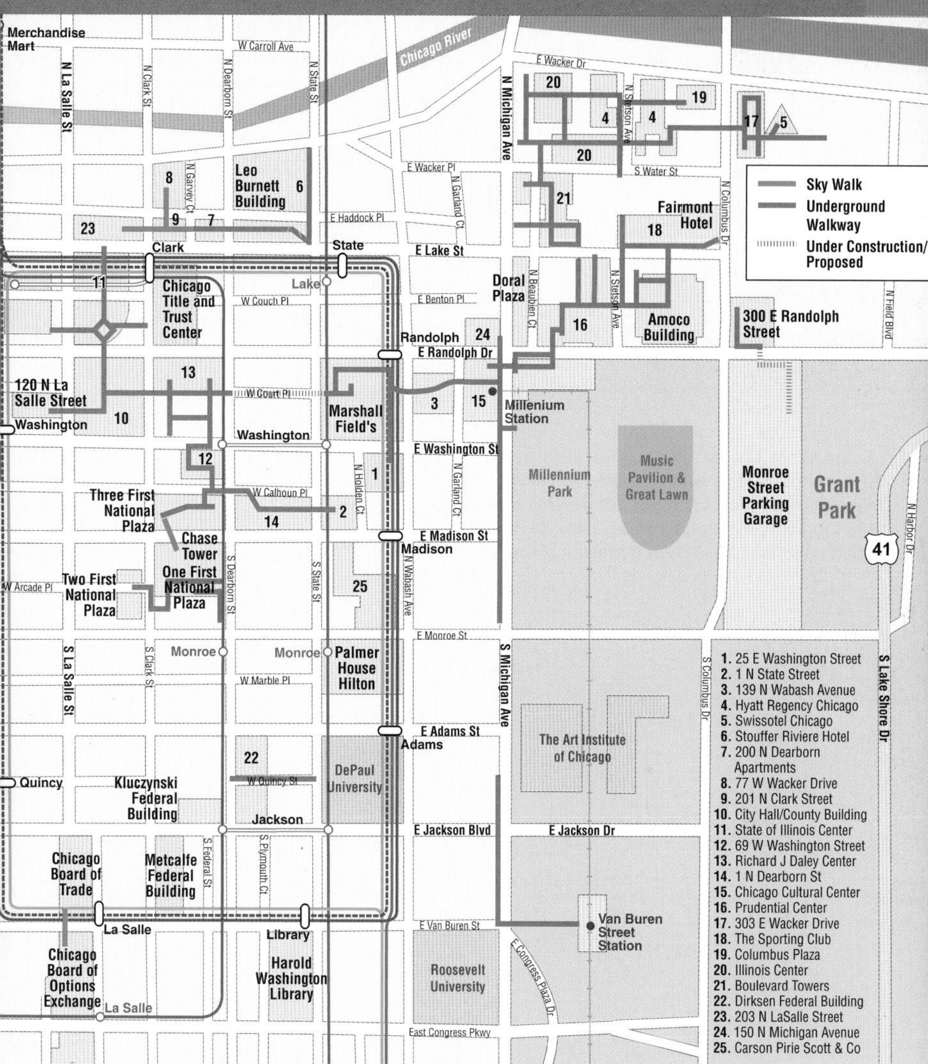

While a number of cold-weather cities are known for their above-ground walkways, Chicago is known for its Pedway, a 40-block network of tunnels and overhead bridges that connects important public, government, and private sector buildings with retail stores, major hotels, rapid transit stations, and commuter rail stations. A subterranean city with shops, restaurants, services, and public art works, the Pedway is a welcome alternative to navigating trafficked intersections on foot and walking outdoors in Chicago's frigid winters. The underground walkway system is open 24 hours; however, access to a number of the buildings is limited after standard business hours. The first Pedway links were built in 1951 to connect the State Street and Dearborn Street subways at Washington Street and Jackson Boulevard. Today, Chicago's Pedway continues to grow as city government and the private sector cooperate to expand it. Those planning on making a subterranean trip to experience the Pedway in its glory would do well to click on over to www.spiegl.org/pedway/pedway.html for a map of the whole lair.

General Information

Address:	10000 W O'Hare Chicago, IL 60666
Phone:	773-686-2200; 800-832-6352
Website:	www.ohare.com
Ground Transportation:	773-686-8040
Lost & Found:	773-894-8760
Parking:	773-686-7530
Traveler's Aid:	773-894-2427
Police:	773-686-2385
Customs Information:	773-894-2900

Overview

O'Delay might be a more fitting name for O'Hare, although Beck might take exception to such a name change. What else can we say about the world's busiest airport? To its credit, O'Hare, located in one of the country's most unpredictable weather zones, serves more than 190,000 travelers daily. While the airport is located just 17 miles northwest of the Loop, it's wise to leave the better part of a day to locate and arrive at your departure gate. Commuter traffic, airline snafus, parking, security checks, snowstorms, airport construction, and roadwork can make traveling from O'Hare as pleasurable as a migraine.

Expansion spells relief, according to Mayor Daley, who is pushing a controversial $6.6-billion plan designed to double O'Hare's capacity and secure its "busiest" title for the rest of the 21st century. The plan calls for building another runway, reconfiguring the other seven, building an additional entrance on the airport's west side, and spending millions soundproofing area homes and schools. Recently political opposition has thrown up hefty lawsuits to block legislation that would cement the deal into federal law.

Meanwhile, the rest of us are stuck in traffic, in line, on the runway, etc...

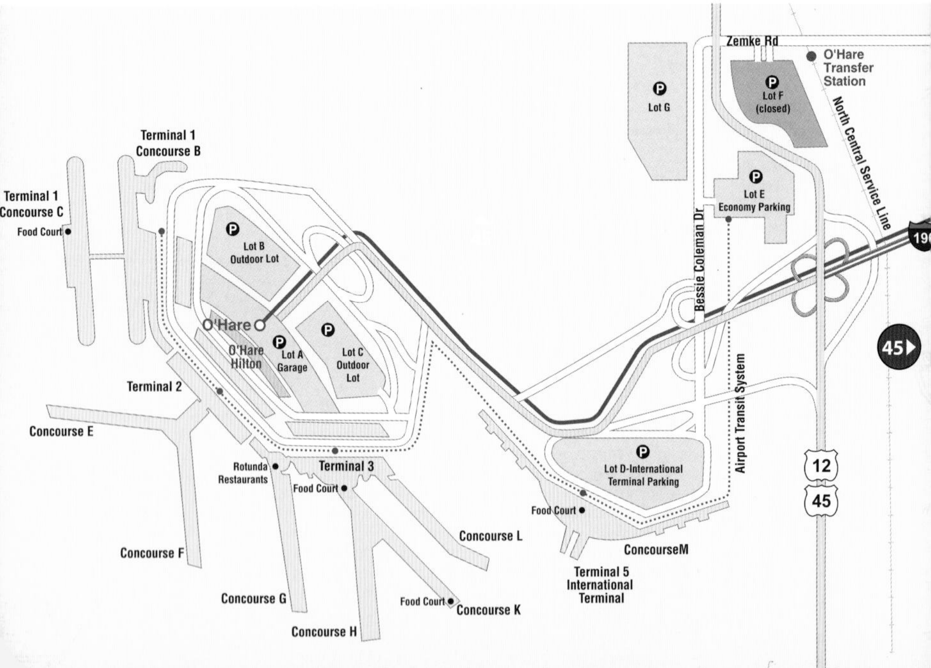

How to Get There

By Car: If you must drive, pack aspirin in your glove compartment along with your favorite CDs because the crawl down the Kennedy will probably be the most grueling part of your entire trip. To be on the safe side, allow over an hour just for the drive (more during rush hours). From the Loop to O'Hare, take I-90 W. From the north suburbs, take I-294 S. From the south suburbs, take I-294 N. From the west suburbs, take I-88 E to I-294 N. Get off all of the above highways at I-190, which leads you directly to the airport. All of the major routes have clear signage, easily legible when you're moving at a snail's pace.

Parking: O'Hare Airport's parking garage reflects its hometown's passion for sports. All levels of the Main Parking Garage are "helpfully" labeled with Chicago sports teams' colors and larger-than-life logos (Wolves, Bulls, Blackhawks, White Sox, Bears, and Cubs). Annoying elevator muzak whines each team's fight song. If this isn't enough to guide you to your car, we can't help you, because the garage's numbering-alphabetical system is more aggravating than the tinny elevator tunes.

If you're parking for less than three hours, go to Level 1. Parking costs $4 for the first 3 hours, $21 for up to 4 hours, and a deterring $50 per day. Overnight parking close to Terminals 1, 2, and 3 on Levels 2 through 6 of the garage or in outside lots B and C costs $26 a day. For flyers with cash to burn, valet parking is available on Level 1 of the garage for $10 per hour or $32 per day (8–24 hours). Parking in the International Terminal 5's designated Lot D costs $3 per hour for the first two hours and $2 per hour thereafter; the daily rate is $30. Incoming international passengers always disembark in Terminal 5 (even if the airline departs from another terminal) because passengers must clear customs.

Long-term parking lots are Economy Lots E and G, which cost $13 per day. From Lot E, walk or take the free shuttle to the free Airport Transit System (ATS) train station servicing all terminals. From Lot G, the shuttle will take you to the ATS stop in Lot E. Budget-conscious frequent flyers may want to purchase a prepaid Lot E "ExpressLane Parking" windshield tag for hassle-free, speedy departure from the airport. Lot F is currently closed until further notice.

How to Get There—*continued*

By Bus: CTA buses 220 and 330 stop at the airport. If you're not near either of those bus lines, your best bet is to take your nearest bus line north or south to one of the O'Hare Blue Line train stations. The CTA also offers a special door-to-door service to and from the airport for Chicago-area residents and out-of-towners needing extra assistance. Call 312-663-4357 for additional information.

By Train: The odds of the Metra's schedule conveniently coinciding with your flight time are only slightly better than those of the Bulls winning the championship this year. The Wisconsin North Central Line departs Union Station for Antioch with a stop at the O'Hare Transfer station five times a day, starting in the afternoons on weekdays only ($3.30 one-way). Travel time is 30 minutes.

By L: We recommend the Blue Line as the best transportation method if you don't have several large bags or dependents in tow. The train runs between downtown Chicago and O'Hare 24 hours a day every 8 to 10 minutes ($2.00 one-way or $1.75 with Chicago Card). Travel time from the Loop is 45 minutes. The train station is on the lowest level of the airport's main parking garage. Walk through the underground pedestrian tunnels to Terminals 1, 2, and 3. If you're headed for the International Terminal 5, walk to Terminal 3 and board the free Airport Transit System (ATS) train.

By Cab: Join the cab queue at the lower level curb-front of all terminals. There are no flat rates, as all of the cabs run on meters, but you probably won't have to spend more than $40. Beware if you're traveling to certain suburbs, though. Fare rules allow cabbies to raise your fare for these routes by 50%! Ask what the fare will be when you enter the cab. Some cab companies servicing O'Hare include American United, 773-262-8633; Flash Cab, 773-878-8500; Jiffy Cab, 773-487-9000; Yellow Cab, 312-808-9130; and Dispatch, 312-829-4222.

By Kiss & Fly: The Kiss & Fly is a convenient drop-off and pick-up point for "chauffeurs" who want to avoid the inevitable chaos at the terminal curb-side. Flyers should leave enough time for the ATS transfer to their terminals. The Kiss & Fly zone is off Bessie Coleman Drive. Take I-190 to the International Terminal exit to Bessie Coleman Drive. Turn left at the light and follow Bessie Coleman Drive north to the Kiss & Fly entrance and ATS stop.

By Shuttle: Continental Airport Express (773-247-1200 or 888-2-THEVAN) provides a daily shuttle service between O'Hare and downtown Chicago from 6 am until 11:30 pm with departures approximately every 10–15 minutes. Shuttles stop at all major downtown hotels. Tickets cost $23 one-way ($42 return) for individuals, $16 per person ($30 return) for pairs going to the same destination and returning together, and $12 per person ($23 return) for three or more going to the same downtown destination and returning together. Shuttle ticket counters are located in the baggage claim areas of Terminal 1 by Door 1E and Terminal 3 at Door 3E; however, shuttles pick up passengers at Terminals 1, 2, 3, and 5. If you haven't pre-purchased a ticket at a counter, have cash ready for the driver.

Omega Airport Shuttle offers hourly service between O'Hare and Midway beginning around 7 am each day 'til about 11:45 pm and between Hyde Park and O'Hare from 5 am to 11:45 pm. The shuttle leaves from the International Terminal's outside curb by Door 5E and from the airport's Bus Shuttle Center in front of the O'Hare Hilton Hotel by Door 4. Allow at least an hour for travel time between the airports and expect to pay $17 for a one-way fare. Omega also has over 20 pickup and drop-off locations on the South Side serving O'Hare and Midway Airports. (773-483-6634; www.omegashuttle.com).

By Limousine: Sounds pricey, but depending on where you're going and how many people you are traveling with, it may be cheaper to travel by limo than by cab or shuttle. Advance reservations recommended. Limo services include O'Hare-Midway Limousine Service, 312-558-1111 (or 800-468-8989 for airport pick-up), www.ohare-midway.com; and My Chauffeur/American Limo, 847-376-6100, www.americanlimousine.com.

Airlines

Airline	*Terminal*	*Phone*
Aer Lingus	5	888-474-7424
Air Canada	2	888-247-2262
Air Canada Jazz	2	888-247-2262
Air France	5	800-237-2747
Air India	5	800-621-8231
Air Jamaica	5	800-523-5585
Alaska Airlines	3	800-426-0333
Alitalia	5	800-223-5730
America West Airlines	2	800-235-9292
American Airlines:		800-443-7300
Domestic	3	
International	3 dep/5 arr	
American Eagle	3	800-433-7300
Asiana Airlines	5	800-227-4262
Aviacsa	5	888-528-4227
British Airways	5	800-247-9297
BMI British Midland	5	800-788-0555
Cayman Airways	5	800-422-9626
Continental Airlines	2	800-525-0280
Delta Airlines	3	800-221-1212
El Al	5	800-223-6700
Iberia Airlines	3 dep/5 arr	800-772-4642
Japan Airlines JAL	5	800-525-3663

Airline	*Terminal*	*Phone*
KLM Royal Dutch Airlines	5	800-374-7747
Korean Air	5	800-438-5000
Kuwait Airways	5	800-458-9248
LOT Polish Airlines	5	800-223-0593
Lufthansa	1 dep/5 arr	800-645-3880
Mexicana Airlines	5	800-531-7921
Northwest KLM Airlines:		
Domestic	2	800-225-2525
International	5	800-447-4747
Pakistan International Airlines	5	800-221-6024
Royal Jordanian	5	800-223-0470
Scandinavian Airlines SAS	5	800-221-2350
Spirit Airlines	3	800-772-7117
Swiss International Airlines	5	877-359-7947
TACA Airlines	5	888-337-8466
Ted Airlines	1	800-225-5833
Turkish Airlines	5	800-874-8875
United Airlines:	2	800-241-6522
Domestic/International dep	1	
International arr	5	
United Express	1	800-241-6522
US Airways	2	800-428-4322
USA 3000	5	877-872-3000

Car Rental

Alamo • O'Hare Intl Arpt, 800-327-9633
Avis • 10000 Bessie Coleman Dr, 800-331-1212/ 773-825-4600
Budget • 580 Bessie Coleman Dr, 800-527-0700
Dollar • O'Hare Intl Arpt, 800-800-4000/773-471-3450
Enterprise • 4025 Mannheim Rd, 847-928-3320
Hertz • 10000 Bessie Coleman Dr, 800-654-3131
National • 560 Bessie Coleman Dr, 800-227-7368
Thrifty • 3901 N Mannheim Rd, 847-928-2000

Hotels

All shuttles to airport hotels depart from the Bus Shuttle Center in front of the O'Hare Hilton Hotel in the center of the airport.

Best Western • 10300 W Higgins Rd, 847-296-4471
Clarion • 5615 N Cumberland Ave, 773-693-5800
Courtyard • 2950 S River Rd, 847-824-7000
Crown Plaza • 5440 N River Rd, 847-671-6350
Days Inn • 1920 E Higgins Rd, 847-437-1650
Days Inn • 2175 E Touhy Ave, 847-635-1300
DoubleTree • 5460 N River Rd, 847-292-9100
Embassy Suites • 5500 N River Rd, 847-678-4000
Four Points Sheraton • 10249 W Irving Park Rd, 847-671-6000
Hampton Inn • 3939 N Mannheim Rd, 847-671-1700
Hampton Inns Suites • 5201 Old Orchard Rd, 847-583-1111
Hawthorn Suites • 1251 American Ln, 847-706-9007
Hilton • O'Hare Intl Arprt, 773-686-8000
Holiday Inn • 8201 W Higgins Rd, 773-355-5070
Hotel Sofitel • 5550 N River Rd, 847-678-4488
Hyatt Regency • 9300 W Bryn Mawr Ave, 847-696-1234
Hyatt Rosemont • 6350 N River Rd, 847-518-1234
La Quinta Inn • 1900 E Oakton St, 847-439-6767
Marriott Suites • 6155 N River Rd, 800-228-9290
Marriott Hotel • 8535 W Higgins Rd, 773-693-4444
Ramada Plaza • 6600 N Mannheim Rd, 847-827-5131
Residence Inn • 7101 Chestnut St, 800-331-3131
Sheraton Suites • 6501 N Mannheim Rd, 847-699-6300
InTown Suites • 2411 Landmeier Rd, 847-228-5500
Super 8 • 2951 Touhy Ave, 847-827-3133
Travelodge • 3003 Mannheim Rd, 847-296-5541
Westin • 6100 N River Rd, 847-698-6000
Wyndham • 6810 N Mannheim Rd, 847-297-1234

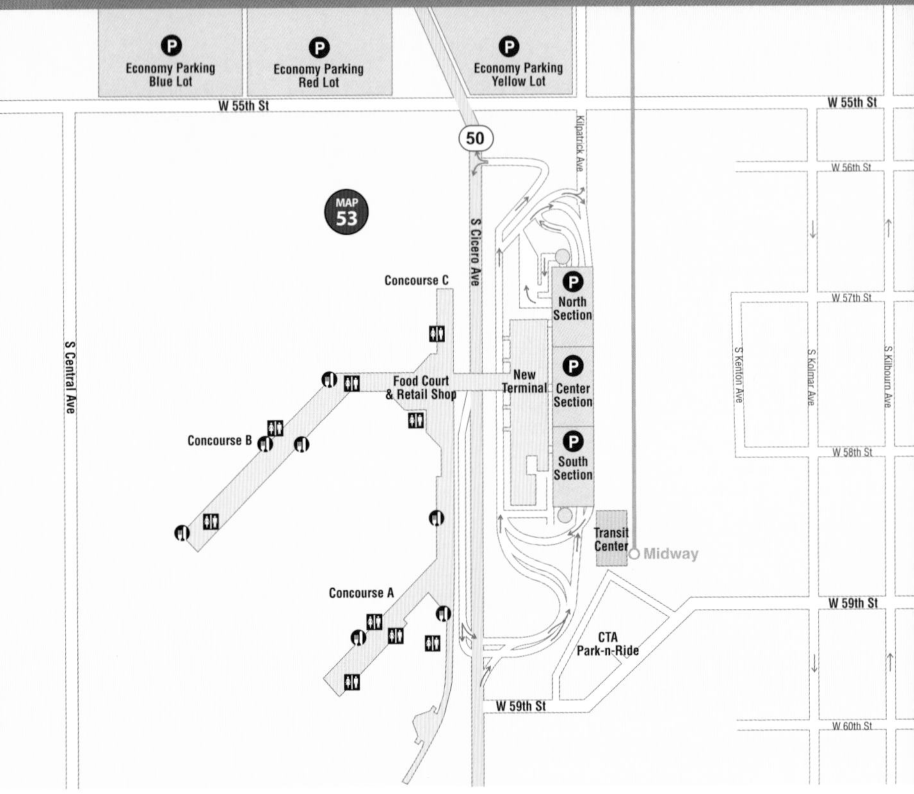

General Information

Address:	5757 S Cicero Ave Chicago, IL 60638
Phone:	773-838-0600
Website:	www.midwayairport.org
Police:	773-838-3003
Parking:	773-838-0756
Customs:	773-948-6330

Overview

Located just ten miles southwest of downtown Chicago is Midway—one of the fastest-growing airports in the country serving 47,000 passengers daily. Considered the city's outlet mall of airports, Midway primarily provides service from budget carriers like Southwest Airlines and ATA. On the plus side, it is an easy alternative to the nightmare named O'Hare. Plus the bars for pre-flight entertainment are not as crowded.

Expect Midway to gain altitude in national airport rankings with the recent completion of its $793 million terminal development. After ten years of planning and construction, the new features include a swank new terminal building, new concourses, a 3,000-space parking facility, food court, retail corridor, and a customs facility to facilitate international flights. In 2003, Concourses G and H were demolished to allow for the expansion of Concourse B. All the changes have upped Midway's jet gate count from 29 to 41.

Note for the superstitious, do not fly on December 8th. In 1972 a Boeing 737 crashed into a residential area during landing. Exactly 33 years later on this date in 2005, another Boeing slid off the runway in a landing attempt.

How To Get There

By Car: From downtown, take I-55 S. From the northern suburbs, take I-290 S to I-55 N. From the southern suburbs, take I-294 N to I-55 N. From the western suburbs, take I-88 E to I-294 S to I-55 N. Whether you're traveling north or south along I-55, look for the Cicero Avenue/South/ Midway Airport exit.

By Bus: CTA buses 55, 59, and 63 all run from points east to the airport. Take the Green Line or the Red Line to the Garfield Station and transfer to bus 55 heading west ($1.75 one-way including transfer). If you're coming from the south on the Red Line, get off at the 63rd Street stop and take bus 63 westbound ($1.80 one-way). Other buses that terminate at the airport include 54B, 379, 382, 383, 384, 385, 386, 831, and 63W.

By L: A 30-minute train ride on the Orange Line is the most convenient and cost-effective method for travel between the Loop and Midway Airport ($1.75 one-way). The Orange Line's first train departs from Midway Station (last stop on the line's southern end) for the Loop at 3:55 am daily and 5:35 am on Sundays and holidays. The first train of the day from the Loop's Adams/Wabash Station at 4:29 am arrives at Midway at 4:54 am, well in advance of the airport's first early bird flight. The last train from Midway to the Loop departs at 12:56 am and arrives at 1:23 am. The final Midway-bound owl train departs from the Adams/Wabash stop around 1:29 am, arriving at Midway by 1:53 am. Trains run every five to seven minutes during rush hours, ten minutes most other times, and fifteen minutes late evenings. We recommend that wee-hours travelers stay alert at all times.

By Cab: Cabs depart from the lower level of the main terminal and are available on a first-come-first-served basis. There are no flat rates (all cabs run on meters), but you can plan on paying around $25 to get to the Loop. Some cab companies servicing Midway include American United, 773-262-8633; Flash Cab, 773-878-8500; Flash Dispatch, 773-561-1444; Jiffy Cab, 773-487-9000; and Yellow Cab, 312-808-9130.

By Shuttle: Continental Airport Express (773-247-1200 or 888-2-THEVAN) travels between Midway and downtown and some northern suburban locations from 6 am until 10:30 pm. Shuttles depart every 15 minutes and make stops at all major downtown hotels. Tickets cost $18 one-way ($32 roundtrip) for individuals, $24 per person for pairs going to the same destination ($40 roundtrip), and $10 per person for three or more going to the same downtown destination ($18 roundtrip). The ticket counter and loading zone are in the terminal's lower level across from the baggage claim area by door LL3. To calculate a shuttle fare to north suburb locations, use the online fare calculator at www.airportexpress.com.

Omega Airport Shuttle (773-483-6634; www.omegashuttle.com) offers service leaving every 45 minutes or so between Midway and O'Hare beginning around 7 am each day with the final shuttle departing around 10 pm. Allow at least an hour for travel time between the airports and expect to pay $15 one-way. Contact Omega for information on more than 20 pickup locations on the South Side, to confirm schedules, to make reservations, and to prearrange home pickups.

By Limousine: Sounds pricey, but depending on where you're going and how many people you are traveling with, it may be cheaper to travel by limo than by cab or shuttle. Advance reservations recommended. Limo services include O'Hare-Midway Limousine Service, 312-558-1111 (or 800-468-8989 for airport pick-up), www.ohare-midway.com; and My Chauffeur/American Limo, 847-376-6100, www.americanlimousine.com

Parking

Short-term parking is on the third floor. Parking is free for the first ten minutes then $4 for 30 minutes to an hour. Add an additional $2 for every hour thereafter, up to $50 for 24 hours. Levels 1, 4, 5, and 6 have the same rates for short-term parking, but the prices level off after four hours so that it only costs $25 per day. If you're planning on parking for a while, the best option is the economy lot for $12 a day on Cicero Avenue at 55th Street, a quarter-mile away. Allow extra time to take the free shuttle between the lot and the terminal.

A new 6,300-space economy parking garage opened in December 2005 at the northwest corner of 55th Street and Laramie Avenue. Rates start at $2 for the first hour, $5 for the first two hours, and $12 for two to 24 hours.

Airlines

Concourse A

ATA	800-225-2995
ATA Connections/Chicago Express	800-225-2995
Southwest	800-435-9792
Ted	800-225-5833

Concourse B		**Concourse C**	
Southwest	800-435-9792	American	800-433-7300
AirTran	800-825-8538	Continental	800-525-0280
ComAir	800-927-0927	Frontier	800-432-1359
ATA	800-225-2995		
Northwest	800-225-2525		
Delta	800-221-1212		

Car Rental

Alamo	800-327-9633	Enterprise	800-566-9249
Avis	800-331-1212	Hertz	800-654-3131
Budget	800-527-7000	National	800-227-7368
Dollar	800-800-4000	Thrifty	800-527-7075

Hotels

Best Western • 8220 S Cicero Ave, 708-497-3000
Fairfield Inn • 6630 S Cicero Ave, 708-594-0090
Hampton Inn • 6540 S Cicero Ave, 708-496-1900
Hampton Inn • 13330 S Cicero Ave, 708-597-3330
Hilton • 9333 S Cicero Ave, 708-425-7800
Holiday Inn Express • 6500 S Cicero Ave, 708-458-0202
Howard Johnson • 4140 W 95th St, 708-425-7900
Holiday Inn Select • 6520 S Cicero Ave, 708-594-5500
Courtyard Midway • 6610 S Cicero Ave, 708-563-0200
Sleep Inn • 6650 S Cicero Ave, 708-594-0001

General Information

Mailing address: Chicago Transit Authority
Merchandise Mart Pl, 7th Fl
PO Box 3555
Chicago, IL 60654
Phone: 312-664-7200
CTA information: 888-YOUR-CTA (968-7282)
Website: www.transitchicago.com

Overview

According to the Chicago Transit Authority bureaucracy, the sky is always falling. The CTA is forever threatening complete collapse to justify constant fare hikes and service cuts. From our perspective, there's never been a better argument for privatization of a civic service than this woefully mismanaged rattling fleet of dinosaurs. In the meantime, CTA users grit their teeth and bear yet another fare overhaul. On a more positive side, CTA service will, eventually, get you relatively close to where you need to go (most of the time), and sometimes the city's trains and buses are even on schedule!

For location-to-location CTA directions and schedules, we honestly and without irony recommend the useful CTA trip planner at tripsweb.rtachicago.com. It allows you to plan your course by either estimated departure times or desired arrival times.

Fares and Fare Cards

CTA's buses cart about one million sweaty, crabby fares and fare cards around Chicago and its surrounding suburbs every day.

In an effort to woo passengers away from cash payment and toward the new Chicago Card fare system, the city has created a tiered, pain-in-the-ass approach to fare payment that makes it more expensive to pay with cash and easier to pay with cards. They don't call Chicago "the city that works your nerves" for nothing.

In a nutshell, you must use a card to ride the L train or to transfer. You can use a card or pay cash on the bus, but you cannot transfer with a cash purchase. Furthermore, cash fares are $2 per each leg of the journey whereas card fares are $1.75 and an additional 25 cents for up to three more transfers within two hours (the transfer rate is deducted from your card on the next leg of your journey). Reduced fares are available for qualified passengers—children under 12, senior citizens, and the disabled. Go to the CTA website for more information about reduced fare applicability at www.transitchicago.com.

Here's a breakdown on the benefits, limitations, and rules for each possible fare method:

Cash: Cash fares are $2 and only available on city busses. You must use a fare card to ride the L. You cannot buy a transfer with a cash fare. Each leg of the journey will cost $2 ($1 for applicable reduced-fare passengers). To pay with cash, insert bills or change into the money eater inside the bus. You must use exact change. No change will be given.

Fare Card: You can purchase the standard paper fare card at any L station from the big blue fare card machines. Fare cards can be purchased in any amount (fare minimum is $1.75) and used on the bus or L. Fares are $1.75, plus 25 cents to transfer. Purchasing a fare card is easy—insert the amount of money you want on your card into the money-eater (whether it will actually accept your crinkly or faded dollar bills or spit them back out at you is entirely another matter), and push the "vend" button. Your card will pop out of the slot (at roughly waist level) below the money eater. Lost or stolen fare cards are not replaceable. Money can be added at any fare card machine. To use a fare card, insert it into the card reader on CTA turnstiles or inside the bus (next to the bus money-eater). No change is given from CTA fare card machines.

Chicago Card: The Chicago Card can be purchased online (allow about a week for delivery) or at participating Jewel and Dominick's locations and some currency exchanges (go to their website for addresses of participating vendors). Chicago Cards can be purchased for predetermined amounts ($10, $20) or for specific amounts. Balances can be checked and Chicago Cards can be reloaded at CTA Fare card machines. Touch the card to the Chicago Card sensor, enter your reload amount into the money eater, and retouch your card to the sensor until the readout says, "Thank you." Do not forget to retouch your card to the sensor after adding money or the money will not be added to your card. There is a 10% bonus for every increment of $20 added to your card—for $20, you get a $2 bonus, for $40, a $4 bonus and so on. To use the Chicago Card, simply press it against the sensor at the turnstile or on the bus. Lost or stolen Chicago Cards can be replaced with their remaining value for $5 if you chose the option to register the card (optional card registration is free, so why not?). There is a one-time fee of $5 for the purchase of a Chicago Card.

Chicago Plus Card: The Chicago Plus card is like the Chicago Card except for a few key differences. Registration of the Chicago Plus card is mandatory. Card balances can only be checked and/or have money added (credit card only) online or by calling CTA customer service. With the Chicago Plus card, you have the option of choosing pay-as-you-go or purchasing a monthly pass. You must have an e-mail address to use a

Chicago Plus Card. Like the regular Chicago Card, Plus Card requires a one-time $5 purchase fee as well as a $5 replacement fee if cards are lost or stolen.

Pass Back Option: At any time, you can share your CTA card with up to six other people traveling with you by passing the card back over the turnstile. The full fare for each rider will be deducted from your card.

Pace Suburban – Chicago Buses

Pace buses serve over 35 million passengers in the Chicago suburbs and some parts of the city. With 240 routes covering 3,446 square miles, Pace provides a vital transportation service to commuters traveling between suburbs, within suburbs, to Metra train stations, and into the city. Buses usually run every 20–30 minutes and service stops by mid-evening. Special express service is offered to Chicago-area entertainment and cultural venues. Contact Pace for specific bus route and schedule information (847-364-PACE; www.pacebus.com).

Park-n-Ride Stations: Pace has 11 Park-n-Ride stations located throughout Pace's six-county coverage area (check the Pace website for locations).

Fares: Pace fares cost $1.25 for local service and $1.50 for express or expanded service. The one-way fare on express routes 210, 355, 855, and 1018 costs $3. CTA Transit Cards may be used on Pace buses. Pace offers discounts for students, children, seniors, and disabled riders, as well as several bus pass package purchase options. Pass options include the Pace 30-Day Commuter Club Cards (CCC) which allows unlimited Pace rides for $50. A combined Pace/CTA 30-day unlimited pass costs $75 and can be used on all Pace buses and CTA trains and buses. The PlusBus Sticker (sold by Metra with a Metra Monthly Train Pass) costs $30 and allows unlimited Pace bus use.

Greyhound Buses

Greyhound is the rock-bottom traveler's best friend. The bus line offers dirt-cheap fares, the flexibility drifters prefer, basic station amenities (i.e. dirty toilets and vending machines that steal your money), and the gritty, butt-busting experience of traveling America's scenic blue-line highways and rural byways with some colorful characters.

Tips on riding "the Dog" out of town:

- Pack your own toilet paper and Wet Ones.
- Air freshener, deodorant, a pillow, and earplugs make being bused more bearable.
- Pack a cooler. Then padlock it.
- Charge your iPod. Seriously.
- Bring a cushion.
- Get your shots.

Stations: Greyhound's main train station is south of Union Station at 630 W Harrison St in West Loop (312-408-5800). CTA buses 60, 125, 156, and 157 make stops near the terminal. The closest L stop is on the Blue Line's Forest Park Branch at the Clinton Street Station on Congress Parkway. Additional Chicago-area Greyhound stations are located within L train stations: 14 W 95th St in the Red Line's 95th Street/Dan Ryan Station (312-408-5999), and 5800 N Cumberland Ave on the Blue Line's O'Hare Branch in the Cumberland Station (773-693-2474). The general aura of the Chicago Greyhound Station is one of seediness and squalor. Keep your belongings with you at all times.

Shipping Services: Greyhound Package Xpress offers commercial and personal shipping services and is available at all three Chicago bus stations. Packages are held at the station for pick-up. The main terminal in South Loop also houses a UPS shipping office that provides door-to-door package delivery.

Fares: Tickets can be purchased on the phone or online with a credit card, or at a station with cash, travelers' checks, or credit cards.

Regular fare pricing applies for both individual advance ticket sales and minutes-before-departure sales. Tickets can be used for travel to the designated destination on any day or at any departure time. Because Greyhound does not reserve seats, boarding occurs on a first-come-first-served basis, so get in line at the boarding zone for a choice seat. However, Greyhound's bark is bigger than its bite—if a significant number of passengers turn out for the same bus, Greyhound rolls another bus, or two, or three out on the spot. Good dog.

Children under 12 receive 40% discounts off of regular fares, seniors 62 and older receive 5% discounts, military members receive 10% discounts, and patients of Veteran's Administration Hospitals receive a 25% discount. Other discounts are available online. The cost for an individual return ticket is always deeply discounted if it is purchased at the same time as a departure ticket.

Tickets purchased three days in advance earn a half-price companion ticket (no age restrictions). Passengers accompanying someone with a disability always ride at a reduced rate.

Super Friendly Fares offer the greatest savings for travelers who can purchase seven days in advance of travel. For example, a regular one-way ticket from Chicago to New York City costs $90 and a regular-fare round-trip ticket costs $159. But booking a round-trip Super Friendly Fare costs $89. You do the math.

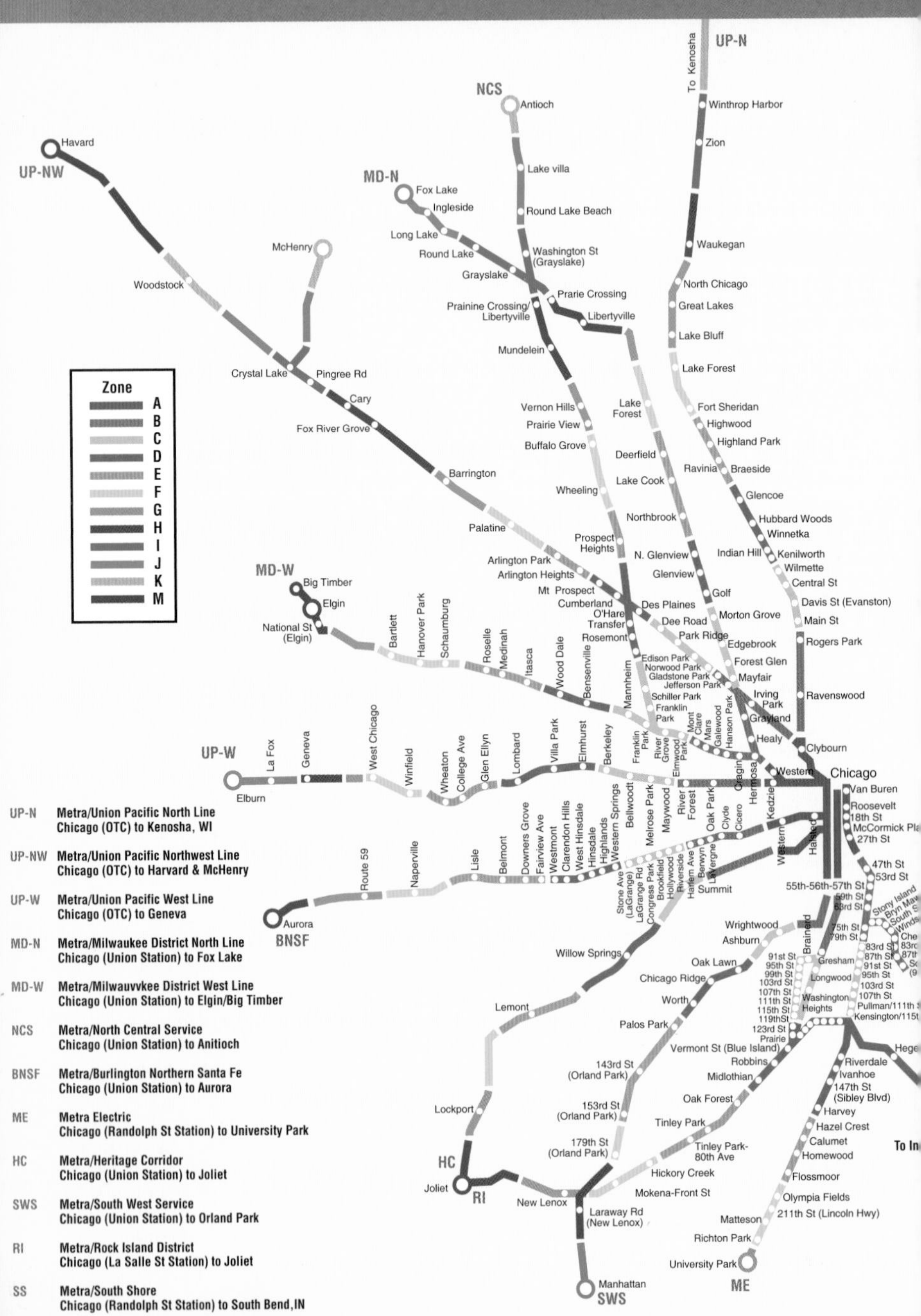

Zone
A
B
C
D
E
F
G
H
I
J
K
M
UP-N
To Kenosha
Winthrop Harbor
Zion
Waukegan
North Chicago
Great Lakes
Lake Bluff
Lake Forest
Fort Sheridan
Highwood
Highland Park
Ravinia
Braeside
Glencoe
Hubbard Woods
Winnetka
Indian Hill
Kenilworth
Wilmette
Central St
Davis St (Evanston)
Main St
Rogers Park
Ravenswood
Clybourn
Chicago
NCS
Antioch
Lake villa
Round Lake Beach
Washington St (Grayslake)
Prarie Crossing
Prainine Crossing/ Libertyville
Libertyville
Mundelein
Vernon Hills
Prairie View
Buffalo Grove
Wheeling
Prospect Heights
MD-N
Fox Lake
Ingleside
Long Lake
Round Lake
Grayslake
Lake Forest
Deerfield
Lake Cook
Northbrook
N. Glenview
Glenview
Golf
Morton Grove
Edgebrook
Forest Glen
Mayfair
Grayland
Healy
Western
UP-NW
Havard
McHenry
Woodstock
Crystal Lake
Pingree Rd
Cary
Fox River Grove
Barrington
Palatine
Arlington Park
Arlington Heights
Mt Prospect
Cumberland
O'Hare Transfer
Rosemont
Des Plaines
Dee Road
Park Ridge
Edison Park
Norwood Park
Gladstone Park
Jefferson Park
Irving Park
MD-W
Big Timber
Elgin
National St (Elgin)
Bartlett
Hanover Park
Schaumburg
Roselle
Medinah
Itasca
Wood Dale
Bensenville
Mannheim
Schiller Park
Franklin Park
Franklin Park
River Grove
Elmwood Park
Mont Clare
Mars
Galewood
Hanson Park
UP-W
Elburn
La Fox
Geneva
West Chicago
Winfield
Wheaton
College Ave
Glen Ellyn
Lombard
Villa Park
Elmhurst
Berkeley
Bellwood
Melrose Park
Maywood
River Forest
Oak Park
Cragin
Hermosa
Kedzie
Clyde
Cicero
Western
Halsted
BNSF
Aurora
Route 59
Naperville
Lisle
Belmont
Downers Grove
Fairview Ave
Westmont
Clarendon Hills
West Hinsdale
Hinsdale
Highlands
Western Springs
Stone Ave (LaGrange)
LaGrange Rd
Congress Park
Brookfield
Hollywood
Riverside
Harlem Ave
Berwyn
LaVergne
Summit
Van Buren
Roosevelt
18th St
McCormick Pla
27th St
47th St
53rd St
55th-56th-57th St
59th St
63rd St
Stony Island
Bryn Maw
South S
Winds
Che
83rd
87th
75th St
79th St
83rd St
87th St
91st St
95th St
103rd St
107th St
Pullman/111th
Kensington/115t
Gresham
Longwood
Washington Heights
Brainerd
91st St
95th St
99th St
103rd St
107th St
111th St
115th St
119thSt
123rd St
Prairie
Wrightwood
Ashburn
Oak Lawn
Chicago Ridge
Worth
Palos Park
Vermont St (Blue Island)
Robbins
Midlothian
Oak Forest
Tinley Park
Tinley Park-80th Ave
Hickory Creek
Mokena-Front St
Willow Springs
Lemont
Lockport
HC
Joliet
RI
New Lenox
Laraway Rd (New Lenox)
143rd St (Orland Park)
153rd St (Orland Park)
179th St (Orland Park)
Manhattan
SWS
Hege
Riverdale
Ivanhoe
147th St (Sibley Blvd)
Harvey
Hazel Crest
Calumet
Homewood
Flossmoor
Olympia Fields
211th St (Lincoln Hwy)
Matteson
Richton Park
University Park
ME
To In
UP-N Metra/Union Pacific North Line Chicago (OTC) to Kenosha, WI
UP-NW Metra/Union Pacific Northwest Line Chicago (OTC) to Harvard & McHenry
UP-W Metra/Union Pacific West Line Chicago (OTC) to Geneva
MD-N Metra/Milwaukee District North Line Chicago (Union Station) to Fox Lake
MD-W Metra/Milwauvvkee District West Line Chicago (Union Station) to Elgin/Big Timber
NCS Metra/North Central Service Chicago (Union Station) to Anitioch
BNSF Metra/Burlington Northern Santa Fe Chicago (Union Station) to Aurora
ME Metra Electric Chicago (Randolph St Station) to University Park
HC Metra/Heritage Corridor Chicago (Union Station) to Joliet
SWS Metra/South West Service Chicago (Union Station) to Orland Park
RI Metra/Rock Island District Chicago (La Salle St Station) to Joliet
SS Metra/South Shore Chicago (Randolph St Station) to South Bend,IN

General Information

Metra Address:	Metra Passenger Services 547 W Jackson Blvd Chicago, IL 60661
Phone:	312-322-6777
Website:	www.metrarail.com
Metra Passenger Service:	312-322-6777
South Shore Metra Lines:	800-356-2079
RTA Information Center:	312-836-7000; www.rtachicago.com

Overview

With a dozen lines and roughly 495 miles of track overseen by the RTA, Metra does its best to service Cook, DuPage, Lake, Will, McHenry, and Kane counties with 230 stations scattered throughout the city and 'burbs. The rails emanating from four major downtown stations are lifelines for commuters traveling to and from the Loop.

The good news for Metra is that ridership is strong. The bad news for riders is that parking at popular stations is difficult. In an attempt to resolve its parking issues, Metra is purchasing land surrounding many suburban stations and constructing new parking facilities. Check out Metra's website for updates on development plans.

Loop Stations

There are four major Metra train stations in the Loop from which 12 train lines emanate. Here's a chart to help clear up any possible confusion:

Station	**Line**
Richard B. Ogilvie T.C.	Union Pacific Lines
Union Station	Milwaukee District Lines North Central Service Southwest Service Burlington Northern Heritage Corridor Amtrak
La Salle Street Station	Rock Island Line
Randolph Street Station (Millennium Station)	South Shore Railroad Metra Electric—Branches: Main Line, South Chicago, Blue Island

Fares

Depending on the number of Metra zones you traverse, one-way, full-fare tickets cost between $1.95 and $6.95. To calculate a base one-way fare, visit www.metrarail.com/Data/farechk.html. Tickets may be purchased through a ticket agent or onboard the train (with a $2 surcharge if the ticket windows were open at the time you boarded the train). There is no reserved seating.

Metra offers a number of reasonably priced ticket packages, including a Ten-Ride Ticket (which saves riders 15% off of one-way fares) and a Monthly Unlimited Ride Ticket (the most economical choice for commuters who use Metra service daily). If your commute includes CTA and/or Pace bus services, consider purchasing the Link-Up Sticker ($36) for unlimited connecting travel on CTA and Pace buses. Metra's Weekend Pass costs $5 and includes unlimited rides on Saturday and Sunday, with the exception of the South Shore route. You can buy all the aforementioned tickets in person, through the mail, or online at www.metrarail.com/TBI/index.html.

Children under age seven ride free. Children ages 7–11 ride for half-price on weekdays and for free on the weekends. Children ages 12–17 ride for half-price on weekends. Full-time grade school or high school students are eligibile to receive 50% off the cost of regular one-way fares. Senior citizens/disability fares are approximately half of the regular fare. US Military Personnel in uniform also ride Metra for half-price. Anyone wearing capri pants after Labor Day will be charged double.

Wendella RiverBuses

Spring through fall, commuters can get to North Michigan Avenue quickly on a Wendella RiverBus plying the Chicago River during rush hours, leaving from Transportation Center at the dock on the northwest corner of Madison Street. RiverBuses run daily from April 1 through November 29. The trip takes nine minutes one-way. The first boat leaves the train station dock at 7 am; the last boat departs from the dock at 400 N Michigan Avenue,at the base of the Wrigley Building at 7 pm. The fare is $2 one-way. Discounted Monthly and Ten-Ride fares are also available (312-337-1446; www.wendellariverbus.com).

Baggage & Pets

While Metra may be "the way to really fly," Metra's restrictions on baggage are more stringent than those of most airlines, though they now allow bicycles on weekday off-peak hours and on weekends (details on the "Bikes on Trains" program are divulged at metrarail.com/Special_Promotions/bikes_on_trains.html). Skis, golf clubs, non-folding carts, water buffaloes, and other large luggage items can never be transported on trains. Pets, with the exception of service animals, are also prohibited aboard trains.

General Information

Loop Station Address:	Millennium Station at Randolph Street 151 E Randolph St Underground at N Michigan Ave & E Randolph St Chicago, IL 60601
Phone:	312-782-0676
Lost & Found:	219-874-4221 x205
Website:	www.nictd.com

Overview

Although the historic South Shore train lines were built in 1903, they still get you from the Loop to Indiana's South Bend Airport in just 2.5 hours. The Northern Indiana Commuter Transportation District (NICTD) oversees the line and its modern electric trains, which serve as a vital transportation link for many northwest Indiana residents working in the Loop.

The South Shore's commuter service reflects its Indiana ridership. Outbound heading from the Loop, there are limited stops before the Hegewisch station, close to the Indiana state line. When traveling by train to Chicago's South Side, you're better off on an outbound Metra Electric Line train departing from the Randolph Street Station (see Metra page). Taking a trip on the South Shore is a rather cheap form of post-industrial voyeurism, as a complete round-trip from the Loop all the way to South Bend can be had for around $20. Along the way you will pass by dozens of antiquated factories, one of the longest stretches of sand-dunes in the Great Lakes region, and, of course, oh-so charming Gary, Indiana.

Fares

Regular one-way fares can be purchased at the stations (with cash or personal check) or on the train (cash only). Ticket prices vary with distance traveled. Tickets purchased onboard the train cost $1 more if the station's ticket windows were open at the time of departure.

Special South Shore fares and packages include commuter favorites: 10-Ride and 25-Ride tickets and the Monthly Pass which is good for unlimited travel. These can be purchased in person at stations staffed with ticket agents, station vending machines, and via the mail. Senior citizens/ disability fares offer savings for persons aged 65 and older with valid identification and for disabled passengers. Students with school identification qualify for student fares, including reduced one-way tickets and discounted 25-Ride Tickets good for travel during weekdays. Youth fares include free passage for infants under two years (who must sit in a paying passenger's lap) and half off a regular fare for children aged two to 13 years. Family fares are available on weekends and holidays as well as off-peak times on weekdays. Each fare-paying adult (minimum age 21) may take up to two children (age 13 and under) with them free of charge. Additional children will be charged the reduced youth fare. There are no published fare discounts for military personnel.

Baggage & Pets

Any accompanying baggage must be placed in the overhead racks. No bicycles are permitted onboard. Apart from small animals in carry-on cages, the only pets allowed onboard are service dogs accompanied by handlers or passengers with disabilities. Animals must not occupy seats.

General Information

Amtrak Reservations:	1-800-USA-RAIL (872-7245)
Website:	www.amtrak.com
Union Station:	225 S Canal St, Chicago, IL 60606
Phone:	312-322-6900

Overview

Chicago is the nucleus for Amtrak's 500-station national rail network, which covers 46 states (every state but Alaska, Hawaii, South Dakota, and Wyoming). Departing from Chicago's Union Station, Amtrak trains head west to Seattle, Portland, and San Francisco, east to New York City and Boston, north to Ontario, and south to New Orleans and San Antonio.

Fares

Amtrak offers affordable fares for regional travel, but their prices can't compete with airfares on longer hauls. But just as airlines offer deeply discounted fares, so does Amtrak. Ask Amtrak's sales agents about special fares and search Amtrak's website for the best deals. (Booking in advance does present some savings.) We recommend the website route, as callers run the risk of being on hold longer than it takes to ride a train from Chicago to Los Angeles.

Amtrak offers special promotional fares year-round targeting seniors, veterans, students, children under 16, and groups of two or more persons traveling together. The "Rail SALE" page on Amtrak's website lists discounted fares between certain city pairs. Amtrak has hooked its sleeper cars up with plenty of travel partners to create interesting packages. The Air-Rail deals, whereby you rail it one way and fly back the other, are attractive for long distance travel. Surf the "Amtrak Partners" webpage for partner promotional fares.

Service

Those who can claim to have arrived on-time traveling Amtrak are few and far between, so tell whoever is picking you up you'll call them on your cell phone when you're close. Pack food on your ride as dining-car fare is mediocre and pricey. On the upside, Amtrak's seats are comfortable and roomy, some have electric sockets for computer hookups, bathrooms are in every car, and the train is almost always clean. Just be wary of strangers wanting to "switch" murders.

Within Illinois: Four main Amtrak lines travel south through Illinois on a daily basis: The "State House" travels to St. Louis, MO; the "Illinois Zephyr" travels to Quincy, IL; the "Illini Service" travels between Chicago and Carbondale, IL; and the "Ann Rutledge" travels to Kansas City, MO. The prices listed here are only quotes and are subject to change. Check Amtrak's website for updates.

Going to New York City or Boston: If you're heading east, the "Lake Shore Limited" breaks off at Albany and goes to New York (21 hours) and Boston (24 hours). One-way tickets cost between $94 and $147.

Going to Seattle or Portland: The "Empire Builder" takes passengers to Seattle and Portland and everywhere in between. With the journey to Seattle taking around 44 hours, we definitely recommend dropping some additional dollars on a sleeper car. A one-way fare costs between $134 and $168.

Going to San Francisco: You'll spend two solid days and then some riding the rails during the 52-hour journey on the "California Zephyr" to San Francisco (Emeryville). The fare costs approximately $122 to $238 one-way. "Zephyr" passes through Lincoln, Denver, and Salt Lake City and makes a whole host of small town America stops along the way.

Going to New Orleans: The "City of New Orleans" line runs from Chicago via Memphis to New Orleans in roughly 20 hours. The fare is approximately $91 to $174 one-way.

Going to San Antonio: The mighty "Texas Eagle" glides across the Alamo and stops at 40 cities on its way from the Midwest to the South. The 32-hour trip will cost approximately $98 to $191 each way (Look at it this way: You're paying less than six bucks an hour!). However, why anyone would want to go to San Antonio is unclear.

Going to Milwaukee: "Hiawatha Service" runs seven times daily to Milwaukee, leaving Chicago approximately every two hours. The 90-minute trip costs $20 each way (a good alternative to driving from Chicago on busy weekends and rush hours).

Going to Kansas City: The "Missouri Routes" line terminates in Kansas City while the "Southwest Chief" passes through it on the way to Los Angeles. "Missouri" departs daily at 8:25 am and travels via St. Louis to Kansas City in just over 12 hours. The fare is about $38 one-way. "Southwest Chief" departs daily at 3:15 pm and reaches Kansas City in just over seven hours.

Going to Los Angeles: The "Southwest Chief" departs for Los Angeles, travels via Albuquerque, takes almost 42 hours, and costs $122–$166 one-way.

Union Station

210 S Canal St at E Adams St and E Jackson Blvd • 312-322-4269

An innovation for both design and travel, Chicago's Union Station is the "Grand Dame" of rail service in a city once considered to be the undisputed rail center of the United States. Designed by the architects Graham, Anderson, Probst, and White and built between 1913 and 1925, Union Station is a terminus for six Metra lines and a major hub for Amtrak's long-distance services. In its peak (1940s), this local transportation treasure handled as many as 300 trains and 100,000 passengers on a daily basis. While today's volume is just half that, this monumental station stands as the last remaining grand station still in use in the City of Chicago and was given landmark status in 2002. Most commuters don't take the time to gaze skyward when rushing through the Great Hall of Union Station (who really has the time to stop and assess their surroundings beyond that of their intended use?), but by not doing so, they are missing something special. Take the time to look up at the magnificent light-swathed ceiling and maybe then it will become clear why Union Station's ornate Great Hall is considered one of the United States' great interior public spaces. Union Station is also a premiere location for formal functions as it annually plays host to a multitude of private affairs and black-tie gatherings.

Both Metra's and Amtrak's train services are on the Concourse Level (ground floor) of the station. This level is then further divided into the North Concourse and South Concourse. Although not always adequately staffed, there is an information desk located between the concourses on this level. And while there is signage throughout Union Station, the many escalators, stairways, and multiple entrances/exits can make navigating the block-long building somewhat of a challenge.

Ticket Windows: The easiest way to get to Metra ticket agents is to enter Union Station at the Clinton Street entrance near East Jackson Boulevard and go down into and through the Grand Hall. Metra's ticket agents will be on your left in the North Concourse. Metra's ticket office is open weekdays 6 am–11:00 pm, Saturday 6:30 am–11:00 pm, and Sunday 7 am–11:00 pm. Metra Lines that terminate at Union Station are Milwaukee District East and West Lines, North Central Service, Burlington Northern Santa Fe, Heritage Corridor, and South West Service.

To get to the Amtrak action, enter Union Station off Canal Street, take the escalator down into the Grand Hall, and turn left. Amtrak's attractive, vintage ticket agent desk straddles the two concourses and is open daily 6:30 am–8:30 pm. Amtrak's waiting rooms and baggage claim are in the South Concourse. For more detail on Amtrak service, call 800-872-7245 or visit www.amtrak.com

Services: On the Mezzanine/Street Level, there is a plethora of convenience stores, newsstands, and eateries. ATMs are located in both concourses on this level.

Public Transportation: The closest L stop to Union Station is Clinton Street on the Blue Line, which stops two blocks south of the station. The Orange, Brown, and Purple lines stop three blocks east of the station at the Quincy stop on Wells Street. CTA buses 1, 151, 157, and 125 all stop at Union Station. Most commuters heading to work in the Loop enter and exit the station from the Madison Street, Adams Street, and Jackson Boulevard doorways where cabs line up.

Richard B. Ogilvie Transportation Center

500 W Madison St at S Canal St • 312-496-4777

Built in 1911 and known locally as the North Western or Madison Street Station, the Metra's Union Pacific Lines originate from the Richard B. Ogilvie Transportation Center. Where Union Station is about form and function, Ogilvie focuses solely on function. Overtly stark and sterile, the tall, smoky-glass-and-green-steel-girder building replaced what was once a classic grand train station similar to the ornate, Beaux Arts-inspired Union Station. Though most of the historic fixtures have been removed, some of the original clocks remain and serve as a reminder of earlier days. Even though promised renovations of the unused historic sub-level areas have yet to come to fruition (it is hoped that the empty space under the tracks can be turned into 120,000 square feet of shops and restaurants), this highly trafficked station remains quite active. Roughly 40,000 passengers pass through the Richard B. Ogilvie Transportation Center on a daily basis.

Ticket Windows: Metra's ticket office is on the Upper Level, across from the entrance to the train platform and is open 5:30 am–12:40 am Monday–Saturday, and 7 am–12:40 am Sundays. ATMs can be found on the Upper Level at Citibank and next to the currency exchange. Public phones are also by the currency exchange in the southeast corner of the Upper Level. Trains depart from this level and the smoking waiting room looks out onto the platform.

Services: Loads of junk food options are available on the Street Level food court, which also serves as a make-shift waiting room for commuters. If you want healthier fare, try the Rice Market and Boudin Sourdough Bakery on the east side of the building. There is available shopping about if you're killing time or wanting to pick up a last-minute gift. An interesting and annoying amenity footnote: the only restrooms in the station are on the Street Level, which is a LONG escalator ride from the train platform. There are no plans for this to change until the proposed renovations are completed, so it's best to "go before you go."

Public Transportation: The closest L station is the Green Line's Clinton Street stop at Lake Street, several blocks north of the station. CTA buses 20, 56, and 157 board at Washington and Canal Streets and travel to North Michigan Avenue and the Loop. Coming from the Loop, take the same bus lines west across Madison Street. If you're after a cab, you'll find other like-minded commuters lining up in front of the main entrance on Madison Street between Canal and Clinton Streets.

Millennium Station

151 E Randolph St at N Michigan Ave • 312-322-7819

Nicknamed the "Triple S" (South "Start" Station), the Millennium Station serves Metra's three electric commuter rail lines in Chicago (Main Line, South Chicago Branch, Blue Island Branch) in addition to several diesel lines. The underground station, centrally located in the Loop, services up to 100,000 commuters daily. This is also the station where the South Shore Line to South Bend, Indiana originates. Schedules for all are somewhat sporadic except during weekday rush hour commutes. The Van Buren Street Station also serves both the Metra Electric and South Shore lines and is located at East Jackson Boulevard and Van Buren Street (312-322-6777). When planning train travel from the Randolph Street and Van Buren Street stations, it's best to verify schedules and stops with the RTA Information Center (312-836-7000; www.rtachicago.com) before committing to a travel plan.

Ticket Windows: Enter the Millennium Station at East Randolph Street and North Michigan Avenue. The ticket office is immediately visible upon descending the steps off Michigan Avenue or entering via the Pedway, which tunnels around the Loop and east under Michigan Avenue, ending at the station. Ticket office hours are 6 am–10:20 pm daily. The waiting room is open 5 am–12:50 am daily.

Services: The continuing Millennium Station renovation efforts have thrown a kink in the otherwise generous amenity offerings usually in place at this pinnacle station. Until the updates are completed, the best way to describe the amenities at the Millennium Street Station is "self-serve."

Public Transportation: Millennium Station is served by CTA buses 56, 151, 157 and on days when there are events at the United Center, express bus 19 becomes available. A little over one block west of the train station in the Loop is the Randolph Street L station, serviced by the Orange, Green, Purple, and Brown lines.

La Salle Street Station

414 S La Salle St at E Congress Pkwy • 312-322-8957

The La Salle Street Station, located underneath the Chicago Stock Exchange, serves the Metra Rock Island District Line's passengers. This former behemoth of a station has been greatly reduced in both size and stature, handling roughly 15,000 commuters daily. The service has 11 main line stops and 10 south suburban stops on its way to Joliet.

Ticket Windows: Enter the station off La Salle Street, take the escalator one floor up, walk through the lobby past the bar to an open area where there are tracks and the ticket office. Agents are on duty 7 am–8 pm weekdays, 10:30 am–6:30 pm on Saturday, and closed on Sunday.

Services: There are no shops to speak of at the La Salle Street Station, but there IS a bar! During the week the small waiting room is less crowded than the bar (go figure), especially after the markets close. Footnote: the worst time to be in or around the Chicago Stock Exchange is after the markets close, so the best advice is to avoid this area until later in the day. The waiting room is open 6 am–12 am daily.

Public Transportation: The Blue Line's La Salle Street stop at Congress Parkway and the Orange, Purple, and Brown lines' La Salle Street stop at Van Buren Street drop L riders right in front of the train station. CTA buses 6 and 146 stop near the station, as well.

Transit • The L

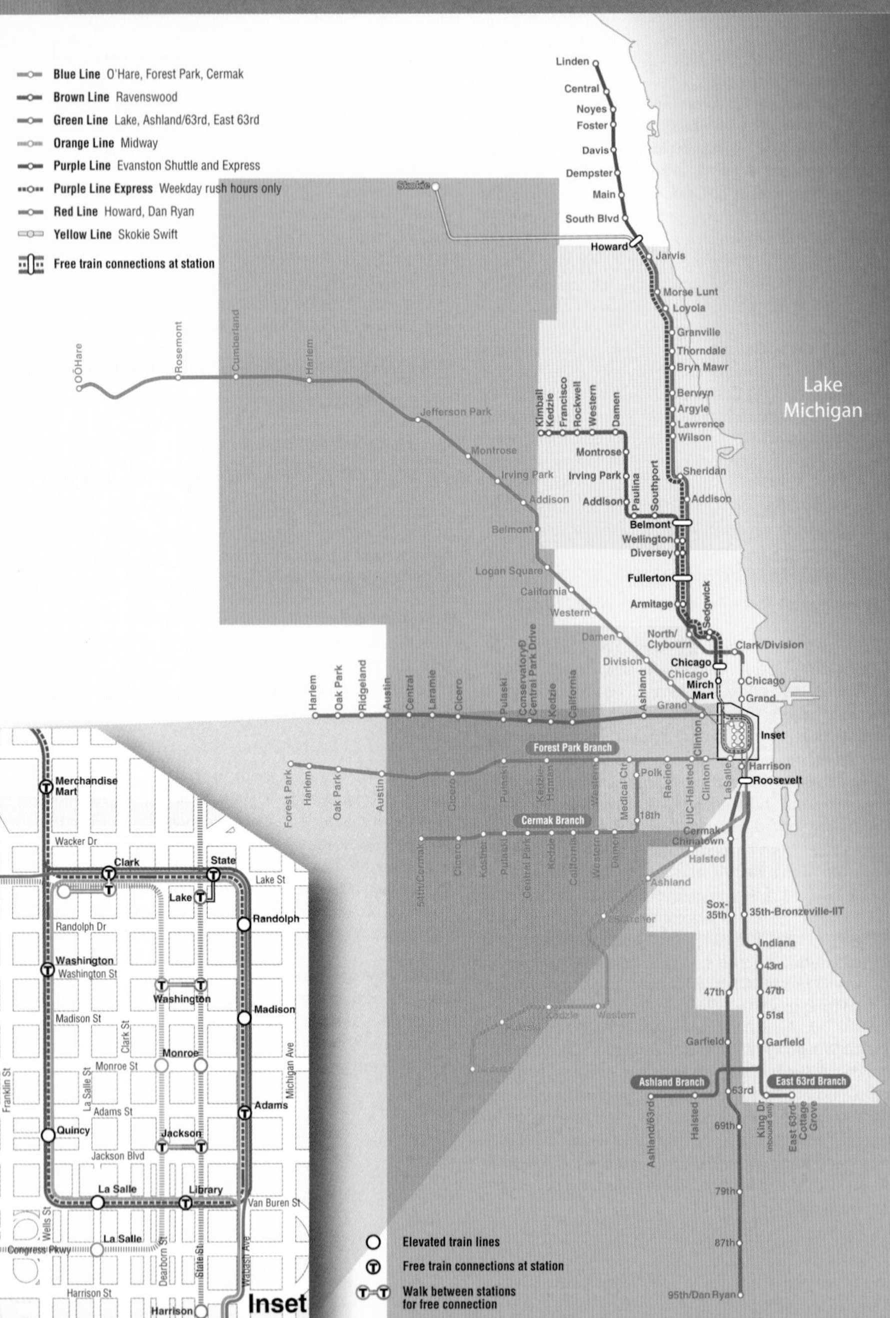

Overview

Whether traveling underground, on street level, or above the sidewalk, Chicagoans refer to their rapid transit system as the "L." (Though some prefer to call it the "Smell.") No matter which one you choose, either name says Chicago as loud and clear as the high-pitched whine, guttural grumble, and steely grind of the train itself. L tracks lasso Chicago's heart creating The Loop, where five of the seven L lines ride side-by-side above the pulsating business and financial district.

L trains make 1,452 trips each day and serve 143 stations in the Chicago Metropolitan Area. The numerous track delays and stalls in service are a burden to thousands of daily commuters. Nonetheless, due to the general directness of the L routes, easy station-to-station transfers, and the difficulties of parking (especially near popular destinations such as Grant Park and Wrigley Field), the benefits of L transportation usually outweigh the discomforts and inconveniences.

Fares

The standard full fare on CTA trains is $1.75. A 25¢ transfer allows two additional rides within two hours of issuance. Transfer rates are automatically deducted from your fare card when reused within the time limit. Transferring within the rail network is free at determined, connected transfer stations.
To ride the L, you need a farecard. Read the CTA Overview for a thorough discussion on the merits of each farecard option, or got to the CTA website at www.transitchicago.com.

Frequency of Service

CTA publishes schedules that say trains run every 3 to 12 minutes during weekday rush hours and every 6 to 20 minutes all other times. But service can be irregular, especially during non-rush hours, after-hours, and in bad weather. While the system is relatively safe late at night, stick to stations in populated areas as much as possible. Buses with Owl Service may be better options in the wee hours.

L Lines

Blue Line: Comprises the O'Hare, Forest Park, and Cermak branches traveling west; O'Hare and Forest Park run 24-hours, while Cermak is operational only on weekdays.

Pink Line: Chicago's newest rail line will take over the blue line route from the loop to 54th and Cermak. At the time of this writing, the Pink Line is not yet operating. Check into its status before traveling if you are heading in that direction.

Red Line: Runs north-south from the Howard Street station down to the 95th Street/Dan Ryan station; operates 24-hours.

Brown Line: Starts from the Kimball Street station and heads south with service to the Loop and sometimes just to Belmont Avenue. On weekdays and Saturdays, the first Loop-bound train leaves Kimball Street at 4:01 am; the last train to leave the Loop is at 12:18 am. Sunday service begins at :46 am and ends at 11:40 pm. After that, take the Red Line to Belmont Avenue, and transfer to the Brown Line where the last train leaves at 2:25 am (12:55 am on Sundays). The Brown Line also runs between Kimball Street and Belmont Avenue from 4 am to 2:04 am weekdays and Saturdays; and from 5:01 am to 2:04 am on Sundays. **Countdown to a new Brown:** The 4-year Brown Line station renovation project is underway and the agonizing delays have already begun. At present, most of the affected stations are west of Western Avenue. Check the CTA website for the latest station closings.

Orange Line: Travels from Midway Airport to the Loop and back. Trains depart from Midway beginning at 3:55 am weekdays and Saturdays and at 7 am on Sundays; the last train leaves the Loop for the airport at 1:29 am daily.

Green Line: Covers portions of west and south Chicago. The Harlem/Lake Street branch travels straight west. The Ashland Avenue/63rd Street and E 63rd Street/Cottage Grove branches go south and split east and west. Depending on the branch, service begins around 4 am weekdays with the last trains running around 1 am. Weekend schedules vary.

Purple Line: Shuttles north-south between Howard Street and Linden Place in suburban Evanston, Chicago's northernmost station. Service starts at 4:35 am and ends at 12:55 am weeknights, 1:45 am on weekends, and 12:55 am Sundays. Weekdays, an express train runs between Linden Place and the Loop between 6:25 am and 10:10 am and then again between 2:55 pm and 6:15 pm. At all other times, take the **Purple Line Express** to the Howard Street station, and transfer to the Red Line to reach the Loop.

Yellow Line: Runs between the north suburban Skokie station and Chicago's Howard Street station on weekdays from 4:50 am to 10:18 pm. On weekends, take CTA bus 97 from Skokie station to Howard Street and catch the Red Line to the Loop.

Bicycles

Bicycles ride free and are permitted onboard at all times except weekdays from 7 am to 9 am and 4 pm to 6 pm. Only two bikes are allowed per car, so survey the platform for other bikes and check out the cars as they pull into the station for two-wheelers already onboard. When entering a station, either use the turnstile or ask an attendant to open the gate. Don't try to take your bike through the tall steel gates—it WILL get stuck!

General Information

City of Chicago Department of Transportation (DOT)

Non-Emergency/
24-Hour Road Conditions Phone: 311
Street Closings Hotline: 312-787-3387
Website: www.cityofchicago.org

Illinois Department of Transportation (IDOT)

Phone:	217-782-7820
IDOT Traffic Hotline:	312-368-4636
Website:	www.dot.state.il.us/news.html
Chicago Skyway Bridge:	312-747-8383
Road Conditions:	800-452-4368
WBBM-AM 780:	Traffic updates every eight minutes

Orientation

Driving in Chicago has the potential to skyrocket your blood pressure as high as the Sears Tower. We highly recommend taking public transportation whenever possible, especially since Chicago has such strong bus and rail systems. But if you must drive in the city, Chicago's grid system makes it relatively easy to navigate.

The intersection of State and Madison Streets in the Loop serves as the base line for both Chicago's street and house numbering system. Running north and south is State Street—the city's east/west dividing line. Madison Street runs east and west and divides the city into north and south. Street and building numbers begin at "1" at the State and Madison Streets intersection and numerically increase going north, south, east, and west to the city limits. Street signs will let you know in what direction you're heading. The city is divided into one-mile sections, or eight square blocks, each with a consecutively higher series of "100" numbers. This explains why Chicagoans numerically refer to street locations such as Irving Park Road as "40 hundred north" rather than "four thousand north."

Buildings with even number addresses are on the north and west sides of streets; odd numbers sit on the south and east sides. Chicago's diagonal streets also follow the grid numbering system. Generally, the South Side's north-south streets have names and the east-west streets mostly go by numbers, such as 30th Street located at 3000 or 30 hundred south. Once you get out of the city limits, good luck. Often times you will find that our suburban friends like to refer to the same road by two different names. Roads will also magically turn into something different for no apparent reason. And sometimes they don't bother putting up street signs at all.

Bridge Lift Season

While bridges spanning the Chicago River contribute to the city's architectural fame, they also serve as a major source of traffic congestion. Boating season demands that bridges lower and rise, so as to allow Chicago's elite access to Lake Michigan in their sailboats. Chicago's bridge lift season runs from early April until June. Each month has designated lift days. Lifts generally begin at 9:30 am and affect the entire downtown area between 11:30 am and 1 pm. During May, more lifts are scheduled on Saturdays between 2 pm and 4 pm. The schedule intensifies on holiday weekends to include evening rush hours. Check out the DOT's website for detailed schedules.

Snow Routes

Failure to efficiently handle city snow removal seals the re-election fate of Chicago's mayors. The Department of Streets and Sanitation manages the ice and snow removal on Chicago's streets. Over 280 salt spreaders/plows cruise 607 miles of arterial streets divided into 245 designated snow routes. Parking is automatically restricted on these routes when snow is piled at least two inches on the pavement. Unfortunately, the two-inch snow routes are a crap-shoot. Tow trucks will enforce these restrictions by their own rules, it seems. On a snow route, you will either find your car gone or buried by a passing plow. Safety dictates you keep your car off of these routes even if only an inch and a half are predicted. Priority arteries also restrict parking daily from 3 am until 7 am between December 1 and April 1, whether or not snow is present (but it usually is).

Major Expressways and Tollways

While the city's grid system is logical, the interstate highway system feeding into the city is confusing for those who don't travel it often. Chicago has free expressways and tollways which require paying a fee. Roads often transition from one to the other. The I-PASS speeds up the life of frequent tollway users and can be purchased through the Illinois State Toll Highway Authority located in Downers Grove (773-242-3620).

DMVs

The Illinois Department of Motor Vehicles (DMV) is one of life's unavoidable hassles. But you'd be pleasantly surprised to see how many of your car-related responsibilities (like renewing your driver's license, getting vehicle registrations, etc.) can be completed online (www.dmv.org). Unless you're British and enjoy standing in line for hours. Visit the website, or call 312-793-1010 for more information.

Chicago DMVs	*Map*	*Hours*
100 W Randolph St	5	Mon–Fri: 8 am–5 pm
69 W Washington St, Concourse Level	5	Mon–Fri: 8 am–5 pm
17 N State St, Ste 1000	5	Mon–Fri: 8 am–4:30 pm
5401 N Elston Ave	46	Mon–Tues: 8:30 am–5 pm; Wed: 10 am–7 pm; Thurs–Fri: 8:30 am–5 pm
9901 S Martin Luther King Dr	59	Mon–Tues: 8:30 am–5 pm; Wed: 10 am–7 pm; Thurs–Fri: 8:30 am–5 pm
5301 W Lexington Ave	49	Tues: 9 am–7 pm; Wed–Fri: 8 am –5:30 pm; Sat: 8 am–12 pm

General Information

Office of the City Clerk—Parking Permits

Mailing Address: City Hall
121 N La Salle St, Rm 107
Chicago, IL 60602
Phone: 312-744-6861
Hours: Weekdays, 8 am–5 pm
Website: www.chicityclerk.com

Department of Revenue (DOR)—Parking Ticket Payments

Mailing Address: PO Box 88292
Chicago, IL 60680-1292
Phone: 312-744-0512
Website: www.cityofchicago.org/revenue
Parking Ticket Assistance & "Boot" Inquiries:
312-744-PARK (7275)
Auto Pound Headquarters: 312-744-4444
(for towed vehicles)
City Non-Emergency Phone: 311

City Stickers

Residents of Chicago who own motor vehicles must have an annually renewed city sticker for their cars. All classes of city vehicle stickers can be purchased from the Office of the City Clerk through the mail (by returning the renewal application you've received in the mail), in person at one of their offices, or online. Stickers may also be purchased at local currency exchanges; however, added fees may apply. New residents are required to purchase their sticker in person with a proof of residency at one of the offices within 30 days of their move-in date. A four-passenger vehicle sticker for long-time residents costs $75, while new residents get a price cut at $37. Senior citizens are also eligible for discounts. After March 1st of each year, half-year stickers are available at half-price for new city residents or current residents who've recently purchased a car. For more information on office locations and pricing, call 312-742-9200 or visit the City Clerk's website.

Residential Zone Permit Parking

Chicago's Residential Parking Permit program reserves street parking during peak parking hours for neighborhood residents and those who provide a service to the residents. Cars in violation of this ordinance will be ticketed. Permits cost $25 annually and are available through the Office of the City Clerk via mail, online, and in person. Applicants must have a valid Chicago City Sticker and an Illinois State license plate. One-day guest passes may also be purchased and distributed by qualified residents. Fifteen 24-hour passes cost $5 per pack at a two-pack limit, so choose your guests wisely and frugally. Check out the City Clerk website or call 312-744-5346 for more information.

Parking Tickets

The Department of Revenue (DOR) handles the payment of parking tickets. You can pay parking tickets by mail, online, or in person. For the addresses and hours of payment processing and hearing facilities, see the DOR website.

Your car gets fitted with the boot when you accrue three or more unpaid tickets. Ten or more tickets and the entire car is encased in molybdenum steel. If the violations are not paid within 24 hours of booting, your vehicle will be towed...maybe. In addition to the boot fee, towing and storage fees must be paid to retrieve your car from a City Auto Pound. If your car is towed due to a boot, contact the City of Chicago's Ticket Help Line (312-744-7275). All payments for outstanding parking ticket debt must be made to a DOR Payment Center, NOT at the pound. The city has two payment plans available for motorists with large ticket fines. The General Payment Plan requires either a deposit of $500 or 25% of your parking debt (whichever is greater) in addition to all outstanding boot, towing, and storage fees. If you qualify for the Hardship Parking Payment Plan, you can make a deposit of $250 or 25% of your debt, whichever is lower. Visit the DOR website for further requirements.

Auto Pounds

To locate your towed vehicle, contact the City of Chicago Auto Pound Headquarters (312-744-4444). There are six auto pounds in addition to the O'Hare Auto Pound (10000 W O'Hare at Remote Lot E, 773-694-0990).

For a standard vehicle, the towing fee is a hefty $150 plus a $10 per day storage fee for the first five days then $35 per day thereafter. Fees are paid at the pound where they accept cash, VISA, MasterCard, Discover, American Express, and first-born children.

Failure to claim vehicles or request a hearing within 21 days of notification can result in your convenient mode of transportation being sold or destroyed and, even then, you still owe the city for the outstanding fines. In that case, see the rest of the Transit section for alternate ways of navigating your way through Chicago.

Important note: Typically on the streets of Chicago, minor street repairs or construction will occur. Signs are taped or tacked to a tree or parking meter nearby. If you leave your car in such an area your car will be towed. However, DO NOT contact the city pound. They will have no idea what you are talking about! Before freaking out, save yourself the embarrassment of reporting your car stolen, and call the number posted on the sign where your car once was. Chances are your car was "temporarily" moved to another location...however, it may not have been by the city. Operators should be able to tell you the general location of your car through your license plate number. City code mandates that the moving of a car must be reported within a few hours whether it be by the city or the other parking powers that be. Otherwise, you can always walk around your neighborhood aimlessly searching for your car.

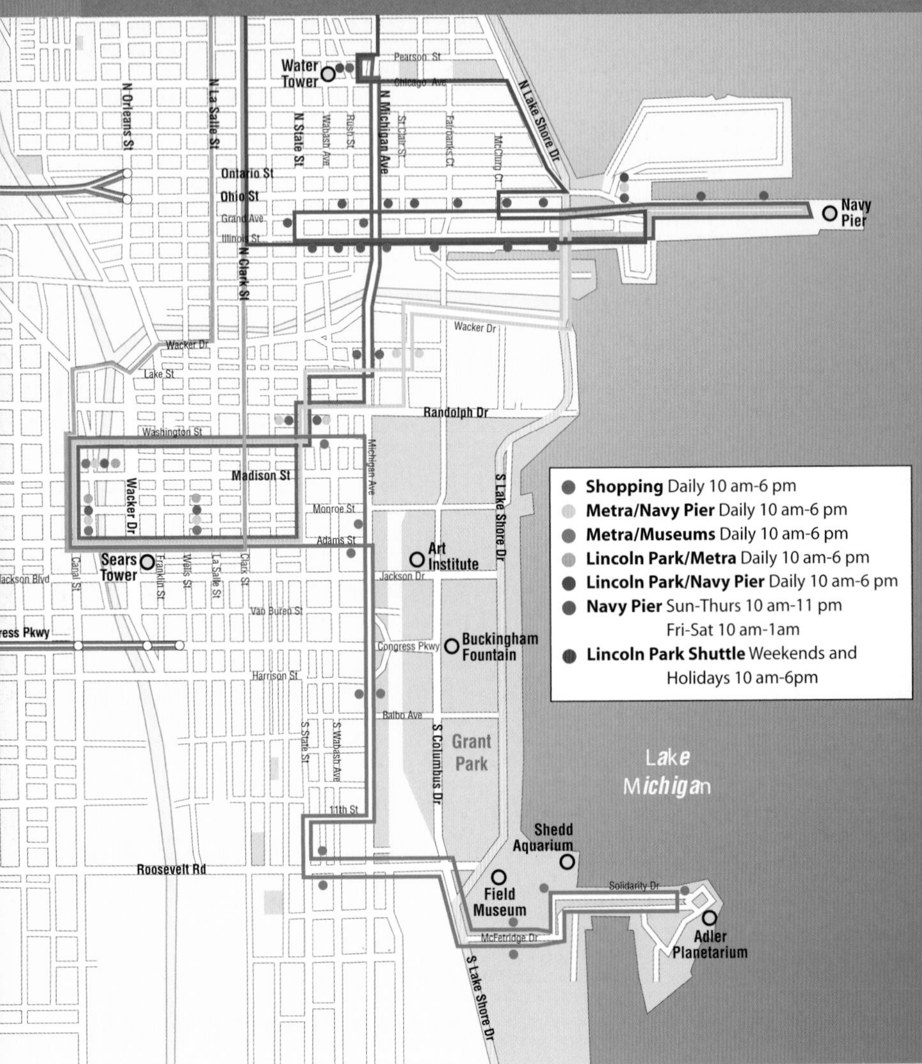

The city of Chicago runs a free trolley service from Memorial Day through Labor Day every year. Most trolleys run every 20–30 minutes from 10 am–6 pm daily (check map for specific line hours). The six color-coded trolley routes dovetail with CTA bus routes, make stops at major Loop L stations and Metra stations, and travel to and from Chicago's most popular attractions. Trolley stops are identifiable by graphic, color-coded signage. Because fare-based trolley companies also roam the streets, be sure to look for the "Free Trolley" sign in the front window. You don't need a ticket to ride; just hop on and off as you please.

For more information, contact: 877-244-2246; www.cityofchicago.org/Transportation

Lake Michigan
Diversey Harbor
North Pond
Lincoln Park
Lincoln Park Lagoon
South Pond
South Pond
41
MAP 29
MAP 30
MAP 31
MAP 32
W Diversey Pkwy
W Diversey Ave
W Schubert Ave
W Drummond Pl
W Wrightwood Ave
W Deming Pl
W St James Pl
W Roslyn Pl
W Arlington Pl
W Fullerton Pkwy
W Kemper Pl
W Belden Ave
W Grant Pl
W Webster Ave
W Dickens Ave
W Armitage Ave
W Wisconsin St
W Menomonee St
W Willow St
W St Paul Ave
W Eugenie St
W Concord Pl
W Concord Ln
W Lutz Pl
W Weed St
W Blackhawk St
W Eastman St
W Schiller St
W North Ave
E North Ave
W Germania Pl
W Burton Pl
E Burton Pl
E Schiller St
N Halsted St
N Clark St
N Lincoln Ave
N Lake Shore Dr
N Cannon Dr
N Stockton Dr
Stockton Dr
N Lincoln Park W
N Ridge Dr
N La Salle St
N State Pkwy
N Dearborn Pkwy
N Sandburg Ter
N Astor St
N Wieland St
N North Park Ave
N Orleans St
N Sedgwick St
N Hudson Ave
N Mohawk St
N Cleveland Ave
N St Michaels Ct
N Meyer Ct
N Larrabee St
N Vine St
N Frontier Ave
N Burling St
N Dayton St
N Fremont St
N Howe St
N Orchard St
N Pearl Ct
N Edward Ct
N Geneva Ter
N Lakeview Ave
N Commonwealth Ave
N Clark St
N Hampden Ct
N Pine Grove Ave
N Lehmann Ct
W Drummond Pl
N Mildred Ave
N Crilly Ct
N Fern Ct
N Sheridan Rd

Useful Phone Numbers

City Board of Elections	312-269-7900
State Board of Elections	312-814-6440
ComEd	800-334-7661
Peoples Gas Billing	312-240-4350
Peoples Gas Emergencies	312-240-7001
Drivers Licensing Facilities	312-793-1010
Office of Mayor Richard Daley	312-744-5000
Governor's Office	217-782-6830
General Aldermanic Information	312-269-7900

Helpful Websites

Angie's List • www.angieslist.com
Membership-driven list rating local contractors and other services. Great for home repair, caterers, etc.

Metromix • www.metromix.com
City guide put out by the *Trib*.

Centerstage Chicago • www.centerstagechicago.com
Chicago's original online guide.

Citysearch Chicago • www.chicago.citysearch.com
Restaurants, clubs, etc.

City of Chicago • www.ci.chi.il.us
Helpful all-purpose guide to city services.

Spacefinder • www.chireader.com/spacefinder
The source for apartment rentals.

Taxi Cabs

Checker	312-243-2537
American United	773-248-7600
Flash Cab	773-898-8500 or 773-561-4444
Yellow Cab	800-829-4222

We're Number One!!!

World's Busiest Airport: O'Hare International
World's Largest Public Library: Harold Washington Library
World's Largest Aquarium: Shedd Aquarium
World's Largest Free Public Zoo: Lincoln Park Zoo
World's Largest Modern Art Museum:
Museum of Contemporary Art
Worlds Largest Commercial Office Building:
Merchandise Mart, 222 Merchandise Mart Plaza
World's Longest Street: Western Avenue
World's Busiest Roadway: The Dan Ryan Expressway
World's Largest Food Festival: Taste of Chicago

Chicago Timeline

1779: Jean-Baptiste Point du Sable establishes Chicago's first permanent settlement.
1803: U.S. Army constructs Fort Dearborn. It is destroyed during conflicts with Native Americans in 1812 and rebuilt in 1816.
1818: Illinois is admitted into the union.
1833: Chicago incorporates as a town of 350 people, bordered by Kinzie, Des Plaines, Madison, and the lakefront.
1837: Chicago incorporates as a city. The population is 4,170. Ogden becomes the city's first mayor.
1851: Northwestern University is founded.
1856: Fort Dearborn is demolished.
1860: Republican Party nominates Abraham Lincoln for president at Chicago's first political convention.
1865: Merry Christmas! Union Stockyards open on Christmas Day.
1869: Water tower is completed.
1871: Great Chicago Fire!
1885: World's first "skyscraper," the 9-story Home Insurance building, goes up on La Salle Street.
1886: Haymarket Riots. Eight Chicago policemen are killed.
1889: Jane Addams opens Hull House.
1892: World's first elevated trains begin operation.
1893: Columbia Exposition celebrates 400th anniversary of Columbus's discovery of America.
1907: Chicago physicist Abraham Michelson is first American to win Nobel Prize.
1910: Original Comiskey Park opens.
1914: Wrigley Field opens.
1927: $750,000 donated to city to build fountain in honor of Clarence Buckingham.
1929: John G. Shedd presents Shedd Aquarium as a "gift to the Chicago People."
1930: Adler Planetarium opens through a gift from Max Adler.
1930: Merchandise Mart built by Marshall Field.
1931: Chicagoan Jane Addams becomes first woman to win Nobel Peace Prize.
1931: Al Capone sent to prison for 11 years for evading taxes.
1934: John Dillinger shot by FBI outside Biograph Theater.
1955: O'Hare International Airport opens.
1958: End of the line: Last streetcar in Chicago stops operating.
1968: Democratic National Convention riots.
1971: Chicago Union Stock Yards are closed.
1974: Sears Tower is completed.
1983: Harold Washington elected first black mayor.
1995: A heat wave contributed to the death of over 700 Chicagoans.
1997: City Council absolves Mrs. O'Leary's cow of blame for Great Chicago Fire.
1998: Six-peat! Chicago Bulls win their sixth world championship in eight years.
2003: Four-peat! Richard M. Daley re-elected for historic fourth term!
2005: White Sox win World Series; various plagues averted by miracle.

12 Essential Chicago Movies

Northside 777 (1948)
Man with the Golden Arm (1955)
Raisin in the Sun (1961)
Medium Cool (1969)
Blues Brothers (1980)
Risky Business (1983)
Ferris Bueller's Day Off (1986)
The Untouchables (1987)
Hoop Dreams (1994)
My Best Friend's Wedding (1997)
High Fidelity (2000)
Barbershop (2002)

Overview

WGN is the classic Chicago TV station. Its radio affiliate at 720 AM *is* Chicago talk radio. WGN isn't a bad place to find intelligent conversation, particularly through the long-running "Extension 720" program hosted by Milt Rosenberg. **WXRT** is the city's independent rock station—one of the few remaining stations still free from the smothering embrace of Clear Channel Communications. Their Sunday morning Beatles Brunch with host Terri Hemmert (a Chicago institution in her own right) is heaven for fans of the Fab Four. In general the station is a little heavy on the white-boy blues (think Clapton and Stevie Ray Vaughan) and crunchy rock ala Dave Matthews and Hootie—if that's your thing. Midway down the dial, alt-music station **Q101's** morning host Mancow Muller is a more immature version of Howard Stern—less sex, more body secretions. In terms of print media, we'll put it this way: the ***Tribune*** appeals to Cubs fans, while the ***Sun-Times*** is favored by White Sox fans. ***Time Out*** is the latest alt entertainment weekly to come to Chicago and the ***Reader*** is the essential paper for slacker job seekers and apartment hunters. The *Reader* also is known for its investigative pieces that take on everything from the daily life of dogcatchers to the seamy world of local politics.

Television

	CLTV	(Cable)
2	WBBM	(CBS)
5	WMAQ	(NBC)
7	WLS	(ABC)
9	WGN	(WB)
11	WTTW	(PBS)
20	WYCC	(PBS)
23	WFBT	(Brokered—ethnic)
26	WCIU	(Independent)
32	WFLD	(Fox)
38	WCPX	(PAX)
44	WSNS	(Telemundo)
50	WPWR	(UPN)
60	WEHS	(Home shopping)
66	WGBO	(Univision)

Radio

AM

560	WIND	Spanish
620	WTMJ	News/Talk
670	WMAQ	Sports
720	WGN	Talk
780	WBBM	Talk
820	WCSN	Sports
850	WAIT	Standards
890	WLS	News/Talk
1000	WLUP	Sports
1110	WMBI	Religious
1200	WLXX	Spanish
1280	WBIG	Talk
1390	WGCI	Gospel
1450	WVON	Talk (Black-oriented)
1490	WPNA	Polish
1510	WWHN	Gospel
1570	WBEE	Jazz

FM

88.1	WCRX	Columbia College
88.5	WHPK	U of Chicago
88.7	WLUW	Loyola U
89.3	WNUR	Northwestern
90.1	WMBI	Christian
90.0	WDCB	Jazz
91.5	WBEZ	National Public Radio
93.1	WXRT	Rock
93.5	WJTW	Adult Contemporary
93.9	WLIT	Adult Contemporary
94.7	WZZN	Modern Rock
95.1	WIIL	Rock
95.5	WNUA	New Age
95.9	WKKD	Oldies
96.3	WBBM	Dance
97.9	WLUP	Rock
98.7	WFMT	Classical
99.5	WUSN	Country
100.3	WNND	Adult Contemporary
101.1	WKQX	Modern Rock
101.9	WTMX	Adult Contemporary
102.7	WVAZ	Urban Contemporary
103.1	WXXY	Latin Pop
103.5	WKSC	Top 40
104.3	WJMK	Oldies
105.1	WOJO	Spanish
105.9	WCKG	Rock
106.7	WYLL	Christian
107.5	WGCI	Urban Contemporary

Print

Chicago Defender	2400 S Michigan Ave	312-225-2400	Black community newspaper.
Chicago Free Press	3845 N Broadway St	773-868-0005	Gay community news.
Chicago Magazine	500 N Dearborn St	312-222-8999	Upscale glossy mag.
Chicago Reader	11 E Illinois St	312-828-0350	Free weekly with listings.
Chicago Reporter	332 S Michigan Ave	312-427-4830	Investigative reporting on issues of race, poverty, and social justice.
Chicago Sun-Times	401 N Wabash Ave	312-321-3000	One of the big dailies.
Chicago Tribune	435 N Michigan Ave	312-222-3232	The other big daily.
Crain's Chicago Business	740 N Rush St	312-649-5200	Business news.
Daily Herald	PO Box 280, Arlington Hts	847-427-4300	Suburban news.
Daily Southtown	6901 W 159th St, Tinley Pk	708-633-6700	News for southsiders.
Ebony	820 S Michigan Ave	312-322-9200	National glossy about African Americans.
Hyde Park Herald	5240 S Harper Ave	773-643-8533	Local for Hyde Parkers.
Korea Times	4447 N Kedzie Ave	773-463-1050	Daily Korean-language newspaper.
La Raza	3909 N Ashland Ave	773-273-2900	Hispanic community paper.
Lerner-Booster-Skyline	7331 N Lincoln Ave, Lincolnwood	847-329-2000	Conglomeration of neighborhood papers.
N'Digo	401 N Wabash Ave	312-321-2800	Black community weekly.
New City	770 N Halsted Ave	312-243-8786	Alternative free weekly.
The Onion	47 W Division St	312-751-0503	Local listings in AV Club insert.
Red Eye	435 N Michigan Ave	312-222-4970	Commuter-deigned offshoot of the *Trib* for 20- and 30-somethings.
Red Streak	401 N Wabash Ave	773-321-3000	Where goest the *Tribune*, there goest the *Sun-Times*.
Time Out Chicago	247 S State St	312-924-9555	Glossy arts and entertainment weekly.
Today's Chicago Woman	233 E Ontario St	312-951-7600	Weekly for working women.
Windy City Times	1940 W Irving Park Rd	773-871 7610	Gay-targeted news weekly.

20 Essential Chicago Books

Native Son, by Richard Wright. Gripping novel about a young black man on the South Side in the '30s.

Neon Wilderness, by Nelson Algren. Short story collection set in Ukrainian Village and Wicker Park.

One More Time, by Mike Royko. Collection of Royko's *Tribune* columns.

The Boss: Richard M. Daley, by Mike Royko. Biography of the former Mayor.

The Jungle, by Upton Sinclair. Gritty look at the life in the meat-packing plants.

Adventures of Augie March, by Saul Bellow. More Chicago in the '30s.

V.I. Warshawsky mystery series, by Sara Paretsky. Series firmly rooted in Chicago landscape.

50 Years at Hull House, by Jane Addams. Story of the Near West Side.

Secret Chicago, by Sam Weller. Off-the-beaten path guidebook.

Ethnic Chicago, by Melvin Holli & Peter D'A. Jones. Insider's guide to Chicago's ethnic neighborhoods.

House on Mango Street, by Sandra Cisneros. Short story collection about a Latina childhood in Chicago.

Our America: Life and Death on the South Side of Chicago, by Lealan Jones, et al. Life in the Chicago Projects as told by two schoolchildren.

The Coast of Chicago, by Stuart Dybek. Short stories of Chicago denizens.

Hairstyles of the Damned, by Joe Meno. Teen angst and punk rock in '80s Chicago.

Never a City So Real: A Walk in Chicago, by Alex Kotlowitz. Modern reflection on the city of big shoulders.

American Pharaoh: Mayor Richard J. Daley, by Adam Cohen and Elizabeth Taylor. Recent work that explores the life and works of Hizzoner the First.

Studs Lonigan, by James T. Farrell. Growing up gritty and Irish in Washington Park, circa the early 20th century.

Chicago: The Second City, by A. J. Liebling. Legendary *New Yorker* columnist and curmudgeon comes to the Windy City, gives it a new sobriquet, and tells all.

A Guide to Chicago's Murals, by Mary Lackritz Gray. Murals, murals, and more murals.

The Pig and the Skyscraper, by Marco D'Eramo. Wandering Italian sociologist comes to Chicago and explores the wide world of capitalism through Chicago's radical history, skyscrapers, and meat-processing plants.

From May to September, every corner of the city is hopping with all manner of block parties, church carnivals, neighborhood festivals, and all-out hootenanny. Contact the Mayor's Office of Special Events for a complete list of the city's 100+ festivals.

Event	When & Where	Description
Chinese New Year	Sunday after the Chinese New Year (late-January or mid-February), Chinatown	2007 is the year of the Boar. Celebrate!
Chicago Auto Show	Early February, McCormick Place	The nation's largest auto show celebrates its 99th year.
Women in the Director's Chair Festival	Two weeks in March, Chicago Cultural Center	Femme films. www.widc.org
Expo For Today's Black Woman	Friday to Sunday, first weekend of March, McCormick Place North, 2301 S Lake Shore Dr	A sister can certainly exhale like a villain there! http://merrygreenpromotions.com/upcomingevents/etbw.html
St Patrick's Day Parade	Saturday prior to St Paddy's, Columbus Ave, Balbo to Randolph	The Chicago River turns green. On purpose.
Chicago Flower Show	Mid-March, Navy Pier	Escape from winter.
Chicago Latino Film Festival	Early-April, various venues	20+-year-old festival screens the best in local and international Latino film. www.latinoculturalcenter.org/Filmfest
Great Chicago Places & Spaces	Weekend in Mid-May, various venues	An architectural love-fest with dozens of free tours around the city.
Bike Chicago	May-September, various venues	More than 100 events including "Bike the Drive" and the midnight LATE Ride.
Printers Row Book Fair	Second weekend in June, Dearborn St, b/w Harrison St & Balbo Dr	Watch for Booksellers Gone Wild coming soon to pay-per-view.
Andersonville Midsommarfest	Second weekend in June, Clark St, b/w Foster & Balmoral Aves	Ain't it Swede?
Old Town Art Fair	Mid-June, 1800 N Orleans St, Menominee St, Lincoln Ave	Arts and crafts.
Taste of Chicago	Last week in June, first week in July, Grant Park	Why go to a restaurant when you can eat standing up in the hot sun in a crowd?
Country Music Fest	Last weekend in June, Grant Park	Annual Lakeside hoe-down. www.cityofchicago.org/specialevents
Gay Pride Parade	Last Sunday in June, Halsted/Broadway Sts b/w Halsted & Grace Sts	200,000 of the city's gay community and their fans take it to the streets. www.chicagopridecalendar.org
43rd Street BluesFest	Mid-June, Oakwood & Cottage Grove	The warm-up for the Grant Park Blues fest.
Beverly Arts Fair	Third week in June, Beverly Arts Center, 2407 W 111th St	Family fun in Beverly.
Juneteenth Celebration	Third Saturday in June, 79th & Stony Island	African American Pride celebration includes parade, music, and lots of barbeque at Rainbow Beach.
57th Street Art Fair	First week in June, 57th & Kimbark	Oldest juried art fair in the Midwest. www.57thstreetartfair.org
Jeff Fest	Late June, Jefferson Park	Neighborhood festival of guys named Jeff. We kid you not.
Bronzeville House Tours	Late June, 3402 S King Dr	The best way to peek into Chicago's African-American history.
Gospel Music Festival	First weekend in June, Grant Park	As much about the soul food as the music.
Chicago Blues Festival	Second weekend in June, Grant Park	Drawing the top names in blues for 21 years.
Old Town Art Fair	Mid-June, 1800 N Orleans St, Menominee St, Lincoln Ave	Arts and crafts.
Independence Eve Fireworks	July 3, Grant Park	Real fireworks occur when a million spectators try to leave Grant Park.
Chicago Hip-Hop Heritage Month	July 1-31, various venues	Where "New Beat" culture celebrates its past, present, and future, www.chihiphop.org.
Venetian Night	Third weekend in July, Monroe Harbor	Wow! Decked out boats!
Outdoor Film Festival	Tuesdays, Mid-July to mid-August, Grant Park	Classic movies, a carafe of vino, and KFC. Life is good.

Event	When & Where	Description
2006 National Hip-Hop Political Convention	July 19-23 NIEU Carruthers Center for Inner City Studies, 700 E Oakwood Blvd	The foundation on which grassroots hip-hop organizing will become a house united, www.chiloc.com.
Rock Around the Block	Second weekend in July	Lots of street-festival quality live music. Expect Bumpus and Underwater People.
Taste of Logan Square	Mid-July, Fullerton & Kedzie	It tastes cement-y.
Korean Street Festival	Mid-July, 3200–3400 W Bryn Mawr	One-stop shopping for your bibimbap, juk, and kimbap.
Fiesta Del Sol	Last weekend in July, Cermak Rd, b/w Throop & Morgan Sts	One of the most festive of the fests.
Bud Billiken Parade	Second Saturday in August, King Dr	World's biggest African-American parade. www.budbillikenparade.com
Black Harvest International Film & Video Festival	First two weeks of August, Gene Siskel Film Center, 164 N State St	Where the substance and form of black filmmaking knows no boundaries, www.siskelfilmcenter.org.
North Halsted Market Days	Second weekend in August, Halsted St b/w Belmont Ave & Addison St	See Gay Pride Parade. Add beer and live music.
Air and Water Show	Third weekend in August, lakefront	The Stealth Bombers never fail to thrill.
Viva Chicago Latin Music Fest	Last weekend in August, Grant Park	Salsa under the stars.
Taste of Polonia	Last weekend in August, 5200 W Lawrence Ave	Polka and keilbasa! Heaven! Pierogis! Paradise!
Gold Coast Art Fair	Early August, Wells St	Fine arts in a fancy neighborhood.
Summer Dance	August, Grant Park	Kick up your heels under the stars. Free lessons and free DJs on Wednesday nights.
African Festival of the Arts	Friday to Sunday, Labor Day weekend, Washington Park, 5531 S King Dr	Last and biggest major afrocentric expo of the year, www.africainternationalhouse.org.
Celtic Fest	Second weekend in September, Grant Park	Clog dance in the bonny heath.
German-American Fest	Early September, Lincoln & Leland	Octoberfest in Lincoln Square. Bring your own leiderhosen.
World Music Festival	Late September, Grant Park	Music acts from around the world, plus beer.
57th St Children's Book Fair	Late September, b/w Kimbark & Dorchester Aves	Lots of kids. Lots of books.
Chicago International Film Festival	October, various locations	Worthy display of the best in international cinema. www.chicagofilmfestival.org
Chicagoween	Mid to Late October, Daley Plaza	Daley Plaza becomes Pumpkin Plaza with trick-or-treating, pumpkin carving, and story-tellers.
Halloween Parade	Halloween day, Halsted b/w Belmont & Addison	Flamboyant Boystown costume extravaganza.
Tree Lighting	Day after Thanksgiving, Daley Plaza	Decking the halls by City Hall.
Mag Mile Lights Festival	Saturday evening before Thanksgiving, Michican Ave	Festive celebration of obligatory consumption.
Thanksgiving Parade	Thanksgiving Day morning, 8:30 am, State St	8:30 am? Yeah, as if.
Christkindlmarket	Thanksgiving Day–December, Daley Plaza	A German village appears for traditional Christmas shopping, food, and songs.

*All dates subject to change. For more up to date information and a schedule of neighborhood festivals, contact the Mayor's Office of Special Events at www.cityofchicago.org/specialevents.

With 13,705 sworn-in police officers, Chicago's crime incidence keeps dropping. Index crime numbers are the lowest in every category since 1984.

Statistics	*2005*	*2004*	*2003*	*2002*	*2001*
Murders	447	448	599	651	665
Criminal Sexual Assault	1,618	1,678	1,836	2,024	1,933
Robbery	15,961	15,914	17,328	18,530	18,450
Aggravated Assault and Battery	17,934	18,746	19,812	22,905	25,544
Burglary	25,298	24,425	25,151	25,613	26,009
Theft	83,235	93,245	97,921	97,468	97,939
Motor Vehicle Theft	22,491	22,803	22,729	25,098	27,689
Arson	683	782	947	1,016	1,004

Departments	*Address*	*Phone*	*Map*
1st District (Central)	1718 S State St	312-745-4290	11
9th District (Deering)	3501 S Lowe Ave	312-747-8227	13
21st District (Prairie)	300 E 29th St	312-747-8340	14
2nd District (Wentworth)	5101 S Wentworth Ave	312-747-8366	15
13th District (Wood)	937 N Wood St	312-746-8357	21
12th District (Monroe)	100 S Racine Ave	312-746-8309	24
14th District (Shakespeare)	2150 N California Ave	312-744-8290	27
18th District (Near North)	1160 N Larrabee St	312-742-5870	31
24th District (Rogers Park)	6464 N Clark St	312-744-5907	34
20th District (Foster)	5400 N Lincoln Ave	312-742-8714	35
19th District (Belmont)	2452 W Belmont Ave	312-744-5983	42
23rd District (Town Hall)	3600 N Halsted St	312-744-8320	44

Chicago hospitals are as varied and interesting as the citizens they serve. Although you don't have to go far to find medical facilities in this city, finding quality medical care is another story.

The Illinois Medical District on the near southwest side is one of the largest healthcare centers in the world. Here you will find the brand-new **Stroger (Map 25)** hospital (basically the infamous Cook County Hospital with a facelift), home to the nation's first and oldest trauma unit. It is by far the busiest hospital in the area and serves a large and mostly indigent population. Unless you are in danger of certain demise, avoid Stroger's emergency department since waits of up to 12 hours for a non-life-threatening reason may bore you to death. The medical campus is also home to the **University of Illinois Medical Center (Map 25)**, **Rush University Medical Center (Map 25)**, and several smaller hospitals.

On the north side, your best bet is to go to **Illinois Masonic Medical Center (Map 43)** for anything serious or **St. Joseph's Hospital (Map 44)** where you might get a room with a view of Lake Michigan. **Northwestern Memorial Hospital (Map 3)** is also a good choice if you are closer to downtown and/or if you have really good insurance. They also house several hospitals in the same campus, and if you break your neck craning to look up at all the pretty skyscrapers in the Streeterville 'hood, they have a first-rate spinal cord unit.

On the south side, the **University of Chicago (Map 19)** hospitals are second to none. A large and imposing set of buildings set in a somewhat dubious neighborhood, the hospital has a first-rate children's emergency department, world-renowned staff, and an excellent reputation. Park on the street at your own risk—the garage may be expensive, but so is replacing your car stereo.

Emergency Rooms	*Address*	*Phone*	*Map*
Northwestern Memorial	251 E Huron St	312-926-2000	3
Mercy	2525 S Michigan Ave	312-567-2000	11
Michael Reese	2929 S Ellis Ave	312-791-2000	14
Provident	500 E 51st St	312-572-2000	16
University of Chicago	858 E 58th St	773-702-1000	19
University of Chicago Children's	5721 S Maryland Ave	773-702-1000	19
St Elizabeth's	1431 N Claremont Ave	773-278-2000	21
St Mary of Nazareth	2233 W Division St	312-770-2005	21
John H Stroger	1901 W Harrison St	312-864-6000	25
Rush-Presbyterian St Luke's	1750 W Harrison St	312-942-6428	25
St Anthony's	2875 W 19th St	773-484-1000	25
University of Illinois at Chicago	1740 W Taylor St	312-355-4000	25
VA Medical Center	820 S Damen Ave	312-569-8387	25
Children's Memorial	2300 Children's Plz	773-880-4000	30
Lincoln Park	550 W Webster Ave	773-883-2000	30
Swedish Covenant	5145 N California Ave	773-878-8200	38
Methodist Hospital of Chicago	5025 N Paulina St	773-271-9040	39
Louis A Weiss Memorial	4646 N Marine Dr	773-878-8700	40
Thorek	850 W Irving Park Rd	773-525-6780	40
Advocate Illinois Masonic Medical Center	836 W Wellington Ave	773-975-1600	43
St Joseph's	2900 N Lake Shore Dr	773-665-3086	44

Other Hospitals	*Address*	*Phone*	*Map*
Rehabilitation Institute of Chicago	345 E Superior St	312-238-1000	3
VA Lakeside Medical Center	333 E Huron St	312-569-8387	3
Advocate Health Center Sykes Center	2545 S Dr Martin L King Jr Dr	312-842-7117	11
Advocate Health Center Lincoln Park	2400 N Sheffield Ave	773-880-0320	29
Kindred Chicago-Lakeshore	6130 N Sheridan Rd	773-381-1222	37
Kindred	2544 W Montrose Ave	773-267-2622	38
Advocate Health Center Irving & Western	4025 N Western Ave, Bldg E	773-275-7700	39
Neurologic & Orthopedic Institute	4501 N Winchester Ave	773-250-0000	39
Ravenswood	4550 N Winchester Ave	773-878-4300	39
Chicago Lakeshore	4840 N Marine Dr	773-878-9700	40

The Chicago Public Library System has 75 branches serving Chicago citizens. Much to the delight of many Windy City book-borrowers, the city has recently constructed several new branches and renovated over 55 existing neighborhood branches with the help of a huge capital improvement program.

With the **Harold Washington Library (Map 5)** as their anchor, two regional libraries, **Sulzer Regional Library (Map 39)** in Lincoln Square and the Southwest side's **Woodson Library (9525 S Halstead St, Map 59),** serve as backup reference and research collections. It is worth noting that Harold Washington Library has a few stand-out exhibits, including one of the history of the blues in the city and, of course, one on the man himself, Chicago's first African-American mayor. Neighborhood branches are geared towards the communities they serve: **Chinatown (Map 10)** has an impressive collection of Asian studies material and literature, the **Roger's Park (Map 34**) branch features a significant Russian-language selection, and Boystown's **John Merlo (Map 44)** collection houses a considerable offering of gay literature and studies. Many of the smaller branches have a decent selection of juvenile materials as well as career guidance and adult popular literature (and Internet access). Architecturally, some of the more interesting branches include the **Chicago Bee (Map 14)** branch, the former newspaper headquarters that serves as a neighborhood landmark for Bronzeville, and the historic **Pullman** branch, specializing in the history of the Pullman district. Chicago's first library branch, the neo-classical **Blackstone (Map 17)** library, is named after the Stockyards magnate. Families and schools should take advantage of the Chicago Public Library System's "Great Kids Museum Passports" available only to adult Chicago residents with a valid library card. You can check out any of their free passports using your library card just like you would any other item, and the loan is good for one week. The pass entitles entry for up to 8 people to any one of the eleven participating cultural institutions in the city. If you don't have access to a library card, you can still partake in a bit of book-love by checking out one of the many free lectures or readings that take place at the Harold Washington Library and the galaxy of branch outposts throughout the year. For more information, call your local library or visit the general website at www.chipublib.org.

Chicago also has many excellent research libraries and university libraries, one of which is the independent **Newberry Library (Map 32)** established in 1887. It shelves rare books, manuscripts, and maps, and hosts the raucous annual Bughouse Square debates in late July. Chicago's universities and colleges generally welcome the public to their libraries during specified hours, but it's best to call first and check.

Library	*Address*	*Phone*	*Map*
Albany Park Public Library	5150 N Kimball Ave	312-744-1933	38
Asher Library-Spertus Institute	618 S Michigan Ave	312-322-1749	9
Bessie Coleman Public Library	731 E 63rd St	312-747-7760	18
Bezazian Public Library	1226 W Ainslie St	312-744-0019	40
Blackstone Public Library	4904 S Lake Park Ave	312-747-0511	17
Budlong Woods Public Library	5630 N Lincoln Ave	312-742-9590	35
Canaryville Public Library	642 W 43rd St	312-747-0644	15
Chicago Bee Public Library	3647 S State St	312-747-6872	14
Chinatown Public Library	2353 S Wentworth Ave	312-747-8013	10
Daley Public Library	3400 S Halsted St	312-747-8990	13
Eckhart Park Branch	1330 W Chicago Ave	312-746-6069	24
Edgewater Public Library	1210 W Elmdale Ave	312-744-0718	37
Hall Public Library	4801 S Michigan Ave	312-747-2541	16
Harold Washington Public Library (Chicago Public Library Central Branch)	400 S State St	312-747-4300	5
Humboldt Park Public Library	1605 N Troy St	312-744-2244	27
John Merlo Public Library	644 W Belmont Ave	312-744-1139	44
King Public Library	3436 S Dr Martin L King Jr Dr	312-747-7543	14
Library of Columbia College	624 S Michigan Ave	312-344-7906	9
Lincoln Park Public Library	1150 W Fullerton Ave	312-744-1926	29
Lincoln-Belmont Public Library	1659 W Melrose St	312-744-0166	42
Lozano Public Library	1805 S Loomis St	312-746-4329	26
Mabel Manning Public Library	6 S Hoyne Ave	312-746-6800	23
Malcolm X College Library	1900 W Van Buren St	312-850-7244	23
Midwest Public Library	2335 W Chicago Ave	312-744-7788	23
Near North Public Library	310 W Division St	312-744-0992	31
Newberry Library	60 W Walton St	312-943-9090	32
Northtown Public Library	6435 N California Ave	312-744-2292	33
Rogers Park Public Library	6907 N Clark St	312-744-0156	34
Roosevelt Public Library	1101 W Taylor St	312-746-5656	26
Sulzer Public Library	4455 N Lincoln Ave	312-744-7616	39
University of Chicago Harper Memorial Library	1116 E 59th St	773-702-7959	19
University of Illinois at Chicago Library	801 S Morgan St	312-996-2726	26
Uptown Public Library	929 W Buena Ave	312-744-8400	40
US Library	77 W Jackson Blvd	312-353-2022	5

60648
60631
60656
60646
60630
60645
60626
60659
60660
60625
60640
60634
60641
60618
60613
60657
60635
60639
60647
60614
60651
60622
60610
60644
60624
60612
60606
60607
60650
60623
60608
60616
60632
60609
60653
60615
60638
60629
60636
60621
60637
60652
60620
60619
60649
60642
60643
60655
60628
60617
60658
60633
60611
60601
60602
60603
60604
60605

The last FedEx drop in Chicago is at 10 pm at O'Hare Airport. Get off the Kennedy at Manheim Road South. Go to Irving Park Road and head west to the first light. Make a right on O'Hare Cargo Area Road. FedEx's address is Building 611, O'Hare Cargo Area Road (800-463-3339; www.FedEx.com).

***=Pick-up time, pm; WSC=World Service Center**

Map 1 • River North / Fulton Market District

Self Service	400 W Erie St	7 PM
Self Service	401 W Superior St	7 PM
Self Service	430 W Erie St	7:30 PM
Self Service	445 W Erie St	7 PM
Self Service	600 W Chicago Ave	7:30 PM
Self Service	770 N Halsted St	7 PM

Map 2 • Near North / River North

FedEx Kinko's	222 Merchandise Mart Plz	9 PM
FedEx Kinko's	350 N Clark St	9 PM
FedEx Kinko's	444 N Wells St	8:45 PM
Image Direct Express	211 W Wacker Dr	4:30 PM
Self Service	1 E Erie St	7 PM
Self Service	1 W Superior St	7 PM
Self Service	20 W Kinzie St	7 PM
Self Service	205 W Wacker Dr	8 PM
Self Service	215 W Superior St	7 PM
Self Service	223 W Erie St	7:45 PM
Self Service	225 W Wacker Dr	7:30 PM
Self Service	300 N State St	7 PM
Self Service	308 W Erie St	7:30 PM
Self Service	311 W Superior St	7:30 PM
Self Service	320 W Ohio St	7 PM
Self Service	325 N Wells St	6 PM
Self Service	330 N Wabash Ave	8 PM
Self Service	343 W Erie St	7:30 PM
Self Service	35 E Wacker Dr	7 PM
Self Service	405 N Wabash Ave	7:30 PM
Self Service	414 N Orleans St	7:30 PM
Self Service	420 N Wabash Ave	8 PM
Self Service	515 N State St	7:30 PM
Self Service	54 W Hubbard St	8 PM
Self Service	540 N Dearborn St	6:30 PM
Self Service	55 W Wacker Dr	7 PM
Self Service	56 W Illinois St	8 PM
Self Service	640 N La Salle St	7 PM
Self Service	65 E Wacker Dr	6:30 PM
Self Service	730 N Franklin St	7:30 PM
Self Service	77 W Wacker Dr	8 PM

Map 3 • Streeterville / Mag Mile

FedEx Kinko's	500 N Michigan Ave	9 PM
FedEx Kinko's	540 N Michigan Ave	6 PM
Self Service	142 E Ontario St	7 PM
Self Service	150 E Huron St #160	7:30 PM
Self Service	211 E Chicago Ave	7 PM
Self Service	211 E Ontario St	7:30 PM
Self Service	233 E Erie St	8 PM
Self Service	251 E Huron St	7:30 PM
Self Service	333 E Ontario St	7:30 PM
Self Service	400 N Michigan Ave	7:30 PM
Self Service	401 N Michigan Ave	8 PM
Self Service	430 N Michigan Ave	7:15 PM
Self Service	444 N Michigan Ave	7:30 PM
Self Service	541 N Fairbanks Ct	8 PM
Self Service	625 N Michigan Ave	7:30 PM
Self Service	633 N St Clair St	7:30 PM
Self Service	645 N Michigan Ave	7:30 PM
Self Service	676 N Michigan Ave	7 PM
Self Service	676 N St Clair St	8 PM
Self Service	737 N Michigan Ave	8 PM

Map 4 • West Loop Gate / Greek Town

FedEx Kinko's	127 S Clinton St	8:45 PM
FedEx Kinko's	500 W Madison St	9 PM
FedEx Kinko's	843 W Van Buren St	6 PM
Self Service	10 S Riverside Plz	7 PM
Self Service	100 N Riverside Plz	7 PM
Self Service	120 S Riverside Plz	7 PM
Self Service	130 S Jefferson St	6 PM
Self Service	2 N Riverside Plz	7 PM
Self Service	216 S Jefferson St	5:30 PM
Self Service	222 S Riverside Plz	7 PM
Self Service	300 S Riverside Plz	8:30 PM
Self Service	322 S Green St	7 PM
Self Service	500 W Monroe St	6:30 PM
Self Service	547 W Jackson Blvd	7 PM
Self Service	550 W Jackson Blvd	7 PM
Self Service	550 W Washington Blvd	8 PM
Self Service	555 W Madison St	8 PM
Self Service	600 W Jackson Blvd	6:30 PM
Self Service	619 W Jackson Blvd	6:30 PM
Self Service	641 W Lake St	7 PM
Self Service	651 W Washington Blvd	5:30 PM
Self Service	730 W Randolph St	6 PM
Self Service	820 W Jackson Blvd	7 PM
Self Service	833 W Jackson Blvd	7:30 PM
Self Service	850 W Jackson Blvd	7 PM

Map 5 • The Loop

FedEx Kinko's	101 N Wacker Dr	7 PM
FedEx Kinko's	111 W Washington St	9 PM
FedEx Kinko's	2 N La Salle St	9 PM
FedEx Kinko's	200 W Jackson Blvd	9 PM
FedEx Kinko's	203 N La Salle St	8 PM
FedEx Kinko's	227 W Monroe St	9 PM
FedEx Kinko's	29 S La Salle St	8 PM
FedEx Kinko's	400 S La Salle St	7 PM
FedEx Kinko's	55 E Monroe St	8 PM
Self Service	1 E Jackson Blvd	6:30 PM
Self Service	1 N Franklin St	8 PM
Self Service	1 N State St	7 PM
Self Service	1 S Clark St	7:30 PM
Self Service	1 S Wacker Dr	8 PM
Self Service	10 S La Salle St	8 PM
Self Service	10 S Wacker Dr	7:30 PM
Self Service	100 N La Salle St	7 PM
Self Service	100 W Monroe St	8 PM
Self Service	100 W Randolph St	7 PM
Self Service	105 W Madison St	7 PM
Self Service	11 E Adams St	7 PM
Self Service	11 S La Salle St	7 PM
Self Service	111 S Wacker Dr	8 PM
Self Service	111 W Jackson Blvd	8 PM
Self Service	115 S La Salle St	8 PM
Self Service	120 N La Salle St	8 PM
Self Service	125 S Wacker Dr	8 PM
Self Service	134 N La Salle St	8 PM
Self Service	135 S La Salle St	7:30 PM
Self Service	140 S Dearborn St, Ste 109	6 PM
Self Service	150 N Wacker Dr	7:30 PM
Self Service	150 S Wacker Dr	8 PM
Self Service	155 N Wacker Dr	7:30 PM
Self Service	171 N Clark St	8 PM
Self Service	175 W Jackson Blvd	8 PM
Self Service	180 N Wabash Ave	7 PM
Self Service	190 S La Salle St	8 PM
Self Service	191 N Wacker Dr	7 PM
Self Service	20 N Michigan Ave	7 PM
Self Service	20 N Wacker Dr	8 PM
Self Service	20 S Clark St	7 PM
Self Service	200 N La Salle St	8 PM
Self Service	200 S Wacker Dr	8 PM
Self Service	200 W Adams St	7 PM
Self Service	200 W Madison St	8 PM
Self Service	200 W Monroe St	7 PM
Self Service	205 W Randolph St	8 PM
Self Service	208 S La Salle St	8 PM
Self Service	209 S La Salle St	6 PM
Self Service	210 S Clark St	8 PM
Self Service	219 S Dearborn St	5:30 PM
Self Service	222 N La Salle St	8 PM
Self Service	225 W Washington St	8 PM
Self Service	230 S Dearborn St	5:45 PM
Self Service	230 W Monroe St	8 PM
Self Service	233 S Wacker Dr	8:30 PM
Self Service	247 S State St	7 PM
Self Service	25 E Washington St	7 PM
Self Service	250 S Wacker Dr	8 PM
Self Service	29 E Madison St	7 PM
Self Service	29 N Wacker Dr	7 PM
Self Service	30 N La Salle St	8 PM
Self Service	30 N Michigan Ave	8 PM
Self Service	30 S Wacker Dr	8 PM
Self Service	30 W Monroe St	7 PM
Self Service	300 S Wacker Dr	7 PM
Self Service	303 W Madison St	8 PM
Self Service	309 W Washington St	7 PM
Self Service	311 S Wacker Dr	7:45 PM
Self Service	33 N Dearborn St	7 PM
Self Service	333 W Wacker Dr	9 PM
Self Service	36 S Wabash Ave	7:30 PM
Self Service	401 S State St	7 PM
Self Service	407 S Dearborn St	7:30 PM
Self Service	53 W Jackson Blvd	7 PM
Self Service	55 E Jackson Blvd	7 PM
Self Service	55 W Monroe St	7 PM
Self Service	70 E Lake St	7 PM
Self Service	71 S Wacker Dr	8 PM

Map 6 • The Loop / Grant Park

FedEx Kinko's	111 E Wacker Dr	7 PM
FedEx Kinko's	130 E Randolph St	9 PM
FedEx Kinko's	34 S Michigan Ave	9 PM
Self Service	150 N Michigan Ave	8 PM
Self Service	155 N Michigan Ave	7:30 PM
Self Service	200 E Randolph St	4:30 PM
Self Service	200 S Michigan Ave	8 PM
Self Service	224 S Michigan Ave	8 PM
Self Service	300 E Randolph St	8 PM
Self Service	310 S Michigan Ave	7 PM
Self Service	332 S Michigan Ave	8 PM
Self Service	360 N Michigan Ave	7 PM
Self Service	430 S Michigan Ave	7 PM
Self Service	8 S Michigan Ave	7:30 PM

Map 8 • South Loop / Printers Row / Dearborn Park

FedEx Kinko's	700 S Wabash Ave	8:45 PM
Self Service	47 W Polk St	8 PM
Self Service	536 S Clark St	7:30 PM
Self Service	542 S Dearborn St	7 PM
Self Service	600 S Federal St	7 PM
Self Service	800 S Wells St	7:30 PM
Self Service	819 S Wabash Ave	5 PM

Map 10 • East Pilsen / Chinatown

FedEx Kinko's	1242 S Canal St	8 PM
Self Service	329 W 18th St	7:30 PM

Map 11 • South Loop / McCormick Place

Self Service	1211 S Michigan Ave	7 PM
Self Service	2035 S State St	5 PM

Map 12 • Bridgeport (West)

Self Service	970 W Pershing Rd	6 PM

Map 13 • Bridgeport (East)

Business Services	3201 S Halsted St	6 PM
Self Service	3300 S Federal St	6 PM
Self Service	710 W 31st St	6 PM

Map 14 • Prairie Shores / Lake Meadows

Self Service	10 W 35th St	6 PM

Map 19 • Hyde Park

FedEx Kinko's	1315 E 57th St	7 PM
Self Service	1126 E 59th St	6:30 PM
Self Service	1155 E 60th St	7 PM
Self Service	1525 E 53rd St	7 PM
Self Service	1554 E 55th St	7 PM
Self Service	5801 S Ellis Ave	7 PM
Self Service	5841 S Maryland Av	6:45 PM
Self Service	956 E 58th St	6:30 PM
Self Service	E 57th St & S University Ave	6:30 PM
Self Service	E 59th St & S Kimbark Ave	6:30 PM

Map 20 • East Hyde Park / Jackson Park

Post Link	1634 E 53rd St	5:30 PM

Map 21 • Wicker Park / Ukrainian Village

Copy Max	1573 N Milwaukee Ave	6 PM
FedEx Kinko's	1800 W North Ave	8:45 PM
Self Service	1520 N Damen Ave	7 PM
Self Service	1608 N Milwaukee Ave	8 PM

Map 22 • Noble Square / Goose Island

Self Service	1467 N Elston Ave	7 PM
Self Service	848 W Eastman St	6:45 PM
Self Service	875 W Division St	8 PM
Self Service	935 W Chestnut St	7:30 PM
Self Service	939 W North Ave	7 PM

Map 23 • West Town / Near West Side

Packaging & Shipping Special	2002 W Chicago Ave	6 PM
Self Service	1700 W Van Buren St	7 PM
Self Service	2023 W Carroll Ave	7 PM

Map 24 • River West / West Town

Pak Mail	1461 W Chicago Ave	4:30 PM
Self Service	1030 W Chicago Ave	5 PM
Self Service	1260 W Madison St	8 PM
Self Service	1500 W Carroll Ave	6:30 PM
Self Service	400 N Noble St	7 PM

Map 25 • Illinois Medical District

Self Service	1725 W Harrison St	7 PM
Self Service	715 S Wood St	4 PM
Self Service	820 S Damen Ave	6 PM
Self Service	840 S Wood St	7 PM

Map 26 • University Village/ Little Italy / Pilsen

Self Service	1100 W Cermak Rd	7 PM
Self Service	1201 W Harrison St	6:30 PM
Self Service	851 S Morgan St	5:30 PM
University Village	1258 S Halsted St	5 PM
Windy City Pack & Ship	1100 W Cermak Rd, Ste B423	3 PM

Map 28 • Bucktown

Self Service	1829 W Fullerton Ave	7 PM
Self Service	1965 N Milwaukee Ave	4 PM
Self Service	2211 N Elston Ave	6 PM
Self Service	2349 N Elston Ave	7 PM
Self Service	2525 N Elston Ave	7:30 PM

Map 29 • DePaul / Wrightwood / Sheffield

FedEx Kinko's	2300 N Clybourn Av	8:45 PM
Self Service	1117 W Wisconsin St	4:15 PM
Self Service	1918 N Mendell St	6 PM
Self Service	2000 N Racine Ave	7 PM
Self Service	2323 N Seminary Ave	7 PM
Self Service	990 W Fullerton Ave	5:30 PM

Map 30 • Lincoln Park

Self Service	1749 N Wells St	7 PM
Self Service	2500 N Clark St	7 PM
Self Service	802 W Belden Ave	7:15 PM

Map 31 • Old Town / Near North

Cleaners Mail	900 N Kingsbury St	5:30 PM
Self Service	1333 N Kingsbury St	7 PM
Self Service	1350 N Wells St	7 PM
Self Service	213 W Institute Pl	7:30 PM
Self Service	820 N Orleans St	7:30 PM
Self Service	900 N Franklin St	8 PM

Map 32 • Gold Coast / Mag Mile

FedEx Kinko's	1201 N Dearborn St	8:45 PM
FedEx Kinko's	875 N Michigan Ave	9 PM
Global Postal & Shipping	1151 N State St	5 PM
Self Service	1 E Delaware Pl	7:30 PM
Self Service	100 E Walton St	7:30 PM
Self Service	1165 N Clark St	6:30 PM
Self Service	844 N Rush St	6 PM
Self Service	900 N Michigan Ave	7 PM
Self Service	919 N Michigan Ave	7 PM
Self Service	980 N Michigan Ave	7 PM

Map 33 • West Rogers Park

Self Service	7555 N California Ave	7:15 PM
Unik Business	2337 W Devon Ave	7 PM

Map 34 • East Rogers Park

Self Service	1723 W Devon Ave	7 PM
Self Service	6355 N Broadway St	6:30 PM
Self Service	7056 N Clark St	6 PM

Map 36 • Bryn Mawr

Self Service	5215 N Ravenswood Ave	6 PM

Map 37 • Edgewater / Andersonville

Bedmar Courier Express Service	5655 N Clark St	7 PM
Postal Mart	5250 N Broadway St	5 PM
Self Service	5419 N Sheridan Rd	7:30 PM

Map 38 • Ravenswood / Albany Park

Self Service	2522 W Lawrence Ave	7 PM

Map 39 • Ravenswood / North Center

Remesas Montrose	1924 W Montrose Ave	6 PM
Self Service	1700 W Irving Park Rd	6:30 PM
Self Service	1807 W Sunnyside Ave	7:30 PM
Self Service	4001 N Ravenswood Ave	6:30 PM
Self Service	4619 N Ravenswood Ave	7 PM

Map 40 • Uptown

Dcii	4539 N Sheridan Rd	5 PM
Mailstop & More	1338 W Irving Park Rd	5:30 PM
Self Service	4753 N Broadway St	7 PM
Self Service	4850 N Broadway St	6:30 PM

Map 41 • Avondale / Old Irving

Self Service	2630 W Bradley Pl # 2650	6:30 PM
Self Service	2704 W Roscoe St	7 PM
Self Service	3401 N California Ave	7 PM
Self Service	3611 N Kedzie Ave	7 PM

Map 42 • North Center / Roscoe Village / West Lakeview

FedEx Kinko's	3435 N Western Ave	8 PM
Mailbox Plus	2248 W Belmont Ave	6 PM
Self Service	1800 W Larchmont Ave	7:30 PM
Self Service	3717 N Ravenswood Ave	7 PM

Map 43 • Wrigleyville/ East Lakeview

FedEx Kinko's	3524 N Southport Ave	8 PM
Self Service	1300 W Belmont Ave	7:30 PM
Self Service	3024 N Ashland Ave	6 PM

Map 44 • East Lakeview

FedEx Kinko's	3001 N Clark St	8 PM
Postal Place	3304 N Broadway St	6:30 PM
Postal Plus	559 W Diversey Pkwy	6 PM
Self Service	2800 N Sheridan Rd	7 PM
Self Service	3660 N Lake Shore Dr	7:30 PM

Chicago's lesbian and gay communities are a diverse, politically influential presence within the city. Just look to the pride pylons lining North Halsted Street, the city's officially recognized gay ghetto, as well as the numerous city politicians who vie for a prime spot in the city's annual gay pride parade, that attracts over 400,000 spectators and participants on the last Sunday in June. Also in East Lakeview (aka Boystown), the North Halsted Street Market Days function as a second gay pride celebration, but this time all the gays' funky straight friends are invited.

Chicago's gay and lesbian community has also carved out a niche in the more residential and low-key Andersonville neighborhood. Anchored by the venerable Women & Children First bookstore, Clark Street, Andersonville's main drag, is a queer corridor of gay and gay-friendly shops, restaurants, and nightlife. Unlike Boystown, which is dominated by, well, boys, Andersonville is known for its female-friendly vibe. Every June, Chicago's lesbians take it to the streets in the annual Dyke March, trouncing, stomping, and twirling through Andersonville on the Saturday before the "official" gay pride parade.

Gay life in Chicago is not just limited to Halsted Street and Andersonville though, nor is it relegated to a few summer street fairs. From Edgewater to South Shore to Humbolt Park, gays and lesbians have become visible entities in many of Chicago's far-reaching 'hoods, notwithstanding the hundreds who live quietly in domestic bliss from Edison Park to Pullman.

With such a diverse array of lesbigay life thriving in the city, it's no wonder that the city's lesbigay offerings are equally diverse. Whether your interests are activism or acupuncture, draperies or drag kings, literature, liturgies, or leather bars, or some combination of the above, you can find your niche in Chicago.

Publications/Media

Pick up a copy of the following publications, log onto a website, or tune in to find out what's happening around town, from the current political headlines to the hottest clubs. Gay rags can be found in gay-friendly book stores, cafés, bars, and shops.

The Field Guide to Gay and Lesbian Chicago • by Kathie Bergquist and Robert McDonald. This comprehensive guide to gay and lesbian life in Chicago is available at bookstores everywhere.

Windy City Times • www.wctimes.com • Gay and Lesbian news weekly—check this site for a calendar of events.

Identity • A cross-cultural GLBT monthly, focusing on race, gender, and culture published by Windy City Media Group.

OUT! Guide • Comprehensive GLBT resource guide with listings for services including therapists, carpenters, real estate brokers, accounting services, social services, restaurants, and much, much more. Indispensable!

Chicago Free Press • www.chicagofreepress.com • Weekly publication with features on political issues, arts, culture, spiritual life, entertainment, and resource lists.

Gay Chicago • www.gaychicagomag.com • One of the city's oldest gay publications, with events listings, columns, news, astrology, and reviews. Male-focused.

Boi • Heavily advertising-based guide to the club scene for circuit boys.

Dyke Diva • www.dykediva.com • An online guide, for gals, of Chicago events and happenings.

Windy City Radio • Tune in Sunday nights, 11 pm–midnight, on WCKG, 105.9 FM, or tune in online at www.windycityradio.com anytime.

Think Pink at WLUW Radio • Queer radio every Tuesday 6:30–8 pm.

Arts & Culture

Women & Children First Books • 5233 N Clark St 773-769-9299 • This 27-year-old lesbian resource in Andersonville is the largest feminist bookstore in the world. Hosts events and discussions regularly.

Unabridged Books • 3251 N Broadway St 773-883-9119 • Largest gay selection in the city, located in the heart of Boystown. You will find a well-annotated book selection, as well as calendars and magazines.

Gerber/Hart Gay and Lesbian Library and Archives • 1127 W Granville St • 773-381-8030 This amazing library houses more than 10,000 books, magazines, newspapers, and videos. Regularly hosts both gay and lesbian book discussion groups. For special events including readings and screenings, check the website at www.gerberhart.org.

Barbara's Bookstore • 1110 N Lake St, Oak Park Gay-friendly bookstore with a large selection of gay and lesbian fiction and non-fiction titles.

Seminary Cooperative Bookstore
5757 University Ave • 773-752-4381
Located in Hyde Park, this bookstore has sections on GLBT studies.

57th Street Books • 1301 E 57th St • 773-684-1300
Another Hyde Park bookstore with a strong GLBT section.

Specialty Video • 3221 N Broadway St • 773-248-3434; 5307 N Clark • 773-878-3434
Huge selection of gay and lesbian videos and DVDs. Dirty movies in the back.

Chicago Filmmakers • 5243 N Clark St • 773-293-1447 • Sponsors of Reeling, the Chicago Lesbian and Gay International Film Festival.

Chicago Lesbian & Gay International Film Festival • www.chicagofilmmakers.org/reeling • Movies by and about LGBT.

Facets Multimedia • 1517 W Fullerton Ave
773-281-9075 • Large selection of gay arthouse films.

About Face Theatre • 773-784-8565
Roving gay & lesbian theater company.

Bailiwick Repertory Theater • 1229 W Belmont Ave • 773-883-1090 • Sponsors annual Gay Pride theater festival.

Theatre Building • 1225 W Belmont Ave • 773-327-5252 • Many gay theatre productions are mounted here.

Aldo Castillo Gallery • 230 W Huron St
312-337-2536 • Fine arts gallery with lesbigay latino/a bent.

Woman Made Gallery • 2418 W Bloomingdale
773-489-8900 • www.womanmade.org
Regularly features lesbian artists.

Las Manos Gallery • 5220 N Clark St • 773-728-8910 • Lesbian-owned and -operated, regularly features gay and lesbian artists.

Literary Exchange • PO Box 438583, 60643
773-509-6881 • Black lesbian writers' group publishes the 'zine *Literary Express*.

Blithe House Quarterly • www.blithe.com • Online gay & les literary journal published in Chicago.

Artemis Singers • PO Box 578296, 60657
773-764-4465 • Lesbian-feminist chorus.

Chicago Gay Men's Chorus • 3540 N Southport Ave, PO Box 333, 60657 • 773-296-0541
www.cgmc.org • The name says it all. Mounts fun, campy annual Christmas concert.

Windy City Gay Chorus • 3023 N Clark St
773-404-WCGC• Sponsors four different gay choruses, including UNISON and The Slickers.

Lakeside Pride Freedom Band •
www.lakesidepride.org • 773-381-6693
Chicago's gay & lesbian marching band. Doesn't every city have one?

Homelatte • www.scottfree.net • Weekly queer reading series with writers and musicians, hosted by Out Music 2005 Artist of the Year Scott Free.

Sports & Recreation

Chi-Town Squares • PO Box 269149 • 773-339-6743 • Gay and lesbian square dancing—what else?

Chicago Metropolitan Sports Association •
www.chicagomsa.com • 312-409-7932
Organizes all varieties of gay and lesbian competitive athletics: bowling, softball, etc.

Chicago Smelts • 3712 N Broadway St • 312-409-4974 • www.chicagosmelts.org • Gay & lesbian swim club.

Frontrunners/Frontwalkers •
www.frfwchicago.org • 312-409-2790
Weekly LBG running and walking group sponsors annual "Proud to Run" race.

Windy City Rodeo • 312-409-3835 • www.ilgracom•
Rope 'em up, rough riders.

Thousand Waves Spa • 1212 W Belmont
773-549-0700 • Women-only spa offers herb wraps and massages along with jacuzzi, steam room, and sauna.

Windy City Athletic Association • www.wcaa.net
773-327-WCAA • Also organizes gay and lesbian competitive sports.

Social Groups/Organizations

Affinity: Advocates for African-American Lesbians • www.affinity95.org • 773-324-0377

Men of All Colors Together (MACT) • PO Box 408922, 60640 • 312-409-6916

Amigas Latinas Lesbianas/Bisexuales •
www.AmigasLatinas.org • 312-409-5697

Association of Latin Men for Action (ALMA) •
info@almachicago.org • www.almachicago.org •
773-929-7688

Asians & Friends, Chicago • www.afchicago.org •
312-409-1573

P-FLAG • Parents & Friends of Lesbians and Gays •
www.pflag.org

Chicagoland Bisexual Network • www.bisexual.org/chicagoland

Chicago Gender Society • PO Box 578005, 60657 •
708-863-7714 • www.chicagogender.com

Political Groups/Activism

Equality Illinois • 3712 N Broadway St, #125, 60613 • 773-477-7173

Human Rights Campaign Chicago • 800-777-4723

Illinois G&L Political Action Network 847-856-0064

Oak Park Area Lesbians/Gays • 1145 Westgate St, Ste 206, 60301 • 708-848-0273

Stonewall Democrats • 3712 N Broadway • 773-573-8838

Religious Services

AIDS Pastoral Care Network • APCN@aol.com 4753 N Broadway St, #400, 60640 • 773-334-5333

Archdiocesan Gay and Lesbian Outreach (AGLO) 711 Belmont Ave, #106, 60657 • www.aglochicago.org • 773-525-3872 Roman Catholic

Broadway United Methodist Church 3344 N Broadway St • 773-348-2679 • Reconciling

Church of the Open Door • 5954 S Albany Ave, 60629 • 773-778-3030 • Black LBGT church

Congregation Or Chadash • 656 W Barry Ave, 60657 • 773-271-2148 • www.orchadash.org • LBGT synagogue

Dignity Chicago • www.dignitychicago.org 312-458-9438 • LBGT Catholic

Good Shepherd Parish and Christ the Redeemer MCC • 7045 N Western Ave, 60645 • 773-275-7776 Non-denominational

Integrity/Chicago • PO Box 3232, Oak Park, 60303 • 773-348-6362 • Episcopal, meets 3rd Friday for Eucharist/reception

Lake Street Church of Evanston • 607 Lake St, Evanston • 847-864-2181 • www.lakestreet.org • Inside/Out GL group

Pilgrim Congregational Church • 460 Lake St, Oak Park • 708-848-5860 • www.afterhours.com • Actively inclusive

Resurrection MCC • 5757 S University Ave, 60637 • 773-288-1535 • Non-demominational

Vajrayana Buddhist Center • 3534 N Hoyne Ave, 60618 • 773-529-1862

Health Center & Support Organizations

Horizons Community Services www.horizonsonline.org • The Midwest's largest lesbian, gay, bisexual, and transgendered social service agency.

- **Lesbian and Gay Help Line** • 773-929-HELP (6 pm until 10 pm)
- **The Crisis Hotline/Anti-Violence Project** 773-871-CARE
- **Legal Services** • 773-929-HELP legal@horizonsonline.org
- **Mature Adult Program** • 773-472-6469 x245 perryw@horizonsonline.org
- **Psychotherapy Services** • 773-472-6469 x261 sarag@horizonsonline.org
- **Youth Services** • 773-472-6469 x252 premp@horizonsonline.org

Illinois State HIV/AIDS/STD Hotline 772-AID-AIDS

AIDS Foundation of Chicago • 411 Wells St, Ste 300, Chicago, IL 60607 • 312-922-2322 • www.aidschicago.com A charitable foundation, not a direct service provider.

AIDSCARE • 315 W Barry Ave, Chicago, IL 60657 773-935-4663

GLAAD Chicago • PO Box 46343, Chicago, IL 60614 • 773-871-7633

PFLAG Chicago • PO Box 11023, Chicago, IL 60611 • 773-472-3079

Howard Brown Health Center • 4025 N Sheridan Rd • 773-388-1600 • General counseling as well as anonymous, free AIDS-testing and GLBT Domestic Violence Counseling and Prevention Program. Also provides general practitioner care for men and women, on a sliding fee scale.

Lesbian Community Cancer Project • Howard Brown Health Center • Support and resources for lesbians with cancer. Free quit-smoking clinics.

AA – New Town Alano Club • 909 W Belmont Ave, 2nd Fl • 773-529-0321 • Gay and lesbian AA, CA, OA, ACOA, Coda, etc.

Support Groups • Many support groups exist for men, women, and families in Chicago. Call Howard Brown or Horizons for referrals.

Bars & Clubs

Gay

- **Annex 3** • 3160 N Clark St • 773-327-5969 • Video bar.
- **Anvil** • 1137 W Granville St • 773-973-0006 Leather/Levis old-school joint.
- **Bucks Saloon** • 3439 N Halsted St • 773-525-1125 Typical gay watering hole.
- **Cell Block** • 3702 N Halsted St • 773-665-8064 Leather bar.
- **Charlie's** • 3726 N Broadway St • 773-871-8887 Country & Western.
- **Chicago Eagle** • 5015 N Clark St • 773-728-0050 Leather bar with back room.
- **Hunter's** • 1932 E Higgins Rd, Elk Grove Village 847-439-8840 • Dance/video bar in the 'burbs.
- **Little Jims** • 3501 N Halsted St • 773-871-6116 Neighborhood bar, 4 am license.
- **Lucky Horseshoe** • 3169 N Halsted St • 773-404-3169 Male dancers.
- **Madrigals** • 5316 N Clark St • 773-334-3033 Women welcome, male dancers.
- **Manhandler** • 1948 N Halsted St • 773-871-3339 Country & Western.
- **North End** • 3733 N Halsted St • 773-477-7999 Another bar on the strip.
- **Nutbush** • 7201 W Franklin St, Forest Park 708-366-5117 • Video bar in the 'burbs.
- **Second Story Bar** • 157 E Ohio St • 312-923-9536 • Streeterville hideout.
- **Sidetrack** • 3349 N Halsted St • 773-477-9189 • Huge video bar, women welcome.
- **Touché** • 6412 N Clark St • 773-465-7400 • Far North leather bar.
- **StarGaze** •5419 N Clark St • 773-561-7363 • Restaurant, dancing, Salsa nights.
- **Temptations** • 10235 W Grand Ave, Franklin Park • 847-455-0008 • Entertainment and dancing in the land of the big hair.

Lesbian

- **The Closet** • 3325 N Broadway St • 773-477-8533 4 am license, men welcome.
- **Chix Mix** • www.chixmixproductions.com Roving women's dance parties.
- **Club Intimus** • 312 W Randolph St • 312-901-1703 Roving women's dance party. Call for info.
- **Lost & Found** • 3058 W Irving Park Rd 773-463-7599 • Old-school women's bar with door buzzer and billiards.
- **The Patch** • 201 155th St, Calumet City 708-891-3980 • 4 am license, entertainment sometimes.

Both

- **Atmosphere** • 5355 N Clark St • 773-784-1100 Neighborhood bar, dancing.
- **Berlin** • 954 W Belmont Ave • 773-348-4975 • Mixed dance clubs. Women-only nights every first and third Wednesday.
- **Big Chicks** • 5024 N Sheridan Rd • 773-728-5511 Mostly men. Very crowded on weekends.
- **Circuit/Rehab** • 3641 N Halsted St 773-325-2233 • Big nightclub. Women's nights on some Fridays.
- **Clark's on Clark** • 5001 N Clark St • 773-728-2373 4 am license, mostly men.
- **Club Escape** • 1530 E 75th St • 773-667-6454 Mixed dance venue, some entertainment.
- **Cocktail** • 3359 N Halsted St • 773-477-1420 Dancing plus male dancers.
- **Escapades** • 6301 S Harlem Ave • 773-229-0886 4 am license, dancing, videos.
- **Gentry on Halsted** • 3320 N Halsted St 773-348-1053 • Cabaret shows, piano bar.
- **Gentry on State** • 440 N State St • 312-836-0933 Cabaret shows, piano bar.
- **Hydrate** • 3458 N Halsted St • 773-975-9244 Mostly guys but girl friendly.
- **Jeffery Pub** • 7041 S Jeffery Blvd. • 773-363-8555 4 am, Southside institution, dancing.
- **Pour House** • 103 155th St, Calumet City 708-891-3980 • 4 am, dancing.
- **Roscoe's** • 3356 N Halsted St • 773-281-3355 Mostly men, cavernous, dancing, videos, café.
- **Scot's** • 1829 W Montrose Ave • 773-528-3253 Mostly men, friendly neighborhood bar.
- **Spin Nightclub** • Halsted St & Belmont Ave 773-327-7711 • Mostly men, dancing.
- **T's Bar & Restaurant** • 5025 N Clark St 773-784-6000 • Not gay-exclusive, *very* gay-friendly. Bar food.

Forget **Wrigley Field (Map 43),** the **Water Tower (Map 32)**, and **Buckingham Fountain (Map 9)**. All right, maybe we didn't forget those emblems of the city in the listings below. Nonetheless, some of the city's landmarks nearest to locals' hearts are those obscure sites only known by insiders. Whose instructions for anything in Uptown don't include its proximity to the **Uptown Theatre (Map 40)**? Who doesn't look for the **Morton Salt Girl (Map 22)** when traversing Elston? For years, Chicago lesbians have used the **Totem Pole (Map 44)** at Waveland and the lake as a rallying point for weekend softball games, and **St. Ben's Church (Map 39)** has become an anchor for an entire neighborhood.

The **Pacific Garden Mission (Map 8)** (which recently announced plans to relocate to a plot at 14th Place and Canal Street…in two years) keeps trying to lure unwitting audiences with free tickets to the long-running radio drama *UNSHACKLED!* Eventually, everyone ends up sopping up the booze in their stomach with a late-night or early morning omelet, flaming saganaki, and giant piece of cake in Greektown. The **Marina Towers (Map 2)** reach for the sky like two heaven-bound corn cobs. The **Union Stockyard Gates (Map 15)** and the memory of bubbly creek where all the butchered remains were disposed of, remind us of our less than savory industrial past. A reminder of another kind comes with the moving **Monument to the Great Northern Migration (Map 14)** located at 26th and King Drive, celebrating the historic migration of African Americans who traveled from the south looking for opportunities.

The giant, neon-lit hot dog sweethearts on top of the Northwest Side's **Superdawg** have been winking at passersby for decades. On the Southwest Side, the not-quite-p.c. dime-store Indian atop **Capital Cigar Store** has been enticing would-be smokers for at least as long.

Map 1 • River North / Fulton Market District

The Blommer Chocolate Co	600 W Kinzie St • 312-226-7700	Opened in 1939. Eventually became the largest commercial chocolate manufacturer in the US.

Map 2 • Near North / River North

Courthouse Place	54 W Hubbard St	This Romanesque-style former courthouse has witnessed many legendary trials.
House of Blues	329 N Dearborn St • 312-923-2000	Branch location of well-known chain o' blues clubs; music is far better than the crap-filled interior suggests…
Marina Towers	300 N State St	Bertrand Goldberg's riverside masterwork. Love the parking.
Merchandise Mart	222 Merchandise Mart Plz • 312-527-7600	Houses furniture showrooms and a small mall.
Sotheby's	215 W Ohio St • 312-396-9599	Renowned auction house. We bid $5.

Map 3 • Streeterville / Mag Mile

Tribune Tower	435 N Michigan Ave • 312-222-2116	Check out the stones from famous buildings around the world—including a real-life rock from the moon!
Wrigley Building	400 N Michigan Ave	Monument to chewing gum.

Map 4 • West Loop Gate / Greek Town

Dugan's Drinking Emporium	128 S Halsted St • 312-421-7191	Sports bar in Greektown. Fantastic beer garden and favorite cop hangout.
Union Station	200 S Canal St • 312-322-4269	Built in 1925, the architecture is not to be missed!

Map 5 • The Loop

Chicago Board of Trade	141 W Jackson Blvd • 312-435-3590	The goddess Ceres tops this deco monolith.
Chicago Board Options Exchange	400 S La Salle St • 312-786-5600	The world's largest options market.
Chicago Cultural Center	78 E Washington St • 312-744-FINEART	The spot for free lectures, exhibits, concerts, and movies.
Chicago Mercantile Exchange	20 S Wacker Dr • 312-930-1000	Economics at work in polyester jackets.
Chicago Stock Exchange	440 S La Salle St • 312-663-2222	The second largest stock exchange in the country.
Daley Civic Plaza	50 W Washington St • 312-443-5500	Home of Picasso sculpture, Christmas tree ceremony, and alfresco lunches.
Harold Washington Library Center	400 S State St • 312-747-4300	The world's largest public library building; nearly 100 works of art on every floor.
Sears Tower	233 S Wacker Dr • 312-875-9696	Tallest building in the US, with a cool skydeck.

Map 6 • The Loop / Grant Park

Art Institute of Chicago	111 S Michigan Ave • 312-443-3600	World-class art museum.
Auditorium Building	430 S Michigan Ave • 312-431-2354	Designed by Louis Sullivan; on National Register of Historic Places.
Fine Arts Building	410 S Michigan Ave • 312-427-7602	Frank Lloyd Wright had an office here.
Symphony Center	220 S Michigan Ave • 312-294-3000	Classical music headquarters.

Map 7 • South Loop / River City

New Maxwell Street Market	548 W Roosevelt Rd • 312-922-3100	Historical market that reinforces the American dream; holds sway only on Sundays.
Old Post Office	404 W Harrison St	This massive, vacant edifice straddling I-90/94 and I-290 is a benchmark for traffic reports.
River City	800 S Wells St	A fluid cement design experiment built by architect Bertrand Goldberg in the '80s; considered a flop, but actually brilliant.
US Postal Distribution Center	433 W Harrison St • 312-983-8391	The city's main mail routing center, employing over 6,000 people and operating 24 hours a day.

Map 8 • South Loop / Printers Row / Dearborn Park

Columbia College Center for Book & Paper Arts	1104 S Wabash Ave, 2nd Fl • 312-344-6630	Two galleries feature changing exhibits of handmade books, paper, letterpress, and other related objects.
Former Elliot Ness Building	618 S Dearborn St	If he sends one of yours to the hospital, you send one of his to the morgue...
Old Dearborn Train Station	47 W Polk St	Turn-of-the-century train station with a lighted clocktower visible for several blocks. Al Capone took a train to prison from here.
Pacific Garden Mission	646 S State St • 312-922-1462	America's oldest continuously-operating rescue mission with free showings of long running radio drama *Unshackled!*

Map 9 • South Loop / South Michigan Ave

Buckingham Fountain	Columbus Dr & E Congress Pkwy	Built of pink marble; inspired by Versailles.
Chicago Hilton and Towers	720 S Michigan Ave • 312-922-4400	Check out the frescoes in the lobby; sneak a kiss in the palatial ballroom.
Johnson Publishing Headquarters	820 S Michigan Ave • 312-322-9200	Largest African-American-owned publishing company, home of *Ebony* and *Jet* magazines.
Shedd Aquarium	1200 S Lake Shore Dr • 312-939-2435	Marine and freshwater creatures from around the world are on view in this 1929 Classical Greek–inspired Beaux Arts structure.
Spirit of Music Garden	601 S Michigan Ave	Where the city struts during Chicago SummerDance.

Map 10 • East Pilsen / Chinatown

Chinatown Gate	S Wentworth Ave & W Cermak Rd	Built in 1976. The characters on the gate read "The world belongs to the people."
Chinatown Square	S Archer Ave	Restaurants, bakeries, gift stores, and herb shops.
On Leong Merchants Association Building	2216 S Wentworth Ave • 312-328-1188	1926 building inspired by architecture of the Kwangtung district of China. Now the home of the Pui Tak Center.
Ping Tom Memorial Park	300 W 19th St • 312-747-7661	Park with Chinese landscape elements.
Raymond Hillard Apartments	211 S Clark St	Another Bertrand Golberg gem going from subsidized senior housing to mixed income residential.

Map 11 • South Loop / McCormick Place

Adler Planetarium & Astronomy Museum	1300 S Lake Shore Dr • 312-922-7827	Depression era wonder that thrilled millions at 1933 Century of Progress Exposition.
America's Courtyard	South of Adler Planetarium on the lakefront	A spiral of stones that echoes both the milky way and ancient structures. Designed by Denise Milan and Ary R. Perez.
Clarke House	1827 S Indiana Ave	Built in 1836 by an unknown architect, this Greek Revival–style home has been relocated twice and is now an official Chicago landmark.
Field Museum	1400 S Lake Shore Dr • 312-922-9410	Go to see Sue, world's largest known T. Rex; stay for the jam-packed halls of vaguely macabre taxidermy.
Hillary Rodham Clinton Women's Park and Gardens of Chicago	S Prairie Ave, b/w 18th St & 19th St	A garden from a former first lady.
Hyatt Regency McCormick Place	2233 S Dr Martin L King Jr Dr • 312-567-1234	The only hotel attached to the city's main convention center.
McCormick Place	2301 S Lake Shore Dr • 312-791-7000	Hard to miss.
Merill C Meigs Field	n/a	Used to be an airport, now being developed into a park.
National Vietnam Veterans Art Museum	1801 S Indiana Ave • 312-326-0270	Features art about the war created by Vietnam veterans from all sides of the conflict.
Northerly Island Park	Lakefront, south of Adler Planetarium	Greenspace now encompassing former site of Meigs Field airport.
Quinn Chapel, African Methodist Episcopal Church	2401 S Wabash Ave • 312-791-1846	Built in 1892, this Victorian Gothic–style church houses Chicago's oldest African-American congregation.

Map 11 • South Loop / McCormick Place *-continued*

Second Presbyterian Church	1936 S Michigan Ave • 312-225-4951	Reconstructed in 1900 by Howard Van Doren Shaw, this ponderous Gothic Revival–style church has stained glass by Tiffany.
Soldier Field	425 E McFetridge Dr • 312-747-1285	A once-antiquated arena is now a world-class stadium for Da Bears and concert events.
The Chicago Daily Defender	2400 S Michigan Ave • 312-225-5656	Founded in 1905, it was the country's most influential black newspaper through the '50s. Still in operation, but much-diminished.
The Chicago Legend	2109 S Wabash Ave • 312-326-0300	Boasts R&B and hip-hop programming, not particularly open-minded toward hip-hop patrons.
The Wheeler Mansion	2020 S Calumet Ave • 312-945-2020	This Second Empire–style mansion now houses a boutique hotel for high-end travelers.
Willie Dixon's Blues Heaven Foundation	2120 S Michigan Ave • 312-808-1286	Former Chess Records studio. Tours, exhibits, workshops, and performances.

Map 12 • Bridgeport (West)

Library Fountain	W 34th St & Halsted St	Pretty water.
Monastery of the Holy Cross	3111 S Aberdeen St • 773-927-7424	Have your breakfast served by monks in this bed-and-breakfast monastery.
St Mary of Perpetual Help	1039 W 32nd St	Built in the 1880s, this was the first Polish Roman Catholic Church in the US to be consecrated.
Wilson Park	S May St & W 34th Pl	A nice respite in the middle of the city.

Map 13 • Bridgeport (East)

McGuane Park	W 29th St & S Halsted St	A park for playing.
Old Neighborhood Italian American Club	3031 S Shields Ave • 312-326-6420	Founded by Angelo LaPietra, a former high-ranking Chicago mobster, after his release from Leavenworth.
Richard J Daley House	3536 S Lowe Ave	Childhood home of Mayor Richard J Daley.

Map 14 • Prairie Shores / Lake Meadows

Bee Branch Public Library	3647 S State St • 312-747-6872	Originally home of black newspaper, *Chicago Bee*.
Black Metropolis Convention & Tourism Council	3501 S King Dr, Ste 1E • 773-373-2865	Information central for questions on everything Bronzeville.
Bronzeville Bed & Breakfast	3911 S King Dr • 773-373-8081	Fine lodging in the old Goldblatt Mansion.
Chicago Bee Building	3647 S State St	Formerly the HQ of the *Chicago Bee* newspaper; now offices.
Douglas Tomb	E 35th St & Lake Park Ave	Resting place of Lincoln's nemesis, the Little Giant, overlooking tracks of Illinois Central railroad and the subdivision he founded. The entrance is on the east side of Lake.
Dunbar Park	S Indiana Ave & E 31st St	Dunbar High's girl's softball team plays here.
Early Chicago Defender Building	3435 S Indiana Ave	Originally an 1899 synagogue, was home of *Chicago Defender* from 1920–1940.
Eighth Regiment Armory	3533 S Giles Ave	First armony built in US for a black regiment, 1914–11918, now a Chicago public high school.
Griffin Funeral Home	3232 S King Dr • 312-842-2422	Site of Civil War–era Camp Douglas, with Civil War museum, founder forefather drilled there.
Ida B Wells / Barnett Home	3624 S King Dr	Former home of the journalism and civil rights pioneer.
Interesting Benches	S Dr Martin L King Jr Dr b/w E 33rd St & E 35th St	13 artists created these 24 unique bench sculptures. Sit on Theme.
Monument to the Great Northern Migration	S Dr Martin L King Jr Dr & E 26th St	Statue by Alison Sarr depicts a man with a briefcase atop a pile of old shoes. Represents the journey of African Americans from the south.
Olivet Baptist Church	3101 S King Dr • 312-538-0124	Church with a longstanding tradition of civil rights organizing ranging from abolitionist and feminist mass meetings to Black Panther Party programs.
Overton Hygenic Building	3619 S State St	Former headquarters of foremost producer of black cosmestics.
St James Catholic Church	2929 S Wabash Ave • 773-534-9281	Tradition of community caretaking that included caring for Confederate POWs at Camp Douglas
Sunset Café	315 E 35th St	One of Chicago's earliest and most legendary jazz venues.
Supreme Life Insurance Company Head Office	3501 S King Dr	Built in 1921 and remodeled–1950, This former major black insurance company, enjoys new life as a mixed commercial structure.
Victory Monument	35th St & King Dr	Early postwar tribute to WWI's black Eighth Regiment of the Illinois National Guard that served as part of the US 370th Infantry in France.
Wabash Avenue YMCA	3763 S Wabash Ave	Since 1913 provided housing and job training for new black arrivals from the South, where the Association for the Study of Negro Life and History, the first group devoted to black studies, was founded in 1915.

Map 15 • Canaryville / Fuller Park

Union Stockyard Gate	Exchange Ave & Peoria St	This limestone gate marks the place that made Chicago the "Hog Butcher to the World."

Map 16 • Bronzeville

Corpus Christi Church	4920 S King Dr • 773-285-7720	Built in 1921 for a predominately Irish parish that rapidly evolved into a predominately black parish.
Drexel Fountain	S Drexel Blvd & E Oakwood Blvd	The city's oldest remaining fountainl
Jamaican Consulate/ Jamaican Market Place	4655 S King Dr, Ste 104 • 773-624-092	A bit of Kingston on the Old South Side.
Liberty Baptist Church	4849 S King Dr • 773-268-6757	An afrocentric 1958 Go-Go styled temple considered King's original Chicago workshop.
Provident Hospital	500 E 51st St • 312-527-2000	Now county controlled, this century-old, hospital was the first to train black doctors and nurses and the site of the first successful open heart surgery.
Robert S Abbott Home	4742 S King Dr	Former home of *Chicago Defender* founder.
Steelife Gallery	4655 S King Dr • 773-538-4773	House of art that inspires the people.

Map 17 • Kenwood

Drexel Square Park	Drexel Blvd, from 51st St to 39th St	Victorian gem boasting city's oldest suriving fountain donated by prominent banking family.
Louis Farrakhan Home	4855 S Woodlawn Ave	Well-guarded home of the leader of the Nation of Islam.
Rainbow/PUSH Coalition Headquarters	930 E 50th St • 773-373-3366	Originally the1924 home of KAM Isaiah Israel, Chicago's oldest Jewish congreation, with late 1940s addition.
South Kenwood Mansions	b/w S Dorchester Ave (east), S Ellis Ave (west), E Hyde Park Blvd (south), & E 47th St (north)	Built in the early 1900s by wealthy businessmen looking to flee the cramped North Side. Once in a state of disrepair, the mansions have (mostly) been rehabbed and are still the Jewels of the South Side.

Map 18 • Washington Park

Aquatic Center & Refectory	5531 S Martin Luther King Jr Dr • 773-256-1248	Designed by Daniel Burnham's firm, the Refectory now holds locker rooms for the Aquatic Center and its 36-foot waterslide.
DuSable Museum of African-American History	740 E 56th Pl • 773-947-0600	Founded in 1961 and dedicated to preserving and honoring African-American culture. The oldest non-profit institution of its kind.
Former Home of Jesse Binga	5922 S Dr Martin L King Jr Dr	Home of nation's first African-American banker.
Washington Park	E 60th St thru E 51st St, from S Cottage Grove Ave to	A sprawling 367-acre park with beautiful lagoons and fields. Check out the "Fountain of Time" sculpture in the southeast corner of the park.

Map 19 • Hyde Park

Frederick C Robie House	5757 S Woodlawn Ave	Designed by Frank Lloyd Wright; renovations proceeding, stay tuned.
Midway Plaisance Park & Skating Rink	S Ellis Ave & S University Ave, from E 59th St to E 60th St • 312-747-0233	Olympic-sized outdoor skating rink.
Nichols Park	1300 E 55th St	Home of the Parrots of Hyde Park.
Nuclear Energy Sculpture	5600 S Ellis Ave	Birthplace of the Atomic Age.
Rockefeller Memorial Chapel	5850 S Woodlawn Ave • 773-702-2100	Built in 1928, this English Gothic–styled cathedral contains one of the world's largest carillons.

Map 20 • East Hyde Park / Jackson Park

Osaka Garden/Wooded Island	just south of the Museum of Science and Industry, b/w the West and East Lagoons	A Japanese garden in the middle of Jackson Park—why not?
Promontory Point Park	5491 S Shore Dr	Picnic with a view.

Map 21 • Wicker Park / Ukrainian Village

Coyote Building	1600 N Milwaukee Ave	This 12-story Art Deco building was constructed in 1929.
Crumbling Bucktown	1579 N Milwaukee Ave	Structural icon visible from miles away; nucleus of Around the Coyote Arts Festival.
Division Street Russian Bath	1916 W Division St • 773-384-9671	Treat yourself to an old-school day at the spa, complete with Swedish massages and a granite heating room.

Map 21 • Wicker Park / Ukrainian Village *-continued*

Flat Iron Building	1579 N Milwaukee Ave	This distinct triangular-shaped building is a part of the Chicago Coalition of Community Cultural Centers and houses artist studios.
Holy Trinity Orthodox Cathedral and Rectory	1121 N Leavitt St • 773-486-6064	Designed by Louis Sullivan to look like a Russian cathedral.
Wicker Park	Pierce St & Hoyne St	The homes in this district reflect the style of Old Chicago.

Map 22 • Noble Square / Goose Island

House of Crosses	1544 W Chestnut St	Eccentric owners have covered the property with hundreds of wooden crosses.
Morton Salt Elston Facility	Elston Ave & Blackhawk St	Has a painting of the famous salt girl, and hey: Acres of salt!
Nelson Algren Fountain	Division St & Ashland Blvd	Has a recent controversial addition.
North Avenue Bridge	W North Ave	Wretched traffic jams; river view.
Polish Museum of America	984 N Milwaukee Ave • 773-384-3352	Right-to-life painting on the side.
Pulaski Park/Pulaski Fieldhouse	Blackhawk St & Cleaver St	Has an outdoor swimming pool.
St Stanislaus Kostka Church	1351 W Evergreen Ave • 773-278-2470	One of the oldest in Chicago.
Weed Street District	b/w Chicago River & Halsted St	Several bars and clubs in one area. Party on.

Map 23 • West Town / Near West Side

First Baptist Congregational Church	1613 W Washington Blvd • 312-243-8047	Can seat 20000 people and houses one of the largest totally enclosed organs in the country.
Metropolitan Missionary Baptist Church	2151 W Washington Blvd • 312-738-0053	An attempt to find an appropriate design for the then-new Christian Science religion. Sold to Baptists in 1947.
Ukrainian Cultural Center	2247 W Chicago Ave • 773-384-6400	A gathering place to share and celebrate Ukrainian culture.
Ukrainian National Museum	721 N Oakley Blvd • 312-421-8020	Museum, library, and archives detail the heritage, culture, and people of the Ukraine.
United Center	1901 W Madison St • 312-455-4500	Statue of His Airness still draws tourists.

Map 24 • River West / West Town

Eckhart Park/Ida Crown Natatorium	Noble St & Chicago Ave • 312-746-5553	One of two swimming pools in the area.
Harpo Studios	1058 W Washington Blvd • 312-591-9222	Home of the Oprah Winfrey Show.

Map 25 • Illinois Medical District

18th St L station	W 18th St & S Paulina St	Gateway to Pilsen features colorful murals celebrating Mexican culture.
Bowler Row Houses	2148 W Bowler St	Historical row houses that have survived the wrecking ball.
Oakley Row Houses	801 S Oakley Ave	Italianate row houses that date back to 1870's.
Vietnam Survivors Memorial	815 S Oakley Ave	Privately funded memorial erected by Vets.

Map 26 • University Village / Little Italy / Pilsen

National Italian American Sports Hall of Fame	1431 W Taylor St	How many Italian American sports stars do you know? DiMaggio is right out front.

Map 27 • Logan Square

Illinois Centennial Monument	3100 W Logan Blvd	Every city needs an obelisk or two…
Logan House	2656 W Logan Blvd	Renowned for over-the-top holiday décor.

Map 28 • Bucktown

Margie's Candies	1960 N Western Ave • 773-384-1035	The Beatles ate here.

Map 29 • DePaul / Wrightwood / Sheffield

Biograph Theater	2433 N Lincoln Ave • 773-348-4123	Site of the gangster John Dillinger's infamous death in 1934, currently closed for renovation.
Cortland Street Drawbridge	1440 W Cortland St	Built in 1902 by John Ernst Erickson, this innovative leaf-lift bridge changed the way the world built bridges.

McCormick Row House District	W Chalmers Pl, W Belden Ave, & W Fullerton Pkwy	Quaint example of late 19th-century urban planning and architecture.
Pumpkin House	1052 W Wrightwood Ave	A Halloween spectacle of lighted pumpkins.

Map 30 • Lincoln Park

Dewes Mansion	503 N Wrightwood Ave • 773-477-3075	Ornate historic home done in the German Baroque style and built in 1896.
Kauffman Store and Flats	2312 N Lincoln Ave	One of the oldest existing buildings designed by Adler and Sullivan. It's amazing that its characteristic features have survived.
Lincoln Park Boat Club	N Cannon Dr & Fullerton Pkwy • 773-549-2628	Paddling, rowing, and sculling since 1910.
Lincoln Park Conservatory	2391 N Stockton Dr • 312-742-7736	Sister to Garfield Park Conservatory. Built in 1891.
Lincoln Park Cultural Center	2045 N Lincoln Park W • 312-742-7726	Programming in visual arts for all ages.
Lincoln Park Zoo	N Cannon Dr, south of W Fullerton Pkwy • 312-742-2000	Oldest free zoo in the U.S.
Midwest Buddhist Temple	435 W Menomonee St	Enter their annual Haiku contest.
Peggy Notebaert Nature Museum	2430 N Cannon Dr • 773-755-5100	An oasis for adults and kids to reconnect with nature by playing with wildflowers and butterflies.
Theurer-Wrigley House	2466 N Lakeview Ave	Early Richard E. Schmidt (and maybe Hugh H. G. Garden) based on late–Italian Renaissance architecture.

Map 32 • Gold Coast / Mag Mile

Water Tower Place and Park	845 N Michigan Ave • 312-440-3165	Huge shopping—6 floors—Marshall Field's…er, Macy's.

Map 33 • West Rogers Park

Bernard Horwich JCC	3003 W Touhy Ave • 773-761-9100	Community center with programming for kids/adults, pool/fitness center, senior center, and sports leagues.
Croatian Cultural Center	2845 W Devon Ave • 773-338-3839	A place where families can relax, socialize and congregate. Intended to benefit the Croatian community in Chicago (duh).
High Ridge YMCA	2424 W Touhy Ave • 773-262-8300	Community center with programming for kids/adults, summer activities, child care programs, sport teams, and a pool.
India Town	W Devon Ave, near Washtenaw Ave	Features Indian and Pakistani shops, grocery stores, restaurants, and more.
Indian Boundary Park	2500 W Lunt Ave • 773-742-7887	Petting zoo, tennis courts, chess tables, ice rink, skate park, batting cages, spray pool, with seasonal community center classes.
Rogers Park/West Ridge Historical Society	7344 N Western Ave • 773-764-4078	Photos/memorabilia/historical documents of the community's history detailing its ethnic diversity.
Thillen's Stadium	Devon & Kedzie Ave	Chicago landmark. 16 softball fields. Features little league baseball and various other games and benefits.
Warren Park	6601 N Western Ave • 312-742-7888	Seasonal free entertainment, pony rides, ethnic food festivals, amusement park rides, arts and crafts, winter sledding hill, baseball diamond, picnic pavilions, and dog play areas.

Map 34 • East Rogers Park

Angel Guardian Croatian Catholic Church	6346 N Ridge Ave • 773-262-0535	1905 red-brick Romanesque church. Turn-of-the-century German stained glass windows by Franz Mayer and F. X. Zettler.
Robert A Black Golf Course	2045 W Pratt Blvd • 773-764-4045	The newest Chicago Park District course. 2,300-yard, par 33 layout for all skill levels.

Map 35 • Arcadia Terrace / Peterson Park

Lincoln Avenue Motels	N Lincoln Ave b/w W Foster Ave & W Devon Ave	Seedy vice dens with cool vintage signs are falling prey to the wrecking ball.

Map 36 • Bryn Mawr

Rosehill Cemetery and Mausoleum	5800 N Ravenswood Ave	Chicago's historical glitterati entombed among unsurpassed sculpture and architecture.

Map 37 • Edgewater / Andersonville

Ann Sather's Restaurant	5207 N Clark St • 773-271-6677	More than a restaurant; a cultural field trip.
Edgewater Beach Apartments	5555 N Sheridan Rd	The big pink building symbolizing the end of the lakeshore bike path.

Map 37 • Edgewater / Andersonville *-continued*

Philadelphia Church	5437 N Clark St • 773-728-5106	Complete with can't-miss neon sign.
Swedish American Museum	5211 N Clark St • 773-728-8111	Everything you want to know about Swedish culture, which is more than you thought.
The Belle Shore Hotel Building	1062 W Bryn Mawr Ave	Former homes of roaring 1920s nightlife, now historic landmarks restored to their former glory as apartments.

Map 38 • Ravenswood / Albany Park

Albany Park Community Center	3401 W Ainslie St • 773-509-5650	Local community center at SW corner of Ainslie and Kimball.
Fish Furniture Co Building	3322 W Lawrence Ave	Striking 1931 Art Moderne building with fish motif, currently houses Interstate Blood Bank.
North Branch Pumping Station	Lawrence Ave & the Chicago River	With its 1930s Art Deco facade, it seems like something prettier should be happening than North Side sewage pumping…
Paradise	2916 W Montrose Ave • 773-588-1989	It's a sushi restaurant. It's a beauty shop. It's a sauna ($12, unlimited time). It's Paradise. Of course, it's a neighborhood landmark.
Ravenswood Manor Park	4626 N Manor Ave	It's just a tiny triangle wedged between the non-elevated L and several streets, but it's ground zero for garden sales, neighborhood associations, dogs, kids, and community activity.
River Park	5100 N Francisco Ave	More than 30 acres of park, including one of the few city canoe launches.
Ronan Park Walking Trail	3000 W Argyle St	1924 Renaissance Revival building designed by Jens Jensen.

Map 39 • Ravenswood / North Center

Lincoln Square	4800 N Lincoln Ave	A virtual tour through a European-style neighborhood.
Old Town School of Folk Music	4544 N Lincoln Ave	Northern expansion of beloved Chicago institution. Classes and concert venue.
St Benedict's Church	2215 W Irving Park Rd • 773-588-6484	The namesake of the St. Ben's neighborhood.

Map 40 • Uptown

Aragon Ballroom	1106 W Lawrence Ave • 773-561-9500	One of the better smaller music venues in the city.
Graceland Cemetery	4001 N Clark St • 773-525-1105	Chicago's famous buried in a masterpiece of landscape architecture.
Green Mill Pub	4802 N Broadway St • 773-878-5552	Live jazz seven nights a week. Capone drank here.
St Augustine College	1333 W Argyle St • 773-878-756	Episcopalian bilingual training school occupying original headquarters of Essanay Studios, where Chaplin, Broco Billy, and Swanson made films before moving to Southern Cali.
Tattoo Factory	4441 N Broadway St • 773-989-4077	Tattoos for the famous and the infamous.
Uptown Theatre	4816 N Broadway St	An acre of seats in a magic city.

Map 41 • Avondale / Old Irving

Com-Ed Plant	N California Ave & W Roscoe St	What's that humming sound in Avondale? Must be this ginormous electrical plant.

Map 42 • North Center / Roscoe Village / West Lakeview

19th District Police Headquarters	2452 W Belmont Ave • 312-744-5983	Going to "Western & Belmont" is synonymous for being in deep sh#*.

Map 43 • Wrigleyville / East Lakeview

Southport Lanes	3325 N Southport Ave • 773-472-6600	Four hand-set lanes. Eat a Honeymooner while you wait.
Vic Theatre	3145 N Sheffield Ave • 773-472-0449	Drink, watch films, and take in an occasional band at this old theatre.
Wrigley Field	1060 W Addison St • 773-404-CUBS	Charm-filled and crumbling ballpark that remains indifferent to wins or losses on the field.

Map 44 • East Lakeview

Belmont Rocks	W Briar Pl at the lake	Popular lakefront hangout.
Dog Beach	Northern tip of Belmont Harbor	Fun and frolic with your pup.
The Giraffes	N Elaine Pl & W Roscoe Ave	Iconic public art.
Totem Pole	W Waveland Ave & N Belmont Harbor Dr	Where did it come from? Why is it there? Nobody knows.

Maps 45–48 • Northwest Chicago

Copernicus Center	5216 W Lawrence Ave • 773-777-9184	Jefferson Park's cultural hub.
Eugene Field Park	5100 N Ridgeway Ave • 773-478-9744	Features a 1928 Tudor Revival fieldhouse, the Eugene Field Cultural Center (home of the Albany Park Theater Project).
Gompers Park	4222 W Foster Ave • 773-685-3270	Large riverfront park.
Hanson Park Fieldhouse	5501 W Fullerton Ave	Very old fieldhouse with WWII barracks.
Harlem CTA Station	N Harlem Ave & The Kennedy Expy	One of the more "el"egant stations.
Logan Square Column	3100 W Logan Blvd	It's just like Paris, yet different.
Superdawg Drive-In	6363 N Milwaukee Ave	Everyone knows the Superdog and his sexy girlfriend.
The Admiral Theater	3940 W Lawrence Ave	Built in 1928, this former vaudeville theater is now a well-known "gentlemen's club."
Walt Disney House	2156 N Tripp Ave	Where old Walt learned to ride his bike.

Maps 49–52 • West Chicago

Austin Town Hall	5610 W Lake St	115-year-old former town hall; now a public recreation building.
Bison Statues at Humboldt Park	1400 N Sacramento Ave	Meet up by the Bison.
Columbus Park Refectory	Columbus Park, 500 S Central Ave	Historic refectory now available for weddings and other fetes.
Delta Fish Market	228 S Kedzie Ave	Defunct fish fry-up features live blues in its parking lot.
Engine 44 Firehouse Mural	412 N Kedzie Ave	When kids do it, it's called graffiti.
Garfield Park Conservatory	300 N Central Park Ave	Tropical oasis in the midst of the urban jungle.
Our Lady of Sorrows School	3121 W Jackson Blvd	Unsung treasure built in the late 19th century.

Maps 53–56 • Southwest Chicago

Adams House	9326 S Longwood Dr	A 1901 Frank Lloyd Wright gem.
Arnett Chapel, African Methodist Episcopal Church	11218 S Bishop St • 773-238-0670	One of oldest black congregations in historically black Morgan Park.
Bell Tower Condos	10321 S Longwood Dr	Built in 1916 for 13th Church of Christ Science, retains many original architectural features including mother-of-pearl stained glass.
Beverly Arts Center	2407 W 111th St • 773-445-3838	Still creatively thriving in its new home further up Blue Island Ridge.
Blackwelder Summerling House	10910 S Prospect Ave	Built in sections from 1865 to 1873, was once Morgan Park's social center and home to Morgan Park's first village president, Isaac Blackwelder.
Bohn Park	111th St & Prospect Ave	Just off Rock Island Monterey Ave station, originally known as Depot Park and sometimes called the Commons, features street lamps from 1893 World's Columbian Exposition.
Bronzeville Children's Museum	9500 S Western Ave • 708-636-9504	The romper room for learning black history for kids of all ages.
Burhans-Ellinwood Model House	10410 S Hoyne Ave	One of two 1917 models designed by Wright for a subdivision of prefabricated American-System Built Houses.
Campbell House	9250 S Damen Ave	An 1896 Tudor designed for the founder of the John H. Vanderpoel Collection.
Capital Cigar Store	6258 S Pulaski Rd	World's most conspicous cigar-store Indian.
Edward L Roberts House	10134 S Longwood Dr	An 1892 Queen Anne, now St. Barnabas's rectory, built by a lumber-milling magnate to exhibit decorative architectural details from his catalogue.
Edwin C Young House	9215 S Pleasant Ave	Robust Queen Anne with tower, front porch, and portcochiere.
Evans House	9914 S Longwood Dr	A 1908 Prairie Style gem designed by Frank Lloyd Wright.
Ferguson House	10954 S Prospect Ave	An 1873 Italianate beauty; built for the manager of Lancaster Fire Insurance.
Frank Anderson House	10400 S Pleasant Ave	Elegant-renaissance house now the residence of Chicago State University's president.
Gately House	10655 S Hoyne Ave	A 1927 neo-classical, recalling classical revival mansions of English Regency; was home of founder of Gately's People Store based in Roseland.
Givens Irish Castle	10244 S Longwood Dr	Seminal grand dame of the mansion district in the original Beverly Hills.
Godspeed House	11216 S Oakley Ave	Farmhouse built in 1876 for the Rev. Thomas Goodspeed, pastor of Morgan Park Baptist Church and professor at Baptist Theological Seminary.
Graffiti Mural	W 59th St & S Damen Ave	An example of when it's public "art" not public "nuisance."
Harris House	10856 S Longwood Dr	A 1906 hilltop Tudor built for the founder of Rotary International.
Holy Name of Mary Church	1423 W 112th St • 773-238-6800	Opened in 1947, once Morgan Park's oldest black parish.
Hopkinson House	10820 S Drew St	Italianate built for real estate dealer, grounds designed by parks landscape architect Jens Jensen.
Horton Mansion	10200 S Longwood Dr	An 1890 Colonial Revival built for the founder of Chicago Bridge & Iron.

Maps 53–56 • Southwest Chicago *-continued*

Howe House	10208 S Wood St	An 1881 Stick Style designed for one of area's oldest residents by a family friend, Daniel H. Burnham.
JB Chambers House	10330 S Seeley Ave	A 1871 blend of Gothic, Italianate, and French Empire styles.
Karge House	2035 W 99th St	A 1926 Spanish Colonial, known for distinctive stone construction with ornate detailing and medallions with scuplted Indian heads.
Lackmore House	10956 S Prospect Ave	Built 1801–1872 by relative of the area's first settler, DeWitt Lane.
McCumber House	10305 S Seeley Ave	A 1911 Colonial Revival once used as a Marshall Field & Co. Showcase House.
Metra 103rd/Washington Heights Rock Island District Branch Line Station	103rd St & Vincennes Ave	Refurbished, handsome late Victorian gem that originally served the village of Washington Heights.
Metra Rock Island Main Line 111th St/Monterey Ave Station		A restored at-grade Victorian gem from early 1892, built to replace 1870 station after Rock Island railroad expanded its suburban service.
Midway Airport	5700 S Cicero Ave	World's Busiest Airport…in 1932. Today a place to fly and land cheaply, surrounded by tiny bungalows filled with various Eastern European types.
Morgan Park Apostolic Penecostal Church	11401 S Vincennes Ave • 773-239-9586	One of oldest black congregations in Morgan Park.
Morgan Park United Methodist Church	11030 S Longwood Dr • 773-238-2600	Early Prairie School treasure along the Blue Island Ridge.
Oakdale Park	956 W 95th St • 312-747-6569	A post–WWII greenspace with oak-shaded walking trails.
Original Rainbow Cone	9233 S Western Ave	People line up day and night in the summer.
Ridge Historical Society	10621 S Seeley Ave • 773-881-1675	Blue Island Ridge history is preserved in the old Walgreen mansion.
Ridge Park	9625 S Longwood Dr • 773-779-0007	Fieldhouse houses John H. Vanderpoel Art Association, comprising 600 pieces dedicated to renowned instructor at Art Institute of Chicago.
St Walter Catholic Church	11722 S Oakley Ave • 773-779-1515	Half-century-old Catholic community with modern approach to traditional values.
Walter Burley Griffin Place	W 104th Pl, Wood St to Prospect Ave	Largest concentration of Prairie Style homes in Chicago, built from 1910 to 1914.
William MR French House	9203 S Pleasant Ave	An 1894 Colonial Revival mansion built for the first director of the Art Institute of Chicago; sculpture by brother David Chester French.

Maps 57–60 • South Chicago

Carter G Woodson Regional Library	9525 S Halsted St • 312-747-6900	Named for the "Father of Black History," houses Vivian Harsh black history collection.
Cedar Park Cemetery & Funeral Home	12540 S Halsted St • 773-785-8840	Final resting place where deer, geese, and other wildfile play in peace.
Chicago Skyway	8801 S Anthony St • 312-747-8383	Soar 125 feet over the southside on this thrilling overpass!
Chicago State University	9501 S King Dr • 773-995-2000	Metropolitan Chicago's oldest public university.
Lilydale First Baptist Church	649 W 113th St • 773-785-1976	Another cultural anchor for Roseland's historically black community.
Lilydale Progressive Missionary Baptist Church	10706 S Michigan Ave • 773-785-8623	Serving the historically black community on Roseland's northern end since the end of WWI.
Market Hall	E 112th St & Champlain Ave	George M. Pullman built colonnaded apartments surrounding a prototype shopping mall in 1893 to house friends visiting the World's Columbian Exposition.
New Regal Theatre	1645 E 79th St	80-year-old former movie house.
Oak Woods Cemetery	1035 E 67th St	Former Mayor Washington and civil rights activist Ida B. Wells rest here.
Palmer Park	201 E 111th St • 312-747-6576	Created in 1904 to integregate social services with recreation for congested tenement districts. Features three WPA-comissioned murals by James Edward McBurney.
Pullman Clock Tower	11141 S Cottage Grove Ave • 773-785-8901	This beacon of Pullman can be seen from far and wide.
Robert S Abbott Park	49 E 95th St • 312-737-6100	Created in 1949 to serve the rapidly growing black community near 95th St & Michigan Ave; one of first parks named after a promiment African American.
South Shore Cultural Center	7059 South Shore Dr • 773-747-2536	A glittering pearl on the south lakefront.
Trinity United Church of Christ	400 W 95th St • 773-962-5650	Where US Senator Barack Obama worships.
West Pullman Elementary School	11941 S Parnell Ave • 773-535-5500	Mammoth 1894 structure featuring Romanesque stylings.
West Pullman Park	401 W 123rd St • 312-727-7090	A 1915 greenspace created to Americanize an industrializing community.

Evanston

Evanston Historical Society	225 Greenwood St • 847-475-3410	Explore Evanston's history. Closed Monday and Tuesday.
Light Opera Works	927 Noyles St • 847-869-6300	26 seasons of musical theater.

Make no bones about it, Chicago is a dog's kind of town. More than 750,000 canines live and play in the Windy City. Dogs socialize and exercise their owners daily at designated Dog-Friendly Areas (DFAs), shady parks, and sprawling beaches.

Dog-Friendly Areas

DFAs are off-leash areas reserved just for canines. Amenities vary by park but often include: doggie drinking fountains; agility equipment; wood chips, pea pebble, and asphalt surfaces; "time out" fenced-in areas for shy or overexcited dogs; trash receptacles and doggie bags for, well, not take-out; and bulletin boards and information kiosks to post animal lovers' announcements.

DFAs are managed jointly by the neighborhoods' dog owners' councils and the Chicago Park District. These spaces are essential to the happiness of Chicago dogs and their owners, as police are notorious for dealing out hefty fines and even arresting dog owners who fail to clean up after or leash their dogs. But at the DFA, canines run free and poop where they please. Just remember to clean up after your pooch, ensure that your dog is fully immunized, de-wormed, licensed, and wearing ID tags. There are limits on how many pups one person can bring at once and please no puppies under four months, dogs in heat, dogs with the name "Killer," or children under 12.

- **Challenger Park**, 1100 W Irving Park Rd (Map 40)
  Nestled next to a cemetery and under the EL tracks, this relatively new DFA has plenty of amenities and neighborhood action. Avoid at all costs during Cubs games.
- **Churchill Field Park**, 1825 N Damen Ave (Map 28)
  This triangular space next to the train tracks is covered with pea gravel and asphalt and many abandoned tennis balls (Golden Retrievers can't get enough).
- **Coliseum Park,** 1466 S Wabash Ave (Map 11)
  Long, narrow, and fenced-in park where dogs race the overhead trains. Nothing to write home about, but, hey, it's legal.
- **Hamlin Park**, 3035 N Hoyne Ave at Wellington Ave (Map 42)
  Located in the shady southwest corner, this active L-shaped park appeals to tennis-ball chasers and fetching owners.
- **Margate Park**, 4921 N Marine Dr (Map 40)
  Called "Puptown" by the Uptown canine-loving community, this beloved DFA is usually packed with doggone fun. Locals are diligent about keeping the pea gravel picked up.
- **Noethling (Grace) Park,** 2645 N Sheffield Ave (Map 29)
  Dogs and owners from the Lincoln Park area love to hang out at the "Wiggley Field" dog run—Chicago's pilot pooch park. Wiggley's got a doggy obstacle course, an asphalt surface, drinking fountain, "time out" area, and info kiosk.
- **Ohio Place Park,** N Orleans St and W Ohio St (Map 2)
  Next to the I-90/94 exit ramp, this fenced-in strip of concrete flanked by bushes isn't pretty, but a dog can play fetch here without a leash. Careful: As the lot is not a Chicago Park District facility, it is not double-gated.
- **River Park**, 5100 N Francisco Ave (Map 38)
  The city's newest DFA.
- **Walsh Playground Park,** 1722 N Ashland Ave (Map 29)
  A 4,500-square-foot park with a small off-leash area for fetching with pea gravel and shade.
- **Wicker Park**, 1425 N Damen Ave (Map 21)
  Popular pooch as well as dog owner pick-up park. Often packed with dog-walkers wrangling fleets of frisky canines.

Creating a DFA takes a serious grass-roots effort spearheaded by the neighborhood's dog owners. They must organize themselves to get the community to bow to their desires through site surveys and three community meetings and raise one-half of the funds needed to build the DFA. Most importantly, they must unleash the support of their alderman, police precinct, and park district. For information on DFAs, call the Park District at 312-742-7529. Chicago's Dog Advisory Work Group, DAWG, (312-409-2169) also assists neighborhood groups in establishing DFAs

Top Dog Parks and Beaches

Leashed dogs and well-behaved owners are welcome in most of Chicago's parks and on its beaches, except during the height of swimming season when the sands are off-limits. Here are some local canines' top picks.

- **Calumet Park and Beach (9800 South)**
  A 200-acre beach and park getaway in the city with tennis courts, baseball fields, basketball courts, water fun, and plenty of parking.
- **Dog Beach (3200 N Lake Shore Dr)**
  This crescent of sand at the north corner of Belmont Harbor is separated from the bike path by a fence, making it an unofficial dog sand box. But the water is dirty, and the police do ticket, so it's not the most ideal dog-frolicking area.
- **Horner Park (2741 W Montrose Ave)**
  Dog heaven with lots of trees, grass, squirrels to chase, and other pups to meet, particularly after work.
- **Lincoln Park (2045 Lincoln Park W)**
  Paws down, the best dog park in town for romping, fetch, and Frisbee. Unofficial "Bark Park" where pet lovers congregate is a grassy area between Lake Shore Dr and Marine Dr.
- **Montrose/Wilson Avenue Beach (MonDog) (4400 North)**
  The city's only legal off-leash beach, MonDog is perfect for pooches to practice dogpaddling. Lake water is shallow and the beachfront is wide.
- **Ohio Street Beach and Olive Park (400 N Lake Shore Dr)**
  The perfect combo for cross-training canines: Olive Park's fenced-in grassy areas for running and neighboring Ohio Street Beach's calm waters for swimming.
- **Promontory Point (5401 South Shore Dr)**
  Radical run for daring, buff dogs that dive off the scenic picnic area's rocks into the deep water below.
- **Sherman Park (1301 W 52nd St)**
  The best place in the city for a Victorian-style stroll over picturesque bridges and through lagoons.

More Doggie Information

Chicago's canine community keeps up to sniff on doggie doings through *Chicagoland Tails Magazine*, www.chicagolandtails.com and the Chicago Canine website, www.chicagocanine.com. The definitive local resource for all things dog is Margaret Littman's book *The Dog Lover's Companion to Chicago* (Avalon Travel Publishing).

In a city with the nation's busiest convention center, it's no wonder that Chicago hotels are designed for the business traveler with expense account prices to boot. Really, the price of even an average downtown room can be outrageous. For a special urban splurge, book a suite at one of Chicago's premier palace hotels—the **Ritz-Carlton (Map 32)**, **Four Seasons (Map 32)**, **Le Meridien (Map 2)**, or **Peninsula (Map 2)**. Hip hoteliers will want to stay at one of downtown's two "**W**" hotels, **Hotel 71 (Map 2)**, or the **The Hard Rock Hotel (Map 6)** located in the vintage Union Carbide building on Michigan Avenue.

Also located in a historic landmark, the **Hotel Burnham (Map 5)** is a lovely boutique hotel near the heart of Chicago's theater district. Burnham and its Kimpton Hotel Group sister **Hotel Allegro (Map 5),** also in the theater district, feature free wine receptions every evening for hotel guests. The **Blake Hotel (Map 8)** on Printer's Row offers boutique-type amenities with handsome Arts & Crafts inspired rooms (even if some of the views can be less than inspiring).

Book budget-minded out-of-town guests at the **Chicago Travelodge Downtown (Map 8)**. It's not much to look at, but the location just off Michigan Avenue between Millennium Park and the Museum Campus can't be beat for the price.

Around the corner at the **Congress Plaza Hotel (Map 9)**, picketers have been marching with placards for what seems like forever—the Hotel Workers Union is on strike with the management and it seems unlikely that their dispute will be settled anytime soon. The strike has hurt business, so some good deals can be had—let your conscience be your judge and brace yourself for heckling strikers should you take the plunge (and remember that Upton Sinclair would *not* approve).

Good values can also be had away from downtown. **City Suites (Map 43)** and its "Neighborhood Inns of Chicago" partners **The Majestic (Map 44)** and **Willows (Map 44),** offer small-hotel charm at reasonable rates. If they are still too rich for your blood, **Heart o' Chicago Motel (Map 37)** is skipping distance from the Edgewater White Castle—and a short walk to the life-affirming Andersonville community. **Sheffield House (Map 43)**, once a transient hotel, offers spare, cheap rooms appealing to the backpacking European traveler, and is only a stone's throw from Wrigley Field.

For such a large city, Chicago doesn't have much to offer by way of B&B's. **The Wheeler Mansion (Map 11)** near McCormick Place is luxurious and antique-filled with fireplaces, custom baths and bedding, and ridiculously high ceilings. The more modest **Wicker Park B&B (Map 21)** gives good breakfast—the owners also own the nearby Alliance Bakery where morning sweets are baked fresh daily. **The Flemish House B&B (Map 32)** is on a quiet, tree-lined street right in the middle of the hullabaloo of Rush Street and the Oak Street Beach. **The Old Town Bed and Breakfast**, run by the friendly and eccentric Serritela family, features contemporary, masculine bedrooms and a common area that includes a grand piano, formal dining room, and deluxe gourmet kitchen available for guests to use.

Finally, there are three youth hostels in Chicago open to the public with rates as low as $15 a night for card-carrying international youth hostel members. For deals, Hot Rooms is a Chicago-based reservation service offering low-rates on undersold rooms: www.hotrooms.com.

Map 2 • Near North / River North

			Pricing	*Rating*
Amalfi Hotel	20 W Kinzie St	312-395-9000	353	***
Best Western Inn	125 W Ohio St	312-467-0800	124	***
Cass Hotel	640 N Wabash Ave	312-787-4031	89	
Club Quarters	75 E Wacker Dr	312-357-6400	94	
Comfort Inn & Suites	15 E Ohio St	312-894-0900	177	**
Courtyard by Marriott	30 E Hubbard St	312-329-2500	189	****
Embassy Suites Hotel	600 N State St	312-943-3800	225	***
Four Points	630 N Rush St	312-981-6600	130	**
Hampton Inn	33 W Illinois St	312-832-0330	157	***
Hilton Garden Inn	10 E Grand Ave	312-595-0000	199	***
Holiday Inn	350 N Orleans St	312-836-5000	135	***
Homewood Suites	40 E Grand Ave	312-644-2222	172	***
Hotel 71	71 E Wacker Dr	312-346-7100	185	****
House of Blues Hotel Loews	333 N Dearborn St	312-245-0333	175	****
Le Meridien	521 N Rush St	312-645-1500	219	****
Lenox House Suites	616 N Rush St	312-337-1000	134	***
Ohio House Motel	600 N La Salle Dr	312-943-6000	85	
Peninsula Chicago Hotel	108 E Superior St	312-337-2888	490	*****
Westin River North Chicago	320 N Dearborn St	312-744-1900	247	***

Map 3 • Streeterville / Mag Mile

			Pricing	Rating
Allerton Crowne Plaza	701 N Michigan Ave	312-440-1500	259	***
Best Western Inn	162 E Ohio St	312-787-3100	159	***
Courtyard Magnificent Mile	165 E Ontario St	312-573-0800	189	***
Embassy Suites Lakefront	511 N Columbus Dr	312-836-5900	218	***
Fairfield Inn	216 E Ontario St	312-787-3777	193	**
Fitzpatrick Chicago Hotel	166 E Superior St	312-787-6000	295	****
Holiday Inn	300 E Ohio St	312-787-6100	189	***
Hotel Inter-Continental	505 N Michigan Ave	312-944-4100	236	****
Marriott	540 N Michigan Ave	312-836-0100	220	***
Omni Chicago Hotel	676 N Michigan Ave	312-944-6664	310	****
Park Hyatt Hotel	800 N Michigan Ave	312-335-1234	377	*****
Radisson Hotel	160 E Huron St	312-787-2900	189	***
Red Roof Inn	162 E Ontario St	312-787-3580	95	
Sheraton Hotel & Towers	301 E North Water St	312-464-1000	139	****
W Chicago Lakeshore	644 N Lake Shore Dr	312-943-9200	234	****
Wyndham Chicago	633 N St Clair St	312-573-0300	206	****

Map 4 • West Loop Gate / Greek Town

			Pricing	Rating
Crowne Plaza Mid City Plaza	1 S Halsted St	312-829-5000	114	****
Old Town Bed and Breakfast	1442 N Park Ave	312-440-9268	175	

Map 5 • The Loop

			Pricing	Rating
Club Quarters Central Loop	111 W Adams St	312-214-6400	129	
Crowne Plaza Silversmith	10 S Wabash Ave	312-372-7696	163	****
Hilton Palmer House	17 E Monroe St	312-726-7500	151	****
Hotel Allegro	171 W Randolph St	312-236-0123	179	***
Hotel Burnham	1 W Washington St	312-782-1111	185	****
Hotel Monaco	225 N Wabash Ave	312-960-8500	195	****
Renaissance Chicago Hotel	1 W Wacker Dr	312-372-7200	299	****
W Chicago City Center	172 W Adams St	312-332-1200	195	****

Map 6 • The Loop / Grant Park

			Pricing	Rating
Fairmont Hotel	200 N Columbus Dr	312-565-8000	344	****
Hard Rock Hotel	230 N Michigan Ave	312-345-1000	383	****
Hyatt Regency Chicago Hotel	151 E Wacker Dr	312-565-1234	243	****
Swissotel Chicago	323 E Wacker Dr	312-565-0565	276	****

Map 7 • South Loop / River City

			Pricing	Rating
Holiday Inn	506 W Harrison St	312-957-9100	131	***

Map 8 • South Loop / Printers Row / Dearborn Park

			Pricing	Rating
Blake Hotel	500 S Dearborn St	312-986-1234	279	
Ho Jo Inn	720 N La Salle St	312-664-8100	139	
Hostelling International	24 E Congress Pkwy	312-692-1560	35	
Travelodge	65 E Harrison St	312-427-8000	114	***

Map 9 • South Loop / South Michigan Ave

			Pricing	Rating
Best Western Grant Park Hotel	1100 S Michigan Ave	312-922-2900	112	**
Congress Plaza Hotel	520 S Michigan Ave	312-427-3800	142	***
Essex Inn	800 S Michigan Ave	312-939-2800	85	**
Hilton & Towers Chicago	720 S Michigan Ave	312-922-4400	186	****

Map 11 • South Loop / McCormick Place

			Pricing	Rating
Hyatt Regency at McCormick Place	2233 S Dr Martin L King Jr Dr	312-567-1234	197	***
Wheeler Mansion	2020 S Calumet Ave	312-945-2020	297	****

Map 12 • Bridgeport (West)

			Pricing	Rating
Benedictine Bed and Breakfast	3111 S Aberdeen St	773-927-7424	145	

Map 14 • Prairie Shores / Lake Meadows

			Pricing	Rating
Amber Inn	3901 S Michigan Ave	773-285-1000	59	
Bronzeville's First Bed & Breakfast	3911 S Dr Martin L King Jr Dr	773-373-8081	175	

Map 17 • Kenwood

			Pricing	Rating
Ramada Inn Lake Shore	4900 S Lake Shore Dr	773-288-5800	99	**

Map 20 • East Hyde Park / Jackson Park

			Pricing	Rating
Wooded Isle Suites	5750 S Stony Island Ave	773-288-5578	151	

Map 21 • Wicker Park / Ukrainian Village

			Pricing	Rating
Wicker Park Inn B&B	1329 N Wicker Park Ave	773-486-2743	131	

Map 22 • Noble Square / Goose Island

			Pricing	Rating
House of Two Urns B&B	1239 N Greenview Ave	773-235-1408	105	

Map 24 • River West / West Town

			Pricing	Rating
Viceroy Hotel	1519 W Warren Blvd	312-421-4611	78	

Map 26 • University Village / Little Italy / Pilsen

			Pricing	Rating
Lugo Hotel	2008 S Blue Island Ave	312-226-5818	34	
Marriott	625 S Ashland Ave	312-491-1234	170	***

Map 27 • Logan Square

			Pricing	Rating
Milshire Hotel	2525 N Milwaukee Ave	773-384-7611	30	

Map 30 • Lincoln Park

			Pricing	Rating
Arlington House International Hostel	616 W Arlington Pl	773-929-5380	58	
Belden Stratford Hotel	2300 N Lincoln Park W	773-281-2900	193	
Days Inn	1816 N Clark St	312-664-3040	109	
Days Inn Gold-Coast	1800 N Lincoln Ave	312-664-7624	99	
Windy City Urban Inn	607 W Deming Pl	773-248-7091		

Map 31 • Old Town / Near North

			Pricing	Rating
Marshall Hotel	1232 N La Salle Dr	312-664-3080	45	

Map 32 • Gold Coast / Mag Mile

			Pricing	Rating
Ambassador West	1300 N State St	312-787-3700	259	****
Doubletree Guest Suites	198 E Delaware Pl	312-664-1100	206	***
Drake Hotel	140 E Walton St	312-787-2200	295	
Flemish House	68 E Cedar St	312-664-9981	145	
Four Seasons Hotel Chicago	120 E Delaware Pl	312-280-8800	383	*****
Millenium Knickerbocker	163 E Walton St	312-751-8100	214	****
Omni Ambassador East Hotel	1301 N State Pkwy	312-787-7200	202	****
Raphael Hotel	201 E Delaware Pl	312-943-5000	193	***
Residence Inn	201 E Walton St	312-943-9800	228	***
Ritz Carlton Hotel	160 E Pearson St	312-266-2343	363	*****
Seneca Hotel	200 E Chestnut St	312-787-8900	169	***
Sofitel Water Tower	20 E Chestnut St	312-324-4000	245	****
Sutton Place Hotel	21 E Bellevue Pl	312-266-2100	257	****
Talbot Hotel	20 E Delaware Pl	312-943-0161	169	****
Tremont	100 E Chestnut St	312-751-1900	177	***
Westin	909 N Michigan Ave	312-943-7200	285	****
Whitehall Hotel	105 E Delaware Pl	312-944-6300	226	****

Map 34 • East Rogers Park

			Pricing	Rating
Super 8 Motel	7300 N Sheridan Rd	773-973-7440	99	

Map 35 • Arcadia Terrace / Peterson Park

			Pricing	Rating
Apache Motel	5535 N Lincoln Ave	773-728-9400	50	
Diplomat Motel	5230 N Lincoln Ave	773-271-5400	75	
Lincoln Inn	5952 N Lincoln Ave	773-784-1118	49	
Lincoln Motel	5900 N Lincoln Ave	773-561-3170	47	
O'Mi Motel	5611 N Lincoln Ave	773-561-6488	55	
Summit Motel	5308 N Lincoln Ave	773-561-3762	50	
Tip Top Motel	6060 N Lincoln Ave	773-539-4800	55	

Map 37 • Edgewater / Andersonville

			Pricing	Rating
Chicago Lodge	920 W Foster Ave	773-334-5600	80	
Heart O'Chicago Motel	5990 N Ridge Ave	773-271-9181	64	
Lakeside Motel	5440 N Sheridan Rd	773-275-2700	58	
The Ardmore House	1248 W Ardmore Ave	773-728-5414	89	

Map 43 • Wrigleyville/ East Lakeview

			Pricing	Rating
Ambers Hotel	1632 W Belmont Ave	773-248-1740	40	
Bellwood Hotel	1409 W Diversey Pkwy	773-404-6000	46	
City Suites Hotel	933 W Belmont Ave	773-404-3400	181	***
Diplomat Hotel	3208 N Sheffield Ave	773-549-6800	50	
Sheffield House	3834 N Sheffield Ave	773-248-3500	55	

Map 44 • East Lakeview

			Pricing	Rating
Abbott Hotel	721 W Belmont Ave	773-248-2700	65	
Belair Hotel	424 W Diversey Pkwy	773-248-4000	85	
Best Western	3434 N Broadway St	773-244-3434	169	***
Days Inn	644 W Diversey Pkwy	773-525-7010	187	
Hotel Majestic	528 W Brompton Ave	773-404-3499	175	***
Inn at Lincoln Park	601 W Diversey Pkwy	773-348-2810	100	**
Majestic Hotel	528 W Brompton Ave	773-404-3499	159	
Willows	555 W Surf St	773-528-8400	173	***

Chicago is a kid's kind of town. From sandy beaches and leafy parks to diverse downtown museums, concerts, and suburban attractions, Chicago's options for family fun are non-stop—just like your kids.

The Best of the Best

The best part about Chicago family-style is that lots of stuff is *free*...or practically free. Great entertainment and educational venues keep cash in parents' pockets for school supplies, groceries, gas, and an occasional adult night out.

- **Top Park:** Lincoln Park (Lake Shore Dr & North Ave, 312-742-7529; www.chicagoparkdistrict.com). From an expansive sandy beach, baseball diamonds, basketball courts, and bike paths to grassy meadows, fishing lagoons, museums, and the nation's oldest free zoo, Lincoln Park promises a full day of outdoor activity.
- **Generations of Amusement:** Kiddieland (8400 W North Ave, Melrose Park, 708-343-8000; www.kiddieland.com). Before Disney and Six Flags, there was Kiddieland, one of the nation's oldest family-owned and operated amusement parks. Many of the over 30 rides and attractions are original to this wholesome, 77-year-old icon of fun including the jelly-bean-colored bumper cars, carousel, swirling tea cups, and "Little Dipper" rollercoaster. Thrill-seeking tweens scream on the "Log Jammer" and high-flying "Galleon." Kids need more steam? Free Pepsi served all day. Unlimited rides for $20.75 admission fee (ages six and up); $17.75 (ages 3–5, seniors); free under age two; discounted admission after 5 pm. Open April–October. Call for seasonal schedule.
- **Spellbinding Story Time:** Lincoln Park Zoo (2200 N Cannon Dr, 312-742-2000; www.lpzoo.com). Donning safari khakis and pith helmet, Professor Bonnie spins adventurous tales and sings for preschoolers at the *Farm-in-the-Zoo*. Wildly popular, this story hour is the toughest ticket in town. Arrive early to secure admission (donation suggested). At the free *Second Sunday Stories,* children's book authors read their works about life on the farm followed by activities and tours of the *Farm-in-the-Zoo*. Call for schedule.
- **Slickest Sledding Hill:** Soldier Field Lakefront Park (312-742-7529; www.chicagoparkdistrict.com). The best part of the Soldier Field's pretty 17-acre park is the free, giant sledding hill with frozen lake views. BYO ride and bundle up for frigid lakefront winds. In warmer months, check out the Children's Garden.
- **Coolest Ice Rink:** McCormick Tribune Ice Rink in Millennium Park (55 N Michigan Ave, 312-742-7529; www.chicagoparkdistrict.com). Skate hand-in-hand in the shadow of architectural landmark buildings lining the Mag Mile. Open daily, admission is free to the 16,000-square-foot rink; skate rental available and warming room on-site.
- **Best-Kept Secret:** Chicago Public Library's "Kraft Great Kids Museum Passport" (Main Branch at 400 S State St, 312-747-4300 and branches city-wide; www.chipublib.org). Families can't afford not to know about the passports on loan for one week that gets family members free admission to over a dozen of Chicago's premier cultural institutions including the biggies at the Museum Campus plus the Art Institute, Peggy Notebaert Museum, and Chicago Historical Society. Available only to Chicago Public Library card-carrying adult Chicago residents. See website for participating institutions and details.
- **Railroad Shop That Rocks:** Berwyn's Toy Trains & Models (7025 Ogden Ave, Berwyn, 708-484-3882). A roundhouse of activity, this hobby shop is the best reason to go to Berwyn, besides all the dollar stores. Engineers of all ages play at the many display train tables. Don't miss the charming, 7-by-14-foot tooting train layout in the backroom.
- **WOW Waterparks:** (312-742-7529; www.chicagoparkdistrict.com). The Chicago Park District operates over 20 free waterparks with arching jets, umbrella sprays, pipe falls, and bubble jets in Chicago's neighborhood parks and beaches. All facilities open daily in summer 11 am to 8 pm.
- **Best Beach:** North Avenue Beach (1600 North Ave, 312-742-7529; www.chicagoparkdistrict.com). From swimming, spiking volleyballs, and kickboxing to sunbathing and sipping sun-downers, this expansive beach on Lake Michigan rivals any on the California coast. The tug-boat shaped beach house has locker facilities and rents volleyball equipment, roller blades, and bikes. On the upper deck is Castaways restaurant and ice cream parlor. There's also a full outdoor fitness center with weights and spin cycles plus a roller blade rink for pick up hockey under the summer sun.
- **Sensational Soda Fountain:** Margie's Candies (1960 N Western Ave, 773-384-1035). Celebrating 85 years of scoop, this old-fashioned ice cream parlor serves yummy frozen treats like soda fountains of yesteryear. Kids who flash report cards with an A get a free ice cream cone.

- **A Child's Choice Bakery:** Sweet Mandy B's (1208 W Webster Ave, 773-244-1174). Trendy and tasty, this cheery bakery's kid confections include awesome cupcakes, chunky whoopee pies, and whimsical cut-out frosted cookies. Signature sweet: "Dirt Cups"—a cake, crushed Oreo cookie, and whipped cream combo crawling with psychedelic gummy worms.
- **Teen Scene:** Jive Monkey (854 W Belmont Ave, 773-404-8000, ext. 229). Hipsters come from across the urban jungle to buy, sell, and swap all things cool including fashionable vintage T-shirts, jewelry, Mod Squad mushroom hats, and the latest Levi's. Best buys are used T-shirts, $3 each.
- **Coolest Family Concerts:** Joe Segal's Jazz Showcase (59 W Grand Ave, 312-670-2473; www.jazzshowcase.com). Hipster kids and jiving parents and grandparents hang out at this swank, serious jazz club's Sunday 4 pm matinee performances where top musicians jam. Non-alcoholic beverages and snacks served. Discount adult admission; children under 12 free. All Ages Blue Chicago Show (736 N Clark St, 312-661-1003; www.bluechicago.com) on Saturday nights from 8 pm to 3 am where families rock to the Gloria Shannon Blues Band in the basement of the Blue Chicago store. Adult admission $8; kids under age 11 free. No alcohol or smoking allowed.
- **Flying High:** Mayor Daley's Kids and Kites Festival (Alternating lakefront locations, 312-744-3315; www.cityofchicago.org/specialevents). Every spring and fall, the Windy City lives up to its blow-hard reputation, lifting kids' spirits and kites to new heights along the lakefront. Kite flying professionals and instructors help enthusiasts of all ages construct kites and fly them for free. Complimentary kite kits provided or bring your own. Free family entertainment, crafts, and storytelling on-site.
- **Not So Little League:** Chicago White Sox FUNdamentals Field (U.S. Cellular Field, 333 W 35th St, 312-674-1000; www.whitesox.com). Little sluggers age three and up play ball in a 15,000-square-foot field of their own within the White Sox's home park. While junior trains, parents spy the pro game going on below from the new, kid-friendly interactive baseball diamond and skills area perched above the left-field concourse. Budding all-stars hone their pitching, batting, and base-running techniques under the sharp eyes of college and pro coach-instructors from the year-round Chicago White Sox Training Academy in Lisle. Batter yet, it's all free with ball-park admission.
- **Masterpiece Portraits:** Classic Kids (917 W Armitage Ave, 773-296-2607; 566 Chestnut St, Winnetka, 847-446-2064). Pricey but priceless photos from this studio capture your kid at his or her model best. Pay a $300 sitting fee plus cost for handcrafted prints and treasure your tyke forever.
- **Weirdest City Sight:** Chicago River runs green (Chicago River downtown along Wacker Dr). No, it's not algae or bile, but bio-degradable green dye. Every St. Patrick's Day, the city turns the Chicago River emerald green like the Incredible Hulk.
- **Parents' Parking Dream:** Little Parkers Program, Standard Parking Garages (888-700-7275; www.standardparking.com). Select garages downtown specially equip families for road trips home with puzzles, crayons, and coloring books. Family-friendly garage amenities include spacious bathrooms with diaper-changing stations. Some rent family videos to monthly parkers. Participating garages: Grant Park North Garage, 25 N Michigan Ave; East Monroe Garage, 350 E Monroe St; Chicago Historical Society Garage, 1730 N Stockton Dr; Huron-St. Claire Self Park near Northwestern Memorial Hospital; Erie-Ontario Self Park in Streeterville neighborhood; and 680 N Lake Shore Dr Self Park.
- **Finest Family Festivals:** Tall Ships (312-744-3370; www.cityofchicago.org/specialevents). Ahoy there, matey! In early August, over 25 old-world sailing vessels drop anchor along the lakeshore at Navy Pier, DuSable Harbor, and the Chicago River filling the skyline with billowing sails. There are daily deck tours ($10 boarding fee) as well as free entertainment and fireworks.
- **Kudos Kids' Theatre:** Marriott Theatre for Young Audiences (Marriott Lincolnshire Resort, 10 Marriott Dr, Lincolnshire, 847-634-0200; www.marriotttheatre.com). Not a bad seat in the house at this intimate arena theater where actors welcome pint-sized audience participation and roam the aisles interacting with kids. Post-performance, the actors conduct Q&A answering kids' theatrical questions. Family productions run year-round. Tickets $10 per person; free parking.
- **Oscar Performances:** Children's International Film Festival (city-wide, 773-281-9075; www.cicff.org). For over two weeks each fall, Chicago's theater venues feature hundreds of witty, ingenious long- and short-form children's movies from around the world, some created by kids. Filmmakers, directors, and animators teach seminars for movie-lovers of all ages.

- **Hippest Halloween Happening:** Chicago Symphony Orchestra's Hallowed Haunts Concert (220 S Michigan Ave, 312-294-3000; www.cso.org). Skeletons rattle and ghosts boogie to classical morbid music at the Chicago Symphony Orchestra's creepy family concert featuring hair-raising Romantic-Era pieces and medieval chants. Come in costume to the concert and ghoulish pre-performance party. Tickets: $7–$45.
- **Perfect Pumpkin Patch:** Sonny Acres Farm (29 W 310 North Ave, West Chicago, 630-231-9515; www.sonnyacres.com). During October, the Feltes family homestead has it all for fall: jack-o-lanterns for carving, homemade pies, decorative Thanksgiving and Halloween displays, and a killer costume shop. Kids love the mountains of pumpkins, crunchy caramel apples, scary hay rides, youngster carnival rides, and haunted barns (one for tiny tikes and another for blood-thirsty teens). Free farm admission and parking; purchase tickets for attractions.
- **Fields of Dreams:** Of course Wrigley Field, but a family outing at the venerable ballpark amounts to a month's down payment on a mini van. For $10 or less per ticket, take the family to the 'burbs' farm league games at pristine ballparks complete with entertainment, eats, and fireworks: Kane County Cougars (34W002 Cherry Ln, Geneva, 630-232-8811; www.kccougars.com) and Shaumburg Flyers (1999 S Springinsguth Rd, Schaumburg, 847-891-2255; www.flyersbaseball.com).
- **No-Flab Family Workout:** Tri-Star Gymnastics' Family Fun Night (1401 Circle Ave, Forest Park, 708-771-7827; www.tri-stargym.com). Families bounce on trampolines, swing on bars, tumble across mats, and climb ropes together at Tri-Star's warehouse-sized gymnastic training facility. Held from 4:30 pm to 5:30 pm on Saturday nights during the school year, admission is $5 per child and parents get in free. Parental supervision (no more than two kids per adult) and signed waiver required.
- **Musical Marathon Encounter:** Chicago Symphony Orchestra's Day of Music (220 S Michigan Ave, 312-294-3333; www.cso.org). A free live music marathon lasting eight hours held each fall. In addition to the world-renowned Chicago Symphony Orchestra, hear the city's top musicians perform classical, jazz, blues, world music, plus lively family entertainment. For year-round family concert performances, check out the orchestra's Kraft Matinee Series.
- **Horse'n Around:** Arlington Park Race Track's Family Day (2200 W Euclid Ave, Arlington Heights, 847-385-7500; www.arlingtonpark.com). From mid-May through mid-September it's a sure bet you'll win big with the kids on a Sunday afternoon at the horse races. Wild West, luau, and circus-themed family activities surround the seriously fun thoroughbred racing action at this swank, clean track. Pony rides, face painters, and petting zoo on-site. From noon to 4 pm, attend the free Junior Jockey Club events (847-385-7706) including educational equine care talks and behind-the scenes track tours (children 12 and under).
- **Brightest Christmas Lights:** Cuneo Museum and Gardens' Winter Wonderland Holiday Light Festival (1350 N Milwaukee Ave, Vernon Hills, 847-362-3042; www.cuneomuseum.org). The largest drive-through Christmas display in Northern Illinois twinkles with millions of lights creating dazzling holiday scenes. Superhero and storybook light sculptures dance in the woods. Festival runs first Friday after Thanksgiving through New Year's weekend from 6 pm to 10 pm. Admission per car is $10 on weekends, $5 weekdays.
- **Winter Blahs Buster:** Fantasy Kingdom (1422 N Kingsbury St at Evergreen St, 312-642-5437). When Chicago's plunging temps prevent playground play, take tykes to this warehouse-turned-play-space magic kingdom to blow off steam. Kids clamor through a giant castle fitted with slides and tunnels (socks required) while donning Camelot costumes for dress-up fun. $12 per child.
- **Shadiest Theme Park:** Pirate's Cove (901 Leicester Rd, Elk Grove Village, 847-437-9494; www.elkgroveparks.org). On the other hand, when Chicago's soaring temps make playing outdoors as appealing as a trip down the Styx, hit this blessedly small-scale, low-tech theme park. Your (10-and-under) mateys will scramble up the Smugglers Cove, ride a rope-and-pulley griffin, and paddle around a wee lagoon, all while you actually keep cool in this heavily-shaded treasure. Great low-cost birthday party site. $6 for residents, $8 for nonresidents.

Rainy Day Activities

Art Institute of Chicago, 111 S Michigan Ave, 312-443-3600; www.artic.edu. While kids find the doll house–sized Thorne Miniature Rooms and shiny medieval armor very cool, they also discover artistic expression from around the world at the Kraft Education Center. Interactive exhibitions introduce children to art from other cultures, time periods, and world-wide geographic regions. "Edutaining" art books and masterpiece puzzles in the children's library reinforce visual learning. Free kids' programs and drawing workshops are also held throughout museum galleries. Admission is free on Tuesdays (however, donation strongly suggested); children under 5 always free.

Cernan Earth and Space Center, Triton College Campus, 2000 Fifth Ave, River Grove, 708-456-0300, ext. 3372; www.triton.edu/cernan. Named after Apollo astronaut Eugene Cernan, a native Chicagoan and the last man on the moon, this cozy planetarium's intimate dome theater features kids' star programs ($5), earth and sky shows, and laser light shows. Monthly sky watch and lectures hosted. Mini space-related museum (free admission) and great celestial gift shop.

Chicago's Museum Campus, 1200–1400 S Lake Shore Dr. The closest you'll come to an educational amusement park. Dinosaurs, live sharks, giant mechanical insects, ancient mummies, and exploding stars are just a handful of adventures your kids will encounter on the lakefront's brainy peninsula home to the Field Museum (312-922-9410; www.fieldmuseum.org), Adler Planetarium & Astronomy Museum (312-922-7827; www.adlerplanetarium.org), and John G. Shedd Aquarium (312-939-2426; www.shedd.org). Check with each institution for its free admission days and special family programs.

Diversey River Bowl, 2211 W Diversey Pkwy, 773-227-7057. Families, couples, and serious bowlers mix it up at this upbeat city alley. Decent grilled food served and full bar on-site. Wednesday through Sunday nights at 8 pm, glow-in-the-dark bowling known as Rock'in Bowl goes well past the little one's bedtime but is fun for teens with chaperones.

DuPage Children's Museum, 301 N Washington St, Naperville, 630-637-8000; www.dupagechildrensmuseum.org. The 45,000-square-foot museum loaded with hands-on, action-packed exhibits keeps pre-schoolers with nano-second attention spans exploring until exhaustion.

Exploritorium, 4701 Oakton St, Skokie, 847-674-1500, x2700; www.skokieparkdistrict.org/facilities.asp. From finger paints and water games to costumes and a multi-storied jungle gym, this facility tuckers tykes out. The climbing gym outfitted with twisting ropes, tubes, and tunnels even brings out the Tarzan in parents. Miniscule admission fee; free for Skokie adult residents and kids under 3.

Federal Reserve Bank of Chicago Visitors' Center, 230 S LaSalle St, 312-322-5322; www.chicagofed.org. The buck stops here where kids learn the power of pocket change through hands-on and computerized exhibits explaining the Fed's role in managing the nation's money. Kids love the rotating, million-dollar cube of cash and $50,800 coin pit. Sneak a peak into the vault stocked with $9 million, trace our country's currency history, and learn how to identify fake bills. Free admission. Open weekdays 9 am–1 pm; free guided tours on Mondays at 1 pm.

Garfield Park Conservatory, 300 N Central Park Ave, 312-746-5100; www.garfield-conservatory.org. Kids really dig Plants Alive!, the free, landmark Conservatory's 5,000-square-foot greenhouse blooming with child-friendly vegetation. Kids climb a two-story twisting daisy stem that doubles as a slide and come nose-to-stinger with a Jurassic-sized bumble bee. Attend story-telling, plant seeds, and dig in the soil pool.

Kohl Children's Museum of Greater Chicago, 165 Green Bay Rd, Wilmette, 847-256-6600; www.kohlchildrensmuseum.org. Kids climb the rigging of a pirate ship, "ride" an L train, meander through mazes, and push mini carts through a fully stocked grocery store.

Milano Model & Toy Museum, 116 Park Ave, Elmhurst, 630-279-4422; www.toys-n-cars.com. Magical place for motor heads and rail buffs of all ages featuring hundreds of rail-related toys and models. Adults, $4; kids under 10, free.

Mitchell Museum of the American Indian, 2600 Central Park Ave on Kendall College Campus, Evanston, 847-475-1030; www.mitchellmuseum.org. From real teepees and dug-out canoes to bow-and-arrows and tom-toms, this compact sensory museum's engaging hands-on exhibits and craft sessions teach kids about the rich Native American life and culture. During the school year, sessions are offered semi-monthly on Saturdays, and on Tuesdays, Wednesdays, and Thursdays in summer. All programs held from 10:30 am to noon.

Museum of Science and Industry, 57th St at S Lake Shore Dr, 773-684-1414; www.msichicago.org. The ultimate hands-on learning experience for families, this massive museum is a tsunami of scientific exploration. Favorite kid exhibits are the 3,500 square-foot The Great Train Story model railroad, the United Airlines jet, a walk-through human heart, a working Coal Mine, and the Idea Factory workshop packed with gears, cranks, and water toys. OMNIMAX Theater on-site. Call for free day schedule.

Navy Pier, 600 E Grand Ave, 312-595-7437; www.navypier.com. A mega-sized free entertainment emporium jutting into Lake Michigan, Navy Pier has an IMAX Theater and tons of carnival-like attractions. The renowned Shakespeare Theater performs kid-friendly shorts of Willy's works. The 57,000-square-foot Chicago Children's Museum has 15 permanent engaging exhibits for toddlers to pre-teens (312-527-1000; www.chichildrensmuseum.org). Museum admission free on Thursday nights from 5 pm to 8 pm.

Oak Brook Family Aquatic Center, 1450 Forest Gate Rd, Oak Brook, 630-990-4233; www.obparks.org. Wet, wild fun for the whole family at this splashy indoor aquatic facility. They've got a zero-depth pool and slide for tadpoles as well as an Olympic-sized pool for bigger fish. Special swim events include watery holiday-themed parties, arts and crafts, water sports days, and dive-in movie nights where you can watch a family flick from your inflatable raft.

Peggy Notebaert Nature Museum, 2430 N Cannon Dr, 773-755-5100; www.naturemuseum.org. Kids delight in Butterfly Haven, a soaring tropical greenhouse habitat, home to hundreds of exotic winged beauties from around the world. The Children's Gallery replicates prairie and wetland habitats. Hands-on, free scientific activities and animal feedings always scheduled. Chicago residents enjoy a $1 discount on admission fee. On Thursdays, admission is free; however donations are strongly suggested.

Pelican Harbor Indoor/Outdoor Aquatic Park, 200 S Lindsay Ln, Bolingbrook, 630-739-1705; www.bolingbrookparks.org. Chicago area's only indoor/outdoor waterpark open year-round. Kids zip down six thrilling water slides (one 75-foot tall), float on inner tubes, and plunge into the diving well. There is a large zero-depth pool for little swimmers, lap pool, sand volleyball, whirlpool, and concessions.

Shops at Northbridge, 520 N Michigan Ave, 312-327-2300; www.westfield.com/northbridge. The entire third floor is not only lined with child apparel, toy, and accessory stores, but has The LEGO Store with play stations and a spacious LEGO building zone. Best part is parents don't have to clean up those blasted colored blocks!

Spertus Museum of Judaica, 618 S Michigan Ave, 312-322-1700; www.spertus.edu/museum. The Children's ARTiFACT Center recreates an impressive archeological site where kids dig up artifacts from ancient Middle East civilizations and experiment with writing in Cuneiform. Free admission on Fridays; all-inclusive, $10 family pass sold the rest of the week.

Wonder Works, 6445 W North Ave, Oak Park, 708-383-4815; www.wonder-works.org. About half a mile west of Chicago's city limits, this modest children's museum is far more accessible for many city families than the Chicago Children's Museum at Navy Pier and boasts the triple advantages of being low-cost ($5 admission + free street parking), low-key, and packed with friendly volunteers. Usually closed on Mondays and Tuesdays, Wonder Works often makes an exception for school holidays (call to confirm, though).

Outdoor *and* Educational

Fresh air family fun venues that work your kids' muscles and minds pack the city and suburbs. Here are some of the best:

Brookfield Zoo, First Ave & 31st St, Brookfield, 708-485-0263; www.brookfieldzoo.org. Chicago's largest zoo spanning 216 wooded acres is home to over 2,500 animal residents from around the world. Hamill Family Play Zoo and the Children's Zoo offer interactive programs on animal antics and opportunities to pet kid-friendly creatures babysat by helpful docents. Several dolphin shows daily. Family and child educational classes offered, plus summer camps and special holiday events. Explore the woodsy Indian Lake district where a life-sized dinosaur "lives." Open daily. Admission is free October through March on Tuesdays and Thursdays and January through February on Saturdays and Sundays.

Cantigny Park, 1 S 151 Winfield Rd, Wheaton, 630-668-5161; www.rrmtf.org/cantigny. The 15-acre complex named after a World War I battle is home to the First Division Museum showcasing the history of the famed U.S. Army's 1st Infantry Division and *Chicago Tribune* founder's Robert R. McCormick Mansion Museum. After clamoring over the cannons, kids can stop to smell the flowers blooming in the manicured gardens. Family programs and concerts scheduled year-round. Park opens Tuesday through Sunday 9 am to sunset; museum is open 9 am–4 pm. Park and museum admission free; car parking fee, $7. Nearby is the top-rated, public Cantigny Golf Course (630-260-8197) offering junior golf instruction and a 9-hole Youth Links Course (630-260-8270).

Chicago Botanic Garden, 1000 Lake Cook Rd, Glencoe, 847-835-5440; www.chicagobotanic.org. Open daily, admission is free to this 385-acre living preserve with more than 1.2 million plants rooted in 23 gardens, three tropical greenhouses, three natural habitats, eight lagoons, and bike paths. Kids love the winding, willow-branch tunnel in the Children's Garden where they can dig for worms and plant seeds. On Monday nights in summer, picnickers listen to the resonating chimes of carillon bell concerts on Evening Island. Late May through October, come for the Jr. Railroad where model trains puff through a garden of America's best loved landmarks (exhibit admission charged); in early December, make sure to check out the Reindog Parade (think bassets with antlers), with or without a Fido of your own.

Cuneo Museum and Gardens, 1350 Milwaukee Ave, Vernon Hills, 847-362-3042; www.cuneomuseum.org. Kids romp through the 75-acre wooded estate's formal gardens, animal sanctuaries, and deer park surrounding a palatial Italianate mansion. Open Tuesday–Sunday 10 am–5 pm; $5 grounds admission fee; mansion tours cost $12 for adults, $7 for children.

Fermi National Accelerator Laboratory, Kirk Rd & Pine St, Batavia, 630-840-8258; www.fnal.gov. Release energy outdoors biking, hiking, and rollerblading the nature trails at the nuclear plant's 680-acre campus. Rare species of butterflies, plants, birds, and baby buffalos live on the rural grounds. Guided prairie tours offered in summer. Picnickers welcome and lake fishing available. Open daily; admission free. Kids power up their nuclear knowledge at the Leon M. Lederman Science Education Center learning about nature's secrets and how the universe began. Admission free; open weekdays. Fermilab physicists conduct behind-the-scenes lab tours and Q&A with guests the first weekend of every month.

Graceland Cemetery, Clark St & Irving Park Blvd, 312-922-3432; www.architecture.org. Eerie and educational, the famous 119-acre necropolis built in 1860 is a national architectural landmark filled with palatial mausoleums, haunting headstones, and reportedly disappearing angelic statues marking the graves of Chicago's rich, famous, and infamous. The Chicago Architecture Foundation's (312-922-3432; www.architecture.org) spine-chilling cemetery tour is a drop-dead Halloween family favorite.

Grosse Pointe Lighthouse, Sheridan Rd & Central St, Evanston, 847-328-6961; www.grossepointelighthouse.net. The pretty grounds surrounding the charming, white, tapering lighthouse built in 1873 and fairy-tale stone cottage are open year-round. Tours of both structures are offered weekends June through September for children aged 8 and up. A wooded trail twists down a grassy slope to the isolated Lighthouse Landing Beach.

Tempel Lipizzans Farm, Wadsworth Rd & Hunt Club Rd, Wadsworth, 847-623-7272; www.tempelfarms.com. Trained in the centuries-old tradition of the Spanish Riding School in Vienna, dancing, white Lipizzaner stallions fly through the air performing fancy four-footed feats. Performances are Wednesdays and Sundays, June through August. Tours of the historic stables offered year-round.

Lambs Farm, 14245 W Rockland Rd, Libertyville, 847-362-4636; www.lambsfarm.org. Over 40 years old, this is Chicagoland's favorite farmyard, a non-profit residential farm for persons with developmental disabilities. Animal petting zoo, mini-golf, and vintage carousel open in season. Year-round feel-good family events include an old-fashioned Breakfast with Santa, Easter Brunch, fall festival, and more. Shops and kid-friendly country restaurant open Tuesday through Sunday.

Lincoln Park Zoo, 2200 N Cannon Dr, 312-742-2000; www.lpzoo.com. The nation's oldest free zoo recently opened the new Ape House, Regenstein African Journey habitat, and North American animal exhibit at the Pritzker Family Children's Zoo. Kids love the graceful giraffes, lumbering elephants, and giant hissing Madagascar cockroaches. Additional family favorites are the Farm-in-the-Zoo, lion house, sea lion pool, and old-fashioned carousel (summer). Call for information on family programs including the ever popular Night Watch where families sleep over at the zoo!

Morton Arboretum, 4100 Illinois Rte 53, Lisle, 630-968-0074; www.mortonarb.org. Forests, meadows, gardens, and wetlands cover 1,700 acres of this outdoor tree and plant museum with paved roads and 14 miles of trails for hiking and biking. Kids dig the new Children's Adventure Garden and Maze. Overall, a great place to tromp around and picnic. Food service on-site. Guided tours and kid/family nature classes offered year-round. Favorite family fall activities include leaf collecting and the "Scarecrow Trail." Open daily. Discounted admission on Wednesdays.

Naper Settlement, 523 S Webster St, Naperville, 630-420-6010; www.naper.settlement.museum. Kids experience life on the Midwestern prairie of the past at this re-creation of a 19th-century agrarian community. Working blacksmith shop, post office, and school house manned by costumed interpreters. The living history village's seasonal programs cater to kids with games, pony rides, and entertainment.

North Park Village Nature Center, 5801 N Pulaski Rd, 312-744-5472; www.cityofchicago.org/environment. You'll think you're a hundred miles west of the city at this 46-acre rolling woods and wetlands where deer roam and owls screech. Nature paths throughout. Admission free; open year-round. Popular week-long EcoExplorers summer camps for kids aged five to 14 years also offered.

Sears Tower Skydeck, 233 S Wacker Dr, 312-875-9696; www.theskydeck.com. OK, so only a pane of glass separates your baby from the sky blue. But the Knee-High Chicago kids' exhibit is worth the parental panic. Interactive displays tell tales of Chicago from a bird's eye view. A touch-and-talk computer explains city landmarks.

Classes

Many of the city's fine cultural institutions have stellar, kid-focused curricula and host popular summer camps. Chicago and suburban park districts offer solid sports instruction, dance, and crafts classes. But private specialty schools also instruct many pint-sized prodigies. Here are some of the most popular and pedigreed organizations:

Academy of Movement and Music, 605 Lake St, Oak Park, 708-848-2329. This 33-year-old school offers popular dance and movement classes. The cool, creative Boys Production class for guys ages five to nine focuses on high-energy body movement practically applied to mini-manly visual arts projects, including mazes, puzzles, murals, sculptures, and machinery.

Alliance Francaise, 810 N Dearborn St, 312-337-1070; www.afchicago.com. Cultivating everything French in Chicagoans of all ages since 1897, this institution breeds petite Francophiles through intense language classes, camps, and cultural programs.

Bubbles Academy, 1504 N Fremont St, 312-944-7677. Yoga for youngsters taught with a creative twist in an open, airy studio.

Dennehy School of Irish Dance, 2555 W 111th St, 773-881-3990; www.dennehydancers.com. A South Side Irish institution, Dennehy has churned out high-stepping Irish dancers for over forty years. Its most-famous pupil so far is egomaniac, foot-pounding Michael Flatley of stage hits *Riverdance* and *Lord of the Dance*.

Flavour Cooking School, 7401 W Madison St, Forest Park, 708-488-0808; www.flavourcookingschool.com. Kids learn to really stir it up from scrambled eggs and lasagna to stir-fry and California cuisine at this cozy cooking school and culinary cookware shop. Class content determined by chefs' ages: Kitchen Helpers (age 4–6); Young Chefs (age 7–11); Sous Chefs (age 12+). Kids' summer cooking camps are also offered.

Gallery 37, 66 E Randolph St, 312-744-8925; www.gallery37.org. Spearheaded by Maggie Daley, as in Mayor Richie's wife, Gallery 37's creative curriculum provides 14- to 21-year-old Chicago residents with educational on-the-job training in the visual, literary, media, culinary, and performing arts. Under the direction of professional artists, apprentices are paid while creating art projects throughout the city such as bench-painting, sculpture, play-writing, and multicultural dance. Eight-week summer program and limited programming during school year. Applications required.

Illinois Rhythmic Gymnastics Center, 491 Lake Cook Rd, Deerfield, 847-498-9888; www.multiplexclubs.com. This top flexible factory turns out more national and Olympic gymnastic team members than any other in the country.

Language Stars, locations city-wide, 866-557-8277; www.languagestars.com. Children aged one through 10 are instructed in foreign language through play-based immersion.

Lou Conte Dance Studio, 1147 W Jackson Blvd, 312-850-9766; www.hubbardstreetdance.org. The dance studio of esteemed Hubbard Street Dance Chicago offers killer classes for teens (aged 11 to 14) in hip-hop, tap, jazz, ballet, African, modern, and more. Also teaches children and teen dance classes through the new, thriving Beverly Arts Center (2407 W 111th St, 773-445-3838; beverlyartcenter.org).

Merit School of Music, 47 W Polk St, 312-786-9428; www.meritmusic.org. This tuition-free conservatory provides economically disadvantaged youth with excellent instruction in playing classical and jazz instruments. An answer to the public school system's sad arts education cuts.

Music Institute of Chicago, 1490 Chicago Ave, Evanston, 847-905-1500; www.musicinst.com. Students of all ages flock to this esteemed school specializing in the Suzuki Method for many instruments. Group and private instruction in string, wind, brass, and percussion instruments offered.

Old Town School of Folk Music, 4544 N Lincoln Ave & 909 W Armitage Ave, 773-728-6000; www.oldtownschool.org. Opened in 1957, this is Chicago's premier all-American music center specializing in lessons on twangy instruments. The school is best known for its Wiggleworms music movement program catering to the under-five folk. Engaging teen curriculum in music, theater, dance, and art is also offered. Kids' concerts, actually all concerts, rock.

Ruth Page Center for the Arts, 1016 N Dearborn St, 312-337-6543; www.ruthpage.com. Prima ballerina classes for beginners to advanced students offered at this fine school whose graduates dance for the American Ballet Theatre, the New York City Ballet, and professional companies world-wide.

Second City Training Center, 1616 N Wells St, 312-664-3959; www.secondcity.com. Sign up your bucket of laughs for famed Second City's improvisational classes. Hilarious kids ages 4–12 attend hour-long sessions on Saturdays. Teen improv program is also offered.

Sherwood Conservatory of Music, 1312 S Michigan Ave, 312-427-6267; www.sherwoodmusic.org. Over-a-century-old Sherwood Conservatory specializes in the Suzuki Method for children ages three to 12 in cello, violin, viola, flute, piano, harp, and guitar. Also teaches classes at the South Side's Beverly Arts Center (2407 W 111th St, 773-445-3838; beverlyartcenter.org).

The Chopping Block, 4747 N Lincoln Ave, 773-472-6700; www.thechoppingblock.net. The Lincoln Square neighborhood store and kitchen complex of this sophisticated culinary store hosts cooking classes for kids ages 7–12 two times a week. Four-day cooking camp for two hours a day held in summers.

Tri-Star Gymnastics, 1401 Circle Ave, Forest Park, 708-771-7827; www.tri-stargym.com. This women-run gym pumps out gymnastic champs ages 18 months through teens. Flexing its muscle since 1987, the not-for-profit center offers caring instruction for boys and girls in gymnastics, tumbling, and trampoline. The center is home to a GIJO Team (Junior Olympics) and USGA Teams.

Shopping Essentials

Designer duds, high-style child furniture, imaginative toys, and kids' tunes—Chicago stores have it all for newborns to teens. Here's just a sampling of the top shops:

- **Active Kids** • 838 W Armitage Ave • 773-281-2002 • Child sportswear.
- **Alamo Shoes** • 5321 N Clark St • 773-334-6100; 6548 W Cermak Rd, Berwyn • 708-795-818 • Experienced staff for toddler shoe fittings.
- **American Girl Place** • 111 E Chicago Ave • 312-943-9400 • Dolls and books.
- **The Baby's Room** • 640 N LaSalle St • 312-642-1520 • Every furniture need fulfilled.
- **Bearly Used** • 401 Linden Ave, Wilmette • 847-256-8700 • Fab deals on duds and furniture.
- **Bellini** • 2100 N Southport Ave • 773-880-5840 (stores also in Highland Park and Oak Brook) • High-end, custom bedding, furniture, and clothes.
- **Building Blocks Toy Store** • 3306 N Lincoln Ave • 773-525-6200 • Old-fashioned, brain-building toys.
- **Carrara Children's Shoes** • 2506 N Clark St • 773-529-9955 • Tot soles from Italy.
- **Children in Paradise** • 909 N Rush St • 312-951-5437 • Personable kids' bookseller.
- **Cut Rate Toys** • 5409 W Devon Ave • 773-763-5740 • Discounted favorites.
- **Disney Store** • 717 N Michigan Ave • 312-654-9208 • Princess paraphernalia and Mouse gear.
- **Forest Bootery** • 492 Central Ave, Highland Park • 847-433-1911; 284 E Market Sq, Lake Forest • 847-234-0201 • Great but pricey shoe store.
- **Galt Toys + Galt Baby** • 900 N Michigan Ave • 312-440-9550; Northbrook Court, Northbrook • 847-498-4660 • High-end toy store and baby supplies.
- **Gymboree** • 835 N Michigan Ave • 312-649-9074 • Designer preemie and kids' clothes.
- **Kozy's Bike Shop** • 601 S LaSalle St • 312-360-0020 • Everything for biking families.
- **LMNOP** • 2572 N Lincoln Ave • 773-975-4055 • Hip, fun kids' clothes.
- **Land of Nod** • 900 W North Ave • 312-475-9903 (stores also in Oak Brook Center and Northbrook Court) • Cute kids' furniture.
- **Lazar's Juvenile Furniture** • 6557 N Lincoln Ave, Lincolnwood • 847-679-6146 • Tried-and-true children's furniture store.
- **Little Strummer** • 909 W Armitage Ave • 773-751-3410 • Kids' tunes.
- **Madison and Friends** • 940 N Rush St • 312-642-6403 • Designer clothes.
- **Mini Me** • 900 N Michigan Ave • 312-988-4011 • European designer clothes.
- **Oilily** • 520 N Michigan Ave • 312-527-5747 • Colorful patterned kids' clothes.
- **Pottery Barn Kids** • 2111 N Clybourn Ave • 773-525-8349 (stores also in Oak Brook Center, Old Orchard Center, and Deer Park Town Center) • Furnishings for the completely coordinated kid's boudoir.
- **POSH Skate Shop** • 628 Church St, Evanston • 847-424-8605 • Cool skateboarders' shop.
- **Psycho Baby** • 1630 N Damen Ave • 773-772-2815 • Funky kids' clothes.
- **Pumpkin Moon** • 1028 North Blvd, Oak Park • 708-524-8144 • Funky, vintage toys.
- **Red Balloon Company** • 2060 Damen Ave • 773-489-9800 • Toys, clothes, furniture.
- **The Right Start** • 2121 N Clybourn Ave • 773-296-4420 • Baby equipment galore.
- **Uncle Fun** • 1338 W Belmont Ave • 773-477-8223 • Hilarious novelties and vintage tin wind-up toys.
- **Shops at Northbridge** • 520 N Michigan Ave • 312-327-2300 • Entire third floor is kids' clothing, toys, and accessories, including Nordstrom.
- **Saturday's Child** • 2146 N Halsted St • 773-525-8697 • Creative toys.
- **The Second Child** • 954 W Armitage Ave • 773-883-0880 • Gently used designer clothes.
- **Timeless Toys** • 4749 N Lincoln Ave • 773-334-4445 • Old-fashioned, hand-crafted toys.
- **Toyscape** • 2911 N Broadway St • 773-665-7400 • Toys galore.
- **U.S. Toy–Constructive Playthings** • 5314 W Lincoln Ave, Skokie • 847-675-5900 • Educational toys favored by teachers.
- **Zany Brainy** • 2163 N Clybourn Ave • 773-281-2371 • Imagination-igniting toys.

Where to go for more information

Chicago Parent Magazine •
www.chicagoparent.com

Oaklee's Guide for Chicagoland Kids •
www.OakleesGuide.com

Internet

Internet		Phone	Map
Caribou Coffee	600 N Kingsbury St	312-335-0576	1
Bean Addiction	555 W Madison St	312-474-9140	4
Caribou Coffee	500 W Madison St	312-463-1130	4
Caribou Coffee	10 S La Salle St	312-609-5108	5
Caribou Coffee	55 W Monroe St	312-214-0852	5
Intelligentsia Coffee & Tea	53 W Jackson Blvd	312-253-0594	5
Lavazza	27 W Washington St	312-977-9971	5
Caribou Coffee	20 N Michigan Ave	312-456-0751	6
The Coffee Beanery	150 N Michigan Ave	312-781-9970	6
Caribou Coffee	800 S Wabash Ave	312-786-9205	8
Gourmand	728 S Dearborn St	312-427-2610	8
Panera Bread	501 S State St	312-922-1566	8
Café Au Lait	1900 S State St	312-225-3940	11
Bridgeport Coffeehouse	3101 S Morgan St	773-247-9950	12
Einstein Bros Bagels	5706 S University Ave	773-834-1018	19
Istria Café	1520 E 57th St	773-955-2556	19
Third World Café	1301 E 53rd St	773-288-3882	19
Alliance Bakery	1736 W Division St	773-278-0366	21
Barista Café	852 N Damen Ave	773-489-2010	21
Café Ballou	939 N Western Ave	773-342-2909	21
Filter	1585 N Milwaukee Ave	773-227-4850	21
Letizia's Natural Bakery	2144 W Division St	773-342-1011	21
Windy City Cyber Café	2246 W North Ave	773-384-6470	21
Coffee on Milwaukee	1046 N Milwaukee Ave	773-276-3200	22
Atomix	1957 W Chicago Ave	312-666-2649	23
Bialy's Café	1421 W Chicago Ave	312-733-7165	24
Corduroy's Espresso Spot	1650 W Ogden Ave	312-455-2989	24
Muse Café	817 N Milwaukee Ave	312-850-2233	24
Sip Coffee House	1223 W Grand Ave	312-563-1123	24
Swim Café	1357 W Chicago Ave	312-492-8600	24
West Gate Coffeehouse	924 W Madison St	312-829-9378	24
Café Frida	739 S Western Ave	312-455-9422	25
Netccino	2234 W Taylor St	312-492-8900	25
Café Jumping Bean	1439 W 18th St	312-455-0019	26
Efebos Internet Café	1640 S Blue Island Ave	312-633-9212	26
Kristoffer's Café & Bakery	1733 S Halsted St	312-829-4150	26
Mi Cafetal	1519 W 18th St	312-738-2883	26
Art Gallery Kafe	1907 N Milwaukee Ave	773-235-2351	28
Coffee Beanery	2158 N Damen Ave	773-278-4200	28
Ambrosia Café	1963 N Sheffield Ave	773-404-4450	29
Bean Café	2235 N Sheffield Ave	773-325-4577	29
Panera Bread	2070 N Clybourn Ave	773-325-9035	29
Savor the Flavor	2545 N Sheffield Ave	773-883-5287	29
Bourgeois Pig Café	738 W Fullerton Ave	773-883-5282	30
Caribou Coffee	2453 N Clark St	773-327-9923	30
Screenz Digital Universe	2717 N Clark St	773-348-9300	30
Cyber Café	25 E Pearson St	312-915-8595	32
Kaffeccino	6441 N Sheridan Rd	773-508-1888	34
Starbuck's	6738 N Sheridan Rd	773-743-0417	34
Worlds Fair Coffee	7603 N Paulina St	773-381-9999	34
Coffee Chicago	5256 N Broadway St	773-784-1305	37
Pause	1107 W Berwyn Ave	773-334-3686	37
Chicago Espresso Co	4645 N Kedzie Ave	773-478-8554	38
Café Marrakech Expresso	4747 N Damen Ave	773-271-4541	39
Perfect Cup	4700 N Damen Ave	773-989-4177	39
Red Eye Café	4164 N Lincoln Ave	773-327-9478	39
So Addictive	4805 N Damen Ave	773-561-3210	39
Corona's Coffee Shop	909 W Irving Park Rd	773-529-1886	40
Dollop Coffee CO	4181 N Clarendon Ave	773-755-1955	40
Urban Tea Lounge	838 W Montrose Ave	773-907-8726	40
MoJoe's Hot House	2849 W Belmont Ave	773-596-5637	41
Mojoe's Café Lounge	2256 W Roscoe St	773-388-1236	42
Caribou Coffee	3240 N Ashland Ave	773-281-3362	43
Mellow Grounds Coffee Lounge	3807 N Ashland Ave	773-528-2877	43
Caribou Coffee	3025 N Clark St	773-529-6366	44
Caribou Coffee	3300 N Broadway St	773-477-3695	44
Caribou Coffee	3500 N Halsted St	773-248-0799	44
House of Hookah	607 W Belmont Ave	773-348-1550	44
Intelligentsia Coffee Roasters	3123 N Broadway St	773-348-8058	44
Panera Bread	616 W Diversey Pkwy	773-528-4556	44
Euro Café	3435 N Harlem Ave	773-286-8544	200
J Bean Coffee & Café	7221 W Forest Preserve Ave	708-583-2245	200
Open Hearth Coffee Shop	5207 N Kimball Ave	773-279-9686	200
Panera Bread	6059 N Lincoln Ave	773-442-8210	200
Humboldt Pie	1001 N California Ave	773-342-4743	201
Café Luna	1742 W 99th St	773-239-8990	202
Café Mozart	600 Davis St	847-492-8056	204

Wi-Fi

Wi-Fi		Phone	Map
Windy City Cyber Café	2246 W North Ave	773-384-6470	21
Efebos Internet Café	1640 S Blue Island Ave	312-633-9212	26
Screenz	5212 N Clark St	773-334-8600	37
Ignite Center	3171 N Clybourn Ave	773-404-7033	42

Pharmacies

		Phone	Map
Walgreens	641 N Clark St	312-587-1416	2
Walgreens	757 N Michigan Ave	312-664-8686	3
Walgreens	111 S Halsted St	312-463-9142	4
Walgreens	501 W Roosevelt Rd	312-492-8559	7
Jewel-Osco	1224 S Wabash Ave	312-663-4646	8
Walgreens	316 W Cermak Rd	312-791-0392	10
Walgreens	3405 S Dr Martin L King Jr Dr	312-326-4058	14
Walgreens	1554 E 55th St	773-667-1177	19
Walgreens	1931 W Cermak Rd	773-847-5781	25
Walgreens	2001 N Milwaukee Ave	773-772-2370	28
CVS Pharmacy	1714 N Sheffield Ave	312-640-5161	29
Walgreens	1520 W Fullerton Ave	773-929-6968	29
Walgreens	1601 N Wells St	312-642-4008	31
CVS Pharmacy	1201 N State Pkwy	312-640-2842	32
Walgreens	1200 N Dearborn St	312-943-0973	32
Walgreens	7510 N Western Ave	773-764-1765	33
Jewel-Osco	5516 N Clark St	773-784-7348	37
Walgreens	5625 N Ridge Ave	773-989-7546	37
Walgreens	3153 W Irving Park Rd	773-588-9196	38
Walgreens	4343 N Kedzie Ave	773-604-4419	38
CVS (10 pm)	3411 W Addison St	773-279-8005	41
Jewel-Osco	3572 N Elston Ave	773-583-9858	41
Walgreens	3302 W Belmont Ave	773-267-2328	41
CVS Pharmacy	2815 N Western Ave	773-486-4102	42
CVS Pharmacy	3944 N Western Ave	773-279-7600	42
Jewel-Osco (10 pm)	3400 N Western Ave	773-327-2723	42
Jewel-Osco	2940 N Ashland Ave	773-348-4155	43
Walgreens	3046 N Halsted St	773-325-0413	44
Walgreens	3201 N Broadway St	773-327-3591	44

Copy Shops

		Phone	Map
FedEx Kinko's	444 N Wells St	312-670-4460	2
FedEx Kinko's	127 S Clinton St	312-258-8833	4
24 Seven Copies	222 N La Salle St	312-704-0247	5
FedEx Kinko's	29 S La Salle St	312-578-8520	5
FedEx Kinko's	1242 S Canal St	312-455-0920	10
FedEx Kinko's	1800 W North Ave	773-395-4639	21
FedEx Kinko's	2300 N Clybourn Ave	773-665-7500	29
FedEx Kinko's	3524 N Southport Ave	773-975-5031	43
Kinko's	3001 N Clark St	773-528-0500	44

Restaurants

		Phone	Map
Plymouth Restaurant	327 S Plymouth Ct	n/a	5
White Palace	1159 S Canal St	312-939-7167	7
Kevin's Hamburger Heaven	554 W 39th St	773-924-5771	13
Hollywood Grill	1601 W North Ave	773-395-1818	28
Tempo	6 E Chestnut St	312-943-4373	32
Deluxe Diner	6349 N Clark St	773-743-8244	34
Huddle House	4748 N Kimball Ave	773-588-5363	38
IHOP	2818 W Diversey Ave	773-342-8901	41
Clark's Diner	930 W Belmont Ave	773-348-5988	43
Golden Apple	2971 N Lincoln Ave	773-528-1413	43
Clark Street Dog	3040 N Clark St	773-281-6690	44
Melrose	3233 N Broadway St	773-327-2060	44
Nookie's Tree	3334 N Halsted St	773-248-9888	44
Blue Angel	5310 N Milwaukee Ave	773-631-8700	NW

Delivery & Messengers

	Address	Phone	Map
Deadline Express	449 N Union Ave	312-850-1200	1
On The Fly Courier	131 N Green St	312-738-2154	4

Gyms

	Address	Phone	Map
XSport Fitness	230 W North Ave	312-932-9100	31
Chicago Fitness Center	3131 N Lincoln Ave	773-549-8181	43
XSport Fitness	3240 N Ashland Ave	773-529-1461	43

Locksmiths

	Phone
A-AAround the Clock	800-281-5445
A-ABC 24-hour Locksmith	773-772-3930
Aabbitt	312-719-8200
Always Available	773-478-1960
Five Star Lock & Key	773-778-2066
Gateway Locksmith	800-964-8282
Safemasters	312-627-8209

Plumbers

	Phone
A-AAAA Plumbing & Sewer	773-282-2878
A Better Man Plumbing & Sewer	773-286-9351
A Metro Plumbing & Sewer Service	877-872-3060
Action Plumbing & Sewer	773-376-6666
Apex Plumbing & Sewer	773-477-7714
Emergency Response	773-736-3247
FPS	773-268-4604
O'Bannon Plumbing & Sewer (Northside)	773-486-5748
O'Bannon Plumbing & Sewer (Southside)	773-862-5112
Roto-Rooter	800-438-7686
Sears HomeCentral	773-737-3580
Sunrise Plumbing & Sewer	773-960-6462
Top Quality Plumbing & Sewer	773-523-1160

The impeccably restored **Music Box Theatre** (Map 43), built in 1929, features fantastic Moorish architecture, floating clouds on the ceilings, and live organ music at many weekend screenings. Specialties include the latest art house and international releases, as well as restored classics and weekend matinee double–features that follow monthly themes. Holiday season sing–alongs of White Christmas are huge hits that sell out in advance. The Music Box is also the major screening ground for International Film Festival and Gay and Lesbian Film Festival releases.

Other worthy art–house screening rooms include the **Landmark Century Centre Cinema** (Map 44) at the Century Mall and **Lowes Piper's Alley Theater** (Map 31) in Old Town. For even more esoteric options, pick up a schedule for the **Gene Siskel Film Center** (Map 5) of the Art Institute or **Facets Multimedia** (Map 29) on Fullerton in the DePaul neighborhood.

The latest action features should be seen at **Loews** (Map 29) at Webster Place, which offers ample theaters and show times. Cheap seats on relatively new releases can be had at the **3 Penny Cinema** (Map 30) on Lincoln and Lincoln Square's **Davis Cinema** (Map 39).

One of Chicago's most notorious places to catch a flick is **The Vic's** (Map 43) "Brew and View," where the drunken frat boy audiences are almost as annoying as the movies that they show.

Theater	*Address*	*Phone*	*Map*
AMC	2600 N Western Ave	773-394-1601	28
AMC Ford City 14	7601 S Cicero Ave	773-582-1839	SW
AMC River East	322 E Illinois St	312-596-0333	3
Beverly Arts Center	2407 W 111th St	773-445-3838	SW
Chicago Cultural Center	78 E Washington St	312-744-6630	5
Chicago Filmmakers	5243 N Clark St	773-293-1447	37
Davis Theater	4614 N Lincoln Ave	773-784-0893	39
Facets Multimedia Theatre	1517 W Fullerton Ave	773-281-4114	29
Gene Siskel Film Center	164 N State St	312-846-2800	5
Henry Crown MSI Omnimax	Museum of Science & Industry, 5700 S Lake Shore Dr	773-684-1414	20
ICE 62nd St & Western	2258 W 62nd St	773-476-4959	SW
ICE Chatham 14	210 87th St	773-783-8711	S
ICE Lawndale Cinemas	3330 W Roosevelt Rd	773-265-1010	W
La Salle Bank Cinema	4901 W Irving Park Rd	312-904-9442	NW
Landmark Century Centre Cinema	2828 N Clark St	773-248-7759	44
Loews	600 N Michigan Ave	312-255-9347	3
Loews	1471 W Webster Ave	773-327-3100	29
Loews Norridge 10	4520 N Harlem Ave	708-452-6677	NW
Loews/AMC Garden Cinema	175 Old Orchard Ctr	847-673-4105	Skokie
Logan Theater	2646 N Milwaukee Ave	773-252-0628	27
Lowes Esquire	58 E Oak St	312-280-1205	32
Lowes Piper Alley Theater	1608 N Wells St	312-642-6275	31
Museum of Contemporary Art	220 E Chicago Ave	312-397-4010	3
Music Box Theatre	3733 N Southport Ave	773-871-6604	43
Navy Pier IMAX Theatre	600 E Grand Ave	312-595-5629	Navy Pier
The Alliance Francaise	810 N Dearborn St	312-337-1070	32
Three Penny Cinema	2424 N Lincoln Ave	773-525-3449	30
University of Chicago Doc Films	1212 E 59th St	773-702-8575	19
Vic Theatre Brew & View	3145 N Sheffield Ave	773-929-6713	43
Village North Theaters	6746 N Sheridan Rd	773-764-9100	34
Village Theater	1548 N Clark St	312-642-2403	32

This past year has been an interesting one for the artists and art lovers in Chicago—newer galleries and local art fairs have pumped fresh energy into the scene. The perception of Chicago as an incubator for emerging start-ups is well-deserved—there are more alternative spaces than ever before.

As for where all this is happening, there continues to be a shift in the art districts in the city. In search of larger, cheaper, and more contemporary gallery spaces, River North galleries flocked to the West Loop. Now the West Loop has solidly positioned itself as the center for more cutting-edge contemporary spaces and has a large enough number of them to make the trip to the neighborhood well worth your time. (Public transportation in the area is not great, but certainly do-able.) Though there are still some impressive hold-outs in River North, namely **Zolla-Lieberman Gallery (Map 2)**, **Zg Gallery (Map 2)**, and the newly expanded **Catherine Edelman Gallery (Map 2)** for photography, most of the scene can be found about a mile-and-a-half southwest.

The intersection of Peoria and Washington Streets serves as the axis for the West Loop Galleries. **Carrie Secrist Gallery (Map 2)** and **Kavi Gupta Gallery (Map 24)** at 835 W Washington are good starting points for the emerging and established variety, while a half block north, buildings on either side of the street are home to a gaggle of smaller spaces such as **Aron Packer Gallery (Map 24)**, **Peter Miller Gallery (Map 24)**, **ThreeWalls (Map 24)**, **Bodybuilder & Sportsman Gallery (Map 24)**, and **Bucket Rider (Map 24)** to name a few standouts. Get ambitious and walk several more blocks northwest to find **Lisa Boyle Gallery (Map 24)** and **Western Exhibitions (Map 24)**, and you will be rewarded with quality work by emerging artists in the ever-expanding movement to the Fulton Street Market District.

Finally, for the most adventurous, be sure to try and feel out some of the many alternative part-time gallery spaces in the city. Though they are a little dicier as far as the exhibition scheduling and location, they often pay off with some of the most unusual and thought-provoking stuff Chicago has to offer. **Deadtech (Map 27)**, **Polvo Art (Map 26)**, **Dogmatic (Map 10)**, and **Heaven Gallery (Map 21)** are a few examples—check www.chicagoart.net for more info on galleries in the city.

Map 1 • River North / Fulton Market District

Northeastern Illinois University Fine Arts Center Gallery	5500 N St Louis Ave	773-442-4944
Woman Made Gallery	685 N Milwaukee Ave	312-738-0400

Map 2 • Near North / River North

Alan Koppel Gallery	210 W Chicago Ave	312-640-0730
Aldo Castillo Gallery	233 W Huron St	312-337-2536
Andrew Bae Gallery	300 W Superior St	312-335-8601
Ann Nathan Gallery	212 W Superior St	312-664-6622
Byron Roche Gallery	750 N Franklin St, Ste 105	312-654-0144
Carl Hammer Gallery	740 N Wells St	312-266-8512
Carrie Secrist Gallery	835 W Washington Blvd	312-491-0917
Catherine Edelman Gallery	300 W Superior St	312-266-2350
Galeria Gala	708 N Wells St	312-640-0517
Gwenda Jay/ Addington Gallery	704 N Wells St	312-664-3406
Habatat Galleries	222 W Superior St	312-440-0288
Hildt Galleries	617 N State St	312-255-0005
I Space	230 W Superior St	312-587-9976
Jean Albano Gallery	215 W Superior St	312-440-0770
Judy A Saslow Gallery	300 W Superior St	312-943-0530
Kass Meridian Gallery	325 W Huron St	312-266-5999
Lydon Fine Art	309 W Superior St	312-943-1133
Marx-Saunders Gallery	230 W Superior St	312-573-1400
Mary Bell Gallery	740 N Franklin St	312-642-0202
Maya Polsky Gallery	215 W Superior St	312-440-0055
Melanee Cooper Gallery	740 N Franklin St	312-202-9305
Mongerson Gallery	704 N Wells St	312-943-2354
Nicole Gallery	230 W Huron St	312-787-7716
NIU Art Gallery	215 W Superior St	312-642-6010
Northern Illinois University Art Gallery	215 W Superior St	312-642-6010
Oskar Friedl Gallery	1029 W 35th St	312-493-4330
Perimeter Gallery	210 W Superior St	312-266-9473
Peter Bartlow Gallery	9 E Huron St	312-337-1782
Portals	742 N Wells St	312-642-1066
Primitive Art Works	706 N Wells St	312-943-3770
Printworks	311 W Superior St	312-664-9407
RH Love Galleries	645 N Michigan Ave	800-437-7568
Richard Norton Gallery	612 Merchandise Mart Plz	312-644-8855
Rita Bucheit Fine Art & Antiques	449 N Wells St	312-527-4080
Robert Henry Adams Fine Art	715 N Franklin St	312-642-8700
Rosenthal Fine Art	3 E Huron St	312-475-0700
Roy Boyd Gallery	739 N Wells St	312-642-1606
Russell Bowman Art Advisory	311 W Superior St, Ste 115	312-751-9500
Schneider Gallery	230 W Superior St	312-988-4033
Stephen Daiter Gallery	311 W Superior St	312-787-3350
Trowbridge Gallery	703 N Wells St	312-587-9575
Vale Craft Gallery	230 W Superior St	312-337-3525
Zg Gallery	300 W Superior St	312-654-9900
Zolla-Lieberman Gallery	325 W Huron St	312-944-1990
Zygman Voss Gallery	222 W Superior St	312-787-3300

Map 3 • Streeterville / Mag Mile

The Arts Club of Chicago	201 E Ontario St	312-787-3997
City Gallery	806 N Michigan Ave	312-742-0808
Inspire Fine Art	435 E Illinois St, Ste 131	312-595-9475
Joel Oppenheimer Gallery	Wrigley Bldg, 410 N Michigan Ave	312-642-5300
Lora D Art Gallery	435 E Illinois St	312-245-9005
Ogilvie/Pertl Gallery	435 E Illinois St, Ste 151	312-321-0750
RS Johnson Fine Art	645 N Michigan Ave, Ste 234	312-943-1661

Map 4 • West Loop Gate / Greek Town

Gallery 2	847 W Jackson Blvd	312-563-5162
Thomas McCormick Gallery	835 W Washington Blvd	312-226-6800

Map 5 • The Loop

Donald Young Gallery	933 W Washington St	312-455-0100
Illinois State Museum Chicago Gallery	100 W Randolph St, 2nd Fl	312-814-5322

Map 6 • The Loop / Grant Park

Beacon Street Gallery	410 S Michigan Ave	312-212-1323
Cliff Dwellers Gallery	200 S Michigan Ave	312-922-8080
Fine Arts Building Gallery	410 S Michigan Ave	312-913-0537
Hilligoss Gallery	520 N Michigan Ave	312-755-0300

Map 10 • East Pilsen / Chinatown

Dogmatic	1822 S Des Plaines	

Map 13 • Bridgeport (East)

MN Gallery	3524 S Halsted St	773-847-0573

Map 19 • Hyde Park

Artisans 21	5241 S Harper Ave	773-288-7450

Map 20 • East Hyde Park / Jackson

Hyde Park Art Center	5307 S Hyde Park Blvd	773-324-5520

Map 21 • Wicker Park / Ukrainian

Carlos E Jimenez Gallery	2301 W North Ave	773-235-5328
David Leonardis Gallery	1346 N Paulina St	773-278-3058
Gallery 203	1579 N Milwaukee Ave	773-252-1952
Heaven Gallery	1550 N Milwaukee Ave	773-342-4597

Map 22 • Noble Square / Goose Island

1112 Gallery	1112 N Milwaukee Ave	773-486-9612
Madron LLC	1000 W North Ave, 3rd Fl	312-640-1302

Map 23 • West Town / Near West Side

Open-End Art Gallery	2000 W Fulton St	312-738-2140

Map 24 • River West / West Town

ARC Gallery	734 N Milwaukee Ave	312-733-2787
Aron Packer Gallery	118 N Peoria St	312-226-8984
Bodybuilder and Sportsman Gallery	119 N Peoria St, #2C	312-492-7261
Bucket Rider Gallery	119 N Peoria St #3D	312-421-6993
Douglas Dawson Gallery	400 N Morgan St	312-226-7975
Flatfile Galleries	217 N Carpenter St	312-491-1190
Frederick Baker Gallery	1230 W Jackson Blvd	312-243-2980
Function + Art	1046 W Fulton Market	312-243-2780
Gescheidle	118 N Peoria St	312-226-3500
GR N'Namdi Gallery	110 N Peoria St	312-563-9240
Kavi Gupta Gallery	835 W Washington Blvd	312-432-0708
Klein Art Works	400 N Morgan St	312-243-0400
Linda Warren Gallery	1052 W Fulton Market	312-432-9500
Lisa Boyle Gallery	1648 W Kinzie St	773-655-5475
Monique Meloche Gallery	118 N Peoria St	312-455-0299
Peter Miller Gallery	118 N Peoria St	312-951-1700
Rhona Hoffman Gallery	118 N Peoria St	312-455-1990
Richard Milliman Fine Art	1364 W Grand Ave	312-432-9900
Rogeramsay Gallery	711 N Milwaukee Ave	312-491-1400
Schopf Gallery on Lake	942 W Lake St	312-432-1630
Stolen Buick Studio	1303 W Chicago Ave	312-226-5902
ThreeWalls	119 N Peoria St	312-432-3972
Walsh Gallery	118 N Peoria St, 2nd Fl	312-829-3312
Western Exhibitions	1648 W Kinzie St	312-307-4685

Map 26 • University Village / Little Italy / Pilsen

Gallery 400	1240 W Harrison St	312-996-6114
Polvo Art Studio	1458 W 18th St	773-344-1940

Map 27 • Logan Square

Deadtech	3321 W Fullerton Ave	

Map 28 • Bucktown

Art Gallery Kafe	1907 N Milwaukee Ave	773-235-2351
Gallery 1633	1633 N Damen Ave	773-384-4441
Morlen Sinoway-Atelier	1052 W Fulton Market	312-432-0100

Map 29 • DePaul / Wrightwood / Sheffield

Chicago Center for the Print	1509 W Fullerton Ave	773-477-1585
DePaul University Art Museum	2350 N Kenmore Ave	773-325-7506
Havana Gallery	1139 W Webster Ave	773-549-2492
La Llorona Gallery	1474 W Webster Ave	773-281-8460

Map 30 • Lincoln Park

Contemporary Art Workshop	542 W Grant Pl	773-472-4004
Old Town Triangle	1763 N North Park Ave	312-337-1938

Map 31 • Old Town / Near North

Thomas Masters Gallery	245 W North Ave	312-440-2322

Map 32 • Gold Coast / Mag Mile

Armstrong Fine Arts	200 E Walton St	312-664-9312
Billy Hork Galleries	109 E Oak St	312-337-1199
Colletti Gallery	67 E Oak St	312-664-6767
FL Braswell Fine Art	73 E Elm St	312-636-4399
Galleries Maurice Sternberg	John Hancock Ctr, 875 N Michigan Ave	312-642-1700
Richard Gray Gallery	John Hancock Ctr, 875 N Michigan Ave, Ste 2503	312-642-8877
Valerie Carberry Gallery	John Hancock Ctr, 875 N Michigan Ave, Ste 2510	312-397-9990

Map 36 • Bryn Mawr

X Gallery	5233 N Damen Ave	773-728-2663

Map 37 • Edgewater / Andersonville

Las Manos Gallery	5220 N Clark St	773-728-8910

Map 39 • Ravenswood / North Center

Peter Jones Gallery	1806 W Cuyler Ave	773-472-6725

Map 42 • North Center / Roscoe Village / West Lakeview

August House Studio	2113 W Roscoe St	773-327-5644

Map 43 • Wrigleyville/ East Lakeview

Bell Studio	3428 N Southport Ave	773-281-2172
Fourth World Artisans	3727 N Southport Ave	773-404-5200

Map 44 • East Lakeview

Leigh Gallery	3306 N Halsted St	773-472-1865

Homage to the Neighborhood Lounge

Chicago is a city of neighborhoods, and as such, we are a city of great little neighborhood taverns. These are the places where the beer you drink is on tap, the bartender throws a basket of pretzels in front of you when you grab your stool, and on any given weekday between 5 and 7 you're likely to see the same sad sacks you see every night, stealing precious time between the bossman and the kids. And then there's the jukebox. The best ones feature all your favorite bar songs, from Hank Williams to The Cars, Blondie to Sly and the Family Stone, and "My Way" sung in Polish or Korean just for the hell of it.

Rub shoulders with the characters from a Nelson Algren story at any of the following joints. **Cal's (map 5)** in the South Loop attracts local winos along with shaggy looking roadies and local slummers from the nearby University Center. In Old Town, the **Old Town Ale House (map 30)** was once voted best dive bar in the country by someone-mumblemumble-we-forget-who. **Stadium West (map 41)** in Avondale, previously the dictionary definition of non-descript, has stepped up its act to attract the fresh young blood streaming into that 'hood. They have a new façade including a glowing neon sign for Blue Moon beer. In Rogers Park, **The Lamp Post (map 34)** has long drawn a friendly crowd of boozy locals.

Young urban arty types have carved out their kitsch-embracing niches at Ukrainian Village and Wicker Park spots such as **Club Foot (map 21)**, **The Gold Star Bar (map 21)**, **The Inner Town Pub (map 21)**, **Lava Lounge (map 21)**, **Rainbo Club (map 21)**, and **Small Bar (map 21)** while their Pilsen and River West brethren drink their PBR at **The Skylark (map 26)** and **The Fulton Lounge (map 24)**, respectively. On the west side, **The California Clipper (West Chicago)** appeals to today's rat pack wannabe's, and on the north side, get drunk with happy hipsters and local punters at **The Village Tap (map 42)**, **The Long Room (map 39)**, and the **Edgewater Lounge (map 37)**.

On the south side, Bridgeport denizens cheer on the home team at neighborhood spots **Schaller's (map 13)** and **Jimbo's Lounge (map 13)**, Further south, University of Chicago Poindexters have been sipping suds at **The Woodlawn Tap (map 19)** and **The Cove (map 20)** since the ivy was only neigh high.

Some of Chicago's best live music venues are also neighborhood spots. **The Velvet Lounge (map 11)**, in the near south side, is a legendary avant-garde jazz dive of the old school tradition. **Katerina's (map 39)**, on an unassuming stretch if Irving Park in North Center, features regualr live gypsy music along with local acts. In the West Village, the **Empty Bottle (map 21)** is the place to catch touring indie bands. Further west, **Rosa's Lounge (Northwest Chicago)** is a friendly venue for live blues. Catch jazz legend Von Freeman jamming at **Chatham's New Apartment Lounge (South Chicago)** every Wednesday night, or live jazz any night of the week at **Uptown's Green Mill Lounge (map 40)**. In the northwest side, **The Abbey Pub (Northwest Chicago)** features everything from alternative rock acts like The Breeders and Peaches, to singer-songwriter showcases and burlesque, while in the South Loop, **Hothouse (map 8)** introduces Chicago audiences to the best in world music acts. If you want to put some twang in your thang, alt-country acts from the Bloodshot Records label regularly perform at Bucktown's **Hideout (map 29)**.

In Chicago, even the best place to get your groove on is often the one right around the corner. Despite the concentration of huge, dazzling and super expensive high-concept nightclubs in River North and River West, (which are typically the domain of tourists and suburbanites), many local folk prefer smaller, friendlier, more intimate, and cheaper local options to catch Saturday (or Monday, or Thursday) night fever. In Lincoln Park, **Neo (map 30)** attracts children of the Eighties and their wannabes with retro dance tunes ranging from goth to new wave. Legendary gay bar **Berlin (map 43)**, in Lakeview, draws a pansexual crowd for there ever-rotating array of theme nights. In the East Village, **Sonotheque (map 24)** is the place to catch the latest beats.

Of course, sometimes a neighborhood lounge becomes so popular that it starts to attract folks from outside its zip code range. **Delilah's (map 29)** in Lincoln Park draws aging punkers from all over the city for their excellent punk rock jukebox, occasional celebrity guest dj's, and great selection of scotches. And speaking of selections, the selection of Belgian beers at Andersonville's **Hopleaf (map 40)** is hard to beat. Finally, a couple honorable shout-outs to Michelle Fire's **Big Chicks (map 40)**, a welcoming gay club in Uptown featuring Michelle's outstanding original artwork collection, and **Chief O'Neill's (map 41)**, an Avondale pub with live Irish music, great pub grub, and loads of craic.

Map 1 • River North / Fulton Market District

Emmit's Irish Pub & Eatery	495 N Milwaukee Ave	312-563-9631	An old-school Chicago establishment.
Funky Buddha Lounge	728 W Grand Ave	312-666-1695	See and be seen at this trendy live music lounge.
The Motel Bar	600 W Chicago Ave	312-822-2900	Hotel bar without the hourly rates!
Rednofive & Fifth Floor	440 N Halsted St	312-733-6699	Two levels of existence; downstairs=dancing, upstairs=posing.
Rive Gauche	306 N Halsted St	312-738-9971	Late night dancing in lavish setting.

Map 2 • Near North / River North

Andy's	11 E Hubbard St	312-642-6805	Old-school jazz…a Chicago legend.
Bin 36	339 N Dearborn St	312-755-9463	Wineology 101.
Blue Chicago	736 N Clark St	312-642-6261	Touristy blues bar.
Blue Frog Bar & Grill	676 N La Salle Dr	312-943-8900	Chutes and Ladders, Howdy Doody, and Karoake.
Brehon Pub	731 N Wells St	312-642-1071	Irish Pub, lots of TVs for sports.
Excalibur	632 N Dearborn St	312-266-1944	Touristy club in a historic castle building that survived the Chicago Fire.
Gentry	440 N State St	312-836-0933	A piano bar is one of the many features of this multi-themed gay club.
Green Door Tavern	678 N Orleans St	312-664-5496	A Chicago landmark; old-school classic.
House of Blues	329 N Dearborn St	312-923-2000	Dan Akroyd's vision of the Blues. Dig deep people.
Howl at the Moon	26 W Hubbard St	312-863-7427	Late night dinner and pianists who encourage patrons to sing.
Martini Ranch	311 W Chicago Ave	312-335-9500	Martinis and after-work mingling.
Minx	111 W Hubbard St	312-828-9000	Nibble upstairs on Pan-Asian food, and recline downstairs to lounge.
Mother Hubbard's	5 W Hubbard St	312-828-0007	Chicago's premier frat-boy tourist trap.
Narcisse	710 N Clark St	312-787-2675	Posh champagne and caviar club.
Pippin's Tavern	806 N Rush St	312-787-5435	Old union haunt = lots of beer.
Pops for Champagne	601 N State St	312-266-POPS	Jazz and champers.
Redhead Piano Bar	16 W Ontario St	312-640-1000	Snug piano bar favorite of the area.
Rock Bottom Restaurants & Brewery	1 W Grand Ave	312-755-9339	Micro-brewery in the heart of downtown.
Spy Bar	646 N Franklin St	312-587-8779	Basement club, house music, fashionable crowd, pricy drinks.
Streeter's Tavern	50 E Chicago Ave	312-944-5206	Ritzy dive bar for students and tourists.
Vision	640 N Dearborn St	312-266-1944	Attached to Excalibur, the venue offers a modern alternative to the oxygen bar.

Map 3 • Streeterville / Mag Mile

Billy Goat Tavern	430 N Michigan Ave	312-222-1525	Cheesboigas, cheeps, pepsi!
Dick's Last Resort	435 E Illinois St	312-836-7870	Between Mardi Gras and Hell.
O'Neill's Bar & Grill	152 E Ontario St	312-787-5269	A touristy joint with pub food.
Timothy O'Toole's Pub	622 N Fairbanks Ct	312-642-0700	Irish sports bar with tons of TV space.

Map 4 • West Loop Gate / Greek Town

Reserve	858 W Lake St	312-455-1111	Trendy, upscale lounge…if you can get in.
Reunion	811 W Lake St	312-491-9600	Mainly a fashionable black crowd, but Thurs and Sats it's rainbow (gay).
Snuggery Saloon & Dining Room	Union Station, 225 S Canal St	312-441-9334	Commuter bar inside Union Station.

Map 5 • The Loop

Cal's	400 S Wells St	312-922-6392	Dictionary definition of "dump" that draws grungy rockers and neighborhood drunks.
Exchequer Pub	226 S Wabash Ave	312-939-5633	Loop location for the working class.
Manhattans	415 S Dearborn St	312-957-0460	Tired of martini bars? Try small but fun Manhattans.
Miller's Pub	134 S Wabash Ave	312-263-4988	A Loop tradition.

Map 6 • The Loop / Grant Park

Houlihan's	111 E Wacker Dr	312-616-FOOD	Trendy, semi-obnoxious sports bar.

Map 7 • South Loop / River City

Scarlett's Gentleman's	750 S Clinton St	312-986-1300	One of the city's few flesh palaces.

Map 8 • South Loop / Printers Row / Dearborn Park

Buddy Guy's Legends	754 S Wabash Ave	312-427-0333	One of the oldest blues clubs in Chicago, and the hardest to get a drink in.
George's Cocktail Lounge	646 S Wabash Ave	312-427-3964	Columbia students and faculty quaff in this dive between classes.
HotHouse	31 E Balbo Ave	312-362-9707	Funky world music and jazz venue.
Kasey's Tavern	701 S Dearborn St	312-427-7992	108-year-old neighborhood oasis.
South Loop Club	701 S State St	312-427-2787	There's something creepy about this place.
Tantrum	1023 S State St	312-939-9160	Tucked-away, nicely appointed bar that attracts a lively South Loop following.

Map 9 • South Loop / South Michigan Ave

Kitty O'Shea's	720 S Michigan Ave	312-294-6860	Cool Irish spot…may turn your hair green.
Savoy Bar and Grill	800 S Michigan Ave	312-939-1464	Serious drinking in a kooky '50s hotel; early morning breakfast.

Map 11 • South Loop / McCormick Place

Chicago Legends	2109 S Wabash Ave	312-326-0300	25-and-over cocktail lounge / nightclub.
Velvet Lounge	2128 1/2 S Indiana Ave	312-791-9050	Raw, gritty jazz haven.
Wabash Tap	1233 S Wabash Ave	312-360-9488	South Loop, no ties, relax-after-work joint.

Map 13 • Bridgeport (East)

Cobblestone's Bar and Grill	514 W Pershing Rd	773-624-3630	Keep it down during a Sox game.
Jimbo's Lounge	3258 S Princeton Ave	312-326-3253	Walk in with a Cub hat…we dare you!
Puffer's Bar	3356 S Halsted St	773-927-6073	A Southside standby.
Schaller's	3714 S Halsted St	773-376-6332	Neighborhood Sox bar with grub.

Map 14 • Prairie Shores / Lake Meadows

Bossman Blues Center	3528 S Indiana Ave	312-326-4046	Garfield Park's answer to dirty blues.

Map 15 • Canaryville / Fuller Park

Kelley's Tavern	4403 S Wallace St	773-924-0796	A neighborhood place.

Map 16 • Bronzeville

Jokes & Notes	4641 S King Dr	773-373-3390	Upscale comedy/jazz club on fire, with stainless steel bar.

Map 19 • Hyde Park

Seven Ten Lanes	1055 E 55th St	773-347-2695	1920s décor in Hyde Park haven.
Woodlawn Tap	1172 E 55th St	773-643-5516	U of Chicago legend.

Map 20 • East Hyde Park / Jackson Park

Bar Louie	5500 S South Shore Dr	773-363-5300	Corporate chain martini bar.
The Cove	1750 E 55th St	773-684-1013	Down-and-outers meet life-of-the-minders.

Map 21 • Wicker Park / Ukrainian Village

Borderline	1954 W North Ave	773-278-5138	When you really shouldn't have one more, but you do anyway, you have it here.
Club Foot	1824 W Augusta Blvd	773-489-0379	Play Tetris and listen to Prince.
D'Vine	1950 W North Ave	773-235-5700	Wicker Park Hip Hop…is this necessary?
Davenport's	1383 N Milwaukee Ave	773-278-1830	Once legendary skanker bar, now yuppy fern bar. Whattya gonna do?
Double Door	1572 N Milwaukee Ave	773-489-3160	Top local and national alt-rock acts.
Empty Bottle	1035 N Western Ave	773-276-3600	Avant-garde jazz and indie rock. Smells like cat.
Estelle's Café & Lounge	2013 W North Ave	773-782-0450	Cool little inexpensive drinking spot.
Gold Star Bar	1755 W Division St	773-227-8700	Hear the Cars and Cash in under an hour.
Iggy's	1840 W North Ave	773-227-4449	Martini bar and lounge. Sunday movie-night with vintage horror flicks.
Inner Town Pub	1935 W Thomas St	773-235-9795	Wicker Park art dorks.
Innjoy	2051 W Division St	773-394-2066	WP Scene-ster place for drinking and local acts.
Lava Lounge	859 N Damen Ave	773-772-3355	Casual, club-type drinker's bar.
Marshall McGearty Tobacco Lounge	1553 N Milwaukee Ave	773-772-8410	Newest advance of the pro-smokers union!

Map 21 • Wicker Park / Ukrainian Village–*continued*

The Note	1565 N Milwaukee Ave	773-489-0011	Eclectic jazz-type fare.
Phyllis' Musical Inn	1800 W Division St	773-486-9862	Divey hot-spot for local music acts.
Pint	1547 N Milwaukee Ave	773-772-0990	Have a pint in this swanky saloon.
Pontiac Café	1531 N Damen Ave	773-252-7767	Redneck Bingo on Sundays!
Rainbo Club	1151 N Damen Ave	773-489-5999	Cool-kid mecca and favorite hang of local celeb John Cusack. Enough said.
Rodan	1530 N Milwaukee Ave	773-276-7036	Ultra modern lounge—video mirrors in the bathrooms.
Salud Tequila Lounge	1471 N Milwaukee Ave	773-235-5577	Tequila lounge…Salud!
Small Bar	2049 W Division St	773-772-2727	Small is the new big at this hipster-cool, cozy hang.
Subterranean Cabaret & Lounge	2011 W North Ave	773-278-6600	Semi-cool music spot.
Vintage Wine Bar	1942 W Division St	773-772-3400	Way-cool retro-look wine bar with solid wine list.

Map 22 • Noble Square / Goose Island

Biology Bar	1520 N Fremont St	312-397-0580	Latin beat music in a science lab environment—a chemistry of its own.
Crobar	1543 N Kingsbury St	312-266-1900	Club creatures come for the music, tourists come for the creatures.
Exit	1315 W North Ave	773-395-2700	Ooohhh. Dark and scary. Eighties punk/goth throwback.
Four	1551 W Division St	773-235-9100	Formally Big Wig—got a facelift and four rooms to play in.
Hot Shots	1440 N Dayton St	312-654-8204	Romanian music.
Jet Vodka Lounge	1555 N Sheffield Ave	312-440-9140	Jet-themed bar.
Joe's	940 W Weed St	312-337-3486	Huge sports bar and music venue for national bands and drunk people.
Slow Down, Life's Too Short	1177 N Elston Ave	773-384-1040	Drinking right on the river.
Zentra	923 W Weed St	312-787-0400	Image is everything. National DJ acts, fashionable crowd, and hookahs.

Map 23 • West Town / Near West Side

Darkroom	2210 W Chicago Ave	773-276-1411	No flash is necessary; artsy crowd, electro music, and industry parties.
Sak's Ukrainian Village Restaurant	2301 W Chicago Ave	773-278-4445	One of the few bastions of the old country remaining in the Village.
Tuman's	2159 W Chicago Ave	773-782-1400	Revived local legend. Cheap beer and comfort food.

Map 24 • River West / West Town

Babalu	1645 W Jackson Blvd	312-733-3512	Live Latin bands and DJs on the weekends.
Betty's Blue Star Lounge	1600 W Grand Ave	312-243-1699	Where hipsters get drunk and f*ck.
Café Fresco	1202 W Grand Ave	312-733-6378	Comfy, local environs.
Chromium	817 W Lake St	312-666-7230	Is just how it sounds—chromy.
Fulton Lounge	955 W Fulton Market	312-942-9500	Hip but laid back, cool music, outside seating.
J Patricks	1367 W Erie St	312-243-0990	Irish flags, beers, and accents.
Jack's Tap	901 W Jackson Blvd	312-666-1700	From the good folks who brought us the Village Tap.
Matchbox	770 N Milwaukee Ave	312-666-9292	Chicago's smallest bar…bar none.
Players Bar & Grill	551 N Odgen Ave	312-733-2121	Hard-core sports bar.
Rhythm	1108 W Randolph St	312-492-6100	Create your own rhythm with a set of drums and a drink.
Sonotheque	1444 W Chicago Ave	312-226-7600	Super sleek: the design, the crowd, the music.
Tasting Room	1415 W Randolph St	312-942-1313	Swank, low-key wine bar.
Transit	1431 W Lake St	312-491-8600	It'll keep you moving.
Twisted Spoke	501 N Ogden Ave	312-666-1500	$2 Jim Beams served by suicide girls and free porn on Saturday nights.
West Town Tavern	1329 W Chicago Ave	312-666-6175	Upscale comfort food.

Map 26 • University Village / Little Italy / Pilsen

Bar Louie	1321 W Taylor St	312-633-9393	Generally good music and decent entrees.
Bevi Amo Wine Bar	1358 W Taylor St	312-455-8255	Good selection, if a bit pricey.
Hawkeye's Bar & Grill	1458 W Taylor St	312-226-3951	Quality bar food (including the healthy side).
The Illinois Bar & Grill	1421 W Taylor St	312-666-6666	Great greasy food and burgers.
Junior's Sports Lounge	724 W Maxwell St	773-276-7582	Sports bar with upscale pretensions.
Skylark	2149 S Halsted St	312-948-5275	Hip hangout for Pilsen arty crowd.

Map 27 • Logan Square

Fireside Bowl	2648 W Fullerton Ave	773-486-2700	No longer a punk rock venue, it's just bowling now.
Streetside Café	3201 W Armitage Ave	773-252-9700	Micro-brews, DJs spin smooth house, ample ambiance.
The Winds Café	2657 N Kedzie Blvd	773-489-7478	Neighborhood bar smack dab in the middle of the 'hood.

Map 28 • Bucktown

Bar Louie	1704 N Damen Ave	773-645-7500	Beer, wine, mammoth sandwiches.
Cans	1640 N Damen Ave	773-227-2277	Canned beers galore! Loud crowd, loud music, great hot wings!
Charleston Tavern	2076 N Hoyne Ave	773-489-4757	Yuppie dive.
Danny's	2222 N Western Ave	773-489-3622	Once was a quirky hipster place.
Darwin's	1935 N Damen Ave	773-252-8530	Evolve in this great little dive bar.
Gallery Cabaret	2020 N Oakley Ave	773-489-5471	Hip dive bar with local acts, attracts plenty of wannabe barflies.
Lemmings	1850 N Damen Ave	773-862-1688	Lite Brite works of art.
The Liar's Club	1665 W Fullerton Ave	773-665-1110	Only sometimes overly hipster, otherwise rad music and good times.
Lincoln Tavern	1858 W Wabansia Ave	773-342-7778	Neighborhood bar.
The Map Room	1949 N Hoyne Ave	773-252-7636	Global theme mixed with the occasional free buffet.
Marie's Rip Tide Lounge	1745 W Armitage Ave	773-278-7317	Drunk wannabes welcome here.
The Mutiny	2428 N Western Ave	773-486-7774	All bands start somewhere…unfortunately it's here.
Northside Café	1635 N Damen Ave	773-384-3555	Popular Wicker Park pick-up bar.
Quenchers Saloon	2401 N Western Ave	773-276-9730	Crowded on the weekends, but ultra comfy couches and free popcorn.

Map 29 • DePaul / Wrightwood / Sheffield

Big House	2354 N Clybourn Ave	773-435-0130	A Tiger Woods type of place: martinis and a Golden Tee course.
Charlie's Ale House	1224 W Webster Ave	773-871-1440	Bad restaurant, sports bar nightmare.
Deliliah's	2771 N Lincoln Ave	773-472-2771	Punk rock dive showing cult classic flicks.
Gin Mill	2462 N Lincoln Ave	773-549-3232	Ever see a college kid drink gin?
Green Dolphin Street	2200 N Ashland Ave	773-395-0066	Big band and jazz venue that serves late-night dinner and vibrations.
Hideout	1354 W Wabansia Ave	773-227-4433	Haven for alt-country and other quirky live tune-age.
Hog Head McDunna's	1505 W Fullerton Ave	773-929-0944	Lincoln Parksy music spot…for the not so musically inclined.
Irish Eyes	2519 N Lincoln Ave	773-348-9548	…are often crying.
Kincade's	950 W Armitage Ave	773-348-0010	Happy-hour sports bar.
Local Option	1102 W Webster Ave	773-348-2008	Neighborhood hole-in-the-wall and proud of it.
Nic and Dino's Tripoli Tavern	1147 W Armitage Ave	773-477-4400	Quality bar food.
The (Prop) House	1675 N Elston Ave	773-486-2086	In the middle of an industrial area; house beats resonate.
Red Lion Pub	2446 N Lincoln Ave	773-348-2695	It's haunted!
Webster Wine Bar	1480 Webster Ave	773-868-0608	Perfect place for "getting to know you" while enjoying flights and pairings.
Wrightwood Tap	1059 W Wrightwood Ave	773-549-4949	Neighborhood feel-good spot.
Zella	1983 N Clybourn Ave	773-549-2910	Great summer seating.

Map 30 • Lincoln Park

B.L.U.E.S.	2519 N Halsted St	773-528-1012	Smaller but notorious blues bar with an older African-American crowd.
Bacchus	2242 N Lincoln Ave	773-477-5238	Yup-to-be dance club.
Bar Louie	1800 N Lincoln Ave	312-337-9800	Another outpost of the chain.
Blu	2247 N Lincoln Ave	773-549-5884	Lincoln Park nightclub…need I say more?
Corner Pocket	2610 N Halsted St	773-281-0050	Student-y billiards bar.
Gamekeepers	345 W Armitage Ave	773-549-0400	Where young singles mingle.
Glascott's	2158 N Halsted St	773-281-1205	Wannabe Irish joint with frat-boy written all over it.
GoodBar	2512 N Halsted St	773-296-9700	Candles, DJ, wine bar.
Griffin's Public House	2710 N Halsted St	773-525-7313	Sports bar for the loyal Michiganians rehashing the ol' days.
Hidden Shamrock	2723 N Halsted St	773-883-0304	We played darts with Joe Walsh here one night.
Katacomb	1909 N Lincoln Ave	312-337-4040	Late night lounge with private nooks resembling catacombs!
Kingston Mines	2548 N Halsted St	773-477-4646	Chicago Blues bar in a neighborhood safe for tourists.
Lion Head Pub & The Apartment	2251 N Lincoln Ave	773-348-5100	DePaul nightspot.
Neo	2350 N Clark St	773-528-2622	Popular eighties retro night. Gag me with a spoon.
Park West	322 W Armitage Ave	773-929-1322	Costs extra to reserve a table.
Sauce	1750 N Clark St	312-932-1750	Sleek, chic place to drink.
Second City	1616 N Wells St	312-664-4032	Drama and food in front of you.
Tequila Roadhouse	1653 N Wells St	312-440-0535	Nightmarish.
Wise Fools Pub	2270 N Lincoln Ave	773-929-1300	Vibes are high for live local legends and jam sessions.

Map 31 • Old Town / Near North

Burton Place	1447 N Wells St	312-664-4699	Great late night; good bar food.
Dragon Room	809 W Evergreen Ave	312-751-2900	Asian-inspired dance club, sushi served, young yuppyish crowd.
North Park Tap	313 W North Ave	312-943-5228	Laid-back crowd.
Old Town Ale House	219 W North Ave	312-944-7020	Crusty old-timers meet performing arts crowd.
Spoon	1240 N Wells St	312-642-5522	Trendy young crowd.
Weeds	1555 N Dayton St	312-943-7815	Pinball, bras, shoes, poetry, and free tequila: anything but ordinary.
Zanies Comedy Club	1548 N Wells St	312-337-4027	After a few drinks, everything is funny. Well, almost.

Map 32 • Gold Coast / Mag Mile

Backroom	1007 N Rush St	312-751-2433	Old jazz club w/ lots of baby boomers.
Bar Chicago	9 W Division St	312-654-1120	Dancing of sorts.
Butch McGuire's	20 W Division St	312-337-9080	Wet T-shirt contests anyone?
Cru Wine Bar	888 N Wabash Ave	312-337-4078	Another little wine bar.
Dublin's	1050 N State St	312-266-6340	Gold Coast pub.
Jilly's Retro Club	1007 N Rush St	312-664-1001	Gold digger's haven. Jerry Springer's old hangout.
Le Passage	937 N Rush St	312-255-0022	Super chic.
Leg Room	7 W Division St	312-337-2583	Bar food and funky music.
Mothers	26 W Division St	312-642-7251	The mother of frat-boy shenanigans.
She-nanigans	16 W Division St	312-642-2344	Another Rush vicinity hellhole.
Signature Lounge	John Hancock Ctr, 875 N Michigan Ave	312-787-9596	Unbelievable view from the women's room.
The Hunt Club	1100 N State St	312-988-7887	The ultimate yuppy sports bar.
The Whisky	1015 N Rush St	312-475-0300	Sutton Place Hotel.
Underground Wonder Bar	10 E Walton St	312-266-7761	Mostly jazz.
Zebra Lounge	1220 N State St	312-642-5140	Garish, cramped piano bar—in other words, it's a hit.

Map 33 • West Rogers Park

Cary's Lounge	2251 W Devon Ave	773-743-5737	Locals' place to go for a nightcap.
McKellin's	2800 W Touhy Ave	773-973-2428	Cozy neighborhood Irish bar.
Mullen's Sports Bar and Grill	7301 N Western Ave	773-465-2113	Food until 1 am (10 pm on Sundays).

Map 34 • East Rogers Park

Hamilton's Pub	6341 N Broadway St	773-764-8133	Watering hole popular with Loyola students.
Heartland Café	7000 N Glenwood Ave	773-465-8005	Like the Grateful Dead parking lot scene.
Jackhammer	6406 N Clark St	773-743-5772	Gay bar with a welcoming neighborhood vibe.
Lamp Post	7126 N Ridge Blvd	773-465-9571	Friendly place to catch a game or toss darts.
No Exit	6970 N Glenwood Ave	773-743-3355	Standard coffee house.
Poitin Stil	1502 W Jarvis Ave	773-338-3285	What's in a name? Cozy little neighborhood Irish joint.
Touche	6412 N Clark St	773-465-7400	Drunken gay leather bar.

Map 35 • Arcadia Terrace / Peterson Park

Emerald Isle	2537 W Peterson Ave	773-561-6674	Ahh, the Emerald Isle!
Hidden Cove	5338 N Lincoln Ave	773-275-6711	Sports bar with trivia, darts, and karaoke.

Map 36 • Bryn Mawr

Big Joe's 2 & 6 Pub	1818 W Foster Ave	773-784-8755	Corner bar endorsed by the Windy City Darters.
Claddagh Ring	2306 W Foster Ave	773-271-4794	Traditional Irish-American bar with plentiful pub fare.
K's Dugout	1930 W Foster Ave	773-561-2227	Drink and watch sports, drink and watch sports, drink and…
Leadway Bar & Café	5233 N Damen Ave	773-728-2663	Artsy bar with free picture-painting and pool-playing.

Map 37 • Edgewater / Andersonville

@tmosphere	5355 N Clark St	773-784-1100	Trendy gay bar with dance floor and DJs.
Charlie's Ale House	5308 N Clark St	773-751-0140	Andersonville's newest yuppie gathering spot.
Edgewater Lounge	5600 N Ashland Ave	773-878-3343	Alehouse with open-mike on Tuesdays for singers.
Farraguts Tavern	5240 N Clark St	773-728-4903	Neighborhood dive, less yuppy than Simon's.
Granville Anvil	1137 Granville Ave	773-973-0006	Gay old-timers drink here.
Joie de Vine	1744 W Balmoral Ave	773-989-6846	Wine and wide screen TV.
Madrigals	5316 N Clark St	773-334-3033	A gay bar with imported male dancers.
Marty's Wine and Martini Bar	1511 W Balmoral Ave	773-561-6425	Compact and classy.
Moody's Pub	5910 N Broadway St	773-275-2696	Best beer garden in the city. Long wait times.
Ole St Andrew's Inn	5938 N Broadway St	773-784-5540	Food and spirits…of the haunted sort.
Ollie's	1064 W Berwyn Ave	773-784-5712	A rare quiet neighborhood joint.
Simon's	5210 N Clark St	773-878-0894	Casual joint replete with thrift-store-attired hipsters.
StarGaze	5419 N Clark St	773-561-7363	Lesbian bar with salsa on Friday nights.

Map 38 • Ravenswood / Albany Park

Brisku's Bistro	4100 N Kedzie Ave	773-279-9141	Croatian bar food and pool.
Lincoln Square Lanes	4874 N Lincoln Ave	773-561-8191	Brews and bowling above a hardware store. Cheap date.
Lost & Found	3058 W Irving Park Rd	773-463-7599	Cozy lesbian bar. Knock to get in.
Montrose Saloon	2933 W Montrose Ave	773-463-7663	Classic Chicago "Old Style." No cell phones, please.
Peek Inn	2825 W Irving Park Rd	773-267-5197	Cool little dive worth a peek.
Skadarlija	4024 N Kedzie Ave	773-463-5600	Smoky Croatian supper club with live music.

Map 39 • Ravenswood / North Center

Celtic Crown Public House	4301 N Western Ave	773-588-1110	Great specials without over-Irishing it!
Chicago Brauhaus	4732 N Lincoln Ave	773-784-4444	More German than Germany...even in Oktober.
Daily Bar & Grill	4560 N Lincoln Ave	773-561-6198	Bar food in retro ambiance.
Foley's	1841 W Irving Park Rd	773-929-1210	Cool little neighborhood spot...when the owner pays the rent.
The Globe Pub	1934 W Irving Park Rd	773-871-3757	Great music venue gone sportsbar.
Heuttenbar	4721 N Lincoln Ave	773-561-2507	German-town favorite with great beer selection.
Katerina's	1920 W Irving Park Rd	773-348-7592	Live jazz, gypsy music, and local rock at this European lounge.
Laschet's Inn	2119 W Irving Park Rd	773-478-7915	Pull on the Lederhosen!
Margie's Pub	4145 N Lincoln Ave	773-477-1644	Bikers and burnouts and boozers...oh my!
O'Donovan's	2100 W Irving Park Rd	773-478-2100	Once the best German restaurant in town...fine, still cool.
O'Lanagan's	2335 W Montrose Ave	773-583-2252	Not an Irishman in sight!
The Rail	4709 N Damen Ave	773-878-9400	One-time dive, the rail rocks in Ravenswood.
Resi's Bierstube	2034 W Irving Park Rd	773-472-1749	Wear your leiderhosen.
Wild Goose	4265 N Lincoln Ave	773-281-7112	Guy's bar. Cheap eats, TVs and games.
Windy City Inn	2257 W Irving Park Rd	773-588-7088	Nice family feel...if you're from Kentucky.

Map 40 • Uptown

Big Chicks	5024 N Sheridan Rd	773-728-5511	Neighborhood gay bar.
Carol's Pub	4659 N Clark St	773-334-2402	Hillbillies gone yuppie...thanks to a little press.
Crew Bar & Grill	4804 N Broadway St	773-784-CREW	Gay sports bar with 50 beers and several televisions, or vice versa.
Green Mill Pub	4802 N Broadway St	773-878-5552	Chicago legend...Al Capone's old hangout.
Hopleaf	5148 N Clark St	773-334-9851	Tons of imports if you can get a seat.
Max's Place	4621 N Clark St	773-784-3864	At $1.25 per draft, who wouldn't pass out?
Nick's Uptown	4015 N Sheridan Rd	773-975-1155	Open late with a great beer selection.
Riviera	4746 N Racine Ave	773-275-6800	Rock out and revel at the old architecture.
T's	5025 N Clark St	773-784-6000	Lesbians lounge in style.
The Uptown Lounge	1136 W Lawrence Ave	773-878-1136	Former dump becomes trendy lounge in up-and-coming neighborhood.

Map 41 • Avondale / Old Irving

Chief O'Neill's	3471 N Elston Ave	773-473-5263	Celtic music and top-of-the-line pub food.
Christina's Place	3759 N Kedzie Ave	773-463-1768	$2 Guinness/4 am/karaoke/dive/awesome.
N	2977 N Elston Ave	773-866-9898	Argentine flair with electro grooves.
Nelly's Saloon	3256 N Elston Ave	773-588-4494	Romanian hangout with occasional live music.
Stadium West	3188 N Elston Ave	773-866-2450	Neighborhood dive with occasional local DJ sets.

Map 42 • North Center / Roscoe Village / West Lakeview

Art of Sports	2444 W Diversey Ave	773-276-7298	More sports than art.
Beat Kitchen	2100 W Belmont Ave	773-281-4444	Hip music spot in a not so hip hood.
Black Rock	3614 N Damen Ave	773-348-4044	Not sure what this place is.
Cody's Public House	1658 W Barry Ave	773-528-4050	Named after the owner's dog.
Four Moon Tavern	1847 W Roscoe St	773-929-6666	This is not four regulars dropping their pants!
Four Treys	3333 N Damen Ave	773-549-8845	One of 5,000 drinking options in this area.
G&L Fire Escape	2157 W Grace St	773-472-1138	Attention ladies! It's a fireman's hangout!
Martyrs'	3855 N Lincoln Ave	773-404-9494	Great stage for live acts.
Mulligan's Public House	2000 W Roscoe St	773-549-4225	Villagers do not go thirsty.
Riverview Tavern & Restaurant	1958 W Roscoe St	773-248-9523	Another Roscoe Village watering hole.
Seanchai	2345 W Belmont Ave	773-549-4444	DJ in back room, drunk locals in front room.
Waterhouse	3407 N Paulina Ave	773-871-1200	Local lounge aiming for a classy feel.
The Village Tap	2055 W Roscoe St	773-883-0817	Neighborhood icon with a touch of class.
Xippo	3759 N Damen Ave	773-529-9135	Martini lounge in unlikely 'hood.

Map 43 • Wrigleyville/ East Lakeview

Bar Celona	3474 N Clark St	773-244-8000	Two bars, one in the basement, DJ spins upstairs.
Berlin	954 W Belmont Ave	773-348-4975	Tiny classic "pansexual" dance club.
Bernie's	3664 N Clark St	773-525-1898	Best bar in Wrigleyville…hands down.
Blarney Stone	3424 N Sheffield Ave	773-348-1078	Cool place where the not-so-beautiful Cub fans hang.
Bungalow Bar and Lounge	1622 W Belmont Ave	773-244-0400	Quirky lounge in a blue-collar neighborhood.
Cherry Red	2833 N Sheffield Ave	773-477-3661	Red lighting, huge dance floor and space, red-hot.
Cubby Bear	1059 W Addison St	773-327-1662	Where the real drunk Cubbie wannabees go.
Dark Horse	3443 N Sheffield Ave	773-248-4400	Different bar music. In a good way. Think "Africa" by Toto.
Elbo Room	2871 N Lincoln Ave	773-549-5549	Didn't RATT play here?
Fizz Bar and Grill	3220 N Lincoln Ave	773-348-6000	Good specialty drinks. Tiki nights and more.
Fly Me to the Moon	3400 N Clark St	773-528-4033	Swanky piano bar turns nightclub.
Ginger Man Tavern	3740 N Clark St	773-549-2050	Not bad when there's no Cubs game.
Goose Island Brewery	3535 N Clark St	773-832-9040	Get a microbrew…and goosed if you're lucky.
Gunther Murphy's	1638 W Belmont Ave	773-472-5139	German beers, German cheers.
Guthrie's Tavern	1300 W Addison St	773-477-2900	Comfortable atmosphere, good drinks, a range of board games to play with.
Higgins' Tavern	3259 N Racine Ave	773-281-7637	Yuppies and drunks.
Improv Olympic	3541 N Clark St	773-880-0199	Get laughs and drunk.
Jack's Bar & Grill	2856 N Southport Ave	773-404-8400	Classy wine bar.
John Barleycorn	3524 N Clark St	773-549-6000	Another chain for frat-boy types.
Justin's	3358 N Southport Ave	773-929-4844	Great bar for Sunday football.
Lincoln Tap Room	3010 N Lincoln Ave	773-868-0060	Great mix of people, comfortable couches.
Metro	3730 N Clark St	773-549-0203	Internationally renowned venue for top local and touring rock music.
Moxie	3517 N Clark St	773-935-6694	Trendy, narrow bar with expensive fancy drinks.
Murphy's Bleachers	3655 N Sheffield Ave	773-281-5356	Outdoor Cubbie haven with drunks galore.
Raw Bar	3720 N Clark St	773-348-7291	Post-Metro rock star hangout.
Schuba's	3159 N Southport Ave	773-525-2508	Top live music staple with new restaurant.
Sheffield's	3258 N Sheffield Ave	773-281-4989	Outdoor area attracts afternoon revelers.
Slugger's	3540 N Clark St	773-248-0055	Batting cages—some people's heaven, others' hell.
Smart Bar	3730 N Clark St	773-549-4140	Club kids unite!
Ten Cat Tavern	3931 N Ashland Ave	773-935-5377	Artsy type relaxing spot.
Trace	3714 N Clark St	773-477-3400	There is more than the Cubs in Wrigleyville.
Trader Todd's	3216 N Sheffield Ave	773-975-8383	Pitcher of beer and karaoke South Beach style.
Uncommon Ground Café	3800 N Clark St	773-929-3680	Local acts play while sipping a latte.
Underground Lounge	952 W Newport Ave	773-327-2739	Cool music spot tucked away below the street.
Wild Hare	3530 N Clark St	773-327-4273	Attire: Dreads, beads, and beanies.
Y*k-zies-Clark	3710 N Clark St	773-525-9200	Loud post-Cubs hangout.

Map 44 • East Lakeview

Charlie's Chicago	3726 N Broadway St	773-871-8887	Gay country and western bar. That's right.
Circuit	3641 N Halsted St	773-325-2233	Huge Boystown dance club—recently remodeled.
The Closet	3325 N Broadway St	773-477-8533	Boy-friendly lesbian bar, 4 am license.
Cocktail	3359 N Halsted St	773-477-1420	Small dance floor, occasional male strippers.
Duke of Perth	2913 N Clark St	773-477-1741	Shades of Edinburgh, along with requisite whiskies and haddock.
Gentry on Halsted	3320 N Halsted St	773-348-1053	A upscale gay piano bar that boasts "classy."
Hydrate	3458 N Halsted St	773-975-9244	Just what Boystown needs—a gay-friendly fern bar!
Jacquelines	3420 N Broadway St	773-404-5149	Gays and straights are united by booze at this neighborhood drunk spot.
Kit Kat Lounge	3700 N Halsted St	773-525-1111	Live drag queen shows.
Little Jim's	3501 N Halsted St	773-871-6116	Chicago's only gay dive.
minibar	3341 N Halsted St	773-871-6227	Fancy cocktails in a smoke-free lounge.
Monsignor Murphy's	3019 N Broadway St	773-348-7285	Irish Pub with plenty of board games.
Roscoe's	3356 N Halsted St	773-281-3355	Cavernous mingling for the gay sweater set.
Sidetrack	3349 N Halsted St	773-477-9189	Popular showtune sing-a-longs!
Spin	800 W Belmont Ave	773-327-7711	Lots of theme days throughout the week.
Town Hall Pub	3340 N Halsted St	773-472-4405	Unassuming, mixed clientele, live music.

Maps 45–48 • Northwest Chicago

5th Province Pub	Irish-American Heritage Ctr, 4626 N Knox Ave	773-282-7035	Authentic pub located in the Heritage Center.
Abbey Pub	3420 W Grace St	773-478-4408	Reputable live music venue.
Emerald Isle	6686 N Northwest Hwy	773-775-2848	The brothers and sisters of Kerry gather here.
Fischman Liquors	4780 N Milwaukee Ave	773-545-0123	We call beer "piwo" 'round here.

Hollywood Lounge	3301 W Bryn Mawr Ave	773-588-9707	Friendly neighborhood bar with extensive beer selection.
Little Rascals	4356 W Belmont Ave	773-545-1416	Neighborhood dump with a grill and a colorful cast of regulars.
Moretti's	6727 N Olmstead Ave	773-631-1223	Sports-guy type of hangout.
New Polonia Club	6101 W Belmont Ave	773-237-0571	A polish bar on the NW side? Go figure.
Old Irving Park Sports Bar & Grill	4217 W Irving Park Blvd	773-725-5595	Hole-in-the-wall sports bar.
Rosa's Lounge	3420 W Armitage Ave	773-342-0452	Chicago's lesser-known Blues staple.
Vaughan's Pub	5485 N Northwest Hwy	773-631-9206	Cozy neighborhood joint with nice beer selection and Irish food.

Maps 49–52 • West Chicago

Black Beetle	2532 W Chicago Ave	773-384-0701	Displaced suburbanites in the heart of Humbolt Park.
California Clipper	1002 N California Ave	773-384-2547	An art-dork and hipster haven.
Freddie's Pepper Box	4501 W Madison St	n/a	No lights...and no strangers please.
La Justicia	3901 W 26th St	773-522-0041	Live rock-en-espanol on Friday nights only!
Ms Carol's Place	3858 W Madison St	n/a	Cozy, smoky and inexpensive. What else do you need?
Red's Lounge	3479 S Archer Ave	773-376-0517	Seediest, smokiest, hardest-to-find dive in Chicago.

Maps 53–56 • Southwest Chicago

Cork & Kerry	10614 S Western Ave	773-445-2675	We think we've actually seen a Leprechaun here.
Groucho's	8355 S Pulaski Rd	773-767-4838	Mainstream and big-hair live rock venue.
Jeremy Lanigan's Irish Pub	3119 W 111th St	773-233-4004	Live celtic music from time-to-time.
Keegan's Pub	10618 S Western Ave	773-233-6829	Another Irish joint on the South Side. Go figure.
Mrs O'Leary's Dubliner	10910 S Western Ave	773-238-0784	Quaint, with locals and expats and hand-carved booths. Sing along to old Irish jukebox tunes.
Sean's Rhino Bar	10330 S Western Ave	773-238-2060	The new kid on the block (1999) offers darts, pool, drink specials and decent pub grub.

Maps 57–60 • South Chicago

Jeffrey Pub	7041 S Jeffery Blvd	773-363-8555	Gay men and lesbians mingle at this southside dance club.
New Apartment Lounge	504 E 75th St	773-483-7728	Where Von Freeman jams every Tuesday night.
Pullman's Pub	611 E 113th St	773-568-0264	Pre-Prohibition watering hole.
Reds	6926 S Stony Island Ave	773-643-5100	Popular place to mack on the opposite sex.

Evanston

1800 Club	1800 Sherman Ave	847-733-7900	Always busy, thanks to cheap drinks and trivia night.
Bill's Blues Bar	1029 Davis St	847-424-9800	Chicago transplant Bill Gilmore invades Evanston.
Keg of Evanston	810 Grove St	847-869-9987	DJ on the weekends. Dollar drafts on Wednesdays!
Prairie Moon	1502 Sherman Ave	847-864-8328	Weekly drink specials.
The Stained Glass Wine Bar	1735 Benson Ave	847-864-8600	240 varieties of wine, braised rabbit, and frog legs.
Tommy Nevin's Pub	1450 Sherman Ave	847-869-0450	Evanston's answer to live music joints.

Oak Park

Avenue Ale House	825 S Oak Park Ave	708-848-2801	Really great place to grab a beer (or frozen margarita or sangria) and watch a game. Tasty grub. Great patio.

Skokie

Chammps	134 Old Orchard Ctr	847-673-4778	Sports bar chain.
Don's Tavern	9335 Skokie Blvd	847-677-3424	Yuppy watering hole connected to Don's Fishmarket.
Principal's Pub	4249 Main St	847-675-7773	Local beer and shot option.
Rick's Place	8266 Lincoln Ave	847-675-1545	Friendly dive.

MAP 6

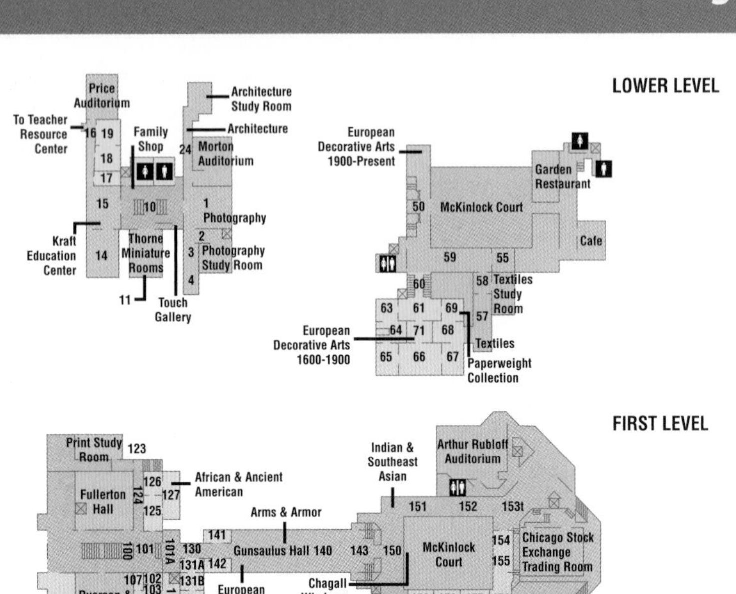
LOWER LEVEL
Price Auditorium
To Teacher Resource Center
Family Shop
Architecture Study Room
Architecture
Morton Auditorium
Photography
Photography Study Room
Kraft Education Center
Thorne Miniature Rooms
Touch Gallery
European Decorative Arts 1900-Present
McKinlock Court
Garden Restaurant
Cafe
Textiles Study Room
Textiles
European Decorative Arts 1600-1900
Paperweight Collection

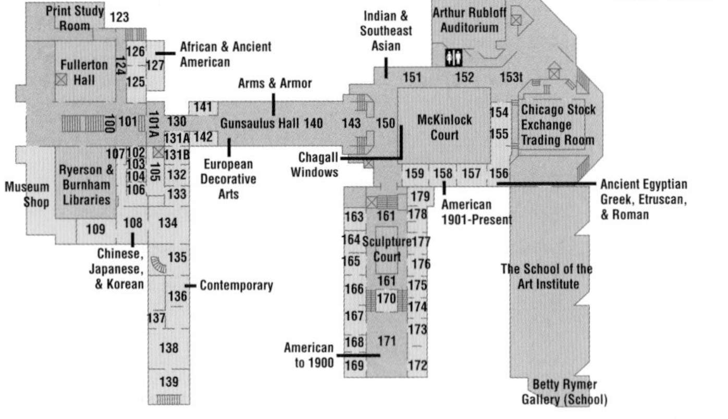
FIRST LEVEL
Print Study Room
Fullerton Hall
African & Ancient American
Arms & Armor
Gunsaulus Hall
Indian & Southeast Asian
Arthur Rubloff Auditorium
McKinlock Court
Chicago Stock Exchange Trading Room
Chagall Windows
European Decorative Arts
Museum Shop
Ryerson & Burnham Libraries
Ancient Egyptian Greek, Etruscan, & Roman
American 1901-Present
Chinese, Japanese, & Korean
Sculpture Court
Contemporary
The School of the Art Institute
American to 1900
Betty Rymer Gallery (School)

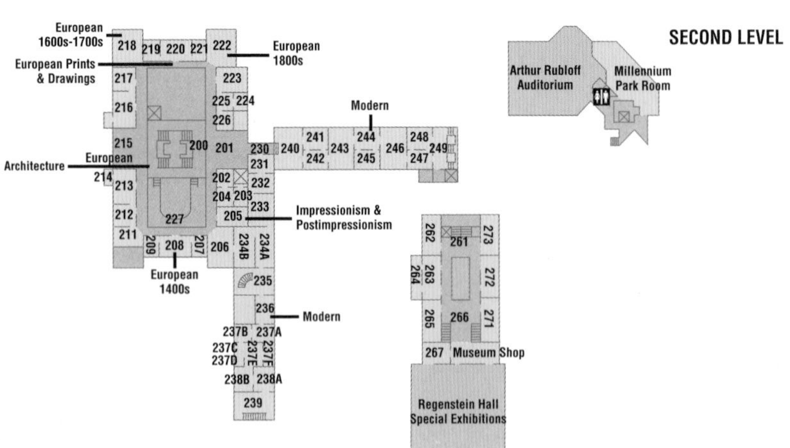
SECOND LEVEL
European 1600s-1700s
European Prints & Drawings
European 1800s
Arthur Rubloff Auditorium
Millennium Park Room
Modern
Architecture
European
Impressionism & Postimpressionism
European 1400s
Modern
Museum Shop
Regenstein Hall Special Exhibitions

General Information

NFT Map: 6
Address: 111 S Michigan Ave
Chicago, IL 60603
Phone: 312-443-3600
Website: www.artic.edu
Hours: Mon–Wed & Fri: 10:30 am–4:30 pm; Thurs: 10:30 am–8 pm; Sat & Sun: 10 am–5 pm; Thanksgiving & Christmas: closed
Admission: $12 for adults, $7 for students/ children/seniors, free for kids under five, free for all on Tuesdays
Call for summer hours.

Overview

Built in 1892 as the only permanent structure of the 1893 Columbian Exposition, the Classical Revival Allerton Wing of the Art Institute of Chicago began life as the "Palace of Culture" for the World's Fair. (The lions were added two years later.) Today the Art Institute is one of the preeminent art museums in the country, housing the largest collection of 19th–century French art outside of Paris (and its modern art collection isn't anything to sneeze at, either). Walking up the grand staircase in the main entrance, visitors are presented with an eclectic collection of architectural fragments wrenched from Chicago buildings that were standing in the way of, well, you know: "progress." There are also impressive exhibitions such as the Japanese wood block prints, the Touch Gallery designed specifically for the visually impaired, as well as really, really old vases and things, but who are we kidding? Everyone comes here for an up–close and personal look at such celebrated paintings as Caillebotte's *Paris Street; Rainy Day,* Seurat's *Grand Jatte,* Grant Wood's *American Gothic,* and Hopper's *Nighthawks,* along with their impressive collection of Monets, Manets, Van Goghs, and Picassos.

Construction of the new $198 million Renzo Piano wing is well underway. The modern addition, as well as its surrounding gardens, has been designed to harmonize with the adjoining Millennium Park. Construction is slated to be finished in 2007. If the new addition has anything more than just its backyard in common with the Millennium Park project, we'll put off buying our gown for the opening until closer to 2010. Fortunately, Piano's work will probably be worth the wait…

Restaurants and Services

The Cafe, on the lower–level of the Rubloff Building, offers self–service dining with burgers, pizza, and deli sandwiches at reasonable prices 11 am–4 pm daily. For a more elegant lunch, dine next door at the Garden Restaurant. Now open year–round from11:30 am to 3 pm daily, the restaurant features patio dining with seasonal cuisine and a full bar. The museum also offers free jazz concerts for Garden diners with their Jazz in the Garden program on Thursday evenings from July to September.

While postcards, books, and magnets may be purchased at kiosks throughout the museum, the Museum Shop, just off the main lobby, offers an extensive collection of art–oriented gifts and souvenirs (and you don't have to pay admission to shop there!). The lower–level Woman's Board Family Shop, adjacent to the Kraft Education Center and the Touch Gallery, hawks kid–oriented goodies.

School of the Art Institute of Chicago

Boasting such illustrious alumni as Georgia O'Keefe, Claes Oldenburg, Laurie Anderson, and David Sedaris, the School of the Art Institute of Chicago (SAIC) offers a fine–art higher education for tomorrow's budding Renoirs for just $14,475 per semester.

Gene Siskel Film Center

160 N State St, 312–846–2600; www.siskelfilmcenter.org
The film branch of the Art Institute offers art house, foreign films, and revivals, with frequent lectures by academics and industry professionals.

How to Get There

By Car: The Art Institute is located on Michigan Avenue between Monroe and Jackson. From I-90/94 N (the Dan Ryan), exit to Congress East (Loop exit). From I–90/94 S (Kennedy Expressway), exit Monroe Steet East. Affordable parking is located underground at Millennium Park garages (enter at Columbus and Monroe) and Grant Park garages (enter on Michigan, either between Madison and Randolph or between Van Buren and Adams).

By Metra: Nearest stops are the Randolph and Van Buren stations served by the Metra Electric and South Shore Lines. For other Metra lines, transfer to the 151 Sheridan Avenue bus at Union Station.

By Bus: Numerous lines serve this strip of Michigan Avenue. Important buses include (from the south) the 3 King Drive, the 4 Collage Grove, and the 6 Jackson Park Express, (from the west) the 126 Jackson and 20 Madison, and (from the north) the 151 Sheridan, the 145 Wilson–Michigan Express, and the 146 Inner Drive/Michigan Express.

By L: From the Red and Blue lines, exit at Monroe. Brown, Orange, Purple and Green exit at Adams and Wabash.

The Grande Dames of Chicago's museum scene, **The Art Institute of Chicago (Map 6)**, the **Museum of Science and Industry (Map 20)**, and the Museum Campus's **Adler Planetarium (Map 11)**, **Field Museum (Map 11)**, and **Shedd Aquarium (Map 9)**, may offer a lifetime of wonder, speculation, and enrichment; but impressive as they are, these cultural epicenters are only the tip of the iceberg when it comes to our city's museum offerings.

Art Museums

Although the Art Institute's collection *is* undeniably impressive (see the preceding page), Chicago's true art lovers know to look past the lions to some of Chicago's less- celebrated treasures.

Columbia College's **Museum of Contemporary Photography (Map 9)** is one of two accredited photography museums in the nation. Other campus-linked art museums include University of Chicago's **David and Alfred Smart Museum (Map 19)**, where the collection spans some 5,000 years. Catch the Lunch at **Loyola University Museum of Art (Map 34)** series for a quick bite with artists and experts on exhibits. Artwork created by and commemorating veterans (from both sides) of the Vietnam War hangs on the walls of the **National Vietnam Veterans Art Museum (Map 11)**.

One of the country's largest collections of art post-1945 is housed at the always eye-opening **Museum of Contemporary Art (Map 3)**. The first Friday of the month, twenty-something singles converge here for cocktails, live entertainment, and friendly flirtation.

History

The **Chicago History Museum (Map 32)** (previously the Chicago Historical Society) is a tremendous archive of the city's past and present. African-American history is celebrated at the nation's oldest museum focusing on the black experience, the **DuSable Museum of African-American History (Map 18)**. The **Oriental Institute (Map 19)** specializes in artifacts from the ancient Near-East, including Persia, Mesopotamia, and Egypt. Nobel Prize-winning sociologist **Jane Addams's Hull-House (Map 26)** examines Chicago's history of immigration, ethnic relations, and social work. "Artifacts" such as a John Lennon guitar and song lyrics by Bono are highlights of the collection at **The Peace Museum (West)**. Exhibits focus on individual peacemakers and artists, human rights, women's leadership, and the horrors of war. Big thoughts behind little objects like Mother Theresa's coffee mug, Martin Luther King Jr.'s toothbrush, and Nelson Mandela's sunglasses.

Science and Technology

As if the aforementioned **Adler Planetarium (Map 11)**, **Shedd Aquarium (Map 9)**, and **Field Museum (Map 11)** (all of which get special treatment within the Parks & Places listings under "Museum Campus") and the **Museum of Science and Industry (Map 20)** (listed with "Jackson Park") weren't enough to keep your head spinning, Chicago is also home to a handful of quirky, smaller science museums. The **International Museum of Surgical Science (Map 32)** offers a window to the world of questionable surgical practices of yore. The **Museum of Holography (Map 24)** examines the art and technology of making things appear 3-D. For kids, the **Children's Museum (Navy Pier)** presents a hands-on approach to learning about science and geography. Conservation and the environment are the focus of the **Peggy Notebaert Nature Museum (Map 30)**, which also features a butterfly haven, delighting the child in us all.

Architecture

The city itself is perhaps one of the best architecture museums in the world. Examine it yourself by embarking on one of the tours offered by the **Chicago Architecture Foundation (Map 6)**. Frank Lloyd Wright's influence on Chicago architecture can be examined at the **Robie House (Map 19)** in Hyde Park and the Frank Lloyd Wright Home and Studio in Oak Park. Chicago's Prairie Avenue District offers an architectural glimpse at Chicago's Victorian Golden Age. Joint tours of the oldest house in Chicago, the **Clarke House (Map 11)** (c. 1836), and the neighboring **Glessner House (Map 11)** offer the curious an interesting inside peek.

Ethnic Museums

Immigration made Chicago into the "City of Neighborhoods." The **Swedish American Museum Center (Map 37)**, the **Chinese American Museum of Chicago (Map 10)**, the **Balzekas Museum of Lithuanian Culture (Map 53)**, and the **Polish Museum of America (Map 22)** all explore the impact of immigration on Chicago. The **Hellenic Museum and Cultural Center (Map 6)** is a celebration of all things Greek. The **Mexican Fine Arts Center (Map 25)** is the largest such museum in the country and examines the Mexican experience through art and culture. The **Spertus Museum (Map 9)** specializes in Jewish history and heritage. Its hands-on reproduction of an archeological dig is eternally popular with kids.

Miscellaneous

Housed in the former home of the legendary, influential blues label, Chess Records, Willie Dixon's **Blues Heaven Foundation (Map 11)** offers tours of where Chuck Berry, Muddy Waters, and even the Rolling Stones once recorded. (The site is memorialized in the Stones' song "2120 South Michigan.")

For the darker side of sightseeing, the **Leather Archives and Museum (Map 34)** exhibits eight galleries of fetish, bondage, and S&M artifacts including photographs, clothing, toys, and more. The **Antiques Fabricare Museum (Map 48)** offers a seemingly "cleaner" afternoon out with the chance to view antique irons, washing machines, and decades-old washing powders.

The **Museum of Broadcast Communications (Map 2)**, one of only three broadcast museums and home to the only Radio Hall of Fame in the nation, recently moved from the Chicago Cultural Center to its own space on State Street.

Museum	*Address*	*Phone*	*Map*
A Philip Randolph Pullman Porter Museum	10406 S Maryland Ave	773-928-3935	S
ABA Museum of Law	321 N Clark St	312-988-6222	32
Adler Planetarium and Astronomy Museum	1300 S Lake Shore Dr	312-922-STAR	11
Antiques Fabricare Museum	4213 W Irving Park Rd	773-282-6216	48
The Art Institute of Chicago	111 S Michigan Ave	312-443-3600	6
Balzekas Museum of Lithuanian Culture	6500 S Pulaski Rd	773-582-6500	SW
Bronzeville Children's Museum	9600 S Western Ave	708-636-9504	SW
Chicago Architecture Foundation	Santa Fe Bldg, 224 S Michigan Ave	312-922-3432	6
Chicago Children's Museum	Navy Pier, 700 E Grand Ave	312-527-1000	Navy Pier
Chicago History Museum	1601 N Clark St	312-642-4600	32
Chicago Maritime Society	Helix Bldg, 310 S Racine Ave	312-421-9096	24
Chinese Historical Society of America	238 W 23rd St	312-949-1000	10
Clarke House Museum	1827 S Indiana Ave	312-745-0040	11
Columbia College for the Book and Paper Arts	Ludington Bldg, 1104 S Wabash Ave	312-344-6630	8
DePaul University Museum	2350 N Kenmore Ave	773-325-7506	29
DL Moody Museum	Smith Hall, 820 N La Salle Dr	312-329-4000	32
DuSable Museum of African-American History	740 E 56th Pl	773-947-0600	18
The Field Museum	1400 S Lake Shore Dr	312-922-9410	11
Frank Lloyd Wright Home and Studio	951 Chicago Ave	708-848-1976	Oak Park
Glessner House Museum	1800 S Prairie Ave	312-326-1480	11
Hellenic Museum and Cultural Center	Greek Island Bldg, 801 W Adams St	312-655-1234	6
Holocaust Memorial Foundation of Illinois	4255 Main St	847- 677-4640	Skokie
International Museum of Surgical Science	1524 N Lake Shore Dr	312-642-6502	32
Intuit: Center for Intuitive and Outsider Art	756 N Milwaukee Ave	312-243-9088	24
Jane Addams Hull-House Museum	800 S Halsted St	312-413-5353	26
Jazz Institute of Chicago	410 S Michigan Ave	312-427-1676	6
Leather Archives & Museum	6418 N Greenview Ave	773-761-9200	34
Loyola University Museum of Art	Lewis Towers, 820 N Michigan Ave	312-915-7600	32
Mexican Fine Arts Center	1852 W 19th St	312-738-1503	25
The Museum of Broadcast Communications	400 N State St	312-245-8200	2
Museum of Contemporary Art	220 E Chicago Ave	312-280-2660	3
Museum of Contemporary Photography	600 S Michigan Ave – Columbia College	312-663-5554	9
Museum of Holography-Chicago	1134 W Washington Blvd	312-226-1007	24
Museum of Science and Industry	5700 S Lake Shore Dr	773-684-1414	20
National Vietnam Veterans Art Museum	1801 S Indiana Ave	312-326-0270	11
The Newberry Library	60 W Walton St	312-943-9090	32
Oriental Institute Museum	University of Chicago, 1155 E 58th St	773-702-9514	19
The Peace Museum	Gold Dome Bldg, 100 N Central Park Ave	773-638-6450	W
Peggy Notebaert Nature Museum	2430 N Cannon Dr	773-755-5100	30
Polish Museum of America	984 N Milwaukee Ave	773-384-3352	22
Robie House	5757 S Woodlawn Ave	773-834-1847	19
Rogers Park/West Ridge Historical Society	7344 N Western Ave	773-764-4078	33
Shedd Aquarium, John G	1200 S Lake Shore Dr	312-939-2438	9
Skokie Heritage Museum	8031 Floral Ave	847-677-6672	Skokie
Smart Museum of Art	University of Chicago, 5550 S Greenwood Ave	773-702-0200	19
Smith Museum of Stained Glass	Navy Pier, 700 E Grand Ave	312-595-5024	Navy Pier
Spertus Museum	618 S Michigan Ave	312-322-1700	9
Swedish American Museum	5211 N Clark St	773-728-8111	37
Ukrainian Institute of Modern Art	2320 W Chicago Ave	773-227-5522	23
Ukrainian National Museum of Chicago	721 N Oakley Blvd	312-421-8020	23
Willie Dixon's Blues Heaven Foundation	2120 S Michigan Ave	312-808-1286	11

Is the "city of big shoulders" also the city of big readers? Oprah and Da Mare would have you think so, what with their "One Book, One City" and "Oprah's Book Club" campaigns. To be sure, there's no lack of bookshops in the city, and Chicago's multitude of quirky, independent stores stand defiantly side–by–side with the bookselling super chains that continue to pop up every day.

For general, all–purpose bookshops, **Barbara's (Map 3, Map 5)** is a Chicago Institution, as is 26–year–old **Unabridged Books (Map 44)** with its specialties in literary fiction, kids' books, travel, cookbooks, and gay and lesbian titles. Down by the University of Chicago campus, **57th Street Books (Map 19)** and **Seminary Co–op Bookstore (Map 19)** both appeal to the brainiac set, whereas **Beck's Book Store (Map 2, Map 5, Map 34, Map 40)** specializes in textbooks for Chicago's community colleges.

Specialty stores abound in the city. We think **Women & Children First (Map 37)** may have the largest selection of feminist and woman–focused books in the country, and their children's section is also top notch. **Afrocentric Bookstore (Map 16)** specializes in black literature and culture. Heal thyself at **Transitions Bookplace (Map 22)**—a peaceful, feng shui enclave in the chaotic Clybourn corridor shopping district. **Soliloquy (Map 42)** will appeal to your inner thespian with their fine selection of scripts and monologues, while the **Occult Bookstore (Map 21)** on Milwaukee Avenue offers everything a budding witch or warlock could desire.

Quimby's (Map 21) in Wicker Park specializes in esoteric small–press books and 'zines with a marked counter–culture feel. You'll find your John Fante, Kathy Acker, and Georges Bataille here. **Printer's Row Fine & Rare Book**s **(Map 8)** specializes in architecture titles. Travelers would be wise to pay a visit to **Savvy Traveler (Map 6)** before setting sail. They carry all manner of travel related books as well as maps, passport cases, fanny packs, and more.

Shuffle through the used stacks at **Bookworks (Map 43)** on North Clark or **Myopic (Map 21)** in Wicker Park. **Selected Works (Map 44)** on Broadway sells used books and sheet music. **Powell's (Map 8, Map 19, Map 43)** has made a name for itself for its great selection of remaindered and off–price lit.

If you must chain it, the **Barnes & Noble (Map 29)** near the Webster Place cinema has a convenient parking lot. **Borders (Map 32)** on North Michigan is accessible for Mag Mile shoppers, ditto the address at 150 North State **(Map 5)** for State Street excursions.

Map 1 • River North / Fulton Market District

N Fagin Books	459 N Milwaukee Ave	312–829–5252	Social sciences.

Map 2 • Near North / River North

Abraham Lincoln Book Shop	357 W Chicago Ave	312–944–3085	History and military specialty store.
After–Words	23 E Illinois St	312–464–1110	New and used.
B Dalton	222 Merchandise Mart Plz	312–329–1881	Chain.
Beck's Book Store	50 E Chicago Ave	312–944–7685	Where there's a Beck's, there's a campus.

Map 3 • Streeterville / Mag Mile

Abbott Hall Book Center	710 N Lake Shore Dr	312–503–8486	Textbooks.
Barbara's	201 E Huron St	312–926–2665	Branch of local chain.
University of Chicago	450 N Cityfront Plz Dr	312–464–8650	Textbooks.

Map 4 • West Loop Gate / Greek Town

Waldenbooks	500 W Madison St	312–627–8334	Chain.

Map 5 • The Loop

Barbara's	111 N State St	312–781–3033	Branch of local chain.
Barbara's	Sears Tower, 233 S Wacker Dr	312–466–0223	Branch of local chain.
Beck's Book Store	209 N Wabash Ave	312–630–9113	Where there's a Beck's, there's a campus.
Beck's Book Store	315 S Plymouth Ct	312–913–0650	Where there's a Beck's, there's a campus.
Books–a–Million	144 S Clark St	312–857–0613	Chain.
Borders	150 N State St	312–606–0750	State Street books.
Brent Books & Cards	309 W Washington St	312–364–0126	General.
Culture	100 W Randolph St	312–263–4514	African–American culture.
Graham Crackers Comics	77 E Madison St	312–629–1810	Comics.
Prairie Avenue Bookshop	418 S Wabash Ave	312–922–8311	Le Corbusier, you say? Architecture bookstore and more.
Tower Records Video Books	214 S Wabash Ave	312–663–0660	Chain.

Map 6 • The Loop / Grant Park

Chicago Architecture Foundation	224 S Michigan Ave	312–922–3432	Lots of pretty pictures.
Phillips & Fort	410 S Michigan Ave, Ste 541	312–697–0700	Rare books.
Rain Dog Books	408 S Michigan Ave	312–922–1200	Small selection of used books plus a cozy café.
Savvy Traveller	310 S Michigan Ave	312–913–9800	Travel books, maps, money belts.

Map 8 • South Loop / Printers Row / Dearborn Park

Books In The City South Loop	545 S State St	312–291–1111	Textbooks.
Powell's	828 S Wabash Ave	312–341–0748	Used and remainders.
Printers Row Fine & Rare Books	715 S Dearborn St	312–583–1800	The name says it all.
Sandmeyer's	714 S Dearborn St	312–922–2104	General.

Map 9 • South Loop / South Michigan Ave

Columbia College	624 S Michigan Ave	312-344-7406	Some general books, mostly textbooks.
L Wiley Book Store	816 S Michigan Ave	312-583-0640	Textbooks.

Map 10 • East Pilsen / Chinatown

Chinese Champion Book & Gift	2167 S China Pl	312-326-3577	Chinese books.
World Journal	2116 S Archer Ave	312-842-8005	A world of Chinese books.

Map 11 • South Loop / McCormick Place

Paragon Book Gallery	1507 S Michigan Ave	312-663-5155	Asian arts.

Map 16 • Bronzeville

Afrocentric Bookstore	4655 S King Dr	773-924-3966	Celebrates the African-American literary tradition.

Map 19 • Hyde Park

57th Street Books	1301 E 57th St	773-684-1300	Frequented by U of C brainiacs.
Borders	1539 E 53rd St	773-752-8663	General/chain.
O'Gara & Wilson	1448 E 57th St	773-363-0993	Used books.
Powell's	1501 E 57th St	773-955-7780	Remainders and off-price books. Mostly scholarly.
Seminary Co-op Bookstore	5757 S University Ave	773-752-4381	Underground trove of scholarly books for all.
University of Chicago Bookstore	970 E 58th St	773-702-8729	Textbooks.

Map 21 • Wicker Park / Ukrainian Village

Brainstorm	1648 W North Ave	773-384-8721	Comic books.
Hejfina	1529 N Milwaukee Ave	773-772-0002	Fine art and Architecture.
Myopic Books	1564 N Milwaukee Ave	773-862-4882	Rare and collectable books.
Occult Bookstore	1579 N Milwaukee Ave, Ste #321	773-292-0995	I put a spell on you.
Quimby's	1854 W North Ave	773-342-0910	Edgy, counter-culture bookshop.

Map 22 • Noble Square / Goose Island

Revolution Books	1103 N Ashland Ave	773-489-0930	Radical and revolutionary books.
Transitions Book Place	1000 W North Ave	312-951-7323	Heal thyself.

Map 23 • West Town / Near West Side

CNW Book Store	1900 W Van Buren St	312-829-6482	Get your Malcolm X College textbooks here.

Map 24 • River West / West Town

Joyce & Company	400 N Racine Ave	312-738-1933	Out of print books.

Map 25 • Illinois Medical District

Logan Medical Bookstore	600 S Paulina St	312-733-4544	Medical books.
UIC Medical Bookstore	828 S Wolcott Ave	312-413-5550	Reading material for when you're laid up.

Map 26 • University Village / Little Italy / Pilsen

Chicago Textbook	1076 W Taylor St	312-733-8398	Textbooks.
Libreria Giron	1443 W 18th St	312-226-2086	Spanish.

Map 28 • Bucktown

Libreria Nsra De Lourves	1907 N Milwaukee Ave	773-342-8890	Spanish books.
Micro Center	2645 N Elston Ave	773-292-1700	Department store chain.

Map 29 • DePaul / Wrightwood / Sheffield

Barnes & Noble	1441 W Webster Ave	773-871-3610	Convenient for the run-in-and-grab-something shopper.

Map 30 • Lincoln Park

Books in the City	2428 N Lincoln Ave	773-472-2665	Textbooks.
Graham Crackers Comics	2562 N Clark St	773-665-2010	Where good and evil meet.
Tower Records	2301 N Clark St	773-477-5994	Chain.

Map 31 • Old Town / Near North

Borders	755 W North Ave	312-266-8060	General/chain.

Map 32 • Gold Coast / Mag Mile

Barnes & Noble	1130 N State St	312-280-8155	Chain.
Borders	830 N Michigan Ave	312-573-0564	Mag Mile books.
Children In Paradise	909 N Rush St	312-951-5437	Kids' books.
Europa Books	832 N State St	312-335-9677	Foreign language books.
Newberry Bookstore	60 W Walton St	312-255-3520	Connected to the cultural library.
Waldenbooks	900 N Michigan Ave	312-337-0330	Chain.

Map 33 • West Rogers Park

India Book House & Journals	2551 W Devon Ave	773-764-6567	Spiritual/cultural.
Iqra Book Center	2751 W Devon Ave	773-274-2665	Islamic books.
Russian American Book Store	2746 W Devon Ave	773-761-3233	Floor to ceiling with musty books, as it should be.
U Arbat-Cobecedhnk	2810 W Devon Ave	773-262-1846	Russian books.

Map 34 • East Rogers Park

Armadillos Pillow	6753 N Sheridan Rd	773-761-2558	General used.
Beck's Book Store	6550 N Sheridan Rd	773-743-2281	Where there's a Beck's, there's a campus.
Under the Table Books	1443 W Jarvis Ave	773-743-3728	General used.

Map 35 • Arcadia Terrace / Peterson Park

Korean Books	5773 N Lincoln Ave	773-769-1010	Korean books.

Map 37 • Edgewater / Andersonville

Ginkgo Leaf Books	1759 W Rosehill Dr	773-989-2200	Rare and collectable books.
Heritage Books	1135 W Granville Ave	773-262-1566	Books of African-American interest.
Kate The Great's Book Emporium	5550 N Broadway St	773-561-1932	Used and New.
Women & Children First	5233 N Clark St	773-769-9299	Spacious feminist bookshop.

Map 39 • Ravenswood / North Center

Book Cellar	4736 N Lincoln Ave	773-293-2665	General books and café.
Variety Comic Book Store	4602 N Western Ave	773-334-2550	

Map 40 • Uptown

Beck's Book Store	4520 N Broadway St	773-784-7963	Where there's a Beck's, there's a campus.
Book Box – Shake, Rattle and Read	4812 N Broadway St	773-334-5311	Weird little store. Mostly used, some new.
Borders	4718 N Broadway St	773-334-7338	General/chain.
Libreria de Hable Hispana	4441 N Broadway St	773-878-2117	Spanish-language bookstore.
Libreria & Ueba Esperanza	1230 W Wilson Ave	773-561-4641	Used and rare books.
Stern's Psychology Book Store	1256 W Victoria St	773-506-0683	Psychology books.

Map 41 • Avondale / Old Irving

Devry Follett Bookstore-Chicago	3300 N Campbell Ave	773-477-2600	Textbooks, etc.

Map 42 • North Center / Roscoe Village / West Lakeview

Galaxy Comic Zone	3804 N Western Ave	773-267-1043	Comic books.

Map 43 • Wrigleyville/ East Lakeview

Beasley Books	1533 W Oakdale Ave, 2nd Fl	773-472-4528	Jazz/Blues, Labor History.
Bookworks	3444 N Clark St	773-871-5318	Used and rare books.
Chicago Comics	3244 N Clark St	773-528-1983	Fun! Not geeky, really. . .
Gallery Bookstore	923 W Belmont Ave	773-975-8200	Used books.
Hanley's	923 W Belmont Ave	773-281-9999	General used books.
Healing Earth Resources	3111 N Ashland Ave	773-327-8459	New Age books.
Powell's	2850 N Lincoln Ave	773-248-1444	Remainders and off-price books. Large art, architecture, photography and rare departments.

Map 44 • East Lakeview

Barnes & Noble	659 W Diversey Pkwy	773-871-9004	Chain.
Bookleggers Used Books	2907 N Broadway St	773-404-8780	Used books.
Bookman's Corner	2959 N Clark St	773-929-8298	Used non-fiction.
Borders	2817 N Clark St	773-935-3909	Behemoth on Clark and Broadway.
Selected Works Bookstore	3510 N Broadway St	773-975-0002	Quirky, junky used book store.
Unabridged Books	3251 N Broadway St	773-883-9119	Great literary bookshop, best gay selection in town.

Overview

Chicago is widely regarded as a world-class food destination, and rightly so, we say. Midwestern stereotypes of super sports fans inhaling Italian beefs and hot links notwithstanding, Chicago is a goldmine for foodies whether they are searching for culinary nirvana at one of the city's big name, high price gastro-palaces where you have to wait weeks, or even months, to get a seat, or at one of the myriad mom-and-pop neighborhood ethnic spots where you may be the only English speaker in the place and you know that the best dishes are not always listed in the menu.

In the past few years, Chicago's adventuresome appetite has come to life. After about a decade of complacency, during which the city's top dining emporiums basically rested on their laurels, a whole new school of Chicago restaurant has come to the fore. Once fueled by students of the masters: Bayless, Trotter, Gordon Sinclair, and so on, the Chicago dining renaissance is already in its second or third generation, and it's now the students of the students, those who honed their skills at places like Trio and Tru, that are taking the reins as we charge into Chicago's culinary future.

Of course there have been casualties along the way, and along with many upstarts, some giants have fallen. Auf weidersehn, we say to The Berghoff, a Chicago landmark since 1890 that closed its doors in 2006. The downtown satellite of Bob Chinn's Crab House also closed up shop, as did Evanston's aforementioned Trio. Other old-school establishments are taking note: places like Cité (which is evolving into the more contemporary and youthful "City" as we type), the Signature Room, and even the revered institution Everest are realizing that you have to offer more than a million dollar view to please Chicago's increasingly sophisticated palates.

And anyways, you gotta problem with hot links?

What follows is a breakdown of some of our current favorite spots, old and new. Of course, with every new restaurant opening, it is likely another one is closing. Therefore, we offer this caveat: phone first.

That's Chicago

Some restaurants are more than just places to grab a bite. They're defining institutions for the city. The original **Billy Goat Tavern (Map 3, Map 5, Map 24)** is known to baby boomers as the birthplace of John Belushi's "cheezeboiga" skit, but Chicagoans appreciate it as the dank, smoky watering hole where reporters from the *Tribune* and *Sun-Times* would gather after work to talk shop. Today it's more frequented by wide-eyed tourists who play at slumming it. "The true originator of Chicago-style pizza" is a title claimed by nearly every pizza shack in town. Of the lot, **Pizzeria Uno's (Map 2)** claim seems the most legit—their recipe dates back to 1943. Other Chicago pizza institutions include **Lou Malnati's (Map 2)** and **Gino's East (Map 2, Map 43)**. Equally important is the Chicago Dog—that is, a hot dog on a steamed bun with a virtual salad on top—onions, relish, tomatoes, pickle spears, sport peppers, mustard (no ketchup, thank you very much), and a dash of celery salt. Post-pub dogs at **Weiner's Circle (Map 30)** are a Lincoln Park right-of-passage—the servers are infamous for their saucy attitudes. Masochists line up for their abuse. On the Northwest side, **Superdawg** is a landmark. The vintage dog spot offers classic drive-in (not drive-thru) service. **Manny's Coffeeshop (Map 7)** in the South Loop is where local politicos go to make deals over breakfast or lunch. For dinner they head for homestyle Italian at **Taylor Street's Rosebud (Map 2)**. Finally, two Chicago institutions put the city on the international culinary radar. **Frontera Grill (Map 2)** packs 'em in for creative and upscale Mexican fare in a festive environment. For a more subdued experience, **Charlie Trotter's** (**Map 30**) pushes the culinary envelope with precious and exquisite creations.

The New Garde

Homaru Canto, who wet his feet at Charlie Trotter's, and Grant Achatz, hailing from Trio, push the food frontiers with their high-concept, scientific approach to haute cuisine. Canto's **MOTO (Map 24)** and Achatz's **Alinea (Map 30)** follow a global trend of clever (and pricey) deconstructions and reconceptions of such mundane ideas as peanut butter and jelly or a margarita with chips and salsa. Meanwhile, does Shawn McClain aspire to be the next Rich Melman? He garnered raves with his Asian-inspired menu at **Spring (Map 21)**, and then wowed veggie lovers with his second venture, **Green Zebra (Map 24)**. Now McClain takes on meat at **Printer's Row's Custom House (Map 8)**. What's next: A retro-styled diner or a pan-Latin party room?

Trendspotting

More Small Plates

Last year when we observed the widespread proliferation of small plate cuisine, from sushi to tapas and everything in between, we had no idea. No idea that the trend would last this long, spread so far and wide, and take on so many varied incarnations. Since then, Chicagoans have welcomed the arrival of small platers **Quartino (Map 2)**, **Volo** (**Map 42**), **Del Toro (Map 21)**, **People's Lounge (Map 21)**, and **Extra Virgin (Map 4)**, to name a few. On the raw fish front, newcomers include Uptown's **Agami (Map 40)**, **Butterfly Sushi (Map 24)**, **Hachi's Kitchen (Map 2**7), **Wakamono (Map 44)**, **Japonica (Map 26)**, **Touch of Sushi (Map 21)**, **Kohan (Map 26)**, and **T-Spot Sushi (Map 42)**. Perhaps the small plate extreme is best summed up by Lincoln Park's **Minnies (Map 30)**, which features bite-sized pub grub.

Pizza Pizza Pizza

No, not the cake-crusted, goopy Chicago style. We're talking super thin crust brick oven or wood-burning oven styles authentic from Italy with ingredients such as gorgonzola, artichokes, prosciutto, and crème fraiche. Not the kind of pizza you order in a dark booth with the buddies or the wife and kids in tow, the extra-large sausage and mushroom that you douse with crushed red pepper and wash down with pitchers of Coke and Old Style. We're talking your own whole pizza pie plopped down on a plate in front of you that you eat all fancy-like with a knife and a fork, while sipping oh la la Peroni beer or a glass of Chianti. With the insanely popular **Pizza D.O.C. (Map 39)** leading the way, new European-style pizza places have been cropping up everywhere. As we write this, these include **Spacca Napoli (Map 39)**, **Piece (Map 21)**, **Capi's Italian (Navy Pier)**, **Frasca (Map 42)**, **Mangia Roma (Map 31)**, **Pizza Rustica (Map 43)**, and **Café Restaurant Art (Map 38)**.

The Return of the Steak

Okay, it never really left us. Chicago is a steak house city. For as long as we can remember, **Morton's (Map 32)** has been the Chicago gold standard for steak houses, with **Gibson's (Map 32)** following close behind. A few newcomers are trying to give these two stalwarts a run for their money. **David Burke's Primehouse (Map 2)** and **Fulton's on the River (Map 2)** both specialize in prime aged steaks. We also recommend Fulton's delectible selection of East and West Coast oysters. Shawn McClain's **Custom House (Map 8)** adds refinement to the "men's club" Chicago steak house scene, while New Yorker **Il Mulino (Map 32)** wows us with high-falutin' New York-style prices.

Turnover in Lincoln Square

Lincoln Square and North Center have been a bustle of new restaurant activity for the past few years. We attribute the trend to the concentration of successful and arty young microbrew-drinking, NPR-listening professionals who call this 'hood home, combined with a friendly, crunchy community vibe that welcomes and supports independent entrepreneurship. In any case, the past year has seen more than its share of per capita restaurant action. For starters, She-She, a Lincoln Square pioneer, closed shop, and **Soiree (Map 39)** soon opened in her place. Two of last year's buzz spots, Aqualina and Charlie's on Leavitt seemed to fold prematurely. **Block 44 (Map 39)**, an American restaurant with small plate options that opened in the Aqualina space is now generating buzz of its own. Tournesol dabbled in the small plate wine bar concept before throwing in the kitchen towel, and last year's Caribbean upstart Toucan has morphed into contemporary Mexican spot **Brioso (Map 39)**. **Tagine** (Map 38) and **T-Spot Sushi (Map 42)** are also newcomers to the Lincoln Square scene. Our heads are still spinning.

The Best of the Rest

Wherein we give a run down of some of our perhaps less trendy but no less worthy dining options…

Vegging Out in Chicago

The phrase "vegetarian" and Chicago has often seemed oxymoronic, but just as more and more mainstream restaurants have been introducing more interesting veggie items than a pasta or risotto dish, so, too, have more genuine, bona-fide vegetarian restaurants been sprouting up on our beefy shores. The **Chicago Diner (Map 44)** and the **Heartland Café (Map 34)** (which does serve some meat) are the crunchy old-school standard bearers. New spots include Roger's Park **Lake Side Café (Map 34)**, the Turkish-turned raw food **Cousin's Incredible Vitality (Map 38)**, and **Alice and Friends Vegetarian Restaurant (Map 37)**, home of the mock meat. **Karyn's (Map 30)** in Lincoln Park attracted such a following for its raw food menu that Karyn opened **Karyn's Cooked (Map 2)** in Old Town. On Devon, **Mysore Woodlands (Map 33)** serves vegetarian food from southern India, while **Arya Bhavan (Map 33)** specializes in Indian vegetarian food from the north and south. **Amitabul** does Vegan Thai on the Northwest side, and **Soul Vegetarian East** does soul vegetarian in the Southside Chatham neighborhood. For upscale vegetarian, try the **Green Zebra (Map 24)**. In Logan Square, down-to-earth scenester spot **Lula (Map 27)** is known for being particularly vegetarian friendly. For a very special night, chose the fixed-price vegetarian tasting menus at **Arun's (Map 38)** or **Charlie Trotter's (Map 30)**. Finally, vegetarians and non-vegetarians alike line up for the vegtarian breakfasts served by followers of Sri Chimnoy at Roscoe Village's popular **Victory's Banne**r **(Map 42)**.

Poor Man's Steak and Other Meaty Matters

Lots of northsiders will swear that the best burgers in Chicago are grilled at **Moody's Pub (Map 37)**, while southsiders know that **Beverly's Top Notch Beefburger (South)** takes the honors. For our part, we sing the praises of the oft-overlooked char-grilled delights at **South Loop Club (Map 8)**. If, on the other hand, you like your meat served on the bone with a tangy sauce, head to the **Gale Street Inn (Northwest)** in Jefferson Park, street-festival mainstay **Robinson's (Map 4, Map 30)**, southside stalward **Leon's Barbeque (South)**, or Logan Square newcomer**Calvin's BBQ (Map 27)**. For encased meats, Chicago has no lack of options—just follow the Vienna Beef signs. For something different, try encased exotic meats such as ostrich or wild boar at **Hot Doug's (Map 41)**, or try one of their names specials such as the "mighty mighty hot" Jennifer Garner (formerly the Britney Spears). On weekends, they feature french fries cooked in duck fat.

Soul Food and Southern Cooking

We say soul food is the most American of American cuisines. On the south side, you can't go wrong with **Army & Lou's (South)**—it's a Chicago legend. **Valois (Map 19)** serves no frills–cafeteria–style soul food. **Miss Lee's Good Food (Map 18)** offers gut–busting southern food for carry–out only, or bring your family and eat in at **Captain Hard Times Dining (South)**. **Soul Queen (South)** cafeteria may have seen better days, but history is written in the photos on the walls. On the west side, stuff yourself silly at **Edna's** on Madison **(West)**. For Cajun food, try Chicago breakfast staple **Wishbone (Map 24, Map 42)** or Jimmy Banno's famous **Heaven on Seven (Map 3, Map 5, Map 43)**. **Dixie Kitchen and Bait Shop (Map 19)** serves up soul and Cajun, as does Bronzeville's **Negro League Café (Map 16)**. Or opt for Cajun and Indian food at Hyde Park's quirky **Rajun Cajun (Map 19)**.

Passport to Good Eating

Culinarily, you can travel the world and never leave Chicago. While some of Chicago's ethic dining emporiums fly high on the local radar, we have a soft spot for the ramshackle storefronts where the real home cooking is happening. Here's a grab bag of our favorite ethnic eats:

African: **Mama Desta's Red Seas (Map 43)**, **Ethiopian Diamond (Map 37)**, **Ras Dashen (Map 37)**

Caribbean: **Calypso Café (Map 19), La Palma (West), Coco (West), Tropic Island Jerk Chicken (South)**

Chinese: **Phoenix Café (Map 10)**, **Evergreen (Map 10)**, **Furama (Map 40)**

Cuban: **Café 28 (Map 39)**, **Café LaGuardia (Map 28)**

Eastern European: **Paprikash (Northwest), Red Apple (Northwest), Sayat Nova (Map 3)**, **Adria Mare (Map 37)**

English / Irish: **Red Lion Pub (Map 29)**, **Chief O'Neill's (Map 41)**, **Mrs. Murphy and Sons (Map 42)**

French: **Café Matou (Map 28)**, **Bistro Campagne (Map 39)**, **La Tache (Map 37)**, **Avec (Map 4)**, **La Creperie (Map 44)**

German: **Mirabell (Northwest), Chicago Brauhaus (Map 39)**, **Glunz Bavarian Haus (Map 39)**

Greek: **Costa's** (**Map 4**), **Santorini (Map 4)**, **Athena (Map 4)**

Indian: **Mysore Woodlands (Map 33)**, **Udupi Palace (Map 33)**, **Arya Bhavan (Map 33)**

Italian: **Ignotz (West), Brunas (West), Angelina (Map 44)**

Japanese: **Tank Sushi (Map 39)**, **Agami (Map 40)**, **Mirai Sushi (Map 21)**, **Katsu (Map 35)**, **Chiyo (Northwest)**

Korean: **Jin Ju (Map 37)**, **San Goo Gap San (Map 36)**, **Hama Matsu** (**Map 40**), **So Gong Dong Tofu House (Northwest)**

Mexican: **Nuevo Leon (Map 26)**, **Tecalitlan (Map 23)**, **Taqueria Trespasada (Map 41)**, **Las Palmas (Map 21)**, **Maiz (West)**, **Los Nopales (Map 39)**

Middle Eastern: **Sahar Pita (Map 38)**, **Semiramis (Map 38)**, **City Noor Kebab (Map 38)**, **Noon O' Kebab (Map 38)**

North African: **Tassili Café (Map 48)**, **Tagine (Map 38)**, **Tizi Melloul (Map 2)**

Nuevo Latino: **Meztiso (Map 2)**, **Cuatro (Map 11)**, **Carnivale (Map 1)**

Scandinavian: **Tre Kroner (West), Svea (Map 37)**, **Wickstrom's (Map 37)**

Spanish: **Del Toro (Map 21)**, **Arco de Cuchlleros (Map 44)**

Thai: **Amarind's (West), Opart (Map 39)**, **Thai Valley (Map 38)**, **Arun's (Map 38)**

Breakfast

Okay, so you're one of those annoying people who manage to be up, dressed, and ready to go before noon. Good for friggin' you. Why don't you get out of my face and go eat at one of these popular breakfast and brunch spots: **Sweet Maple Café (Map 26)**, **Orange (Map 43)**, **Over Easy Café (Map 39)**, **Ina's (Map 24)**, **Flo (Map 24)**, **Hot Spot (Map 27)**, or **Tweet (Map 40)**.

Diners

Because sometimes you just want a cup of joe and a patty melt, we recommend: **Salt and Pepper Diner (Map 29, Map 43)**, **Nookie's Tree (Map 44)**, **Ramova Grill (Map 13)**, **Salonica Grill (Map 19)**, **Clara's (Map 41)**, **Manny's Coffee Shop (Map 7)**, **Hollywood Grill (Map 28)**, **The Golden Apple (Map 43)**, **The Golden Angel (Map 39)**, and, last but in no way least, **The S&G (Map 43)**, a.k.a. Sam and George's.

Foodies on the Web

Need a recommendation?

Both professional food critics and the vox populi weigh in on the popular restaurant sites of the *Chicago Reader* and the *Chicago Tribune*'s Metromix. Both offer search categories, so you can find places by location, price, type of cuisine, etc. If you're going somewhere obscure or off–the–beaten path, however, be sure to phone first—Metromix, in particular, often seems to be out–of–date.

www.chicagoreader.com

www.metromix.com

Stay Hip to What's Hot

Chicago Magazine's food editors will deliver the latest Chicago food gossip directly to your inbox every week or so, along with chef interviews, links, and whatever food ephemera amuses them. Subscribe to Dish for free at the *Chicago Magazine* website:

www.ChicagoMagazine.com

Professional chefs and passionate lay folk chat about both the latest hot spots and hidden neighborhood gems on the LTH Forum. The foodie debates, all in the spirit of fun, can get raucous, and sometimes even local celebrity chefs enter the fore to throw down. A warning: Regular posting on the LTH Forum is a tell–tale sign of your descent down the slippery slope of food geekdom.

www.lthforum.com

Key: $: Under $10 / $$: $10–$20 / $$$: $20–$30 / $$$$: $30–$40 / $$$$$: $40+
** : Does not accept credit cards. / † : Accepts only American Express. / † †: Accepts only Visa and Mastercard*
Time listed refers to kitchen closing time on weekend nights.

Map 1 • River North / Fulton Market District

Carnival	702 W Fulton St	312-850-5050	$$$	11:30 pm	Authentic, soulful Latin fusion cuisine.
Iguana Café	517 N Halsted St	312-432-0663	$	2 am	Internet cafe with bagels and such.
Japonais	600 W Chicago Ave	312-822-9600	$$$	11:30 pm	Elegant, way-upscale Asian.
La Scarola	721 W Grand Ave	312-243-1740	$$	11 pm	Authentic Italian in a super-close atmosphere.
Reza's	432 W Ontario St	312-664-4500	$$$	12 am	Huge portions of Persian fare.
Scoozi!	410 W Huron St	312-943-5900	$$	10 pm	Once-trendy Italian has had its day.
Timo	464 N Halsted St	312-226-4300	$$$	11 pm	Eclectic eating in funky atmosphere.
Tony Rocco's River North	416 W Ontario St	312-787-1400	$$	11:30 pm	Italian home cooking and roasted chicken.
Zealous	419 W Superior St	312-475-9112	$$$$	10 pm	Over-the-top gourmet from Trotter protégé.

Map 2 • Near North / River North

1492 Tapas Bar	42 E Superior St	312-867-1492	$$	2 am	Tasty tapas in River North graystone.
Allen's New American Café	217 W Huron St	312-587-9600	$$$	11 pm	Innovative New American cuisine.
Avenues	Peninsula Hotel, 108 E Superior St	312-573-6754	$$$$$	11 pm	Sophisticated menu with a view.
Ballo	449 N Dearborn St	312-832-7700	$$$	12:30 am	Loud and clubby. Nonetheless, Italian food here is actually decent.
Ben Pao	52 W Illinois St	312-222-1888	$$	11 pm	Upscale Chinese spot.
Bijan's Bistro	663 N State St	312-202-1904	$$	3:30 am	Light, contemporary American fare.
Bin 36	339 N Dearborn St	312-755-9463	$$$	11 pm	Wine tastings and pairings.
Brasserie Jo	59 W Hubbard St	312-595-0800	$$$	11 pm	Swanky French.
Brett's Kitchen	233 W Superior St	312-664-6354	$	4 pm	Charming breakfast and sandwich stop.
Café Iberico	739 N La Salle Blvd	312-573-1510	$	1:30 am	Shoulder-to-shoulder tapas joint.
Carson's Ribs	612 N Wells St	312-280-9200	$$	11:30 pm	Immense barbecue pork chops that last for days!
Cerise	Le Meridien Hotel, 521 N Rush St	312-645-1500	$$$	11 pm	Precious, pretty food.
Chicago Chop House	60 W Ontario St	312-787-7100	$$$$$	11:30 pm	Old-school steaks meet old-school politicos and similar characters.
Club Lago	331 W Superior St	312-951-2849	$$	11 pm	Generous servings of basic Italian.
Coco Pazzo	300 W Hubbard St	312-836-0900	$$$$$	11 pm	Hearty, high-end Italian.
Crofton on Wells	535 N Wells St	312-755-1790	$$$	11 pm	Pushing the envelope with some top regional cuisine.
Cyrano's Bistrot & Wine Bar	546 N Wells St	312-467-0546	$$	10:30 pm	Steak frites!
David Burke's Primehouse	616 N Rush St	312-660-6000	$$$$$	12 am	Aged steaks by former Smith & Wollensky VP.
F212	401 N Wells St	312-670-4212	$$$	12 am	Scientific approach to dessert and espresso.
Fogo De Chao	661 N La Salle St	312-932-9330	$$$$	10 pm	The meatiest place on earth!
Frontera Grill	445 N Clark St	312-661-1434	$$	11 pm	Rick Bayless's famous cantina—expect to wait awhile.
Fulton's on the River	315 N La Salle St	312-822-0100	$$$$	11 pm	Best. Oysters. In. Chicago.
Gaylord Fine India Cuisine	678 N Clark St	312-664-1700	$	10 pm	Indian buffet.
Gene & Georgetti	500 N Franklin St	312-527-3718	$$$$$	12 am	Big steaks.
Gino's	633 N Wells St	312-943-1124	$$	11 pm	Legendary deep dish pizza since 1966.
Harry Caray's	33 W Kinzie St	312-828-0966	$$	11 pm	Tourist trap for suburban punters.
House of Blues	329 N Dearborn St	312-923-2007	$$	11 pm	Sunday gospel brunch buffet.
India House	59 W Grand Ave	312-645-9500	$$	11 pm	Best lunch buffet. Wear stretch pants.
Joe's Seafood, Prime Steak & Stone Crab	60 E Grand Ave	312-379-5637	$$$	11 pm	Part of popular Miami beach chain. Whatever.
Karyn's Cooked	738 N Wells St	312-587-1050	$$	10 pm	Hot food by the queen of raw food.
Keefer's	20 W Kinzie St	312-467-9525	$$$	11:30 pm	French-influenced steakhouse.
Kevin	9 W Hubbard St	312-595-0055	$$$		Promising new fusion.
Kinzie Chophouse	400 N Wells St	312-822-0191	$$$	11 pm	Neighborhood steak house.
Klay Oven	414 N Orleans St	312-527-3999	$$	10 pm	Upscale Indian buffet.
L8	222 W Ontario St	312-266-0616	$$$	3 am	Small plate cuisine in River North.
Lawry's The Prime Rib	100 E Ontario St	312-787-5000	$$$	11 pm	Carnivore's delight.
Lou Malnati's Pizzeria	439 N Wells St	312-828-9800	$	12 am	Famous in a city famous for pizza.
Maggiano's Little Italy	516 N Clark St	312-644-7700	$$	11 pm	Gut-busting family-style Italian.
Meztiso	710 N Wells St	312-274-9500	$$	12 am	Spanish-Mexican fusion spells Nuevo Pan Latino to me.
Mr Beef	666 N Orleans St	312-337-8500	$	2 pm	Get your Italian beef fix at this tried-and-true Chicago classic.
Nacional 27	325 W Huron St	312-664-2727	$$$	11 pm	Pan-Latin supper club with dance floor.

					Babaloo
Naha	500 N Clark St	312-321-6242	$$$$	n/a	Mediterranean-inspired luxury.
Narcisse	710 N Clark St	312-787-2675	$$$$	1 am	Dripping in luxury in a champagne, foie gras way.
Original Gino's East	633 N Wells St	312-943-1124	$	9 pm	Great for teenagers.
Osteria Via Stato	620 N State St	312-642-8450	$$$$	11 pm	Menu-oriented Italian. Fancy, but reasonably priced.
Oysy	50 E Grand Ave	312-670-6750	$$$	11:30 pm	River North sleek sushi outpost.
Pizzeria Due	619 N Wabash Ave	312-943-2400	$	2:30 am	Sister to Pizzeria Uno.
Pizzeria Uno	29 E Ohio St	312-321-1000	$	1 am	Legendary Chicago pizza.
Quartino	626 N State St	312-698-5000	$$$	12 am	Trendy Italian small plates and house-cured salami.
Redfish	400 N State St	312-467-1600	$$	12 am	Fun Cajun; free beads and good drinks.
Rosebud on Rush	720 N Rush St	312-266-6444	$$	12 am	A branch of Chicago's legendary, old-school Italian.
Roy's	720 N State St	312-787-7599	$$$	10 pm	Pretty Hawaiian contemporary cuisine.
Rumba	351 W Hubbard St	312-222-1226	$$	12 am	Burgers, fries, the regular.
Ruth's Chris Steak House	431 N Dearborn St	312-321-2725	$$	11:30 pm	Consistent steak chain.
Shanghai Terrace	Peninsula Hotel, 108 E Superior St	312-573-6744	$$$$	11 pm	The city's most extravagant Chinese restaurant.
Shaw's Crab House & Blue Crab Lounge	21 E Hubbard St	312-527-2722	$$$$	11 pm	A seafood destination.
Smith & Wollensky	318 N State St	312-670-9900	$$$$	11 pm	Chicago branch of New York steak emporium.
Sorriso	321 N Clark St	312-644-0283	$$$	11 pm	Uninspired Italian with Riverfront view.
Star of Siam	11 E Illinois St	312-670-0100	$	10:45 pm	Thai—heard the quality's gone down.
Sullivan's Steakhouse	415 N Dearborn St	312-527-3510	$$$$	11 pm	Another upscale steakhouse.
Sushi Naniwa	607 N Wells St	312-255-8555	$$	11 pm	Quality sushi. Great outdoor.
Sushisamba Rio	504 N Wells St	312-595-2300	$$$	2 am	Riding the Brazilian sushi craze.
Tizi Melloul	531 N Wells St	312-670-4338	$$$	11 pm	Exotic setting for Moroccan tangines.
Topolobampo	445 N Clark St	312-661-1434	$$$$	10:30 pm	Standard bearer for upscale Mexican.
Vermillion	10 W Hubbard St	312-527-4060	$$$	11 pm	Indian-Latin fusion—what next?
Vong's Thai Kitchen	6 W Hubbard St	312-644-8664	$$	11 pm	Thai with a satisfying kick.
Weber Grill	Hilton Garden Inn, 539 N State St	312-467-9696	$$	11:45 pm	Weird Weber Grill-themed concept place.
Wildfire	159 W Erie St	312-787-9000	$$	11 pm	Fun, trendy American.

Map 3 • Streeterville / Mag Mile

Bandera	535 N Michigan Ave	312-644-3524	$$	11 pm	Lunch above Mag Mile.
Benihana of Tokyo	166 E Superior St	312-664-9643	$$	11 pm	Tepanyaki chain.
Billy Goat Tavern	430 N Michigan Ave	312-222-1525	$*	2 am	Cheezboiga; no fries, chips; pepsi, no coke.
Capital Grille	633 N St Clair St	312-337-9400	$$$$	11 pm	Macho steak and zin.
City	Lake Point Tower, 505 N Lake Shore Dr, 70th Fl	312-644-4050	$$$$	11 pm	Contemporary with a view.
Copperblue	505 N Lake Shore Dr	312-527-1200	$$$$	11:30 pm	Contemporary American in chic locale yet not crazy pretentious.
Dick's Last Resort	435 E Illinois St	312-836-7870	$$	1:45 am	Tourist's last memory of the night.
Emilio's Tapas Sol y Nieve	215 E Ohio St	312-467-7177	$$$	12 am	One of the nicest branches of the local tapas chain.
Fox & Obel Café	401 E Illinois St	312-379-0112	$$	9 pm	Creative café grub with gourmet ingredients from next-door market.
Heaven on Seven	600 N Michigan Ave	312-280-7774	$$	11 pm	Cajun grub and cocktails.
Hot Diggity Dogs	251 E Ohio St	312-943-5598	$*	5 pm	Walk-up chicawga dawgs.
Indian Garden	247 E Ontario St	312-280-4910	$$	10:30 pm	Good veggie options.
Kamehachi	240 E Ontario St	312-587-0600	$$	12 am	Old school sushi spot.
Les Nomades	222 E Ontario St	312-649-9010	$$$$$	10 pm	Deluxe haute cuisine.
Nomi	Park Hyatt 800 N Michigan Ave	312-239-4030	$$$$$	12 am	Deluxe French fusion.
Ron of Japan	230 E Ontario St	312-644-6500	$$$	10 pm	Guilty pleasure teppanyaki.
Sayat Nova	157 E Ohio St	312-644-9159	$$	10 pm	Armenian.
Tru	676 N St Clair St	312-202-0001	$$$$$	11 pm	Dazzling contemporary cuisine.
Volare	201 E Grand Ave	312-410-9900	$$$	11 pm	Casual Italian.
Wave	644 N Lake Shore Dr	312-255-4460	$$$	11 pm	Trendy W Hotel gruberie is making a...you guessed it.

Map 4 • West Loop Gate / Greek Town

Artopolis Bakery & Café	306 S Halsted St	312-559-9000	$$	1 am	Frappes to Mediterranean pizza.
Athena	212 S Halsted St	312-655-0000	$$$	1 am	Goddess Athena-inspired outdoor and indoor.

Map 4 • West Loop Gate / Greek Town*-continued*

Avec	615 W Randolph St	312-377-2002	$$	1 am	Small plates, big flavors, chefs' hangout.
Blackbird	619 W Randolph St	312-715-0708	$$$$	11:30 pm	Chic les plus ultra.
Butter	130 S Green St	312-666-9813	$$$$	11 pm	As in "smooth as…" at this upscale eatery.
Costa's	340 S Halsted St	312-263-9700	$$$	12 am	Greece at its warmest. Have the octopus.
Dine	733 W Madison St	312-602-2100	$$$	11 pm	Martinis and comfort food at the Crowne Plaza.
Extra Virgin	741 W Randolph St	312-474-0700	$$	12 am	Italian wine bar/small plates.
Gold Coast Dogs	Union Station, 225 S Canal St	312-258-8585	$*	10 pm	Gotta have the dogs.
Greek Islands	200 S Halsted St	312-782-9855	$$$	1 am	Greek Heaven—not to be missed.
J&C Inn	558 W Van Buren St	312-663-4114	$$$	2 pm	Dingy outside—best sandwiches in town inside.
Lou Mitchell's	565 W Jackson Blvd	312-939-3111	$*	3 pm	Rub shoulders with local pols at this legendary grill.
Nine	440 W Randolph St	312-575-9900	$$$	12 am	Toast marshmallows at the table at this ultra-trendy contemporary spot.
Nine Muses	315 S Halsted St	312-902-9922	$$$	1 am	Brick bars and backgammon.
Parthenon	314 S Halsted St	312-726-2407	$$$	1 am	Creators of flaming saganaki!
Pegasus Restaurant and Taverna	130 S Halsted St	312-226-4666	$$$	12:45 am	Rooftop garden—Chicago secret!
Red Light	820 W Randolph St	312-733-8880	$$$$	12 am	Fusion of Asian dishes in a oriental atmosphere.
Robinson's No 1 Ribs	Union Station, 225 S Canal St	312-258-8477	$*	7:30 pm	Dress down and dig in.
Rodity's	222 S Halsted St	312-454-0800	$$$	1 am	Greek lamb since 1972.
Santorini	800 W Adams St	312-829-8820	$$$	1 am	Fish, shellfish, and roasted chicken. Yum.
Starfish	804 W Randolph St	312-997-2433	$$	11:30 pm	Flamboyant sushi place.
Sushi Wabi	842 W Randolph St	312-563-1224	$$$	12 am	Self-consciously chic sushi.

Map 5 • The Loop

Atwood Café	1 W Washington St	312-368-1900	$$$	11 pm	High tea with contemporary flair.
Barro Cantina	73 E Lake St	312-346-8457	$$	10 pm	Standard Mexican margarita grub.
Billy Goat Tavern	330 S Wells St	312-554-0297	$*	4 pm	Cheezboiga joint made famous by SNL. Awesome.
Everest	440 S La Salle St	312-663-8920	$$$$$	10:45 pm	Classic fine dining experience with a knock-out view.
Gold Coast Dogs	159 N Wabash Ave	312-917-1677	$*	6 pm	Classic dog joint.
Gold Coast Dogs	17 S Wabash Ave	312-578-1133	$*	7 pm	Onion peppers, pickle spear, tomato, celery salt, mustard.
Hannah's Bretzel	180 W Washington St	312-621-1111	$	6 pm	Homemade pretzels and organic lunch fare.
Heaven on Seven	111 N Wabash Ave	312-263-6443	$$	5 pm	Cajun Chicago classic. Closed for dinner.
Italian Village	71 W Monroe St	312-332-4040	$$$	1 am	Comprised of three Italian restaurants.
Kamehachi	311 S Wacker Dr	312-765-8700	$$	3 pm	South Loop outpost of popular local sushi chain.
La Cantina Enoteca	Italian Village Restaurant Complex, 71 W Monroe St	312-332-7005	$$	12 am	Casual Italian with seafood specialty.
La Rosetta	70 W Madison St	312-332-9500	$$	9 pm	Family-style Italian.
Miller's Pub	134 S Wabash Ave	312-263-4988	$$	2 am	Down-to-earth grub in a pub.
Mrs Levy's Delicatessen	Sears Tower, 233 S Wacker Dr	312-993-0530	$		No surprises here.
Nick's Fishmarket & Grill	51 S Clark St	312-621-0200	$$$	11 pm	Power lunch.
Oasis Café	21 N Wabash Ave	312-558-1058	$$*	4 pm	Middle Eastern hideout inside of a jewelry store.
Plymouth Restaurant	327 S Plymouth Ct		$	24 hrs	24-hour diner with bar and grill.
Rhapsody	Symphony Ctr, 65 E Adams St	312-786-9911	$$$	9 pm	Upscale pre-symphony grub.
Russian Tea Time	71 W Monroe St	312-360-0000	$$$	12 am	Rich food. Richer interior. Copious amounts of vodka.
Spa Café	112 W Monroe St	312-551-0000	$	4 pm	It's like you're staying at an exclusive spa, except, not quite.
Trattoria No 10	10 N Dearborn St	312-984-1718	$$$	10 pm	Elegant Italian.
The Village	Italian Village	312-332-7005	$$	12:30 am	Quaint, casual Italian looks like a village.
Vivere	71 W Monroe St	312-332-4040	$$$	10:30 pm	Dated Italian luxury.

Map 6 • The Loop / Grant Park

Aria	Fairmont Chicago Hotel, 200 N Columbus Dr	312-444-9494	$$$$	11 pm	Artistic, creative pan-global grub.
Artist's Café	412 S Michigan Ave	312-939-7855	$$†	11 pm	Sit at the counter. They've got the chattiest waiters in town.
Bennigan's	150 S Michigan Ave	312-427-0577	$$	1:30 am	The busiest Bennigan's in the world! Yetch.
China Grill	Hard Rock Hotel, 230 N Michigan Ave	312-334-6700	$$$$$	11 pm	Les So Very Tres.
Park Grill	11 N Michigan Ave	312-521-7275	$$$	10:30 pm	Contemporary American cooking in Millenium Park.

Map 7 • South Loop / River City

Bake for Me	608 W Roosevelt Rd	312-957-1994	$	2 pm	Good coffee and pastries.
Manny's Coffee Shop	1141 S Jefferson St	312-939-2855	$	4 pm	Famous deli—popular with politicians.
White Palace Grill	1159 S Canal St	312-939-7167	$	24 hrs	An ode to grease, and some fine omelettes to boot.

Map 8 • South Loop / Printers Row / Dearborn Park

Blackie's	755 S Clark St	312-786-1161	$*	10 pm	A famous burger, lesser-known best breakfast in South Loop on Fri, Sat, Sun.
Custom House	500 S Dearborn St	312-523-0200	$$$$	10 pm	Shaun McClain does steak house.
Eleven City Diner	1112 S Wabash Ave	312-212-1112	$$	3 am	Traditional Jewish deli.
Hackney's	733 S Dearborn St	312-461-1116	$$	11:30 pm	A specialty burger and onion loaf; a northshore legend since 1939.
South Loop Club	701 S State St	312-427-2787	$††	4:30 am	Very casual bar restaurant with surprisingly good kitchen.
SRO	610 S Dearborn St	312-360-1776	$$*	8 pm	Great kitchen boasting Chicago's #1 Turkey Burger.
Trattoria Caterina	616 S Dearborn St	312-939-7606	$$	9 pm	A little touch of Italy, and a great value for Italian cuisine.

Map 9 • South Loop / South Michigan Ave

Oysy	888 S Michigan Ave	312-922-1127	$$$	11 pm	Chic, industrial sushi setting.

Map 10 • East Pilsen / Chinatown

Emperor's Choice	2238 S Wentworth Ave	312-225-8800	$	12 am	Start with seafood; finish with tea.
Evergreen	2411 S Wentworth Ave	312-225-8898	$$	12 am	More upscale than most Chinatown grub.
Happy Chef Dim Sum House	2164 S Archer Ave	312-808-3689	$	2 am	Entrees priced to try several dishes.
Joy Yee's Noodle Shop	2159 Chinatown Sq	312-328-0001	$	10:30 pm	Huge portions of Korean and Chinese, plus bubble tea.
Lao Sze Chuan Spicy City	2172 S Archer Ave	312-326-5040	$	12 am	Authentic Chinese dishes plus great evening karaoke.
Penang	2201 S Wentworth Ave	312-326-6888	$	1 am	Malaysian favorites.
Phoenix	2131 S Archer Ave	312-328-0848	$	11 pm	The best Chinese breakfast in town.
Three Happiness	209 W Cermak Rd	312-842-1964	$	7 am	Long waits for dim sum.
Won Kow	2237 S Wentworth Ave	312-842-7500	$	12 am	Cheap, tasty dim sum.

Map 11 • South Loop / McCormick Place

Chef Luciano	49 E Cermak Rd	312-326-0062	$*	7 pm	Walk-in restaurant with eclectic entrees; Italian/African/Cajun influences.
Chicago Firehouse Restaurant	1401 S Michigan Ave	312-786-1401	$$$$	10:30 pm	Transformed Chicago firehouse complete with pole and fine dining.
Cuatro	2030 S Wabash Ave	312-842-8856	$$$	11 pm	Trendy atmosphere for pan-Latin grub.
Gioco	1312 S Wabash Ave	312-939-3870	$$$	12 am	Great Italian dining.
Kroll's	1736 S Michigan Ave	312-235-1400	$$	2 am	Chicago outpost of Green Bay grill. Packers Backers better watch their backs.
NetWorks	Hyatt Regency, 2231 S Dr Martin L King Jr Dr	312-567-1234	$$	10 pm	Contemporary American with a focus on Chicago specialties.
Opera	1301 S Wabash Ave	312-461-0161	$$$	12 am	Theatrical Asian grub.
Triad	1933 S Indiana Ave	312-225-8833	$$$	11:30 pm	Guess what? Another sleek sushi lounge.
Wells on Wells	1617 N Wells St	312-944-1617	$$	2 am	Two words: pretzel buns.
Zapatista	1307 S Wabash Ave	312-435-1307	$$	11 pm	Fancified Mexican food in big, loud environment.

Map 13 • Bridgeport (East)

Franco's Ristorante	300 W 31st St	312-225-9566	$$	10 pm	Family-style Italian near Sox park.
Freddie's Pizza & Pasta Parlor	701 W 31st St	312-808-0149	$	11 pm	Italian ice, beef sandwiches, and appropriate attitude.
Gio's	2724 S Lowe Ave	312-225-6368	$	9 pm	BYO Italian deli with groceries.
Kevin's Hamburger Heaven	554 W 39th St	773-924-5771	$*	24 hrs	Hamburgers and milkshakes.
Metropolis Rotisseria	924 W Armitage Ave	773-868-9000	$$	9:30 pm	Chicken shack next to the train tracks.
Phil's Pizza	3551 S Halsted St	773-523-0947	$*	1:30 am	Pizza-rific.
Ramova Grill	3510 S Halsted St	773-847-9058	$*	5 pm	Old-school diner.
Wing Yip Chop Suey	537 W 26th St	312-326-2822	$*	9 pm	Nader bumper sticker on window.

Map 14 • Prairie Shores / Lake Meadows

Blue Sea Drive Inn	427 E Pershing Rd	773-285-3325	$*	12 am	Fast food and carry out.
Chicago Rib House	3851 S Michigan Ave	773-268-8750	$*	11:30 pm	It is named like that for a reason. All day lunch.
Hong Kong Delight	327 E 35th St	312-842-2929	$$*	10 pm	Not quite like being there, but close enough.
McDonald's	207 E 35th St	312-842-8040	$	10 pm	Features memorabilia from mid-20th century civil rights movement, owner marched with King.

Map 16 • Bronzeville

Barbara's	353 E 51st St	773-624-0087	$*	6 pm	Soul breakfast and lunch.
Harold's Chicken Shack	108 E 47th St	773-285-8362	$*	4 am	It may say #7 but it is #1 around here.
Harold's Chicken Shack	307 E 51st St	773-373-9016	$*	4 am	Fries, bread, and chicken.
Negro League Café	301 E 43rd St	773-536-7000	$$$	2 am	Where black baseball history stokes up a new Bronzeville Renaissance.

Map 17 • Kenwood

Fung's Chop Suey	1400 E 47th St	773-924-2328	$*	10:30 pm	When you're thinking delivery.
Kenny's Ribs & Chicken	1461 E Hyde Park Blvd	773-241-5550	$	2 am	Cheap and good to go.
Lake Shore Café	4900 S Lake Shore Dr	773-288-5800	$$	10 pm	Basic hotel food.
The Original Pancake House	1517 E Hyde Park Blvd	773-288-2323	$*	5 pm	A pancake style for every person.

Map 18 • Washington Park

Ms Lee's Good Food	205 E Garfield Blvd	773-752-5253	$*	11 pm	Soul food carry-out by ex-Gladys' Luncheonette.
Rose's BBQ Chicken	5426 S State St	773-268-3401	$*	1 am	Don't mind the floor, it's the sauce.

Map 19 • Hyde Park

Bonjour Café Bakery	1550 E 55th St	773-241-5300	$	6 pm	Have a pastry and be seen.
C'Est Si Bon	5225 S Harper Ave	773-363-4123	$$	3 pm	Go for Sunday Brunch.
Calypso Café	Harper Ctr, 5211 S Harper Ave	773-955-0229	$$	11 pm	Good Caribbean. Great drinks.
Cedars Mediterranean Kitchen	1206 E 53rd St	773-324-6227	$$	10 pm	Great food, horrible service.
Daley's Restaurant	809 E 63rd St	773-643-6670	$$*	9 pm	The mayor ought to try this place.
Dixie Kitchen and Bait Shop	5225 S Harper Ave	773-363-4943	$$	11 pm	A little taste of the South.
Hyde Park Gyros	1368 E 53rd St	773-947-8229	$*	10 pm	Gyros and Fried Mushrooms—yum!
Kikuya Japanese Restaurant	1601 E 55th St	773-667-3727	$$	9:30 pm	Best sushi in the neighborhood.
La Petite Folie	Hyde Park Shopping Ctr, 1504 E 55th St	773-493-1394	$$$$	8:30 pm	The only haute cuisine in the neighborhood. Expensive and worth it.
Maravilla's Mexican Restaurant	5211 S Harper Ave	773-643-3155	$	11 pm	Cheap, good Mexican. Stinging salsa. Open real late.
Medici on 57th	1327 E 57th St	773-667-7394	$	12 am	The essence of life at U of C.
Mellow Yellow	1508 E 53rd St	773-667-2000	$	11 pm	Comfort food for morning and night.
Nathan's	1372 E 53rd St	773-288-5353	$	10 pm	A taste of Jamaica.
Noodles Etc	1333 E 53rd St	773-947-8787	$	10 pm	More collegiate than the original.
Ribs N Bibs	5300 S Dorchester Ave	773-493-0400	$	1 am	Finger lickin'. Wear the bib.
Salonica	1440 E 57th St	773-752-3899	$*	9:30 pm	Where to go the morning after.
Thai 55 Restaurant	1607 E 55th St	773-363-7119	$	10 pm	Good Americanized Thai.
Valois	1518 E 53rd St	773-667-0647	$*	10 pm	See Your Food.

Map 20 • East Hyde Park / Jackson Park

Café Corea	1603 E 55th St	773-288-1795	$*	9 pm	Cozy café.
Marina Café	6401 S Coast Guard Dr	773-947-0400	$$$	10 pm	Boaters order dockside. Live jazz on Weekends.
Morry's Deli	5500 S Cornell Ave	773-363-3800	$*	7:45 pm	Good on the go.
Nile Restaurant	1611 E 55th St	773-324-9499	$	9 pm	Varied Middle Eastern.
Orly's Café	1660 E 55th St	773-643-5500	$	n/a	Stick to the Mexican. Have a margarita.
Piccolo Mondo	1642 E 56th St	773-643-1106	$$	9:30 pm	Best Italian in the area.
Siam Thai Cuisine	1639 E 55th St	773-324-9296	$	10 pm	More Thai in Hyde Park.
Snail's Thai Cuisine	1649 E 55th St	773-667-5423	$††	10 pm	Great Hyde Park Thai.

Map 21 • Wicker Park / Ukrainian Village

Adobo Grill	2005 W Division St	773-252-9990	$$$$	11:30 pm	Upscale Mexican for yuppies.
Bin Wine Café	1559 N Milwaukee Ave	773-486-2233	$$	2 am	Casual swirl and nosh.
Blue Line Club Car	1548 N Damen Ave	773-395-3700	$$	2 am	Mix a diner with a Martini club and here you go.
Bluefin	1952 W North Ave	773-394-7373	$$$	11 pm	Upscale, trendy sushi bar.
Bob San	1805 W Division St	773-235-8888	$$$$	12:30 pm	Youthful sushi joint.
The Bongo Room	1470 N Milwaukee Ave	773-489-0690	$	2 pm	Great breakfast spot, expect to wait on weekends.
Café Ballou	939 N Western Ave	773-342-2909	$*	7 pm	Old-world-style coffeehouse.
Cleo's	1935 W Chicago Ave	312-243-5600	$	1 am	Off the beaten Wicker Park/East Village path. Polished with local attitude.
Cold Comfort Café & Deli	2211 W North Ave	773-772-4552	$$	4 pm	Freshly made deli sandwiches; groceries.
Cooking Fools	1916 W North Ave	773-276-5565	$$	9 pm	Gourmet café/catering.
D'Vine Restaurant & Wine Bar	1950 W North Ave	773-235-5700	$$$$	3 am	Another place to be seen and blow your paycheck.
Del Toro	1520 N Damen Ave	773-252-1500	$$$	2 am	Hipster spot for small plate Spanish kweezine.
Dodo	935 N Damen Ave	773-772-3636	$	4 pm	Adventurous breakfast and lunch options.
Earwax	1561 N Milwaukee Ave	773-772-4019	$††	10:30 pm	Wicker Park staple and eclectic health food mecca.
Enoteca Roma Winebar & Bruschetteria	2144 W Division St	773-342-1011	$$	11 pm	Wine bar/ Italian café.
Feast	1616 N Damen Ave	773-772-7100	$$$	11 pm	Popular for Sunday brunch.
Flash Taco	1570 N Damen Ave	773-772-1997	$*	5 am	Cheap late-night tacos.
Francesca's Forno	1576 N Milwaukee Ave	773-770-0184	$$$	12 am	Rustic Italian from the Mia Francesca empire.
Green Ginger	2050 W Division St	773-486-6700	$$$	11 pm	Asian-fusion as hip as it is tasty.
Half & Half	1560 N Damen Ave	773-489-6220	$$	7 pm	Breakfast "cuisine."
Handlebar	2311 W North Ave	773-384-9546	$$	12 am	Bicycle-themed (largely) vegetarian restaurants decorated with off-duty messengers.
Hilary's Urban Eatery	1630 W Division St	773-235-4327	$$	10 pm	Salmon cakes to die for.
Iggy's	1840 W North Ave	773-227-4449	$$$	2 am	Old-world bordello meets new-world metal and neon.
Las Palmas	1835 W North Ave	773-289-4991	$	12 pm	Great al fresco dining and atrium seating.
Leona's	1936 W Augusta Blvd	773-292-4300	$	12 am	Local chain restaurant. Sub-par food, even worse service.
Mas	1670 W Division St	773-276-8700	$$	11:30 pm	Stylish Latin cooking, dinner only.
Milk & Honey	1920 W Division St	773-395-9434	$	5 pm	Heaven for breakfast.
Mirai Sushi	2020 W Division St	773-862-8500	$$	11 pm	Chic dining and good sushi.
Moonshine	1824 W Division St	773-862-8686	$$	12:30 am	Auto repair garage turned vintage barn with neon lights and televisions!
Oberweis Ice Cream and Dairy Store	1293 N Milwaukee Ave	773-276-9006	$	11 pm	Ice cream hot spot owned by conservative Republican gubernatorial also-ran.
Pacific Café	1619 N Damen Ave	773-862-1988	$$	11 pm	Inexpensive sushi/Japanese.
Papajin Chinese & Sushi Bar	1551 N Milwaukee Ave	773-384-9600	$$	12 am	Chinese/sushi.
Parlor	1745 W North Ave	773-782-9000	$$$	3 am	Pseudo-swank, contemporary-classic, American eater with mostly American wine list.
Paje	1332 N Milwaukee Ave	773-395-1313	$$	n/a	Upmarket soul food for R Kelly's *Trapped in the Closet* cohorts.
Penny's Noodle Shop	1542 N Damen Ave	773-394-0100	$	10:30 pm	Cheap Thai.
People Lounge	1560 N Milwaukee Ave	773-227-9339	$$	2 pm	Traditional tapas with international groove.
Picante	2016 W Division St	773-328-8800	$*	3:30 am	Very very very very very small taqueria.

Map 21 • Wicker Park / Ukrainian Village–*continued*

Piece	1927 W North Ave	773-772-4422	$$	12:30 am	"Designer" pizza joint.
Pot Pan Thai	1750 W North Ave	773-862-6990	$	11 pm	Cheap noodle shop.
Sigara Hookah Café & Lounge	2013 W Division St	773-292-9190	$	2:30 pm	Middle Eastern coffee, smokes, and eats.
Smoke Daddy	1804 W Division St	773-772-6656	$	1 am	Barbecue and blues.
Spring	2039 W North Ave	773-395-7100	$$$$	10:30 pm	Vogue, overpriced Asian-inspired seafood by Shaun McClain.
Sultan's Market	2057 W North Ave	773-235-3072	$*	9 pm	Cheap Middle Eastern, groceries.
Thai Lagoon	2322 W North Ave	773-489-5747	$$	11 pm	Great Thai, funky atmosphere.
Thai Village	2053 W Division St	773-384-5352	$		Cheap, tasty, and great outdoor seating.
Tre Via	1575 N Milwaukee Ave	773-227-7990	$$$	1 am	Ambitious Italian with many comfort-food options.

Map 22 • Noble Square / Goose Island

Corosh	1072 N Milwaukee Ave	773-235-0600	$$	1 am	Italian and pub fare, great patio.
El Barco Mariscos Seafood	1035 N Ashland Blvd	773-486-6850	$$	12 am	Outdoor seating, terrific ceviche.
Luc Thang	1524 N Ashland Blvd	773-395-3907	$††	11 pm	Thai with Chinese and Vietnamese touches.
NYC Bagel	1001 W North Ave	312-274-1278	$	5 pm	NY-style deli, best egg salad in the city.
Rudy's Taste	1024 N Ashland Ave	773-252-3666	$$	10 pm	Tasty, cheap, authentic Guatemalan home cooking.
Sangria Restaurant and Tapas Bar	901 W Weed St	312-266-1200	$$	2 am	Specialty sangria and contemporary tapas in bright, lively room.
Schwa	1466 N Ashland Ave	773-252-1466	$$$$	10:30 pm	Innovative fine dining with a hipster vibe.

Map 23 • West Town / Near West Side

A Tavola	2148 W Chicago Ave	773-276-7567	$$$	10:30 pm	Upscale Italian charm in an intimate setting.
China Dragon Restaurant	2008 W Madison St	312-666-3766	$$*	10:30 pm	Dependably fantastic Chinese.
Il Jack's Italian Restaurant	1758 W Grand Ave	312-421-7565	$$	11:30 pm	Neighborhood Italian with Sopranos feel.
Old Lviv	2228 W Chicago Ave	773-772-7250	$*	8 pm	Eastern European buffet.
Tecalitlan Restaurant	1814 W Chicago Ave	773-384-4285	$	2 am	Popular family-style, Mexican restaurant.

Map 24 • River West / West Town

160 Blue	1400 W Randolph St	312-850-0303	$$$	11 pm	Ameri-French owned by Michael Jordan.
Amelia's Mexican Grille	1235 W Grand Ave	312-421-2000	$$	11 pm	OK food, outside seating can get quite noisy.
Amore Ristorante	1330 W Madison St	312-829-3333	$$$	2 am	Eat Italian cuisine while listening to live music.
Aroma	941 W Randolph St	312-492-7889	$	11 pm	Busy Thai Restaurants serving up the yummies. They do delivery.
Avenue M	695 N Milwaukee Ave	312-243-1133	$$$$	2 pm	High-end steaks and chops.
Bella Notte	1374 W Grand Ave	312-733-5136	$$$$	11:30 pm	Romantic, Italian, and schmoozy.
Billy Goat Tavern	1535 W Madison St	312-733-9132	$*	11 pm	Cheezeboiga chain.
Bombon Café	38 S Ashland Ave	312-733-8717	$	8 pm	Upscale tortas in a bright sunny setting!
Breakfast Club	1381 W Hubbard St	312-666-3166	$$	3 pm	Brunch and then some.
Buongiorno Café	1123 W Grand Ave	312-829-7433	$	5 pm	Yet another Italian café to choose your paninis from your ponzeros.
Burger Baron	1381 W Grand Ave	312-733-3285	$	8:30 pm	Burgers and beer for the Everyman.
Butterfly Sushi Bar and Thai Cuisine	1156 W Grand Ave	312-563-5555	$$	11 pm	Cute BYOB sushi storefront in the East Village.
Cannella's on Grand	1132 W Grand Ave	312-433-9400	$$$$	11 pm	Long standing fine-dining favorite.
Carmichael's Chicago Steak House	1052 W Monroe St	312-433-0025	$$$$	12 am	Great steaks in a vintage style dining room.
D'Agostino's Pizzeria	752 N Ogden Ave	312-850-3247	$	12 am	Cheezy take on the Italian family restaurants.
D'Amotos Italian Bakery	1124 W Grand Ave	312-733-5456	$*	6 pm	Old Italy's finest baked goods to go, amazing focaccia bread.
De Cero	814 W Randolph St	312-455-8114	$$$	11 pm	Made-to-order tacos, fresh fruit cocktail, Mexican heaven.
Dragonfly Mandarin Restaurants	832 W Randolph St	312-787-7600	$$$	3 am	This place can't seem to land anywhere; more dance club than anything.
Fan Si Pan	1618 W Chicago Ave	312-738-1405	$$$††	9 pm	Extra-fresh Vietnamese and Laotian food.
Flo	1434 W Chicago Ave	312-243-0477	$$	n/a	Mexican-influenced breakfast in a relaxed atmosphere.
Follia	953 W Fulton St	312-243-2888	$$$	1 am	Swanky, upscale Italian.

Green Zebra	1460 W Chicago Ave	312-243-7100	$$$$	11 pm	Innovative and mostly vegetarian, by Spring's Shawn McClain.
Hacienda Tecalitlan	820 N Ashland Blvd	312-243-6667	$$	12 am	Beautiful, authentic interior with amazing margaritas.
Ina's	1235 W Randolph St	312-226-8227	$$$	10 pm	Special occasion breakfasts. Try the scrapple—it's better than it sounds.
Jak's Tap	901 W Jackson Blvd	312-666-1700	$$	2 am	College kids blend with businessmen over a pitcher of beer
Jerry's Sandwiches	1045 W Madison St	312-563-1008	$	4 pm	Fresh and slightly gourmet concoctions.
La Sardine	111 N Carpenter St	312-421-2800	$$	11 pm	Tuesdays fixed price for $20!
Le Peep Grill	1000 W Washington Blvd	312-563-9990	$	2:30 pm	Flurry of brunch options, sunny color scheme, outdoor seating.
Marche	833 W Randolph St	312-226-8399	$$$	12 am	Theatrical French brasserie dining.
May Street Market	1132 W Grand Ave	312-421-5547	$$$	11 pm	American / Global fusion with foam and such.
Misto	1118 W Grand Ave	312-226-5989	$$$$	11 pm	Contemporary Italian cuisine, but more popular bar.
Moretti's	1645 W Jackson Blvd	312-850-0208	$	4:30 am	Pizzeria with garden patio.
Moto	945 W Fulton Market	312-491-0058	$$$$	11 pm	Conceptual laboratory food creations.
Oggi Trattoria Café	1378 W Grand Ave	312-733-0442	$$	9 pm	One of the godfathers of the neighborhood.
Rushmore	1023 W Lake St	312-421-8845	$$$$	10:30 pm	Sophisticated comfort.
Salerno's Pizza and Pasta	1201 W Grand Ave	312-666-3444	$	11 pm	Tony Soprano would be proud, and full.
Saultaus	1350 W Randolph St	312-455-1919	$$$$	12:30 pm	Pretentious lounge with fancy food.
Silver Palm	768 N Milwaukee Ave	312-666-9322	$$$	2 am	Dine in a 1940s train car on upscale American food.
Sushi X	1136 W Chicago Ave	312-491-9232	$$	12 am	Speakeasy sushi bar with fish so fresh they swim to your plate. BYOB.
Swim Café	1357 W Chicago Ave	312-492-8600	$	6 pm	Fresh, homemade breakfast and lunch fair with aquatic theme.
Twisted Spoke	501 N Ogden Ave	312-666-1500	$	3 am	Famous for serving smut movies and eggs simultaneously.
Union Park	228 S Racine Ave	312-243-9002	$	12 am	Clubby groove with bar food.
Vinnie's Sandwich Shop	1204 W Grand Ave	312-738-2985	$	5 pm	No frills, handy for construction workers.
Vivo	838 W Randolph St	312-733-3379	$$$$	12 am	Restaurants Row's first residence of Italian dining.
West Town Tavern	1329 W Chicago Ave	312-666-6175	$$$	10 pm	Home cooking if you're fancy and have a lot of time on your hands.
Windy City Café	1062 W Chicago Ave	312-492-8010	$	4 pm	Small town diner feel and menu, grab a booth.
Wishbone	1001 W Washington Blvd	312-850-2663	$$	10 pm	Comfort food, comfort folks.

Map 25 • Illinois Medical District

Carnitas Uruapan Restaurant	1725 W 18th St	312-226-2654	$*	5 pm	Carnitas muy necesitas.
Chicago Chocolate Café	847 W Randolph St	312-738-0888	$	12 am	Hot chocolate served five ways.
Damenzo's	2324 W Taylor St	312-421-1142	$	1 am	Pizza, pizza puffs, small bar.
El Charco Verde	2255 W Taylor St	312-738-1686	$	10 pm	A Mexican favorite.
Ferrara Bakery	2210 W Taylor St	312-666-2200	$	6 pm	Serving Italian pastries since 1908.
Lu-Lu's Hot Dogs	1000 S Leavitt St	312-243-3444	$*	1 am	Hot Dawg!
TJ's Family Restaurant	1928 W Cermak Rd	773-927-3349	$*	10 pm	Neighborhood diner.

Map 26 • University Village/ Little Italy / Pilsen

Al's Number 1 Italian Beef	1079 W Taylor St	312-226-4017	$*	1 am	Where's the beef? Right here.
Birreria Reyes de Ocotlan	1322 W 18th St	312-733-2613	$$*	9 pm	Mexican.
Caffe La Scala	626 S Racine Ave	312-421-7262	$$$	11 pm	Upscale Italian near United Center.
Carm's Beef and Snack Shop	1057 W Polk St	312-738-1046	$*	4:30 pm	Italian subs and sausages.
Chez Joel	1119 W Taylor St	312-226-6479	$$$	11 pm	Delicious French cuisine in Little Italy.
Couscous	1445 W Taylor St	312-226-2408	$$††	9:30 pm	Middle Eastern and Maghrebin Cuisine. Unique falafel.
De Pasada	1519 W Taylor St	312-243-6441	$	12 pm	Inexpensive, good quality Mexican—friendly staff.
Demitasse	1066 W Taylor St	312-226-7669	$	3 pm	Delightful breakfast spot.
Francesca's	1400 W Taylor St	312-829-2828	$$	11 pm	Loud, bustling dining room.
Golden Thai	1509 W Taylor St	312-733-0760	$	10 pm	Always busy, but there's better Thai out there.
Japonica	1422 W Taylor St	312-421-3288	$$	11 pm	Sushi ventures into Little Italy.
Kohan Japanese Restaurant	730 W Maxwell St	312-421-6254	$$	11 pm	Sushi for UIC students.
La Cebollita	1723 S Ashland Ave	312-492-8443	$*	10 pm	Gorditas, sopas, to dine-in or carry out.
La Vita	1359 W Taylor St	312-491-1414	$$$	11 pm	Date-spot for northern Italian
Mario's Italian Lemonade	1068 W Taylor St	n/a	$*	n/a	Seasonal '60s lemonade shack.

Map 26 • University Village/ Little Italy / Pilsen—*continued*

May Street Café	1136 W Cermak Rd	312-421-4442	$	10:30 pm	Inexpensive, super casual pan-Latin.
New Rosebud Café	1500 W Taylor St	312-942-1117	$	11:30 pm	Popular with the United Center crowd.
Nuevo Leon	1515 W 18th St	312-421-1517	$*	4 am	Real-deal Mexican grub in Pilsen.
Pizza Tango	1013 W 18th St	312-421-2111	$	10 pm	Argentinean-style thin crust pizza.
Playa Azul	1514 W 18th St	312-421-2552	$$*	12 am	Seafood à la Mexicaine.
Sweet Maple Café	1339 W Taylor St	312-243-8908	$	2 pm	Super-homey breakfast, homemade biscuits.
Taj Mahal	1512 W Taylor St	312-226-6546	$$††	10 pm	Affordable Indian.
Taqueria Los Comales	1544 W 18th St	312-666-2251	$*	1 am	Mexican fast food in cheerful environment.
Taylor Street Taco Grill	1412 W Taylor St	312-850-9717	$	10 pm	On the cheaper end, but not bad.
Tuscany	1014 W Taylor St	312-829-1990	$$	11 pm	Elegant Taylor Street Italian.
WOW Café & Wingery	717 W Maxwell St	312-997-9969	$	12 am	N'awlins wing joint with a plethora of sauces.

Map 27 • Logan Square

Buona Terra Ristorante	2535 N California Ave	773-289-3800	$$	11 pm	Logan Square shmoozy Italian.
Café Bolero	2252 N Western Ave	773-227-9000	$$	12 am	Tasty Cuban fare.
Calvin's BBQ	2540 W Armitage Ave	773-342-5100	$$	11 pm	All-American home cooking: ribs, meatloaf and the like.
Choi's Chinese Restaurant	2638 N Milwaukee Ave	773-486-8496	$$	9 pm	Good, fresh Chinese food.
Dunlay's on the Square	3137 W Logan Blvd	773-227-2400	$$	3 am	American food and sports viewing.
El Cid	2115 N Milwaukee Ave	773-252-4747	$	1 am	Authentic Mexican for the masses.
El Nandu	2731 N Fullerton Ave	773-278-0900	$$	12 am	Argentine delicacies mixed with music.
El Pollo Loco	2715 N Milwaukee Ave	773-394-5626	$*	10 pm	Lots to cluck about with this cheap flame-grilled chicken.
Hachi's Kitchen	2521 N California Ave	773-276-8080	$$	12 am	Locals rave over this Logan Square sushi spot.
Hot Spot	2824 W Armitage Ave	773-770-3838	$††	2 am	Sunny hipster brunch spot.
Johnny's Grill	2545 N Kedzie Blvd	773-278-2215	$*	10 pm	Diner food for the grunge crowd.
Lula Café	2537 N Kedzie Blvd	773-489-9554	$$	10 pm	Pan-ethnic nouveau for hipsters.
Mama's Apple	2139 N Milwaukee Ave	773-252-2807	$$	11 pm	Mama's in the kitchen cooking up Latin comfort food.

Map 28 • Bucktown

Café De Luca	1721 N Damen Ave	773-342-6000	$$	9 pm	Café and Italian sandwiches.
Café Laguardia	2111 W Armitage Ave	773-862-5996	$$	11 pm	Cuban food like you wouldn't believe.
Café Matou	1846 N Milwaukee Ave	773-384-8911	$$$	11 pm	Fantastic French food, dodgy locale.
Club Lucky	1824 W Wabansia Ave	773-227-2300	$$	12 am	Age-old Italian joint.
Coast Sushi Bar	2045 N Damen Ave	773-235-5775	$$	12 am	BYOB sushi.
Darwin's	1935 N Damen Ave	773-252-8530	$$††	11 pm	Grown-up bar food.
Hollywood Grill	1601 W North Ave	773-395-1818	$	24 Hrs	24-hour Wicker Park dive.
Honey 1 BBQ	2241 N Western Ave	773-227-5130	$$	12 am	BBQ cooked in a big ole smoker. Yum.
Hot Chocolate	1747 N Damen Ave	773-489-1747	$$	12 am	Much more than just hot chocolate.
Il Covo	2152 N Damen Ave	773-862-5555	$$$	11 pm	Italian spot with upstairs lounge.
Irazu	1865 N Milwaukee Ave	773-252-5687	$*	9 pm	Hipsters and bikers gather 'round for Central American staples.
Ixcapuzalco	2165 N Western Ave	773-486-7340	$$$$	11 pm	Haute tamales in cantina ambience.
Jane's	1655 W Cortland St	773-862-5263	$$$	11 pm	Good-for-you gourmet.
Le Bouchon	1958 N Damen Ave	773-862-6600	$$	12 am	Affordable, crowded French.
Margie's Candies	1960 N Western Ave	773-384-1035	$	11 pm	Immense ice cream concoctions.
Meritage Café & Wine Bar	2118 N Damen Ave	773-235-6434	$$$$	12 am	Great food, great domestic wine list. A real neighborhood eatery.
Miko's Italian Ice	1846 N Damen Ave	773-645-9664	$*	9 pm	Italian ice storefront.
My Pie Pizza	2010 N Damen Ave	773-394-6900	$	10:15 pm	A.Y.C.E. pizza and salad bar.
Northside Bar & Grill	1635 N Damen Ave	773-384-3555	$$	2:30 am	Bucktown institution; outdoor seating.
Rinconcito Sudamericano	1954 W Armitage Ave	773-489-3126	$$	9:30 pm	Yummy South American food.
Roong Thai Restaurant	1633 N Milwaukee Ave	773-252-3488	$$	10 pm	Tasty Thai.
Scylla	1952 N Damen Ave	773-227-2995	$$$	11 pm	Seafood in Bucktown.
Silver Cloud Club & Grill	1700 N Damen Ave	773-489-6212	$$	12 am	Comfort food and drinks.
Think Café	2235 N Western Ave	773-394-0537	$$$	11 pm	Gourmet Italian—reasonable prices.
Toast	2046 N Damen Ave	773-772-5600	$	4 pm	Simple but chic breakfast. Killer food.

Map 29 • DePaul / Wrightwood / Sheffield

Ambrosia Café	1963 N Sheffield Ave	773-404-4450	$	3 am	Smoothies and hookahs? Huh.
Buffalo Wild Wings	2464 N Lincoln Ave	773-868-9453	$	1:30 am	Sports bar with wings.
Clarke's Pancake House & Restaurant	2441 N Lincoln Ave	773-472-3505	$		Great pancake and omelette spot.
Goose Island Brewing Company	1800 N Clybourn Ave	312-915-0071	$	1 pm	Pub grub at its best.

Green Dolphin Street	2200 N Ashland Ave	773-395-0066	$$$$	11 pm	Live jazz club and contemporary American.
John's Place	1200 W Webster Ave	773-525-6670	$$	11 pm	Healthy comfort food.
Red Lion Pub	2446 N Lincoln Ave	773-348-2695	$	12 am	It's haunted!
Sai Café	2010 N Sheffield Ave	773-472-8080	$$$	12 am	Traditional sushi place.
Salt & Pepper Diner	2575 N Lincoln Ave	773-525-8788	$*	4 pm	Cheap breakfasts in an area with few such options.
Shine & Morida	901 W Armitage Ave	773-296-0101	$$	11 pm	Chinese and Japanese all-in-one.
State	935 W Webster Ave	773-975-8030	$$$	12 am	Flashy service-oriented spot with concierge service.
Sweet Mandy B's	1207 W Webster Ave	773-244-1174	$	7 pm	Picture-perfect sweet shoppe.
Taco & Burrito House	1548 W Fullerton Ave	773-665-8389	$*	5 am	Super-cheap burrito shack, open very late.
Tsuki	1441 W Fullerton Ave	773-883-8722	$$	12 am	It was bound to happen: tapas + sushi.
Twisted Lizard	1964 N Sheffield Ave	773-929-1414	$$	12 am	Yuppie Mexican.
Vosges	951 W Armitage Ave	773-296-9866	$	8 pm	Gourmet chocolates.

Map 30 • Lincoln Park

Aladdin Café	2269 N Lincoln Ave	773-871-7327	$	10 pm	Dine-in or take-out hummos hut.
Alinea	1723 N Halsted St	312-867-0110	$$$$$	10 pm	Conceptual experiments in fine dining.
Ambria	2300 N Lincoln Park W	773-472-5959	$$$$$	10:30 pm	Luxe French with impeccable service.
Athenian Room	807 W Webster Ave	773-348-5155	$††	10:30 am	Casual Greek cuisine.
Austrian Bakery & Deli	2523 N Clark St	773-244-9922	$	8:30 pm	Low-carb diets are over. Celebrate here.
Ben & Jerry's	338 W Armitage Ave	773-281-5152	$*	11 pm	Gourmet ice cream.
Boka	1729 N Halsted St	312-337-6070	$$$	12 am	Ambitious menu, swank décor.
Brick's Chicago	1909 N Lincoln Ave	312-255-0851	$$	9 pm	Thin-crust pizza and Trappist ales hold sway here.
Café Ba-Ba-Reeba!	2024 N Halsted St	773-935-5000	$$$	12 am	Noisy, bustling tapas joint.
Café Bernard	2100 N Halsted St	773-871-2100	$$	11:30 pm	Charming French.
Charlie Trotter's	816 W Armitage Ave	773-248-6228	$$$$$	10:30 pm	World-famous nouvelle cuisine.
Deli Boutique	2318 N Clark St	773-880-9820	$	8 pm	Euro grocery/sandwich shop.
Duke's Bar and Grill	2616 N Clark St	773-248-0250	$$	1 am	Burger-lovers paradise.
Dunlay's	2600 N Clark St	773-883-6000	$$$	11 pm	Upscale American.
Emilio's Tapas	444 Fullerton Pkwy	773-327-5100	$$$	12 am	Cavernous branch of local tapas chain.
Ethel's Chocolate Lounge	819 W Armitage Ave	773-281-0029	$	11 pm	Chocolate lounge.
Fattoush	2652 N Halsted St	773-327-2652	$$	11 pm	Nicely priced Middle-East nosh.
Frances' Deli	2552 N Clark St	773-248-4580	$	9 pm	Inventive deli.
Geja's Café	340 W Armitage Ave	773-281-9101	$$$	12:30 am	Romantic fondue with live flamenco.
Hema's Kitchen II	2411 N Clark St	773-529-1705	$$	11 pm	Almost as good as original on Devon.
Hey Sushi	2630 N Clark St	773-248-3900	$$	10 pm	Clubby sushi spot.
Itto Sushi	2616 N Halsted St	773-871-1800	$$	12 am	Your typical sushi spot.
Karyn's	1901 N Halsted Ave	312-255-1590	$$	10 pm	The queen of raw food.
King Crab	1816 N Halsted St	312-280-8990	$$$	12 pm	Reliable fish and seafood.
Landmark	1633 N Halsted St	312-587-1600	$$$$	12 pm	Cavernous club restaurant for Lincoln Parkers.
Minnies	1969 N Halsted St	312-943-9900	$	1 am	Mini-burgers and mini-sandwiches served hot or cold.
Mon Ami Gabi	2300 N Lincoln Park W	773-348-8886	$$$	11 pm	Ambria's more casual neighbor.
My Pie Pizza	2417 N Clark St	773-929-3380	$	10:30 pm	A.Y.C.E. pizza and salad bar.
Nookies	1746 N Wells St	312-337-2454	$*	9:45 pm	Inventive omelettes with some strong coffee.
Nookies, Too	2114 N Halsted St	773-327-1400	$*	12 am	Inventive omelettes with some strong coffee.
North Pond	2610 N Cannon Dr	773-477-5845	$$$$	10 pm	Earthy contemporary American.
O' Fame	750 W Webster Ave	773-929-5111	$$	11 pm	Nice, neighborhood casual Italian.
Original Pancake House	2020 N Lincoln Park W	773-929-8130	$$*	4 pm	Breakfast-y grill.
Piattini	934 W Webster Ave	773-281-3898	$$	11 pm	Italian tapas.
PS Bangkok	2521 N Halsted St	773-348-0072	$	11 pm	Popular Thai with delivery.
Ranalli's	1925 N Lincoln Ave	312-642-4700	$	1 am	Huge patio for summertime quaffing.
Ranalli's	2301 N Clark St	773-529-3168	$	2 am	Local chain with 100+ beers.
Ritter's Breakfast Delivery	2665 N Clark St	773-665-4700	$	2 pm	Hit the snooze botton. Have breakfast in bed.
RJ Grunt's	2056 N Lincoln Park W	773-929-5363	$$		Great grub.
Robinson's No 1 Ribs	655 W Armitage Ave	312-337-1399	$*	10 pm	Down home ribs in Lincoln Park.
Salvatore's Ristorante	525 W Arlington Pl	773-528-1200	$$$	10 pm	Cute neighborhood Italian.
Sedgwick's Bar & Grill	1935 N Sedgwick St	312-337-7900	$	12 am	Home-style breakfast buffet.
Sushi O Sushi	346 W Armitage Ave	773-871-4777	$$	11 pm	Newly remodeled fresh seafood.
Sushi Para II	2256 N Clark St	773-477-3219	$$	10:30 pm	A.Y.C.E. sushi that's good. No, really.
Taco Burrito Palace #2	2441 N Halsted St	773-248-0740	$*	5 am	Speedy Mexican.
Tilli's	1952 N Halsted St	773-325-0044	$$	11 pm	Cute staff and good food.
Toast	746 W Webster Ave	773-935-5600	$	3 pm	Trendy breakfast.

Map 30 • Lincoln Park–*continued*

Treats Frozen Desserts	2200 N Clark St	773-472-6666	$*	12 am	Guilt-free ice cream.
Twin Anchors	1655 N Sedgwick St	312-266-1616	$$	12 am	Sinatra came for the ribs, stayed for the drinks and atmosphere.
Vinci	1732 N Halsted St	312-266-1199	$$$	11:30 pm	Homemade pasta raises the bar.
Wiener's Circle	2622 N Clark St	773-477-7444	$*	5 am	Classic dogs served with a generous helping of sass.

Map 31 • Old Town / Near North

Bistrot Margot	1437 N Wells St	312-587-3660	$$$$	11 pm	Great date place.
Chic Café	Cooking and Hospitality Institute, 361 W Chestnut St	312-873-2032	$$	8 pm	Gourmet prix fixe by culinary students.
Cucina Bella Osteria & Wine Bar	1612 N Sedgwick St	312-274-1119	$$*	11 pm	Solid Italian; wine bar.
Dinotto Ristorante	215 W North Ave	312-202-0302	$$	12 am	Everyone's a regular at this neighborhood Italian joint.
Fireplace Inn	1448 N Wells St	312-664-5264	$$$	1:30 pm	Popular spot to watch sports.
Flat Top Grill	319 W North Ave	312-787-7676	$$	11 pm	Choose yer own adventure or stir-fry, as it were.
Fresh Choice	1534 N Wells St	312-664-7065	$*	10 pm	Sandwich and smoothie king.
Kamehachi	1400 N Wells St	312-664-3663	$$$	1:30 am	Sushi favorite with upstairs lounge.
Kiki's Bistro	900 N Franklin St	312-335-5454	$$$$	11 pm	Stylish French.
Las Pinatas	1552 N Wells St	312-664-8277	$$	n/a	Festive atmosphere, fantastic food.
Mangia Roma	1623 N Halstead St	312-475-9801	$$	10:30 pm	Casual Roman spot with pizza.
Michael's	101 W North Ave	312-642-5246	$	n/a	Classic diner, great sundaes.
Mizu	315 W North Ave	312-951-8880	$$	5 pm	Sushi and skewered meats with dipping sauces.
MK	868 N Franklin St	312-482-9179	$$$$	10 pm	Very stylish.
O'Brien's	1528 N Wells St	312-787-3131	$$$	12:30 pm	Best outdoor in Old Town.
Old Jerusalem	1411 N Wells St	312-944-0459	$$	11 pm	Cheap, good food.
Salpicon	1252 N Wells St	312-988-7811	$$	11 pm	Colorful Mexican with tequila tastings.
Topo Gigio Ristorante	1516 N Wells St	312-266-9355	$$$	11 pm	Crowded reliable Italian. Big outdoor.

Map 32 • Gold Coast / Mag Mile

Ashkenaz	12 E Cedar St	312-944-5006	$	7 pm	Chicago's true Jewish deli.
Bistro 110	110 E Pearson St	312-266-3110	$$$	11 pm	Popular Sunday jazz brunch.
Bistrot Zinc	1131 N State St	312-337-1131	$$	11 pm	Quiet elegance.
Café des Architectes	Sofitel Chicago Water Tower, 20 E Chestnut St	312-324-4063	$$$	11 pm	French Mediterranean with late kitchen.
Café Spiaggia	980 N Michigan Ave	312-280-2750	$$	10:30 pm	More casual and less pricey than its Spiaggia forebear.
Cape Cod Room	Drake Hotel, 140 E Walton Pl	312-787-2200	$$$$	11 pm	Over-the-top nautical décor.
Carmine's	1043 N Rush St	312-988-7676	$$$	12:30 pm	Crowded and pricey italian.
Cheesecake Factory	John Hancock Ctr, 875 N Michigan Ave	312-337-1101	$$	12:30 am	40+ kinds of cheesecake.
Cru Wine Bar & Café	888 N Wabash Ave	312-337-4001	$$$	2 am	Cool, funky wine and cheese.
Dave & Buster's	1030 N Clark St	312-943-5151	$$	12:15 am	Chuck E. Cheese for grown-ups.
Foodlife	835 N Michigan Ave	312-335-3663	$$	9 pm	Le food court deluxe.
Gibson's Steakhouse	1028 N Rush St	312-266-8999	$$$$$	1 am	If you love steak, get a reservation.
Hugo's Frog Bar & Fish House	1024 N Rush St	312-640-0999	$$$	12 am	Hearty seafood.
Il Mulino New York	1150 N Dearborn St	312-440-8888	$$$$$	11 pm	Top NYC Italian w/ top NYC prices.
Johnny Rockets	901 N Rush St	312-337-3900	$	2 am	Jukebox and malts—outdoor seating, late night eating.
Le Colonial	937 N Rush St	312-255-0088	$$$	12 am	Indochine comes to the Second City. Very nice.
McCormick & Schmick's	41 E Chestnut St	312-397-9500	$$$$	12 am	Seafood chain that outdoes itself on portions and taste.
Mike Ditka's	100 E Chestnut St	312-587-8989	$$$	11 pm	The place for Ditka, Chicago sports, and meat.
Morton's of Chicago	1050 N State St	312-266-4820	$$$$$	11 pm	The steakhouse standard.
Mr. J's Dawg & Burger	822 N State St	312-943-4679	$	11 pm	Tasty greasy pit.
Original Pancake House	22 E Bellevue Pl	312-642-7917	$$*	5 pm	The apple waffle/pancake is right!
Pane Caldo	72 E Walton St	312-649-0055	$$$$	11 pm	Tucked-away genius Italian trattoria.
PJ Clarke's	1204 N State Pkwy	312-664-1650	$$	11:30 pm	Sandwiches and such.
Pump Room	Omni Ambassador East Hotel, 1301 N State Pkwy	312-266-0360	$$$$$	12 am	Chicago old-school tradition. Dress code.
Ra Sushi	1139 N State St	312-274-0011	$$$	1 am	Rock-n-roll sushi bar.
Ritz-Carlton Dining Room	160 E Pearson St	312-573-5223	$$$$$	11 pm	Hotel dining deluxe.
Signature Room	John Hancock Ctr, 875 N Michigan Ave	312-787-9596	$$$$	11 pm	It's the view. Proposal hot spot.

Spiaggia	980 N Michigan Ave	312-280-2750	$$$$$	10:30 pm	One of Chicago's best—gorgeous lake view and Italian cuisine.
Tavern on Rush	1031 N Rush St	312-664-9600	$$$$	1 am	Summer mainstay, American menu.
Tempo	6 E Chestnut St	312-943-4373	$$*	24 hrs	24/7 patio seating and huge menu.
Tsunami	1160 N Dearborn St	312-642-9911	$$$	11:30 pm	Sushi and sake in a club-like atmosphere.
Whiskey Bar and Grill	1015 N Rush St	312-475-0300	$$	12 am	Great summer place where hip and trendy folks abound.

Map 33 • West Rogers Park

Afghan Restaurant	2818 W Devon Ave	773-262-8000	$	2 pm	Afghan gyro for "hunger", whole baby goat for "starving."
Annapurna	2608 W Devon Ave	773-764-1858	$		Vegetarian fast food.
Arya Bhavan	2508 W Devon Ave	773-274-5800	$$	11 pm	Northern Indian all-vegetarian.
Café Montenegro	6954 N Western Ave	773-761-2233	$*	12 am	Greek-accented coffeeshop.
Candlelite	7452 N Western Ave	773-465-0087	$	2 am	Rogers Park pizza institution, with cocktails.
Ghandi India Restaurant	2601 W Devon Ave	773-761-8714	$$	11 pm	Family-style North and South Indian fare.
Good Morgan Kosher Fish Market	2948 W Devon Ave	773-764-8115	$$*	2 am	Fish market/restaurant in the Devon kosher strip.
Hashalom	2905 W Devon Ave	773-465-5675	$*	9 pm	Israeli/Moroccan, kosher, BYOB, closed Sat/Sun.
Hema's Kitchen	6406 N Oakley Ave	773-338-1627	$$	9:15 pm	Indian comfort food.
Indian Garden	2546 W Devon Ave	773-338-2929	$$	10:15 pm	Get your tandoori here.
Mysore Woodland's	2548 W Devon Ave	773-338-8160	$$	10 pm	Yummy Indian.
Sher a Punjab	2525 W Devon Ave	773-764-9392	$	9:30 pm	Lunch and dinner buffets.
Sukhadia's	2559 W Devon Ave	773-338-5400	$	9:30 pm	Indian sweet maker and caterer.
Tiffin	2536 W Devon Ave	773-338-2143	$$	10:30 pm	Most upscale Indian restaurant on Devon, yet moderately priced.
U Lucky Dawg	6821 N Western Ave	773-274-3652	$*	11 pm	"Famous" hot dog joint. Breakfast, lunch, and dinner, outdoor seating.
Udupi Palace	2543 W Devon Ave	773-338-2152	$	9:30 pm	Pure vegetarian Indian food, low-fat, not too spicy.
Viceroy of India	2520 W Devon Ave	773-743-4100	$$	10:30 pm	Popular Indian restaurant, vegetarian options.

Map 34 • East Rogers Park

A&T Restaurant	7026 N Clark St	773-274-0036	$††	9 pm	Classic diner-grill.
Buffalo Joe's	1841 W Howard St	773-764-7300	$*	11 pm	Wings and fast food carryout spot, with a soul food flava.
Café Suron	1146 W Pratt Blvd	773-465-6500	$$$	11 pm	Lebanese fine dining. BYOB.
Capt'n Nemos	7363 N Clark St	773-973-0570	$*	7 pm	Free soup while you wait at this always-jovial local sandwich chain.
Caribbean American Bakery	1539 W Howard St	773-761-0700	$††	8 pm	Jamaican bakery featuring meat pies, pastries, and jerk chicken for carryout.
Deluxe Diner	6349 N Clark St	773-743-8244	$*	24 hrs	Retro-styled greasy spoon.
El Famous Burrito	7047 N Clark St	773-465-0377	$*	1 am	Best greasy burrito in Chicago.
Ennui Café	6981 N Sheridan Rd	773-973-2233	$*	12 am	Tasty tidbits.
Ghareeb Nawaz	2032 W Devon Ave	773-761-5300	$*	12 am	Indo-Pakistani lunch counter on the east side of the strip.
Grande Noodles and Sushi Bar	6632 N Clark St	773-761-6666	$$††	10 pm	Damn fine pot stickers.
Heartland Café	7000 N Glenwood Ave	773-465-8005	$$	11 pm	Brown rice, socialist newspapers, and vegetarian tidbits reign here.
La Cazuela Mariscos	6922 N Clark St	773-338-5425	$	10 pm	Taqueria specializing in seafood.
Lake Side Café	1418 W Howard St	773-262-9503	$$	10 pm	Vegetarian restaurant specializing in organic grub.
Morseland	1218 W Morse Ave	773-764-8900	$$$	2 am	Rogers Park café with ambitious fare.
Panini Panini	6764 N Sheridan Rd	773-761-4110	$$*	11 pm	Italian flavor for the North Side.
Quesadillas y Mariscos Dona Lolis	6924 N Clark St	773-761-5677	$*	10 pm	Authentic quesadillas and gorditas with interesting ingredients.
Speakeasy Supperclub	1401 W Devon Ave	773-338-0600	$$	11 pm	Dino would have enjoyed the live music and eclectic menu.
Taste of Peru	6545 N Clark St	773-381-4540	$††	12 am	Barebones spot for cheap. authentic Peruvian food.
Thai Spice	1320 W Devon Ave	773-973-0504	$	11 pm	Look beyond the grim exterior for freshly prepared Thai.
Tickie's Belizean Cuisine	7605 N Paulina St	773-973-3919	$	8 pm	Authentic Caribbean food in cheerful storefront across from the Howard L.

Map 35 • Arcadia Terrace / Peterson Park

Aztecas Mexican Taqueria	5421 N Lincoln Ave	773-506-2052	$	12 am	Standard Mexican fare.
Café Orange	5639 N Lincoln Ave	773-275-5040	$$	2 am	Korean and Japanese fare with a hip vibe and occasional karaoke.
Charcoal Delights	3139 W Foster Ave	773-583-0056	$††	11 pm	Great gyros to go.
Fondue Stube	2717 W Peterson Ave	773-784-2200	$$	12 am	Fun fondue!
Garden Buffet	5347 N Lincoln Ave	773-728-1249	$	11 pm	Korean/Japanese with huge buffet and sushi bar.
IHOP	5929 N Lincoln Ave	773-769-1550	$	12 am	It's an IHOP for pete's sake. What else do you need to know?
Katsu	2651 W Peterson Ave	773-784-3383	$$$	10 pm	Familiar, family sushi place.
Pueblito Viejo	5429 N Lincoln Ave	773-784-9135	$$	2:20 am	Adorable Columbian village-theme with live music on weekends.
Solga	5828 N Lincoln Ave	773-728-0802	$$$††	11 pm	Korean BBQ with charcoal grill.
Tom Yum Thai & Japanese	3232 W Foster Ave	773-442-8100	$$	10 pm	Courteous, competent, good value Thai and sushi.
Wolfy's	2734 W Peterson Ave	773-743-0207	$	9 pm	Dine in and carry out dogs, burgers, and such.
Woo Chon	5744 N California Ave	773-728-8001	$††	12 am	Authentic Korean BBQ. Brusque but oddly fun service.

Map 36 • Bryn Mawr

Delisi's Pizzeria	5806 N Western Ave	773-784-6320	$	10:30 pm	Chicago memorabilia, great pizza and complimentary Tootsie Rolls.
Fireside Restaurant & Lounge	5739 N Ravenswood Ave	773-878-5942	$$	3 am	Diverse crowd and eclectic menu from ribs to pizza.
Greenhouse Inn	6300 N Ridge Ave	773-273-4182	$	2:30 pm	Church and bridge groups meet for homemade soups.
Max's Italian Beef	5754 N Western Ave	773-989-8200	$$*	7 pm	Chicago institution; home of the pepper-and-egg sandwich.
San Soo Gab San	5247 N Western Ave	773-334-1589	$$	6 am	Do-it-yourself Korean barbeque at 4 am.
Yes Thai	5211 N Damen Ave	773-878-3487	$	10:30 pm	Noodles and curries in a cozy atmosphere.

Map 37 • Edgewater / Andersonville

Adria Mare	5401 N Broadway St	773-989-4511	$$	10 pm	Croatian home cooking.
Alice and Friends Vegetarian Café	5812 N Broadway St	773-275-8797	$$$*	10 pm	Veggie to vegan.
Andie's	5253 N Clark St	773-784-8616	$$	1 am	Fresh Middle Eastern in airy atmosphere.
Angel's	5403 N Clark St	773-271-1138	$$	11 pm	Best huevos rancheros in town.
Ann Sather	5207 N Clark St	773-271-6677	$	4 pm	Andersonville landmark with Swedish-inspired food.
Col-Ubas Steak House	5665 N Clark St	773-506-1579	$$	10 pm	Skip the steak but try the authentic Columbian and Cuban fare.
Corner Grille	5200 N Clark St	773-271-3663	$	4 pm	Breakfast and lunch spot.
Ethiopian Diamond	6120 N Broadway St	773-338-6100	$$$	11 pm	Visit for jazz on Fridays.
Francesca's Bryn Mawr	1039 W Bryn Mawr Ave	773-506-9261	$$	11 pm	Dined in an SRO before?
Huey's Hot Dogs	1507 W Balmoral Ave	773-293-4800	$	8 pm	Enjoy a dog al fresco.
Indie Café	5951 N Broadway St	773-561-5577	$$	10:30 pm	Thai and sushi. Yummy and cheap.
Jin Ju	5203 N Clark St	773-334-6377	$$$	12 am	Upscale Korean.
La Fonda Latino	5350 N Broadway St	773-271-3935	$$	9:30 pm	Real tasty pan-Latin.
La Tache	1475 W Balmoral Ave	773-334-7168	$$	11 pm	Neighborhood French bistro.
M Henry	5707 N Clark St	773-561-1600	$$	3 pm	Stylish brunch option in Andersonville.
Moody's Pub	5910 N Broadway St	773-275-2696	$*	2 am	Burgers only, but the best.
Pasteur	5525 N Broadway St	773-878-1061	$$$$	10:30 pm	Easy to imagine you're in Vietnam 50 years ago.
Patio Beef	6022 N Broadway St	773-764-8500	$*	9:30 pm	Bacon double cheese and lotto to go.
Pauline's	1754 W Balmoral Ave	773-561-8573	$*	3 am	Weekend breakfast hotspot; try the famous five-egg omelette.
RAS Dashen Ethiopian	5846 N Broadway St	773-506-9601	$$	11 pm	Traditional Ethiopian comfort food; vegan-friendly
Reza's	5255 N Clark St	773-561-1898	$$	12 am	Many Persian options, leftovers for lunch the next day.
Standee's	1133 W Granville Ave	773-743-5013	$	11 pm	Loyola students and others congregate here for diner fare.
Sushi Luxe	5204 N Clark St	773-334-0770	$$		Sushi and bar.
Svea	5236 N Clark St	773-275-7738	$*	11 pm	Adorable, tiny Swedish diner.
Swedish Bakery	5348 N Clark St	773-561-8919	$*	5 pm	Famous tasty pastries and cakes.
Sweet Occasions and More	5306 N Clark St	773-275-6526	$$	11 pm	Good desserts, awful name.
Tanoshii	5547 N Clark St	773-878-6886	$$	12 am	Order from the chef for innovative sushi.

Taste of Lebanon	1509 W Foster Ave	773-334-1600	$*	7:30 pm	Casual Lebanese.
Tomboy	5402 N Clark St	773-907-0636	$$$	11 pm	Loud, hip and fun, BYOB
Wickstrom's Swedish Deli	5247 N Clark St	773-275-6100	$$††	6 pm	Swedish deli and gourmet shop

Map 38 • Ravenswood / Albany Park

Al-Khaymeih	4742 N Kedzie Ave	773-583-0999	$	11 pm	Lebanese eatery with better-than-average vegetarian appetizers.
Arun's	4156 N Kedzie Ave	773-539-1909	$$$$$	10 pm	Worldwide rep for four-star prix fixe Thai.
Brasa Roja	3125 W Montrose Ave	773-866-2252	$$	10 pm	Friendly Columbian place specializing in flame-roasted chicken.
Café Restaurant Art	4658 N Rockwell St	773-539-0645		$	11 pm European-style pizza joint that also serves Middle Eastern food.
City Noor Kebab	4714 N Kedzie Ave	773-267-9700	$$	12 am	Middle Eastern food galore!
Cousin's IV (Incredible Vitality)	3038 W Irving Park Rd	773-478-6868	$$	11:30 pm	Overcooking not a prob at this raw restaurant.
Dharma Garden Thai Restaurants	3111 W Irving Park Rd	773-588-9140	$††	10 pm	Thai vegetarian and seafood dishes. Karaoke some evenings.
Feed the Beast	4300 N Lincoln Ave	773-588-4280		n/a	Affordable italian food.
Golden Crust Italian Pizzeria	4620 N Kedzie Ave	773-539-5860	$	2 am	Honkin' portions of the Italian-American comfort food of yore.
Great Sea Chinese Restaurants	3254 W Lawrence Ave	773-478-9129	$$††	10:30 pm	Otherwise basic Chinese locally famous for its hot wings.
Golden Angel Restaurant	4340 N Lincoln Ave	773-583-6969	$	24 hrs	Diner; eggs, pancakes, and pies on the run.
Han Bat	2723 W Lawrence Ave	773-271-8640	$$$*	9:30 pm	Very traditional Korean. The seollongtang is reportedly sublime.
Huddle House	4748 N Kimball Ave	773-588-5363	$*	24 hrs	This cozy diner open 24 hours.
Jimmy's Fast Food	4810 N Drake Ave	773-267-0247	$*	10 pm	Unpretentious diner; Mexican and American.
Kang Nam	4849 N Kedzie Ave	773-539-2524	$$	10:30 pm	Could be the best Korean BBQ in town. Crazy excellent.
Kitchen Chicago	4664 N Manor Ave	773-463-0863	$	2 pm	Café food: soup, sandwiches, sweets.
Lutz Continental Café	2458 W Montrose Ave	773-478-7785	$$	10 pm	If Grandma was German, she would serve these pastries.
Manzo's Ristorante	3210 W Irving Park Rd	773-478-3070	$$	1:30 am	Do not miss the Sunday buffet. Tasty, plentiful and cheap Italian.
Mi Rancho / Angelo's	3026 W Montrose Ave	773-588-6211	$	2 am	Pizza and Mexican for carry-out and delivery.
Noon O Kabab	4661 N Kedzie Ave	773-279-8899	$	11 pm	Bring a doggie bag for day-after lunch.
Paradise Japanese	2916 W Montrose Ave	773-588-1989	$$	10:30 pm	Competent sushi connected to a Korean spa.
Penguin	2723 W Lawrence Ave	773-271-4924	$	1 pm	High-fat, authentic Argentine ice cream (empanadas and pizza, too, but go straight for dessert).
Rockwell's Neighborhood Grill	4632 N Rockwell St	773-509-1871	$	11 pm	Familiar bar food and brunchtime favorites in a friendly atmosphere.
Sahar Pita	4835 N Kedzie Ave	773-583-6695	$$	11 pm	Tasty Middle Eastern carry-out by the Sahar meat folks.
Salam	4636 N Kedzie Ave	773-583-0776	$*	10 pm	Home of the 19-cent falafel.
Santa Rita Taqueria	2752 W Lawrence Ave	773-784-1522	$*	12 am	Inexpensive tasty fare open late. Weekend pastor is fantastic.
Semiramis	4639 N Kedzie Ave	773-279-8900	$$††	10 pm	Lebanese with great value to quality ratio. Try the sumac fries.
Shelly's Freez	5119 N Lincoln Ave	773-271-2783	$*	10 pm	Classic Italian beef and dipped soft-serve.
Tagine	4749 N Rockwell St	773-989-4340	$$	11 pm	Moroccan BYOB with savory stews.
Thai Little Home Café	4747 N Kedzie Ave	773-478-3944	$††	9 pm	Two rooms + one lunch buffet = less than $10.
Thai Valley	4600 N Kedzie Ave	773-588-2020			BYOB Thai restaurant with lunch specials.

Map 39 • Ravenswood / North Center

Alps East Restaurant	2012 W Irving Park Rd	773-975-0527	$	4 pm	Cheap breakfasts are your best bet here.
Bistro Campagne	4518 N Lincoln Ave	773-271-6100	$$	10:30 pm	Organic French fare in a cozy room.
Block 44	4365 N Lincoln Ave	773-868-4404	$$$	11 pm	Rave reviews for small plate fare in Lincoln Square.
Brioso	4603 N Lincoln Ave	773-989-9000	$$	11 pm	Lively neighborhood spot for tasty Mexican.
Café 28	1800 W Irving Park Rd	773-528-2883	$$	10:30 pm	Trendy Cuban.
Café Selmarie	4729 N Lincoln Ave	773-989-5595	$$	11 pm	Bakery/café.
Chicago Brauhaus	4732 N Lincoln Ave	773-784-4444	$$	12 am	Live German music in beerhouse atmosphere.
Chicago Joe's	2256 W Irving Park Rd	773-478-7000	$	2 am	Casual little North Center spot. It was in Wayne's World!

Map 39 • Ravenswood / North Center–*continued*

Cy's Steak & Chop House	4138 N Lincoln Ave	773-404-5800	$$$	11 pm	Now that's what I call a steak!
Daily Bar & Grill	4560 N Lincoln Ave	773-561-6198	$	11 pm	Bar food in retro ambiance.
Essence of India	4601 N Lincoln Ave	773-506-0002	$$	10:30 pm	Traditional northern Indian cuisine.
First Slice Pie Café	4401 N Ravenswood Ave	773-506-7380	$$*	6 pm	Upscale café benefiting the hungry in more ways than one.
Garcia's	4749 N Western Ave	773-769-5600	$	4 am	Mexican/Tex-Mex with great shakes.
Glenn's Diner	1820 W Montrose Ave	773-506-1720	$$	9 pm	Fish-focused American fare.
Glunz Bavarian Haus	4128 N Lincoln Ave	773-472-4287	$$	11 pm	Weiner schnitzel and beer.
Jury's Food & Drink	4337 N Lincoln Ave	773-935-2255	$	11 pm	Neighborhood pub.
La Boca della Verita	4618 N Lincoln Ave	773-784-6222	$$	11 pm	Cozy Italian café.
Lincoln Restaurant	4008 N Lincoln Ave	773-248-1820	$$	11 pm	Old-school family joint. Been there forever.
Los Nopales	4544 N Western Ave	773-334-3149	$$††	10 pm	Creative, cheap Mexican BYOB.
Margie's Candies	1813 W Montrose Ave	773-348-0400	$	11 pm	Ridiculously decadent sundaes and homemade confections.
O'Donovan's	2100 W Irving Park Rd	773-478-2100	$	3 am	Three words: Dollar Burger Night.
Opart Thai House	4658 N Western Ave	773-989-8517	$††	10:45 pm	Local favorite for fresh Thai. BYOB.
Orange Garden	1942 W Irving Park Rd	773-525-7479	$$††	10 pm	Over seventy years of Cantonese cooking.
Over Easy Café	4943 N Damen Ave	773-506-2605	$	3 pm	Bright breakfast spot.
Pizza DOC	2251 W Lawrence Ave	773-784-8777	$$	11 pm	European-style, wood-oven pizza.
Roong Petch	1828 W Montrose Ave	773-989-0818	$	10 pm	One of many Thai options in Lincoln Square.
Royal Thai	2209 W Montrose Ave	773-509-0007	$	10 pm	Vegetarians get their own special menu.
Smokin' Woody's	4160 N Lincoln Ave	773-880-1100	$$	11 pm	Ribs 'n' wings 'n' other sticky eats.
Soiree Bar and Restaurant	4539 N Lincoln Ave	773-293-3690	$$	10:30 pm	Fancy food at realistic prices.
Spacca Napoli	1769 W Sunnyside Ave	773-878-2420	$$	11 pm	Neapolitan styles pizza in Ravenswood.
Spoon Thai	4608 N Western Ave	773-769-1173	$*		Departure from the standard Thai fare.
Tank Sushi	4514 N Lincoln Ave	773-769-2600	$$	11:30 pm	Fresh sushi with Latin flair.
Thai Oscar	4638 N Western Ave	773-878-6220	$	9:45 pm	Thai and Sushi, neither that great.

Map 40 • Uptown

Agami	4712 N Broadway St	773-506-1845	$$$	2 am	Swanky sushi.
Andie's	1467 W Montrose Ave	773-348-0654	$$	11 pm	Middle Eastern food in Babylonian surroundings.
Anna Maria Pasteria	4400 N Clark St	773-506-2662	$$	11 pm	Cute, neighborhood Italian, casual date spot.
Bale French Bakery	5018 N Broadway St	773-561-4424	$*	8 pm	French/Asian bakery and sandwiches.
Café Too	4715 N Sheridan Rd	773-275-0626	$	8 pm	Uptown café provides job training for the homeless.
Deleece	4004 N Southport Ave	773-325-1710	$$	11 pm	Ambitious global fare in cute storefront.
Don Quijote	4761 N Clark St	773-769-5930	$*	n/a	Burritos as big as your head.
Furama	4936 N Broadway St	773-271-1161	$$	10 pm	Dim sum with karaoke.
Golden House Restaurant	4744 N Broadway St	773-334-0406	$*	6:30 pm	Pancakes and ambience in Uptown.
Hai Yen Restaurant	1055 W Argyle St	773-561-4077	$$	10:30pm	Chinese and veggie pho.
Hama Matsu	5143 N Clark St	773-506-2978	$$$	10:30 pm	Japanese and Korean fare.
Holiday Club	4000 N Sheridan Rd	773-348-9600	$$*	2 am	The Rat Pack is back! With food.
JJ Fish & Chicken	4515 N Sheridan Rd	773-275-3474	$*	9 pm	Fried catfish, perch and okra…a heart attack waiting to happen.
La Donna	5146 N Clark St	773-561-9400	$$	12 am	Friendly, tasty Italian.
Magnolia Café	1224 W Wilson Ave	773-728-8785	$$	11:30 pm	Magnolias in an American bistro.
Nhu Hoa	1020 W Argyle St	773-878-0618	$	10 pm	Vietnamese.
Pho Xe Lua	1021 W Argyle St	773-275-7512	$	9:30 pm	Over 200 Vietnamese and Chinese dishes.
Pho Xe Tang	4953 N Broadway St	773-878-2253	$††	n/a	Bigger and brighter. Vietnamese and Chinese cuisine all day.
Riques	5004 N Sheridan Rd	773-728-6200	$	11 pm	Inexpensive and creative Mexican BYOB.
Siam Noodle & Rice	4654 N Sheridan Rd	773-769-6694	$††	9:30 pm	Damn fine Thai food.
Silver Seafood	4829 N Broadway St	773-784-0668	$	1 am	Asian delights from the sea.
Smoke Country House	1467 W Irving Park Rd	773-327-0600	$$	10 pm	Great barbecue on the north side (huh…imagine that!).
Thai Pastry	4925 N Broadway St	773-784-5399	$	11 pm	Free pastry with every order!
Tokyo Marina	5058 N Clark St	773-878-2900	$	10:30 pm	Sushi in a pinch.
Tweet	5020 N Sheridan Rd	773-728-5576	$$*	10:30 pm	Gourmet food without pretension.

Map 41 • Avondale / Old Irving

Chief O'Neill's	3471 N Elston Ave	773-583-3066	$	10 pm	Excellent traditional pub fare.
Clara's	3159 N California Ave	773-539-3020	$*	2 am	Ultimate cheap greasy spoon.
Eat First Chinese Restaurant	3337 W Belmont Ave	773-588-7071	$	11 pm	No dining room to speak of, but super-fast delivery of standard Chinese.
Fierro's Argentine Grill	2550 W Addison St	773-305-3333	$$*	10 pm	Don't blink or you'll pass up this cheery Argentine spot.
Hot Doug's	3324 N California Ave	773-279-9550	$*	4 pm	Get your weird game dogs at this

					campy encased meat emporium.
IHOP	2818 W Diversey Ave	773-342-8901	$	24 Hrs	Open 24 hrs, go for the International Passport breakfast.
Kuma's Corner	2900 W Belmont Ave	773-604-8769	$$	1 am	Bar and grill with upscale fare such as Kobe beef burgers.
La Finca	3361 N Elston Ave	773-478-4006	$††	10 pm	Friendly, family run servicable Mexican and margaritas.
Sunshine Restaurant	3521 N Kedzie Ave	773-267-1578	$	3 pm	Grill grub.
Taqueria Trespazada	3144 N California Ave	773-539-4533	$*	2 am	Tasty, cheap tacos and salsas—no atmosphere.

Map 42 • North Center / Roscoe Village / West Lakeview

Brett's Café Americain	2011 W Roscoe St	773-248-0999	$$$	10 pm	Go for brunch or dessert. Great bread basket.
Carreno's Pizzeria	1955 W Addison St	773-248-0455	$*	12 am	Take-out pizzas a little on the salty side.
Costello Sandwich & Sides	2015 W Roscoe St	773-929-2323	$	9 pm	Yummy baked sandwiches.
El Tinajon	2054 W Roscoe St	773-525-8455	$$	n/a	Good, cheap Guatemalan. Great mango margaritas.
Four Moon Tavern	1847 W Roscoe St	773-929-6666	$	1 am	Neighborhood tavern. Cozy back room. Thespian crowd.
Frasca	3358 N Paulina St	773-248-5222	$$	11 pm	European-style pizza with a cozy wine bar and outdoor seating.
Gino's	2801 N Lincoln Ave	773-327-3737	$$	11 pm	Legendary deep dish pizza since 1966.
Kaze Sushi	2032 W Roscoe St	773-327-4860	$$	11:30 pm	Innovative, gourmet sushi.
Kitsch'n on Roscoe	2005 W Roscoe St	773-248-7372	$$	10 pm	Clever retro food and tiki bar. Friendly staff.
La Mora	2132 W Roscoe St	773-404-4555	$$	11 pm	Neighborhood Mediterranean-influenced Italian fare.
Lee's Chop Suey	2415 W Diversey Ave	773-342-7050	$*	10 pm	Chop suey and booze.
Mrs Murphy and Sons	3905 N Lincoln Ave	773-248-3905	$$$	11 pm	Fancy Irish food: An oxymoron, or reality? Decide for yourself here.
Piazza Bella Trattoria	2116 W Roscoe St	773-477-7330	$$$	11 pm	Neighborhood Italian.
Rajun Cajun	1459 E 53rd St	773-955-1145	$$	9:30 pm	Lots of rajun but no more cajun.
Riverview Tavern & Grill	1958 W Roscoe St	773-248-9523	$$	11 pm	Frat food and beer.
Sola	3868 N Lincoln Ave	773-327-3868	$$$	11 pm	Contemporary American with Polynesian flair.
T-Spot Sushi	3925 N Lincoln Ave	773-549-4500	$$	11 pm	Good sushi and tea in small Euro-fancy room. BYOB.
Terragusto	1851 W Addison St	773-248-2777	$$	9:30 pm	Italian market with café.
Thai Linda Café	2022 W Roscoe St	773-868-0075	$$	9:45 pm	Standard-issue neighborhood Thai.
The Village Tap	2055 W Roscoe St	773-883-0817	$	n/a	Beer garden and good bar food.
Turquoise Restaurant on Roscoe	2147 W Roscoe St	773-549-3523	$$	12 am	Fresh and creative Middle-Eastern fare.
Victory's Banner	2100 W Roscoe St	773-665-0227	$	3 pm	Best vegetarian in the city complete with toga-clad waitstaff.
Volo Restaurant and Wine Bar	2008 W Roscoe St	773-348-4600	$$$	12:30 pm	New American small plates with swirl.
Wishbone	3300 N Lincoln Ave	773-549-2663	$$	10 pm	Overrated Cajun spot popular for brunch.

Map 43 • Wrigleyville/ East Lakeview

A La Turka	3134 N Lincoln Ave	773-935-6101	$$	2 am	Hookahs, shish kebabs, and belly-dancing.
Ann Sather	3416 N Southport Ave	773-404-4475	$$	2 pm	Huge cinnamon rolls and great omlettes.
Ann Sather	929 W Belmont Ave	773-348-2378	$	9 pm	Warm, family friendly ambience, Swedish comfort food.
Art of Pizza	3033 N Ashland Ave	773-327-5600	$	11 pm	Deep dish pizza by the slice. Slow delivery but worth the wait.
Blue Bayou	3734 N Southport Ave	773-871-3300	$$	11 pm	New Orleans-themed, in case you couldn't guess.
Bolat	3346 N Clark St	773-665-1100	$$	11 pm	West African cuisine—try the okra with rice.
Capt'n Nemos	3650 N Ashland Ave	773-929-7687	$††	9 pm	Great sandwiches and yummy soup.
Clarke's Diner	930 W Belmont Ave	773-348-5988	$$	24 Hrs	All night, alright and helluv kitschy diner fun.
Coobah	3423 N Southport Ave	773-528-2220	$$	2 am	Trendy Latin spot near Music Box.
Cy's Crab House	3819 N Ashland Ave	773-883-8900	$$	12 am	Persian-tinged seafood emporium.
Duck Walk	919 W Belmont Ave	773-665-0455	$	11 pm	Your basic Thai, cheap but good.
Fundajo Grill	3140 N Lincoln Ave	773-404-4500	$$$	11 pm	Contemporary American with retro lounge flair.
Golden Apple	2971 N Lincoln Ave	773-528-1413	$	24 hrs	24-hour greasy hangover food.
Heaven on Seven	3478 N Clark St	773-477-7818	$$	11 pm	An epicurean jaunt to N'awlins. Yum.
House of Sushi & Noodles	1610 W Belmont Ave	773-935-9110	$$	10:30 pm	Cheap sushi, huge menu with polaroids of customers on walls.

Map 43 • Wrigleyville/ East Lakeview–*continued*

Julius Meinl	3601 N Southport Ave	773-868-1857	$	11 pm	Pastries and coffee, served in the Viennese manner.
Lucky's	3472 N Clark St	773-549-0665	$	3 am	They put fries IN the sandwich. Genius.
Mama Desta's Red Sea	3216 N Clark St	773-935-7561	$$	11:30 pm	No forks at this authentic Ethiopian restaurant.
Matsu Yama	1059 W Belmont Ave	773-327-8838	$$	12 am	Lovely, fresh sushi.
Matsuya	3469 N Clark St	773-248-2677	$$	11:30 pm	One of the best on Sushi Row.
Menagerie	1232 W Belmont Ave	773-404-8333	$$$	10:30 pm	Styish fusion.
Mia Francesca	3311 N Clark St	773-281-3310	$$	11 pm	Contemporary Italian date place.
Moe's Cantina	3518 N Clark St	773-281-8399	$$$	2 am	Updated Mexican place with a contemporary "concept."
Orange	3231 N Clark St	773-549-4400	$$	2:30 pm	Super stylish brunches.
Original Gino's East	2801 N Lincoln Ave	773-327-3737	$$	12 am	Family-style sit-in pizza joint.
Panes	3002 N Sheffield Ave	773-665-0972	$	10 pm	Homemade sandwiches, muffins, cookies, and brownies.
Penny's Noodle Shop	3400 N Sheffield Ave	773-281-8222	$$	10:30 pm	Pad thai, pad see ew, popular place for a lite lunch.
Penny's Noodle Shop	950 W Diversey Ave	773-281-8448	$$	10:30 pm	Pad thai, pad see ew, popular place for a lite lunch.
Pepper Lounge	3441 N Sheffield Ave	773-665-7377	$$	1 am	Loungey late-night dining. Smoker friendly.
Pick Me Up	3408 N Clark St	773-248-6613	$††	24 hrs	Best place for late night veggies or meat.
Pizza Rustica	3913 N Sheridan Rd	773-404-8955	$$	11 pm	Super-thin crust-pizza.
Platiyo	3313 N Clark St	773-477-6700	$$	11 pm	Festive and contemporary Mexican.
PS Bangkok	3345 N Clark St	773-871-7777	$	11:30 pm	Popular neighborhood Thai that delivers.
Rise	3401 N Southport Ave	773-525-3535	$$	11:30 pm	Sushi nightspot.
S&G	3000 N Lincoln Ave	773-935-4025	$	24 hrs	Cop hangout with chintzy decorating and fake plants.
Salt & Pepper Diner	3537 N Clark St	773-883-9800	$*	12 am	Old-school greasy-spoon diner.
Shiroi Hana	3242 N Clark St	773-477-1652	$$	10:30 pm	Tastiest sushi ever.
Socca	3301 N Clark St	773-248-1155	$$	11 pm	Tasty, satisfying Mediterannean.
Standard India	917 W Belmont Ave	773-929-1123	$††	11 pm	Yet another Indian buffet.
Strega Nona	3747 N Southport Ave	773-244-0990	$$	11 pm	Casual Italian near the Music Box.
Tango Sur	3763 N Southport Ave	773-477-5466	$$	11:30 pm	Vegetarian's vision of hell: big juicy Argentinean steaks.
Taqueria El Milagro	1434 W Belmont Ave	773-975-2348	$	4 am	Friendly staff caters to late night drunks.
Tombo Kitchen	3244 N Lincoln Ave	773-244-9885	$$	2 am	Modern, very good sushi.
Twisted Spoke	3365 N Clark St	773-525-5300	$	1 am	Plays porn and serves eggs late night on weekends, slow service.
Vines on Clark	3554 N Clark St	773-327-8572	$$	11 pm	Upscale sandwich menu vying for the Wrigley buck.
Wrigleyville Dog	3737 N Clark St	773-296-1500	$*	5 am	Hot dog heaven.

Map 44 • East Lakeview

Aladdin's Eatery	614 W Diversey Pkwy	773-327-6300	$	11 pm	Fresh Middle-Eastern.
Angelina Ristorante	3561 N Broadway St	773-935-5933	$$$	11 pm	Casual, romantic Italian.
Ann Sather	3411 N Broadway St	773-305-0024	$	4 pm	Airy branch of local comfort food chain.
Arco de Cuchilleros	3445 N Halsted St	773-296-6046	$$$	12 am	Intimate tapas; great sangria.
Café Blossom	608 W Barry Ave	773-935-5284		$	11 pm Tiny sushi spot.
Chicago Diner	3411 N Halsted St	773-935-6696	$$	11 pm	A vegetarian institution.
Clark Street Dog	3040 N Clark St	773-281-6690	$*	3 am	24-hour hot dogs and cheese fries.
Cornelia's Restaurant	750 W Cornelia Ave	773-248-8333	$$	11 pm	Tres Gay Boystown ski lodge / cabaret lounge.
Cousin's	2833 N Broadway St	773-880-0063	$$	11:30 pm	Veggie-friendly Turkish food.
Duke of Perth	2913 N Clark St	773-477-1741	$	12 am	Fish and chips.
eatZi's	Century Mall, 2828 N Clark St	773-832-9310	$	8 pm	Gourmet grub to go.
Erwin, An American Café & Bar	2925 N Halsted St	773-528-7200	$$$$	10 pm	Elegant.
Firefly	3335 N Halsted St	773-525-2505	$$	1 am	Upscale neighborhood joint.
Half Shell	676 W Diversey Pkwy	773-549-1773	$$$*	11:30 pm	Casual raw bar.
Jack's on Halsted	3201 N Halsted St	773-244-9191	$$$$	11:30 pm	Great wine list.
Kit Kat Lounge & Supper Club	3700 N Halsted St	773-525-1111	$$	1 am	Drag shows while you dine.
Koryo	2936 N Broadway St	773-477-8510	$$	11 pm	Upscale Korean.
La Creperie	2845 N Clark St	773-528-9050	$$	11 pm	Live French music. Shabby, but cute.
Las Mananitas	3523 N Halsted St	773-528-2109	$$*	12 am	Lethal margaritas.
Mark's Chop Suey	3343 N Halsted St	773-281-9090	$	11 pm	The BEST eggrolls.
Mars	3124 N Broadway St	773-404-1600	$$	11 pm	White tablecloth Chinese.
Melrose	3233 N Broadway St	773-327-2060	$$††	24 hrs	24-hour diner.
Nancy's Original Stuffed Pizza	2930 N Broadway St	773-883-1977	$	2 am	Seedy pizza parlor.
Nookie's Tree	3334 N Halsted St	773-248-9888	$*	24 hrs	24-hour diner.
Renaldi's Pizza Pub	2827 N Broadway St	773-248-8903	$$	2 am	"You're too thin, eat something!"
The Bagel	3107 N Broadway St	773-477-0300	$	11 pm	Great deli fare.

Wakamono	3317 N Broadway St	773-296-6800	$$	11:30 pm	Sushi and Japanese small plates.
X/O	3441 N Halsted St	773-348-9696	$$	2 am	Small plate cuisine in Boystown.
Yoshi's Café	3257 N Halsted St	773-248-6160	$$$	11 pm	Franco-Japanese fusion.

Maps 45–48 • Northwest Chicago

Amitabul	6207 N Milwaukee Ave	773-774-0276	$$	10 pm	Buddha-inspired Korean Vegan.
Birria Huentitan	4019 W North Ave	773-276-0768	$*	24 hrs	Cheap late night eats and huge burritos.
Blue Angel	5310 N Milwaukee Ave	773-631-8700	$	24-hrs	Chicago's only stunt-flier-themed 24-hour diner.
Chiyo	3800 W Lawrence Ave	773-267-1555	$$$	12 am	Order their 7-course kaiseki menu a few days in advance.
Don Juan	6730 N Northwest Hwy	773-775-6438	$$	11 pm	Popular Mexican spot.
Edgebrook Coffee Shop	6322 N Central Ave	773-792-1433	$*	2 pm	Old school homemade diner grub.
Elephant	5348 W Devon Ave	773-467-1168	$††	9 pm	Thai.
Fonda Del Mar	3749 W Fullerton Ave	773-489-3748	$$††	11 pm	Stylish Mexican food minus the price tag.
Fontana	3424 W Irving Park Rd	773-279-9359	$	8 pm	One-stop shop for Balkan baked goods, grill items, and stews.
Gale Street Inn	4914 N Milwaukee Ave	773-725-1300	$$$	10:30 pm	Classy ribs 'n' jazz joint.
Grota Smorgasborg	3112 N Central Ave	773-622-4677	$$††	10 pm	All-you-can-eat chow in medieval-feeling banquet hall.
Halina's Polish Delights	5914 W Lawrence Ave	773-205-0256	$*	9 pm	Tiny authentic Polish diner.
Hiromi's	3609 W Lawrence Ave	773-588-6764	$	2 am	Phillipine and Japanese food. Tagalong karaoke (English on request).
Joy Ribs	6320 N Lincoln Ave	773-509-0211	$$	12 pm	Korean BBQ done one better with a zingy marinade.
Mario's Café	5241 N Harlem Ave	773-594-9742	$	2:30 am	Need a quick Bulgarian fix? Mario's is the place.
Mayan Sol	3830 W Lawrence Ave	773-539-4398	$$*	10 pm	Upscale Central American and South American cuisine.
Mirabell	3454 W Addison St	773-463-1962	$$	11 pm	Adorable German tavern.
Montasero's Ristorante	3935 W Devon Ave	773-588-2515	$$	10 pm	Don't be surprised to find an envelope full of unmarked bills in the toilet tank.
Noodles	5956 W Higgins Ave	773-775-7525	$$	10 pm	Come for the Italian, stay for the dancing old folks.
Paprikash	5210 W Diversey Ave	773-736-4949	$$	11 pm	Heavy, Hungarian comfort food.
Pollo Campero	2730 N Narragansett Ave	773-622-6657	$	10 pm	Guatemalan fried-chicken chain.
Red Apple	3121 N Milwaukee Ave	773-588-5781	$††	9:30 pm	Polish comfort food. Is there any other kind?
Ristorante Agostino	2817 N Harlem Ave	773-745-6464	$$	11 pm	Elegant date place for impeccable Italian.
Sabatino's	4441 W Irving Park Rd	773-283-8331	$$	12:30 am	Romantic date place.
Seo Hae	3534 W Lawrence Ave	773-539-2444	$$††	10 pm	No frills family-owned Korean place.
So Gong Dong Tofu House	3307 W Bryn Mawr Ave	773-539-8377	$$††	10 pm	Yummy Korean tofu soup spot.
Taqueria La Oaxaquena	6113 W Diversey Ave	773-637-8709	$$	10 pm	Fancy and innovative Mexican.
Tassili Café	4342 N Elston Ave	773-685-6773	$$	12 am	Algerian food
Teresa II Polish Restaurants & Lounge	4751 N Milwaukee Ave	773-283-0184	$$*	11 pm	Clean your plate or Teresa will scold you.
Trattoria Pasta D'Arte	6311 N Milwaukee Ave	773-763-1181	$$	11 pm	Upscale, creative Italian.
Tre Kronor	3258 W Foster Ave	773-267-9888	$$	10 pm	Swedish institution.

Maps 49–52 • West Chicago

Amarind's	6822 W North Ave	773-889-9999	$$	10 pm	People drive from all over for awesome Thai food.
Bacchanalia Ristorante	2413 S Oakley Ave	773-254-6555	$$*	11 pm	Cozy Italian spot.
Bruna's	2424 S Oakley Ave	773-254-5550	$$	11 pm	Cozy old-school Italian.
Coco	2723 W Division St	773-384-4811	$$$	1 am	Upscale contemporary and classic Puerto Rican.
Coleman's Hickory House	5754 W Chicago Ave	773-287-0363	$	3 am	Killer chicken and ribs at dirt cheap prices.
Edna's Restaurant	3175 W Madison St	773-638-7079	$*	7 pm	Best soul food on the west side.
Falco's Pizza	2806 W 40th St	773-523-7996	$*	1:30 am	Popular casual Italian spot.
Feed	2803 W Chicago Ave	773-489-4600	$$*	10 pm	Tasty grilled chicken.
Flying Saucer	1123 N California Ave	773-342-9076	$$††	10 pm	Creative diner fare at hipster hangout.
Haro	2436 S Oakley Ave	773-847-2400	$$	1 am	The small plate madness is spreading!!!
Ignotz	2421 S Oakley Ave	773-579-0300	$$*	11 pm	Northern Italian in cozy setting.
La Palma	1340 N Homan Ave	773-862-0886	$††	8 pm	Authentic Puerto Rican grub at no-frills cafeteria.
Lalo's	3515 W 26th St	773-522-0345	$$	10 pm	Local chain popular for their margaritas.
Lindy's and Gertie's	3685 S Archer Ave	773-927-7807	$††	11:30 pm	Local chili and ice-cream chain.Try the chili-ice-cream sundae.
MacArthur's	5412 W Madison Ave	773-261-2316	$*	9 pm	Sweet potatoes, collard greens and grits, cafeteria style.

Maps 49–52 • West Chicago-*continued*

Maiz	1041 N California Ave	773-276-3149	$*	10 pm	Homemade corn masa antojito heaven.
New Submarine Pier	4048 S Archer Ave	773-890-4733	$*	10 pm	Best subs on this side of town.
Pico Rico	4107 W North Ave	773-252-7426	$*	10 pm	Ecuadorian rotisserie chicken joint.
Taqueria Puebla Mexico	3625 W North Ave	773-772-8435	$*	9 pm	Authentic Mexican from the Puebla region.
Taquerias Atotonilco	3916 W 26th St	773-762-3380	$*	n/a	Quick, friendly eat-in or take-out hangovercure-all.
Tommy's Rock-n-Roll Café	2548 W Chicago Ave	773-486-6768	$	4 pm	Homemade donuts, sandwiches, and guitars.

Maps 53–56 • Southwest Chicago

Beverly Woods Restaurant	11532 S Western Ave	773-233-7700	$$$	8 pm	Banqueting traditional in original Beverly Hills.
Bobak's	5725 S Archer Ave	773-735-5334	$	9 pm	A melange of Polish buffet and supermarket, Chicago style.
Franconello's Italian Restaurant	10222 S Western Ave	773-881-4100	$$	11 pm	Peek-a-boo with the chefs in the exhibition kitchen as they crank out old-world class.
Hoe China Tea	4020 W 55th St	773-284-2463	$	9:30 pm	Come for the fruity cocktails.
Jack's Java	9500 S Western Ave	708-422-4995	$$	9 pm	Very jazzy New Bronzeville café.
Janson's Drive-In / Snyder's Red Hots	9900 S Western Ave	773-238-3612	$*	10 pm	No indoor seating at this classic drive-thru.
Leona's Restaurant	11015 S Western Ave	773-881-7700	$$	11 pm	Relatively pricey, but tasty dining.
Lume's	11601 S Western Ave	773-233-2323	$	3:45 pm	Where the beautiful people breakfast and lunch.
Tatra Inn	6040 S Pulaski Rd	773-582-8313	$	8 pm	Eastern European smorgasbord.
Top Notch Beefburger	2116 W 95th St	773-445-7218	$*	8:30 pm	Burgers and fries in 50's environment—very Happy Days.
Uncle Joe's Jerk	10210 S Vincennes Ave	773-779-9966	$	8 pm	Beverly Plaza location, where jerk salad is to slay for.

Maps 57–60 • South Chicago

Army & Lou's	422 E 75th St	773-483-3100	$$	10 pm	Southside soul food.
Atomic Sub	6353 S Cottage Grove Ave	773-684-2602	$*	3 pm	Watch out, the bomb has hit!
Cal Harbor Restaurant	546 E 115th St	773-264-5435	*	6 pm	Omelettes, burgers, etc. at family grill.
Captain Hard Times	436 E 79th St	773-487-2900	$$$	12 am	Southside date destination.
Chatham Pancake House	700 E 87th St	773-874-0010	$	3 pm	Cheap, hearty breakfast.
Dat's Donuts	8251 S Cottage Grove Ave	773-723-1002	$*	10 pm	Krispy Kreme, eat your heart out.
Helen's Restaurant	1732 E 79th St	773-933-9871	$*	7 pm	Even James Brown goes to Helen's when he wants down-home cooking.
Leon's Bar-B-Que	8249 S Cottage Grove Ave	773-488-4556	$*	3 am	Southside BBQ fixture.
Phil's Kastle	3532 E 95th St	773-734-9591	$*	n/a	50s soda shop with prices to match.
Seven Seas Submarine	11216 S Michigan Ave	773-785-0550	*	8 pm	Dine in or take out at this tiny sandwich shop.
Soul Queen	9031 S Stony Island Ave	773-731-3366	$*	12 am	Inexpensive comfort food.
Soul Vegetarian East	205 E 75th St	773-224-0104	$$	11 pm	Vegetarian soul food? SVE pleases even the skeptics.
Tropic Island Jerk Chicken	1922 E 79th St	773-978-5375	$††	11 pm	Caribbean carry-out.

Evanston

Asada Brazilian Grill	1012 Church St	847-425-4175	$$$	11 pm	40 item salad bar and 18 tableside carved, roasted meats.
Blind Faith Café	525 Dempster St	847-328-6875	$$	10 pm	Vegetarian. Healthy, fiber-filled fare for the Birkenstock set. Food so earthy, you'll need to floss the dirt from your teeth.
Buffalo Joe's	812 Clark St	847-328-5525	$*	n/a	Kick-ass wings and more!
Café Mozart	600 Davis St	847-492-8056	$††	11 pm	Wireless Internet, leopard couch, snarky staff.
Clarke's	720 Clark St	847-864-1610	$	2 am	Inexpensive sandwiches and omelettes.
Dixie Kitchen	825 Church St	847-733-9030	$$	11 pm	Hot cornmeal johnnycakes, fried green tomatoes, corn fritters, North Carolina pulled pork and black eyed peas. Lawd!
Dozika	601 Dempster St	847-869-9740	$$	10 pm	Pan-Asian cuisine. Expensive, but nice variety.
Hecky's Barbeque	1902 Green Bay Rd	847-492-1182	$$	10 pm	It's the sauce that's the boss.
Jamaica Gates	618 1/2 Church St	847-869-1629	$	10 pm	Jerk chicken joint.
Joy Yee Noodle Shop	521 Davis St	847-733-1900	$$	10:30 pm	Pricey, trendy "bubble tea" specialists.
Kafein Café	1621 Chicago Ave	847-491-1621	††	2 am	Open 'til 2 am on weeknights and 3 am on weekends, perfect for those late-night cram sessions.
Las Palmas	817 University Pl	847-328-2555	$$	11 pm	High-priced margaritas; fresh Mexican fare.

Lulu's Dim Sum and Then Sum	804 Davis St	847-869-4343	$$	11 pm	Best Pad Thai in Evanston. Huge portions, reasonably priced.
Mt Everest	630 Church St	847-491-1069	$$$	10 pm	Nepalese and Indian food with lunch buffet.
Narra	1710 Orrington Ave	847-866-8700	$$$$	10 pm	Unpretentious fine dining in the Hotel Orrington.
Noodles & Company	930 Church St	847-733-1200	$$	10 pm	Thai noodles, pasta, even mac and cheese!
Olive Mountain	610 Davis St	847-475-0380	$$	10:30 pm	Middle Eastern specialties.
Pete Miller's Original Steakhouse	1557 Sherman Ave	847-328-0399	$$$$	1:30 am	American. Beef bubbas stake out this joint.
Tapas Barcelona	1615 Chicago Ave	847-866-9900	$$$	11 pm	Spanish. Lick your fingers with friends over tasty tapas and sangria.
Trattoria Demi	1571 Sherman Ave	847-332-2330	††	10 pm	Good Italian food in a cozy setting.
Unicorn Café	1723 Sherman Ave	847-332-2312	*	12 am	Quaint and reasonably priced.
Va Pensiero	Margarita Inn, 1566 Oak Ave	847-475-7779	$$$$$	10 pm	Italian. Classy, romantic supper club offering over 250 Italian wines. A "pop the question" kind of place.

Oak Park

Buzz Café	905 S Lombard Ave	708-524-2899	n/a	9 pm	Neighborhood-centric, good food, quirky art, live story-telling, and music. Nuff said!
Café Le Coq	734 Lake St	708-848-2233	$$$$	10 pm	French Bistro wows Oak Park foodies, just down the street from many of Oak Park's sites.
Cucina Paradiso	814 North Blvd	708-848-3434	$$$ ††	10:30 pm	Italian. Fork-twirling Oak Parkers come a-datin' at this friendly pasta place and bar.
Jeruselum Café	1030 Lake St	708-848-7734	$$	n/a	Terrific Middle Eastern food, with an extensive juice bar.
Khyber Pass	1031 Lake St	708-445-9032	$$	10 pm	Indian. Taxi drivers and curry-loving locals fill up on lunch and dinner buffets.
Mama Thai	1112 W Madison St	708-386-0100	$$	10 pm	Inexpensive, charming, and delicious.
Marion Street Grill	189 N Marion St	708-383-1551	*	10 pm	Inviting, upscale restaurant featuring fresh seafood, steaks, and chops. Impressive wine list.
New Rebozo	1116 Madison St	708-445-0370	$$$	10:30 pm	Best Mexican in town with a delicious upscale tweak to the specials.
Oak Park Abbey	728 Lake St	708-358-8840	$$	11 pm	Small plates have struck Oak Park and continue to spread!
Pete's Red Hots	6346 W Roosevelt Rd	708-383-6122	$*	12 am	Fast food at its finest. Best fries ever.
Petersen Ice Cream	1100 Chicago Ave	708-386-6131	$$	10 pm	American. Comfort food and silky ice cream make this diner a popular destination.
Philander's Oak Park	Carlton Hotel, 1120 Pleasant St	708-848-4250	$$$$	11:30 pm	Seafood. Marine cuisine served in handsome atmosphere; nightly, fishtail to live jazz.

Navy Pier

Bubba Gump Shrimp Co	700 E Grand Ave	312-252-4867	$$	12 am	Navy Pier tourist trap.
Capi's Italian Kitchen	700 E Grand Ave	312-276-0641	$$††	10 pm	Hand-tossed brick oven pizza.
Riva	700 E Grand Ave	312-644-7482	$$$	11 am	Touristic fine dining on the Pier.

Skokie

Barnum and Bagel	4700 Dempster St	847-676-4466	$	9 pm	Eat-in deli popular with families.
Don's Fishmarket	9335 Skokie Blvd	847-677-3424	$$$	11 pm	Popular seafood restaurant features "Shrimp Extravaganza," "Crabfest," and "Lobsterfest."
El Tipico	3341 Dempster St	847-676-4070	$$	11:30 pm	Skokie's favorite margarita and burrito joint.
Grecian Kitchen Delights	3938 Dempster St	847-677-5507	$	9 pm	Mostly carryout with good value Greek Chicken.
Hub's Ribs	3727 Dempster St	847-673-9409	††	12 am	Nothing kosher or vegetarian-friendly about this local bbq favorite.
Hy Life Bistro	4120 Dempster St	847-674-2021	*	9 pm	Kosher restaurant that is vegetarian-friendly.
Kabul House	3320 Dempster St	847-763-9930	$$	10 pm	One of Chicagoland's few Afghani restaurants.
Kaufman's Deli	4905 Dempster St	847-677-9880	$	8 pm	This is THE deli that people return to. Best bagels in the Midwest.
Papillon	5111 Brown St	847-763-1322		10 pm	French fine dining in downtown Skokie.
Pita Inn	3910 Dempster	847-677-0211	$	12 am	Local favorite for cheap, speedy falafel and shawerma.
Ruby of Siam	9420 Skokie Blvd	847-675-7008	$$	11 pm	Authentic and appealing Thai food.
Shallots Bistro	4741 Main St	847-677-3463	$$$$	10 pm	Kosher fine dining—closed Fridays and Saturdays.
Slice of Life	4120 W Dempster	847-674-2021	$$$	9 pm	Vegetarian-friendly kosher deli.

Charge up your Chicago Card, or if you're ready for traffic battles, don't forget the quarters. This city has something to offer shoppers of every taste and budget. Whether you're perusing by neighborhood or with a list in hand, comfortable shoes aren't a bad idea, either.

Downtown and High–End

Chicago is made up of several small shopping districts (and a few rather huge ones), each with its own distinct character. North Michigan Avenue, a.k.a the Mag Mile, features superstore after superstore, from the **Virgin Megastore (Map 3)** to **Niketown (Map 3)** to the **Apple Store (Map 3)** (iPod central) to **The Disney Store (Map 3)**, as well as the gamut of high–end powerhouses (**Gucci (Map 32)**, **Tiffany (Map 3)**, **Hermes (Map 32)**...). Tucked on a side street off Michigan, a two–block strip of Oak Street houses some of the city's most chi–chi boutiques, including **Prada (Map 32)**, **Nicole Miller (Map 32)**, **Ultimo (Map 32)**, and **BCBG (Map 32)**. Most of Chicago's department stores also appear on the Michigan strip. **Bloomingdale's (Map 32)**, **Neiman–Marcus (Map 3)**, and **Lord & Taylor (Map 32)** can all be found here. The old State Street district still features the gorgeous **Marshall Field's (Map 5)** flagship building and **Carson Pirie Scott (Map 5)**, but pricier retailers have cleared out and given way to such staunchly proletariat meccas as **Sears (Map 5)**.

Armitage Street in Lincoln Park is home to exclusive boutiques a–plenty. People flock from all corners to shop at **Lori's Designer Shoes** (Map 30) or browse the racks at **Cynthia Rowley (Map 30)**. Be sure to check out **Lush (Map 29, Map 32)** for body products so yummy you'll want to eat 'em. If it's chic you seek, find it on Division Street in Wicker Park. Featuring ultra–hip women's clothing stores such as **Penelope's (Map 21)**, French housewares at **Porte Rouge (Map 21)**, and **Ruby Room (Map 21)**, a spa bridging the body/ spirit connection.

Low–Key Hip

Ravenswood/North Center (known as Lincoln Square along the strip of Lincoln Avenue) offers up old world German charm at **Merz Apothecary (Map 39)** and **Delicatessen Meyer (Map 39)**, as well as some new–age choices like **Gallimaufry Gallery (Map 39)**. Beverly's is more arty–crafty. Here you can gear up to make your own green brew at **Bev Art Brewer and Winemaker Supply (Beverly / Morgan Park)**.

Vintage and More, North Side Style

Antique and thrift lovers can do their thing all over the city. **The Salvation Army (Map 25, Map 40)**, **Village Discount Outlet (Map 28, Map 38, Map 40, Map 42)**, and **Unique Thrift Store (Map 40)** (featuring half–price Mondays!) offer locations in several neighborhoods. Charity–based stores such as **Brown Elephant (Map 21, Map 37)** and **White Elephant (Map 30)** provide newer, cleaner merchandise at a slightly higher price. It's a mod, mod world in Edgewater, home to both **Broadway Antique Market (Map 37)** and **Edgewater Antique Mall (Map 37)**, two multi–dealer facilities within blocks of each other featuring the best of the 20th century. While you're on the north side, head to Andersonville and get in touch with your naughty side with a stop at **Bon Bon (Map 37)** for a decadent chocolate treat or **Tulip (Map 37, Map 44)**, a toy gallery of a strictly adult persuasion.

Calling All Rock Stars

For those who prefer their shopping on the funkier side, Wrigleyville/East Lakeview offers a variety of used book and record stores, as well as great little shops that skillfully combine vintage and retail clothing and accessories. **Strange Cargo (Map 43)**, **Hollywood Mirror (Map 43)**, and **Ragstock (Map 21, Map 43)** are top picks, and make sure you stop by **The Alley (Map 43)** for any black or leather needs. Preferably both.

Some of Chicago's best shopping treasures are the unique little stores that anchor every neighborhood. From housewares shops in Chinatown to Sari palaces and authentic chai on Devon, from academic bookshops in Hyde Park to the West Side's Harlem Irving Plaza, Chicago offers the willing consumer plenty of opportunities to burn through their credit limits.

Map 1 • River North / Fulton Market District

Doolin's	511 N Halsted St	312-243-9424	Party decorations galore, closed Sundays.

Map 2 • Near North / River North

American Girl Place	111 E Chicago Ave	817-247-5223	Stepford dolls for your 'tween.
Jazz Record Mart	27 E Illinois St	312-222-1467	Jazz-lover's emporium.
Mig and Tig Furniture	540 N Wells St	312-644-8277	Classic well-made furniture.
Montauk	401 N Wells St	312-951-5688	The most comfortable sofas.
Orange Skin	223 W Erie St	773-394-4500	Objects of desire and high design.
Paper Source	232 W Chicago Ave	312-337-0798	Great paper and invitations.

Map 3 • Streeterville / Mag Mile

Apple Store	679 N Michigan Ave	312-981-4104	All of their newest and shiniest offerings, plus classes and seminars.
Chicago Place	700 N Michigan Ave	312-266-7710	Upscale mall.
Disney Store	717 N Michigan Ave	312-654-9208	M-i-c-k-e-Why?
Garrett Popcorn Shop	670 N Michigan Ave	312-944-4730	Everything you could possibly think of related to popcorn.
Neiman-Marcus	737 N Michigan Ave	312-642-5900	Affectionately known as "Needless Mark-up" by those who can afford it anyway.
Niketown	669 N Michigan Ave	312-642-6363	Nike label sports clothing.
Ralph Lauren	750 N Michigan Ave	312-280-1655	If you love those little polo horses...
Tiffany & Co	730 N Michigan Ave	312-944-7500	Deluxe jeweler.
Virgin Megastore	540 N Michigan Ave	312-645-9300	Music, books, videos, DVDs.

Map 4 • West Loop Gate / Greek Town

Athenian Candle Co	300 S Halsted St	312-332-6988	Candles, curse-breakers, Greek trinkets, and much more.
Greek Town Music	330 S Halsted St	312-263-6342	Music, T-shirts, hats—everything Greek!

Map 5 • The Loop

American Music World	111 N State St	312-781-4050	The place to go if you're looking to buy an instrument.
Carson Pirie Scott	1 S State St	312-641-7000	Department store.
Gallery 37 Store	66 E Randolph St	312-744-7274	Speciality gifts.
Kramer's Health Food Center	230 S Wabash Ave	312-922-0077	Healthy hippie heaven.
Marshall Field's	111 N State St	312-781-1000	Department store.
Rock Records	175 W Washington St	312-346-3489	Good CD store.
Sears	2 N State St	312-373-6000	Blue-collar stalwart.

Map 6 • The Loop / Grant Park

Art & Artisans	108 S Michigan Ave	312-641-0088	Art gallery.
Museum Shop of the Art Institute	111 S Michigan Ave	800-518-4214	Art Institute gift shop.
Poster Plus	200 S Michigan Ave	800-659-1905	Vintage posters and custom framing.
Precious Possessions	28 N Michigan Ave	312-726-8118	Mineral shop.
The Savvy Traveller	310 S Michigan Ave	312-913-9800	Travel goods for the Phineas Fogg in us all.

Map 7 • South Loop / River City

Adam Joseph's Hats	544 W Roosevelt Rd	312-913-1855	Haberdashery and menswear.
Fishman's Fabrics	1101 S Des Plaines St	312-922-7250	Huge fabric wholesaler.
Lee's Foreign Car Service	727 S Jefferson St	312-663-0823	Import parts and service.
Morris & Sons	555 W Roosevelt Rd	312-243-5635	Mostly men, off-price Italian designers.

Map 8 • South Loop / Printers Row / Dearborn Park

Kozy's Bike Shop	601 S La Salle St	312-360-0020	Bikes and accessories in a fun loft setting.
Printer's Row Fine and Rare Books	715 S Dearborn St	312-583-1800	Fine and rare books.
Sandmeyer's Book Store	714 S Dearborn St	312-922-2104	Dream come true if you love books and atmosphere.

Map 9 • South Loop / South Michigan Ave

Bariff Shop	618 S Michigan Ave	312-322-1740	Unique Hanukkah gifts include yiddishwear and the Moses action figure.

Map 10 • East Pilsen / Chinatown

Chinatown Bazaar	2221 S Wentworth Ave	312-225-1088	Part clothing store, part knick-knack shop.
Pacific Imports	2200 S Wentworth Ave	312-808-0456	Mostly home furnishings.
Sun Sun Tong	2260 S Wentworth Ave	312-842-6398	Stock up on Chinese herbs and teas.
Ten Ren Tea & Ginseng Co	2247 S Wentworth Ave	312-842-1171	The only place to buy ginseng.
Woks 'n' Things	2234 S Wentworth Ave	312-842-0701	Stir-fry utensils and cookware.

Map 11 • South Loop / McCormick Place

Blue Star Auto Stores	2001 S State St	312-225-0717	All your auto needs.
Cycle Bicycle Shop	1465 S Michigan Ave	312-987-1080	Bike shop, obviously.
Waterware	1829 S State St	312-225-4549	Designer plumbing fixtures.

Map 12 • Bridgeport (West)

Best's Kosher Outlet Store	1000 W Pershing Rd	773-650-6338	Packaged deli meats and made-to-order sandwiches.
Bridgeport Antiques	2963 S Archer Ave	773-927-9070	Old stuff.

Map 13 • Bridgeport (East)

Ace Bakery	3241 S Halsted St	312-225-4973	Excellent breads and pastries.
Augustine's Spiritual Goods	3327 S Halsted St	773-843-1933	Mystical and religious knick-knacks.
Bridgeport News Travel & Tours	3252 S Halsted St	312-225-6311	Travel store.
Health King Enterprises Chinese Medicinals	238 W 31st St	312-567-9978	Natural remedies.
Henry's Sports & Bait Shop	3130 S Canal St	312-225-8538	Fishing mecca.
Let's Boogie Records & Tapes	3321 S Halsted St	773-254-0139	Music.

Map 14 • Prairie Shores / Lake Meadows

Ashley Stewart	3455 S Dr Martin L King Jr Dr	312-567-0405	Women's clothing.
Avenue	3429 S Dr Martin L King Jr Dr	312-808-1492	Modern plus-size clothes.

Map 16 • Bronzeville

Afrocentric Bookstore	4655 S King Dr	773-924-3966	The authority on Afrocentic literature.
Issues Barber & Beauty Salon	3958 S Cottage Grove Ave	773-924-4247	Beauty salon.
Leaders 1354	4351 S Cottage Grove Ave	773-285-1067	The place for hip-hop fit and skateboards and spray-pained murals of Harold Washington, Marley, Che, and Malcolm.
Parker House Sausage Co	4605 S State St	773-538-1112	All types of sausages.
Sensual Steps	4518 S Cottage Grove Ave	773-548-FEET	A sanctuary for fancy kicks, handbags, camisoles, jewelry, and shawls by mainstream and black designers.

Map 17 • Kenwood

Coop's Records	1350 E 47th St	773-538-5277	Music.
South Shore Décor	1328 E 47th St	773-373-3116	Wall coverings, paint, blinds, and window treatments galore.

Map 19 • Hyde Park

57th Street Books	1301 E 57th St	773-684-1300	Brainy, independent bookstore.
The Baby PhD Store	5225 S Harper Ave	773-684-8920	For the smart kid.
Borders	1539 E 53rd St	773-752-8663	Check out the outside Patio.
Coconuts	1506 E 53rd St	773-667-2455	Mainstream music anyone?
Cohn & Stern for Men	1500 E 55th St	773-752-8100	Men's accessories.
Dr Wax Records and Tapes	5225 S Harper Ave	773-493-8696	Old-style vinyl.
Futons N More	1370 E 53rd St	773-324-7083	Futons 'n more.
House of Africa	1510 E 63rd St	773-324-6858	Afrocentric everything.
Hyde Park Records	1377 E 53rd St	773-288-6588	Buy/sell vintage LPs.
O'Gara and Wilson	1448 E 57th St	773-363-0993	Rare and out-of-print books.
Powell's Bookstore	1501 E 57th St	773-955-7780	Famous bookstore.
Toys Et Cetera	5211 S Harper Ave	773-324-6039	Just for fun.
Wesley's Shoe Corral	1506 E 55th St	773-667-7463	Shoes.
Wheels and Things	5210 S Harper Ave	773-493-4326	Bike sales and repairs.

Map 20 • East Hyde Park / Jackson Park

Art's Cycle Sales & Service	1652 E 53rd St	773-363-7524	Bike sales and repairs.

Map 21 • Wicker Park / Ukrainian Village

American Apparel	1563 N Milwaukee Ave	773-235-6778	Sweatshop-free clothes Wicker Park boutique.
Asrai Garden	1935 W North Ave	773-782-0680	Flowers and garden.
The Brown Elephant	1459 N Milwaukee Ave	773-252-8801	Resale boutique benefits Howard Brown Health Center.
Casa de Soul	1919 W Division St	773-252-2520	Asian/African-inspired global lifestyle boutique for men and women.
Cattails	1935 W Division St	773-486-1621	A unique flower market.
City Soles	2001 W North Ave	773-489-2001	Up to $600 a pop for the latest European soles.
DeciBel Audio	1407 N Milwaukee Ave	773-862-6700	New and used stereo equipment.
Habit	1951 W Division St	773-342-0093	Indie/local designer's collective.
hejfina	1529 N Milwaukee Ave	773-772-0002	Sleek, sophisticated boutique.
Jade	1557 N Milwaukee Ave	773-342-5233	Hip women's boutique.
Lille	1923 W North Ave	773-342-0563	Great little things for the home.
Lilly Vallente	1746 W Division St	773-645-1537	Vintage/thrift store.
Modern Times	1538 N Milwaukee Ave	773-772-8871	Vintage mid-century modern funishings.
Myopic Bookstore	1564 N Milwaukee Ave	773-862-4882	A Wicker Park brainy-hipster institution.
Nina	1655 W Division St	773-486-8996	Yarn shop includes delicate, frayed thread from old saris.
Paper Doll	1747 W Division St	773-227-6950	Paper and cards.
Penelope's	1913 W Division St	773-395-2351	Casual, stylish women's clothes.
Plein Aire	2036 W Division St	773-227-3722	Cute, affordable boutique.
Porte Rouge	1911 W Division St	773-269-2800	Fancy French housewares and free tea.
Quimby's Bookstore	1854 W North Ave	773-342-0910	Books and music.
Ragstock	1433 N Milwaukee Ave	773-486-1783	Funky vintage clothes and trendy irregulars.
Reckless Records	1532 N Milwaukee Ave	773-235-3727	Mostly indie music-new and used.
Ruby Room	1743 W Division St	773-235-2323	A "spa for the spirit" of the chic.
Silver Moon	1755 W North Ave	773-235-5797	Amazing vintage.
The Silver Room	1442 N Milwaukee Ave	773-278-7130	Clothing and accessories.
Symmetry	1925 W Division St	773-645-0502	Upscale/modern furniture and décor featuring Tibetan rugs.
Tatine	1742 W Division St	773-342-1890	Fancy candle/soap store.
Una Mae's Freak Boutique	1422 N Milwaukee Ave	773-276-7002	A Wicker Park staple—vintage and new clothing.
Untitled	1941 W North Ave	773-342-0500	Uber-hipster clothing.
Wag Artworks	2121 W Division St	773-772-2922	Gallery featuring wall art, jewelry, and various other forms of artwork.

Map 22 • Noble Square / Goose Island

Best Buy	1000 W North Ave	312-988-4067	Electronics and home appliances monolith.
Cost Plus World Market	1623 N Sheffield Ave	312-587-8037	Like Pier One, but with food and wine.
Dusty Groove Records	1120 N Ashland Ave	773-342-5800	Vinyl and CDs. Specializes in funk, soul, rare groove, now sound, and world music.
Irv's Luggage Warehouse	820 W North Ave	312-787-4787	Carries some discounted luggage and briefcases.
J Crew	929 W North Ave	312-951-0784	We've mastered the fine art of breaking in chinos.
Old Navy	1596 N Kingsbury St	312-397-0485	Inexpensive fashion chain.
Olga's Flower Shop	1041 N Ashland Ave	773-645-9160	Flowers for all occasions.
Restoration Hardware	938 W North Ave	312-475-9116	Fancy housewares.
Right-On Futon	1184 N Milwaukee Ave	773-235-2533	Need a new bed? Check this place out!
Transitions Bookplace	1000 W North Ave	312-951-7323	Books on spirituality, health, etc. Has a café.
Wax Addict Records	1014 N Ashland Ave	773-772-9930	Popular with DJs and other wax addicts.

Map 23 • West Town / Near West Side

Alcala's	1733 W Chicago Ave	312-226-0152	Western-wear emporium sells boots, jeans and cowboy hats.
Bleeding Heart Bakery	2018 W Chicago Ave	773-278-3638	Proof that politically-correct pastry—organic, sustainable— tastes good.
Decoro Studio	2000 W Carroll St	312-850-9260	Lot filled with Asian antiques and furniture.
Donofrio's Double Corona Cigars	2058 W Chicago Ave	773-342-7820	Brian Donofrio sells very fine imported cigars.
H&R Sports	1739 W Chicago Ave	312-226-8737	Soccer gear.
Rotofugi	1953 W Chicago Ave	312-491-9501	Really cool toy store with urban vinyl figures.
Salvage One Architectural Elements	1840 W Hubbard St	312-733-0098	Warehouse of antique, vintage and salvaged architectural pieces for home/loft restoration.
Sprout Home	745 N Damen Ave	312-226-5950	Plants and gardening supplies meet modernism.
Tomato Tattoo	1855 W Chicago Ave	312-226-6660	Every hip strip needs a tattoo parlor.

Map 24 • River West / West Town

3 Design Three	1431 W Chicago Ave	312-738-0333	Funky furniture with style, open by appointment.
Aesthetic Eye	1520 W Chicago Ave	312-243-1520	Art gallery, irregular hours.
Casati	949 W Fulton Market	312-421-9905	Mid-century Italian furniture and accessories.
Chicago Avenue Discount	1637 W Chicago Ave	312-226-0004	Shoes for $1.93!
Design Inc	1359 W Grand Ave	312-243-4333	Architecturally centered home design.
Douglas Dawson Gallery	400 N Morgan St	312-226-7975	Fancy artifacts from around the world.
Jan's Antiques	225 N Racine Ave	312-563-0275	Mind-boggling antique emporium.
MK Brody	1101 W Randolph St	800-652-7639	Piñatas and balloons.
PakMail	1461 W Chicago Ave	312-664-2866	Packing supplies, FedEx, UPS.
Pet Care Plus	1212 W Grand Ave	312-397-9077	For the pet-obsessed.
The Realm	1430 W Chicago Ave	312-491-0999	Exotic furniture from far-away places.
Roots	1140 W Grand Ave	312-666-6466	Trendy hair salon.
RR#1 Chicago Apothecary	814 N Ashland Blvd	312-421-9079	Old-school pharmacy.
Snap	470 N Ogden Ave	312-226-5110	Hair and nail salon.
Upgrade Cycle Works	1130 W Chicago Ave	312-226-8650	Bikes, accessories and servicing.
Xyloform	1423 W Chicago Ave	312-455-7949	Furniture store.

Map 25 • Illinois Medical District

Accents Flowers and Gifts	2246 W Taylor St	312-850-4438	Flower shop conveniently located near major hospitals.
Salvation Army Thrift Store	2024 S Western Ave	773-254-1127	Good 'ol fashioned thrifting.

Map 26 • University Village/ Little Italy / Pilsen

Conte Di Savoia	1438 W Taylor St	312-666-3471	European and Italian specialties.
Lush Wine and Spirits	1306 S Halsted St	312-738-1900	Wine, microbrews, and booze.
Scafuri Bakery	1337 W Taylor St	312-733-8881	The secret's in the bread.

Map 27 • Logan Square

Fleur	3149 W Logan Blvd	773-395-2770	Not your mother's floral arrangements, plus handmade goods from locals.
Provenance Food and Wine	2528 N California Ave	773-384-0699	Reasonably priced wines and unreasonably priced groceries.
Threads, Etc	2327 N Milwaukee Ave	773-276-6411	Resale clothes and furniture.

Map 28 • Bucktown

Bleeker Street Antiques	1946 N Leavitt St	773-862-3185	Fine selection of antiques.
G Boutique	2131 N Damen Ave	773-235-1234	Lingerie and bedroom accessories.
Goddess and the Grocer	1646 N Damen Ave	773-342-3200	Gourmet groceries and take-out.
Jean Alan	2134 N Damen Ave	773-278-2345	House and home.
Jolie Joli	1623 N Damen Ave	773-342-7272	Clothing and accessories.
Mark Shale Outlet	2593 N Elston Ave	773-772-9600	Great deals on grown-up clothes.
p.45	1643 N Damen Ave	773-862-4523	Edgy women's boutique.
Pagoda Red	1714 N Damen Ave	773-235-1188	Fine Asian antiques.
Pavilion Antiques	2055 N Damen Ave	773-645-0924	Antique furniture.
Red Balloon Company	2060 N Damen Ave	773-489-9800	A unique store for children—toys, clothes and furniture.
Robin Richman	2108 N Damen Ave	773-278-6150	Arty, indie boutique.
T-Shirt Deli	1739 N Damen Ave	773-276-6266	Pricey—but quality—custom-made t-shirts.
Tangerine	1719 N Damen Ave	773-772-0505	Feminine women's boutique.
Vienna Beef Factory Store	2501 N Damen Ave	773-278-7800	Here's the beef.
Village Discount Outlet	2032 N Milwaukee Ave	866-545-3866	Tons of clothes and weekly specials.
Vive La Femme	2115 N Damen Ave	773-772-7429	Style beyond size.

Map 29 • DePaul / Wrightwood / Sheffield

Active Endeavors	853 W Armitage Ave	773-281-8100	Playing sports or heading into the great outdoors? This is your place for gear.
Dirk's Fish	2070 N Clybourn Ave	773-404-3475	Carry out fresh fish and seafood spot.
Eskell	953 W Webster Ave	773-477-9390	Local/indie designer boutique.
Isabella Fine Lingerie	1101 W Webster Ave	773-281-2352	Fine after-hours wear.
Jayson Home & Garden	1885 N Clybourn Ave	773-248-8180	Flowers and garden.

Map 29 • DePaul / Wrightwood / Sheffield–*continued*

Left Bank	1155 W Webster Ave	773-929-7422	Jewelry and home décor.
Lush Cosmetics	859 W Armitage Ave	773-281-5874	Handmade soaps and natural cosmetics—too bad they aren't edible.
Sam's Wine and Liquor Warehouse	1720 N Marcey St	312-664-4394	Great selection, accessories, classes, and free samples.
Tabula Tua	1015 W Armitage Ave	773-525-3500	Housewares.
Uncle Dan's	2440 N Lincoln Ave	773-477-1918	One-stop shopping for survivalists.
Vosges Haut Chocolat	951 W Armitage Ave	773-296-9866	Delicious exotic gourmet chocolates flavored with Indian spices, whiskey, etc.
Wine Discount Center	1826 N Elston Ave	773-489-3454	Wine warehouse—free tastings every Saturday.

Map 30 • Lincoln Park

Art & Science	1971 N Halsted St	312-787-4247	Beauty salon.
Barneys New York Co-Op	2209 N Halsted St	773-248-0426	Barney's "affordable" sister.
Buy Popular Demand	2629 N Halsted St	773-868-0404	Consignment shop offering affordable fashions.
Cynthia Rowley	808 W Armitage Ave	773-528-6160	Apparel and accessories.
Dave's Records	2604 N Clark St	773-929-6325	All LPs, from Janacek to Jay-Z.
Ethan Allen	1700 N Halsted St	312-573-2500	Furniture store.
Gallery 1756	1756 N Sedgwick St	312-642-6900	Fine art.
GNC	2740 N Clark St	773-883-3008	General nutrition center.
Hi Fi Records	2568 N Clark St	773-880-1002	Pint-sized music store with a style for everyone.
Lori's Designer Shoes	824 W Armitage Ave	773-281-5655	Designer shoes.
Sally Beauty Supply	2727 N Clark St	773-477-6222	Wholesale for stylists, but open to the public.
Triangle Gallery of Old Town	1763 N North Park Ave	312-337-1938	Don't miss their openings.
White Elephant	2300 Children's Plz	773-880-4237	Resale shop at the Children's Memorial Hospital.

Map 31 • Old Town / Near North

Crate & Barrel Outlet Store	1864 N Clybourn Ave	312-787-4775	Housewares.
Etre	1361 N Wells St	312-266-8101	Upscale boutique.
Fleet Feet Sports	210 W North Ave	312-587-3338	The staff watches you run to make sure the shoes fit.
Fudge Pot	1532 N Wells St	312-943-1777	A chocolate institution.
Jumbalia	1429 N Wells St	312-335-9082	Great gift store.
Old Town Gardens	1555 N Wells St	312-266-6300	Beautiful plants and flowers.
The Spice House	1512 N Wells St	312-274-0378	Spice up your cooking.
Up Down Tobacco	1550 N Wells St	312-337-8025	Great selection of cigars, cigarettes, and accessories.
Village Cycle	1337 N Wells St	312-751-2488	Good urban cycling store.

Map 32 • Gold Coast / Mag Mile

Anthropologie	1120 N State St	312-255-1848	Hip clothing and knick-knacks.
Barney's New York	25 E Oak St	312-587-1700	Upscale boutique, clothing and accessories.
BCBG	55 E Oak St	312-787-7395	Apparel and accessories.
Bloomingdale's	900 N Michigan Ave	312-440-4460	Upscale department store.
Bravco Beauty Center	43 E Oak St	312-943-4305	For those who like to be pampered.
Chanel at the Drake Hotel	935 N Michigan Ave	312-787-5000	Classic, expensive clothing, accessories, and fragrances.
Club Monaco	900 N Michigan Ave	312-787-8757	Fashion-forward clothing that doesn't try too hard.
Elements	102 E Oak St	312-642-6574	Cool house-y stuff.
Europa Books	832 N State St	312-335-9677	International magazines.
Fitigues Surplus	50 E Oak St	312-943-8676	Outlet store of women's designer gear.
Frette	41 E Oak St	312-649-3744	European furniture and accessories.
G'bani	949 N State St	312-440-1718	Shoes.
Gucci	900 N Michigan Ave	312-664-5504	Tom Ford's alluring and provocative clothes and accessories.
H&M	840 N Michigan Ave	312-640-0060	European department store taking Chicago by storm.
Hermes	110 E Oak St	312-787-8175	Fancy scarves and more.
Hershey's Chicago	822 N Michigan Ave	312-337-7711	Dumb and fun chocoholic tourist trap.
Lush Cosmetics	835 N Michigan Ave	312-573-1805	Handmade soaps and natural cosmetics—too bad they aren't edible!
Lord & Taylor	835 N Michigan Ave	312-787-7400	You'd have to be a lord to shop here.
MAC	40 E Oak St	312-951-7310	Fabulous make-up.
Nicole Miller	63 E Oak St	312-664-3532	Female fashion.
Paul Stuart X/S	John Hancock Ctr, 875 N Michigan Ave	312-640-2650	Located on the second floor, one of only two Paul Stuart outlets in the world. So far.
Prada	30 E Oak St	312-951-1113	Expensive, but delightful clothing and accessories.
Pratesi	67 E Oak St	312-943-8422	Linens.
Tod's	121 E Oak St	312-943-0070	Clothing.
Ultimate Bride	106 E Oak St	312-337-6300	Bridal gear.
Ultimo	114 E Oak St	312-787-1171	Apparel and accessories.
Urban Outfitters	935 N Rush St	312-640-1919	Retro clothing, nifty gifts, and cool accessories.
Water Tower	845 N Michigan Ave	312-440-3166	Marshall Fields, er, Macy's.

Map 33 • West Rogers Park

Argo Georgian Bakery	2812 W Devon Ave	773-764-6322	Some Russian baked goods for your trouble?
AutoZone	2555 W Touhy Ave	773-764-5277	Stuff for your car.
Cheesecakes by JR	2841 W Howard St	773-465-6733	Over 20 flavors of cheesecakes.
Chicago Harley Davidson	6868 N Western Ave	773-338-6868	Hogs, gear, etc.
Levinson's Bakery	2856 W Devon Ave	773-761-3174	Always fresh!
Office Mart	2801 W Touhy Ave	773-262-3924	Combination office supply store and Internet coffee shop.
Raj Jewels	2652 W Devon Ave	773-465-5755	For all your Indian wedding needs.
Resham's	2540 W Devon Ave	773-764-9692	Saris and fabric fill the store.
Taj Sari Palace	2553 W Devon Ave	773-338-0177	Beautiful Indian clothing and accessories.
Tel-Aviv Kosher Bakery	2944 W Devon Ave	773-764-8877	Under the supervision of Rabbi Chaim Goldzweig!
Three Sisters Deli	2854 W Devon Ave	773-973-1919	Russian deli with fresh herring, smoked meats, and caviar.

Map 34 • East Rogers Park

Mar-Jen Discount Furniture	1536 W Devon Ave	773-338-6636	Cheap futons, dorm furniture.

Map 35 • Arcadia Terrace / Peterson Park

Grazer's Gourmet	5333 N Lincoln Ave	773-561-5500	Homemade granola minus the macramé.

Map 36 • Bryn Mawr

Easy Street	5206 N Damen Ave	773-728-6978	Antiques and collectibles, you know the drill.
Target	2036 W Peterson Ave	n/a	All you need, under one roof.

Map 37 • Edgewater / Andersonville

Alamo Shoes	5321 N Clark St	773-334-6100	Large selection for the soles from local retailer.
Alchemy Arts	1203 W Bryn Mawr Ave	800-WITCHES	Old-school occult shop.
Blue Hydrangea	1113 W Berwyn Ave	773-293-1113	Friendly flower shop.
Bon Bon	5410 N Clark St	773-784-9882	Sweet handmade chocolate boutique.
Broadway Antique Market	6130 N Broadway St	773-743-5444	BAM! Calling all mallrats and antique freaks—one of America's most reviewed antique stores.
Brown Elephant	5404 N Clark St	773-271-9382	Resale shop benefits local HIV clinic.
Cassona	5241 N Clark St	773-506-7882	Gorgeous home furnishings.
Early to Bed	5232 N Sheridan Rd	773-271-1219	Woman-oriented grown-up toys. Boy friendly.
Edgewater Antique Mall	6314 N Broadway St	773-262-2525	20th century antiques and vintage.
Elda de la Rosa	5555 N Sheridan Rd	773-769-3128	Custom gowns and dresses.
Erickson Jewelers	5304 N Clark St	773-275-2010	Large selection of jewelry.
Gethsemane Garden Center	5739 N Clark St	773-878-5915	Like mini-trip to a botanical garden; but you can take it home.
Johnny Sprocket's	1052 W Bryn Mawr Ave	773-293-1695	Caters to all your bicycle needs.
Kate the Great Bookstore	5550 N Broadway St	773-561-1932	Friendly staff actually knows something about books.
Middle East Bakery	1512 W Foster Ave	773-561-2224	So good, so cheap.
Paper Trail	5309 N Clark St	773-275-2191	Paper boutique and cards galore.
Presence	5216 N Clark St	773-989-4420	Cool boutique for young women.
Scout	5221 N Clark St	773-275-5700	Beautiful urban antiques.
Soothe Your Senses Day Spa	6260 N Broadway St	773-262-4246	Bringing Southern charm to Chicago.
Surrender	5225 N Clark St	773-784-4455	Health and beauty.
Toys & Treasures	5311 N Clark St	773-769-5311	Educational toys and quality books for kids.
Tulip Toy Gallery	1480 W Berwyn Ave	773-275-6110	Woman-owned, inviting sex paraphenalia shop.
White Attic	5408 N Clark St	773-907-9800	Clean home furnishings and art work.
Wikstrom's Scandinavian Foods and Gifts	5247 N Clark St	773-275-6100	The Swedish epicenter of Andersonville.
Women & Children First	5233 N Clark St	773-769-9299	World's biggest feminist book and music store.

Map 38 • Ravenswood / Albany Park

Lincoln Antique Mall	3115 W Irving Park Rd	773-604-4700	Mid-sized antique mall.
The Music Store	3121 W Irving Park Rd	773-478-7400	Guitars and other musical instruments.
Odin Tatu	3313 W Irving Park Rd	773-442-8288	Get inked.
Rave Sports	3346 W Lawrence Ave	773-588-7176	Athletic shoes and clothing.
Sassy Boutique	3210 W Lawrence Ave	773-539-1738	Cute partywear for 20-somethings. (Sign on store inexplicably reads "Tomato").
Scents & Sensibility	4654 N Rockwell St	773-267-3838	Cards. And things to put your cards and candles and flowers into.
Village Discount Outlet	3301 W Lawrence Ave	866-545-3866	Tons of clothes and weekly specials.
Village Discount Outlet	4027 N Kedzie Ave	866-545-3866	Tons of clothes and weekly specials.

Map 39 • Ravenswood / North Center

Angel Food Bakery	1636 W Montrose Ave	773-728-1512	Whimsical bakery with interesting sandwiches to go.
Architectural Artifacts	4325 N Ravenswood Ave	773-348-0622	Renovator's dream.
Book Cellar	4736 N Lincoln Ave	773-293-2665	Book store/coffee shop/wine bar. Also has sandwiches.

Map 39 • Ravenswood / North Center—*continued*

The Cheese Stands Alone	4547 N Western Ave	773-293-3870	Artisinal cheeses from Europe and America in this delightfully stinky shop.
The Chopping Block	4747 N Lincoln Ave	773-472-6700	Gourmet cooking utensils and cooking classes.
Delicatessen Meyer	4750 N Lincoln Ave	773-561-3377	German delicatessen, excellent sausage, German wines and beers, etc.
Different Strummer	4544 N Lincoln Ave	773-751-3398	Guitars and such.
East Meets West	2118 W Lawrence Ave	773-275-1976	Handpicked fair-trade global wares.
European Import Center	4752 N Lincoln Ave	773-561-8281	Beer steins and other gifts from Bavaria.
Evil Clown Records	4314 N Lincoln Ave	773-509-0708	Evil clowns disguised as savvy music clerks.
Gallimaufry Gallery	4712 N Lincoln Ave	773-728-3600	Artisan crafts including instruments, incense, stone fountains.
Glass Art & Decorative Studio	4507 N Lincoln Ave	773-561-9008	Stained glass and gifts.
Griffins & Gargoyles Antiques	2140 W Lawrence Ave	773-769-1255	Pine furniture from Europe.
Hazel	1902 W Montrose Ave	773-769-2227	Stylish gifts and jewelry, plus an extensive stationery section.
Laurie's Planet of Sound	4639 N Lincoln Ave	773-271-3569	Funky CD shop.
Margie's Candies	1813 W Montrose Ave	773-348-0400	Second generation of a Chicago classic.
Martin's Big & Tall Store for Men	4745 N Lincoln Ave	773-784-5853	The name says it all.
Merz Apothecary	4716 N Lincoln Ave	773-989-0900	German and other imported toiletries, herbal supplements, etc. The original.
Quake Collectables	4628 N Lincoln Ave	773-878-4288	Vintage toys and fun!
Timeless Toys	4749 N Lincoln Ave	773-334-4445	Old-fashioned toys.

Map 40 • Uptown

Eagle Leathers	5005 N Clark St	773-728-7228	Come to daddy.
Play It Again Sports	3939 N Ashland Ave	773-463-9900	Sporting goods.
Salvation Army Thrift Store	4315 N Broadway St	773-348-1401	Good 'ol fashioned thrifting.
Shake Rattle and Read Book Box	4812 N Broadway St	773-334-5311	Funky used bookstore; great finds, but cluttered.
Tai Nam Market Center	4925 N Broadway St	773-275-5666	Vietnamese. Very good.
Unique Thrift Store	4445 N Sheridan Rd	773-275-8623	Half-price Mondays.
Village Discount Outlet	4898 N Clark St	866-545-3866	Tons of clothes and weekly specials.
Wilson Broadway Mall	1114 W Wilson Ave	773-561-0300	Socks, shoes, ethnic shopping, music, luggage—it's all here.

Map 42 • North Center / Roscoe Village / West Lakeview

Antique Resources	1741 W Belmont Ave	773-871-4242	Large inventory of antique furniture.
Father Time Antiques	2108 W Belmont Ave	773-880-5599	Antiques store.
Glam to Go	2002 W Roscoe St	773-525-7004	Girly-girls get pampered.
Good Old Days Antiques	2138 W Belmont Ave	773-472-8837	Antiques and treasures.
Lynn's Hallmark	3353 N Lincoln Ave	773-281-8108	Cards, stationery, and gift wrap.
My Closet	3350 N Paulina St	773-388-9851	Marked-down designer wear from Bloomingdale's and Macy's.
Village Discount Outlet	2043 W Roscoe St	866-545-3866	Tons of clothes and weekly specials.

Map 43 • Wrigleyville/ East Lakeview

The Alley	3228 N Clark St	773-883-1800	Skulls, tattoos, big boots.
Belmont Army Surplus	855 W Belmont Ave	773-549-1038	Combo of name brand, trendy men's and women's clothing, and army surplus wear.
Bookworks	3444 N Clark St	773-871-5318	Friendly, well-organized used books.
Disgraceland	3338 N Clark St	773-281-5875	Two floors of decent resale clothing.
Fashion Tomato	937 W Belmont Ave	773-281-2921	Cheap, trendy clothes for girls who go to clubs and like to "party."
Hollywood Mirror	812 W Belmont Ave	773-404-2044	Vintage clothes and kitschy doo-dads.
Krista K	3458 N Southport Ave	773-248-1967	Snobby clothes for snobby women but good selection of jeans.
Midwest Stereo	1613 W Belmont Ave	773-975-4250	DJ equipment, fog machines, strobe lights.
Namaskar Boutique	3950 N Southport Ave	773-472-0930	Yoga accessories.
Never Mind	953 W Belmont Ave	773-472-4922	Trendy accessories and clothes for trixie girls.
Ragstock	812 W Belmont Ave	773-868-9263	Vintage resale and trendy off-price clothes.
Shane	3657 N Southport Ave	773-549-0179	High-end trendy clothing for 20-somethings.
Strange Cargo	3448 N Clark St	773-327-8090	Hip affordable threads for the 20-somethings.
Uncle Fun	1338 W Belmont Ave	773-477-8223	Cramped and crazy retro toys and novelties.

Map 44 • East Lakeview

Borderline	3333 N Broadway St	773-975-9533	Dance music store named after Madonna song.
The Brown Elephant Resale	3651 N Halsted St	773-549-5943	Resale boutique benefits Howard Brown Health Clinic.
Century Mall	2828 N Clark St	773-929-8100	Most notable occupants include the cinema and Bally's Fitness.
Clothes Optional	2918 N Clark St	773-296-6630	Funky thrift store.
Cupcakes	613 W Briar Pl	708-525-0817	Just fancy cupcakes.
Equinox	3401 N Broadway St	773-281-9151	Gifts and glassware—great Xmas ornament selection.
GayMart	3459 N Halsted St	773-929-4272	Gay Barbie and other homo kitsch and gifts.
Onu Asian Mart	3310 N Broadway St	773-880-9280	All your Asian staples.

Pastoral Artisan	2945 N Broadway St	773-472-4781	Fancy cheese, wine, and other gourmet items to go.
The Pleasure Chest	3155 N Broadway St	773-525-7151	Sextastic adult store.
Reckless Records	3161 N Broadway St	773-404-5080	Oldies and new releases on vinyl.
Spare Parts	2947 N Broadway St	773-525-4242	Cool bags, purses, and man purses.
Tulip Toy Gallery	3448 N Halsted St	773-975-1515	Woman-owned, inviting sex paraphenalia shop.
Unabridged Bookstore	3251 N Broadway St	773-883-9119	Helpful bookstore with great travel, kids and gay sections.
Windy City Sweets	3308 N Broadway St	773-477-6100	Old-fashioned candy shop with homemade fudge.

Maps 45–48 • Northwest Chicago

Albany Office Supply	3419 W Lawrence Ave	773-267-6000	A substantial portion of the store is devoted to Hello Kitty. Some other stuff too, but who cares about that?
American Science & Surplus	5316 N Milwaukee Ave	773-763-0313	Your one-stop obscure gizmo shop.
El Mundo Del Dulce (Candy World)	4806 N Drake Ave	773-866-0659	Candy for children, pinatas, party supplies.
Harlem Irving Plaza	N Harlem Ave & W Irving Park Blvd	773-625-3036	Every tacky, low-end, wholesale-to-public you could ever want.
NY Shoes Imports	3546 W Lawrence Ave	773-509-9903	Has slightly fetishistic edge; interesting lingerie in back.
Perfumes R' Us	3608 W Lawrence Ave	773-463-9575	Well-known name brand perfumes including Nina Ricci, Chanel, DNKY, etc., discounted and wholesale.
Rolling Stone Records	7300 W Irving Park Rd	708-456-0861	The place to rock, with lots of big-haired in-store appearances.
Salvation Army Thrift Store	3837 W Fullerton Ave	773-276-1955	Good 'ol fashioned thrifting.
Srpska Tradicija	3615 W Lawrence Ave	773-588-7372	Music, books, religious icons and gifts from Serbia and Montenegro.
Sweden Shop	3304 W Foster Ave	773-478-0327	Gifts from Scandinavia.
Village Discount Outlet	4635 N Elston Ave	866-545-3866	Tons of clothes and weekly specials.

Maps 49–52 • West Chicago

Buyer's Flea Market	4545 W Division St	773-227-1889	A weekend bargain hunter's dream.
Family Dollar	5410 W Chicago Ave	773-287-7050	All your convenient(ce) store needs for under a dollar.
Moo & Oink	4848 W Madison St	773-473-4800	A barbeque enthusiast's Mecca.
Village Discount Outlet	2514 W 47th St	866-545-3866	Tons of clothes and weekly specials.
Village Discount Outlet	4020 W 26th St	866-545-3866	Tons of clothes and weekly specials.

Maps 53–56 • Southwest Chicago

African American Images Bookstore	1909 W 95th St	800-552-1991	Books, art, and jewelry with an African-American theme.
The Beverly Cigar Company	10513 S Western Ave	773-239-3264	More than 65 types of stogies, including a Honduras-rolled house brand.
Beverly & Novelty Costume Shop	11626 S Western Ave	773-779-0068	Lifeline of trick-or-treaters and masquerade ballers on Far Southwest Side.
Beverly Records	11612 S Western Ave	773-779-0066	Flip through actual vinyl here. Remember that stuff?
Bobak's	5275 S Archer Ave	773-735-5334	A melange of Polish buffet and supermarket, Chicago style.
Borders Book, Music, Movies & Café	2210 W 95th St	773-445-5471	The hub of Beverly's literary universe.
Calabria Imports	1905 W 103rd St	773-396-5800	Italian deli foodstuffs.
County Fair	10800 S Western Ave	773-238-5576	Classic family-owned market with produce, organics, butcher & deli!
Ford City Shopping Center	7601 S Cicero Ave	773-767-6400	One-stop shopping for everyone on the Southwest Side and Suburbs. Multiplex cinema shows blockbusters.
Grich Antiques	10857 S Western Ave	773-233-8734	Furniture, housewares, and vintage electronics.
Izzy Rizzy's House of Tricks	6356 S Pulaski Rd	773-735-7370	Where to get your whoopy cushions, hand-buzzers, and fake puke.
Mr Peabody Records	11832 S Western Ave	773-881-9299	One of two black-owned, thriving retailers of rare vinyl in the world.
Ms Priss	9915 S Walden Pkwy	773-233-7747	Clubby young woman's fashion haven.
Optimo Hat	10215 S Western Ave	773-238-2999	Custom-made men's hats.
Reading on Walden	9913 S Walden Pkwy	773-233-7633	Hidden neighborhood bookstore right off the Metro Rock Island line.
Village Discount Outlet	6419 S Kedzie Ave	866-545-3866	Tons of clothes and weekly specials.
Village Discount Outlet	7443 S Racine Ave	866-545-3866	Tons of clothes and weekly specials.
World Folk Music	1808 W 103rd St	773-779-7059	Weird instruments and lessons for kids and adults.

Maps 57–60 • South Chicago

Halsted Indoor Mall	11444 S Halsted St	773-995-0265	Lots of bargains under one roof in historically black Morgan Park, on site of former golf course.
Underground Afrocentric Bookstore	1727 E 87th St	773-768-8869	New and used books of African-American interest.

Evanston

Active Endeavors	901 Church St	847-869-7070	New Evanston location for casual chic clothing.
Art & Science Hair Salon	811 Church St	847-864-4247	Beakers bring you back to science class. Student discounts available.
Asinamali Women's Boutique	1722 Sherman Ave	847-866-6219	Great clothes in a reasonable price range.

If you live in Chicago, you know a few things for sure: Hot dogs should have sweet relish, pickles, tomato, onion, sport peppers, and yellow mustard; the Cubs always lose; deep-dish is the best kind of pizza; and Chicago is a *theater* town. You can't swing Mrs. O'Leary's cow without hitting a tiny, struggling off-Loop storefront theater. The storefront theaters are so prevalent here that the city's Department of Cultural Affairs, in its effort to bring smaller productions to the newly revitalized "theater district" (more on that later), named its new downtown venue after them (**Storefront Theater (Map 5)**).

General Tips

The Theater section of the *Chicago Reader*, a free weekly available citywide in bookstores, cafés, bars, and in boxes on street corners (or online at www.chicagoreader.com) is the best friend of the Chicago theatergoer-in-the-know. Turn to the Short List, look for "Highly Recommended" status, or search for Critic's Choices to ferret out your best bets. Another source is *New City*'s "Top Five Shows to See Now" list. Look for free copies of *New City* in the same places as the *Reader*. Hottix (www.hottix.org), a program of the League of Chicago Theaters, offers half-price tickets to same-day shows on a first-come-first-served basis. Also, if you are new in town and want to break into the biz, drop by any theater in your 'hood and pick up a copy of *PerformInk*, the Chicago trade paper for theater and the performing arts, or check 'em out online at www.performink.com. Also, for the budget conscious, The Saints (a volunteer usher program used by most of the large and medium-sized theaters in Chicago) offers opportunities to usher and see multiple plays for free. You have to join their ranks for an annual $55 fee, but think of how much you'll save on theater tickets. Check out www.saintschicago.org for more information.

Let's get this out of the way. If you want to see a big, traveling Broadway show, check out www.broadwayinchicago.com. There you can find the listings for **Cadillac Palace Theatre (Map 5)**, **Ford Center for the Performing Arts/Oriental Theatre (Map 5)**, the **LaSalle Bank Theatre (Map 5)**, or the beautiful and historic **Auditorium Theatre (Map 5)** (designed by Louis Sullivan). But Chicago, my friends, offers so much more than just second runs…

Downtown Theaters aka "The Downtown Theater District"

There are many large theaters producing quality work in downtown Chicago. One of the oldest theaters in Chicago, **The Goodman Theatre (Map 5)** is a stalwart of the downtown theater scene. Now in its new location at 170 North Dearborn, the Goodman is a professional theater featuring high-quality plays by well-known and lesser-known playwrights. **Steppenwolf Theatre Co. (Map 30)** in Old Town produces wonderful ensemble productions with notable Chicago actors. Among their famous ensemble members are John Mahoney, John Malkovitch, Laurie Metcalf, Martha Plimpton, and Gary Sinise. Similarly, **Lookingglass Theatre (Map 43)** (known for ensemble member David Schwimmer of *Friends* fame) creates productions with an artistic ensemble. Their new location in Chicago's Water Tower Water Works building, one of the few structures to survive the famous 1871 Chicago fire is well worth a trip downtown. Known as a playwright's theater, **Victory Gardens Theater (Map 30)** produces original works by contemporary, living playwrights. Also worth mentioning in this category, though they run at neighborhood theaters, are the Chicago productions of the *Blue Man Group* (**Briar Street Theatre (Map 44)**); **Chicago Shakespeare Theater (Map 3)** on Navy Pier, offering pricey but elegant productions of the Bard's classics; and *Tony n' Tina's Wedding* (www.tonyntina.com). The latter offers up a live dinner theater event at **Piper's Alley**, complete with a re-enactment of the wedding reception of a loud, dysfunctional Italian family. Finally, the **Storefront Theater (Map 5)** at the Chicago Department of Cultural Affairs remounts the best of the neighborhood theater productions in its state-of-the- art venue at 66 E Randolph.

Medium-Sized Neighborhood Theaters

Really amazing productions can be found at medium-sized neighborhood theaters. Some of the best picks include the longest-running show in Chicago today, *Too Much Light Makes the Baby Go Blind* (at **The Neo-Futurarium (Map 37)**). Proclaiming to perform thirty plays in sixty minutes, the show ends when one or the other is over. Other good bets include **Stage Left Theatre (Map 43)** (whose work has cultivated some of the best national playwrights), **Live Bait Theater (Map 43)** (first-run plays), **About Face Theatre (Map 44)** (high-quality gay/lesbian/bisexual works), **Famous Door Theatre (Map 43)** (original and "seldom-produced" works), **Redmoon Theater (Map 43)** (highly unique large-scale puppetry productions), and **Teatro Luna (Map 36)** (Chicago's only all-Latina performance troupe).

Improv

Chicago is also well known for its improv scene. **The Second City (Map 31),** the famed training ground for most of *Saturday Night Live*'s original cast, keeps on going with many shows at four venues in Chicago. Check out www.secondcity.com for show times. Other improv venues include **The Playground Theater (Map 42)**, **ImprovOlympic Theater (Map 43)** (with its free Friday and Saturday midnight "Cage Match"), **Annoyance Theatre (Map 40)**, **Comedy Sportz (Map 44)**, and **WNEP Theater (Map 39)**. Most of these venues feature improv teams battling against one another for audience approval. Information about all venues can be found on www.improvchicago.com.

Fringe/Performance Art/Other

There is only one organization solely devoted to the presentation of large performance art events in Chicago. It is the **Museum of Contemporary Art (Map 3)** (www.mcachicago.org). Bringing in dance, performance art, theater, film and readings from around the globe, the performance department at the MCA is devoted to presenting the best of the live arts to Chicago audiences.

Some of Chicago's best productions occur in alternative spaces. They are created by smaller companies who don't have a venue, whether by choice or by size. These are the tiny, glittering gems of the Chicago theater scene. Find these productions in the Performance Listings in the *Reader*. Don't shy away from a theater company you've never heard of producing at a rented venue. This is very common in Chicago, and these productions are often worth the trip. We can't list them all here (for they are too numerous), but here are some of our favorites.

For girl–on–girl combat action, check out *Babes with Blades* (www.babeswithblades.com) in semi–regular productions at various venues. 500 Clown (www.500clown.com) produces loose adaptations of classic tales (*Frankenstein, Macbeth*) in original, dangerous clown theater that the authors wouldn't recognize. *Defiant Theatre* (www.defianttheatre.org) subverts the social, moral, and aesthetic expectations of the theater with edgy productions at varied venues. Roadworks Productions (www.roadworks.org) is an outpost for gripping plays by new and overlooked playwrights. Collaboraction (known mainly for its *Sketchbook* series) is a collective comprising cross–disciplinary artists presenting short unique works in all media. Drawing from diverse sources, Goat Island Performance Ensemble (www.goatislandperformance.org) offers up heady movement–based performance created in a lengthy ensemble process. *Plasticene* (www.plasticene.com) confronts audiences with rare physical theater. In the summer, look for remounts of favorite local productions at **Theater on the Lake (Map 30)** (www.chicagoparkdistrict.com), a screened–in theater venue situated near Fullerton Avenue on Chicago's lakefront. Curious Theater Branch (www.curioustheaterbranch.com) has presented original, engaging theater for the last eleven years. **Bailiwick Repertory Theatre (Map 43)** offers up the hit *Naked Boys Singing*, which is pretty much what it sounds like. And finally, the truly horrifying **American Girl Place (Map 2)** offers up *Circle of Friends: An American Girl Doll Musical* inside the American Girl Doll Store. This is not a recommendation for the discerning theatergoer; however, if you want to witness the indoctrination of small girls in American capitalist culture, look no further.

Out of Town

There also are some fantastic theatrical adventures just beyond the borders of our fair city. For outstanding productions of plays that focus on writing and language, check out Writer's Theatre in Glencoe. A little bit closer to home, Evanston offers some quality productions by Next Theatre, Light Opera Works, and the acclaimed theater department at Northwestern University. West of the city, Oak Park offers up gems at the Village Players and the Oak Park Festival Theatre (which offers outdoor plays and musicals during the summer months.) In Wilmette, an annual musical production is presented at the Wallace Bowl in Gillson Park just across the street from the Bahai temple.

A recent count in *PerformInk* listed nearly 200 theaters on its links page, in addition to 30 or so improvisational theater troupes. Large theaters producing traveling shows, off–Loop groups producing original plays of all stripes, improvisational shows at all hours of the night—you name it, Chicago has it. Don't miss the chance to take in some of Chicago's finest performance opportunities.

Theater	*Address*	*Phone*	*Map*
About Face Theatre	1222 W Wilson Ave	773-784-8565	44
American Girl Place	111 E Chicago Ave	877-247-5223	2
American Theater Company	1909 W Byron St	773-929-1031	42
Angel Island Theater	731 W Sheridan Rd	773-871-0442	44
Annoyance Productions	4802 N Broadway St	773-989-9884	40
Apollo Theater Chicago	2540 N Lincoln Ave	773-935-6100	29
Arie Crown Theatre	2301 S Lake Shore Dr	312-791-6190	11
Athenaeum Theatre	2936 N Southport Ave	773-935-6860	43
Auditorium Theatre	50 E Congress Pkwy	312-922-2110	5
Bailiwick Repertory Theatre	1229 W Belmont Ave	773-883-1090	43
Black Ensemble Theater	4520 N Beacon St	773-769-4451	40
Breadline Theatre	1802 W Berenice Ave	773-327-6096	42
Briar Street Theatre	3133 N Halsted St	773-348-4000	44
Cadillac Palace Theatre	151 W Randolph St	312-977-1700	5
Casa Aztlan	1831 S Racine Ave	312-666-5508	26
Chase Park Theater	4701 N Ashland Ave	312-742-7518	40
Chicago Center for the Performing Arts	777 N Green St	312-327-2000	1
Chicago Dramatists	1105 W Chicago Ave	312-633-0630	24
Chicago Shakespeare Theater	800 E Grand Ave	312-595-5600	3
The Chicago Theatre	175 N State St	312-462-6300	5
Chopin Theater	1543 W Division St	773-278-1500	22
Civic Opera House	20 N Wacker Dr	312-419-0033	5
Comedy Sportz	2851 N Halsted St	773-549-8080	44
Cornservatory	4210 N Lincoln Ave	312-409-6435	39
Court Theatre	5535 S Ellis Ave	773-753-4472	19

Theater	*Address*	*Phone*	*Map*
Dance Center of Columbia College	1306 S Michigan Ave	312-344-8300	11
Drury Lane Theatre at Water Tower Place	175 E Chestnut St	312-642-2000	32
Duncan YMCA Chernin Center for the Arts	1001 W Roosevelt Rd	312-421-7800	26
Famous Door Theater	3408 N Sheffield Ave	773-404-8283	43
Ford Center for the Performing Arts/Oriental Theatre	24 W Randolph St	312-782-2004	5
Free Street Theater	1419 W Blackhawk St	773-772-7248	22
Getz Theater (Columbia College)	62 E 11th St	312-663-1124	8
The Goodman Theatre	170 N Dearborn St	312-443-3800	5
Harold Washington Cultural Center	4701 S Dr Martin L King Jr Dr	773-373-1900	16
Harris Theater for Music and Dance	205 E Randolph St	312-334-7777	5
ImprovOlympic Theater	3541 N Clark St	773-880-0199	43
Ivanhoe Theater	750 W Wellington Ave	312-335-8499	44
The Josephinum	1500 N Bell Ave	n/a	21
Kathleen Mullady Memorial Theatre	1125 W Loyola Ave	773-508-3847	34
Lakeshore Theatre	3175 N Broadway St	773-472-3492	44
LaSalle Bank Theatre	22 W Monroe St	312-977-1710	5
Lifeline Theatre	6912 N Glenwood Ave	773-761-4477	34
Links Hall Studio	3435 N Sheffield Ave	773-281-0824	43
Live Bait Theater	3914 N Clark St	773-871-1212	43
Lookingglass Theatre	821 N Michigan Ave	312-337-0665	43
Mercury Theater	3745 N Southport Ave	773-325-1700	43
Merle Reskin Theatre	60 E Balbo Ave	312-922-1999	8
Methadome Theatre	4437 N Broadway St	773-769-2959	40
Museum of Contemporary Art	220 E Chicago Ave	312-280-2660	3
National Pastime Theater	4139 N Broadway St	773-327-7077	40
The Neo-Futurarium	5153 N Ashland Ave	773-275-5255	37
North Shore Center for the Performing Arts	9501 Skokie Blvd	847-673-6300	207
O'Malley Theater-Roosevelt University	430 S Michigan Ave	312-341-3719	6
O'Rourke Center for the Performing Arts	1145 W Wilson Ave	773-878-9761	40
The Playground Theater	3209 N Halsted St	773-871-3793	42
Profiles Theatre	4147 N Broadway St	773-549-1815	40
Prop Theatre	3504 N Elston Ave	773-539-7838	39
Puppet Parlor	1922 W Montrose Ave	773-774-2919	39
Raven Theatre	6157 N Clark St	773-338-2177	33
Red Hen Productions	5123 N Clark St	773-728-0599	40
A Red Orchid Theatre	1531 N Wells St	312-943-8722	31
Redmoon Theater Co	1438 W Kinzie St	312-850-8440	43
Royal George Theatre Center	1641 N Halsted St	312-988-9000	30
Ruth Page Center Theater	1016 N Dearborn St	312-337-6543	32
Second City	1616 N Wells St	312-337-3992	31
Second City etc/Second City Skybox	1608 N Wells St	312-337-3992	31
The Side Studio	1441 W Jarvis Ave	773-973-2105	34
Stage Left Theatre	3408 N Sheffield Ave	773-883-8830	43
Steep Theatre	3902 N Sheridan Rd	312-458-0722	43
Steppenwolf Theatre Co	1650 N Halsted St	312-335-1650	30
Storefront Theater	66 E Randolph St	312-742-8497	5
Strawdog Theatre	3829 N Broadway St	773-528-9696	44
Teatro Luna	5215 N Ravenswood Ave	773-878-5862	36
Theater on the Lake	2400 N Lake Shore Dr	312-742-7994	30
Theatre Building	1225 W Belmont Ave	773-327-5252	43
TimeLine Theatre Co	615 W Wellington Ave	773-281-8463	44
TinFish Theatre	4247 N Lincoln Ave	773-549-1888	39
Trap Door Productions	1655 W Cortland St	773-384-0494	28
UIC Theatre	1044 W Harrison St	312-996-2939	26
Viaduct Theater	3111 N Western Ave	773-296-6024	42
Victory Gardens	2257 N Lincoln Ave	773-871-3000	30
Vittum Theater	1012 N Noble St	773-871-3000	22
WNEP Theater	2131 W Cuyler Ave, #1	773-509-2945	39

Quintessential Columbia College Chicago

1,300,000+
Square feet of classroom, office, and living space in Chicago's South Loop

300,000+
Visitors per year take advantage of campus exhibitions, performances, and special events

10,800+
Students in 2005-2006 school year . . . up from 125 students in 1963

2,500
Faculty and staff – 100 percent of faculty are working professionals in touch with the latest developments in their fields

231
National and international dance companies presented at our Dance Center in the last 30 years

8
2005 Emmy nominations among seven alumni

1
Semester in LA – the only academic program permanently located on a working studio lot

1
The first undergraduate poetry major in the country

0
Other institutions like Columbia College Chicago

create... change

Street Index

Some of the townships and communities immediately adjoining Chicago proper thought it would be a fun joke to restart street numbering at their borders—or name a street exactly the same name as an entirely unrelated Chicago street. These cases are designated with an asterisk.*

A

Street Index

B

C

Street Index

D

E

H

I

L

N

S

Y

Essential Numbers

General

All emergencies **911**
AIDS Hotline 800-342-AIDS
Animal Anti-Cruelty Society 312-644-8338
Chicago Dental Referral Service 312-836-7305
Chicago Department of Housing 773-285-5800
City of Chicago Board of Elections 312-269-7900
Dog License (City Clerk) 312-744-6875
Driver's Licenses 312-793-1010
Emergency Services 312-747-7247
Employment Discrimination 312-744-7584
Gas Leaks 312-240-7000
Income Tax (Illinois) 800-732-8866
Income Tax (Federal) 800-829-3676
Legal Assistance 312-332-1624
Mayor's Office 312-744-4000
Parking (City Stickers) 312-742-9200
Parking Ticket Inquiries 312-744-7275
Report Crime in Your Neighborhood 312-372-0101
Passports 312-341-6020
Police Assistance (non-emergency) 311
Social Security 773-890-2492
Streets and Sanitation 312-744-5000
Telephone Repair Service 888-611-4466
Voter Information 312-269-7900
Water Main Leaks 312-744-7038

Helplines

Alcoholics Anonymous 312-346-1475
Alcohol, Drug and Abuse Helpline 800-234-0420
Alcoholism and Substance Abuse 312-988-7900
Domestic Violence Hotline 800-799-7233
Drug Care, St. Elizabeth's 773-278-5015
Gamblers Anonymous 312-346-1588
Illinois Child Abuse Hotline 800-252-2873
Narcotics Anonymous 708-848-4884
Parental Stress Services 312-372-7368
Runaway Switchboard 800-621-4000
Sexual Assault Hotline 888-293-2080
United Way Community Information
and Referral 312-876-0010
Violence – Anti-Violence Project 773-871-CARE

Complaints

Better Business Bureau of Chicago 312-832-0500
Consumer Fraud Division (Attorney General's Office) 312-814-3000
Chicago Department of Consumer Services 312-744-9400
Citizen's Utility Board 800-669-5556
Department of Housing Inspection Complaints 312-747-9000
Mayor's Office 312-744-4000
Postal Service Complaints 312-983-8400